Books by ROBERT COLES

CHILDREN OF CRISIS: A STUDY OF COURAGE AND FEAR

STILL HUNGRY IN AMERICA

THE IMAGE IS YOU

UPROOTED CHILDREN

WAGES OF NEGLECT
(with Maria Piers)

DRUGS AND YOUTH
(with Joseph Brenner and Dermot Meagher)

ERIK H. ERIKSON:
THE GROWTH OF HIS WORK

THE ,MIDDLE AMERICANS
(with Jon Erikson)

THE GEOGRAPHY OF FAITH
(with Daniel Berrigan)

MIGRANTS, SHARECROPPERS, MOUNTAINEERS
(Volume II of *Children of Crisis*)

THE SOUTH GOES NORTH
(Volume III of *Children of Crisis*)

For Children

DEAD END SCHOOL

THE GRASS PIPE

Migrants, Sharecroppers, Mountaineers

VOLUME II OF CHILDREN OF CRISIS

ROBERT COLES, M.D.

An Atlantic Monthly Press Book

LITTLE, BROWN AND COMPANY • BOSTON • TORONTO

LIBRARY OF CONGRESS CATALOG CARD NO. 76–162331

10   9   8   7   6   5

"Rural Upheaval" is Chapter 6 of *On Fighting Poverty* edited by
James L. Sundquist, © 1969 by the American Academy of Arts
and Sciences, Basic Books, Inc., Publishers, New York.

Part of "Hugh McCaslin" appeared as "Life in Appalachia," ©
June, 1968, by Transaction, Inc., New Brunswick, New Jersey.

ATLANTIC–LITTLE, BROWN BOOKS
ARE PUBLISHED BY
LITTLE, BROWN AND COMPANY
IN ASSOCIATION WITH
THE ATLANTIC MONTHLY PRESS

Published simultaneously in Canada
by Little, Brown & Company (Canada) Limited
PRINTED IN THE UNITED STATES OF AMERICA

*To those many American children whose
parents are migrants, sharecroppers
and mountaineers.*

Isaiah 49:8–11

In an acceptable time have I heard thee, and in a day of salvation have I helped thee: and I will preserve thee, and give thee for a covenant of the people, to establish the earth, to cause to inherit the desolate heritages; that thou mayest say to the prisoners, go forth; to them that are in darkness, show yourselves. They shall feed in the ways, and their pastures shall be in all high places. They shall not hunger nor thirst; neither shall the heat nor the sun smite them: for he that hath mercy on them shall lead them, even by the springs of the water shall he guide them. And I will make all my mountains a way, and my highways shall be exalted.

FOREWORD

A T the end of another foreword, the one that preceded the first volume of this series, I made mention of what I believe was a continuity between my study of school desegregation in the South — and the work I began in Mississippi in the late 1950's with the sit-in movement and with segregationists opposed to it — and other work I have been doing over the past years. I mentioned the migrant farm children I was getting to know, the sharecropper families I was spending time with, the people I was visiting again and again in the hill country immediately to the north of our southern states. Now, I am once more writing a foreword to a volume about "children of crisis," and again I am writing about the "courage and fear" I cited in the first volume's subtitle; but I have decided to give this second volume a title that points out exactly which children of which parents have to struggle for that courage and learn to live with that fear. The children number millions, I regret to say. They live in migrant camps all up and down the Atlantic seaboard, especially in Florida, where thousands and thousands of farm workers harvest winter crops, then leave for the North to do the same kind of work as far away as New York and New England; they live, they still live, throughout Mississippi and Alabama and Georgia and the Carolinas on land that is owned by others but tilled by their parents, who are sharecroppers or tenant farmers; and finally, they live up in the hollows of what is commonly called Appalachia, that is, in West Virginia, eastern Kentucky, and western North Carolina and Virginia.

How those children live, how their parents live, what they all are likely to have on their minds, and what it is like for them to grow up and come to terms with their particular fate — on such "subjects" I will try to shed some light, as much of it as one child psychiatrist can after more than a decade of observations and more observations. But I might just as well, right here and right off, confess the very severe limits that inevitably plague this kind of work. Children who live the lives that are described in this book need what millions of my kind of words simply cannot provide: bread, clean water, decent housing, and in general a world more welcoming, a kinder and more decent kind of world than they now know. No book can provide such things, I realize, but some books — and this is not one of them — can at least offer a social and political analysis of the reasons so many thousands of American families, citizens of the world's mightiest nation, continue to be so desperately needy; and other books can show why it is, historically, that we have continued to permit, perhaps even encourage sharecroppers and tenant farmers and migrant farmers and mountaineers to live as they do, work as they do, get the pittance of wages they get — if indeed they get any wages at all. Such books have been written, as have those that offer first-hand sociological and anthropological descriptions of "life" as it takes place in the "Black Belt" or in Appalachia, and I shall certainly direct the reader to those books and essays and reports. Indeed, some of the references given at the end of this volume, if sought out and consulted, will supply just about everything significant that a generation or two of social scientists have done to document the nature of rural towns, rural folkways, and rural issues or problems of many kinds.

Nevertheless, even though the people written about here have obvious, awful, and crying everyday needs that go unmet, the cast of this particular book has to be inward or psychological, concerning itself with matters of the mind and heart and even the soul or the spirit of hard-pressed people — as did its predecessor and as will its successor, a third volume of *Children of Crisis*, entitled *The South Goes North*. I feel myself every day walking on the edge of things, very near the disciplines of sociology and anthropology, quite close to matters of history and politics; but what I learn grows out of my work as a physician and a child psychiatrist, both of which occupations constantly give form and shape to my questions. It is as a physician that I approach the people whom I at once try to observe, to be with, and to let rest, in the sense of retaining whatever shred of dignity, against great odds, it is possible for such people to have — a dignity that certainly deserves to remain uncontaminated by the careless, self-centered, presumptuous, even barbarous technical vocabularies that flourish all about us these days.

I cannot in a series of books like this embark on an extended theoretical discussion of the relationship between clinical work and social observation, or the relationship between a case history and a life history and indeed history itself. I can only say that I have contended with those matters, not abstractly but out in the "field," amid people, workers, citizens who in their own ways always do contend with such matters as where pain ends and faith begins, or how individuals make their mark on a society, try to change it, try in the face of serious and unyielding opposition to get new policies going. I have, though, tried to draw upon the work of others, and have found it both necessary and desirable to carry my concerns back to the university, where I could sit with them and gain some perspective on them. Needless to say, the "uneducated" or "illiterate" people I have worked with out in those "fields" have also given me some perspective on the university, and on my own profession.

In *Erik H. Erikson: The Growth of His Work* I have tried to examine the theoretical underpinnings of the kind of clinical study described in the present book. Let me repeat here my debt to Erikson the clinician, the thinker, the writer, the fieldworker; it is a debt I believe I share with thousands of clinical workers all over the world.

For many years now, Anna Freud has asked child psychiatrists to look long and hard before leaping to all those formulations that fill up so many pages of so many professional journals. "Direct observation," she calls for — and one can feel her, in her various writings, wondering when it will ever stop, the labeling of children, the constant speculations and prognostications, the endless construction of theories and yet more theories, so often done on the basis of scanty, even flimsy clinical evidence. I have tried, at least I hope I have tried, never to forget her request that we *observe*, do so directly and for many years; and only toward the end of one's studies write, but write with the same directness one tries to demonstrate as an observer.

Other encouragement ought also be mentioned now. From 1961 to 1968 my research was primarily supported by the New World Foundation and the Field Foundation, first with grants to the Southern Regional Council, then to the Harvard University Health Services. From 1968 until the present time the Ford Foundation has supported that research with two grants, again to the Harvard University Health Services. I continue to acknowledge my gratitude to these private foundations, who have never once tried to influence or control my work, my ideas, my manner of writing things up. It has been a pleasure in this day and age to deal with men who will grant money without compelling application forms to be completed, "methodological procedures" to be stated, and finally, conclusions and solutions and "guidelines" and "strategies" to be promised.

Sections of this book have appeared elsewhere in somewhat shorter or different or indeed enlarged form. Much of Chapter III was originally delivered at the University of Pittsburgh as the seventeenth annual Horace Mann Lecture; since the university publishes all such lectures, this one appeared in print in 1969 as *Uprooted Children: The Early Life of Migrant Farm Workers.* The section of Chapter VI devoted to Hugh McCaslin was first published in *Transaction.* Part of Chapter IX was read as the commencement address at Haverford College in May of 1968, and afterwards published in *The American Scholar,* as was a brief part of Chapter X. Chapter XI is also a chapter in *On Fighting Poverty,* edited by James L. Sundquist. A section of Chapter IX was originally read in October of 1969 at the University of West Virginia's centennial year of observance. The paper was first published in a monograph (*The Public University in Its Second Century*) issued by the Office of Research and Development of the West Virginia Center for Appalachian Studies and Development. In revised and expanded form the paper was published in *The Appalachian Review.* A section from Chapter

XII was read in October of 1969 to the Commission on Religion in Appalachia (which met in Asheville, North Carolina) and later the address appeared in *Commonweal.*

I wish more personally to express my thanks for the kindness and assistance, indispensable to this work, I have received from Leslie Dunbar, Vernon Eagle, Dana Farnsworth and Edward Meade. I wish to thank Peter Davison, a fine editor, and Devorah W. Gilbert and Martha Stearns and Elizabeth Garber, helpers in making legible sense out of all this writing. I am once again grateful to Mrs. Pamela Daniels for the help she gave in the preparation of the notes and references at the back of the book. Then, I wish to mention the people who appear in this book — to speak and have their say, to worry or proclaim their hopes, their ambitions, and in spite of everything, their joys. What is there to say? A whole book of thanks would not be enough; and even a few profuse words of thanks are too much, because these migrants, these mountaineers, these sharecroppers know a kind of "score," a kind of scheme of things that makes their help come, finally, to this: "Sure, it's fine to talk with you. I hope all that I say gets heard someplace, but you can't expect too much." I am afraid I thoroughly agree with him, that half-paralyzed coal miner from West Virginia; which means I agree with the sober warning he gave me to keep in mind while writing all these words.

I again have to state that this foreword is a foreword to work in progress. When this volume of *Children of Crisis* appears it will be accompanied by another volume, whose title, *The South Goes North,* describes my attempt to follow the destiny of rural Americans — who by the millions, white and black and from Appalachia and all over the South, have gone North to our cities. In some instances the very people described here have made that move, and I followed them, or pursued some of their relatives, the kinfolk who did not stay, who no longer could take it, who had to go — get out, get far away, try life elsewhere, in Chicago and Cleveland and New York and Boston, "in any place that isn't no place." So, *The South Goes North* completes what has been for me some twelve years of trying to make sense of what takes place at that elusive yet terribly sharp edge where a nation's history becomes, for particular men, women and children a complete life, full of countless stresses, only some of which I could ever hope to notice and understand.

And, speaking of those men, women and children, I have not used the real names of the people I have interviewed, and I have done as much as possible to conceal their real homes and identities. If I have unwittingly used the name of any living person in this book, I offer my apology here. It has been my wish to protect at all costs the privacy of those people, many of them friends, whom I have interviewed over the years.

I mentioned "work in progress." I hope in due course to tell of the children of the West, to document how it goes for a Spanish-speaking child in Texas or New Mexico or California, or an Indian child in the Southwest, or an Eskimo child in Alaska. And the reason I could have hoped to do that, the reason I could ever have hoped to finish what I have achieved so far, has to do with my wife Jane, whose presence and energy has made the traveling and listening and watching and writing somehow possible.

CONTENTS

PART ONE

THE SETTING

I

THE LAND

I AM writing about the land. I am writing about people, of course, about fellow citizens, and particularly about children, who live uprooted lives, who have been stranded, who are hidden from the rest of us. Nevertheless, I am writing about the land, miles and miles of it, the rich American earth. I am also writing about *a* land, the United States of America, some country that is hilly and rocky and often windswept or fog-covered, some that is a plateau, high and leveled-off and dry, some that is low and flat and at the water's edge. More precisely, I suppose, I am trying to approach the lives of certain individuals who may in various ways differ, as members or representatives of this or that "group" of people, but who for all of that share something hard to define exactly or label with a few long and authoritative words, something that has to do with the way people, however unlike in appearance or background, manage to live on the land and come to terms with it, every day of their lives.

The men and women whose lives, I repeat, I can only approach, do not live in cities (though their children and grandchildren may or perhaps will someday) and certainly do not live in the prosperous suburbs that hug those cities so rigidly. People who are called migrant farmers or sharecroppers or tenant farmers or mountaineers or hillbillies are not to be found in the small towns and villages that often are taken to be the reposi-tories of America's rural heritage — by those who live in large,

3

metropolitan centers and are willing to go just so far afield, so far toward the "country" in search of anything, including their nation's history. It can be said that migrants and sharecroppers and mountaineers live both nowhere and everywhere. Their homes, their houses, their cabins (which I fear all too commonly can be appropriately called shacks or huts) are scattered all over. They defy the dots and circles that, with names beside them, appear on maps. I can pick up one of those maps and point my finger at the smallest towns in, say, a county of the Mississippi Delta, or one of Florida's south-central counties or Kentucky's eastern counties, and still know that however large the atlas and however tiny, even microscopic, the places shown, I will not find large numbers of tenant farmers, migrants or mountaineers, respectively, in any of them, be they county seats or the remotest of hamlets.

It is outside the town limits, in between one town and another, straddling county lines, even state lines, that they can be found — settlements of families, as I have come to think of them in my mind. Their cabins, with a protective coloration like that of animals, have almost invariably become part of the land: the wood and metal walls turn rusty brown and dull gray and blend into everything else and successfully camouflage entire settlements. They are often nameless settlements, or if they do have a name it is to set people apart from others, and just as important, attach them to the land's contours, to this particular field or creek or that hollow or bend in a river or valley.

Some of the settlements, of course, move across the land — a caravan of trucks, a few buses, a single car or maybe two, all filled to the brim with migrants. Yet, when the vehicles are brought to a stop it is done beside bushes and under trees. The point is to be inconspicuous, to hide, to disappear from sight; and so a number of families disperse, become little knots of people here and there, anxious for the ground as a resting-place and anxious to blend into things, merge with them, and thereby hide away from the rest of us, from the world that gazetteers and atlases and census bureaus take note of, from the world of the police and the government, but also from the merely curious and even the openly concerned.

The next day, when light comes, the trek is to be resumed and the risks of travel have to be taken. So, they emerge, the migrant settlers. They assemble and move on, and again they are wanderers whose chief purpose is an accommodation of their energies to the earth's needs. If the earth is ready, about to bear its fruits, the migrants try to be there, do their work, then slip away. As some of them have said to me, and will say in these pages, a whole life can be lived away from almost everyone but oneself and one's immediate relatives and companions. One knows hundreds of acres of land well — byroads and side roads and dirt roads and asphalt roads. One recognizes familiar terrain in a dozen states, in places all over. Yet, one is no one: frequently unregistered at birth, ineligible to vote, unprotected by laws that apply to others, often unrecorded as having died, and all during life an actual resident of no municipality or township or state — even stateless in the larger sense of being decidedly unwanted and spurned by a whole nation.

Surely it must be different with sharecroppers and mountaineers, though. If migrants cover the land, cover a virtual continent in search of work, sharecroppers or tenant farmers are by definition rooted to a specific piece of land, as are mountaineers, who after all live up along the sides of particular Appalachian hills. A dazed, rootless itinerant field hand does not to all appearances live like a sharecropper, who may never have left a particular plantation, or like a mountaineer, who stubbornly stays up his hollow, come what may. Yet, for all three the land means everything, the land and what grows on it, what can be found under it, what the seasons do to it, and what man does to it, and indeed what long ago was done to it by a mysterious Nature, or an equally baffling chronicle of events called History, or finally what it was made by God, like the other two inscrutable, but unlike them, at least for the people we are to meet and try to know here, very much present and listening and in fact a person, *the* person: He Who listens and remembers — and Whose land it all really is, something plantation owners and growers and county officials may forget for a while, but will ultimately discover at a given point in eternity's scheme of things, so thousands of harvesters believe.

I am not saying that all these people, so scattered and so different and so removed from one another (but so very much alike) do not share man's general need to confine his fellow man, give him a name, call a certain stretch of territory his, pinpoint him in time and space. The title of this book right away declares that my concern is with people who migrate from one place to another, and people who work the land that ostensibly belongs to others, in exchange for a share of the profits, and people who cling hard indeed to a mighty and prominent range of mountains. And the first pages in the book declare the migrants to be Americans, the sharecroppers to be Americans, and the mountaineers to be perhaps the most typically American of Americans — in the old-fashioned, conventional sense of what has constituted an American for the longest period of time. (Indians and blacks, also here when the Republic was founded, would not become Americans until much later.)

Indeed, it is possible to get quite precise; a variety of names and phrases, like nets, can pull in just about all these people. They live in the "Black Belt" of the South, from Georgia to Louisiana, or near Lake Okeechobee and the Everglades in Florida; or they live on the edge of the Cumberlands, the Alleghenys, the Blue Ridge mountains; or they spend time in the lowlands of the Carolinas, in Virginia's tidewater area, all along a stretch of Long Island, in upstate New York, downstate New Jersey, or in New England, where tobacco grows (in Connecticut) and apples fall from trees (in Massachusetts, for instance) and potatoes cover the ground (Maine's far north Aroostook county). Still, when all that is said, we have only begun. These twentieth-century people, living in the world's richest, strongest twentieth-century nation, are to some extent obeying rituals and commands, are responding to urges and demonstrating rhythms that defy (as well as yield to) the influence of contemporary American life — again, as we the majority know and experience that life. The "migrants, sharecroppers and mountaineers" who are gathered collectively together in this book live not only *on* the land, but *in* a land, one in certain respects all their own. The land all these people know so well has physical boundaries that can be traced out, if we have a mind to do so; but it is just as important for us to know about those psychological boundaries, within which a certain kind of encounter takes place between human hands and the earth; the boundaries between all those fields and meadows and clearings and forests and all those people bent on eating and sleeping and amusing themselves and staking out things for themselves and finding things for themselves.

I would like to begin, in other words, by describing the land and what it is like, what is *there* for men and women to work on, to handle every day. And it should be emphasized that the men and women and children whom we are trying to know here do indeed "handle" the land, do so quite stubbornly and successfully and patiently and cleverly and at times fearfully, but at other times fearlessly and casually and yes almost brazenly, in view of all the threats and the misfortunes, the never-ending dangers and obstacles.

What *is* the land like? To migrants the land is not "like" any-thing; rather, it never stops appearing, waiting, calling, needing, summoning, urging, and then disappearing. To sharecroppers the land is more familiar, but not all that familiar, because it belongs to someone else, and always what is to be done must be settled with that stranger, that boss. To mountaineers the land is almost anything and everything: a neighbor, a friend, a part of the family, handed down and talked about and loved, loved dearly — loved and treasured and obeyed, it can be said, as we agree to do when we get married.

Yet, once more, for all those differences, the three kinds of people are one people; and it is what they do that makes them one. Together they grapple and fight the land, dig into it, try to tame it, exploit it, even plunder it; together they placate the land, bring water to it, spread nourishing substances over it, and in many ways curry its favor. They appeal to it, both openly and more slyly, with rakes that brush and stroke and caress and with hands that pick and pluck, and with words and songs, too — prayers and pleas and cries and requests and petitions. High up the hills of West Virginia men petition for sun; they live nearer the sun than most people, but they can be denied the sun by clouds that hang to the hilltops. In the "Black Belt" men petition for rain; the land is rich and the sun plentiful, but water is needed, and not everywhere has man had the money and ingenuity to bring that water in and keep it at hand, ready and waiting — "the irrigation" as a sharecropper calls it, the pipes and way yonder the dams and artificial lakes he may have heard a plantation owner or his foreman talk about. In southern Florida men petition for peace and quiet of sorts: for an autumn without hurricanes; for a winter that brings no icy blasts, no ruinous frosts; for a spring and summer that offer rain, but not too much rain — though if a choice has to be made, for more rather than less rain, because the droughts are the greatest danger, are a calamity all too familiar in and near the Everglades.

Much of that petitioning takes place right out in the fields themselves, and is done by tenants or itinerant field hands or proud landowners of small plots up in the hills. As with many things that happen in the world, the cliché holds: one has to see something to believe it. In this case one has to hear as well as see: hear the nervous statements and observations, the speculations and predictions, has to hear the doubts and the exasperated, anguished cries which express a sense of futility, foreboding, or distress, a desperate suspicion that all is lost, perhaps only for this year, perhaps even for good. Alternatively, there are the good moments, the occasions when the petitions have been answered, when grateful men and women and children can say thank you or thank You, Almighty God, for befriending us through yet another stretch of time — from planting to plowing to harvesting, from spring through summer and into the autumn, or way down in Florida, from autumn through the winter and into the spring.

The seasons at their worst can bring all but certain defeat, or at their kindest the seasons can offer the distinct likelihood of victory; but most of the time the seasons only begin to influence

the land — do so decisively, but not conclusively. Men, men and
their wives, parents helped by their children, can through work,
hard and tough and backbreaking work, manage to get a reward
for their efforts: "crops" or "produce" or "a harvest," the reward is
called. Their work is called menial; such efforts are considered
automatic and stereotyped — but by whom? Nature is a formidable adversary, most of us will acknowledge in an offhand way,
but we who spend most of our lives in the cities have no reason
to understand just how formidable Nature can be — and therefore cannot know how shrewd and inventive a field hand, yes a
common, ordinary, badly paid, poorly educated field hand has to
be, faced as he is with land that must be coaxed, persuaded and
prompted, aroused and inspired, however much richness and
fertility it possesses.

I have seen those field hands walking the flat land, climbing
patches of hilly land under cultivation, talking to themselves as
they sow seeds, calculating the moment to take it all in, what
they have planted and managed to grow. Later on I will hope to
give some indication of what is thought and said by sowers and
reapers, planters and harvesters, but as a start the majesty of the
challenge to be faced by men who would tame the land had
better be acknowledged. Modestly the men themselves admit
that "it is no mean job," and if they will not advertise the cleverness and ingenuity required, they will most certainly let you
know how fickle spring can be, how disappointing summer sometimes is, how overly prompt and forbidding a particular autumn's
appearance was, and how utterly devastating it turned out, that
last winter.

Joys are to be had, though; and keenly appreciated, too — a
magnificent rural landscape, much of it semitropical, which still
exists, miraculously enough, in this giant of an industrial country.
In winter Alabama's mean temperature is 48 degrees Fahrenheit
and in summer 79 degrees Fahrenheit. On the average, less than
thirty-five days witness temperatures below the freezing point.
Snow falls once or twice a year, and then only in the northern
part of the state. The prevailing winds come from the south. Rain
is generally plentiful, amounting to over fifty inches a year. In

West Virginia, for all the timber-cutting and the depredations of insects, substantial remnants remain of a vast, primeval forest, a blanket of hardwoods and pines that once completely covered the state. Hemlocks, chestnuts and oaks are to be found in abundance. Some tulip poplars stand two hundred feet tall. Some sugar maples stand one hundred feet tall. And there are others: ash trees, whose wood is used in baseball bats, tennis rackets and hockey sticks; or the buckeye; or sourwood trees that supply the sourwood honey that is much loved up the hollows; or those holly trees, the Christmas holly and the mountain holly; or the black cherry tree, whose bark is used in making cough syrup; or the black walnut; or the silver bell; or the spruces so thick, clothing one ridge after another; or the lindens, which stand more alone, and can go dozens and dozens of feet into the air.

What air it is, too! The air up those hills and mountains can be so clear and dry and bracing that the lungs shudder, the head feels much more invigorated than it wants to be. The air can also be raw and wet, or heavy and clammy. Rain is plentiful, at times more than plentiful. Some regions receive seventy or eighty inches a year. Needless to say, trees flourish under such conditions, but incredibly, so do people — the kind who find the brisk winds, the chilly weather, the continual dampness appetizing, and even intoxicating. For such people clouds are no dreaded stranger, thunder and lightning are music, and fog an amusing, welcome visitor. There is enough sun to grow a few vegetables, and the forests — why, without the water, without the mist and the dew and the long "downfalls" and the sudden cloudbursts, there would be no forest worth the name up the side of those hills, only fires and the burned remains that fires leave. Instead, those trees continue to stand; and also around are plants and flowers, hundreds of different kinds, all very much known to mountaineers as well as botanists. The forests are filled with shrubs, lovely ones like azaleas and rhododendrons and wisteria and laurel. A man looking for berries finds huckleberries and strawberries and raspberries. A man wanting to take a look at flowers finds lilies and bloodroot and phlox and the colorfully named lady slipper or bleeding heart or Indian paintbrush or

Devil's walking stick or bee balm. On the other hand, a man who
has more serious things (or simply fauna instead of flora) on his
mind can find foxes, skunks, opossums, racoons, rabbits, beavers
— or frogs and toads and turtles and snakes, plenty of all of
them, and up in the sky, plenty of birds, some that stay year
round, and many that come and stop and leave during and in
between the seasons.

Men who till the soil, who live intimately with a given kind of
terrain, whatever its features, are men who share more than their
particular "culture" or "life-style" may at first glance seem to
indicate. Perhaps most of all there is the vastness of the land, its
size, its expanse, its ability to seem limitless and all-powerful.
The sun rises out of the land tentatively, then with increasing
assurance and influence; the sun goes down into the same land
flaming, even if weak enough, at last, to be stared at. The days
and seasons come and go, but the land stands firm. Snow may
cover the land, water drench it, wind dust it off or try to carry it
off, lightning seem to jab at it, tornadoes bear down on it
mightily and fearfully, the sun warm it up, draw it out, excite it;
whatever happens, the land remains, survives, *is*. Yes, in the
thirties America had its "dust bowl," and its earth still shows the
ravages of man; but by and large the people in this book, plundered and needy though they may also be, live on rich, fertile
land, yielding and bountiful, so blessed as to be for decades and
decades almost defiantly productive, even in the face of preda-
tory man's greed and carelessness, which have been compensated
for only recently and in certain places by chemicals and water
pumped in from afar.

Most of Appalachia and the rural South and for that matter the
rural North is graced with a wonderful, life-giving, utterly reassuring abundance of water, so that the irrigating canals and
pipes that migrants know in central Florida are not part of a
desperate, do-or-die stand, such as a farmer might have to take in
Arizona or parts of California. Water beats down upon the Appalachian mountains, and all over them one sees the result: gorges
and ravines and passageways pouring forth that water; rivers
never very low and in spring almost invariably flooded; rivers

that compete with one another, join and separate, fight for streams and draw competitively upon tributaries. Water comes to Mississippi and Louisiana from the greatest of American rivers, but water comes openly and secretly even to Florida, whose land stretches further south than any other state, whose land also can experience seasons of bad, worrisome drought. As is the case with the Carolinas, sand reefs and generally narrow, elongated islands hug both of Florida's shores, thus making for a whole series of lakes, lagoons, bays and splendid, restful harbors. The state is laced with rivers and lakes, including the very large Lake Okeechobee, near which thousands of migrant farmers spend their winters at work with the crops. The lakes are frequently connected by subterranean channels, and for that matter isolated subterranean springs and streams can be found all over the state. The springs and streams eventually become rivers, and through a system of man-made canals farmers try hard to exert a degree of control over the natural largesse.

More often than not, mountaineers and tenant farmers and migrants can be found living near that water, near creeks and not far from lakes and quite close to the waters of any number of rivers. The mountain settlements are squeezed into a valley a river has carved out, or pressed close to a creek whose banks actually provide a clearing, a way down, a road out of the wilderness; or settlements are crammed near a lake, where a hungry migrant or tenant farmer can search for fish, which is one thing that costs nothing. "We never lose sight of water, and we never lose sight of the sky, and we never lose sight of the land, that's how we live," I was told by a tenant farmer who lives in what history books variously call the Black Belt, the Black Prairie, the Cotton Belt. He actually lives in Alabama, whose land is several colors; black yes, but also red and sand-brown and mixed with green moss and the whiteness of chalk. Along the Gulf of Mexico and some miles north — a so-called "timber belt" — the land is sandy but quite responsive to fertilizers. Then comes the famous black soil: laced with limestone and marl formations; essentially devoid of sand; especially suited to the production of cotton and grains. A little farther north one finds land rich in minerals, rich for instance in the iron that makes Birmingham a steel city. And, finally, Alabama's land becomes part of the Tennessee valley, and there contains red clays and dark loams which, again, can nourish grains and vegetables.

It is, of course, easy for a visitor like me to work himself up into a lather about such things, to become almost euphoric at the variety of trees or birds or types of soil; about striking waterfalls and rapid streams and sluggish rivers and wide estuaries and bayous dripping with Spanish moss; about lonely herons that rise out of mist only to fall quickly and just as quickly disappear. All of that is the heady and maybe corrupt stuff of southern nostalgia or Appalachian romanticism. All of that would seem to border on the bizarre or the Gothic and even the outrageous when it is made to accompany a discussion of how, for example, an extremely poor migrant, most of the time hungry, and without money and maybe even a roof of any kind over his head, manages barely to stay alive. Tourists may hear about those plateaus and mountaintops, those headwaters and ebb tides, those rich clays and silts and peats and gravelly or sandy spots, and all the lovely flowers and shrubs they bear. Tourists, too, may hear about soft white sands and a coast's shallow indentations, which become inviting bays; and tourists love to hear about mild, equable weather or low, marshy tracts that offer surprisingly good fishing. All the while terribly forsaken and just about indigent families live nearby, nearer-by in fact than most tourists will ever realize; and those families have little time to care about such matters, such attractions, or so we might reasonably believe.

Certainly it is true that migrant farm workers don't look upon their experiences the way casual travelers might. Nor do sharecroppers wax lyrical about the South, that haunting, mysterious, strangely uncommon region which has both defied and invited descriptions all through American history. Mountaineers have their ballads to sing, their guitars to "pick" away at, but they don't stand on ridges or the edges of plateaus or way up on peaks in order to get breathtaking views, which are then photographed and thereby carried home, to be shown one evening after another. No, in Logan County, West Virginia, mountaineers don't find themselves quaint; and in Adams County, Mississippi, tenant farmers don't burble about those antebellum homes, or gush in pride and awe at the river, the great god of a river; and in Collier County, Florida, or Palm Beach County, Florida, migrant workers don't join hands with conservationists and worry about wildlife in the beautiful, ever spectacular Everglades.

And yet, I have, I think, learned a few things from these people. I have learned something more than how they live and scarcely stay alive. I have learned what little margin, what little leeway I was prepared to give them. I came ready to comprehend their suffering, their misery, the injustice of their position in our society, and I came prepared to write down my indignation and rage and horror. But I am not sure I was prepared to ask myself a single thing that would upset the central beliefs I brought with me to the "Black Belt" and those migrant camps and the Cumberland Mountains. I believed that these groups are the poorest of our poor, the most overcome, the most broken, the most bowed down; that they are sunk, lost, tired, discouraged; that they are faced every day with dreary work, if indeed any work, and with miserable living conditions and with varying degrees and kinds of hunger, malnutrition and illness; that they are at the mercy of things, compelled to face life passively, fearfully, even automatically; and that finally, if they deserve sympathy and concern and the conscientious efforts of the rest of the nation in their behalf, they also have to be looked at directly and without illusions, for their own sake. There is no use trying to fool ourselves about the seriousness of their problems or the damage done to them over the generations by the circumstances that not only surround but utterly envelop their lives, and there is no use, either, indulging ourselves, by turning such people into storybook characters, full of nobility and interesting, intriguing passions and charming or innocent (hence particularly enviable) virtues.

And yet — I have to say that again — a good portion of this book will, I hope, spell out what goes, what has to go, after "and yet," even as still other parts of the book will confirm quite grimly what has just preceded those two words — confirm human misery, confirm the waste, the outrageous and unconscionable

waste of lives, and particularly of the energy and talent and spirit
that these lives have to offer. Still, right here in the first chapter
of this book I want to quote the words of a man who understands
a lot about the land and a lot about his life — a lot that I found
(and maybe still find) hard to fathom and comprehend, but even
harder to accept and fit into my scheme of things, my political
ideas, my psychological theories and my social values. He works
on the land in between what I suppose could be called the rural
South and Appalachia, in a broad valley at the foot of the hill
country of Tennessee. Although no one man can speak for the
three groups I am concerned with here, this man comes as close
as any in combining elements that belong to all of these groups.
He is a tenant farmer; he practices a kind of sharecropping, by no
means the worst, most exploitative kind, and finally, not uncommonly, he has two close relatives who have joined the eastern
migrant "stream." The man I call a yeoman, a sturdy and almost
fierce small farmer, talks about matters other than his "problems,"
and those other matters, I would argue, ought to get recorded at
the very start of things — much earlier, alas, than I came to grasp
them in the course of my work.

I approach his land (*his* it is, because he so feels it to be) on a
dusty path rather than a road. I get annoyed, because the path is
winding, a bit wind-raked, pitted and creviced. I look for shade;
it is warm and very muggy. I have been there before, but now
that all the crops are "down" — which means all the seeds are in
the earth, the weeds have yet to appear, and time seems a little
more available — there is every hope of the "big talk" the yeoman
himself had once promised we would one day have. This was the
day, and he was ready. He is especially talkative compared to
others who do his kind of work, and for that I am grateful,
though a little suspicious. Maybe silence is all that can be trusted
by me — one who is so at the mercy of words. I am just starting
out, and I have, after all, been warned again and again that this
man should be glum, burdened, restrained, anything but generous with his thoughts. Instead he seems unexpectedly plain-
spoken and outgoing. I have noticed that he drinks rather
copiously, and in ostensible jest but out of genuine candor and

friendliness, he had offered to take me to a still, a place where moonshine is made, "the first one you'll find upon leaving Alabama and coming up the road into the hills of Tennessee, yes sir." Perhaps the drink explains it, then, his voluble, blustery, open, giving manner.

So, as I listened over a long day and several others to the yeoman talking, I wondered: what drives him on, this expansive man, who has so much to be sad about, but insists, protests, protests *too much*, his pleasure in taking on — all of nature, it would seem? And why does he not face up to the substance of his life, the social and economic vulnerability that he experiences, the overwhelming difficulties that drag on, that will not, maybe never can, let go of him? In the next chapter (and perhaps all through this book) I shall discuss some of that; but now is the time to let him talk about what he gets out of life, rather than what he wants out of it or what monstrous evils it most assuredly does visit upon him.

"I can't say I'm pleased with everything," he will say and repeat from time to time. "And yet," he adds and will stubbornly add from time to time — until at last, years after this first conversation, I will have finally been stopped in my tracks and made to hear, made to realize. "And yet, even if you're not pleased, you can still be glad for what you have to be glad for, not much that's big and important, I know, but there's something, there's something good we can tell you we have." Later on he became a little less "defensive," a little less boastful; but now, almost a decade since we first met, I have yet to hear him go back on that kind of affirmation — only progressively expand on it, while at the same time admitting to the obstacles he has to contend with every day of his life.

"I can't say it's not a struggle; it is, a bad one. If I had to choose, I'd not choose this life — maybe another one that's easier. I only know this one here, though. How can you go picking out another kind of life if you only can have the one you have? I can't say I'm a happy man here; we have it bad a lot. I can't say I mind my work, though, and if I had to choose, like I say, I don't think I'd know what to do but tell the Lord that I'll take this one, this life, all over again, with the pain and all. Every morning I wake up and I'm thinking to myself, what should I do today? We have the few chickens and I go and check on them and see if they've given us a few eggs, and I feed them of course. There will be a day or two, and more sometimes, when it's a lot easier to feed the chickens than us.

"I have to get the water, and that comes next. I take my oldest boy with me. He talks about going to a city one day, but I have an answer for him. I say: go, go North, go to Chicago or a place like that, and you'll see, oh will you, and you may not come back here, and you may find yourself a job with good money, but you'll pine for it here and you'll be sorry and you'll ache; you'll hurt, real bad it'll be. I'm not trying to scare him. It sounds like I am, but I'm not. We're born to this land here, and it's no good when you leave. I did once; I was in the Army. I know what I could have done. I know how I could have stayed there, in the state of Indiana, up toward Chicago. But I asked myself if I wanted to be in a place I didn't want to be in — even with a check from the welfare people, or a job if I could get one — or if I wanted to be back here, doing what I was taught by my daddy to do. You can see how I answered myself.

"Now I have the same kind of talks with my boy, especially in the early morning. We're out there walking over to the pump before the sun is all the way up. He'll say to me — he's tired and just waking up, I know — that if we lived in a city, someplace big you know, there would be water there to turn on and we'd be able to sleep later. Yes, true; I admit to him when he's right. I tell him that he's right. But I say, look Jimmy, there are some places where you like to get up, or at least it's not so bad, and there are other places where you could sleep all morning and have a million dollars lying near you, and still you wouldn't want to go out and take a walk there. Maybe with a million dollars I would go anywhere. Jimmy told me I was sure wrong saying I'd turn my back on a million dollars. But he knows what I'm telling him: for us it's a choice we have, between going away or else staying here and not seeing much money at all, but working on the land, like we know how to do, and living here, where you can feel you're you, and no one else, and there isn't the next guy pushing on you and kicking you and calling you every bad name there ever was. If you go, that's what you go to. If you go you can't hardly breathe, there are so many people, and you never see the sun, you *never* do. I used to wake up, when I was in the city on leave, military leave, and I'd ask myself, where is that sun, where does it hide itself from you?

"I've noticed that by the time we're on the way back from the well, Jimmy is persuaded, yes sir. He'll agree with me; he'll say he likes it, going out into the air, first thing in the morning, and toting the water. By the time we've done that, the chickens have eaten up everything and they hear us and they cackle away for more, but they're not going to get it. Momma is all waken up, and she's working to do the best she can for us, for breakfast; and there'll be days when we have eggs and toast and grits and everything, and there'll be other days when it's coffee, thin as can be, and nothing in it, even for the baby. Yes, it gets bad — in winter especially. We make enough to get by, but there's no spare, and if there's an extra expense, then we don't have a single thing to fall back upon. I can't ask for anything. I can't call on anyone — except for God, and sometimes He'll answer. He'll send the minister over with a package for us.

"No matter, though. I always have my work. You can feed off that, you know. In the winter it's the chickens and keeping us supplied with wood and water and all like that. The rest of the year it's much more; it's doing everything, practically anything you could think of. After breakfast I go out and start with the planting, or the weeding or the harvesting; it depends on what season you're in. I know my land, I'll say I do. I know the weather, too. When I've come back with the water I can tell my wife and children what the day will be like. I can say it's going to be a day of sun, all the way; or I can say the clouds are there, thick as can be, but don't be fooled, because they're going to be burned right up, sent running like a pack of squirrels by that foxy old sun; or I can say we're in for it, a heavy day of clouds, or the good rain, lots of it I hope, or maybe just a few drops that won't add up to anything.

"The weather helps make the land what it is, you see. Good weather, any farming man needs that. But to begin with he'll need soil he can work on; and you stop anybody within a hundred or two miles of this place and they'll all agree that hereabouts we've been blessed by Almighty God with good farmland. I talk to my land, you know. I ask it to be good; each year at the start I do. And each year at the end I say, thank you and amen. It's like being in church and talking with God. It's His land, anyway, and I do believe if we could ask Him He'd be in favor of us thanking Him — thanking Him through a little whisper or two while we're out there doing the work. If God sends sun and rain and He's already given you your land that's good, then there's just one more thing needed, and it's not hard to guess what it is: work. Jimmy laughs when I tell him we've got to go and see if we're up to God, if we can do the work He'd expect from us. Jimmy thinks his old daddy is starting to get *real* old, and be like his granddaddy was when he was at the end and ready to pass on. But I've always believed that when we leave our house and start in out there on the land, we're meeting God and doing all we can to show Him we can hear Him and we can believe in Him; and the proof is that He's there, helping us with the gift of His land, you see, and His sun you see, and His good, good rain, His precious rain that He sends us just when we need it and sometimes in-between and to spare. It's up to us to go out and do our best by Him, and work on His land, and take good care that we get everything we can out of it, all the vegetables and the cotton, and the flowers — I'm not forgetting them. My wife takes them over to town and we sell them. We get a good price on them. I hear they go to some man in Birmingham, maybe it is, and he sells them again to anyone who wants to have flowers and likes flowers — and the man who buys them and takes them home probably wishes he was out here and growing them and not in Birmingham, Alabama, paying his dollar for having a look at them, a little look, before the poor flowers go and die.

"When I come home it's a tired man that walks in that door. I'm hungry, because I don't eat all day. It doesn't go down good in my stomach, food doesn't, when I'm sweating and bend-

ing and my back is bent over and my front is all caved in. I get
pains, bad ones all across my middle and up to my chest. We
don't have a doctor near here, and I'm not one to feel sorry for
myself. I told my wife I'd stop having food during the day, and
I'd feel better; she said I was dead wrong, but I wasn't. It's been
two years or so, two summers, since I went back in the middle of
the day for some of her soup that she makes, or the potatoes. She
holds it all for me, and then I'll eat and eat at the end of the day,
and it's like I say, I don't get the pains then, nor at the start of
the day, with breakfast.

"I'll stop when it's hot, bad hot, in the summer. I'll stop around
the middle of the day, when the sun is high — maybe going
down some, but only a little. I have my tree, my favorite tree. It's
my bed away from bed, my wife says; that's what she calls it, my
bed away from bed. And she's all correct, every word. I can doze
off. I can lie there and look up to the sky and have my talk with
God, just like I was in church, or just like I was up there, and
taken in to see Him and hear His judgment, like we all will, one
day. I can lie there and ask myself: James, what have you done
this morning? Then I can say: James, you've done what's waiting
out there for you to do, which is all anyone could have told you
to do and expect it to be finished. The next thing, I can ask: what
is ahead for the afternoon? And you know, I'll have it running
through my mind, as if I had a television camera in my head, and
it could take pictures of what is *going* to happen, way before a
man gets himself up and lifts his arms to start. Lying on my back
over there I have the tree over me, better than any curtain you'll
ever buy, and when I want to turn off what crosses through my
own head, and listen in to someone else, I just do. I say: James,
I'm real tired of you and all the thoughts that's going through
you to worry you. I say: James, there are others in God's Kingdom. The next thing you know, I hear a bird up there, talking to
another bird, and they're just going and going, maybe arguing or
maybe telling each other that it's a good day, and to be glad
for it.

"We have good soil here, and the birds know it; just like you
and I, they try to find the best places to stop and rest. It's fine,

hard soil, but not too hard. There are plenty of worms, and birds like them and I like them too, because I need worms for fishing. That's what I do when I have time; and we need those fish. My wife some of the time says that if it wasn't for the fish I catch, we'd all be gone by now. She's wrong, but it helps to bring her home a good catch. There's hunting a little way north of here in some woods, but I don't have the time. I don't have a car, either. With a car I could go hunting up in the hills. But I put all my time and energy into this land that I've got to use, that's mine to use, and I'm not ready to feel sorry for myself, no I'm not.

"I don't like feeling sorry for myself, and I don't like my wife to get doing that, nor my children. Nor do I like others, anyone else, to say: isn't it sad, how bad off they are out on that farm. We have people who will come by and try to get you feeling all bad about yourself and how you live. I don't like it, not having much money, and being a lot down and out half the year — that's through the winter and the first part of the spring — but I get by, and I'd like to keep trying to get by. I'd like help, of course. I admit to that. I'd like the government people to help the poor, small man, and not only the big boys, the big farmers, who own the Agricultural Department, there in Washington, yes they do. One of the people here, an agricultural agent we have, told me that it's true, that they have a big Agricultural Department in Washington, and it gives men with plantations, the real large ones, lots and lots of money for *not* planting their crops. I came home and told all my family that there might be a lot of hope for us: one day someone out of Washington will discover us, here in Tennessee, and he'll say that we can have plenty of money, the green bills, all we need to live on, if we just sit here and don't lift a finger, just look at the land and don't plant crops in it. But I'll tell you something: I couldn't do it, be here and not do my growing. I'd have to leave here, I would. I'd leave so fast no one would believe I was gone; that's what I'd do if I was told I shouldn't plant, I shouldn't work on my land, and if I don't then I'll be paid for doing nothing.

"I'd about die if I didn't have my work. I wouldn't know what to do with the time; the hours would pass by, one after the next, and I'd be here, sitting and looking at my land with my legs still and my arms just hanging down and I'd be staring — I would be like a scarecrow, that's what. I wouldn't have any life in me left. The money would be welcome, but I know I'd soon die. And the worst of it, the real worst of it, would be knowing that the land is just sitting there, lying out there, not being touched, not being asked to do anything, not being planted, not coming up with the shoots — just those weeds, that are always there. I wouldn't be pushing the shoots along; I wouldn't be telling them to grow and get bigger and try the world out, because it's not bad, what with sun to keep you warm and a good shower you get every once in a while. There will be days when I can almost see my little shoots growing and they're weak and tender, but they're strong, too. It won't be long, I know, before they'll be hardier; they'll be tough, and no weeds can get them, not then. No weeds ever win out around here — not with me around to look at things and do what has to be done. There are times when I wish the good Lord would say to Himself that He should treat us all like we're in His Garden, and He should help the good people along, and take up the bad people, the weeds, and put them someplace else — maybe up on one of the stars, way away. Then the weeds could have another chance there, to start over and not turn into weeds, you might say. I don't want people to be killed, as if they could *only* be weeds and nothing else!"

He doesn't want to harm anyone, not even people who have no great respect for him, and indeed do him and his kind no good, perhaps a lot of harm. "His kind" belongs to the South and to Appalachia both, to a whole half of a nation, really. It so happens that on several counts he is rather in between: he lives at the edge of the rural South, but at the edge of Appalachia; not far from two good-sized cities yet very much in a rural setting; he is a light-skinned black man who appears to be a nicely tanned white man — and, finally, his speech includes elements of the mountaineer's language, of the white yeoman's, and of the black tenant farmer's. Those who have spent any length of time in counties like Buncombe County or Yancey County in North Carolina (to move a little east from Tennessee) will know what I mean.

Certainly he is not Everyman; in this instance, though, I believe a particular person comes rather close to speaking for three large and scattered "groups," which are different in many respects but also alike in many ways. Among migrants, sharecroppers and mountaineers one finds black people and white people — and various shades of both. They are people who stay put in the South with a vengeance, or they wander without respite over a whole wide expanse of this nation. For all the distinctions to be made, the classifications and comparisons, the "cross-cultural" similarities or the psychological and sociological differences, what is shared among these people might be called something of the spirit: a closeness to the land, a familiarity with it, and despite the suffering and sacrifice and rage and hurt and pain, a constant regard for that land, an attachment to that land, a kind of love.

For years I have heard that love emerge, even in the midst of bitterness and frustration. I have watched migrants try to stop being migrants, become instead city folk; and I have watched sharecroppers head joyfully and eagerly North, glad to be rid of plantation owners and foremen and sheriffs, the whole miserable, mean lot of them. I have watched mountaineers slip through mountain passes and valleys toward Dayton, say, or Chicago — all too willingly, because work and the food money can buy is far better than constant and unappeased hunger. As they get ready to leave, those many men and women and children, they deny having any regrets. *And yet* they do: they are losing something; they feel low and sad; more precisely, they anticipate the yearning they may later have, the homesickness, the lovesickness, the sense of bereavement. Dispossessed, they have to leave; they ought to leave. It was an awful life. *And yet* — one more time: "If I don't have to go, maybe it'll be my sons. They'll be the ones to cry and not me. They'll be happy, I know. They'll be looking ahead, I know. But it'll be a shame for us to leave, my family; it's a shame when you leave the only thing you've known, your land — and remember, it's land that's seen you trying and that's tried back, tried to give you all it could. There's no land up there, just people and buildings. I know that. That's too bad. That's the way it has to be; I know it. I do. But I don't have to like it. I don't. I never will, even if I have to say good-bye and go on up the road myself, away from here, from my land."

So far he and hundreds of thousands of others are still there, still migrant farmers, still sharecroppers or tenant farmers, still living up those mountain hollows. They all look for changes, hope for them, dream of them — and at the same time stand their ground, and more literally, walk it, walk that ground and work it, and stay with it and stay on it, and know it as a friend, a giver, a lover, a great protagonist that is ready to bargain, that is ready to resist, that is *there*. The American land.

II

THE METHOD

THIS book contains several elements: first, the words of others, their ideas and feelings, their statements, their assertions, their exclamations; second, my own effort to put in words what I have observed and considered important, whether inspiring, troubling, confusing, or merely worth quiet interest and reflection; and, finally, some discussion and analysis — I suppose those are the two words — of the sharpness of vision and the coherence of mind I have seen and heard others demonstrate. All three elements work together to convey not only *what is* (itself rather a daunting task) but how men and women and children, *who are,* deal with the things of this world, the "reality" or "environment" one hears so many psychiatrists talk about.

I speak as a physician and as a child psychiatrist, and as one who has tried to study not only the illnesses and problems that people have, but also their *lives.* The lives described in this book certainly are ill-favored and maybe misshapen; they must on occasion have to be acknowledged as forbidding or grotesque or ruined almost beyond repair; but they may also give cause for wonder, for more admiration than sorrow. Lives, as opposed to problems, may puzzle the fixed notions of theorists, while at the same time adding confirmation to what has been revealed by such keenly sensitive (if "methodologically untrained") observers as Dostoevski or Zola, Orwell or Agee, who have managed, regardless of time and place, to set down something both comprehensible and enduring about human beings the rest of us have merely pigeonholed as "peasants" or "the rural proletariat" or "the lower class" or, more recently, "the culturally deprived" or "the disadvantaged" — or, here and now, "migrants, share-croppers and mountaineers."[1]

We hunger after certainty. We want "orientations" and "con-ceptual frameworks" and carefully spelled out "methodological approaches." We want things "clarified"; we want a "theoretical structure," so that life's inconsistencies and paradoxes will some-how yield to man's need for a scrupulous kind of "order." For some it is a matter of so-called "objectivity": man's behavior at some "level" can be made utterly straightforward, can be submitted to the linear workings of a particular psychological or sociological theory. For others there may be different reasons to prune things down, forget this fact and emphasize that line of thinking; I refer, of course, to the needs of the politically active person, who wants changes and works for those changes, and who requires all "data," pure though they may be, to pass the muster of a given set of purposes and "objectives."(The resemblance to "objective" is one more irony in our path.) We want to do things *for* people, *with* them, even, alas, *to* them. Therefore, we see what we want to see, and find important. We then justify in any number of ways our reason for not looking at a particular side of a problem: it is "irrelevant," or a waste of time, or politically inexpedient, or not the business of a social scientist or of a doctor. What *really* matters, each of us insists, is one or another emphasis, one or another truth.

Meanwhile, as American southern writers like William Faulk-ner and Flannery O'Connor and James Agee[2] almost drove themselves and their readers crazy trying to say, there are many truths — so many that no one mind or viewpoint or discipline or profession can possibly encompass and comprehend them all, nor do justice to them in words, even intricate and specialized ones, or "neutral" ones.

I mention all of this, none of it new or especially startling, because I want to make it very clear, as clear as I possibly can, how I have gone about doing the work described in this book — which means with what purposes in my mind and what ideas or assumptions as guides. Most especially I want to say, loud and clear, what I have not done, what this book does not lay claim to be, does not make a pretense of offering to its readers. I would suggest that some reasonably representative and suggestive voices are to be found in these pages. The voices are those of migrant farm workers and sharecroppers or tenant farmers and mountaineers — though theirs are not the only voices — and the hopes and fears expressed are also theirs. My own voice is constantly present, even when others speak, and so are some of my own hopes and fears.

Now why do I have to intrude upon this narrative at all, with chapters like this one and the one preceding? Why not let the people speak for themselves? Why interrupt them? Again, during the more general and analytic sections of the book, why let these people interrupt the author? My answer is that as a child psychiatrist I had to learn how important it is not only to "detect" something going on in a child's mind, but to go through certain experiences *with* the child in order to be of help. The doctor does not investigate a case out of scientific curiosity only; he is there to *help*. Clinical "experiences," like a game of tennis, amount to an exchange, a back-and-forth movement of ideas and impressions, a shared earnestness and eagerness. And often on both sides of the net those "experiences," hard to corral in the confines of a particular kind of technical language, happen simultaneously to both physician and patient: a lump in the throat, a moment of vehemence, an outburst of apprehension, a spell of silence, a passionate conviction that must be given utterance, an increasing persuasion that "things" are going well between the doctor and the patient, the little him or little her and "the man who's still a baby and has toys all over his office," as I once heard a child psychiatrist described.

Increasingly these past years psychiatrists and psychoanalysts (some of them, at least) have learned to look upon people as citizens of a nation, as members of a given society, and *particular* members at that, not merely as members of an Oedipal family. That is to say, we become irate, hurt, worried, murderously worked up, decisively bored, or tired and sad because of events that actually take place in the economic market or the political arena. The exchanges we once had with our parents, or continue to have with ourselves in the form of fantasies or nightmares, are not the only things that upset the mind, or drive it to distraction. It is one thing, however, to ask that the windows of clinical offices be opened, so as to be rid of stale, musty air; it is quite another thing to abandon what offices in hospitals and clinics all over the world have furnished us: countless hours of experience, the pursuit of a method of observation, the acquisition of a special if limited kind of coherence — the acquisition, also, of a sensibility the doctor must work for in himself and hopefully bring about in his patients. Although I myself have in a physical sense for the most part left those offices, yet in all the work described in this book I have been working as a clinician. Not as a clinician alone, but perhaps more desperately than ever, trying to do what I have learned to do, been trained to do, in the course of studying medicine and psychiatry.[3]

I take pains to mention all of that because I do not wish to set my kind of work up against more traditional forms of psychiatry in a polemical way; nor do I wish to use the people in this book as a foil or a means of assault on other people — in this case the thousands and thousands of patients who seek psychiatric help in child-guidance clinics or outpatient clinics throughout the nation.[4] The crying needs of one group of people do not make any less real the thoroughly different needs of another group. If one argues that priorities must be established, I would agree; but I am wary of those (perhaps on occasion myself included) who would use a migrant farmer's distress as an excuse to attack and bully and abuse another worried, fearful human being who happens to come from the "middle class" and might consider himself or herself persistently "neurotic." Suffering knows no barriers of color or class. Suffering — real, substantial, hard to bear — can be found among all people, everywhere. This may sound banal, but there is a peculiar arrogance practiced by some of us who talk so proudly about our "work" with "the poor": we praise them to high heaven, and denounce everyone else either casually or mercilessly. There are, I fear, many kinds of exploitation. Certain people in this book — plantation owners or sheriffs — betray by their words the economic and political kind. It may be considerably harder for some of the rest of us to see other forms of inhumanity; it may even be hard for some of us to see what is nearest at hand — our smugness, our blind spots, our self-importance, our presumptuousness, our condescension toward people whose cause we claim to support, our bustling energetic self-righteousness.

I am taking a long time at all this, I know; but it is not an easy subject to explore, at least not for me. Long ago Freud urged all of us who would know how others think and feel to look at our own reactions and responses and styles of thought or feeling. I am not writing an autobiography, nor do I wish this chapter to become an exercise in "self-analysis" or an examination of the "countertransference" at work under particular professional circumstances. I am, however, trying to alert myself and those who read these pages to a danger I certainly do not feel any of us (myself emphatically included) can escape when we spend long stretches of time with people who at once make us feel sad, indignant, giving, resentful, and God knows how many other emotions. What are we to *do*, we begin to ask. All well and good that we feel so inclined; a lot of people had better start asking such a question if there is to be an end to political and economic injustices.

The trouble is that we don't only start asking questions. Something else begins to take place, also. The resentment and outrage we feel for the sake of the people whose lives we have come to witness spills over. The first targets are sheriffs and growers and plantation owners but soon those individuals are not enough. Then the entire nation gets criticized, and more specifically, a "power structure" is blamed, and not once in a while, but incessantly. There are, to be sure, many "power structures," all over the world, and many of them deserve criticism and more criticism, the strongest possible kind that an aroused and indignant public can mobilize. That said, one has to turn inward, and ask oneself whether the suffering a migrant farmer experiences justifies a refusal to look at the various "conditions" that tie others down and prevent them from knowing or caring about migrant farmers — conditions that also allow cruelty to flow not only from the "power structure" on downward, but from all of us to each other, from migrants to migrants, from sharecroppers to sharecroppers, from mountaineers to mountaineers.

Yes, one has to add quickly, even if such things are true, even if men are cursed by their "nature," there is an explicit political and economic "evil" that accounts for the way a sharecropper lives, say, in the Mississippi Delta. Still, I have to ask myself whether the situation in the Delta and my desire to see sweeping changes take place there require of me unequivocal bitterness and contempt toward those who do not happen to share my particular concerns.

Maybe it comes to this: as a citizen I am appalled by the injustice I see about, injustice that is consolidated, injustice that is handed down as a birthright over the generations, injustice whose continuing presence disgraces all human beings everywhere; but as an observer intent on seeing what exactly goes into making up those lives (uprooted lives, brutally exploited lives, dazed lives, unfamiliar lives so far as most of us are concerned) I would only be adding to the injustice just mentioned, were I to translate clear-cut economic and political wrongs into the same kind of psychological alternatives, and paint for you portraits of brutalized and desperate workers, set upon daily and viciously by rich, savage, heartless plunderers or their lackeys. There have been times when I have thought that to be the case, or at least wanted to think so; and I do not now bring up doubts and reservations in order to gloss over the misery and the exploitation one finds in the United States. No, I find it an awful disgrace that men and women whom I have known for so long, and their children, whom I have seen born, helped to be born, who belong to my children's generation — that these children, and *their* children will live (I have no reason to doubt it) a similarly vulnerable, harsh, humiliating existence.

Nevertheless, faced with the most dreary circumstances imaginable, with the humiliating day-to-day existence I just spoke of, not a few individuals, more of them certainly than I once believed, manage to find for themselves moments of satisfaction, accomplishment and self-respect. Those moments can become stabilized in a lasting kind of wry detachment or a plucky feeling of confidence that is not only fatuous or self-deluding but justifies itself all the time through deeds done, statements made, unfavorable odds at least confronted if not overcome. If the work I do has any justification whatever, it comes, I believe, from the capacity a clinician must have to distinguish between the objective conditions that constitute a disease and the range of subjective responses to a disease that particular men, women and children make. In so doing, they, of course, affect the way they perceive and manage their symptoms. There is no point saying that things aren't really so bad because people under great stress, involved in one crisis after another, summon incredible resources of mind and heart and spirit, and emerge finally, in spite of it all, as undestroyed, even if terribly wounded. There is no reason, either, to insist, because things are very, very bad, that any reparative and even redemptive efforts an observer may find are utterly beside the real point, namely that *more* is needed: more bread, more running water, more electricity, more jobs that offer decent wages.

Somehow we all must learn to know one another. I should imagine that a number of the people who speak out in this book feel that they are misunderstood by their friends and supporters and natural allies as well as by their obvious or thinly disguised enemies. Certainly I ought to say that I myself have been gently and on occasion firmly or sternly reminded how absurd some of my questions have been, how misleading or smug were the assumptions they convey. The fact is that again and again I have seen a poor, a lowly, an illiterate migrant worker wince a little at something I have said or done, smile a little nervously, glare and pout, wonder a little in his eyes about me and my purposes, and through his grimace let me know the disapproval he surely has felt; and yes, the criticism he also feels, the sober, thought-out criticism, perhaps not easily put into words — though eventually that will happen, too.

What I have just been discussing has to do with my "method," which I feel inside me, after all, maybe in my bones rather than my head. The work itself is, thank God, easier to describe without a lot of sweaty, worried, and twisted declarations, retractions and qualifications. In 1958 I lived in Mississippi, and it was then that I began the first part of this research. I started making trips to the Delta, at first sight-seeing trips; later on, as racial conflict became more open and prominent in the state, I found it harder and harder not to notice something else besides large, pleasant plantations or cotton growing as far as the eye could reach or levees holding back the great river. In the first volume of *Children of Crisis*[5] I have described what eventually happened, the intersection, really, of my professional life and my personal life with the social and political changes that had come upon the South in the late 1950's. Here it is important to stress that when I started seeing particular black and white people caught up in a phase of historical change I also became determined to do something else as well: observe not only how people participate in a social revolution or how others oppose such changes, but also observe how people live and conduct their affairs and try to make do — those who live out from day to day their own version of history by trying to deal with particular burdens; historical, social, political, and awful economic burdens.

As I indicated in the preface to the first volume of *Children of Crisis* and indicated again in this volume's preface, it was almost inevitable that I would ask myself how sharecroppers and tenant farmers and migrant workers *live*. The families I first knew and studied in New Orleans in the early 1960's, families whose children pioneered school desegregation against fierce and unremitting opposition, had come to the city from rural Louisiana and Mississippi. In each family's case there were relatives who worked the land, who "sharecropped," who rented a few acres and tried to survive on what they grew each year — grew to sell and grew to eat. In some instances a brother or a cousin had left altogether, left not for New Orleans, but left for Florida, to which large numbers of field hands from all over the rural South have gone in search of work and money. I would hear about it: the gradual collapse of yet another small farm; the gradual mechanization of a plantation in this or that parish of Louisiana or county of Mississippi; the gradual loss of what little share-croppers or tenant farmers can fall back upon; their increasingly urgent need to move someplace; and the choice various share-croppers or tenant farmers made — such as to "try Florida, try harvesting the crops over there, and maybe moving around some, to where the crops are, standing and waiting on people to take them all in, like the beans that are there, and cukes, I guess, and like that." There in fact, word for word, was the first description I ever heard of the migrant life; it was offered to me in New Orleans, in February of 1960, now over a decade ago. A mother and housewife was talking about her sister. I never met that particular woman, but I did make my first trip to Belle Glade, Florida (and nearby towns) in 1963, there to see where thou-sands of migrant workers live in the winter and work as har-vesters. By that time I had come to know a good deal of what such people leave behind, the rural landscape of the "Black Belt." By that time I had started visiting with particular frequency (two, maybe three times a week) some ten families, four share-croppers, six tenant farmers.

I would in 1963 begin to do the same with migrant families, start visiting over the months and the years ten families; and eventually start following them up the coast, up North: all through Georgia and through the Carolinas and all through Vir-ginia, and Maryland and New Jersey and Delaware, and finally through New York or Connecticut or even Massachusetts or Maine — through, it so happens, most of the original thirteen colonies.[6] I would in 1963 also start the third part of this study by making several visits to Asheville, and Burnsville, North Carolina, at first in order to find out how school desegregation took place in a small city and rural community of the South in contrast to large cities like New Orleans and Atlanta, and later in order to meet families in the hills of western North Carolina, whose lives in many respects both resembled and were a contrast to the lives of those sharecropper and migrant families I was getting to know.

In 1965 I extended my work in Appalachia further. I started going to eastern Kentucky and West Virginia as a consultant to

the Appalachian Volunteers, a group of young activists who for
years have tried to make political dents that are hard to make in
the region.[7] In a sense my association with the Appalachian
Volunteers very much resembles the work I did during the early
sixties in Mississippi and Georgia with the students who staged
one sit-in after another, rode on "freedom rides" and eventually
initiated the well-known Mississippi Summer Project of 1964. I
have taken up and analyzed all that work in the first volume of
Children of Crisis and have no wish here to discuss the most
recent turns and twists of the South's (not only the black man's
but the white man's) thoroughly unfinished racial struggle. I will
simply say that in the course of my work with the AV's, as they
have come to be called up the hollows, I attempted to be an
observer, a student, a doctor and a child psychiatrist trying to
learn a little; but at times I very much wanted to stand beside
those who cannot tolerate what goes on in many of those
Appalachian counties. I have also written at length in the first
volume of *Children of Crisis* (and elsewhere) about "participant
observation" and there is no need to go over all of that here. I can
only add that for me to work with the Appalachian Volunteers, or
in a different way with the National Sharecroppers Fund, the
National Advisory Committee on Farm Labor, the South Florida
Migrant Legal Services, Inc. has been at once to learn things and
to try to change things.[8] If there is one single fact all the people
described in this book share it is the fact of vulnerability, of
powerlessness; and so it is the duty of people like me, who would
claim some knowledge of how certain people feel way down in
the lowest possible "layers" of their unconscious minds, to witness at first hand the effort made by mountaineers or tenant
farmers or migrants to achieve a kinder, more decent world, and
to witness also the defeats they suffer, the frustrations they have
to meet, the constant insults and intimidations of all kinds that
take place anywhere that a field hand tries to challenge en-
trenched power, change the way a given world is run, or merely
assert his claim to be an American citizen, a human being, a
person.

What sounds like a series of random and unrelated studies or explorations has over a decade gained enough coherence for me to feel I can set down on paper some descriptions of particular lives and some discussions and observations that are tied to those lives and others very much like them. I have used years of conversations and experiences in many counties of many states. The heart of the work has been the thirty families I have visited and worked with and watched and come at times to feel almost joined to — as a doctor, a companion in travel, a friend. Ten of the thirty families belong to the rural South's diminishing but still very active system of sharecropping and farm tenantry; ten other families pursue migrant lives; the final ten live up in the hollows of eastern Kentucky, western North Carolina and in several areas of West Virginia. I have divided up the years with these families. I have spent three or four months with one group, an additional season with another group, and on and on over the years. No family have I now, as I write, known less than six years; some I have known over a decade, and the great majority from seven to nine years. I have, additionally, talked with many, many others whose lives touch upon, bear upon, connect up with, have to do with the people in these thirty families: teachers, employers, merchants, county officials, sheriffs, so-called community organizers — and of course they range from advocates to opponents, from helpers to completely unsympathetic onlookers.

So, what has accumulated in ten years' time can be called thousands of "interviews," done with parents, done with children, done in cabins, done out in fields, done in buses or cars or trucks, done in packing houses, done in schools, done in the offices of growers, the homes of plantation owners, the stores that grocers run or the places that gasoline station owners use. I have used a tape recorder consistently but not always. I realize that in the twentieth century an observer who merely listens and tries to write down in somewhat understandable sentences what he has heard and seen cannot in some circles be considered "objective" or even "scientific." I am sick and tired of calling the interviews I have done "taped" and knowing thereby that they automatically gain a large-size boost in respect and worth so far as certain people are concerned. I want to make this very clear: I use a tape recorder so that I can later have with me the exact voices of the people I have known — their words, their expressions, the moods and the tone that came across in particular conversations. I do not, I hope, go running around the countryside forcing gadgetry on people who are already the victims of various technological "revolutions." I have not, I hope, felt compelled to record every breath and word of every exchange that has been pursued by me these past years. I do not feel it is up to me to judge how I have used those three tape recorders I have at different times used since 1959; rather, it has been up to the people I work with to make an assessment — and they have done so, by showing themselves frightened, amused, beguiled or bored by the machine, or indifferent to it, or utterly oblivious of it, or suspicious of it, or annoyed by it.

For my part, I have tried to be discreet; I have tried to respect the desires and attitudes of the individual families concerned. I have asked them (only after I have known them for months, I hasten to add) whether I might record some of our talks, so that I can have them, as it were, and keep them and go over them — oh, not only to analyze themes and interpret meanings and motives and "goals" and "attitudes," but because after a while a person can get to know another person, feel more and more in touch with him or her, more and more sure why certain words are spoken and with what intent, with what inner conviction. It does help, too — by God it does — to listen to the sounds of those voices, the rhythms and cadences, the pauses, the hesitations that suddenly are overcome, the hurry that is shown, followed by a relaxed stretch. I also take photographs of the people I visit, obviously not to use here, but like the tapes, to hold near me and help guide my mind (and I hope my heart) a little nearer to what I guess has to be called the essence (words simply fail here) of particular lives. And there does come a time, after a few years of visits and more visits, talks and more talks, good talks and rather dismal ones, when something seems to have happened, "clicked," come about, developed; when, that is, on both sides some reasonably reliable and trustworthy impressions begin to congeal and become something else, so that a mountaineer can say: "Well, I guess I know you a small bit and you know me the same, and I sure hope you go and tell those people out over beyond those hills what we're *really* like. But the funny thing is, I don't believe I know myself what it is we're really like, and I don't believe you'll ever know, either, to be frank with you."

So, there it is, the tension and the mystery of things, the beginning of certainty that evaporates in a flash, the confusion that suddenly gives way to a genuinely luminous moment. Though, God knows, it may be an impossible wish, I have wanted all along to remain true to something I can only try to get at, something I can only try to describe with a series of warnings to myself: do not come up with a lot of brittle, pretentious generalizations that explain everything and anything; do not smother with sticky sentiment lives already weak and open to attack; do not refuse those lives their tenacity or shirk from pointing out the price that has to be paid for just such tenacity, for all that goes into remaining, bearing up, continuing and lasting. They have lasted, the families I have known and others who share a similar fate; they have lasted and lasted, endured as Faulkner said they will, prevailed even, if not over their many oppressors, at least over odds like disease, malnutrition, and the extreme hardships that, again, are not only their fate but also their almost inescapable destiny as American citizens. I have gradually found myself more welcome with these families, and at the same time steadily more confused by the stubborn individuality of human beings who might well have been destroyed altogether or at the very least turned into the rural equivalent of "mass men."

The names of the particular people I have known and the specific plantations or hollows or migrant camps obviously must not be given nor can the people I have known in any way at all be revealed. Accordingly, as I mentioned in the introduction, I have changed the names of counties and states, and changed dozens and dozens of other details. Often I have drawn composite pictures; that is, I have combined two or three people into one to make the particular individuals I know unrecognizable, and also to emphasize and highlight the issues for the reader. I suppose I am asking for the writer's privilege to concentrate things, combine meanings, subdue distractions, sharpen what seems central and determining. But I can and should list the "areas" within a reasonable compass: for the sharecroppers and tenant farmers, the Delta of Mississippi, and across the river, two parishes of Louisiana that face the Delta, and two counties in south-central Alabama, and two counties in South Carolina, one to the west of the state, one in the lowlands, and also, two counties in North Carolina, both coastal counties. For migrants, camps all over Florida, particularly Palm Beach and Collier counties — it is practically impossible to disguise the locations of those camps because they are well-known, maybe notorious is the way to put it — and then, with migrant camps located all the way up the Atlantic seaboard, I managed to spend most of my time in upstate New York, lower New Jersey and Massachusetts, and visit more briefly places in the Carolinas and Virginia's eastern shore. Finally, so far as Appalachia is concerned, the families I know best there live in one county in western North Carolina, two in eastern Kentucky and one in West Virginia. A typical recent year was divided into thirds and visits were devoted in that way to one group after another — mountaineers, say in a summer and early autumn, followed by sharecroppers in late autumn and winter, and then in the spring and early summer, migrant farm workers.

If one easily justifies a decision to scramble names and locations, one has a harder time knowing how to present what some speak of as "material" or "data" or sections of "protocols" — "write-ups about people" is what I call them. I have once more decided to do what I did in the first volume of *Children of Crisis* — that is, by and large put the remarks of the people interviewed into what I suppose has to be called the middle-class, grammatical language many Americans and perhaps most book readers learn to use. Part of me has wanted to transcribe those tapes and present them directly, with only minor editing; but three groups of people are involved, and in any case, it is hard to set forth all that is to be heard without constantly explaining particular words and expressions and in a way distracting the reader (and becoming distracted oneself) by dialects, slang, and the strong and suggestive vernacular of uneducated but very perceptive people. Even as I am not writing a history of Appalachia or a sociological description of a rural sharecropping community or an anthropological analysis of life among migrants or a political discussion of the rights given and denied agricultural workers, so I am not presenting here a series of appreciative or critical linguistic essays, or a footnote to the history of "folk music." My job, at least as I see it, is to bring alive to the extent I possibly can a number of lives, and especially to bring alive the "innerness" in those lives: the expectations and assumptions, the vacillations and misgivings and scruples, the rhythm — as it engages with the outside world, with social and political events, with our nation's history; as it takes place in thoughts and feelings, in a child's drawings or games, in a man's imprecations, his casual remarks, his offhand jokes, his private beliefs that are, finally, entrusted to a person like me, an outsider, a stranger, a listener, an observer, a doctor, a curious (in several senses of the word) fellow who one mountaineer described as "always coming back and not seeming to know exactly what he wants to hear or know."

The words, then, belong to the people I have met and heard use them; but the order of the words, of whole sentences and paragraphs and days and days and days of conversation has definitely been my doing, at times I think for the better, certainly so far as pointedness goes, so far as clear-cut, distilled, comprehensible English goes. Whether the loss of many emphatic, even brutal expressions (unfamiliar or obscure to most Americans) is a sacrifice worth making, I cannot judge, having already made the sacrifice. This book is long; were I to offer more and more of the styles of speech I heard, apart from the content expressed, I fear twice this present number of pages might not be enough.[9] I have, though, tried to get across some of the contrasting rhythms to be heard in conversation, for example, in West Virginia, or in Alabama.

In time one's literal-minded, detail-conscious eagerness can be seen for the nervousness it is, the obtuse, pedantic scholasticism it can become, and the condescension it conveys and betrays to others. In time one also begins to learn — maybe the most important thing one *can* learn, that all over the place, in Immokalee, Florida, or Ebenezer, Mississippi, or Stella, North Carolina, or Grassy, West Virginia, people voice the deepest, the most urgent and essential things on their minds in ways that are remarkably similar, that almost seem to transcend not only particular dialects, but even speech itself. I refer not only to gestures and sighs and inarticulate but unmistakable shouts and cries; I refer to the simplicity and directness of words used in cabin after cabin, words that ignore race and caste and section and region, words like *I fear, I love, I hate, I need, I want, I don't* — don't see why and don't understand — and words like *them,* used to signify all those others who are not to be trusted, only feared for their power and influence. Perhaps the narratives I have put together tell something of what prompts those words; if so, the long and perplexing task of editing tapes, of arranging and rearranging sequences of talk, of adding sentences spoken on one or another occasion and noted by me on scraps of paper, has been somewhat successful.

And one more thing: I, the author, keep interrupting, keep on intruding, it seems, with comments and summarizing accounts and various "interpretations," especially when I am writing about children or calling attention to their drawings or paintings. My job has required a meeting of people, if not of worlds, a meeting of me and a migrant child or a sharecropper child or a tall, quiet mountaineer, who teaches me by what he chooses to deliver from himself to me in the way of words. There *is* a clinical dimension to this work, a give and take any doctor knows when he talks with a patient and finds himself learning not only from what he hears, but what he feels, what he hears within himself. I am saying again what I mentioned earlier in this chapter: some weaving in and out by me is required, so that the sense of an encounter is given, one between individuals who get to talk about what certain kinds of living can be like.

Why not, then, devote some chapters to myself, go explicitly and at length into all of the personal reactions and doubts and problems that must have arisen and appeared and loomed heavily indeed over the horizon of such work? I have asked that of myself many times — and been asked that. It may be that I have in a deliberately scattered way done so, here and elsewhere.[10] I do not wish to ignore the obvious fact that an exchange took place, that people were "out there," were come upon, repeatedly called upon, and that their responses reached me, touched me, changed me, even as my visits no doubt changed a number of the people about to speak in this book. Here a chapter given the title "method" ought to turn into one that concerns itself with "purpose." I have attempted to indicate some of the dilemmas that this kind of work inevitably produces, in the people "studied" and also in the observer who calls himself a "student," if not some more high-sounding and pretentious thing. The aim of all these trips and visits can be put like this: to approach certain lives, not to pin them down, not to confine them with labels, not to limit them with heavily intellectualized speculations but again to approach, to describe, to transmit as directly and sensibly as possible what has been seen, heard, grasped, felt by an observer who is also being constantly observed himself — not only by himself but by others, who watch and doubt and fear and resent him, and also, yes, show him kindness and generosity and tenderness and affection. The aim, once again then, is to approach, then describe what there is that seems to *matter*. If all of this sounds increasingly vague and murky and doubtful, I apologize. Perhaps what develops over the course of the book itself will clear things up somewhat.

I do have a few more negatives, though. (Perhaps if I come up with enough of them, *that* will clarify what I positively have wanted to do.) This is not an "attitudinal study." I do not pretend that any assertions made here, by the people quoted or by me, have any "statistical significance," any general or large-scale "validity." I have used no questionnaires. I have not tried to determine whether the people I met and grew to know are in any way accurate reflections of this or that "group" or "segment" of the population. It is all impressionistic, this kind of work, all tied to one person's mind and body; even the tape recorder can only record the answers to the questions I asked, can only convey the

trust that can develop between two people over those much
advertised and dwelled-upon "cross-cultural" barriers. I certainly
do sound "defensive" here; but then, there are too many in my
profession who get "defensive" by calling others names like
"defensive." Once upon a time (a long time ago, it now seems) I
desperately wanted to make sure that I was doing the respectable and approved thing, the most "scientific" thing possible; and
now I have learned, chiefly I believe from these people in this
book, that it is enough of a challenge to spend some years with
them and come out of it all with some observations and con-
siderations that keep coming up, over and over again — until, I
swear, they seem to have the ring of truth to them. I do not know
how that ring will sound to others, but its sound after a while
gets to be distinct and unforgettable to me. Near one of the
towns I just mentioned, near Grassy, West Virginia, I heard it all
said as satisfactorily as my wordy attempts will ever manage:
"When I hear something that strikes me to be right, it sounds
loud and clear to me; when it's a lot of talk, I find my head
shutting up, like a flower does when it gets cold, because I know
it's just a lot of noise, and it'll put you to sleep as much as it'll
bother you."

I have known the mountaineer who spoke those words for
seven years, and I keep going to see him and his wife and his
eight children and his five brothers and his one sister and his
father and his mother and his one little granddaughter and his
many, many cousins. I go to visit them all, him and his kin, every
single year. I try to find out "how it goes," how the children are,
what is coming of them as they steadily grow bigger and feel
more sure of themselves, if not so confident about their future in
that town, that little hollow near the town. I try, most of all, to *be*
there; for all the self-consciousness bound to come with my
presence I still try for that, for as much naturalness as we all can
manage while we talk. Of course it can be hard getting along,
especially on the first few days of each visit. Yet, one can also
become self-conscious about self-consciousness, so to speak. The
point is that after a while a visitor may not be forgotten, but he at
least can be taken for granted somewhat; he can be asked to help

out a little with chores, asked to go for a walk, go to church, go to the store, go to a neighbor's. And he can be taught, he can be shown something up the hollow, a new patch of herbs, a dam being built by beavers, a spot that almost guarantees a good catch of fish, a place with a commanding view. Later, when it is time to say good-bye, there still may be plenty of "gaps" around, a "cultural" gap, a "generational" one, a "socioeconomic" one; but there is also in visitor and visited a touch of sadness, a feeling that attachments have taken place, that separations are painful, that letters ought to be written, and time declared not only an enemy but a friend, because there will be a next visit (won't there?). Another visit means, of course, the promise of yet another occasion for all of us to be courteous and friendly and even enthusiastic, to feel quizzical and perplexed, to ask questions or look interested, to answer questions and appear tired or bored or indifferent, or feel compelled to conceal one's state of mind, one's "attitude."

I cannot put such developments down on paper; they defy words, thank God, because they are the spontaneous, unaffected, unstudied stuff of life. I can only say that they are there, those mountaineers in Grassy, West Virginia, and the sharecroppers or migrants I continue to visit in colorfully named and sad, very sad towns and hamlets and camps and tiny clusters of a house or two. They are there, out on the land. They are always there, as if put there by Nature's very order of things. They are men and women and children whose job it is to take on that land, and who, in so doing, become the people they are.

PART TWO

THE CHILDREN

III

UPROOTED CHILDREN

FOR nine months the infant grows and grows in the womb. The quarters are extremely limited; at the end an X-ray shows the small yet developed body quite bent over on itself and cramped; yet a whole new life has come into being. For some hundreds of thousands of American migrant children that stretch of time, those months, represent the longest rest ever to be had, the longest stay in any one place. From birth on, moves and more moves take place, quick trips and drawn-out journeys. From birth on for such children, it is travel and all that goes with travel — forced travel, by migrant farm workers who roam the American land in search of crops to harvest and enough dollars to stay alive — "to live half right."

How in fact do such children live, the boys and girls who are born to migrant farmers? What do they gradually and eventually learn — and what do they have to teach us, the homeowners and apartment dwellers, the residents of villages and towns and cities and states? To begin with, many migrant children are not born in hospitals, not delivered by physicians, or even carefully trained midwives like those who work with the Frontier Nursing Service in eastern Kentucky. Again and again the migrant mother will casually describe the work she does in the field all during her pregnancy, the travel she undertakes during that same period of time, and finally the delivery itself: done in the rural cabin, or yes, done "on the road" or even in the fields. However indifferent one may be to the cause of such people, it is hard to accept the fact that in the second half of the twentieth century, in the

United States of America, women bear their children on the side of a road, or in a one-room house that lacks running water and electricity — in either case, attended by a friend or neighbor or relative, who is able to offer affection and sympathy, but not medical help.[1] Here is how a rather conservative grower both confirms the existence of and objects to a state of affairs: "Sure, some of them have their babies away from hospitals. I know that. We'd never turn them away from a hospital, here or anyplace. But they have their own life, you know, and they don't do things the way we do. It's ignorance; and it's superstition. A lot of them, they don't know where the hospital is, and they don't want to go there; and some of them, they just want to be with their mother or their aunt, or someone, and they'll scream out there. I've even heard them a couple of times by the side of my fields, and the best thing you can do is leave them alone. Once one of my men went over and tried to take them to the hospital, but they screamed even louder, and he thought they believed he was going to arrest them, or something. It's awful, how ignorant people can be."

Yes, people can be very ignorant. One migrant woman I have come to know is a mother of four children. She attended school for three, maybe four years, and then only "now and then." She admits to knowing very little about any number of things, though she does claim a certain kind of awareness of herself: "Yes sir, I've always had my mother with me, come the time to have the child, except for once, and then my sister, she was real good with me, yes sir. I have them real easy, and it's bad for a little while, but then something happens, and the next thing you know, the baby is crying. I bleed for a week, and I have to keep washing myself, but soon you're not doing so bad, no sir, you're not. The first time and the second time my momma tried to take me to the hospital, you know. She comes from Sylvester, Georgia, yes sir, and she never went to any hospital herself, to have us; but she said I deserved better, and she tried. She just told me when the pains started that I had to come with her, and we went to the hospital, and I got scared, but I went in, and I was shaking real bad, not because of the baby, but I thought they'd arrest us, and I'd end up having the child, my first one, in a jail.

"When we asked to see a doctor and I said I was hurting, and there'd be a baby soon, the way it looked, the nurse said who was my doctor, and my momma she said there wasn't any. Then the nurse said that was too bad, and did we have a deposit for a bed, and it was a lot, more than we ever see, and we said no, but we'd try to pay any bills we ran up, and as fast as possible. Then she shook her head, and she said it was too bad, but we should hurry on up to the other side of the county, to the county hospital, and that was where we might get in, though she wasn't sure, but her hospital, it was an all-private one, and you couldn't come there except if a doctor brought you in, or if there was the money, and only then could she call up a doctor and ask him if he could come over and take the case.

"So that's what happened, and we went back, and it was good that I had my girl real easy-like, my momma said. The next time we tried another hospital, but it was the same thing. So, after that, we knew what to expect, yes sir. You get to know about things after a while."

She had learned something, learned a lot actually. Ignorant, barely able to write her name, never a reader, without a diploma of any kind, even one from a secondary or elementary school, she yet had figured out how certain private hospitals are run, what "criteria" they demand before a potential patient, however much in pain and in serious medical difficulty, becomes an actual patient. She needed no teacher, no social scientist to tell her the economic and political facts of life, of *her* life. I was gently reprimanded when I asked her whether she might not have been helped by a policeman or a fireman, who traditionally (so I thought from my work as a doctor in northern cities) respond to the pleas of women about to deliver babies: "You couldn't be *too* serious, I don't believe, because you must know, you must, that if we ever go near the police, or the fire people, or like that, the sheriff, then it's like asking for trouble, and a lot, too, because they'll tell you, if you pick the crops, they'll tell you to stay away, and if you go asking them for anything, then it won't be but a few seconds, and they'll have you locked up, oh will they."

She has never been locked up, nor does she believe in keeping her children locked up — watched over, carefully controlled, trained to do all sorts of things. "I lets them be," she says when asked how she spends her day with them. In point of fact, like all mothers, she constantly makes choices, or has no choice but to make a particular choice. For instance, I have watched her and other migrant mothers begin to breast-feed their children as a matter of course. For some months I assumed they naturally *had* to do so, because bottled milk is expensive, and certainly there are no physicians around to prescribe this formula and that one, and all the rest of the things American mothers of the middle class come to take for granted. Finally I began to notice how much she enjoyed suckling her child, and how long she went on doing it, and how sad, very sad she became when at a year and a half or so the time came to stop (for what reason, even then, I began to ask myself). So, I went ahead one day and made an observation: "If you had a lot of money, and could buy a lot of milk at the store, would you want to feed your small babies that way, with the bottle?"

She knew exactly what I was getting at, knew it in a sure, self-confident way that did not have to reduce itself into a barrage of nervous, anxious, wordy statements and counter-questions and explanations: "Yes sir, I know what you means. There are times when I find myself wondering if I'll ever get a chance to try one of those bottles out. I'd like to, but you have to keep going to the store then, for the milk, and then I'd run dry — and what if I started with the bottle and I couldn't buy any more milk, because there was no crops, you know, and then I'd be dry, and the baby would be suffering real bad, she would. If I had all that money, like you say, I'd try it, though. But I don't think I'd want to keep away from my baby all the time, like that, and so I don't think I'd try it for so long that I'd run dry, no sir, because I like being near to the baby. It's the best time you ever have with your child, if you ask me. That's right, it's the best time."

She holds the child firmly and fondles her lavishly as she feeds her. She makes no effort to cover her breasts, not before me or her fellow workers. Many times she has carried her infant to a field, done picking, stopped to go to the edge of the field, fed the child, left the child to itself or the care of its grandmother or older sister, and returned to the tomatoes or beans or cucumbers. Many times, too, she has reminded me that picking crops can be boring and repetitive and laborious, and so made very much more tolerable by the presence of good, clean, cool water to drink, and a good meal at lunchtime and best of all, a child to feed lying nearby. She knows that the chances are that good water and food will not be available, but an infant — yes, the presence of an infant is much more likely: "To tell the truth, I do better in the field, when I know my baby is waiting there for me, and soon I'll be able to go see her and do what I can for her. It gives you something to look ahead to."

She plans then. She plans her days around the crops and around the care of her children — she and her mother do that. Sometimes they both pick the crops, and nearby the children play, and indeed upon occasion the oldest child, nine years old, helps out not only with the younger children but the beans or tomatoes also. Sometimes the mother works on her knees, up and down the planted rows, and *her* mother stays with the children, on the edge of the farm or back in the cabin. Sometimes, too, there is no work to be had, and "we stays still and lets the children do their running about."

To my eye, migrant children begin a migrant life very, very early.[2] By and large they are allowed rather free rein as soon as they can begin to crawl. Even before that they do not usually have cribs, and often enough they lack clothes and usually toys of any sort. Put differently, the migrant child learns right off that he has no particular possessions of his own, no place that is his to use for rest and sleep, no objects that are his to look at and touch and move about and come to recognize as familiar. He does not find out that the feet get covered with socks, the body with diapers and shirts and pants. He does not find out that there is music in the air, from mysterious boxes, nor does he wake up to find bears and bunnies at hand to touch and fondle. In sum, he does not get a sense of *his* space, *his* things, or a rhythm that is *his*. He sleeps with his mother at first, and in a few months, with his brothers and sisters. Sometimes he sleeps on a bed, sometimes on the floor, sometimes on the back seat of a car, or on the floor of a truck, and sometimes on the ground. If the locations vary, and the company, so do other things. Unlike middle-class children, the migrant child cannot assume that internal pains will soon bring some kind of relief, or that external nuisances (and worse) will be quickly done away with after a shout, a cry, a scream. One migrant mother described her own feelings of helplessness and eventually indifference in the face of such circumstances: "My children, they suffer. I know. They hurts and I can't stop it. I just have to pray that they'll stay alive, somehow. They gets the colic, and I don't know what to do. One of them, he can't breathe right and his chest, it's in trouble. I can hear the noise inside when he takes his breaths. The worst thing, if you ask me, is the bites they get. It makes them unhappy, real unhappy. They itches and scratches and bleeds, and oh, it's the worst. They must want to tear all their skin off, but you can't do that. There'd still be mosquitoes and ants and rats and like that around, and they'd be after your insides then, if the skin was all gone. That's what would happen then. But I say to myself it's life, the way living is, and there's not much to do but accept what happens. Do you have a choice but to accept? That's what I'd like to ask you, yes sir. Once, when I was little, I seem to recall asking my uncle if there wasn't something you could do, but he said no, there wasn't and to hush up. So I did. Now I have to tell my kids the same, that you don't go around complaining — you just don't."

She doesn't, and a lot of mothers like her don't; and their children don't either. The infants don't cry as much as ours do; or at least the infants have learned not to cry. They are lovingly breast-fed, then put aside, for work or because there is travel to do or chores or whatever. The babies lie about and move about and crawl about, likely as not nude all day and all night. A piece of cloth may be put under them, "to catch their stuff," but not always, and in the outdoors, in the fields, usually not.

As for "their stuff," what we call "toilet training," migrant children on the whole never, never get to see a full-fledged bathroom. They never take a bath or a shower. Sometimes they see their parents use an outhouse; and sometimes they see them use the fields. The children are taught to leave a cabin or car or truck for those outhouses and fields, but the learning takes place relatively slowly and casually, at least to this observer's eye. What takes place rather more quickly has to do with the cabin itself and the car: at about the age of two the child learns he must respect both those places, though not very much else, including the immediate territory around the house — all of which can be understood by anyone who has seen the condition of some outhouses migrants are supposed to use, or the distance between the cabins migrants inhabit and those outhouses, or for that matter, a good serviceable stretch of woods.

They can be active, darting children, many migrant children; and they don't make the mistake of getting attached to a lot of places and possessions. They move around a lot, and they move together, even as they sleep together. They are not afraid to touch one another; in fact, they seek one another out, reach for one another, even seem lost without one another. They don't fight over who owns what, nor do they insist that this is mine and that belongs to someone else. They don't try to shout one another down, for the sake of their mother's attention or for any other reason. At times I have felt them as one — three or four or five or six children, brothers and sisters who feel very much joined and seem very much ready to take almost anything that might come their way. Some might say the children clutch at one another nervously. Some might say they huddle together, rather as Daumier or Käthe Kollwitz showed the poor doing. Some might say they belong to a "community," get along better than middle-class children, grow up without much of the "sibling rivalry" that plagues those more comfortable and fortunate children. Some might say they "adapt" to their lot, "cope" with the severe poverty and disorganization that goes with a migrant life. I find it very hard to say *any one* such thing.[3] At times I see migrant children very close together, it's true, but much too quiet, much too withdrawn from the world. At times I see children together but terribly alone — because they are tired and sick, feverish and hungry, in pain but resigned to pain. Nor does that kind of observation go unnoticed by their mothers, those weary, uneducated, unsophisticated women — who have trouble with words and grammar, who are shy for a long time, then fearfully talkative, then outspoken beyond, at times, the outsider's capacity to do much but listen in confusion and sympathy and anger: "It's hard with the children, because I have to work, and so does my husband, because when the crops are there, you try to make the money you can. So I gets them to be good to one another, and watch out for each other. But a lot of the time, they're not feeling good. I know. They've just run down, the way you get, you know. They don't feel very good. There'll be a pain and something bothering them, and they all look after each other, yes they do. But it's hard, especially when they all goes and gets sick at the same time, and that happens a lot, I'll admit.

"I guess I could be better for them, if I had more to give them, more food and like that, and if I could be a better mother to them, I guess it is. But I try my best, and there's all we have to do, with the crops to work on, and we have to keep on the move, from place to place it is, you know, and there's never much left over, I'll say that, neither money nor food nor anything else. So you have to say to yourself that the little ones will take care of themselves. It's not just you; it's them, and they can be there, to wait on one another. But I'll admit, I don't believe it's the right thing, for them to be waiting on one another so much that — well, there will be sometimes when I tell their father that they're already grown up, the kids, and it's too bad they have to worry so much for each other, because that's hard on a girl of seven or eight, worrying after the little ones, and each of them, looking after the smaller one. Sometimes I think it would be better if we didn't have to keep moving, but it's what we've been doing all these years, and it's the only thing we know, and it's better than starving to death, I tell myself. So I hope and pray my kids won't have to do the same. I tell them that, and I hope they're listening!"

She tells her children a lot, as a matter of fact. She does not spoil them, let them get their way, indulge them, allow them to boss her around and get fresh with her and become loudmouthed and noisy and full of themselves. She can be very stern and very insistent with them. She doesn't really speak to them very much, explain this and that to them, go into details, offer reasons, appeal to all sorts of ideas and ideals and convictions. She doesn't coax them or persuade them or argue them down. She doesn't beat them up either, or threaten to do so. It is hard to *say* what she does, because words are shunned by her and anyway don't quite convey her sad, silent willfulness, a mixture of self-command and self-restraint; and it is hard to *describe* what she does, because whatever happens manages to happen swiftly and abruptly and without a lot of gestures and movements and steps and countersteps. There will be a word like "here" or "there" or "OK" or "now" or "it's time," and there will be an arm raised, a finger pointed, and most of all a look, a fierce look or a summoning look or a steady, knowing look — and the children stir and move and do. They come over and eat what there is to eat. They get ready to leave for the fields. They get ready to come home. They prepare to leave for yet another county, town, cabin, series of fields. They may be sad or afraid. They may be annoyed or angry. They may be troubled; but I have never seen any evidence that they are afraid of being left behind. They may be feeling good, very good — glad to be leaving or arriving. Whatever the mood and occasion, they have learned to take their cues from their mother, and one another, and hurry on. I suppose I am saying that they tend to be rather obedient — out of fear, out of hunger, out of love, it is hard to separate the reasons, the reasons for their obedience or the reasons we also learn to be compliant. I hear just that from the owners of farms and the foremen who manage them — that migrant children are "a pretty good bunch." Well, if the people who employ migrants by the thousands find them "lazy" or "careless" or "shiftless" or "irresponsible" or "ignorant" or "wild" or "animallike," then how is it that their children manage so well, even earn a bit of praise and respect here and there? "I know what you mean," the owner of a very large farm in central Florida says in initial response to the essence of that question. Then he pauses for a minute and struggles with the irony and finally seems to have his answer to it, which is a very good half question indeed: "Well, I don't know, you take children anywhere, and they're not what their parents are, are they?" Then he amplifies: "Sometimes they're better than their parents and sometimes they're worse. You'll find good parents and bad kids and vice versa. As for these migrants, if you ask me, it's the parents who have never amounted to much and maybe they try to do better with their kids, though they're certainly not very ambitious, those parents, so I don't think they push their kids to be successful, the way we might. Maybe it's just they're good and strict with their kids, and if that's the way they treat them, then the kids learn to behave. Of course, they can't really spoil their kids, I'll admit. They don't have much to spoil them with; and what they have, they tend to be wasteful about, you know."

Life is, as the man said, lean and bare for migrant farm workers, and their children find that out rather quickly.[4] Hunger pangs don't always become appeased, however loud and long the child cries. Pain persists, injuries go unattended. The heat does not get cooled down by air conditioners or even fans, and cold air is not warmed by radiators. Always there is the next town, the next county, the next state, and at every stop those cabins — almost windowless, unadorned and undecorated, full of cracks, nearly empty, there as the merest of shelters, there to be left all too soon, something that both parents and children know.

How does such knowledge come alive — that is, get turned into the ways parents treat children, the ways children act, behave, think, get along, grow up? How consciously does a migrant mother transmit her fears to her children, or her weariness, or her sense of exhaustion and defeat, or her raging disappointment that life somehow cannot be better — for her and for the children who confront her every day with requests, questions, demands, or perhaps only their forlorn and all too hushed and restrained presence? I have watched these mothers "interact" with their children, "rear" them, demonstrate this or that "attitude" toward them or "pattern of behavior." Always I have wondered what is *really* going on, what unspoken assumptions work their way continually into acts, deeds, and even occasionally into words — some of them surprisingly and embarrassingly eloquent, to the point that what is revealed has to do not only with their assumptions, but mine, too. For instance, I had known one migrant farm worker, a mother of seven children, a black lady from Arkansas, two years before I finally asked her what she hopes for her children as she brings them up. She smiled, appeared not at all brought up short or puzzled or annoyed. She did hesitate for a few seconds, then began to talk as she glanced at the hot plate in the cabin: "Well, I hope each one of them, my three girls and four boys, each one of them has a hot plate like that one over there, and some food to put on it, and I mean every day. I'd like them to know that wherever they go, there'll be food and the hot plate to cook it. When I was their age, there wasn't those hot plates, and most of the places, they didn't have electricity in them, no sir. We'd travel from one place to the next, picking, taking in the crops, and there'd be a cabin — a lot of the times they'd make the chicken coops bigger to hold us — and the bossman, he'd give you your food, and charge you so much for it that you'd be lucky if you didn't owe him money after a day's work. There'd be hash and hash, and the potatoes, and bread, and I guess that's all, except for the soda pop. There'd be nothing to start the day with, but around the middle they'd come to give you something and at the end, too. A lot of the time we'd get sick from what they'd bring, but you had to keep on picking away or they'd stop feeding you altogether, and then you'd starve to death, and my daddy, he'd say that it's better to eat bad food than no food at all, yes sir. Now no one can deny that, I do believe.

"But now it's changed for the better, the last ten years, I guess, it has. They've put the electricity into some of the cabins — no, not all, but a lot — and they've stopped giving you the food, in return for the deductions. You can get a meal ticket, and keep on eating that way, and they'll give you a sandwich and pop for lunch for a dollar or more, sometimes two, but there's no obligation, and if you save up the money you can get a hot plate and cook your own, and carry the plate up North and back down here and all over the state of Florida, yes sir. And it's better for the children, I think, my cooking. It's much, much better.

"Now, I'd like them to amount to something, my children. I don't know what, but something that would help them to settle down and stop the moving, stop it for good. It's hard, though. They gets used to it, and when I tell them they should one day plan to stop, and find work someplace, in a city or someplace like that — well, then, they'll say that they like the trips we take to here and there and everywhere, and why can't they keep going, like we do. So, I try to tell them that I don't mean they should leave me, and I should leave them, but that maybe one day, when they're real big, and I'm too old to get down on my knees and pick those beans, maybe one day they'll be able to stop, stop and never start again — oh, would that be good for all of us, a home we'd never, never leave.

"You know, when they're real small, it's hard, because as soon as they start talking, they'll want to know why we have to go, and why can't we stay, and why, why, why. *Then* they'd be happy if I didn't get them in the car to move on. But later, I'd say by the time they're maybe five or six, like that, they've got the bug in them; they've got used to moving on, and you can't tell them no, that someday if God is good to us, we'll be able to stop and stay stopped for good. You see, I do believe that a child can get in the traveling habit, and he'll never stop himself and try to get out of it. That's what worries me, I'll admit. I'll hear my oldest one, he's eleven, talk, and he says he thinks he can pick a lot faster than me or anyone else, and he'll one day go farther North than we do, and he'll make more money out of it, and I think to myself that there's nothing I can do but let him do it, and hope one of us, one of the girls maybe, if she meets a good man, will find a home, a real home, and live in it and never leave it.

"We tried three times, you know. My husband and me, we tried to stay there in Arkansas and work on his place, the boss-man's, and we couldn't, because he said we were to stay if we liked, but he couldn't pay us nothing from now on, because of the machinery he'd bought himself. Then we tried Little Rock, and there wasn't a job you could find, and people said go North, but my sister went to Chicago and died there, a year after she came. They said she had bad blood and her lungs were all no good, and maybe it was the city that killed her, my Uncle James said. So, we decided we'd just stay away from there, the city, and then the man came through, from one of the big farms down here, and he said we could make money, big money, if we just went along with him and went down to Florida and worked on the crops, just the way we always did, and that seemed like a good idea, so we did. And with the kids, one after the other, and with needing to have someplace to stay and some food and money, we've been moving along ever since, and it's been a lot of moving, I'll say that, and I wish one day we'd find there was nothing for us to do but stop, except that if we did, there might not be much food for that hot plate, that's what worries me, and I'll tell you, it's what my boy will say and my girl — they tell me that if we didn't keep on picking the crops, well then we'd have nothing to eat, and that wouldn't be worth it, sitting around and going hungry all the time. And I agree with them on that.

"So, we keep going, yes sir, we do. I try to keep everyone in good shape, the best I can. I tell them that it'll be nice, where we're going to, and there will be a lot to see on the road, and there's no telling what kind of harvest there will be, but we might make a lot of money if there's a real good one. I don't believe I should hold out those promises, though — because they believe you, the kids, I know that now, and it just makes them good, happy children, moving along with you, and helping you with the crops. They do a lot, and I'd rather they could be working at something else, later, like I said before, but I doubt they will."

Her children, like others I have seen and like those already described, are in a sense little wanderers from the very start. They are allowed to roam cabins, roam fields, roam along the side of roads, into thickets and bushes and trees. They follow one another around, even as their parents follow the crops, follow the sun, follow the roads. Nor does all that go unnoticed, except by the likes of me: "I lets them have the run of the place, because we'll soon be gone, and they might as well have all the fun they can. They want to go with us and help us with the picking, and they do sometimes, and they learn how to pick themselves, and that's what they say they'll be doing when they get big and grown up, and one will say I'll cut the most celery, and one will say I'll pick more beans than you, and one will say tomatoes are for me, and soon they've got all the crops divided up for themselves, and my husband and me, we say that if the life was better then we wouldn't mind, but you know it's a real hard life, going on the road, and we don't know what to do, whether to tell them, the kids, that it's a bad time they have in store for themselves — and you don't have the heart to do that, say that — or tell them to go ahead and plan on the picking, the harvesting, and tell them it'll be good, just like you kids think. Except that my husband and I, we know it's just not true that it's good. So there it is, we're not telling them the truth, that's a fact."

She does tell them the truth, of course. She tells them that life is hard, unpredictable, uncertain, never to be taken for granted and in fact rather dangerous. She tells them whom to fear: policemen, firemen, sheriffs, people who wear business shirts, people who are called owners or bossmen or foremen or managers. She tells them that no, the rest rooms in the gas stations are not to be used; better the fields or the woods. She tells them to watch out, watch out for just about anyone who is not a picker, a harvester, a farmhand, a migrant worker. She tells them why they can't stop here, or go there, or enter this place or try that one's food. She tells them why sometimes, when they are driving North with others in other cars, the state police meet them at the state line and warn them to move, move fast, move without stopping, move on side roads, move preferably by night. She tells them that no, there aren't any second helpings; no, we don't dress the way those people do, walking on that sidewalk; no, we can't live in a house like that; no, we can't live in any one house, period; no, we can't stay, however nice it is here, however much you want to stay, however much it would help everyone if we did; and no, there isn't much we can do, to stop the pain, or make things more comfortable or give life a little softness, a little excitement, a little humor and richness.

Still, the children find that excitement or humor, if not softness and richness; to the surprise of their parents they make do, they improvise, they make the best of a bad lot and do things — with sticks and stones, with cattails, with leaves, with a few of the vegetables their parents pick, with mud and sand and wild flowers. They build the only world they can, not with blocks and wagons and cars and balloons and railroad tracks, but with the earth, the earth whose products their parents harvest, the earth whose products become, for those particular children, toys, weapons, things of a moment's joy. "They have their good times, I know that," says a mother, "and sometimes I say to myself that if only it could last forever; but it can't, I know. Soon they'll be on their knees like me, and it won't be fun no more, no it won't."

The "soon" that she mentioned is not figured out in years, months or weeks. In fact, migrant children learn to live by the sun and the moon, by day and by night, by a rhythm that has little to do with days and hours and minutes and seconds. There are no clocks around, nor calendars. Today is not this day, of this month, nor do the years get mentioned. The child does not hear that it is so-and-so time — time to do one or another thing. Even Sundays seem to come naturally, as if from Heaven; and during the height of the harvest season they, too, go unobserved. As a matter of fact, the arrival of Sunday, its recognition and its observance can be a striking thing to see and hear: "I never know what day it is — what difference does it make? — but it gets in my bones that it's Sunday. Well, to be honest, we let each other know, and there's the minister, he's the one who keeps his eye on the days, and waits until the day before Sunday, and then he'll go and let one of us know, that tomorrow we should try to stop, even if it's just for a few hours, and pray and ask God to smile down on us and make it better for us, later on up there, if not down here. Then, you know, we talk to one another, and the word passes along, yes it does. I'll be pulling my haul of beans toward the end of the row, to store them, and someone will come to me and say, tomorrow is Sunday, and the reverend, he said we should all be there first thing in the morning, and if we do, then we can be through in time to go to the fields. Now, a lot of the time there's nothing to do in the fields, and then it's a different thing, yes it is; because then we can look forward to Sunday, and know it's going to be a full day, whether in the church, or if the minister comes here, to this camp, and we meets outside and he talks to us and we sing — and afterwards you feel better."

Does she actually forget the days, or not know them, by name or number or whatever? No, she "kind of keeps track" and "yes, I know if it's around Monday or Tuesday, or if it's getting to be Saturday." She went to school, on and off, for three or four years, and she is proud that she knows how to sign her name, though she hasn't done it often, and she is ashamed to do it when anyone is watching. Yet, for her children she wants a different kind of education, even as she doubts that her desires will be fulfilled: "I'd like them all, my five kids, to learn everything there is to be learned in the world. I'd like for them to read books and to write as much as they can, and to count way up to the big numbers. I'd like for them to finish with their schooling. I tell them that the only way they'll ever do better than us, their daddy and me, is to get all the learning they can. But it's hard, you know, it's very hard, because we have to keep going along — there's always a farm up the road that needs some picking, and right away; and if we stay still, we'll soon have none of us, because there won't be a thing to eat, and we'll just go down and down until we're all bones and no flesh — that's what my daddy used to tell me might happen to us one day, and that's what I have to tell my kids, too. Then, they'll ask you why is it that the other kids, they just stay and stay and never move, and why is it that we have to move, and I don't hardly know what to say, then, so I tells them that they mustn't ask those questions, because there's no answer to them, and then the kids, they'll soon be laughing, and they'll come over and tell me that they're real glad that we were going up the road, and to the next place, because they got to see everything in the world, and those other kids — well, they're just stuck there in the same old place."

Space, time and movement, to become conceptual, mean very special things to a migrant child, and so does food, which can never be taken for granted. Many of the children I have studied these past years — in various parts of Florida and all along the eastern seaboard — view life as a constant series of trips, undertaken rather desperately in a seemingly endless expanse of time. Those same children are both active and fearful, full of initiative and desperately forlorn, driven to a wide range of ingenious and resourceful deeds and terribly paralyzed by all sorts of things: the weakness and lethargy that go with hunger and malnutrition, and the sadness and hopelessness that I suppose can be called part of their "preschool education." Indeed the ironies mount the more time one spends with the children, the more one sees them take care of one another, pick crops fast, go fetch water and food at the age of two or three *and* know what size coins or how many dollar bills must be brought back home, talk about the police, listen to a car engine and comment on its strengths or weaknesses, discuss the advantages and disadvantages of harvesting various crops, speak about the way property owners profit from the high rents they charge for their cabins. At the same time, of course, those same children can be observed in different moods, heard making other statements — about how tired they are, about how foolish it is to spend a week in school here and another few days there, and then a couple of weeks "up yonder," about how difficult it is to make sense of people and places and customs and attitudes, about life itself, and yes, about how human beings on this planet treat one another. One of the mothers I came to know best over a period of three years let me know exactly what her children thought and said about such matters: "They'll ask you something sometimes, and you don't know how to answer them. I scratch my head and try to figure out what to say, but I can't. Then I'll ask someone, and there's no good answer that anyone has for you. I mean, if my child looks right up at me and says he thinks we live a bad life, and he thinks just about every other child in the country is doing better than he is — I mean, has a better life — then I don't know what to say, except that we're hardworking, and we do what we can, and it's true we're not doing too well, that I admit. Then my girl, she's very smart, and she'll tell me that sometimes she'll be riding along with us, there in the back seat, and she'll see those houses we pass, and the kids playing, and she'll feel like crying, because we don't have a house to stay in, and we're always going from one place to another, and we don't live so good, compared to others. But I try to tell her that God isn't going to let everything be like it is, and someday the real poor people, they'll be a lot better off, and anyway, there's no point to feeling sorry for yourself, because you can't change things, no you can't, and all you can do is say to yourself that it's true, that we've got a long, hard row to hoe, and the Lord sometimes seems to have other, more important things to do, than look after us, but you have to keep going, or else you want to go and die by the side of the road, and someday that will happen, too, but there's no point in making it happen sooner rather than later — that's what I think, and that's what I tell my girls and my boys, yes sir I do.

"Now, they'll come back at me, oh do they, with first one question and then another, until I don't know what to say, and I tell them to stop. Sometimes I have to hit them, yes sir, I'll admit it. They'll be asking about why, why, why, and I don't have the answers and I'm tired out, and I figure sooner or later they'll have to stop asking and just be glad they're alive. Once I told my girl that, and then she said we *wasn't* alive, and we was dead, and I thought she was trying to be funny, but she wasn't, and she started crying. Then I told her she was being foolish, and of course we're alive, and she said that all we do is move and move, and most of the time she's not sure where we're going to be, and if there'll be enough to eat. That's true, but you're still alive, I said to her, and so am I, and I'm older than you by a long time, and why don't you have faith in God, and maybe do good in your learning, in those schools, and then maybe you could get yourself a home someday, and stay in it, and you'd be a lot better off, I know it, and I wish we all of us could — I mean, could have a home."

The mother mentions schools, not *a* school, not two or three, but "*those* schools." She knows that her children have attended school, at various times, in Florida, Virginia, Delaware, New York, New Jersey and Connecticut. She may not list those states very easily or confidently, but she knows they exist, and she knows she visits them, among others, every year, and she knows that upon occasion her daughter and her sons have gone to elementary schools in those states, and stayed in those schools maybe a few weeks, maybe only a few days, then moved on — to another school, or to no school "for a while," even though during the period of time called "for a while" other children all over the country are at school. What happens to her children in "those schools"? What do they expect to learn when they arrive? What do they actually learn, and how long do they actually stay in school?[5] Rather obviously, migrant children spend relatively little time in classrooms, in comparison to other American children, and learn very little while there. During the two years I worked most closely and methodically with migrant families who belong to the "eastern stream," I had occasion to check on the children's school attendance for ten families. I found that each child put in, on the average, about a week and a half of school, that is, eight days, during the month. Often the children had colds, stomachaches, asthma, skin infections and anemia, and so had to stay home "to rest." Often the children lacked clothes, and so had to await their "turn" to put on the shoes and socks and pants or dresses that were, in fact, shared by, say, three or four children. Often the parents had no real confidence in the value of education, at least the kind they knew their children had to get, in view of the nature of the migrant life, and in view, for that matter, of the demands put upon the migrant farmer who lives that kind of life. Nor did the children usually feel that what they had already learned — rather a lot, if outside the schools — ought to be forsaken in favor of the values and standards and habits encouraged within schools often enough attended, at best, on the sufferance of the teachers and the other children.

Rather obviously, migrancy makes regular school attendance, even if very much desired by a particular set of parents for their children, next to impossible. The most ambitious and articulate migrant farmer I have ever met, a black man originally from northern Louisiana, describes all too precisely the dilemma he must face as a parent, a worker, an American citizen: "You don't realize how hard it is, trying to make sure your kids get a little learning, just a little. I don't expect my oldest boy — he's named after me — to go on and finish school. The little schooling he'll get, it's no good, because he's been in and out of so many of them, the schools, and he gets confused, and it's no good. You'll go from one state to the next, and sometimes the school will remember Peter, and they'll try to pick right up with him, where he left off, and give him special teaching, so he doesn't lose all his time just finding out what's going on, and where the other kids are. But, in a lot of schools, they don't seem even to want you, your kids. They'll give you and them those sour looks when you come in, and they'll act toward you as if you're dirty — you know what I mean? — as if, well, as if you're just no good, and that's that. My boy, he sees it, just like me, even if he's only nine, he does. I try to tell him not to pay attention, but he knows, and he tries to be as quiet and good as he can, but I can see him getting upset, only hiding it, and I don't know what to say. So I just try to make the best of it, and tell him that no matter what, even if it's a little bit here and a little bit there, he's got to learn how to read and how to write and how to know what's happening, not just to himself, but to everyone in the world, wherever they all are. But the boy is right clever, and he says, Daddy, you're not talking the truth at all, no sir; and it don't make any difference, he says, if you get your schooling, because the people who don't want you in school, and don't pay you any attention there, and only smile when you tell them you're sorry, but you won't be there come next week, because you've got to move on with your family — well, those people will be everywhere, no matter where you want to go, and what you want to do, so there's no getting away from them and why even try, if you know you're not going to win much."

Yet, his son Peter does try, and his failure to get a decent education, an even halfway adequate one, tells us, if nothing else, that earnestness and persistence, even on the part of a rather bright child, can only go so far. Peter has always been the quietest of his parents' children, the most anxious to learn things and do things and question things. His younger brothers and sisters tend to be more active, less curious, more impulsive, less contemplative. From the very start Peter wanted to attend school, and worked hard while there. His efforts caught the attention of several teachers, one in Florida and one in Virginia. He has always asked why and indeed proposed answers to his own questions — all of which can annoy his parents, and apparently his teachers, too, upon occasion. I have spent an unusually long period of time with Peter, not only because he and his family have had a lot to teach me, but because sometimes the exceptional child (perhaps like the very sick patient) can demonstrate rather dramatically what others also go through or experience or endure more tamely and less ostentatiously but no less convincingly.

It so happens that I knew Peter before he went to school, and talked with him many times after he had spent a day "in the big room," which is what he often called his classroom when he was six or seven years old. To a boy like Peter a school building, even an old and not very attractively furnished one, is a new world — of large windows and solid floors and doors and plastered ceilings and walls with pictures on them, and a seat that one has, that one is given, that one is supposed to own, or virtually own, for day after day, almost as a right of some sort. After his first week in the first grade Peter said this: "They told me I could sit in that chair and they said the desk, it was for me, and that every day I should come to the same place, to the chair she said was mine for as long as I'm there, in that school — that's what they say, the teachers, anyway."

So, they told him he could not only sit someplace, but he could have something — for himself; and they told him that the next day he would continue to have what was formerly (the previous day) had — and indeed the same would go for the next day after that, until there were no more days to be spent at the school. I believe Peter's remarks indicated he was not quite sure that what he heard would actually and reliably take place. I believe Peter wondered how he could possibly find himself in possession of something and keep it day after day. Peter and I talked at great length about that school, and by bringing together his various remarks, made over many weeks, it is possible to sense a little of what school meant to him, a little of what that abstraction "life" meant (and continually means) to him: "I was pretty scared, going in there. I never saw such a big door. I was scared I couldn't open it, and then I was scared I wouldn't be able to get out, because maybe the second time it would be too hard. The teacher, she kept on pulling the things up and down over the windows — yes, a kid told me they're 'blinds,' and they have them to let the sun in and keep the sun out. A lot of the time the teacher would try to help us out. She'd want to know if anyone had anything to ask, or what we wanted to do next. But she seemed to know what she was going to do, and I'd just wait and hope she didn't catch me not knowing the answer to one of her questions. She said to me that I had to pay attention, even if I wasn't going to be there for very long, and I said I would, and I've tried to do the best I can, and I've tried to be as good as I can. She asked me as I was leaving the other day if I would be staying long, and I said I didn't know, and she said I should ask my daddy, and he'd know, but when I did, he said he didn't know, and it all depended on the crops and what the crew man said, because he's the one who takes us to the farms. Then I told the teacher that, and she said yes, she knew what it was like, but that I should forget I'm anywhere else while I'm in school and get the most I can learned.

"I try to remember everything she says, the teacher. She's real smart, and she dresses good, a different dress every day, I think. She told us we should watch how we wear our clothes, and try to wash ourselves every day and use brushes on our teeth and eat all these different things on the chart she has. I told my momma, and she said yes, what the teacher says is correct, yes it is, but you can't always go along, because there's no time, what with work and like that, and if you haven't got the shower, you can't take it, and maybe someday it will be different. I asked her if we could get some chairs, like in school, and we could carry them where we go, and they'd be better than now, because you sit on the floor where we're staying, and the teacher said a good chair helps your back grow up straight, if you know how to sit in it right. But there's not the money, my daddy said, and it's hard enough *us* moving, never mind a lot of furniture, he said. When I get big, I'll find a chair that's good — but it can fold up. The teacher said you can fold up a lot of things and just carry them with you, so there's no excuse for us not having a lot of things, even if we're moving a lot, that's what she said, and one of the kids, he said his father was a salesman and traveled all over the country — and he said, the kid, that his father had a suitcase full of things you could fold up and unfold and they were all very light and you could hold the suitcase up with one finger if you wanted, that's how light. My daddy said it wasn't the same, the traveling we do, and going around selling a lot of things. He said you could make big money that way, but you couldn't do it unless you were a big shot in the first place, and with us, it's no use but to do what you know to do, and try to get by the best you can, and that's very hard, he says.

"I like going into the school, because it's really, really nice in there, and you can be sure no bugs will be biting you, and the sun doesn't make you too hot, and they have the water that's really cold and it tastes good. They'll give you cookies and milk, and it's a lot of fun sitting on your chair and talking with the other kids. One boy wanted to know why I was going soon — I told him the other day, and he thought I was trying to fool him, I think — and I said I didn't know why, but I had to go because my daddy picks the crops and we moves along, and we have to. The boy, he thought I was trying to be funny, that's what he said first, and then the next time he came over and he said that he'd talked with his daddy and the daddy said that there was a lot of us, the migrant people, and it was true that we're in one city and out, and on to the next, and so I had to go, it's true, if that's what my daddy does. Then he said, the boy said, that his daddy told him to stay clear of me, because I might be carrying a lot of sickness around, and dirt, and like that; but he said, his name is Jimmy, he said I was OK and he wasn't going to tell his father, but we should be friends in the yard during the playtime, and besides he heard his mother say it was too bad everyone didn't have a home and stay there from when he's born until he's all grown up, and then it would be better for everyone.

"I thought I might never see Jimmy again, or the school either, when we drove away, but I thought I might get to see another school, and my momma said that Jimmy wasn't the only boy in the world, and there'd be plenty like him up North, and they might even be better to us up there while we're there, though she wasn't too sure. Then I was getting ready to say we shouldn't go at all, and my daddy told me to shut up, because it's hard enough to keep going without us talking about this friend and the school and the teacher and how we want to stay; so he said if I said another word I'd soon be sorry, and I didn't. Then I forgot — we were way up there, a long way from Florida, I think, and I said something Jimmy said, and they told me I'd better watch out, so I stopped and just looked out the window, and that's when I thought it would be good, like Jimmy said his mother said, if one day we stopped and we never, never went up the road again to the next farm, and after that, the next one, until you can't remember if you're going to leave or you've just come.

"That's what my momma will say sometimes, that she just can't remember, and she'll ask us, and we're not always a help, because we'll just be going along, and not knowing why they want to leave and then stop, because it seems they could just stop and never leave, and maybe someone could find them a job where they'd never have to leave, and maybe then I could stay in the same school and I'd make a lot of friends and I'd keep them until when I was grown up. Then I'd have the friends and I wouldn't always be moving, because they'd help me, and that's what it means to be a friend, the teacher said, and Jimmy told me that if

I'd be staying around, he'd ask his mother if I could come over, and he thought that if I came during the day, and his father wasn't home, then it would be all right, because his mother says she's in favor of helping us out, my people, Jimmy says, and she said if she had the money she'd buy houses for all of us, and she said there must be a way we could stay in one place, but Jimmy said he told her what I said: if we don't keep moving, we don't eat. That's what my daddy says, and I told Jimmy. It's all right to go to school, my daddy says, but they won't feed you in school, and they won't give you a place to sleep, so first you have to stay alive, and then comes school. Jimmy said my daddy was right, but he was making a mistake, too — because his daddy says that if you don't finish school, you'll have nothing to do and you'll starve to death, so it's best to go to school and learn whatever the teacher says, even if you don't like to."

Peter has come to know several Jimmys in his short life, and he has left several schools reluctantly, sadly, even bitterly. On the other hand, he has also been glad to leave many schools. He feels he has been ignored or scorned. He feels different from other schoolchildren — and has felt that one or another teacher emphasizes those differences, makes them explicit, speaks them out, and in a way makes him feel thoroughly unwanted. I knew him long enough and followed his family's travels far enough to get a fairly quick response from him after his first day in a particular school. The experience invariably would either be good or bad, or so Peter judged. He would talk about what he saw and felt, and in so doing reveal himself to be, I thought, remarkably intuitive and perceptive. Yet, he insisted to me on numerous occasions that what he noticed other migrant children also notice, and no less rapidly than he. "I'm a big talker" he told me after one of our "big talks." His younger brother, Tom, would see the same things, though, when he went to school; he might not put what he sees into words, or even be fully aware of what he senses happening, but he would know it all, know the hurt and loneliness and isolation and sadness, know it all in the bones, in the heart, in the back of his mind — wherever such knowledge is stored by human beings. So Peter believed, or so I believe he believed, on the basis of his observations and remarks and complaints and questions, all shared with me during the two years we conversed — in Florida and North Carolina and Virginia and upstate New York, each of which claims to offer children like Peter what every American child presumably is entitled to as a birthright, a free public education: "I always am a *little* scared when I try a new school, yes; but I try to remember that I won't be there long, and if it's no good, I'm not stuck there, like the kids who live there. We'll come in and they'll tell you you're special, and they'll do what they can to make you good, to clean you up, they'll say, and to give you better habits, they'll say. I don't like those kinds of teachers and schools that they're in.

"Yes, I met one today. She wasn't worse than the last one, but she wasn't better, either. We could tell. She started in with what we had on, and how we could at least clean our shoes, even if they weren't good, and all that; and I said in my mind that I wish I was outside, fishing maybe, or doing anything but listening to her. Then I recalled my daddy saying it would only be two or three weeks, so I didn't get bothered, no. She asked me my name, and I told her, and she asked me where I was from, and I told her, and she asked me what I was going to school for, and I told her — that it was because I *had* to — and she smiled. (I think it was because I said what she was thinking, and she was glad, so she smiled.) I told myself later that if I'd gone and told her that I was there at school because I wanted to be a teacher, like her, or even the principal, then she'd have come after me with the ruler or the pointer she has in her hand all the time. Well, I figure we'll get a good rest there, and the chairs are good, and they give you the milk and cookies, and my momma says that's worth the whole day, regardless of what they say, but I think she's wrong, real wrong.

"To me a good school is one where the teacher is friendly, and she wants to be on your side, and she'll ask you to tell the other kids some of the things you can do, and all you've done — you know, about the crops, and like that. There was one teacher like that, and I think it was up North, in New York it was. She said that so long as we were there in the class she was going to ask

everyone to join us, that's what she said, and we could teach the
other kids what we know and they could do the same with us.
She showed the class where we traveled, on the map, and I told
my daddy that I never before knew how far we went each year,
and he said he couldn't understand why I didn't know, because I
did the traveling all right, with him, and so I should know. But
when you look on the map, and hear the other kids say they've
never been that far, and they wish someday they could, then you
think you've done something good, too — and they'll tell you in
the recess that they've only seen where they live and we've been
all over. I told my daddy what they said, and he said it sure was
true, that we've been all over, and he hopes the day will come
when we'll be in one place, but he sure doubts it, and if I wanted
I could tell the teacher he said so — but I didn't. I don't think
she'd know how to answer Daddy, except to say she's sorry, and
she's already told us that, yes she did, right before the whole
class. She said we had a hard life, that's what, the people who do
the picking of the crops, and she wanted us to know that she was
on our side, and she wanted to help us learn all we could, because it would be better for us later, the more we knew, and
maybe most of us would find a job and keep it, and there'd be no
more people following the crops all over, from place to place, and
it would be better for America, she said. Then she asked if I
agreed, and I didn't say one way or the other, and she asked me
to just say what I thought, and I did. I said I'd been doing
enough of traveling, and I'd seen a lot of places, and I wouldn't
mind stopping for a change, no ma'am, and if we just stayed
there, in that town, and I could go to school there — well, that
would be all right by me, and it would be better than some of the
other places we stop, I could say that right off, a real lot better.

"There'll be times when I wish I'd have been born one of the
other kids, yes sir; that's how I sometimes think, yes. Mostly, it's
when the teacher is good to you — then you think you'd like to
stay. If the teacher is bad, and the kids don't speak to you, then
you want to go away and never come back, and you're glad that
you won't stay there too long. Now school is good, because it's a
good school and they pays attention to you; most of the time

though, in other schools, you just sit there, and you want to sleep. Suddenly the teacher will ask you what you're thinking, and you tell her the truth, that you don't know. Then she'll ask you what you want to be, and I don't know what to answer, so I say I'd like to work like my daddy at the crops, and maybe one day get a job in the city, and stay there. Then they'll tell you to study hard, the teachers, but they don't give you much to do, and they'll keep on asking you how the crops are coming, and how long you'll be there, and when are you going to be going, and like that. Sometimes I won't go to school. I tell my momma that I'm not going and can I help take care of my brothers and can I help in the field, or anything, and she'll say yes, mostly, unless she thinks the police will be getting after me, for not being in school — but most of the time they don't care, and they'll tell you you're doing good to be caring for your brother and working. Yes sir, they'll drive by and wave and they don't seem to mind if you're not in school. Once a policeman asked me if I liked school and I said sometimes I did and then he said I was wasting my time there, because you don't need a lot of reading and writing to pick the crops, and if you get too much of schooling, he said, you start getting too big for your shoes, and cause a lot of trouble, and then you'll end up in jail pretty fast and never get out if you don't watch your step — never get out."

Peter seeks consolation from such a future; and he often finds it by looking back to earlier years and occasions. In his own brief life as a young child, a young migrant, a young boy of, say, eight or nine or ten, he has begun to find that the one possession he has and cannot lose is yesterday, the old days, the experiences that have gone but remain — and remain not only in the mind's memories and dreams, but in the lives of others, those brothers or sisters who are younger and who present a child like Peter with themselves, which means all the things they do that remind Peter of what he once did and indeed can continue to do as the older brother becomes a companion of younger children. I found myself concluding and in my notes emphasizing all of that, Peter's tendency to *go back*, to flee the present for the sake of the past. After all, I had to repeat to myself again and again, Peter finds school useless or worse. He finds his parents tired and distracted or worse. He finds himself at loose ends: I am a child, yet today I can work, tomorrow I may be told I'm to attend school, the next day I'll be on the road again and unsure where I shall soon be, when I shall again be still for a while — sitting on the ground, that is, or in a cabin, rather than upon the seat of a car or a bus. In the face of such uncertainties, earlier moments and ways and feelings become things (if such is the word) to be tenaciously grasped and held. And so, Peter will help pick beans, and do a very good job at moving up and down the rows, but soon thereafter be playing on his hands and knees with his younger brothers, and sucking lollipops with them and lying under a tree and crawling about and laughing with them. His mother in her own way takes note of what happens, and needs no prodding from any observer to describe the sequence of events: "I think stooping for those beans can go to your head. You get dizzy after a day of it, and you want to go down on your back and stretch yourself all you can and try to feel like yourself again, and not all curled up on yourself. If Peter goes along with his daddy and me and does the stooping and picking, then he'll be real tired at the end of the day, and it seems he wants to be like my little ones — and I say to myself if it'll help him feel any better, after all that work, then Lord he can do what he likes, and if I had it in me to keep them all little babies, then I'd do it, because that's when they're truly happiest, yes sir."

Yet, it turns out that her children and thousands of other migrant children are not very happy for very long; actually, many of those children have a hard time understanding the many contradictions that plague their lives. For one thing, as already indicated, migrant children of two or three are allowed, in some respects, a good deal of active, assertive freedom. They are encouraged to care for one another, but also encouraged to fend for themselves — go exploring in the woods or the fields, play games almost anywhere and anytime, feel easy and relaxed about time, about schedules, about places where things are done and routines that give order to the doing of those things. Again and again I have seen migrant children leave their cabins for the day

and return anytime, when and if they pleased — to get themselves a bottle of pop and make for themselves a meal of "lun-
cheon meat" and bread and potato chips, or often enough, potato
chips and potato salad and Coke, period. At the same time, however, those very children are also taught obedience and a real
and powerful kind of fatalism: one can only go here, do that, and
most of all, submit to the rigors and demands and confusion and
sadness of travel — always the travel, inevitably the travel, end-
lessly the travel, all of which can amount to a rather inert and
compliant and passive life. Put differently, the child is told the
grim facts of his particular life, but also given dozens of stories
and excuses and explanations and promises whose collective
function, quite naturally and humanly, is to blunt the awful,
painful edges of that very life. It can even be said that migrant
children obtain and learn to live with an almost uncanny mixture
of realism and mysticism. It is as if they must discover how
difficult their years will be, but also acquire certain places of
psychological and spiritual refuge. Naturally, each family has its
own particular mixture of sentiment and hard facts to offer and
emphasize, even as each child makes for himself his very own
nature; he becomes a blend of the assertive and the quiet, the
forceful and the subdued, the utterly realistic and the strangely
fanciful. What I am saying, of course, goes for all children, but at
the same time I must insist that migrant children have a very
special psychological fate — and one that is unusually hard for
them to endure.

For example, I mentioned earlier that migrant children tend to
be close to one another, tend to care very much for one another,
tend almost to absorb themselves in one another, and certainly —
the first observation one like me makes when he comes to know
them — tend to touch one another, constantly and reassuringly
and unselfconsciously and most of the time rather tenderly. At
the same time those same children, so literally touching to each
other, can appear more and more untouched — indifferent, tired,
bored, listless, apathetic, and finally, most ironically, isolated
physically as well as psychologically. Many of them, unlike the

boy Peter, just discussed, abandon themselves to a private world that is very hard for any outsiders to comprehend, even a mother or father. School means nothing, is often forsaken completely, even the pretense of going. Friends are an affair of the moment, to be forsaken and lost amid all the disorder and turmoil and instability that goes with one move after another. Sports, organized and progressively challenging sports, are unknown. Needless to say, the migrant child does not go to restaurants, theaters, movies, museums, zoos and concerts; nor do those television sets he watches work very well; they are old and half broken to start with, purchased secondhand (with a bit of luck) on a never-ending installment basis, and in addition, as Peter's mother puts it, "way out in the country you can't pick up the pictures," particularly when there is no antenna, and the set has been bouncing around for miles and miles, as indeed have its owners.

It is hard to convey such experiences, such a world, to those who don't see it and feel it and smell it and hear it. It is even harder to describe that world as it is met and apprehended and suffered by hundreds of thousands of parents and children. I say this not as a preliminary exercise in self-congratulation — what is hard is being done and therefore deserves admiration — but to warn myself and the reader alike, particularly at this point, against the temptation of psychological categorization, the temptation to say that migrant children are this or that, are "active" or "passive," resort to excessive "denial" and too many "rationalizations" and "projections" or resort to an almost brutal kind of realism, a kind of self-confrontation so devoid of humor and guile and hope and patience as to be a caricature of the analysis the rest of us value, be it psychological or political or philosophical. I am saying that migrant children are many things, and do many things with their brief and relatively sad lives. They can be ingenious and foolish. They can have all sorts of illusions, and they can speak about themselves with almost unbearable candor and severity and gloom. They can feel disgusted with their lot, or they can pay no attention to it, simply endure what has to be; or they can romp and laugh and shout, even though their observer knows how close to the surface are the tears (and fears) and how overworked even the fun seems at times — the kind of thing, of course, that can happen to all of us.

In a sense, as I write about these young children I am lost. How literally extraordinary, and in fact how extraordinarily cruel their lives are: the constant mobility, the leave-takings and the fearful arrivals, the demanding work they often manage to do, the extreme hardship that goes with a meager (at best) income, the need always to gird oneself for the next slur, the next sharp rebuke, the next reminder that one is different and distinctly unwanted, except, naturally, for the work that has to be done in the fields. I also want to emphasize that extremely hard-pressed people can find their own painful, heavyhearted way, can learn to make that way as bearable as possible and can laugh not only because they want to cry and not only in bitter, ironic resignation (the kind melancholy philosophers allow themselves to express with a wan smile) but because it has been possible, after all the misery and chaos, to carve a little joy out of the world. That is to say, they make do, however sullenly and desperately and wildly and innocently and shrewdly, and they teach their children unsystematically but persistently that they, too, must survive — somehow, some way, against whatever odds.

Peter's mother, over the years has essentially told me about that, about the facts of survival, not because I asked her what she has in mind when she punishes or praises her children, or tells them one or another thing, but because she constantly does things — for, with, to — her children. In a moment of quiet conversation her deeds, thousands of them done over many, many years, sort themselves out and find their own pattern, their own sense, their own words — oh, not perfect or eminently logical or completely consistent words, but words that offer vision and suggest blindness and offer confidence and suggest anxiety, the responses of a hardworking and God-fearing mother who won't quite surrender but also fears she won't quite avoid a terrible and early death: "I worry every day — it'll be a second sometime in the morning or in the afternoon or most likely before I drop off to sleep. I worry that my children will wake up one time and find I'm gone. It might be the bus will go crashing, or the car or the truck on the way to the farm, or it might be I've just been called away from this bad world by God, because He's decided I ought to have a long, long rest, yes sir. Then I'll stop and remind myself that I can't die, not just yet, because there's the children, and it's hard enough for them, yes it is — too hard, if you ask me. Sometimes I'll ask myself why it has to be so hard, and why can't we just live like other people you see from the road, near their houses, you know. But who can question the Lord, that's what I think. The way I see it, I've got to do the best I can for my children, all of them. So, I keep on telling them they've got to be good, and take care of each other, and mind me and do what I says. And I tell them I don't want them getting smart ideas, and trying to be wild and getting into any trouble, because you know — well, the way I sees the world, if you're born on the road, you'll most likely have to stay with it, and they're not going to let go of you, the crew man and the sheriff and like that, and if they did, we'd be at a loss, because you go into the city, I hear, and it's worse than anything that ever was, that's what we hear all the time.

"I'm trying to make my children into good children, that's what. I'm trying to make them believe in God, and listen to Him and obey His Commandments. I'm trying to have them pay me attention, and my husband, their daddy, pay him attention, and I'd like for all of them to know what they can, and grow into good people, yes, and be a credit to their daddy and me. I knows it's going to be hard for them, real bad at times, it gets. I tell them that, and I tell them not to be too set on things, not to expect that life is going to be easy. But I tell them that every man, he's entitled to rest and quiet some of the time, and we all can pray and hope it'll get better. And I tell them it used to be we never saw any money at all, and they'd send you up in those small trucks, but now they'll pay you some, and we most often have a car — we lose it, yes sir, when there's no work for a few weeks and then we're really in trouble — and we have more clothes now than we ever before had, much more, because most of my children, they have their shoes now, and clothes good enough for church, most of the time. So you can't just feel sorry about things, because if you do, then you'll just be sitting there and not doing anything — and crying, I guess. Sometimes I do; I'll wake up and I'll find my eyes are all filled up with tears, and I can't figure out why, no sir. I'll be getting up, and I'll have to wipe away my eyes, and try to stop it, so the children don't think something is wrong, and then, you know, they'll start in, too. Yes, that has happened a few times, until I tell us all to go about and do something, and stop, stop the crying right away.

"You can't spend your one and only life wishing you had another life instead of the one you've got. I tell myself that, and then the tears stop; and if the children are complaining about this or that — well, I tell them that, too. I tell them it's no use complaining, and we've got to go on, and hope the day will come when it's better for us, and maybe we'll have a place to rest, and never again have to 'go on the season' and move and keep on moving and get ourselves so tired that we start the day in with the crying. Yes sir, I believe I cry when I'm just so tired there isn't anything else to do but cry. Or else it's because I'll be waking up and I know what's facing us, oh I do, and it just will be too much for me to think about, so I guess I go and get upset, before I even know it, and then I have to pinch myself, the way my own momma used to do, and talk to myself the way she would, and say just like her: 'There's no use but to go on, and someday we'll have our long, good rest.' Yes sir, that's what she used to say, and that's what I'll be saying on those bad mornings; and you know, I'll sometimes hear my girl telling herself the same thing, and I'll say to myself that it's good she can do it now, because later on she'll find herself feeling low, and then she'll have to have a message to tell herself, or else she'll be in real bad trouble, real bad trouble."

Mothers like her possess an almost uncanny mixture of willfulness and sadness.[6] Sometimes they seem to do their work almost in spite of themselves; yet at other times they seem to take the sad and burdensome things of life quite in stride. As they themselves ask, what else can they do? The answer, of course, is that complete disintegration can always be an alternative — helped along by cheap wine, and the hot sun and the dark, damp corners of those cabins, where one can curl up and for all practical purposes die. Migrant mothers know all that, know the choices they have, the possibilities that life presents. Migrant mothers also know what has to be done — so that the children, those many, many children will at least eat something, will somehow get collected and moved and brought safely to the new place, the new quarters, the next stop or spot or farm or camp or field, to name a few destinations such mothers commonly mention when they talk to me about what keeps them in half-good spirits. I will, that is, ask how they feel, and how they and their children are getting along, and they will answer me with something like this: "I'm not too bad, no sir, I'm not. We keeps going, yes sir, we do. If you don't keep going, you're gone, I say. You have to keep moving and so you don't have time to stop and get upset about things. There's always another spot to get to, and no sooner do you get there — well, then you have to get yourself settled. There'll be yourself to settle and there'll be the kids and their daddy, too, and right off the work will be there for you to do, in the fields and with the kids, too. So, the way I see it, a mother can't let herself be discouraged. She's got to keep herself in good spirits, so her children, they'll be doing fine; because if I'm going to get all bothered, then sure enough my kids will, and that won't be good for them or me neither, I'll tell you. That's why I never lets myself get into a bad spell."

Actually, she does indeed get into bad spells, spells of moodiness and suspicion and petulance and rage, and so do her children from time to time, particularly as they grow older and approach the end of childhood. By definition, life for migrants is a matter of travel, of movement; and their children soon enough come to know that fact, which means they get to feel tentative about people and places and things. Anything around is only precariously theirs. Anything soon to come will just as soon disappear. Anything left just had to be left. As a matter of fact, life itself moves, moves fast and without those occasions or ceremonies that give the rest of us a few footholds. The many young migrant children I have observed and described to myself as agile, curious, and inventive are, by the age of seven or eight, far too composed, restrained, stiff and sullen. They know even then exactly where they must go, exactly what they must do. They no longer like to wander in the woods, or poke about near swamps. When other children are just beginning to come into their own, just beginning to explore and search and take over a little of the earth, migrant children begin to lose interest in the world outside them. They stop noticing animals or plants or trees or flowers. They don't seem to hear the world's noises. To an outside observer they might seem inward, morose, drawn and tired. Certainly some of those qualities of mind and appearance have to do with the poor food migrant children have had, with the accumulation of diseases that day after day cause migrant children pain and weakness. Yet, in addition, there is a speed, a real swiftness to migrant living that cannot be overlooked, and among migrant children particularly, the whole business of growing up goes fast, surprisingly fast, awfully fast, grimly and decisively fast. At two or three, migrant children see their parents hurry, work against time, step on it, get a move on. At three or four, those same children can often be impulsive, boisterous, eager, impatient in fact, and constantly ready — miraculously so, an observer like me feels — to lose no time, to make short work of what is and turn to the next task, the next ride.

However, at six or eight or ten, something else has begun to happen; children formerly willing to make haste and take on things energetically, if not enthusiastically, now seem harried as they hurry, breathless and abrupt as they press on. I do not think I am becoming dramatic when I say that for a few (first) feverish years migrant children are hard-pressed but still (and obviously) quick, animated — tenacious of life is perhaps a way to say it. Between five and ten, though, those same children experience an ebb of life, even a loss of life. They keep moving along; they pick themselves up again and again, as indeed they were brought up to do, as their parents continue to do, as they will soon (all too soon) be doing with their own children. They get where they're going, and to a casual eye they seem active enough, strenuous workers in the field, on their toes when asked something, called to do something. Still, their mothers know different; their mothers know that a change is taking place, has taken place, has to take place; their mothers know that life is short and brutish, that one is lucky to live and have the privilege of becoming a parent, that on the road the days merge terribly, that it is a matter of rolling on, always rolling on. So they go headlong into the days and nights, obey the commands of the seasons and pursue the crops; and meanwhile, somewhere inside themselves, they make their observations and their analyses, they take note of what happens to themselves and their children: "My little ones, they'll be spry and smart, yes they will be; but when they're older — I guess you'd say school age, but they're not all the time in school, I'll have to admit — then they're different, that's what I'd say. They'll be drowsy, or they won't be running around much. They'll take their time and they'll slouch, you know. They'll loaf around and do only what they think they've got to do. I guess — well, actually, I suppose they're just getting grown, that's what it is. My boy, he's the one just nine this season, he used to be up and doing things before I even knew what he was aiming to do; but now he'll let no one push him, except if he's afraid, and even then, he'll be pulling back all he can, just doing enough to get by. The crew leader, he said the boy will be 'another lazy picker' and I stood up and spoke back. I said we gets them in, the beans, don't we and what more can he want, for all he pays us? I'll ask you? I guess he wants our blood. That's what I think it is he wants, and if he sees my children trying to keep some of their blood to themselves, then he gets spiteful about them and calls them all his names like that; and there isn't anything you can do but listen and try to go on and forget."

She tries to go on and forget. So do her children, the older they get. Once wide awake, even enterprising, they slowly become dilatory, leaden, slow, laggard and lumpish. Necessarily on the move a lot, they yet appear motionless. Put to work in the fields, they seem curiously unoccupied. The work gets done (and by them) yet they do not seem to work. I suppose I am saying that older migrant children begin to labor, to do what they must do if they are not to be without a little money, a little food; but at the same time the work is not done in a diligent, painstaking and spirited way. Again, it is done, all that hard, demanding work; the crops get taken in. What one fails to see, however, is a sense of real purpose and conviction in the older children who, like their parents, have learned that their fate is of no real concern to others.[7] The point is survival: mere survival at best; survival against great odds; survival that never is assured and that quite apparently exacts its costs. If I had to sum up those costs in a few words I would probably say: care is lost; the child stops caring, hardens himself or herself to the coming battle, as it is gradually but definitely comprehended, and tries to hold on, persist, make it through the next trip, the next day, the next row of crops.

So, all year round, all day long, hour after hour, migrants stoop or reach for vegetables and fruit, which they pull and pick and cut and at the same time those migrants settle into one place or prepare the move to another; and at the same time those migrants try to be parents, try stubbornly to do what has to be done — feed the children and get them to listen and respond and do this rather than that, do it now rather than later. I have described the determination that goes into such a life — of travel and fear and impoverishment and uncertainty. I have described the first and desperate intimacy many migrant children experience with their mothers. I have described the migrant child's developing sense of his particular world — its occasional pleasures, its severe restrictions, its constant flux, its essential sameness. To do so I have drawn upon what can actually be considered the best, the most intact, of the people I have seen and heard. After all, when parents and children together live the kind of life most migrants do, it seems a little miraculous that they even halfway escape the misery and wretchedness — that is, manage to continue and remain and last, last over the generations, last long enough to work and be observed by me or anyone else.

There is, though, the misery; and it cannot be denied its importance, because not only bodies but minds suffer out of hunger and untreated illness; and that kind of psychological suffering also needs to be documented. Nor can an observer like me allow his shame, outrage and compassion to turn exhausted, suffering people into courageous heroes who, though badly down on their luck, nevertheless manage to win a spiritual victory. I fear that rather another kind of applause is in order, the kind that celebrates the struggle that a doomed man tries to put up. Migrant parents and even migrant children do indeed become what some of their harshest and least forgiving critics call them: listless, apathetic, hard to understand, disorderly, subject to outbursts of self-injury and destructive violence toward others. It is no small thing, a disaster almost beyond repair, when children grow up adrift the land, when they learn as a birthright the disorder and early sorrow that goes with peonage, with an unsettled, vagabond life. We are describing millions of psychological catastrophes, the nature of which has been spelled out to me by both migrant parents and migrant children. The father of six of those children — a hard worker but a beaten man — talks and talks about his failures and his sense of defeat, about his sense of ruin at the hands of a relentless fate whose judgment upon him and those near him and like him simply cannot be stayed: "There will be a time, you know, when I'll ask myself what I ever did — maybe in some other life — to deserve this kind of deal. You know what I mean? I mean I feel there must be someone who's decided you should live like this, for something wrong that's been done. I don't know. I can't say it any other way. All I know is that it's no life, trying to pick beans on fifty farms all over the country, and trying to make sure your kids don't die, one after the other. Sometimes we'll be driving along and I say to myself that there's one thing I can do to end all of this for good, and it would save not only me but the children a lot of hardship, a lot. But you can't do that; I can't, at least. So, instead I go and lose my mind. You've seen me, yes you have; and I know I'm going to do it. I start with the wine, when I'm working, just so the hours will go faster, and I won't mind bending over — the pain to my back — and I won't mind the heat. There'll be days when I work right through, and there'll be days when I stop in the middle of the day, because I don't want to get sick. But there will be other days when I hear myself saying that I've got to let go, I've just got to. I've got to get so drunk that I'm dead, dead in my mind, and then if I live after it, that's fine, and if I never wake up, that's fine, too. It's not for me to decide, you see. We can't decide on anything, being on the road, and owing everything to the crew leaders and people like that. The only thing we can decide, my daddy used to tell me, is whether we'll stay alive or whether we won't. He said no matter what, we should keep going; but he got killed when the bus that was taking him and a lot of others got stalled right on a railroad track and it was crushed into little pieces by the train. I'll think of him, you know, when I get full of wine. I'll think of him telling me that you can't figure out what's the reason the world is like it is; you can only try to keep from dying, and it may take you your entire life to do that — and I guess he didn't expect that suddenly he'd be gone, after all the work he put in, just to stay alive."

His wife has some observations to make about him and the effort he makes to stay alive: "My husband, he's a good man a lot of the time. He never talks about the children, not even to me, but he loves them, I know he does. Once he told me that it hurts him every time one of our children is born, because he knows what's ahead for them. You know something? Each time, with each child, he's gone and got worse drunk than any other time. I don't know why, just that it's happened. He almost killed me and all the children the last time. He had a knife and he said he might use it. Then he took us all in the car; he made us get in, and he said if I didn't go along with him, he'd kill me, and if I did, there was a chance I'd live, and the children, too. So, I did, and he drove with his foot pressing on the gas all the way down. I could hear him trying to go faster, pushing on the pedal and trying to force it, and thank God the floor of the car wouldn't let him have his way. Well, he cursed us all, but most of all himself. He was after himself. He was chasing himself. He kept on saying that he had to catch himself and he had to get a hold on himself, and if he didn't, then he might as well die. In between, he'd tell us we were all going to die, and the sooner the better, because the only way for us to have peace, to have rest, was to die. There was no other way, he kept on shouting that to us.

"Then I must have lost my mind, like he had lost his. I started crying, and I can remember screaming to God please to turn my husband and me and the children away from Him, because it wasn't time yet, no it wasn't, for us to see Him. Then I crawled down, I reached down, I don't remember how I did, and pulled his foot away from the gas, and he didn't try to put it back, no he didn't; and the car went on and on, and then it began to slow down, and then it stopped, and then before he had a change of mind, I got out and I got all of us out, all except him, and we didn't leave him, though. Where could we go? I didn't know where we were, and it was dark. We spread ourselves down nearby to the car, and we tried to rest. I looked up at the sky and I couldn't forget it for the rest of my life, what I saw then and what I thought, no sir, I couldn't. When I die I know I'll be thinking like that and I'll be seeing like that: there was the sky, and it was dark, but the moon was there, almost round, and it hung low, real low, and it was colored funny, orange I guess; and all the stars were there, all over, everywhere it seemed. I'd never looked long enough to see so many stars, even though we do a lot of traveling, and we're up through the night, and you might have thought I'd have noticed them, all the stars, before. But moving across the country, you forget about the sky, I guess. I told my boy that, a few days later I did, that we shouldn't forget the sky, because we're going along underneath it a lot of the time, and he said that maybe we forget it because it's like a roof to us, and that if you're under a roof, you never look at it.

"While I was staring up there at the sky, I thought I heard something, a noise. It was the wind, I know, but to me it was God, it was God as well as the wind, and He was there, speaking right into both my ears, telling me to stay where I was, with the children, and near my husband, and He was looking over us, yes, and He'd see that the day would come when we'd have a home — a home that was ours, and that we'd never leave, and that we'd have for as long as God Himself is with us, and that's forever, you know. Maybe it would be up in one of those stars, one of the bright ones, one of the bright stars, maybe the home would be there, I thought — and then I saw one, a real bright star, and I said that's it, that's maybe where we would all go, but not until it's the right time, not a second before, and I was glad then that we stayed around, and didn't all die, and I'm still glad.

"Oh, not all the time, I'm not all the time glad, I'll admit that. I was glad then, when my husband woke up, and he said he was sorry and he was glad, and he'd try to be good and not lose himself on account of wine. I was glad later, too. Most of the time I'm glad, actually. It's just sometimes I don't feel glad. I don't feel glad at all. Like my husband, I sometimes feel myself going to pieces; yes sir, that's how it feels, like you're going to pieces. Once I was real bad — real, real bad — and I thought I'd die because I was in such a bad way. I recall I'd have the same dream every single night, even every time I put my head down, it seemed. It got so that I was scared to sleep, real scared. I'd try sitting up and resting, but not closing my eyes. After a while they'd close, though, and then it would come again, and the next thing I'd know I'd be waking up and shouting and crying and screaming, and sometimes I'd be standing up and even I'd be running around wherever we were staying, and my husband would be shaking me, or my children, they'd be crying and telling me no, no, no it wasn't so and don't be scared, Momma, and it'll be all right, they'd say. But I never believed them when I first woke up, it would take me an hour or so, I'd guess, to shake myself free of that dream, and I'd never really forget it, even when I'd be working. I'd be pulling the beans and putting them in the hamper, and I'd feel myself shaking, and there'd be someone nearby and she'd say, 'Martha, you took too much of that wine last night'; and I'd say no, I didn't touch a single drop, not last night or any other night for a long, long time. I wouldn't tell nobody, except my husband, but it was this dream I was having, and thank God now it's left me, but I can still see it, if I want to.

"There was a road, that's how the dream started, and it was all smoothed out and kept clean, and if you looked down on it you'd see yourself, like it was a mirror or something placed on the top of the road. I'd be standing there, and all of a sudden I'd see one car after the other coming, and inside the car would be one of my little ones, then there'd be the next child, and the next one, and each one had a car all to himself, and they'd be going down the road, almost as though they were going to go racing one another or something. But all of a sudden they'd explode, the cars would, one and then another, and soon they'd all be gone, and I couldn't find the sight of my children, and I'd still be standing there, where I was all the time, and I'd be shaking, whether in the dream or when I was waking up, I don't know. More than anything else, what hurt me was that the last thing that happened in the dream was that I'd see myself, standing on the road. I'd be looking down, and I could see my new child — yes, there'd be one I'd be carrying, and I'd be near the time to have the baby, and I'd be big and I'd be seeing myself, like in a mirror, like I said. But I'd have no other of my children left. They'd all be gone; and my husband, he'd be gone; and there'd be me, and my baby, not born yet, and that would be all. No, there'd be no cars, either. They'd all have gone and exploded, I guess."

How is such a dream to be analyzed or interpreted or made to explain something about her, about her wishes and fears and worries, about those things the rest of us would call her "psychological problems"? Why did the dream plague her then, seize control of her mind for those few weeks, then leave her, never to return? For all the world that separates her from me, for all her naïveté (as it is put by people like me when we talk about certain other people) and my sophistication (as it is also put by people like me when we talk about ourselves) we could pursue the meaning of her dream without too much self-consciousness, and with a minimum of theoretical contrivance, density or speculation. For several years, on and off, I had been telling her that I wanted to know how her children *felt*, how their spirits held up (or didn't) and she knew — right from the start, really — what I meant. In fact, once she told me what I meant: "I know. You want to see if they're scared, or if they're not. You want to see if they feel good, or if they feel lousy, real lousy — the way I guess their mother does a lot of the time!" So, the dream did not puzzle her all that much, only frighten her a lot, make her tremble, because at night she couldn't escape what by day she knew, could not help knowing — in every "level" of her mind, in her unconscious and in her subconscious and in her preconscious and in the thoroughly conscious part of her mind and yes, in her bones and her heart: "I'm always thinking, when I get ready to have another baby, that I wish I could be a better mother to them, and give them a better life to be born into than the one they're going to get on account of being my children, and not some other mother's. It's the worst of being a mother, knowing you can't offer your babies much, knowing there isn't much to offer them — there's really nothing, to be honest, but the little milk you have and the love you can give them, to start them off with. I know it's going to be bad for them when they grow up, and sometimes I wonder why God sends us here, all of us, if He knows how bad it's to be.

"There'll be a moment when I'll look at my children, and I'll wonder if they hold it against me for bringing them into this world, to live like we do, and not the others, with the money you know, and with the places where they can stay and not be always moving. The only rest we'll get, I'm afraid, the only rest we'll get is in the grave. Once, a long time ago, I said so, to my oldest boy, and he'll now and then repeat it to the younger ones. I want to tell him to stop, but I know he's right, and they don't get too upset with what he says, even if it's bad, like that. I think they sometimes don't really mind dying. God knows, they talk about it enough. Maybe it's what they hear from the minister. He's always telling us that everyone has to die, and that if you suffer here on earth you live longer in Heaven; and one of my girls, she said if that was the way, then maybe it was all right to be sick, but when you get to die, then is the time you're going to feel better, and not before then, no matter what you try to do."

Her children see no doctors for their various illnesses, and they don't actually "try to do" (as she put it) very much at all for themselves when they fall sick. They wait. They hope. Sometimes they say their prayers. Their mother also waits and hopes and prays, and apparently worries, too — and dreams and forgets her dreams and once, for a number of days, couldn't quite forget them, the terrible, terrible dreams that reflect in detail and in symbol the hard, hard life migrants live themselves, and see their children also as a matter of course begin to pursue. "I wouldn't mind it for myself," says the mother whose dream stayed with her so long, "but it's not good for the children, being 'on the road,' and when we're moving along I'll catch myself thinking I did wrong to bring all of them into the world — yes sir, I did wrong. But you can't think like that for too long, no sir, you can't; and I do believe the children, if they had their choice between not being born at all and being born and living with us — well, they'd choose to be themselves, to be with us, even if it's not easy for them and us, even so."

Sometimes when a mother like the one just quoted made an assertion like that to me, affirmed herself in spite of everything, said that there was after all a point to it all, a point to life, to life pure (and swift and unlucky) if not so simple, I felt in her the same questions I could not avoid asking myself. What *do* they think, those migrant children — about "life" and its hardships, about the reasons they must constantly travel, about the special future that more than likely faces them, in contrast to other American children? Does a migrant child of, say, seven or eight blame his parents for the pain he continues to experience, day after day, and for the hunger? Does that child see his later life as likely to be very much like his father's, or are there other alternatives and possibilities that occur to him as he goes about the business of getting bigger and working more and more in the fields? "What do *you* think?" I have heard from the mother who was once dream possessed and from other mothers like her; and there does come a time when people like me ought to stop throwing questions like that back at the people who ask them (as if we have some royal privilege that grants us the right to do so) and spell out what exactly (if anything) we do think.

Fortunately, migrant children have been quite willing to let me know what *they* see and think, what *they* believe about a number of matters. Like all children, they don't necessarily get into extended conversations; they don't say a lot, go into wordy descriptions of their moods and fantasies and desires and feelings. They do, however, throw out hints; they use their faces and their hands; they make gestures and grimaces; they speak out, with a phrase here and a series of sentences there. Moreover, it has been my experience that they will also use crayons and paints to great advantage, so that given enough time and trust the observer (become viewer) can see on paper, in outline and in colors and shapes, all sorts of suggestive, provocative, and instructive things. When the migrant child *then* is asked a question or two, about this or that he has portrayed, pictured, given form and made light or dark — well, I believe there is a lot to be heard in those moments, moments in a sense after the deed of creation has been finished, moments when thoughts and (more assertively) opinions can emerge from something concrete, something done, even something achieved, in this case achieved by children not always used to that kind of effort.

So, the children have drawn pictures, dozens and dozens of pictures; particular migrant children whom I came to know for two, maybe three, sometimes four years, and whom, at times, I asked to use paper and pencils and crayons and paints. I might, for instance, want to see a favorite "spot" drawn, a place the child especially liked, a house he might like or a camp he didn't like at all. I might want to know about all those schools, about how they looked and how they seemed from the inside and how they can be compared, one to the other, the good and the bad, the pleasant and the very unpleasant. I might be interested in the crops, in which ones are good and bad to harvest, and how they look, the beans or the tomatoes or the celery or the cucumbers, when they are there, ready and waiting. I might ask about the essence of migratory life, about the way the road appears to the child, about what there is to be seen and avoided and enjoyed on those roads, about what remains in a given child's mind when all the memories are sorted out, and one of them is left — to be chosen, to be drawn, and then reluctantly or shyly or cautiously or openly or even insistently handed to me as "it," the thing that was suggested as a possible subject by me, and therefore to be drawn as a favor or in fear, or resisted out of fear or anger, or refused out of fear or confusion or resentment.

What do they see, then — see in their mind's eye, see casually or intensely, see and through pictures enable others to see? Certain themes do come up repeatedly, no doubt because migrant children share a number of concerns. Tom, for instance, was a seven-year-old boy when he drew for me a rather formless and chaotic and dreary picture (Figure 1) of the fields he already knew as a helper to his parents, a harvester really. When he was five I had seen him race along those rows of beans — picking, picking, picking. Once in a while he would show his age by shouting out his achievements, by pointing to anyone near at hand how much he had just done, how experienced he had become. Children are often like that, a little enthusiastic and a little boastful. They will learn, we tell ourselves, they will learn to take their own abilities for granted, to deal less ostentatiously and noisily with themselves and the world. I knew Tom between the ages of five, when he started working in the fields, and seven, when he still worked at harvesting crops. I spent a lot of time with him and his family during those two years, and since then have made a point of seeing him at least several times each year. (At this writing, he is no longer a child; he is fourteen and he lives with a woman and he is a father and like his parents he is a migrant farm worker — but that will have to be told elsewhere, when I describe the lives of grown-up, yes, at fourteen, grown-up migrants.)

Tom always liked to draw pictures, and in fact knew enough about what some people would call "the problems of representation" to appreciate his own failings: "I'm no good. I'll bet some kids can really do a good picture for you. Each time I try, but when it's done I can't say it looks the way I'd like it to look. It's not like it should be — real, I mean. I know you said it doesn't have to be, but is it a good picture if you have to tell someone what you've tried to draw?" Of course I reassured him. I gave him my prepared speech, full of encouragement and friendliness and praise, all of which, I have to add, I very much meant — be-

cause he did try hard, and his mind had a lot going on "inside" or
"deep down," all of which he very much wanted to put on paper
and afterwards talk about.

The fields, the dark, jumbled, confusing, sunless fields —
guarded, be it noted, by a black fence and the outlines of some
dark faceless men — were nearby when Tom drew the picture.
They were not in sight, those fields, because a strip of pines
intervened — none of which appears on the paper — but as Tom
used his crayons he could hear all sorts of sounds from the
migrants, who were eating their lunches and talking and arguing.
One man was singing. Tom worked on the grass, used a wooden
board I carried around, talked as he drew, interrupted his work
to eat *his* lunch. This is perhaps the moment for me to mention
something about migrant children: in contrast to all other children I have observed and worked with, migrant boys and girls
are quite willing to interrupt their particular tasks — for instance,
drawing a picture or playing various games with me — for any
number of reasons. It is not that they are agitated or anxious or
unable to concentrate and finish what they start. It is not that
they run about helter-skelter because they are confused or
alarmed or afraid. It is not that they don't understand what we
are attempting, and have to move on rather than reveal their lack
of comprehension. Yes, some of them, like many other children,
do have some of the difficulties I have just listed; but I emphatically do not have such essentially psychopathological matters in
mind. The habits of children are vastly responsive to the habits of
their parents. If parents accept (because they have learned they
must) the necessity of constantly moving from one field to
another, from one responsibility to another, each of which can
only be partially fulfilled by any given person and indeed requires a whole field of people, then it is only natural that their
children will experience no great need to stick at things stubbornly or indeed consistently. The child has learned that there is
always the next place, the next journey, the next occasion. The
fields are there, being worked on when the child arrives with his
parents. The fields are still there, and often enough still being
worked on when the child with his family leaves — for another

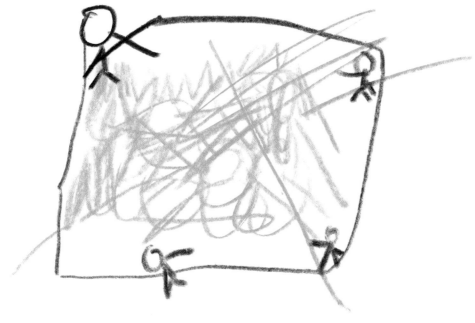

FIGURE 1

FIGURE 2

FIGURE 3

FIGURE 4

location, another cycle of arrival and initiative and involvement and exhaustion and departure, a cycle that, in the words of the Bible, words that in my opinion convey exactly what thousands of children feel, is a "world without end."

If Tom can distract himself, say, for candy and Coke, yet return and finish what he has started, he can also do a quick turn of drawing or sketching and pause for discussion, which itself can be a pleasant distraction to a child not made anxious at the prospect of a change of direction or action: "I'd like to stop for a second, because when we're traveling on a road like that one, we'll have to stop, you know. My daddy, he says that a field isn't so bad when you're resting on it; it's only when you're picking that a field is so bad. No, most of the time we don't stop by the road. My daddy, he says you can get into a lot of trouble that way, because the police are always looking to see if we're not keeping moving, and if they catch you sitting by the road, they'll take you to jail and they won't let you out so easy, either. They'll make you promise to get away and never come back. They'll tell you that if you're going to be picking, you've got to go ahead and pick, and then you've got to get away, fast. That's why you have to watch where you're going when you're on the way to a farm, and you're not sure where it is. You've got to be careful, and the best thing is to follow someone who can lead you there, that's what my daddy says. Then, if you have to stop, you can find a path and go down it, and you'll be safe, and you won't end up being caught."

He does not seem to regard the fields as very safe or pleasant places to be. The more he works on his drawing, the more he seems compelled to talk about the subject: "I like to be moving along. If you keep moving you're safer than if you just stop in a field, and someone comes by, and they can ask you what you're doing, and they can tell you to get back in the car and go away as fast as the motor will go. Once I was really scared, and so was everyone else. We went way down a road that we thought was safe, and there was a little pond there, and we went and played in it, because they said we could, Momma and Daddy did. Then the man came, he was a foreman my daddy told me afterwards.

Then he said we would all be arrested and we were no good, and
we should be in jail and stay there forever. My daddy said we'd
go right away, and we did, and he said — the rest of the day he
said it over and over — that you're in trouble moving from one
state to the other, because the state police, they don't like you,
and the sheriffs, they don't like you, and you know the foremen,
they have badges, and they can arrest you, and they have men
with guns and they'll come along and hold one right to your ears
and your head, and they'll tell you that either you work or you
move on up the road, and if you sit there and try to eat something, or like that, then you'll get yourself in jail, and it won't be
easy to get out, no sir. That's why it's bad luck to stop and rest in
a field, and if you see one that has crops, then it's bad luck,
too — because you're lucky if you'll have any money left, for all
the work you do. I don't like fields, that's what I think."

What else is there to say about Tom's drawing, about the
migrant life he has already become part of? Tom looks upon the
fields and roads, the fields and roads that never really end for
families like his, as both fearful and redemptive: "One thing I'll
tell you, if it's real bad on a farm, if they're watching you too
close and they don't pay you what they should, then you can
sneak away in the middle of the night. Even if they have their
guards looking over where you're staying, the guards will fall
asleep, and before they wake up, you can be on your way, and
then you've got a chance to find a better place to work. That's
why you have to keep your eye on the road, and when you leave
it to stay in a cabin near a field, or in a tent like we were in the
last time, then you should always remember the fastest way to
the main road, and you should point the car so it's ready to go
and all you have to do is get in the car and start the driving. It
wasn't long ago that we did that, just packed up and left. We
pretended we were asleep for a while, in case anyone was looking, and then in the middle of the night we up and went, and
they probably didn't find out until it was morning, and by then
we were a long way and my daddy and the others, they checked
in with this man they knew, and he gave them all work to do,
picking beans, and he said he was glad to have them, and he'd

give them every penny they earned, and not to worry — but my daddy says you never know if you should believe them or not, and a lot of the time they'll just double-cross you and go back on their promise, and you're left with almost nothing, and there isn't much you can do, so you move on and hope it won't keep happening like that, no sir; and sometimes it won't either, because you'll work, and then they'll pay you right what you deserve, and that makes it much better."

Does Tom wonder where it will all end, the travel and the new places to occupy for ever so short a time? Does he dream of some road that will lead to some other way of life? Does the continual motion make him grow weary and resentful, in spite of his own words to the contrary? Does he think about other children, who live not far from the roads he knows so well, children he occasionally, sporadically meets in this school, where he attended classes for a month, and that one, which he liked, but had to leave after two weeks? I have asked him questions like those, but often he condenses his answers in a particular drawing — such as this one (Figure 2): "I don't know where that road is going; I mean, no, I didn't have a road I was thinking of when I drew. I just made the road, and it probably keeps going until it hits the icebergs, I guess. I put some little roads in, but you shouldn't leave the road you're going on. I remember I asked my daddy once if he knew where the highway ends, the one we take North, and he said it probably ended where you get as far North as you can get — and there aren't any crops there, he said, so we'll never see the place, but it's very cold there, and maybe a lot of it has no people, because it's better to live where it's warmer. I said I'd like for us one time to keep going and see an iceberg and see what it's like there. My daddy said maybe we would, but he didn't mean it, I could tell. A lot of the time I'll ask him if we could go down a road further, and see some places, and he says yes, we can, but he doesn't want to — my momma says we've got to be careful and we can't keep asking to go here and there, because we're not supposed to and we'll get in trouble. She says we should close our eyes and imagine that there's a big fence on each side of the road, and that we can't get off, even if we

wanted to and tried to, because of the fence. That's why I put the
fence in, a little, to keep the car there from getting in trouble
with the police.

"No, I didn't mean for there to be a crash, no. It would be bad
if one happened. My daddy's brothers, three of them got killed in
a crash. They were coming back to Florida from up North, from
New Jersey it was, and the bus, it just hit a truck and a lot of
people got killed. They say the bus was old, and once down here
the brakes stopped working, but the crew leader had it fixed, and
it was supposed to be safe. They were younger than my daddy,
yes sir, and he said he didn't see how it could be anything but
God's desire, that they should all, all of them, be saved forever-
more from going up and down through the states and never
being paid enough, except for some food and a place to sleep,
and after that, they don't give you much money for anything else.
I figured that if I was picturing the road and me in the car, I'd
put a truck there, too; because, you know, we see a lot of trucks
and the buses, too, when we go through Florida and then up
North. But I hope the car and the bus in the picture don't crash
like they do a lot of the time.

"Sometimes — yes, sometimes I think to myself when we're
passing a town, that I'd like to look through the place and maybe
stay there — I mean live there, and not go right on to the next
place. I used to ask why, I'd ask my momma and my daddy and
my uncles, but they all said I should stop with the questions, and
stop trying to get a lot of reasons for things, and like that. In
school once, in Florida it was, there was a real nice teacher (it
was last year) and she said to the class that they should all be
nice to me and the rest of us, because if people like us didn't go
around doing the picking, then there'd be no food for everyone to
eat — the fruit and vegetables. A girl laughed and said that was
a big joke, because her daddy had a big farm, and he didn't use
any people, just machines. I nearly asked her what her daddy
was growing, but I didn't. I guess I was scared. The teacher
didn't do anything. She just said we should go on and do our
work, and the less trouble in the class the better it would be all
the way around. I thought afterwards that I'd like to follow her

home, the girl, and see if she was telling the truth; because I didn't believe her.

"I asked my daddy, and he said there are some farms like that, but not many in Florida, because the farmers need us to pick beans and tomatoes, and the machines cost a lot, and you can't get a second crop from the plants after the machine. No, I didn't speak to her, and I didn't follow her either. I mean, I did for a little while, but I got scared, and my friend, he said we'd better turn around or we'd be in jail, and we wouldn't get out of there for a long, long time. Then we did, we turned around, and when I told my sister — she's ten — she said we were lucky we're not there now, in jail, because the police, they keep their eyes on us all the time, if we leave the camps or the fields, to go shopping or to school or like that. I said one of these days I'd slip by. I'd get me a suit or something, and a real shiny pair of shoes, and I'd just walk down the street until I came to where they live, the kids that go to that school, and if someone came up to me and tried to stop me and if he asked me what I was doing, then I'd say I was just looking, and I thought I'd go get some ice cream, and I'd have the money and I'd show it to the policeman, and they couldn't say I was trying to steal something, or I was hiding from them, the policemen and like that. But my sister said they'd just laugh and pick me up, like I was a bean or a tomato, and the next thing I'd know I'd be there, in jail, and they might never let me out, except if one of the growers comes, and he would say it was OK if they let me out, and he'd pay the fine, but then I'd have to work for him.

"That's how you end up, I hear. They never do anything a lot of people, but work for the same man, because they always are owing him money, the grower, and he is always getting them out of jail, and then they owe him more money. My daddy says, and my sister, she says that the grower keeps on giving them the wine, and they drink it, and they'll be drunk, and the police will be called, and arrest them, and then the grower will come, one of his men mostly, and pay to get people out, and then they'll have to work some more — until they get killed. I hope it'll never happen like that to me. I'd like someday, I'll be honest, I'd like to

go to the city, and I could get a job there. Once there was a nice
boy who sat beside me — not long ago, I think it was this same
year — and I was going to ask him if I could get a job from his
father. No, I didn't want to ask him what his father's job was, but
he seemed like he was real rich, the boy, and I thought maybe I
could get a job, and I could maybe live there, in the house there,
you know, where the boy does, and then I wouldn't have to be
going North later this year."

Would he miss his mother and father? "No — I mean, yes. But
I think they could come and see me sometimes. If the people let
me live in their house, maybe they would let my daddy come and
see me, and my mother could come, and they wouldn't stay too
long, I know."

Migrant children see everything as temporary. Places come and
go; and people and schools and fields. The children don't know
what it is, in Tom's words, to "stay too long"; rather, they live in a
world that lacks holidays and trips to department stores and
libraries. Children like Tom, for example, don't see any mail,
because their parents lack an address, a place from which letters
are sent and to which letters come. Children like Tom don't know
about bookshelves and walls with pictures on them and comfortable chairs in cozy living rooms and telephones (which are put
by telephone companies into *residences*) and cabinets full of
glassware or serving dishes or stacks of canned goods. A suitcase
hardly seems like a very important thing to any of us, yet migrant
children have dreamed of having one, dreamed and dreamed and
can say why after they draw a picture, as a girl of nine named
Doris did: "I was smaller when I saw a store, and it had big
suitcases and little ones; they all were made of leather, I think. I
asked my mother if she could please, one day, get one for me; not
a big one, because I know they must cost more money than we
could ever have, but a small one. She said why did I want one,
and I said it was because I could keep all my things together,
and they'd never get lost, wherever we go. I have a few things
that are mine — the comb, the rabbit's tail my daddy gave me
before he died, the lipstick and the fan, and like that — and I
don't want to go and lose them, and I've already lost a lot of

things. I had a luck bracelet and I left it someplace, and I had a scarf, a real pretty one, and it got lost, and a mirror, too. That's why if I could have a place to put my things, my special things, then I'd have them and if we went all the way across the country and back, I'd still have them, and I'd keep them."

She still doesn't have her suitcase. In fact, Doris doesn't have very much of anything, so that when I asked her to draw whatever she wished, she answered as follows: "I don't know if there's anything I can draw." I suggested something from the countryside — she seemed sad, after all, and in no mood for my kind of clever silences, meant to prod children like her into this or that psychological initiative (and revelation). She said no, the countryside was the countryside, and she sees quite enough of it, so there is no need to give those trees and fields and roads any additional permanence. Rather, she said this: "I see a lot of the trees and the farms. I'd like to draw a picture I could like, and I could look at it, and it would be nice to look at, and I could take it with me. But I don't know what to draw." Her judgment on the countryside was fairly clear and emphatic, but so was her sense of confusion. She knew what she didn't want to do, but she was at loose ends, too. She seemed to be asking herself some questions. What *do* I want to see, and carry with me through all those dismal trips and rides and detours and long, long, oh so long journeys? Where can I find a little beauty in the world, a touch of joy, a bit of refreshment and encouragement — and self-supplied at that, through crayons I have myself wielded on paper? Is there anything worth remembering, worth keeping, worth holding onto tenaciously, without any letup whatsoever? Perhaps I am forcing melodrama on Doris's mind, which certainly needs no more worries or fears. Perhaps for her life is a matter of getting up and working in the fields and eating what there is to eat and sleeping and moving on, moving here and there and always, always moving. I don't think so, though. For all the fancy words I use, and all the ambiguities and ironies I hunger after, the little girl Doris has insisted that I also listen to her. She has even made me realize I must do more than listen and observe and collect my "data" and, like her, move on: "If I draw a picture, a good one, I want to keep it. The last time you said you wanted it, and I told my mother I liked it and I wanted to keep it. I asked my mother if I could get some glue and put it on the window of the car, but she said no. She said we'd get stopped and arrested."

So, Doris did two pictures at each sitting, one for herself and another one, as similar as possible, for me — all of which leads me to state another thing I have noticed especially among migrant children: unlike other children I have come to know, girls like Doris and boys like Tom don't want to give up drawings they make, not to me and not even to others in their family or to neighbors. It is not a matter of property; nor does the child cling to the picture because he feels "realized" at last through something artistically done. Nor is he drawn irresistibly to the form and symmetry he has wrought, to all those colors at last made accessible to himself. Doris one day told me why she wouldn't let go, and I will let her explanation — unadorned by my translations and interpretations — stand as quite good enough: "I just want it — because it's good to look at, and it may not be as good as it could be, but it was the best I could do, and I can take it and look at it, and it will be along with me up North, and I can think of being back here where I drew it, and then I'll know we'll be coming back here where I drew it, and I can look ahead to that, you see." Doris did a second drawing, essentially the same, which she gave to me, then put the first version away — with her rabbit tail and other belongings. She had done many other drawings for me, but somehow this one, a picture of the few things she owned, meant more to her than any of the others. It was as if she had finally found some kind of permanence for her meager possessions, and also a talisman of sorts. So long as her things had a new and separate life of their own, in the picture, they would all be collected together, her little world of possessions, as they could not be in the suitcase that has never come. Now she could look ahead and look back and have some sense of direction, some idea of a destination, some feeling that life has its rhythms and sequences and purposes. But I said I would not do what I have just done, speak for her, be her interpreter.

We are all compelled whether we know it or not, and the well-

educated and well-analyzed are not the only ones who comprehend the mind's constraints. I have to make my little and not so
little remarks, and Doris has to carry a few personal effects all
over America. Another child known to me, whom I will call
Larry, can paint the necessities that govern his particular life.
(Figure 3). What would he like to draw above all else, he was
asked, and he said in reply that he didn't want to draw at all this
time. He wanted to paint. Well, why did he want to paint this
time? (We had together been using crayons for over a year.)
"Oh, I don't know — except that tomorrow is my birthday." He
was to be nine. Half because I wasn't actually sure what day
"tomorrow" was, and half because, I suppose, I knew the *reason*
why time had become blurred for me during the weeks I had
moved about with Larry and his family, I asked him what day
his birthday was: "It's in the middle of the summer, on the
hottest day." He was dead serious, and I was both puzzled and
embarrassed, a condition of my mind which he noticed.

He was moved to explain things, to help me — to do what I am
trained to do, formulate and soothe and heal or whatever. "I
don't know the day. The teacher in one of the schools kept saying
I had to bring in a certificate that said where I was born and
gave the day and like that. I asked my mother and she said there
wasn't any. I told the teacher, and she said that was bad, and to
check again. I checked, and my mother said no, and so did my
daddy, and so did the crew leader. He said I should tell the
teacher to shut up, and if she didn't I could just walk out of
school and they wouldn't go after me or give me any trouble at
all. No, I didn't leave, no sir; I stayed there for as long as we did
in the camp. It was the best school I'd ever seen. They had cold
air all the time, no matter how hot it got. I wanted to stay there
all night. They gave you good cookies all the time, and milk; and
the teacher, she said she wanted to buy us some clothes and pay
for it herself. She said I should tell my mother to come to school
and they would have a talk; and she said I should get my birth
certificate and hold on to it. Then one day she brought in hers
and showed it to us; and she said we all should stand up and say
to the class where we were born and on what day of the year; but

I didn't know. She said we should ask where our mothers were born and our fathers. So I did and I told her. I was born here in Florida, and my mother in Georgia and my father there, too; and my mother said it was a hot, hot day, and she thought it was right in the middle of summer, July it must be, she said, around about there, but she wasn't sure. Then I asked her if she'd go register me, like the teacher said, and she said I'd better stay home and help out with the picking, if I was going to go listening to everything and then getting the funny ideas and trying to get us all in trouble, because the crew man, he said if we started going over to the courthouse and asking one thing of them, and then another — well, they'd soon have us all in jail, my mother said."

He painted a picture of his certificate, and thus showed both me and himself that he could persist with an idea, an intention. Paint to him meant a more worthy and lasting commitment. To paint is to emphasize, to declare out loud and for all to hear — or so he feels: "If you paint a certificate it won't rub away, like with the crayons. I don't know how they make the real ones, but they have big black letters and one of them, it has a red circle — and the teacher, she said it was a *seal,* and it belonged to a city and it was put on a lot of important papers." If he had his certificate what would he do with it, once he had shown it to his teacher? He would keep it, treasure it, fasten it to himself in some foolproof way that he himself could only vaguely suggest rather than spell out: "I'd never lose it, like I did my belt. My daddy gave me a belt, and I was afraid if I put it on all the time, it wouldn't look so good after a while; so I kept it with me, and put it with my shoes and when we went to church I'd have on my shoes and my belt. But once in a camp there was a fire, and I lost my belt and my shoes; and I should have worn the belt, my mother said, or carried it with me wherever I went, even to the field. But I didn't, and too bad."

Shoes cannot be taken for granted by children like him, nor belts, nor socks; nor (so it seems) birth certificates, which presumably everyone in America has. Since I know that children like Larry are born in cabins or even in the fields, with no doctors around to help, and since I know that they move all over and have no official address, no place of residence, I should not have been surprised that those same children lack birth certificates — yet, I was indeed surprised. Who am I? Where do I come from? When did it really happen, my entrance into this world? Those are questions which, after all, the rest of us never stop asking, in one form or another; and they are questions Larry asks himself in a specially grim and stark fashion, because he really doesn't have the usual, concrete answers, let alone all the fancy symbolic or metaphysical ones. Since he is, I believe, a bright and shrewd child, he won't quite let the matter drop, as many migrant children seem to do. I'm not at all convinced they actually *do* let "the matter" drop. Given a little acquaintance and the right conversational opening, I have heard other migrant children tell me what Larry has told me: it is hard to settle for near answers and half answers when the issue is *yourself*, your origins as a person and as a citizen.

Put a little differently, it is hard to be an exile, to be sent packing all the time, to be banished, to be turned out and shown the door. In the drawings of migrant children I constantly see, at no one's behest but their own, roads and fields (quite naturally) but also (and a little more significantly) those souvenirs and reminders of other places and times — when a comb was given as a present, when something that at least looked precious was found; and finally other drawings show even more mysterious objects, such as windows that are attached to no buildings, and doors that likewise seem suspended in space. Why, exactly why, should a number of migrant children flex their artistic muscles over windows and doors, over sandboxes, or more literally, over a series of quadrangles? I cannot speak for all the migrant children I know, even as many of them can only stumble upon their words, only stand mute, only look and grimace and smile and frown, only ask questions in reply to questions. Yet, a few of those children eventually and often unexpectedly have managed to have their say, managed to let me know what they're getting at, and by implication, what is preventing me from recognizing the obvious concerns of their lives. I have in mind a girl of eight who spends most of her time in Collier County, Florida, and Palm Beach County, Florida, but manages a yearly trek north to upstate New York and New Jersey and into New England, to the farms of Connecticut. As I became a regular visitor of her family, she above all the other children expressed an interest in the paints and crayons I brought along, as well as the various games. She loved a top I had, and a Yo-Yo. She loved the toy cars and trucks and tractors: "I know about all of those. I know my trucks. I know my tractors. I know the cars, and I've been in a lot of them." She once asked me how fast I've driven. She once asked me what it was like to be on an airplane. She once asked me if an airplane could just take off — and land on the moon or the stars or the sun. She once asked me why there are always clouds up North — and why down South the sun is so mean and hot, so pitiless to people who don't own air conditioners or screens or even mosquito repellents or lotions to soothe burned and blistered skin.

She was, in fact, always asking me questions and making sly, provocative, even enigmatic remarks. "I love the Yo-Yo" she told me, "because it keeps going, up and down, and that's what I do." What did she mean? "Well, we don't stay in one camp too long. When the crops are in, you have to move." As for the pictures she did, she liked to put a Yo-Yo or two in them ("for fun") but most of all she liked to make sure the sun was blocked out by clouds that loomed large over the sketched or painted scene — which frequently would have a door or a window or both, along with, say, a lone tree or some disorganized shrubbery. In one picture (Figure 4) she allowed a door to dominate the paper. I expected her to *do* something with the door, to attach it or use it in some way, but she simply let it be and went on to other things, to the sun and its grim face, to the clouds, those sad, inevitable clouds of hers, and to a sandbox and a Yo-Yo, and finally, to a tall plant which I thought might be a small tree. I asked her about that — the pine tree, as I saw it: "No, no, it's a big, tall corn. We pick a lot of corn up North." She was, in other words, getting ready to go North. It was early May, and soon they would all be on the road. What does that mean, though, to *her*? I've asked her that

question in various ways and she in her own ways has replied —
through her drawings and paintings, and in the games we've
played and finally, with these words: "I hate to go, yes sir, I do. I
found some sand over there, and my brother Billy and my
brother Eddie and me, we like to go and make things there. Soon
we'll be going, I know. I can tell when it's happening. First we
move our things into the car, and then we go in, and then we go
away and I don't know if we'll come back here or not. Maybe, my
mother says — all depending, you know. I try to remember
everything, so I won't leave anything behind. Every time we go,
my daddy, he gets sore at me, because at the last second I'll be
running out of the car and checking on whether I've left any of
my things there. I'll go inside and come out and then I know I
haven't left something."

Twice I watched her do just that, watched her enter the cabin,
look around and leave, watched *her* watch — look and stare and
most of all touch, as if by putting her hands on walls and floors
and doors and windows she could absorb them, keep them, make
them more a part of her. She is a touching girl. She touches. In a
minute or two, while the rest of her family frets and adjusts
themselves, one to the other and all to the car which they more
than fill up, this little girl of theirs scurries about — inspecting,
scanning, brushing her body and especially her hands and most
especially her fingers on a broken-down shack she is about to
leave. When I saw her look out of the window (no screens) and
open and close the door several times (it didn't quite open or
quite close) I realized at last what all those windows and doors
she drew might have meant, and the sandboxes and the corn up
North, the corn that was waiting for her, summoning her family,
drawing them all from the cabins, making an uproar out of their
lives: up and down, to and fro, in and out, here and there, they
would go — hence the Yo-Yo and the windows from which one
looks out to say good-bye and the doors which lead in and out, in
and out, over and over again.

It is hard, very hard to do justice to the lives of such children
with words; and I say that because I have tried and feel decidedly inadequate to the job — of all the jobs I have had, to this

one I feel particularly inadequate. I do not wish to deny these American children the efforts they make every day — to live, to make sense of the world, to get along with one another and all sorts of grown-up people, to find a little pleasure and fun and laughs in a world that clearly has not seen fit to smile very generously upon them. Nor do I wish to deny these children their awful struggles, which in sum amount to a kind of continuing, indeed endless chaos. It is all too easy, as I must keep on saying, for a doctor like me to do either — see only ruined lives or see only the courageous and the heroic in these children. I am tempted to do the former because for one thing there is a lot of misery to see, and for another I have been trained to look for that misery, see it, assess it, make a judgment about its extent and severity; and I want to praise their courage as an act, perhaps, of reparation — because I frankly have often felt overwhelmed by the conditions I have witnessed during seven years of work with migrant farm families: social conditions, medical conditions, but above all a special and extraordinary kind of human condition, a fate really, and one that is terrible almost beyond description.

What Conrad, in "Heart of Darkness," called "the horror, the horror" eventually has its effect on the observer as well as the observed, particularly when children are the observed and a professional observer of children does the observing.[8] "The horror, the horror" refers to man's inhumanity to man, the brutality that civilized people somehow manage to allow in their midst. The crucial word is "somehow"; because in one way or another all of us, certainly including myself, have to live with, contend with even, the lives of migrant children — those I have just attempted to describe and hundreds of thousands of others — who live (it turns out, when we take the trouble to inquire) just about everywhere in the United States: North and South, East and West, in between, near towns or cities and also out of almost everyone's sight.[9]

Somehow, then, we come to terms with them, the wretched of the American earth. We do so each in his or her own way. We ignore them. We shun them. We claim ignorance of them. We declare ourselves helpless before their problems. We say they deserve what they get, or don't deserve better, or do deserve better — if only they would go demand it. We say things are complicated, hard to change, stubbornly unyielding. We say progress is coming, has even come, will come in the future. We say (in a pinch) that yes, it *is* awful — but so have others found life: awful, mean, harsh, cruel, and a lot of other words. Finally, we say yes it *is* awful — but so awful that those who live under such circumstances are redeemed, not later in Heaven, as many of them believe, but right here on this earth, where they become by virtue of extreme hardship and suffering a kind of elect: hard and tough and shrewd and canny and undeluded; open and honest and decent and self-sacrificing; hauntingly, accusingly hardworking. I have many times extolled these children and their people — extolled them all almost to Heaven, where I suppose I also believe they will eventually and at last get their reward, and where, by the way, they will be out of my way, out of my mind, which balks at saying what it nevertheless knows must be said about how utterly, perhaps unspeakably devastating a migrant life can be for children.

I am talking about what I imagine can loosely be called psychological issues, but I do not mean to ignore the bodily ills of these children: the hunger and the chronic malnutrition that they learn to accept as unavoidable; the diseases that one by one crop up as the first ten years of life go by, diseases that go undiagnosed and untreated, diseases of the skin and the muscles and the bones and the vital organs, vitamin- and mineral-deficiency diseases and untreated congenital diseases and infectious diseases and parasitic diseases and in the words of one migrant mother, "all the sicknesses that ever was." She goes on: "I believe our children get them, the sicknesses, and there isn't anything for us to do but pray, because I've never seen a doctor in my life, except once, when he delivered my oldest girl; the rest, they was just born, yes sir, and I was lucky to have my sister near me, and that's the way, you know." She has some idea about other things, too. She thinks her children are living in Hell, literally that. She is a fierce, biblical woman when she gets going — when, that is, she is talking about her children. I have heard the sermons, many of them from her, and I see no reason, after these years of work with mothers like her and children like hers, to refuse her a place in the last, sad summing up that mercifully allows an observer to go on to other matters while the observed, in this instance, pursue the most they can possibly hope for — the barest, most meager fragments of what can only ironically be called *a life*.

"This life," says the mother, "it's no good on me and my husband, but it's much worse than no good on the children we have, much worse than it can be for any of God's children, that's what I believe. I'll ask myself a lot of the time why a child should be born, if this is the life for him; but you can't make it that we have no children, can you? — because it's the child that gives you the hope. I say to myself that maybe I can't get out of this, but if just one, just one and no more of my children gets out, then I'd be happy and I'd die happy. Sometimes I dream of my girl or one of my boys, that they've left us and found a home, and it has a backyard, and we all were there and eating in the backyard, and no one could come along and tell us to get out, because we could tell *them* to get out, because it's our land, and we own it, and no one can shout at us and tell us to keep moving, keep moving. That's the life we live — moving and moving and moving. I asked the minister a little while ago; I asked him why do we have to always move and move, just to stay alive, and not have no money and die, and he said we're seeking God, maybe, and that's why we keep moving, because God, He traveled, you know, all over the Holy Land, and He kept on trying to convert people to be good to Him, you know, but they weren't, oh no they weren't, and He was rebuked, and He was scorned (remember those words?) and He couldn't stay anyplace, because they were always after Him, always, and they didn't want Him here and they didn't want Him there, and all like that, and all during His life, until they punished Him so bad, so bad it was.

"The minister, he said if you suffer — well, you're God's people, and that's what it's about. I told him that once he preached to us and told us all morning that it was God who was supposed to suffer, and He did. Now it shouldn't be us who's going from place to place and, you know, nobody will let us stop and live with them, except if we go to those camps, and they'll take all your money away, that you must know, because they deduct for the food and the transporting, they tell you. Pretty

soon they'll give you a slip of paper and it says you've worked
and picked all the beans there are, and all the tomatoes, and the
field is empty, and you've made your money, but you've been
eating, and they took you up from Florida to where you are, and
it cost them money to transport you, so it's all even, and they
don't owe you and you don't owe them, except that you've got to
get back, and that means you'll be working on the crops to get
back South, and it never seems to stop, that's what. Like I said,
should we be doing it, the crops every last place, and without
anything to have when it's over? They'll come and round you up
and tell you it can be jail or the fields, that's what they will tell
you, if you get a bad crew leader, that's what. Once we had a
nice one, and he was always trying to help us, and he wanted us
to make some money and save it, and one day we could stop
picking and our children, they could just be, in one place they
could be, and they wouldn't always be crying when we leave. But
he died, the good crew man, and it's been bad since. You know,
there comes a time, yes sir, there does, when the child, he'll stop
crying, and then he doesn't care much, one way or the other. I
guess he's figured out that we've got to go, and it's bad all the
time, and there's no getting around it."

That is what the migrant child eventually learns about "life,"
and once learned finds hard to forget. He learns that each day
brings toil for his parents, backbreaking toil: bending and stooping and reaching and carrying. He learns that each day means a
trip: to the fields and back from the fields, to a new county or on
to another state, another region of the country. He learns that
each day means not aimlessness and not purposeless motion, but
compelled, directed (some would even say utterly *forced*) travel.
He learns, quite literally, that the wages of work is more work.
He learns that wherever he goes he is both wanted and unwanted, and that in any case, soon there will be another place
and another and another. I must to some extent repeat and
repeat the essence of such migrancy (the wandering, the disapproval and ostracism, the extreme and unyielding poverty) because children learn that way, learn by repetition, learn by going
through something ten times and a hundred times and a thousand times, until finally it is there, up in their minds in the form

of what me and my kind call an "image," a "self-image," a *notion,*
that is, of life's hurts and life's drawbacks, of life's calamities —
which in this case are inescapable, relentless, unremitting.

By the time migrant children are nine and ten and eleven they
have had their education, learned their lessons. In many cases
they have long since stopped even the pretense of school. They
are working, or helping out with younger children, or playing
and getting ready to go out on dates and love and become
parents and follow their parents' footsteps. As for their emotions,
they are, to my eye, an increasingly sad group of children. They
have their fun, their outbursts of games and jokes and teasing
and taunting and laughing; but they are for too long stretches of
time downcast and tired and bored and indifferent and to themselves very unkind. They feel worthless, blamed, frowned upon,
spoken ill of. Life itself, the world around them, even their own
parents, everything that is, seems to brand them, stigmatize
them, view them with disfavor, and in a million ways call them to
account — lace into them, pick on them, tell them off, dress them
down. The only answer to such a fate is sex, when it becomes
possible, and drink, when it is available, and always the old,
familiar answers — travel, work, rest when that can be had, and
occasionally during the year a moment in church, where forgiveness can be asked, where the promise of salvation can be heard,
where some wild, screaming, frantic, angry, frightened, nervous,
half-mad cry for help can be put into words and songs and really
given the body's expression: turns and twists and grimaces and
arms raised and trunks bent and legs spread and pulled together
and feet used to stamp and kick and move — always that, move.

"I do a lot of walking and my feet are always tired, but in
church I can walk up and down, but not too far; and my feet feel
better, you know. It's because God must be near." So she believes — that God is not far off. So her children believe, too.
What is life like? One keeps on asking those children that question — for the tenth or so time (or is it the hundredth time?) in
the last year or two, because they do seem to want to talk about
what is ahead for them, and *that,* one believes, is a good sign for
them and a helpful thing (it must be acknowledged) for anyone

who wants to find out about such matters, about what people see their life to be, their future to be, their destiny I suppose it could be called. "Well, I'll tell you," the girl says gravely in answer to the question. Then she doesn't say anything for a long time and the observer and listener gets nervous and starts rummaging for another question, another remark, to lighten the atmosphere, to keep things going, to prevent all that awkwardness, a sign no doubt of mistrust or suspicion or a poor "relationship." Yet, once in a while there does come an answer, in fits and starts, in poor language that has to be a little corrected later, but an answer it is — and a question, too, at the very beginning a question: "Well, I'll tell you, I don't know how it'll be ahead for me, but do you think my people, all of us here, will ever be able to stop and live like they do, the rest of the people?" No one knows the answer to that, one says, but hopefully such a day will come, and soon. "No, I don't think so. I think a lot of people, they don't want us to be with them, and all they want is for us to do their work, and then good-bye, they say, and don't come back until the next time, when there's more work and then we'll have you around to do it, and then good-bye again."

There is another pause, another flurry of remarks, then this: "I'd like to have a home, and children, maybe three or four, two boys and two girls. They could all be nice children, and they wouldn't get sick and die, not one. We would have a house and it would have all the things, television and good furniture, not secondhand. If we wanted to work the crops, we'd plant them for ourselves, because the house and the land we'd have would be ours and no one could come and take us away and take the house away, either. I'd make us all go to school, even me; because if you don't learn things, then you'll be easy to fool, and you'll never be able to hold on to anything, my daddy says. He says he tries, and he doesn't get tricked *all* the time, but a lot of the time he does, and he can't help it, and he's sorry we don't just stay in a place and he's sorry my sisters and brothers and me don't go to school until we're as smart as the crew men and the foremen and the owners and the police and everyone. Then we could stop them from always pushing on us and not letting us do anything they don't want us to do. That's why, if I could, I'd like to be in school at the same time my kids would be there, and we'd be getting our education.

"I do believe we could have it better; because if we could get a job in one of the towns, then we could get a house and keep it and not leave and then if I broke my arm, like I did, they would take care of it in the hospital and not send you from one to the other until you pass out because you're dizzy and the blood is all over, and it hurts and like that, yes sir. Also, we could go and buy things in the stores — if we had the money and if they knew you lived there and weren't just passing through. All the time they'll tell you that, they'll say that you're just passing through and not to bother people, and they don't want you to come in and mess things up. But I could have a baby carriage and take my babies to the shopping stores, like you see people do, and we could go into all of them and it would be fun. I'd like that. I'd love it. I'd love to go and shop and bring a lot of things home and they'd be mine and I could keep them and I could fix up the house and if I didn't like the way it looks I could change things and it would look different, and it would be better.

"My mother, she always says it don't make any difference how we live in a place, it don't, because we'll soon be leaving. If it's a real bad place, she'll say, 'Don't worry, because we'll soon be leaving,' and if it's a better one, then she'll say, 'Don't fuss around and try to get everything all fixed up, because we'll soon be leaving.' Once when I was real little, I remember, I asked her why we couldn't stop our leaving and stay where we are, and she slapped me and told me to stop bothering her; and my daddy said if I could find a better way to make some money, then he'd like to know it. But I don't know how he could do any better, and he's the hardest-working picker there is, the crew man told him, and we all heard. My daddy said if he would ever stop picking, he'd never, never miss doing it, but he can't, and maybe I'll never be able to, either. Maybe I'll just dream about a house and living in it. My mother says she dreams a lot about it, having a house, but she says it's only natural we would wish for things, even if you can't have them. But, if you're asking what it'll really be like when I'm much older, then I can tell you it'll be just like now.

Maybe it'll be much better for us, but I don't think so. I think maybe it won't be too different, because my daddy says if you're doing the kind of work we do, they need you, and they're not going to let you go, and besides there isn't much else for us to do but what we're already doing. My brother, he thinks maybe he could learn to drive a tractor and he'd just go up and down the same fields and a few others, and he'd never have to go on the road like we do now; and he says when I think of going with a boy, I should ask him if he's going to go on the road, or if he's going to stay someplace, where he is, and get himself some kind of work that will let him settle down. But every time you try, they have no work but picking, they say, and the foremen, they're around and soon the sheriff and likely as not they'll arrest you for owing them something. If you get away, though, then you have to go someplace, and if you go to a city, then it's no good there, either, from what you hear, and you can't even work there, either; and it's real bad, the living, even if you don't have to be moving on up the road all the time.

"To me it would be the happiest day in the world if one day I woke up and I had a bed, and there was just me and a real nice man, my husband, there; and I could hear my children, and they would all be next door to us, in another room, all their own; and they would have a bed, each one of them would, and we would just be there, and people would come by and they'd say that's where they live, and that's where they'll always be, and they'll never be moving, no, and they won't have to, because they'll own the house, like the foremen do and the crew men and everyone else does, except us. Then we won't be with the migrant people anymore, and we'll be with everyone else, and it'll be real different."

So, it would be, vastly different. She and children like her would see a different world. Unlike migrant children, other children like to draw pastoral landscapes, like to drench them in sun, fill them with flowers, render them anything but bleak. Unlike migrant children, other children don't draw roads that are fenced in and blocked off or lead nowhere and everywhere and never end.[10] Unlike migrant children, most children don't worry about birth certificates, or doors and more doors and always doors —

that belong, even in a few years of experience, to half a hundred or more houses. So again, it would be different if the little girl just quoted could have a solid, permanent home. Her drawings would not be like the four I have selected, or like dozens of others very similar. The themes would be different, because her life would be different. Her days and months and years would have a certain kind of continuity, a kind we all don't think about, because some things are so very important, so intimate to life's meaning and nature that we really cannot bear to think about them; and indeed if we *were* thinking about them we would for some reason have come upon serious trouble.

Even many animals define themselves by where they live, by the territory they possess or covet or choose to forsake in order to find new land, a new sense of control and self-sufficiency, a new dominion. It is utterly part of our nature to want roots, to need roots, to struggle for roots, for a sense of belonging, for some place that is recognized as *mine,* as *yours,* as *ours.*[11] Nations, regions, states, counties, cities, towns — all of them have to do with politics and geography and history; but they are more than that, they somehow reflect man's humanity, his need to stay someplace and live there and get to know something — a lot, actually: other people, and what I suppose can be called a particular environment, or space or neighborhood or world, or set of circumstances. It is bad enough that thousands of us, thousands of American children, still go hungry and sick and are ignored and spurned — every day and constantly and just about from birth to death. It is quite another thing, a lower order of human degradation, that we also have thousands of boys and girls who live utterly uprooted lives, who wander the American earth, who even as children enable us to eat by harvesting our crops but who never, never can think of anyplace as home, of themselves as anything but homeless. There are moments, and I believe this is one of them, when, whoever we are, observers or no, we have to throw up our hands in heaviness of heart and dismay and disgust and say, in desperation: God save them, those children; and for allowing such a state of affairs to continue, God save us, too.

IV

STRANDED CHILDREN

THE cabins; they stand off the highways, way off them, up the dirt roads — and almost always the children linger around those cabins. They sit and play or they run all over and play or they linger about and seem not to be doing much of anything — those boys and girls of, say, Tunica County, Mississippi, or Clarke County, Alabama, or McCormick County, South Carolina. In books read by second- or third-grade students, such children are called "country boys" or "farm girls." In textbooks, such boys and girls are called sharecropper children or the children of tenant farmers or field hands. I suppose, as we now seem to insist, it is a state of mind, a quality of upbringing that characterizes those children: they are seriously "deprived" and "disadvantaged" — "backward," it once was put — and they need so very much that perhaps the easiest way to start is to say they need just about everything.

Many of the cabins have been abandoned, but thousands and thousands of them remain inhabited, and the people who live inside know that. They know they have been left behind; know they often have chosen to be left behind,[1] chosen to remain and feel — perhaps the word is *stranded:* "I don't know why we're still here, but we are; and I guess we always will be, yes sir. There comes a time when you say to yourself that the only thing you can do is whatever there is to do, and if there's nothing more, then there isn't. But a lot of them, a lot of our people, they've left, you know. They'll still be doing it, too — a family here and one over there, and mostly by night. That's the time. It'll be around midnight or into the morning, and you can almost hear them. I *do* sometimes. I'll be turning over in my sleep, and suddenly I'll hear a car coming, or there'll be one over the other side of the plantation, a car being started, and I'll scratch myself and ask if it's a dream I'm having, or if it's another family going up there — to Chicago, likely. That's where I think most of us from here go, if they get there; and you wonder sometimes if they don't get lost or give up and stop someplace by the road and settle into raising some food. But like down here, the people up North whose land it is, they probably don't want us growing a lot of food ourselves there, either. They just want us to sweat for them, grow for them."

So, she is resigned to staying put; she is resigned even though her older sister and her two younger sisters and her brother have left the state of Mississippi and even though they all have at one time or another come back and told her to leave, to leave for good and take their mother along so that none of them would ever again live in or return to the plantation every one of them calls "the place." She is resigned to the kind of life her mother had — though she wonders whether even that kind of life will be permitted: "They said we could stay, especially my mother, but if she goes, then they might make me and my family leave here, and they'll burn down the house, like they've been doing, and like they'd really have done already if it wasn't that my mother waited on them for years and years, and the bossman, his wife said no, they should let us alone. You know she came over here, the missus; she drove up one day. She got out of her car and she started looking around, and we got scared, because from the look on her face we thought she was real sore at us, and she was going to take after us and tell us we were in the wrong for something.

"We just waited, and after a while she came over and she said she was real sorry that we didn't have a better place to live, but it was going to be machines now that harvest the crops, and there wasn't much we could do anymore. She went over and looked my mother straight into her eyes and told her she sure was grateful for all she'd done; and it was too bad about her arthritis and the pain she was having and how sad it was to see her bent over like that, but not to worry, because she can stay here for as long as she wants, my mother can, and not to worry about the house (the big house she meant, yes she did) because there was this nice young girl, and she was working out fine, and they had some other help, too — for the heavy work, a boy I believe she said. Then she turned around fast, all of a sudden, and she just marched out and drove off, and she didn't say good-bye — not until she was in the car. Then she waved, but I don't believe there was a smile on her face, no sir; and my mother, it was she that was smiling, and afterwards saying how nice it was for her, the missus, to come up here."

I described the daughter as resigned, yet her words also convey a certain sense of annoyance, however restrained; or perhaps what I notice is a wry or sardonic quality[2] mixed with an earnest and forthright manner that tempers the underlying resignation. The resignation emerges when least expected: "To be telling you the truth, I'm not sure it's going to be any better for my children, not than it was for me or for my mother, and maybe even for my grandmother, and I can remember a little of her. Sometimes I'll be wondering if maybe I should have said to my mother that we've *got* to go up there to Chicago, and then she would have gone; but I never tried it, and I'm just as glad, actually. The way I see it, my little ones wouldn't have been any better off in the city, and worse, maybe — it might be much worse up there. A nephew of mine, he's my sister's boy, I hear he's in jail, someplace near Chicago. Now, the sheriff, he doesn't put us in jail, so long as we don't bother anyone — yes, I mean the white folks. And you'd be crazy, you'd have to be, to go bothering them, don't you know.

"I tell my boys and I tell my girls that they should stay clear of the white man, unless he beckons you, and then try to be nice and polite and do what he's asking if it's possible to do, and if it's not, then always apologize and say you'll do the best you can, and you'll be sorry if it's not enough. They say up North the colored man doesn't have to be afraid of the white no more, and the colored children, they speak up and say as they please before the white man. But there's my nephew — they put him right into jail. And I'll bet there's a lot more of us in jail up there than down here, though I *do* know we've got plenty of us put away down here. The reason is, a lot of the colored people have gone into the Mississippi towns, don't you know, since they can't stay here on the farms and work for the white people, and so they go to a place like Greenville, and some even to Jackson, and that's where they get into trouble with the law, they sure do. So, I'm afraid to leave and I'm afraid to stay, and whichever I do, I think it might be real bad for my boys and girls — real bad."

She has five children, or five that have so far stayed alive. She has had "three or four" miscarriages and two of her children died, one at seven months, "suddenly and for no reason" and one at age four "of a real bad cold, it seemed like." Over the years I have come to know her as well as someone like me will ever really understand someone like her — which is to say that I do indeed believe that I have learned a lot about her and her family. Yet I worry about those often discussed (maybe too much discussed) barriers that separate observers like me from share-cropper families like hers — and for all their present difficulties, she and her husband and their children are precisely that, share-croppers, or so they think themselves to be: "We've been on shares to the mister and his daddy and before him the old, old gentleman, and I do believe it goes back to when we were all slaves, yes sir. Today there isn't much for my husband to do, except for errands here and there. But until a couple of years ago, we'd work our land, the part the bossman gave to us, and at the end of the year he'd come over and he'd settle up with us. No, there wasn't too much money we'd get; but you know he'd be giving us the house, this one, all along, and they'd supply us our food and like that, and if anything special comes up, something real bad, they're good people, and we could go over there and ask them, and they'd be glad to help. Of course, we don't ask anything big of them, and we never did. It worked out OK, being on shares with him, because he's a fair person, and he'd tell me and my husband to stop standing and sit down, and he'd open his book and point to the page and tell us it was the one with our name on it, and all the figures were there, and that's how it all added up — and he never would be like some of the others. They'll give you nothing, or close to it, and they'll say you're lucky to be getting the food all along, and lucky to have a roof over your head."

They do not feel too lucky these days. They worry about their children, yet don't know how to make those worries less necessary. They care about their children, yet have no conviction that such love and concern will matter.[3] Most of the time they simply go about the business of living, or trying to live, or just barely staying alive: "I'm afraid we're sick a lot of the time, me and my children are. If it's not one thing, it's something else, and according to the minister, we're all of us just as likely to die sooner than later, because God might be waiting on us — you never know. I tell my children, each one of them, that it's better they be good and obey me and do as I say, because they can go fast, just like the older people, and it's a long time to spend in Hell, if they're no good and God turns His back on them.

"They're good, though, my boys — the two of them — and my three girls. They like to go along and help me, and most of the time they don't give me trouble. I try to do the best I can for them, and I tell them they've got to look after one another, because their daddy and me might die one day, and then they'd be alone, except for my mother, and she's sick. Then they'll ask about their cousins, and I'll tell them it's a long way from here to Chicago, and I hope it stays that way, because as bad as it is here, it'll be only worse someplace else; and I say it twice, and sometimes more, so they'll hear and they won't forget. Then, of course, they'll ask why it is that the people are leaving, and I say some are, but some aren't, and we aren't, and that's the answer, and there'll be no other answer, and stop asking. But they do, a little later on, and I'll be repeating the same thing. And you know, a while back my boy Henry, he's seven, wanted to know if there wasn't some chance we'd leave here, and I told him no, and why was he keeping on asking me, and he said that if someday *we* didn't go, then maybe *he* would, but I told him how bad it would be if he was up North, and he listened. I could tell he got scared by what I was saying, and he said maybe I was right and it was bad here, and maybe we could die all of a sudden — like I keep on telling him — but from now on he was going to be happy we're here, and from now on he promised he'd stop talking about the North. Like I said, as bad as it is, there's always worse trouble you can get into."

Such children, sharecropper children, learn that particular kind of self-satisfaction rather early. A child born of a sharecropper or a tenant farmer gradually gets a sense of things, a sense of who he is and where he is and what his life is likely to be like. I cannot emphasize strongly enough how early it is that such a "sense of things," complicated and subtle, yet ultimately all too brutal and clear, begins to develop. For example, the mother I have just quoted has what I suppose can be called an "attitude" toward her children, an attitude that begins to take shape well before the boy or girl is born, and an attitude that upon analysis reveals all sorts of things not only about a particular kind of "child-rearing," but also about a whole region, a whole way of life. At different times the mother and I have talked about her children and her hopes for them and her fears about them and her view of what they will have to learn. Any one conversation has its limits, but over the years particular things occur and occur, are stated and stated; and finally one can somewhat reliably feel certain words and sentiments "coming," or "near expression" in the course of a given talk — in which case the observer feels that he, like the children in question, has a little of that "sense of things" just mentioned. Perhaps I am merely saying that the wife of a sharecropper, like the wife of a lawyer or a businessman or a psychiatrist, needs time and various kinds of occasions if she is ever going to get across either to herself or some observer what can so glibly be called her "philosophy," or again, her "attitudes." A sharecropper's wife does not use those words, but she knows what they are meant to mean, and she has her own words that are not exactly vague or pretentious or incomprehensible: "To me, if you ask me what I believe, it's that God wants us to have children, and not only because without them we'd soon disappear, but because as long as boys and girls keep coming, you know the world might one day get better. I get to feeling better when I'm carrying, yes I do. You know something else — each time I'm carrying, the missus up there will be a little nicer to me, all during the time she will. She'll ask me how I'm getting on; and she'll ask me if it's a boy or a girl I want; and she'll ask me if my legs are swelling up, like the last time, or not; and toward the end, if I don't lose the child, like I have, you know, she'll come over sometime, when I'm working up there for her — in the house, yes sir — and she'll tell me not to be in a hurry and to share my work with Alice and with Lucy, because they're helping her a lot, too.

"She's the one, the missus, who gets us the midwife. They say it's better having a midwife than a doctor — the missus told me that the first time, when she brought the woman over and told me she wasn't going to have any of us delivering without someone who's trained and knows all about things. Then the woman kept on coming back every few weeks — it was for my first one — and when I felt the baby asking to be born, moving hard at me, I did what the missus said and told my husband to go up there to the house, and tell her, the missus, that it was the time. And you know what? Well, it didn't take the missus long to get the midwife, and when she came she stayed with me, and she delivered my Martha, and since then she has delivered my other ones, too — except for the ones I lost, and for James, because he came too quick for anyone to get here.

"I love having the midwife woman come, and my mother says it's a miracle, what a colored lady can learn how to do — just about be a doctor, yes sir. I've never gone to a doctor's place, no I haven't, not for myself. But once I went with the missus, because she was in a bad state. Her head was aching, and she couldn't keep her food down, and she kept on having dizzy spells. She called the doctor, and she called her husband, he was up in Memphis; and then she said I should go with her to the doctor, and if she had trouble in the car, then she could stop and I was to go get help. She lasted through the ride, though; and when we got to the doctor's she had me come in with her, and I've never seen such a place in all my life: there was the desk he had, and a table he had her sit on, and he had the books, and he had medicines and he had things to use on you, every kind you can think of, and soon he was listening to her heart, he said, and her lungs, and he'd test her with one thing and another until she must have had every test there was, and then he wrote her out something, and she got the pills at the store, and later on she said, I heard her tell her husband, that the doctor had helped and made her better, he had. Now, the midwife, she's not like the doctor, because she hasn't got her an office. She's not white, either — and I should say that, I guess — and I don't believe she can get you better so fast, the way the doctors can. But if you're like us, the doctors don't see you, because they're not for the colored. I hear say that even our leading people, the leading colored folks here, they'll be real lucky if the doctor will see them, no matter if they have the money to pay or not. The good doctors, they say, will build themselves a special door for us to use, and they'll be real nice to you, if you can pay them; but there will be others, and they tell you that they're only for the white people, yes sir, and we should try to find someone else.

"I once said to the midwife that she should learn other things besides delivering — that way she could help us all the time. But she said she had all she could do to keep up with the babies, as they come; and even so, with her around for us, a lot of colored people just go and have their babies by themselves, one after the other. It's too bad because women can suffer, they can suffer a lot having a child, and it's bad when there's no one to help them — and that's how it was with my mother, and my mother says that she believes we're lucky to have a missus like we do, who will go and get the midwife and pay for her and like that. My mother admits that's one of the best reasons to leave, to go North. I mean, people say that it can be bad up there, but there are the hospitals and doctors, and they'll take care of a colored person, the doctors, and you have a better chance — I mean with delivering and if your baby gets sick and all the rest, you know. Anyway, if the missus becomes nicer to you when you become heavy, that's a good reason to become heavy! Even if she didn't change her attitude, I'd still be wanting my children. Wouldn't any mother?

"One reason I go along with my mother and agree with her — I mean about staying here and not leaving, like people do — well, it's because even if we have it bad here, it's still what we know, and I'm afraid from what I hear — my sister writes me — that we'd be losing if we left, even if we'd be gaining. Yes sir, that's how I'd add it up. That's what my mother says. She'll say to me: 'Ella, sure we could go up there, but I don't want to go. If I thought it was good for *you*, never mind me, I'd go anyway. But there's a good chance it won't be better — for any of us. Maybe the hospitals are good up there, but I'll bet colored people are pushed around in those hospitals, even if they do take us in and listen to our troubles.' That's what she'll say, my mother. Now, I'll tell you, I feel the same way. My little girl, she'll ask me why so many people keep leaving here, the colored people, and when are *we* going; but I say to her there's a lot of colored people left down here, you bet. And there's a good reason why: they know, we do, that it's no good for us anyplace, and before you go changing one sickness for another, then you stop and think — that's what the midwife says about going to Chicago.

"A lot of what she says, the midwife, I agree with. She'll tell you when she hands you your baby that you can't build Heaven for your child here on earth, here in Mississippi; but you can try your best, and make your child feel he belongs here, belongs to you, even if it's not the best life he's been born to have, and even if he would have been better off to have been born somewhere else to someone else. So, that's what I try to do. I whisper to my little baby that it sure is hot here, and we sure don't have all the good food we should have, and sometimes we don't have a single thing good for them to wear — nothing at all — but it could be worse, and at least we're alive, and we do the best we can. The way I see it, a child is lucky to get born in the first place. Like the midwife will tell you, and I know it, oh do I: a lot just die before ever seeing the sun or the sky or the trees. They die inside you, before they're much of anything, and that's a shame. That's what you have to keep reminding yourself, and that's what you have to

tell your children, or else they'll grow up and they'll feel sorry for
themselves — and you should never let yourself get in low spirits,
never."

Does she, in fact, ever get moody and sad and fearful — for all
her protests that one must not let such things happen? Do her
children, too, begin to wonder just what she means when she tells
them they are lucky — of all ironic things (so people like me
think) *lucky?* Put differently, is such talk from her an effort to
whistle in the dark, an effort to deny or rationalize away the
obvious pain and sorrow and bitterness that must in some way
plague such impoverished sharecropper women? If so, exactly how
long are children, however young and ignorant and naïve, deceived by such obvious (if necessary, some of us hasten nervously to add) psychological maneuvers? I ask those questions
not in order to answer them flatly and unequivocally. I think I
am in fact recording something when I include the questions in
the midst of a particular limited psychological chronicle, when I
spell out some of the doubts and confusions and misgivings I
happened to have felt and tried to resolve as I listened to people
trying to settle and explain a few things for themselves rather
than for me.

To start dealing with — not answering — some questions, I
had better say yes, she and other mothers like her do indeed
become unhappy; they get to feeling "blue," and can be heard
saying they feel "bluer than blue."[4] So it goes, too, with the
children — the thousands of boys and girls who still live in the
rural South, despite all the migration to all the cities all over the
North and way out in the West. They try, those parents and
those children; they try and try not to "get low in spirits." Sadness among the sharecroppers or tenant farmers or field hands I
have met has a peculiar and intense kind of life — and emotions
like sadness *do* have a life, one characterized by growth, change,
development and above all, it seems, persistence.[5] When, for
example, I speak of sadness, I have in mind a number of ways
children or mothers or fathers give expression to what is "inside."
Moreover, with the families I am now discussing, the issue of
sadness — to be more specific, of abandonment — is significant

or important enough, I believe, to stand as the central theme of at least this particular descriptive and analytic effort.

To begin with, there is the rather striking and thoroughly open or explicit *clinging* that mothers such as the one I have already quoted demonstrate toward their infants. Of course, almost all mothers cling to their babies, and I have already described how migrant mothers attach themselves with great intensity to their newborn sons and daughters. In this regard there are differences, though; differences between migrant mothers and sharecropper mothers and differences between both of them on the one hand and many other American mothers, whose position in society goes under the name of middle class. Here, for example, is another mother speaking about her children. She was born a few miles from North Carolina's Atlantic coast, and she expects to die there. She might have been the mother of five, had she not already known a miscarriage and struggled with a dying child: "I did lose my little girl, I did; but you have to expect things like that, you just have to. I recall when I was little, and I'd cry about something, then my mother would get ahold of me and she'd tell me off, she would. She'd say as long as you're going to be living and not dead, you're going to be fighting the tears away, and I'd better start learning right away about how to go ahead and do my work and wipe those tears away. She'd take my hand and make me clear my eyes, and usually, when I think back, I recall her telling me one bad story or another — about how they used to treat us colored people back in the past, and how we didn't disappear from God's earth, even so we didn't, and how I should never forget that for all the bad times there are good times, and it tastes better, something good and juicy, when you've been hungry for a long time.

"When you lose faith in things, you should stop yourself and remember God and remember that there's always hope. That's what my mother always told me. I think I must have listened to her, because most of the time I keep my spirits up, and I'm now telling my children exactly as she told me, even if she is gone — it's now five years I think. Yes, that's right, I start whispering the words to my little baby, the first thing after they're born — because it's not too early, I don't believe. The reason is they've got to know that we may not have a lot of the things they need, but we have each other, that's what I tell them. Bad as it can get, so long as we keep together with each other, then we'll get by, yes I believe we will. Sometimes a child of mine, she'll get to crying real bad, and I know she's hurting and I know she needs something I can't give her; but I'll come over and I'll hold her and I'll hold her and I'll hold her, and I'll tell her, right into her ear, that if she hasn't got anything — nothing to wear and the sicknesses and the food that isn't what she should be having — then even so there's me, and I'll never leave my children, never. If we're to die, we'll all go together, and that is how it has to be.

"I think my children do pay attention. I try to make sure they'll listen to me and do what's right. My mother used to hit me when I was in the wrong, but afterwards she'd draw me to her and she'd tell me she didn't want to hurt me, but the world is full of a lot of trouble for us, that's the truth, and if we made trouble for each other, on top of all the trouble there is — well, then, we sure couldn't expect to last very long. Even so, no matter how much my mother tried, I guess I failed her some of the time; and now I see it in my own kids: they'll go ahead and forget everything I say to them. I don't know how to explain why they do, but if you ask me, I think they're themselves and not me, and I really think they sometimes don't want to hear what I tell them. They don't want to hear that they can't have what they'd like, and what others have. They'll go around hitting at the door and kicking at a pail, and like that, and they'll ask why can't it be this way and the other way and not like it is. And I ask, too. And I lose my temper, too. I'll be holding my little baby as close as can be and all of a sudden I can feel myself getting full of the devil, and I want to say that I shouldn't be saying yes to the bossman, and my baby should be having this and my baby should be having that — and everything, everything a baby needs. But I know I can't get a doctor and I know I can't get the best food and I know I can't dress my children up like the white folks do — nor like some colored, a few, that do good and I hear make as much money as a lot of the whites. That's why for one like me, you

have to talk with yourself as much as with your child. You have
to keep yourself quiet and pinch yourself so you don't go crying
as bad as your little girl will; and your little boy, he will cry just
as much. You see, you're being crossed all the time: there's something else you mustn't do, and there's a reason why you have to
stop here and stay away from the next thing. There'll come a time,
there'll come a day, when you're ready to shout at God Himself
and ask Him why we're on this earth, people like us, if every time
we turn there's a sign that says 'Watch Out' or 'Not For You'
or — oh, like that, I guess!"

She is plagued by frustrations. I declare her frustrated and
emphasize the assertion not because I have any idea that an
interpretation of mine is needed after her perfectly clear remarks.
As for sadness, she denies feeling it when she describes her
various frustrations. She has told me a number of times what
makes her feel sad — feel "low" or feel "bad" — and never does
she consider her intense attachment to her infant child to be
evidence of such a state of mind. Nor does she affirm her sadness
when she indicates how baffled she feels, how undermined by the
world, how cramped in style and thwarted and deterred and
blocked and inconvenienced and restrained and restricted. All
the time the world stands in her way and undoes in fact what she
might think about or dream of. All the time she fights back, holds
and hugs and kisses her children, tells them to submit, to go
along with what simply must be. All the time, as I see it, she
acknowledges in one way or another, with one phrase or another,
her sense of frustration. Willingly or reluctantly (or really, in
both ways) she accommodates. She tries to warn her children
and herself; she tries to speak out the discontent she feels; more
than that, she tries to live the discontent out. That is to say, she
draws as close as she can to her children, and she makes them
right off partners in frustration — and in that way, I believe, she
makes a little less oppressive the very substantial sadness she
somehow must find a way to keep under control.

Once I asked her whether she did in fact get "unhappy" when
one or another frustration came up. She answered me quickly
and with a look that seemed to say that she more or less expected

me eventually to get around to such matters: "No, no I don't let these things get me down. I don't. You can't. My mother said you can't, and I believed her when she said it, and now that I have my own kids I believe her more. I try to forget the misery we have, because if you don't you're lost, and you can feel yourself going down — way under the water it is. I try to be as good as I can, and if there's something I can't do, and something my little girl can't do, then I get us to go and forget and turn our minds elsewhere. There's always the jobs you've *got* to do, and you have to tell your kids that they have eyes so they can look ahead, so that even if there's something stopping you, they can look over it and there must be, there just *must* be a way you can get around trouble and get yourself to where you're going — though, I'll admit, there will be some days when I just can't figure out where we're going and how we'll ever get there or anyplace else."

Frustration, frustration mingled with resignation, can turn to other moods, as we all know. The mothers quoted here often enough become irritable, sullen, annoyed and snappish. They strike out at their children, at their husbands, at themselves. When they do so they describe themselves rather freely as "upset" or "fed up" or "angry," but again, not sad and not overwhelmed or in danger of giving up — and indeed they are not about to surrender, though they may well fear that possibility more than they can bear to realize. I am not at this point trying to get categorical, or make those generalizations that allow us to feel conveniently in control of a bothersome and troubling "problem." Nor do I wish to submit the many and various lives I have met in those rural cabins to a lot of fancy, self-important theoretical language — about the last thing an already burdened and restricted people need. Rather I hope to do whatever justice I possibly can to their lives — and I hesitate to use the word "justice" in this or any other context that has to do with sharecroppers and tenant farmers. I have really wanted the people I have observed to let me know, given enough time and a little trust, how they see their lives unfold or work out or develop.

Sharecroppers, like the rest of us, have an idea about the *trends* in their lives — something that may be obvious, but also something easily forgotten by one like me. If I have ideas about what sharecroppers do with their children, and what they go through in their minds and hearts as their children grow up, then so does a woman like this — who repeatedly objected to remarks I made, remarks full of *my* notions about *her* feelings, and who may well be responsible for this overly long and apologetic preamble: "No sir. No. I'm not going to go along with you on that, no sir. I don't think you've got it right. Maybe I'm just being cross with you because it's a bad day. I have them, you know. I just wake up with the day staring at me and no matter how good I know I should try to feel, all I can say to myself is that it's going to be a bad day. But when you ask me if it bothers me when the little ones get bigger and start running around, then I have to tell you no, it doesn't. A mother, she knows; she'll be giving birth to her little child, and before her eyes she'll be picturing her or him; and if it's a girl the mother will see her when she's little and when she gets bigger, and still bigger, and finally she's all grown up and that's the end of the child. Each time I'll be lying on that bed about to have my child it'll happen like that — with my mind giving me those pictures. When I told my mother, the first time, she said of course I would do that, because when a mother is bringing a baby into the world, she's naturally going to stop and look ahead.

"Now to me it's been good when my girls and my little boy started leaving me. I mean, you can't be together all the time, and after a while you can feel them wanting to get away — in their legs and arms you can. They'll be crawling on you and you know they want to go all over and find out where the floor begins and where it ends and what it's like over there where the crops are, and the pine trees — and you know, like that. I'm happy when they're off looking around for themselves. Yes, I truly am. It's more trouble for me, I'll admit. But I can be free of them longer, and that's good. They'll do a lot of crying, of course, and they'll want to come back to you; but I try to tell them that they should sit over there, in front of the house, and enjoy themselves, because a little later on, it won't be so much fun for them, no sir, it won't. A lot of the time, when they're crawling and when they're learning to stand on their feet and move along, I'll pretend to be busy fixing up something — frying up some grits, or straightening up the room — and I'll follow them with my ears. They'll be fighting and screaming and they'll be teaching the smallest one, and she'll be catching on, and I'll tell myself it's not so bad for the kids, it's not so bad. But I know they're not getting the best there is — for food and like that — and there's not much future here, that's what the bossman says, and he's the one who should know. Then I'll slip, and I'll wonder if maybe we shouldn't have left here, so that my kids could be growing up somewhere that *has* a future to give them. But from what you hear, it's not so good up there, even if they do have a future to offer you, because the kids don't have room to play or hardly to breathe; and I heard from the lady down the road after her daughter came home for a visit that there are no sheriffs around to push on you up there, but you can't let your kids go anyplace, because they'll get killed on the streets. The streets are real mean up there, she told me.

"That's why we can be happy here, because for my little girl there's land outside, and she can't hurt herself too much there, I know that. There'll be times I feel myself getting mad at her and the other kids, I'll admit it, and my mother will see me letting my temper go and she'll tell me that's how she'd be sometimes. First there'll be an irritation, and then all of a sudden, I'm shouting and screaming and I don't know what's come over me. Later on I'll recall bits and pieces of what I said and what happened. My mother says we all have to fall to pieces sometimes, or else we couldn't go on.

"When you ask what I say to the kids during a temper, it's hard to tell, except that I'll say things I never should, and sometimes it's like I'm doing the exact same thing I tell my kids *not* to do, and I should be punished like them — as the minister says, with soap on my tongue, except we don't have soap, no sir, because it costs a lot, and you need a lot of water for it, like she has, the bossman's wife. My husband went in her house once — they'd asked him to carry some furniture down. He said the bossman and his wife and kids leave the water running, and there was soap thrown out in a trash can, and it was a piece you could have used and used.

"I guess the main thing is I tell the kids to stop with their fighting and pushing all over one another. I tell them — I'll be real mad and shouting, yes sir — that they'd better watch out, because it won't be long before they'll be big and grown, and if they start getting fresh then, they'll end up in jail as fast as can be, and that will be the end of them, oh will it. Then I'll speak to them like the sheriff would, I guess, and I'll be telling them what the minister will say — and you know, they've got to learn to pay me attention and obey, and if they don't, they'll suffer for it even more than I tell them they will. And the way I see it, I've got to suffer for them right now. I mean, if they see me getting upset and bothered then they'll stop in their ways and get to behaving themselves, you know. It's too bad, that's what I believe, that I can't have a lot to give them. Maybe if we'd gone North I could be shopping and buying things for them; but we're here, and they'll have to like it. They'll ask me those questions, the children do, and it shows you they peek in on what my mother will be saying, or me. They'll bother you with all the whys, until you're ready to go kill them to stop them from talking, yes sir — and I'm not ashamed to admit it. My mother says they're just learning things and having their fun by teasing me, and that's the way a child will be. They'll be upset by you, and they'll want to get even, so they'll go and upset you right back. My boy used to tell me he was going to go shoot the sheriff, and the bossman too, and take over his plantation and live up there in his house, and he wouldn't let me come in because I was bad, and so was the minister. Then he'd say it over and over again, how bad, bad, bad I was, until I had to shout him down, and I'd be telling him he was bad and he'd be telling me the same thing right back and it'd be a fight we'd have — until I just came and grabbed him and made him stop. I'd put my hand over his mouth, yes that was how.

"Maybe if my children were up North, they'd be out fighting the police, the way they tell me they will when they are little. I don't know. Here, you have to watch your step. Here you have to hit a colored man if you're going to hit someone, and that's the truth. I don't let my children go hitting one another too much. They might get ideas in their heads about a white man, and that would be the end for all of us. I teach them to be quiet, and they get to be quiet, and that's good. Sometimes I think they'd like to be doing more talking and playing, but I don't have the time to be with them and also help in the field sometimes and also go work for the bossman, cleaning up his office; and besides, I have my stomach pains, and there must be something wrong in there, and my legs are bad, the veins. There'll be one day I'm feeling pretty good, then the next I feel as bad as can be, so bad I can't describe it. I take to crying and I don't know why. My head will be aching, and all of a sudden there'll be the tears, and I have to wipe them away, and then there'll be more after those I cleared off. It's my older children, I sometimes think. They don't have much hope, and when they lose it, I lose it with them. I'll tell them that it may get better here, you know, but they don't listen much, and I'll wonder if they're asking themselves why it was we stayed here — being colored for one thing, and not getting much that you can call your own, except the cabin they give us.

"We get enough from work and the 'loans against the crops,' the bossman calls them, to keep from dying. But you feel disappointed sometimes, even if you can scrape up some food; and that's how the kids, my children, they get to be — sort of disappointed. And so am I, except that I can't spend my days feeling I've lost all my hope, and it's never going to get better. So, I'll tell the kids to go outside there and sit under a tree and play and don't just stare and stare, unless they want to be resting. I know they're tired a lot, because it's hot, and the bugs, they eat on them and itch them and it wears them down. If they're staring here, near me, and then they start talking and making me feel I was real bad not to have a better life waiting on them when they got born, then I'll be all upset, and one minute I'll want to sit with them and say yes, you're right, you are; but the next I'll want them to stop with their complaining and leave me alone and stop making themselves upset, and like that. If their daddy comes by, then I'll tell him, and he's very good with them, because he'll just go out after them, and he'll tell them we can't sit back and feel bad, because the only way the colored man has ever amounted to something, it's because he keeps himself going, and you just *have* to, and that's all there is to say, and nothing more."

So she insisted then and so she has many times insisted. Yet, over the years I have learned to doubt her silences and her claims that this or that word (or long speech) represents her final position on a given subject. For a long time she almost literally had nothing to say. She sat out my visits or stood watching me as I anxiously and indeed somewhat desperately tried to talk with and play with her children, who began to take me for a strange white fool — first to be feared, then to be suspected, and finally to be indulged and flattered and really helped along in whatever fuzzy and persistent schemes he had in mind. It took their mother much longer to take my presence for granted, then to assume my presence as in essence a friendly one, and at last to forget my presence for a minute here and for considerably longer than a minute there — or even *use* my presence, apologetically in the beginning and forthrightly later on, three years later on, when a thought or a question or a reminiscence would simply be spoken. Those were the moments I remember best, and they were almost always moments when *she* was remembering something. I think I am being true to the occasions when I say they were almost invariably (I began to feel *inevitably*) nostalgic.

In her own way she, too, felt the persistent force of past events. Both of us knew that she had found in me a listener, and that I was not by any means the first one. There had been her mother, and there was "the reverend." She shouted and "hollered" at them, too — and sometimes, like the rest of us, she stopped in the middle, seized by a moment of self-consciousness, worried by a glimpse of her own petulance, which we all have and which only some people manage to acknowledge. A few times I also raised my voice — I thought because I wanted to get through, be heard by her. She was so absorbed in putting her thoughts to word that I feared she would not hear my remarks, my objections or observations or pleas that one thing or another be considered.

Afterwards, of course, I would have second thoughts about everything said. I would think about our talks, or play them back and try to hear again exactly who said what and when. I would try to figure out why she got so excited and why I did. I would, in fact, be "home," because I was doing what my life had somehow brought me to do: analyzing things and finding reasons and explanations for them or trends and patterns in them. It was a comfortable feeling I had in those small, uncrowded motels — "rural" as the terrain they serve and different indeed from the large noisy motels one finds elsewhere. It was comfortable because I was surrounded by comfort: air conditioning and running water and a bathroom and a good bed and nearby a restaurant that served a reasonable variety of reasonably good food. I was also comfortable because I was now doing something that had continuity.

After all, years of my life had been given over to listening and coming up with interpretations, and in those motel rooms I could sit back and listen to a machine and write things down on sheets of white paper — and do it all under reasonably decent physical circumstances. But I had my doubts in those motel rooms. Should I actually be there at all? Should I be spending all those hours with that woman and her family? Shouldn't I rather be some other place doing some other kind of work? And she had her doubts, too. Although excitement can mask beliefs, it can also make possible their expression — like this: "I've been saying not one good word today, that's what I just realized. I'd better stop. I guess this isn't one of my happy days — but they can't come all the time. I feel happiest after I've gone and spoken my troubles in church. I'm sorry I was having you hear me, but it's no easy time we all have here, and there'll be a minute once or twice a day that I can't be sure I'll last — because there's too much we don't have that we need, and there's not enough of what we do have.

"I get to the point I'm ready to die; I'm ready to say I can't do it any longer, oh Lord, I can't, so You'll have to come and take me, and if it means I'm going to go to Hell, because I can't wait until it's my time to be called, then I guess it'll have to be Hell for me. And you know, sometimes I'll be carrying on a talk with

Him, with God, and all of a sudden I'll feel better, like the reverend said I should. The only trouble is I never do let Him know how really bad it can get for us — and the reverend said I don't have to, because He knows anyway. But when I was hollering just now, that's the same thing my kids will hear sometimes, and they know not to speak back, just listen. Their daddy can holler, too; he'll get all upset, and he'll talk and talk and talk, and you can't follow his every word, and sometimes he'll go outside and start kicking things around, but other times he just stops, and I think maybe he'll begin to cry, but he never does. He just sits there, and after a while he'll shrug his shoulders and go back to doing what he was doing before. Then there will be a time when we both start complaining, but soon we decide, most of the time we do, that if there's trouble we have — well, there's also a lot we can recall that wasn't so bad, no sir. And most of all, you have to remember, like we say to ourselves: here we are. That's what my husband will say, and so will I: *here we are.*

"I guess we mean if we're *here,* then how could it be so bad — because if it had been even worse, then we wouldn't still be here. Then we'll get to thinking, and we'll recall a good time we had once, and then another time — how the girls were born, and the boys, and how my mother has been good to us, and how the bossman came over and said there was nothing to be afraid of, because if the civil rights people or the Klan started getting after us, they wouldn't get on his property. He said he'd go and shoot them himself, if he had to, if they didn't leave. He said he knew we didn't have anything to do with the civil rights people, and that's why we shouldn't be scared. So we weren't, and nothing happened.

"You know, there are more happy times than you might think — once you start looking for them. You have to be in the right mind to go look. That's what I'll say or my husband will say — when we're feeling good. There was a Christmastime a few years back, when my brother sent us more money than we'd ever seen, and I went down to the store and the man, he thought I was losing my mind, because I asked for one thing, and then another, and pretty soon I had a big pile of things, and in the beginning he went along and got them, but after a little, he stared at me and he asked me what I'd been having to drink, and he said if I didn't get out fast, he'd have the sheriff out there, and that would be some Christmas I'd have — in jail. Then I naturally decided to show him the bills, and I did, and he looked at them real long and he asked me — yes, he was getting a little more respectful, he was — if he could just take ahold of one of the ten-dollar bills and see if it was OK. After he saw it was real money I had, then he told me I was the luckiest woman in Tunica County, and maybe the luckiest one in the whole state of Mississippi, and if there was anything he could do to be of help, then he'd go over and deliver and he'd even drive me along, because it sure would be heavy, toting along the packages and more packages, and he could understand I'd be fearful of buying things if I didn't know how I'd get them back to the place.

"Yes, I said, he could drive me and my packages and that would be a relief. So, I bought and I bought. I'd see this and that, and I'd ask for the candy and the cookies and the cheese and the meats, you know, and I knew I was going to have me a time, telling my kids that they should eat the new food and it would be good for them and make them grow bigger. They like Kool-Aid, and it isn't often they can have milk for themselves and there we were, having a chicken on Christmas. I had to tell my kids that you may get used to Kool-Aid and like it, but if you have good luck, like we did that Christmas — well, then you can drink milk and eat the better things and they'll taste just as good and even better, once you get used to them. Of course, one of my girls went and spoiled things; she said we weren't going to be having that food again, so why should we try eating it, just for Christmas. Then, I didn't know what to say. It was my husband who answered; he said we should just forget all we ever ate before and all we'll ever eat later on, and just have ourselves a good Christmas — and you know, we did. It was the best day ever in the world, yes it was."

As a matter of fact there have been other good days, too. The memory of one would trigger the memory of another, and on a few such occasions she allowed herself to get dangerously full of them all, to the point that she would appear euphoric (which I suppose was as "inappropriate" in her as in anyone else) or almost bizarrely contented with her life, her lot, her future as she saw it. I am not necessarily referring to a sort of "religious fugue," as I found myself calling some of the vehement joy, the biblically suffused, highly oratorical transport she could manage. On the contrary, it was nostalgia, pure if not so simple, that would come over her and make her feel quiet and pleased with things, but sad, very sad in a reflective way, sad without hysteria and without desperation.

Maybe I am talking about the kind of sadness the rest of us have heard in the blues and "work songs" and "field songs," an almost distilled sadness that defies the outsider's comprehension and sometimes prompts him to think of Kierkegaard's "resignation" or Buber's "acceptance."[6] There is a passion and a biblical quality to the expression of that sadness — though "the reverend" himself comes in for some fairly sharp if forgiving criticism, which would be retracted, I noticed, not immediately but several days later, when one of his sermons (which I would have heard in church) would be repeated as if in repentance by a parishioner who had listened carefully indeed when she was in church. As a matter of fact, during those nostalgic moments "the reverend" is not really condemned as a person. Once, when the story of the lavish Christmas was fondly recalled for me (the third time it was, in three years), "the reverend" more or less served as a link between that particular memory and the larger mood that was to be expressed: "I don't mean to jump on the reverend, but he was down to see us as soon as we got home. No sooner had the grocery man left, than the reverend was there, and it was the first time I ever saw him bend over and lift his hat and treat us like we were — I guess you'd have to say he was looking at us as though we'd become white folks. Yes, the word spreads fast around here, and I'll tell you what must have happened. The colored people in the store were watching, and when they saw the man, the white man, carry our packages and drive us home, they must have gone running home themselves, and I'll bet everyone a hundred miles around knew what happened, and the reverend included.

"He came, like I said, and he was nice and polite, and he didn't have a cross word to say to us, and he was real obliging and asked if we wanted him to come back later, because he could see how busy we were, and with all those groceries and things — well, it might take a day or two to unload them. So, I told him that there wouldn't be no difference; now or later was all right, and we're always glad to have him around, including that time. Then he said he was always glad to come around and that time especially, because he could see we were really happy and in good luck, he said, and that was how it was meant for us to be around Christmastime, because it was a joyful day, Christ being born and like that. Then I said he was right, and we sure felt glad and pleased by our good luck, and we wanted him to know we would pray and thank the Lord. Then he said he was glad of that, and you mustn't take anything for granted in this world, no sir, and the Lord provides, and now we had proof. So, I said yes, I was sure he was right about the Lord and His providing — but this time it wasn't Him, it was from our family up North, and they'd sent us a lot of money, more than we ever before had seen. As if he didn't know from what he heard!

"Well, he didn't have much more to say, the reverend. My mother asked him if he wanted to come and eat with us on Christmas, and he said no, that he liked to eat with his family, and they would be cooking in their home, and everyone should be in his own place on Christmas. Then he told us again how lucky it was, what happened, and we agreed, and he got up and he was getting ready to go, I thought, except that he wasn't. Instead he walked over and he stared right at me, he did, and then he asked: 'If you have some money left, you can believe that I'll be glad to have it, and I would try to do God's Will with it, and there sure are a lot of people who won't be having the Christmas you're going to have.' It was like that, only he went on and on, and while he was speaking I was thinking and deciding. He'd been staring at me, and the way I figured it, if I stopped

staring back, he'd walk away with everything we had, the few
dollars left, and all the groceries and everything. But if I just
kept on looking right into his eyes, then he wouldn't have me
bowing down before him, and he'd stop and leave us be — and it
wasn't as if we'd had Christmases like that one every year.

"So, I kept hearing him and looking upon him, and he kept
talking and looking upon me, and then he finished with his talk,
and I didn't say a word, and then I did. I said, 'Yes sir,' that's
what I said. Then I said: 'I know what you mean,' that's what I
said. Then I asked him again if he wouldn't like to come and eat
some of the food we'd got, and he said no, he had a lot waiting
for him over there at home, and then I said the same thing again:
'I know what you mean.' In a second he was at the door leaving
us and you know what, he didn't even remember to wish us a
Merry Christmas. I guess he was in a hurry, and people forget a
lot when they've got to rush on.

"The reverend, he's no different than anyone else. I mean, he
is, because he's God's minister; but he's one of us, that's for sure,
and the way I see it, even Jesus had His trouble in the Temple,
so you can't trust ministers any more than the rest of us people.
Remember what happened to Jesus? He ran into enemies all
over, and it was with ministers just like with the other people
who didn't like Him. I guess you're pretty lucky in this world if
you stay alive long enough — I mean so you can grow up, and
not die the first thing when you're born. When you're little and
you don't know much except that you're you, and you've been
born, all you want is to stay here as long as you can, even if the
reverend does say it's better up there in Heaven. I recall when I
became a woman and I went and told my mother, she started to
cry, and I didn't know why. She said she was glad I'd lived as
long as that, so that I could become a woman; and maybe I could
go and live longer and have children and like that. Then she told
me about all the people that died, her sisters and her brothers
and a lot of them before they were ever born in the first place —
and now I know what she was telling me about!

"Most of the time you just go along and you don't think back;
but my little girl — she isn't little any more — came to me a

couple of months back, and told me she was bleeding and what did she do wrong, and I said nothing, and I told her why she was bleeding. I tried to recall what my mother said to me, and I did; and we both sat and talked, and yes sir, we were all filled up with tears, we were. But if you didn't have times like that, then you'd never know you was even living. That's what my mother said when I told her I was bleeding. She said you can't just go along and never have something real important happen.

"Here it's quiet compared to the city, I know. I've never been to a real big city. My uncle, he's been to Jackson and Birmingham and Memphis, because they had him in the Army, you know; and he was up there in New York and then he never did come back. The next thing we knew, he was dead. We got a telegram from a veterans' department of the government, saying he'd been in the hospital and he died there. It was he who was the one that told us all about going to the cities, and that's how my sister and brother happened to leave; in the same year they both left for the North. I thought of going myself, and so did my husband, but why should we, I asked myself. Even if there wasn't my mother or the reverend or the bossman telling you it was no good up there — even so, I would have been smart enough to know it. I mean, is there anyplace on God's earth where a colored man is going to have a real easy time? Is there? I'd like to know where, I would. As I see it, you'll be here or someplace else and it's the same; and you know, I'll picture us all leaving here, and traveling up the road, like the others have done, and I can't see us going too far before I'll want to turn around and get back — because we won't have what we've got and there won't be anything better in its place.

"I recall I went over to Greenville once, with my grandma it was, because she had a sister there. It took the whole day, with the bus late, and we sure had a long walk after the bus. All the time I was missing my home, and I wished I was back there. I'd think of our bed, and my daddy telling us before we fell asleep that we should be good and mind ourselves and not get fresh and if we did he'd hit us bad. I told Grandma I wanted to go home, and she said she did, too, but let's go visit her sister first. Then we did, and her sister said she wished she could go back up with us, but she had to stay, because she came there, to Greenville, with her husband; and he was there because he had a brother who learned to fix automobiles in the Army, and now he wasn't doing so bad, after all.

"That's me, I guess; I'm always looking back on things and recalling them and trying to forget something if it isn't any good. Every time a bad thing happens, I'll try to push myself to think of a good one. Mostly there'll be the Christmastime I told you about, and the times I've been with my grandma — like on the bus, with her looking out of the window and telling me it was real beautiful to look at, the state of Mississippi, even if it didn't treat us the best. That's what I say, too. That's how I believe. I'd be sad if I didn't have those sunflowers around and the pine trees, you know; and even in Greenville, Mississippi, I'll bet we'd have to give up on the flowers we have, and we couldn't have a chicken or two. We bought the chickens with the money we got from Chicago. They sent us a card with the money, and they said they didn't want us eating up everything at once, and we should go buy some chickens, and we did. Then the teacher helped me and my kids write back and thank them; and we couldn't help but add how good the chickens were and wasn't it too bad that they couldn't have them up there in Chicago. And you know, it's not as bad here all the time as it is some of the time, and you have to remember that. We have the seasons, and they change; and so does your luck."

She was smiling when she said that, and she went on in a more or less circular fashion — remembering that Christmas again, not because she was rambling or "senile" or provocative or at loose ends for conversation, but because she wanted to fall back on a few things in her life as long as the spirit moved her to do so. At the same time, I began to realize, she was responding to a moment not only in her life, but her daughter's — a second daughter who had also "become a woman" a little while ago. Sharecropper children, then, like children all over the world, stir their parents, and particularly their mothers, to a variety of responses and states of mind. Sharecropper children can make their parents smile and laugh. Sharecropper children can inspire self-congratulation in their parents. Sharecropper children can cause their parents worry or melancholy. The mood that dominates among those sharecropper children is one of mixed sadness and doubtfulness. I say that not only because I have subjected miles of tapes to something I dubiously call "thematic analysis"; but because I have myself seen what cannot be recorded on a tape recorder, seen gestures and looks and moves and responses to moves and signals made and nods given and arms raised — to express frustration, rage, confusion, hopelessness.

In South Carolina it was once put this way: "I hope maybe you could go tell a lot of people that we never stop trying. I don't have much to offer my kids, but I tell them I'm here and they're here, and it won't be long before we're gone, so the best thing to do is go ahead each day and say thank you, sun, for rising, and good-bye, sun, when it goes down, and I hope to see you tomorrow, and if I don't, then be good to those who stay after me. I do believe the sun must be part of God, because if we didn't have the sun we'd have no crops at all, and then we'd be dead and it's bad enough now even with the sun. All I know is that you can't worry more than from day to day. There'll be times when I start, but I say to myself that I should live by the sun, and not look ahead more than each day, because if I did, I believe my tears would come and they'd come and they'd wash us all away, they would. There'll be sometimes when I recall my mother saying that the sun is meant to dry up all your tears from the night before, that's what — besides making the land grow the crops. So, you see, we'd have a bad time without the sun. If you ask me, we just plain have a bad time all the time. But at least the sun is there, thank God, to help us out. There's just so much helping out that we ever get, and it's not enough; no, it isn't."

For such mothers life has an undeniable sadness to it — interrupted, though, by periods of earnest faith or gaiety or hard work that forces a suspension of all feelings. "When I'm helping out with the cotton and tobacco," says that mother, "I don't keep track of anything, not my kids or the time of day it is or even if I hurt or I don't. It's like you'll be dead for a while — just going along, up and down, doing what you have to do; and then, when you stop, you all of a sudden say to yourself that you're the same old you again, and you have to do this and that, and there's an ache you have, or an errand to get over with. There'll be some afternoons, I'll say so, when I feel real bad, and it's like the whole world has come crashing down on me. But I soon catch my breath and go about my business. I thank God for sparing me trouble while I have to be busy working, and I thank Him for keeping me alive. If I died, there'd be no mother for the kids — my mother died when I was little, and I know — and they'd be even worse off than they already are, and it's pretty bad for them each day, you know."

If it's "pretty bad for them each day," the badness takes both subjective and objective expression. Objectively, there is the cabin, the virtual peonage, the extreme hardship, the absence of money, the presence of hunger and malnutrition and parasites and so many diseases it is hard to know where to begin treating them, because they all really amount to one thing: a mean, terrible, brutish way of life become flesh, become infections and injuries and wasting away and "bad blood" and "weak blood" and "tired blood" and running noses and running sores and draining ears and draining wounds and "poor bones" and "poor teeth" and "poor eyes" — all of which, again, amount to the objective side of being poor, the objective side of what we call "poverty," in this case the extreme rural kind.[7] Yet, in those cabins that are out of just about everyone's sight, there is also a subjective side to things, perhaps less apparent or tangible or dramatic, but nonetheless real and significant for child and adult alike. To begin with, mothers cling to their children not only because they are dear and precious and wonderful to have, and in need of all the protection they can get, but because they may at any moment "go" (stop breathing, burn up with fever and die) and because soon, all too soon, the burdensome world will close in on them. The clinging, then, has its sad side, its grimness and fear. So does the frustration felt by both mother and child a little later on, when the baby is let loose — to become a toddler, to explore and begin to find out the precise nature of his or her inheritance. The mother's sadness now has to do with her realization that the child will indeed find out the truth, and the child's sadness has to do with what he finds out, what he comes to know and learns to live with: soreness and itching that don't go away, that get no treatment; hunger pangs, sometimes relieved by starches and Kool-Aid and candy, but sometimes not; hot nights made no easier by fans (let alone air-conditioners) and tight-fitting screens and trips to lakes or mountains or the sea; and cold nights untempered by heating systems and warm blankets and Shetland wool sweaters.

Put differently, the families are more than "just" frustrated; their sense of frustration has in it a visible, an audible quality of sadness — that so much cannot be done *for* the child, and that so much cannot be done *by* the child. Needless to say, frustration causes parents and children alike to be irritable, to tease one another — and I have found such particularly to be the case among three- or four-year-old children and their sharecropper mothers and fathers. All children have to be told not to go here or there and say this or that, but the special fearfulness of a sharecropper's life settles upon a child rather quickly — and with a struggle. "They do a lot of bothering you, the kids do," I was told by one of the mothers already quoted. I asked her for examples and she answered: "Well, they'll get testy, you know. They'll jump on everything you say to them, so that after a while I try to stay away from them and let them get in trouble for themselves, and then they'll find out. Then they'll come back and try to get *me* in trouble. They'll say the bossman is coming and I'll run to see. They'll tell me someone came by and left us a big pile of food on the table, and he said we can eat all we want, and there will always be more. I guess they do a lot of imagining when they're little. But there'll be another day when all they do is cry and cry, until I don't know what to do, they're so low, their spirit is."

After a while the teasing stops and the "bad spirits" give way to something else, a consolidated and long-lasting kind of bitterness and anger which in turn reflect a deep and abiding sense of disappointment — about life and its interminable miseries, and equally, about themselves, as the ones for some inscrutable reason chosen to live such lives. Five- and six-year-old children become sullen and resentful and feel at a loss about things, and so do their parents, who share what their children go through and can acknowledge the fact: "I used to think maybe it'll get better, maybe it will. I'd hear the minister talk, and I'd think if we can get to Jerusalem after we die — well, who knows, maybe we'll get there before we die, since God can work miracles. But I guess there isn't going to be any miracle, no sir; there isn't. And there isn't going to be anything for us that'll make it easier. I know that, and if my children don't, they'd better; but they do know — I know. They'll give me a clue now and then. They'll say that they wish they had some other mother and daddy, and that me and their daddy, we should have had other mothers and daddys, too — and then we wouldn't be here in this bad state, no sir.

"Sometimes the kids get real fresh, and they want to go and hit someone and get into a fight, but I tell them that if they go and do that, they won't make it any easier for us, worse in fact it would be, and besides they'll go right to jail and they'll spend the rest of their lives there — eating bread and drinking water, if they're lucky, and working on the road gangs, yes sir, like you see them doing when they come by from time to time. I know. My brother is in one of those gangs. He spoke fresh to the bossman, and then he hit him, because he said he didn't get what was owed him -- on shares, it was. He said he worked and worked all the years, and come each Christmastime the bossman, he'd drive up and say, 'Walter, you've done a great job, and I'm going to cancel most of your debts and keep you fed right through the winter.' That's a fact. That's what the bossman would say, and I'd hear it from Walter. I guess one time my brother couldn't stand it any longer, and he took after that bossman, and now poor Walter is in jail. You see, it's no use. That's what I tell the boys. My girls know better, yes sir — though they'll say wild things, too. The only thing for you to do is keep your thoughts to yourself and don't speak, unless you can trust the one you're speaking with, and try to get by each day. Sometimes I'll catch myself adding that you should hope for the best; but as the kids get older, they know it'll never come, *the best,* so you're being foolish to hope for it, because you shouldn't hope for something if you know it's not going to come your way, regardless."

What she knows her children slowly get to know. By the time her children are nine or ten or eleven they share her sentiments. They expect very little and hope for less. They are not quite without hope. They get up in the morning and go through the day. They can smile and find ways to make one another laugh. They can be persistent and industrious when asked or told to do something, to go on an errand, to help out here or there. Yet, they know despair, know how foolish it is to set their minds and hearts upon a very promising future. They have not lost hope about everyday living. They are not necessarily "depressed" or "suicidal." *Almost all* of the sharecropper children I have observed are not psychiatrically "sick," but they are indeed tired and in a very specific sense afflicted by hopelessness. Here is how a mother from Wilcox County, Alabama, describes what I am trying to get at: "Well, he's twelve, my boy, and he's become a man, you know. He doesn't give me trouble; no he doesn't. I told him a long time ago that if you cause trouble, you'll soon be in trouble yourself, and I guess he remembers what I said. I don't believe we want any trouble, and I know my children don't either, not a one of them. As soon as they can really use their heads and are grown up — well, I'd say by the time they're ten, maybe — they're not going to say something or do something that will mean jail, or worse even than that. I mean, I hope they won't.

"As I see it, if a boy is going to keep out of trouble and grow up and stay here in Alabama, then he has to mind himself, and the best way to do that is keep your mouth shut and your ears open and your eyes down and don't expect one single good thing to happen to you and stay with your own people whenever you can — that's what my daddy used to say to us, and that's what I learned, and that's what every one of my children has learned. I pray to God they have. And if they haven't, God save them; and He'd better, because there's nothing I can do to help my children out, besides teach them what I just said. When they get old enough to go to school — that's six or seven — they learn how to do some of the reading and the writing there; but a mother has to teach her children some lessons, even if they are going to school.

"Once a while back, maybe two years it was, my girl came home and said the teacher made them say that everyone here in the country of America is born equal, and we're all the same. Well, I didn't say a word. I was preparing their supper, and I kept on thinking to myself, and I asked myself how I could let my children believe that, when that's not the way they're going to live. So, I called my girl over, and the other children, too; and I told them that there is the white man and the black man, and the rich man and the poor man, and the sheriff and the rest of us, and there's the ones who have got a say and the ones who don't. That's what I told them, and you know what, I had them repeat it to me, out loud, and they did; and I told them they should listen to what they just said, and they'd better keep repeating it to themselves, saying it, until the end of their lives, like we all do.

"Then my son, he was ten I guess then, he said that he knew what I was saying, and he didn't expect one single thing from anyone, and he wasn't going to take anything that wasn't his, and he just would do like he should, and mind himself and be good, and if there was to be a reward, like you hear in church, it would be coming up there in Heaven, and you can't count on anything here, and there's nothing that's promised us, and like my grand-daddy used to tell me and like I would tell my boy, now he was telling me — that if you're out there in the fields and you see a rainbow and you start getting ideas that the rainbow means there'll be good times coming, then you'd better close your eyes for a while, and sure enough when you open them the rainbow will be gone, and no fooling, there'll probably be some white man nearby, telling you to get on it, or you won't have nothing to eat before long. Now, if your son can tell you that, he knows what he has to know; and nothing is going to go swelling his head, and he'll be all right. He won't expect any favors, and he won't get in trouble. Maybe it's different up North, but down here there's only one thing for us to do, and that's stay clear of trouble, if you

know what I mean. My daddy, he'd say that to get yourself
trouble, you've first got to decide to want something you mustn't
want, and then there's trouble that follows, and he knew
Alabama."

   She and thousands of other mothers bring up their children to
expect little, to expect nothing, to have none of the hope other
American children assume, take for granted, never really think
about at all. And it is literally hopelessness that these particular
children learn — in Wilcox County, Alabama, and other counties
in Alabama and other counties in other states. Like their parents
before them, they grow up and learn the facts of life and learn
the necessity of despair. Even so, they learn to find, as I must
repeatedly insist, whatever satisfactions and pleasures are humanly possible or available; and as a result, when they get older
and become parents themselves, they will have some decently
welcome and satisfying memories — yes, nostalgic memories —
to share with their children. Again and again I have heard that
nostalgia, heard it spoken by sharecropper parents and saw it
appreciated by sharecropper children. Nor is someone like me the
only one who gets to appreciate the irony of such nostalgia —
that it should suddenly appear in the mind and heart of a tired
mother whose home is, say a tar-paper shack in Holmes County,
Mississippi: "I don't have any bad feelings toward anyone, no sir,
I don't. Oh yes, I admit I do. There are some mean people that
God put here on this earth, I guess to test us and see if we can be
counted on to be good and not get in trouble. The civil rights
people, they'd come here a few years ago, the young white
people, and they'd tell you that we should start marching to the
courthouse and fight, that's what we should do. When I said no, I
wasn't going to march to the courthouse, the white girl who came
here got upset with me, and after a little while she told me that
being an Uncle Tom wasn't the way. Well, a month later they
were all gone, every one of those civil rights people, and here we
are.
   "Imagine: they were telling us we should be doing this thing
and not that thing. And she kept pointing her finger, all the time

she did, that white girl. I recall one time she came over and she said to me, 'Don't you hate Mississippi, for all it's done to your people?' and I said there sure was a lot of bad things going on here, and she said *everything* was bad here, and I said that wasn't what I said and it wasn't what I believed, either. The next thing, she wanted to know what was good here, and could I just name one thing. Well, I couldn't, not to her I couldn't. I just didn't say nothing after that, and she left, and I heard her say to her friend that they should cross us from their list. Then I sat and I thought to myself, like you find yourself doing for a little while now and then, and I remembered when we were little, how there'd be a holiday and we'd all get together, and there'd be a cake my mother would make, and sometimes there'd be chicken and my daddy loved the beer he'd get. The bossman used to buy a case and we could divide it. But the best times my sister and I had was fishing; we'd go with my brother, and he'd show us how, and we'd stand there and stand there and when we got a fish we were the happiest people in the whole world, and we'd bring it home and Mama would fry it up, and let me tell you, nothing, even if it costs a million dollars, could ever taste better, no sir. And I remember the games we had near the pond and in the woods, and the candy they'd give you, the white people, if you knew them and went up and asked them if you could help them someday; and even if they said no, they'd give you a Life Saver or like that from their pocketbooks or a penny, and we could get those sugar-caps, don't you know. They don't have sugar-caps in the stores anymore, but they were all colors, and on a piece of paper, and you'd eat them off the paper, little round things they were. My mama used to say they was good for stopping the stomach from rolling.

"Oh yes, we'd be hungry a lot. I remember that, too; but there'd be a Coke or the sugar-caps, and like I said, we'd catch a fish sometimes and we always had plenty of grits, and there'd be the holidays, and then we'd have 'treats,' my mama called them, like chicken. Another thing I often think back upon: the old car out there on the side of the plantation. One of the white people left it there, and he said we could all get to use it for fun, the kids, because it wasn't good for driving any more. And we did. We'd be in and out of that car, and there'd be an evening when my mama let us sleep there, and naturally we'd be so excited we couldn't fall asleep. That's how it still is, with my kids; they still can enjoy some of the same things. We have that car over there, just across the field, and my kids play in it just like I used to do. It's a lot bigger than the car we had, and they have fun, yes they do. We have a circus that comes through, and it's good. They don't charge much, and the bossman treats all the kids, and we go, too. I still go fishing, you know. I love fishing more than anything in the whole world, and so does my husband and the kids. Sometimes the whole family will go. My husband's brother, Harold, he went up North, to Cleveland, Ohio, and he hasn't gone fishing once, we heard, since he's been up there. He got a job and he wrote and said we should all come up there, and he sent us a picture postcard of the city, and there was a lake there. My husband, he got the minister to write back and ask Harold if he was fishing in that lake, and the next thing we knew Harold didn't have his job any more, and he said you can't go fishing in the lake, because it's like an ocean, and the fish aren't near the shore and they've been killed off, a lot of them, because there's poison in the lake. So I told our minister how lucky we are down here, with our little pond, and the minister said that's right.

"No, I don't say it's all good here. It's just good some of the time — when you're having yourself a rest out here and you can look at your tall sunflowers, you know, and when you have your good days, not too hot and not too cold, like in winter. Then, you look up and there's not a cloud anywhere, and the sun is smiling down on you, and everything is growing — and it's on those days that the fish will come near and bite, and you can catch them good, and they're not big, no, but if you fix them up, they taste better than anything. There'll be bad times, too — yes. But my mama told me, and I tell my own kids, that when there's a bad time, think of the good times, and when you're having a good time, don't get lost in it, and get all swelled up, because there'll be a bad time coming along next. So, I guess that's how I see it."

From all I can gather, that is indeed how she sees things. Life is hard and on the whole ungenerous, yet sometimes things seem a little easier — a moment here and another there. And those moments are to be remembered, for one thing as solace, and for another out of self-respect. The memories, as I have heard them put to words, are always to a listener like me a little sad, and a little surprising, too: so much apparent pleasure obtained under such hard and frustrating circumstances. Yet, it has to be said that the memories are consistently sad as well as joyful, something the people themselves eventually say to me. Sharecroppers can become nostalgic, but mostly their nostalgia expresses a sense of imminent trouble, which can at least be softened somewhat by a psychological retreat into whatever consolation the past happens to offer.

The psychological story goes something like this: hopelessness by itself is unbearable, so the everyday sadness of life has to be confronted in a number of ways, among them the resort to nostalgia. Perhaps what happens should be characterized as a mixture of stoic indifference (to the enormity of life's burdens) and muted defiance (toward the fate that decrees these burdens) and finally, a stubborn form of gaiety, both ironic and yes, sarcastic — as if the mind (through its powers of selective and tempered recall) can show anyone and everyone that by no means is all lost. "There is always prayer," I hear said again and again in those cabins; and then, often as not, another "always" will crop up: "And there is always the good time we had." Immediately after the second "always" one hears the particular instance or short series of instances spelled out. There was this moment or that one. There was the "spell" here, when such-and-such took place, or the "bout" had with so-and-so, which turned out so unexpectedly well. There was, in sum, the past, the sad past, but the past that one is now around to think back upon, to reflect upon, to talk about, to declare somehow overcome, gone through, endured.

Sadness, then, in and of itself is not the issue, so much as what is *done* with sadness — by people who cannot go to doctors or psychiatrists to discuss their gloom and despair, who with one

another don't take to formal discussions or even prolonged conversations, and who for that matter have learned to appear
utterly mute to outsiders. I cannot repeat often enough how slyly
silent tenant farmers can be, and teach their children to be, when
someone like me approaches. Eventually, though, the silence is
given up, and things like nostalgia can be heard. Eventually too,
the psychological purpose of the nostalgia can be appreciated,
and so far as children go, its definite importance comprehended.
And indeed, most all the nostalgic moments I witnessed and
heard and struggled to understand had to do with children. The
particular remembrance evoked either the speaker's own childhood or someone else's — that of a grown-up friend or neighbor
or relative, or that of a child just old enough to have a substantial
past, one his mother or father could summon and marvel at as
well as be unhappy about. The sharecropper's nostalgia is a kind
of sadness that is at once acknowledged and denied; a sadness
that in a way summarizes other sadnesses, particularly those that
the men and women who live in those rural cabins experience as
parents, as mothers and fathers whose job it is to bring up yet
another generation of field hands: "We just try to stay alive, and
maybe go along, but not very far, not anywhere, I guess." She
meant to say, of course, that there isn't much chance that she and
her family will go very far or get very far. Yet, it can be said that
she had just gone some distance indeed — into a sort of reverie
which enabled her to travel back, back over the hard and bitter
past of her life and her mother's life and her grandmother's life.
And while doing so she even managed to find resting places,
those moments of amusement and joy a mind can recall.

So it goes, the sadness of a sharecropper's life. At birth the
sharecropper child is held and holds on for dear life, already
against great odds. At fourteen and fifteen the young sharecropper or tenant farmer, no longer really a child, begins to have
moods of nostalgia. In between those two times are other times,
times when one or another "attitude" or sentiment or display of
emotion or whatever predominates — a sense of frustration or of
bitterness, the inclination to tease, the wish to strike out, to strike
down, the feeling of hopelessness or loneliness. Not that I want

to separate these children from all other children — who at one time or another go through everything I have just mentioned. But there is, at least in my experience, a certain distinctive pattern or sequence to the lives of sharecropper children, to their growth and development. That is to say, certain things come up: ways of getting along, ways of acting and reacting, ways of speaking about specific themes, which have regularly and predictably to do with the concrete and substantive matters of the share-cropper's world.

When I hear sadness expressed, I often hear something else, something that the children I am describing in this chapter begin to convey almost as soon as they can talk and draw and paint. I am speaking of something that the word "stranded" conveys. It is as if the child right off knows (or comes to know or is taught or learns) that he and his family have little future, no prospects, hardly anything ahead but a mean, even cruel struggle for that very minimum of things, mere existence itself. It is as if the child realizes full well that others by the thousands, even by the millions, have left rather than face what is ahead of him or her. A child of ten managed to tell me about himself and his coming fate: "I don't think it'll be much different, my life and my daddy's; I mean, what he's doing and I will do. The trouble is, Daddy says it may be worse for us. My momma says no, it won't, because it can't be, because we're already as bad off as it can get. I'd like to find me a job that I could keep, and it would be a good one, and near here; but you hear there's no work, except helping with the crops, like my daddy does, and he says that's all I can expect is to do that, unless there's *more* machines, so that the bossman won't need but two or three men. Daddy says the bossman told him that it's still cheaper to have us than the machines, and that's why we're here, I guess.

"Yes, I'll ask my daddy sometimes why we don't just up and leave, like a lot of people have been doing. He says that there's no reason to; and if we did, we'd be going from out of one mess into another one. My brother Billy and me, and my sister Alice, we all asked him once, and when he said the same old thing to us, we said that we heard the bossman kept telling the foreman that the colored people would leave Mississippi, every one of them, and Alabama too, if they know what's best for them, but since they don't then they'd better obey and do what they're told. Daddy didn't say anything back. He nodded his head and he went back to cutting the trees, and we were about to go away, and then he said we should stay right where we are, and listen to him, and he told us if we'd all gone up to Chicago or New York, then we might be dead from some accident or poison or all the things they have up there. He said to grow up in those cities is the worst possible thing that can happen to you, even including Mississippi and Alabama. So that's why he stayed, he said; and he's going to stay until the day he dies, and he told us to watch out and not get a lot of ideas, because the next thing you know we'll be all grown up, and we shouldn't have the idea we can go someplace and it'll be better there. That's a wrong idea.

"No, I haven't been to school this year, because of my momma being sick and then my grandma died; and we don't have the clothes. I help my daddy with the planting and I do errands for the foreman and I help with my little brothers. I'd like to go to a big city, even just to visit. I'd like to go to Birmingham, Alabama. I know a kid, his uncle lives there. He works in a big factory, I think. But he came back last year, the uncle did; and he told my friend there wasn't much reason now to go to Birmingham, because they're cutting back on people unless they've gone to school half their life, almost, and have the papers, you know, to prove it. I hope maybe I can go into the Army. I hear say if they consent to take you, they give you all the clothes you'll ever need in your whole life, and they feed you all the time, with the best food in the whole world and all you want of it, and they'll train you for working in a good job. They say it's hard to get yourself accepted, though, because you can't have any sickness, and they check up on you, how big and strong you are. I have some trouble with breathing, and the man in the grocery store, he said it was probably that my heart didn't grow to the right size and I guess it'll never go away. I asked my momma if it could be cleared away somehow, so that my heart could grow, and she said she didn't think so, because it's too late now. But I hear they may be opening some factories right down here. The minister said they might one day, but you can't be sure when; and he said if we pray, then maybe it'll be sooner and not later. Sometimes all of us try to pray at the same time; my momma makes us. I pray the factories will come down here real soon, when I'll be old enough to go and work in them.

"There'll be times when I hear my daddy say that soon there'll be nothing for us to do here, but there still won't be any point going to another place. So we'll be lost, he says, and left with only this roof to cover us — as long as the bossman says it's OK to stay here. I have my friend Tom, and he says he's going to catch a ride on a freight train one of these days, and he'll end up there, in the North; and then he says he'll go to a policeman and tell him he's lost and do they know where you can get a job and something to eat. It's better up North for the colored people, and there you can go ask for help, that's what Tom says. Tom asked if I wanted to go with him, and I said I'll think about it and make up my mind. I didn't ask my daddy, because I know what he'd say, right away. I asked Mr. Robinson, the funeral man, and he said I would be a fool not to go, because you can always get a meal up there, through welfare, but you can't down here. But then he turned around and said I should be careful, because it was real bad up there, real bad, and getting worse all the time. He said if you went up there around ten or twenty years ago, the colored man, then you were all right; but now it's a different picture. He said you end up all the way across the country, up North, and it can be better than here and it can be worse than here, all depending on a lot of things. You can freeze up there, I know. And my daddy says you live in a room or two, and you see no land. All you can see is the rats; they hide way down under the buildings and they crawl up at night and bite you. But they'll give you good welfare money up North, except that you have to pay most of it for the building you live in. I guess we're just going to stay here, and there's nothing else to do: each way, you've got your troubles, everyone says. My daddy always tells us we're just stuck here, and we'd better stay, because we should have left, maybe, a long time ago; and now if we leave it's like asking for trouble, and there's no guarantee it won't be worse than what we've already got, yes sir."

That is what it feels like to be stranded. The word has come back from the North, the word that lets those hundreds of thousands who are still Southerners know how things have changed, say, since 1940 or 1950. And yet, people continue to leave, but often with grave doubts and fears, and with few illusions about the freedom and wealth of those beckoning cities — which of course, always seemed to promise more than they actually delivered, or so many of those who have stayed behind also somehow knew and insisted, perhaps to make themselves feel better. Even those children who definitely plan one day to leave the countryside and go to a city nearby or far away, have their doubts and can talk about them, as did one girl of nine, alternately naïve and cynical, trusting and suspicious, grave and optimistic: "If you're a girl, I believe you can get yourself a job better, whether you're down here or up North. So, I hope to do that, and maybe if I'm married, my husband will be able to find a job, too — though it's not so easy, I know, for the man. When you ask me what I'll be doing later, and where I'll be living, I don't know the answer. From as far back as I can think, I used to tell my mother that we ought to leave here, and not be always doing what they tell you to do, the people that run this place. My mother used to say that one day we'd leave, but we owed all this money, from borrowing until the crops would come in. Then my aunt and uncle, they owed a lot of money and they came over last year, I think it was, and said we should all just up and leave one night, and the money we owed, we more than made up for with work, and the debt was just the bossman's way of keeping us doing whatever he wants. But we stayed and my aunt and uncle left the state.

"Everyone says I can be a maid and wash dishes, but I'd like to be a teacher, if I could. I don't go to school all the time, but when I do I find myself liking some of the teachers, how they dress up and know what to say. One of them is real nice, and she drives a new car to school, and she'll talk to you about going to a meeting in Memphis, and then there was another meeting in Atlanta, and she's been around and all over and everywhere. I did real good in school, and the teacher said I was coming along fine and I should go there more, and she'd teach me more — but we have to take turns. There's my other sisters and my brother, and we go one after the other to school and to church, and maybe one day we'll all have the right clothes, but until then we just have to go by turns.

"Once another teacher gave me a ride and she wanted to know what I was thinking of, for my future; and I said I don't know, and she said I should get on it, and start thinking. I told my mother what the teacher said, and my mother asked what the teacher expected us to do, since we're not getting all that money from the state of Alabama, like teachers do. When I next went to school, I asked that teacher if she could figure out how me and my sisters and my brother could go ahead and amount to something, like she said we should, if there wasn't a nickel or dime in the place, never mind any dollar bills. Yes sir, that's what I said, and it was just what my mother said. The teacher told me I was getting fresh. But I told her right back. I said it was all right for her telling us what to do, but meanwhile we were out there and we didn't hardly see any money, and it was real bad for my mother, trying to figure if we'd be getting what we should to eat every day. Then the teacher said I was beginning to talk like I was from the civil rights people and to shut my mouth or go and leave; and the next day it wasn't my turn to come there anyway, and I gave the shoes to my sister Mary Jean, and I told her to give the worst look she could to her, Miss Holmes. Mary Jean promised she would, and she did; and I never went back for a long time, and when I did she paid me no attention, Miss Holmes did, but I believe Mary Jean went up and asked if she could speak to the teacher, and she explained that none of us has ever seen a civil rights person hereabouts — never; and we just try to work the land and mind our own business, and they would all testify to it, the foreman and the bossman. My mother wanted the school people to know the truth, so she had Mary Jean tell the teacher.

"I don't trust no one, especially most of the teachers, and the big important people. Once the sheriff came to school, and the teacher told us we'd better not make a single sound, or he'd hear us, and he'd send us right to jail. Then one boy raised his hand, and she called on him, and he asked if it was right that they can put us in jail anytime they please, no matter what we say. Well, the next thing the teacher did was tell us that we should get those silly questions out of our heads, or else we would really end up there, in jail. Then the girl near me raised her hand, and she asked the teacher if it wasn't so, that we should all go away from here because there was nothing to keep us. The teacher said again that we should stop the questions and she was sorry she mentioned the sheriff and let's go back to learning arithmetic. There was a girl who was nodding and saying yes, we should go back to the arithmetic, and you know who she was: Caroline Jones, and her daddy is the richest colored man between here and Chicago, my daddy says. He owns funeral parlors and an insurance company, and if you have a complaint, you're supposed to see him, and then he'll tell you if he's going to talk to the white people about it, or if he won't. His girl, Caroline, comes to school with all different kinds of dresses and shoes, and she walks around as if she owns the school. The teachers, I believe they're scared of her, because if her daddy really wanted to, he could probably get them fired, any teacher that crossed Caroline. The other day I asked Caroline if she really planned to be a teacher, because the teacher told her she'd make a good one. Caroline said no, she'd like to go to Hollywood and get a job in the movies. I said that would be what I'd like, too, but I haven't seen many movies. She said her daddy drives her up to Memphis, I think, and they see them there. A while ago we had a television set, and we'd see movies on it; but it wasn't a good set when we got it, and soon it broke down for good. The man at the store said there was no point trying to fix it. Oh, it was left by a family when they went North.

"If I really could choose, I'd leave here, yes sir, and never come back. I'd try to get my whole family to go with me, though. If they wouldn't leave, I don't know if I could. I'm sure if I stay I'll get some job cleaning up for the white folks, and if you get a good woman to work for, she'll be nice to you and slip you a dress or something, before she throws it out. Maybe I could marry Caroline's brother, except she says he's going to Atlanta to college, and she thinks he'll never come back. If he did, and I married him, I'd be rich! Then we'd have a television that works real good, and I wouldn't need dresses from the white folks, no I wouldn't. I could go and get my own, and I'd wear shoes all the time, like the teachers do — and Caroline."

Such children, like all other children, have their dreams; but sharecropper children also have their doubts, very concrete ones, perhaps more of them than most boys and girls do. The younger sharecropper children I have met and observed can draw or paint pictures that express those doubts, and incidentally, a whole range of other feelings, which in sum constitute, I suppose, a "world view" — though the children themselves might wonder, were they to hear that expression, why I make so much of their halting or casual or eager and enthusiastic efforts.[8] Yet, they *do* manage to "say" a lot in those drawings; and since children of poor, southern rural families are likely to be even more silent (at five or six, for instance) than other children in the presence of someone like me, the use of crayons and paints becomes particularly important and instructive — I believe for them as well as their observer. In any event, Lawrence kept on telling me — briefly, but to the point — that he enjoyed the artwork he was doing, but he also hoped that I would like what I saw and *keep* it, so I "could show all the pictures to the other doctors, and they could see if they are correct."

What does the boy mean by "correct"? Well, of course if asked, he doesn't really know how to answer, or so he says at first. Then he acknowledges he had wondered whether (as in school) someone is grading his work: "I've not been to school much, but my sister has, and she said if you draw something the teacher tells you later if it's good or bad." He is seven, and actually he has been to school for a couple of years — though he does miss many days because he is sick, or because he doesn't have warm enough clothes, or any suitable clothes at all.[9] (Like others who live nearby, he shares a particular set of shoes and a pair of pants with his brothers. They rotate the use of the clothes, and by the same token rotate their attendance at school.) Finally, he lets me know something else: "The best thing would be if you kept the pictures, all the pictures I'm making; and even if they're not so good, they could remind you of the place here, after you go away."

Lawrence always liked to draw "the place," by which he meant the cabin in which he was born and now lives, and the land around it, some of which has pine trees, some of which is planted in cotton, some of which boasts a few flowers grown by his mother — who, incidentally, is not allowed to grow vegetables anywhere on that land. I asked Lawrence about that one day, because he put a few tomato plants and a few pieces of corn near the sunflowers he drew: "Well, it's not our land, except to grow cotton and corn and then share with the bossman, if we make money. The bossman says he doesn't want us using his land to grow a lot of food we could use for ourselves, so he said no to my daddy, and we're only allowed the flowers. My mother likes the flowers, and she grows them, and when the bossman comes by every once in a while, he'll tell us they are real pretty, the flowers she grows, and aren't we glad she's growing them, because they're as good as can be to look at. My mother doesn't answer him, and later she says he is the meanest man who ever smiled — and he's always smiling at us and telling us we're real good colored people, and he wishes everyone else colored was as good as we are, even half as good, he says.

"That's why, in the picture I tried to fool him and put the corn there and the tomato plants. It used to be that my granddaddy grew a little of each, and he'd go and bring some to the missus and she always said his was the best she ever tasted. But after she died and her husband got sick, the son took over, Junior they used to call him — that's what my daddy told me — and he's tough, real bad tough. He comes around on his inspection, that's what he calls it, and wants to make sure we're all being good and not 'sitting in the sun,' he says, and being 'lazy,' he says, and my daddy says he's scared to tell him to leave us alone, because it's his, the land, but if we didn't do anything but sit under the sun, then it would be *us* who'd suffer the worst — that's what my daddy said he'd like to tell him, Mr. Junior, the bossman. But my mother laughs and says he comes around here because he likes to feel big and important, and he likes to feel like his daddy, 'inspecting' us. Each time he comes he'll take and pick one of my mother's little flowers and put it on his jacket, and he won't even thank her. Then the next thing, he'll be sending the maid they have, Ruth, to come over and pick a whole bunch for the house. Once he sent us a dollar, but most of the time he sends us nothing, and there's not a thing we can do, no sir, that's what my daddy says.

"There was a time we might have gone away from here, but my daddy said no, and I'm glad. I sure know a lot of places here, and I'd hate to leave now. I like the woods the best, and next best the road down beside the big house; it goes near the pond, and there's a well there, and I get the water. The teacher told us if you go to a big city, likely as not you'll have water right in your house, and all you do is turn it on and turn it off, and it's always there, and it's as clean as can be. But she says it's real bad up there, and better to stay here; and my daddy says she's right. He says that here you don't have much except plenty of land, and the little you can get from working it, and up there you get your money, but you're like in jail, from all you hear; and that's no place to be."

He has drawn dozens of pastoral scenes, all of them evidence of his familiarity with the land he and his father and indeed everyone in their family knows so well. He has his very own way of approaching the paper, using the crayons, and in general doing his work. Like many sharecropper children I have met, he has done more drawing in school than anything else, and he could even (toward the very end of the time I spent with him and his family) tell me why: "The teacher said the other day that none of us talk right, and we should be ashamed of ourselves, and how could we ever amount to anything if that's how we're going to be speaking later on. That's why she has us make pictures, she said. Then she told us we'll be hopeless on the rest of the lessons, too — the writing and numbers — so maybe we should just wear the crayons down every day."

Actually, Lawrence does rather like drawing, though he does not wear his crayons down in a blind and obliging way. After all the experience he's had with those crayons, he still seems to value the magic they possess, their constant readiness to offer up a variety of colors. For Lawrence it can apparently be remarkable that something in this world is thoroughly reliable, and almost always *there*, to be called upon and applied. On several occasions, as he prepared to work, Lawrence made remarks similar to this: "Don't those crayons lose their color sometime? I mean, you use them and you use them, and they have the same color always. I thought after you used them a while they wouldn't be so red and blue and green and yellow. My daddy says that anything you own gives out after long, and he says that goes for the land we have here to plant. Daddy says we're lucky, because the land is good here, and it's still got a lot of life in it — but one day the life will go away. Maybe that will happen after I'm gone, he says; but a lot of land, it gives out fast, and there isn't anything you can do. Daddy said we're losing our woods, too — and the bossman isn't stopping it, because they cut down the pine trees, and then they send them away, and before you know it, the logs get to be paper, I don't know how. And the bossman makes some money. Up the road they came and put stakes on a big piece of land, and said we were to stay off it, because they'll be planting pine trees and growing them, only to cut them down. The first I heard of it — they were talking at the store, some white men from the city — I came and told my daddy, and he said I make up things in my mind, but they came and did what I heard, and my daddy told me later I was telling the truth, he could see."

Lawrence often begins a drawing with a tree, maybe two of them. Then he moves to the land, the earth he knows so well, the earth he never stops seeing. In the morning, he wakes up and looks through the wide cracks on the floor of the two-room cabin he and his three brothers and two sisters and parents and one aunt and three fatherless cousins and grandmother call home. All during the day he sees the earth as he goes to get water or goes to "help with the planting" or "work on the crops"; and in the evening he finds himself lying on a mattress with two of his brothers and staring down at the darkness of the ground. So, he draws that ground, that earth, that land; and he puts a little grass on it, and some cotton and some corn, and some tomatoes, and sometimes his mother's flowers. He makes the earth prominent, substantial, thick with layers and at times several shades — light brown and dark brown and gray and black. He brings out the consistency of things — the sandiness, the lumps and clods. He brings out the interruptions that rocks make and the intrusions that roots make. He brings out man's artifacts, the ditches that irrigate, the tidy furrows that have to do with cultivation and planting. He brings out the land's larger hospitality to chipmunks and ants and worms as well as to human beings.

While he draws a picture — say, this one (Figure 5) — he is willing to talk about the land he knows so well. That land is all the picture shows, except for a thin blue sky, put in last, and a red-hot sun, which marks the end of a day. There are no people around, no buildings, no evidence of anything human. Or, in fact, *is* Lawrence there, somewhere — and his family, and his neighbors and his father's bosses and just about everyone in the whole Mississippi Delta? Here is what Lawrence at various times said about that drawing and several others almost exactly like it, a "series" I suppose they could be called: "I guess I always draw the same thing. Maybe you draw what you really know, what you know the best. I know this land best, because my daddy started me out from as far back as I can remember helping him do the chores; and he would tell me there's one thing I'll have to know all my life, as long as we stay here, and that's what to do on the land we have to use. The bossman gives it to us, and it's ours, and he doesn't care what we do, so long as we raise what he wants and do it right and bring it all in; and then he takes care of everything, and tells us how we made out. Daddy says you can't but pray, and no matter what happens, the bossman will say that we could have done better, but we can stay through and try again next year, and he'll help us right through, like he always does, and we won't be without food and we can stay where we are. My daddy says it could be worse for us than it is, and we owe what we have each day to the land; and my mother says we should be thanking God for the good land He gave us around — here in this county.

"I'm always asking my daddy something and he's always giving me the right answer — about the land. He'll do a lot of explaining to us while we take the wagon and go for the water. He'll be telling us about how when he was a boy they didn't have the motors and the engines, and the cotton was a lot harder to take in. Now we have other crops, and it's hard with them, Daddy says, but not as bad as it used to be with the cotton; and we have good water for the land — the irrigation, you know. Daddy says he can remember when they came around from Washington or someplace up North and told us how to plant trees and keep the wind from blowing all the good land away, and the bossman's daddy came over and explained everything to my granddaddy and all the others, and my daddy was there. According to what you hear the white people say — the foreman and his helper and like that — we'll be all right here and there's still profits to make. I heard the foreman say in the store last winter that they still needed the niggers in Mississippi to work in the fields and help out with other work, and since a lot of colored people have gone, that's better. But there still are a lot of the colored people here, and we're going to stay for a long time, the foreman said, and we'll help out with the planting and the caring for the crops and getting them in on time, you know. And if you don't get them in real fast, everything is lost.

"My daddy says he'll never leave here, but I don't know if I'll be here all my life. My mother says maybe I will and maybe I won't, when I ask her. She says some go and some stay, and if a lot of us are up there and away, in the North, a lot of us are still here, where we've always been, and it's bad all around, yes sir. If

I could have anything I wanted — like you say — I wouldn't
know what I'd do. I'd sit down under that tree — it's my favorite
place to sit — and I'd try to decide, and then I'd ask everyone I
could, and then I'd make a choice. Sometimes I'll go to school,
and the teacher will tell us to keep on wishing we'll be big and
rich someday, and the minister, he says some people, they're just
chosen by God to have a lot of money, and live real good. Maybe
that's what I wish: some money to have, so I could go and buy
everything in the store — cans of food and a lot of candy and the
curtains my mother has been hoping for, if we ever get the
money. My daddy says the biggest time in the world would be if
we could get some money and we could fix up where we live to
be better, like they did with the church. The lady — she's the
bossman's wife and Daddy says her folks own a real big place, a
plantation, not far away — every time come Christmas, around
then, just before Christmas it is, she'll show up and give us a
ham. She'll do it for a lot of people. She used to have a chicken to
bring us, my daddy says, and then she thought the hams in the
tin can, they're better, so we get them. I wouldn't mind having
them all the time, and maybe that's what I should wish for, if I
could get my wish come true. Last time, I can remember, she
drove up and she told us here we are, a nice ham, and my mother
said thank you, and my daddy and all of us, we had to say thank
you, and she said we were real good, and she was glad to come
by and wish us a merry Christmas, and she hoped we'd be going
to church and praying, and my mother said yes, we would, that's
for sure, and she said that was real good, and as long as you
pray, you'll stay clear of trouble, and that's the truth. Just before
she went back into her car she asked my mother if everything
was going fine, and my mother said, 'Yes ma'am,' it was, and she
got in and drove off, but before that she said, 'Good.' I heard her.
Afterwards, my mother said it was too bad she didn't offer us
some things, and we could have said yes. My mother said she
hears they're always throwing food away up there at the House,
and throwing away clothes, and maybe there would be a few
curtains they could give us. But Daddy said if they gave to us,
there's all the other tenants, and pretty soon they'd be in trouble

with the other white folks for 'pampering the niggers,' that's how they say it. I heard it said once myself in the store that time, like I told you."

Lawrence shows no signs of being pampered. Like everyone else in his family he gets up at sunrise and goes to bed at sunset. There are no clocks to bother him and in general his sense of time has little to do with minutes and hours. He mostly works. He walks for several miles to a pond and fills up with water two buckets he has brought along, all before breakfast. While he is walking he relieves himself. He has never brushed his teeth in his life. There are no toothbrushes in his family's cabin, nor toothpaste. There is one mirror there, a small one, used by Lawrence's mother on Sunday when she "fixes up" herself and "really gets dressed." Lawrence does not regularly wash himself. Sometimes he takes a bar of soap to the pond and washes his hands there. It is a small pond, a shallow pond, and he does not swim in it. I do not believe he should drink the pond's water, but he does drink it; and so does everyone else in his family. For breakfast Lawrence has coffee or Coke and grits, prepared by his mother who is also up at dawn. He has never in his life had bacon and eggs for breakfast; when there are eggs, usually on holidays, they are for dinner, which is the midday meal, and the main one. Usually dinner consists of a glass of Kool-Aid (first) followed by bread spread with margarine, grits again, some greens, and by no means always, a pork chop — or more likely fatback or "streak-meat," which are both more fat than anything else. (The "streak-meat," like the "streak-o-lean" I have noticed particularly among migrants is exactly what the name implies: a hunk of fat streaked occasionally by meat.)

Then comes work for Lawrence, or on relatively rare days, school. There is planting to be done, or chores up where the cattle are. There is fishing, which means food for dinner. There are crops to take in. On school days there are shoes to put on, and the good clothes, which are also worn on Sundays by Lawrence or his brothers, who may be of different ages and sizes, but manage to share clothes without embarrassment or difficulty.

I have never seen them talk or act as if something doesn't fit, and their mother hasn't either. Actually, Lawrence's mother keeps her eyes on her children and would certainly know what they do or say, though not very much conversation goes on in the cabin each morning. It is mostly quiet: "A lot of the time it's hot, you know, or it's cold here in the winter; and when the weather doesn't favor you, there's no reason why you should make it worse by talking a lot — that's what I tell my family. My husband, he's not one for talking, anyhow. He just gets up and tries to forget his aches and pains by going to work. Most of the time he'll miss his breakfast, yes sir, and that gives more for the children; and I do the same. With Lawrence, we don't have much to worry about. He's not as sickly as Ronald, and he'll do almost anything we ask. I don't have to say a word to him, you know. I'll catch myself thinking of something and he'll pick up what's in my mind and go do it, and there's never a word spoken between us. Yes, maybe it *is* in my eyes, that he'll see something. I don't know. Lawrence is a good boy. I only hope he stays good. It gets harder to be good the older you get, that's what I believe. Right now Lawrence is below ten, and he helps us out. Soon he'll be over ten, and getting to be grown up, and he'll be asking all those questions, and I'll be quiet like always, but it won't be because there's no reason to say anything. It'll be because I won't know what to say — because, you know, they'll ask you things, like why should they stay here, and that kind of question, and the best thing is to keep your peace and hope they hear from others that if you go and leave for the North there'll be trouble for you up there."

The silence in the cabin occasionally gets interrupted early in the morning. Birds start their talk and seem to be ignored by Lawrence and everyone else in his family. A few miles away a big truck or two can be heard passing, though the road is no major one and few automobiles use it. Families like Lawrence's make up most of the people nearby, and they don't own cars. Eventually the foreman and one of his assistants arrive; the point, of course, is to see how everything is going. Lawrence, like his father, says little to them, but knows why they have come and what he must do: "Daddy told me when I was little to go call him when they came — when it's the bossman himself or the people who work for him, like the foreman. Now I don't go running for him, because Daddy can hear their car, he says. They used to ride up on a horse. They'll just ask if we're taking care of everything, and I'll say, 'Yes, sir, we are, as best we can.' Then they'll look around and drive off. Daddy says he's not sure how they've got the plantation divided up — and how many of us are working the land for them, but it's big, this plantation. The teacher, she said it's 'real big,' and she said she doesn't like to tell stories, so it's true. what she says. I heard her tell my mother that the sun could rise and fall on all the land on the plantation, and you would still have land left over."

Lawrence is quite aware of the sun; indeed, it enables him to keep time. He watches the sun every hour or so, and he makes predictions about the weather by judging the sun's heat, its intensity, its degree of control over the sky. Somehow he seems to know whether an early morning haze or the clouds of breakfast time will be burned away or remain; and his description can be a military one: "The sun wins a lot, but sometimes it just can't. The clouds, they're just too strong, I guess. The sun will go after them, but no use. Other days, you can tell that nothing is going to get in the way of that Mr. Sun for too long, no sir. Even the night before you can tell those days, because the sun, he'll go down real slow-like, and he's as red as can be; then he'll settle over there on to the other side of the plantation, and it'll be light so long that you know there can't be a cloud the next day, not one cloud in the whole sky."

Lawrence liked to draw the sun for me, and the moon, too. Both of them have a magic for him, the sun because it makes everything grow and the moon because it stands out so prominently in the otherwise rather dark sky. Millions of men, women and children have felt the same way about both of those celestial bodies, but I doubt whether many American children who live in the suburbs or the cities spend much time thinking about the sun or the moon. A child like Lawrence lives by the sun in the day and the moon at night; that is, he is helped to tell time, figure out what he should be doing and where, and yes, he is helped psychologically, too.

Another child I have come to know, the nine-year-old daughter of a tenant farmer in Jones County, North Carolina, talks even more than Lawrence about the sky, the moon, the stars, the sun. Like him, she is moved constantly to draw all of them, so removed in space yet so close to her life. Jeannette is the girl's name; and a smart, winning child she is, full of imagination and wonder and humor — but also confusion and gloom. I had to spend more time than usual with her before I found out a little of what her almost frozen appearance managed to conceal. Eventually I had to face the fact that a girl I initially considered distinctly retarded turned out to be perhaps the brightest of all the so-called "stranded" children I am now trying to describe — children whose fathers, like Jeannette's, still work as sharecroppers or tenant farmers or field hands.

For months Jeannette seemed not only quieter than others in her family, but I have to confess, a little odd. She had a habit of moving near me as I entered the cabin — it can tactfully be called an extremely fragile and vulnerable building, lacking in the appointments Americans usually take for granted. Like a fly or mosquito, I once thought, she would draw close, breathe just hard enough to make a little noise, then withdraw to a distant corner of that one room which eight human beings call "home." Her eyes never stop staring at the visitor. While other eyes, her mother's, say, or those that belong to her sisters or brother or father usually looked down or up or in any direction that amounted to *away*, Jeannette's eyes held fast. Perhaps it was my own nervousness that made me pin words like "retarded" or "inappropriate" or "eccentric" on a girl's open and direct curiosity. In any event, I gradually began to appreciate Jeannette's perceptiveness and the intensity as well as generosity of her mind. She missed little and gave "life" and "nature" the very definite benefit of the doubt. "I know it's not so good for us," she once declared, "but there's never a day I don't see something I like."

Perhaps she is naïve — a child and so childlike. Perhaps "underneath" she is more in despair than she knows or can admit. Perhaps she will soon change her mind, lose what older people like me call her innocence, her exceptionally trusting or confident nature. Yet, I doubt it. After a while one sees how, in the face of great difficulties and recurrent fits of discouragement, a "trait" like Jeannette's optimism has its roots in a˙ long tradition. For example, Jeannette's grandmother, her mother's mother, is the one who inspires the child's spirit of enthusiasm, her sense of expectation about the world. Jeannette's mother, however, is tired and often despondent; like me, I suppose, she finds Jeannette a little unnerving. She once tried to bring alive the child's special qualities: "She's a strange child, my Jeannette is; and I don't know why. I had trouble bearing her, but that's been the case with all my children. She was strong most of the time when she was little, and she was always wanting to eat more and more and more. You have to stop them. You have to tell them you just don't have anything more for them to eat, even if they're as hungry as can be. With Jeannette, I'll say this about her, she was always wondering why — why this and why that. All your kids will do that, but she was worse than the rest of them, yes she was. She'd point to everything and ask me how it all came and from where, and I'd tell her to stop and she didn't. Instead she'd go over to my mother and start talking with her, and my mother was over there on the bed, lying there sick, and she'd try to answer the child, but no one could, I don't believe, with all the learning in the world.

"If you ask me, my mother fell to listening to Jeannette and going along with her. Jeannette would tell her that God was up there in the sun, looking down on us and making the grass grow, and in the night He is in the moon, so we won't be without Him, and my mother would say, 'Yes, child,' and 'You're right, child,' and there wasn't a thing I could say to change their minds, either of them. By now we just know that Jeannette is Jeannette, and she doesn't go to school all the time, but when she does she's good, the teachers say, real good, and why doesn't she come there more, they ask, but they know the answer, I know they do. I haven't clothes for all of them at the same time. And Jeannette isn't that interested in school, because she says she looks around and she sees things, and she learns that way. I guess I see what she means, though I doubt there is much you can see that'll teach you any more than you know already. But you can go ask Jeannette, and she'll one day talk your ear off. She's got a whole lot to say, that girl; I only tell her that me and her daddy and other people, they can't sit and listen all day, not with the chores you have from the first thing you get up to the last second before you fall into bed, and you're as tired as can be, and you're asleep before you know it."

Jeannette has done what her mother predicted, talked and talked with me and asked questions and gladly done drawings and paintings. Her landscapes are her pride, full of trees and flowers. She loves to start with the sky, then come down toward the earth, through trees that are drawn from their top branches first, followed by a sturdy trunk and at last the roots. Most children I know, regardless of race, class, family background or region, begin such drawings the other way around, from the ground on up, with the blue sky and the sun commonly a near afterthought. Eventually, after two pictures were done during the same visit, one with crayons and one with paints, one a daytime scene and one set in the evening (Figures 6 and 7), I felt able to ask Jeannette why she liked to start things up in the sky and work downward. That question marked the beginning of a certain frankness she and I shared with one another, one of the most important, instructive and above all touching experiences I've ever had with any child, any human being anywhere. As I get ready to set forth some of the highlights of Jeannette's remarks, made to me over a period of many months, I wonder how any words can quite convey the liveliness in her, *not* (I must say) easily visible in her face, but in her voice itself. Perhaps the best word is *vibrant;* Jeannette has a vibrant personality, which her voice especially gets across to people.

Jeannette's suns and moons are also particularly alive — full, as a matter of fact, of her own animated self. Certainly she means those suns and moons to be something awesome: "The sun, it's hot, but it's real good. I'll be going outside in the morning and I'll wave to the sun and I'll be glad when he comes to visit us, because if he didn't we'd be in trouble. There wouldn't be the crops, and we'd have no place to live; they'd tell us to leave, and Daddy says we'd probably go to Washington, up there, but he doesn't want for us to go there or anyplace else. I don't like the days when there will only be the clouds all day long. I like it when the sun will break through and start shining down on us, but I like it best of all when there's not a cloud in the sky, and just the sun, and you feel real warm because you're right under it, and you sure know.

"I don't know why I start with the sun up there. I like the colors blue and yellow; maybe that's why. I like to look up at the sky. Grandma says it's where we're all going — sooner or later, she says. If you look at the clouds, you can see they look like people a lot of the time. Sometimes there'll be no clouds; maybe that's when the Lord God has called everyone together and they're out of sight, far away from us, maybe right in the sun. I know it must be really hot there, in the sun, but it doesn't matter when you're dead. Then all that matters is whether the Lord is smiling on you or frowning on you. With the moon it's different. You don't want it so dark that there's no light to see by, and the moon carries you through the night, most nights, if you get scared; that's what Grandma told me and she's right. She said if I wake up and I get to shaking and I'm real scared, then go quietly to the door and find the moon and she'll smile on you and everything will be fine. But if the moon isn't there, don't worry either; because it'll be back real soon, and it's never away for more than a few days. Then try to find a good star, and if you can't because of the clouds, then go wake Grandma — but I've never done that.

"When I get big I'd like to go on one of those big airplanes you see passing over. Grandma said they don't reach the top of the sky, just part of the way. She doesn't know where they're going,

FIGURE 5

FIGURE 6

FIGURE 7

FIGURE 8

FIGURE 9

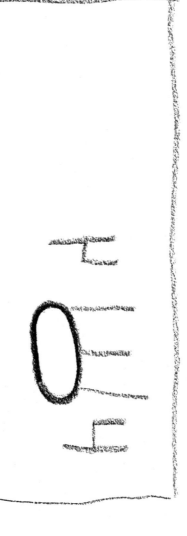

FIGURE 10

FIGURE 11

FIGURE 12

FIGURE 13

just to some cities, she thinks, but which ones you can't tell. The first time I thought they might be some bird, but I don't know what the name would be. Then when I went to school the teacher said maybe I was thinking of an eagle when I saw the airplane. She said she was going to write a letter to some people, the ones that own the plane and fly it, and ask them for a picture postcard — I guess it will show what you'd find it like if you went and got in and went right along with the plane through the sky. Once I was up a tree and I thought I'd try to be a plane, and I did, but I fell down. No, I didn't hurt myself. I just kept on wishing I didn't fall. I wished I was still up there, flying and flying, flying way high and away.

"Grandma told me that the only way for us folks is to go up. If you go sideways, you just end up in another county, and it's no different. If you go down, you're on your way to Hell, like Mr. Sam Pierce, the reverend says. He says you have to lower everybody into the ground after they die, but you should really pray that they never go lower than the hole that's been dug, because then they're really headed for trouble. Way down in the middle of the ground, there's no sun you can see, nor the moon; that's what I hear. It's no good. Grandma will say sometimes that it's just as bad up here in Jones County as down underground, but I can't go along with her on that. Like you hear in church: you mustn't go along and give up and look on only the wrong side of things. If the sun comes up in the morning, it means you have the day coming around the turn, and you can be glad."

Yes, she can get a little maudlin, a little rhetorical; and at nine she is clearly not inventing a great and original vision of things. Yet, Jeannette's world — at least the one outside her mind — is a terribly harsh and bare one, which she is earnestly trying to find at least passably comprehensible. In her own family, in other families a few miles this or that way, one can meet children who are not making the kind of effort Jeannette demonstrates. Her sister, the one nearest in age to her, wonders why Jeannette "troubles" about so much: "I'm older by a year, I believe, and I never have worried like Jeannette. She troubles herself, and she goes to Grandma, and they'll get talking, and we don't know what keeps them together so long. Once my momma said she thinks there's a ghost or something that got stuck in Jeannette, and it makes her do a lot of the talking she does; and she's always asking about something, too. She'll wake up and want you to go looking out there, and when she'll hear a noise she'll know what it is, which of the animals. It doesn't make any difference to me. I guess I'd rather be back to sleep. I'll wake and hear her talking in her sleep; but Grandma says we all talk in the middle of the night, only we don't know it. But I'll bet Jeannette talks more than I do."

Jeannette does indeed talk more than her older sister or her younger ones. She also thinks more about the next few years of life than they do. She has thoughts and wishes and daydreams about those years, even as she spends a lot of time playing in the fields or the woods and helping her mother get the younger children into the house in order to eat or go to bed. She imagines herself living somewhere else, living a life thoroughly different from the one she knows she will actually have. Here is how her mind wonders and wanders and hopes and then gives up hoping and in a flash of bitter irony, a child's kind of "black humor," yields to what psychiatrists call "reality": "I'll be walking sometimes and I say something to myself. I say that maybe one day later on I'll be far away from here, and I'll be a singer or I'll have a job on the radio or the television, and I'll live nice, as nice as you'd like to. I could bring everyone in my whole family to live near me, and they wouldn't always be thinking there's no next meal, and they wouldn't be scared all the time of the bossman and his people; and all of us, we'd be happy, like my grandma says God meant for us to be.

"If I had a good job, and I liked it, I'd have clothes and shoes, so I'd never hurt my feet walking, and they wouldn't get hot and burned, you know, in the summer. I'd have a room and it would be like you see in the stores when you go into New Bern: there would be the rugs and the television and a big mirror and you could see yourself, and anytime you wanted to find out how you are looking, you could just go over and there you'd be, right before yourself, and you could fix yourself up and be real nice.

You know what I'd like a lot, too? I'd like a plant and some flowers, like the teacher, Miss Johnson, has on her desk; and I'd like to have a car, and then I'd learn how to drive it, and I could get inside and start the motor and wherever I'd want to go, I could get there, pretty soon. The other thing I could do would be find me someone who could fix my leg, so it doesn't hurt, and fix my teeth, because they're bad, and I'll wake up in the night, and the tooth will really be giving me a lot of pain. I'd drive from town to town until I met a nice man, a doctor, and he'd give me medicines for all the troubles.

"If I was feeling real good, and if I still could keep on wishing things, then I'd ask how you get to go onto those planes, and I'd go. You can fly all around to everywhere, the teacher said, and I sure would. Before long I'd be seeing the whole world, all the places and the cities, and somewhere there'd be a lot of water and somewhere deserts and no rain. Then I'd come home and I'd tell my sisters and everyone what I saw and how you can do things — if you're not here and instead you're away, and if you've got some money, you know, and if there's no bossman pushing on you, and there aren't a lot of people around, telling you to do what they say."

Who are "they," the oppressors? Are they white only, or only certain whites? Is there any hope right there in North Carolina or in other such states, or must girls like Jeannette go far away if they are to live even half comfortably, and even a little without aches and pain? One thinks about such matters as a Jeannette talks, and sooner or later she provides an answer: "Maybe we could stay here and I could have my house and I would be in a real nice place, but I don't think the white people will let us — let us live so it's real good for us. My daddy says it's the colored people, too; they'll sit on top of one another, and some will take a lot of money from the white man, so they can boss us around worse than the white man does himself. I think if you're going to find something better — I mean, a good house and some money — then like you hear, you've got to leave here. The trouble is, most of the time they'll tell you that after you go away you don't find much that's good, so you might just as well stay, until you know where to go. My grandma says I'll probably be here all my life, like her, and maybe she's right.

"You know what? You know what I'd like to be, if I'm going to be in Jones County all my life? I'd like to be a scarecrow. Yes sir, if I got to be a scarecrow, I'd have the easiest life. I'd just be standing there, and they wouldn't be pushing on me, like they do, and calling me bad names, whispering them, in the store, when I go there. The lady, she said I was an 'uppity little nigger,' I heard her, because of how I look, how I carry my head, or something. I was outside, and she didn't know and she couldn't see me, and I listened to her talking, and I listened until I heard what she said, the whole of it, and then I went away as fast as I could, and she didn't know I was there. If I was a scarecrow, then maybe I could scare all those white people away; if they said something bad, I could be there and they'd want to run. The only thing is, I'd like to be alive and to fly, not just be standing there you know, like scarecrows do. I could be there in the field for some of the time and keep the birds away, but I could be a bird myself and fly around, all over. But I'd always come back here, because my grandma says they don't like blackbirds in the city."

She drew a picture of a scarecrow for me one afternoon and then added those birds a scarecrow is supposed to keep away — blackbirds among others (Figure 8). All her birds were black-birds, and so I asked her whether other birds threaten the crops, too. Yes, they do; but mostly it's the blackbirds. Then she added the reason: "They're hungry, and they don't get much to eat, and they have to try. You can't blame them. A long time ago, I recall, my daddy was fixing the scarecrow, so it would stand straight and keep up and not fall down, and he said he feels bad for the birds, for the blackbirds, because all they're trying to do is get the same thing as we are — food; and it's too bad, but if the birds get all they want, then we'll be on the losing side, and so they have to be scared away, or else we'll starve to death our-selves."

Jeannette's drawing of the scarecrow meant a lot to her. Months later she would mention the drawing, ask me if I still had it, ask me whether anyone else had ever drawn a scarecrow for me. I said no, she was the only one, though other parts of the drawing — the sky and sun and earth and blackbirds — had been done at one time or another by a good number of children I have known. She could understand that. She was glad, though, that she alone had thought to draw a scarecrow. When she was a very little girl she had seen a scarecrow and asked her father whether it talked, and if so, to whom. Well, of course, her father had told her that scarecrows don't talk, though she doubted him at the time and in a way she still does. Oh, she *knows* in her mind that they don't, the scarecrows of Jones County and all the others, all over America; but she would like for them to have a say about various matters and through her (perhaps it can be put like that) they *do* have a say — those lonely, ragged and forlorn things who themselves look scared, who appear more frightened than the birds that fly by and only occasionally ignore the surrounding crops.

"It's talking, the scarecrow," Jeannette told me when I asked the same old question I had asked her so many times: is there anything happening there, in the place you've just drawn? Some children don't like to be bothered with that kind of prodding. They know the inquiry for what it is, an effort to get them to talk about what they have put into a picture, and by doing so reveal a bit of what is on the very young artist's mind. In contrast, Jeannette has never needed much encouragement to set her imagination afire; indeed she welcomes questions — the more the better, it seems. She likes to tell stories. I believe that she was almost waiting for me to be intrigued with her scarecrow. Within seconds of my question she was off running with a story, a reporter's account it almost was: "The scarecrow likes to talk. He talks to the corn and the trees and he talks real loud when the wind comes and blows right through him and shakes him; and then all the birds fly away as fast as they can. A lot of the time the scarecrow wishes there'd be other scarecrows around, and then they could all talk together and have themselves a good time. But there aren't the other scarecrows, so this one talks to himself, and he sings a lot, and that way he doesn't feel too bad.

A lot of the time he's hungry, but he doesn't eat the corn, because he's not supposed to. I don't know how he eats. Maybe he doesn't have to. Everyone has to eat, though. Don't they?"

Jeannette doesn't eat too well. Nor do many, many other children like her. I still find myself surprised and dismayed by a child's drawing in which there is a table but no food, or a plate but no food, a bowl but no food. Unlike other boys and girls, sharecropper children do not draw strong kitchen tables or dining room tables, bedecked with flowers and dishes and fruit and vegetables. Sharecropper children don't supply colorful tablecloths and vases and tall glasses with straws inside, and they don't paint or sketch a refrigerator nearby, full of good things to eat, or a stove where all of that is being prepared. When a sharecropper boy draws a home, it is small and inconsequential in appearance, a mere spot on the thick, powerful earth, and all too faithfully his home (Figure 9). When a sharecropper girl draws a kitchen at mealtime or any other moment of the day it is her kitchen and none other (Figure 10).

A boy of eight who lives in McCormick County, South Carolina, drew the home, and a girl of seven who lives in Holmes County, Mississippi, drew the kitchen — which means in this case the entire house, all of its one room. The boy knew what he was doing, and so did the girl. The boy had this to say: "It's what we have. It's not the best place in the world to live, my mother says so, and if we looked far enough, we might find a better place, but it's ours, and so long as we're here, there's no reason to leave, because before we'd be long on the road, looking for something better, we'd probably get put in jail or get real bad sick, and there'd be no one to help us. Our place — you know, my daddy says he thinks it was built by slaves. All the houses around here, they were all built by the slaves. The Mister, his family has owned most of the county, a lot of it, since before we were freed, the colored; and afterwards, we stayed here, and if it hadn't been for them, the Mister and his family, we'd all have had no place to be, and Lord knows, my mother says, if any of us would be alive today. My brother — he's a couple of years older than me —

thinks he could build us a better place than this one, but it's not our land, and we're lucky to have what we have. The Mister says we're doing good work with the crops, and we can stay here, and if he can help us during the winter, he will. He lets us charge up the groceries, and then when the crops are in he deducts. Last winter it was so cold my daddy said we might as well be up North. The Mister came over and went from place to place, and he said if we needed paper to fill in the cracks we could come over and get the paper, and he would get some more if it ran out; and he told us to sleep right close to the stove, but we knew how to, anyway."

The girl had this to say: "I did my best to make it look good, the table we have. I can't draw good, but I can draw some things better than others. My favorite is to draw a dress, the one that was sent down for us, my sister and me, from Toledo — no sir, I don't know where Toledo is, except that it's far, far off and my aunt is there, and my cousins, too. They all used to live here, you know, and they left. We got the table from them. They took it and brought it here; the day before they left, they did. No, we didn't have our own before then. We had the bed, and we'd eat there. It was better sitting on the bed, but now that we have the table and the two chairs there, we use them sometimes. We put things on the table, the pot with the soup or the grits, and we get our servings from the table, and Daddy will sit there on the chair and rest himself. He says he doesn't want to go to bed just as soon as the sun goes down, and he gets a good rest on the chair. That's why we're glad to have the table and the chairs. Now I have a good dress I can use for church, thanks to our aunt. Daddy says he doesn't think he'll go up to Toledo, though. You have to get a car, and a car can break down, and then you're lost as can be. My aunt saved the fare for a long time and took the bus, but it was because her husband died that they let her go, the bossman did. He said they couldn't be of use to him anymore, so they should leave when they could, but he wouldn't push on them for when. Then my aunt collected on the insurance. It was supposed to be five hundred dollars, the man told her a long time ago, but he came and gave her two hundred. He said the value of insurance policies was going down, and there wasn't anything he could do. My aunt said he must be the richest nigger in America, from all the insurance he collects every time someone dies. He has a big car and it's got the air-cool in it. He keeps the windows closed all the time. My daddy says he comes by all the houses, and like he did with my uncle before he passed, he collects a quarter from you a couple of times in the month. Then, if you die he brings your wife the cash, but not what he told you. He brings something, though, so at least my aunt and my cousins had their bus fare."

In Washington County, Alabama, some white children could tell that black girl how mean and devious white insurance agents and bossmen can be — to the families of white tenant farmers, who by no means are a numerical match for their black counterparts, but who still exist (and suffer terribly) in parts of the South.[10] Tim is six years old. He is thin and tall for his age. He has hazel eyes and light brown hair. He is far from an open, affable boy, but over the years he gets more and more talkative. His schoolteacher thinks he "may be a little smarter than some like him." What does she mean by that? She, too, doesn't talk very much at first, but eventually she lets me know that she simply assumed that I was aware, as she is, that Alabama has its "poor white people" and "they're low on intelligence, a lot of them." Not that she is prejudiced against her own people; and not that she would ever want to use seriously that term "poor white trash"; and not that she doesn't fully understand why things are as they are: "I know why a boy like Tim doesn't take to school and never will. They're dirt poor, and they have no education, his parents, and they live off of Mr. Williams's land. They work it, and they give him a share of what they make and they keep the rest for themselves. It's pitiful, if you ask me — how they live."

I do not believe the word "pitiful" quite describes Tim and his family. They are poor, as "dirt poor" as can be, which they say themselves. They lack good food and decent shelter. They see little that is promising "up ahead," in the years to come. White though they are, there is little reason for them to be grateful for Alabama's agricultural economy, all of which Tim's parents know. So, while we talked about Tim, his father could interrupt this way: "Tim hasn't got a great future, any more than I did. In every county of this state you'll find your rich men, and the few that do well by serving them. I mean, they'll hire their foremen, and they'll have their lawyers and the men who do the insuring, and the county agents, the agricultural agents, and the sheriff — they all work for Mr. Williams, you know, one way or the other they do, just like me. The only difference is that I *really* work for him, from the first of the sunlight to the last; the rest, they'll be in the town, in the Donut Shoppe there, sitting and figuring how they can get some more money out of old man Williams and his boy, Sonny Williams. Tim asked me the other day why I didn't have a job like that, with a necktie and a big new car, and I told him there's the rich and the poor in this county, and only a few in-between, and most of us, we're just poor.

"We're not niggers, though; I'll tell you that. I feel sorry for them. They can't read nor write, and as bad as it is for the white, it's worse for the colored. Old man Williams, he has the colored working on his land, too — on the other side of the county. I hear they have it bad, real bad. My wife says they can't be much worse off than we have it, but I reminded her — they'd be killed if they tried to step in the Donut Shoppe or our church or like that, and we're not going to let one of them in our school, no matter what they try to do up there in Washington, D.C. Sonny Williams, he's my age, born the same year, my mother told me, and he's good and polite and respectful to all of us white men who work his daddy's land; and I hear he hates the niggers and wants to drive them all up North. He says they just live for the next meal, and they've got no ambition in them. I don't see how he can go and get rid of all his colored, though; not with all the land under cultivation. They're still needed around here, yes sir — niggers are. But if they want to go up North, I'm in favor of it. I'd never leave here, but I could understand them leaving. Maybe if they went, there'd be more machines the old man Williams would have to buy, and I could learn to drive one, and he'd pay me. I guess he'd have to be real nice to the white, if more of the colored left.

"Maybe Timmie will keep on going in school, and maybe he can get a job there in town, and he could live better. I always tell my children that they're not me, nor their mother, and they can go and find a better life, maybe; and they're not niggers, either — I tell them that. They should keep their eyes open, and there's no telling what comes up, sometimes — I mean a job or a chance to make some money. I'm afraid I don't see much of that — money."

He doesn't see money at all for weeks at a time. Like black tenant farmers or sharecroppers, Tim's father is part of a virtual barter economy. He seeds the black earth, cares for and harvests cotton and a variety of vegetables, and in exchange he gets a rather broken-down cabin (which has electricity but no running water and no heat except for what a coal stove provides) and a share of the profits, a share of what is sold to a nearby "wholesale produce company" — owned and run, it turns out, by the same family that lets Tim (for the boy at six already knows how to pick weeds and later picks the crops themselves) and his father work their "parcel" of land. Tim knows all of that, at age six knows who he is and who his father is and who the colored man is and who old man Williams is and who Sonny Williams is. Shyly, yet with obvious relish he draws a picture (Figure 11) of a great big hulk of a man, and tells me very explicitly what that man is like: "He's the richest man I'll ever see, my daddy says, unless I go a long way from here. He owns the county, just about, and into the next one, too — they say. Daddy says there could be worse, but sometimes he'll change his mind and say no, there can't be worse — not worse than old man Williams.

Now Mr. Williams does indeed appear threatening and even grotesque when compared to Tim's sketches of his dad (Figure 12) or those the boy did of a black "handyman" (Figure 13) — which is what Tim and his father both choose to call a man who in fact does exactly what they do, work Alabama's generous land for the very ungenerous old man Williams. Tim might be tempted to be as rich and powerful as Mr. Williams, but Tim at six has some ethical concern inside that literally childish and

immature and undeveloped mind of his: "I don't know. I'd like to
be like old man Williams, but if I had all he does, I'd want to
give some of it away. I mean, I could give some of it to my
daddy, and I wouldn't stop there, no. I'd go and give some to Mr.
Howe and Mr. Gurney and Mr. Wallace and Mr. McKeon
and — maybe everyone old man Williams has working for him.
I'd go and give some to his niggers, too; yes, I would. He has
those handymen, you know, and they help him and they are in
the worst shape in the whole world, and if I had the money they
have in the Williams family, I'd share it, that's what I think.

"Daddy says once you get money, you think different; you just
want to hold on to what you have. But if you remember your
own troubles, then you'll be nicer to other people, that's what he
said in his sermon, the minister, and I would, if I became rich.
My brother Richard, he says he would, too; and Daddy agreed.
He said that the trouble is that Mr. Williams has never been poor
a day in his life, and he's never been without anything, so you
can't expect him to think as we do. Then my mother said maybe
they should start rotating around the money, to more and more
people, rather than one man and his family having it, and then
there'd be more people with money, and some of them might be
willing to go and give a little money to others, especially to the
people who work so hard for practically nothing. Then we'd have
a better state of Alabama than we do right now. My brother
Richard must have told the teacher that — she's Miss Wilson,
and she's got the fourth grade all to herself, yes she does — and
she got real upset with him and said to him, 'Richard, you've got
some crazy ideas in your head and where did you get them?' And
my brother didn't lay it on anyone, the blame. My mother said
they'll let us talk like that, because we're in school, but not when
we get to be a man or a woman — then there'd be the sheriff out
after us, and the next thing we'd know, we'd be run out of the
county and maybe the next one, too."

So, Tim's view of the world turns out not to be so different
from that of other children, who, though black, share much of
Tim's experience: with the land, with the bosses and their agents,
with parents who feel hurt and used and put upon and cheated,

yet also feel unable and afraid to do anything but submit and complain and grumble and fret and murmur and at times shout and cry and scream — all that to themselves or among others like themselves. In the end, however strong the protest, there seems no choice but, once again, to submit, to acquiesce, to go along and hope that somehow and in some way there will come an end to it — an end to the hard, mean toil, barely rewarded and performed for the gain of others. Tim's father speaks, I believe, for this nation's thousands of sharecroppers and tenant farmers, men who keep on working and working, compliantly it seems, but feel worried and victimized and ill-used and, during bad moments, broken in mind and spirit: "I'm all right a lot of days. I just do the work that has to be done. There'll be a day or two out of the month, though, that I get wondering too much about things, and I feel I'm slipping into trouble; yes, I do, I'll admit it. I was born and brought up here, and before me there was my daddy and before him there was his daddy, and way back we go. We love Alabama, and I'd never leave, not for anything. I'm a Southerner, I guess you'd say. But there's a lot of unfairness around here, and I don't think it's right. I'll be plowing or picking and I'll say to myself that it's not right for some of us to have almost nothing, and there'll be others who own everything there is to be owned. But you can't think like that, because then you're getting to be dangerous. That's what the teachers will tell your kids when they go repeating you in school, and I guess the teachers are right, because they know a lot more than someone like me does, I'll admit to that. But they've got their salaries, you know, and they live as good as anyone does here, except for Mr. Williams and his people that run things for him. I guess I run things for him, too — just like his foreman Mr. Graves says *he* does; only I get nothing and Graves gets his big fat check. It's enough to break me up sometimes, but you can't let that happen. You'll become someone for the doctor then, and you don't want that. So you go on and work the next mile of land, that's what."

It is always there for them, Tim's father and all the fathers like him, the next mile of land; and for Tim and all the children like him the land also figures prominently — in their words and thoughts and dreams and drawings and paintings. In contrast to migrant children, who also know the land and work on the land, but see it as the cause of their confusing, irregular kind of life, sharecropper children view the fields and the crops as life's one reliable element. When will it all end, migrant children ask in any number of implicit and explicit ways. At least we have the fields out there and what they bring us, sharecropper children feel and often enough even say. Migrant children know that the crops mean money, meager though the amount is, even as sharecropper children associate a harvest with a few if not many meals. On the other hand, the migrant child knows one farm will lead to another, and all of those farms mean, finally, the dazed and bewildered state of mind that goes with such living; whereas sharecropper children have roots — if nothing else, roots. The world may be unfair, the bossman stingy, the children themselves half starved, but at least there is that particular stretch of land out there, familiar and unchanging and yes, full of the miraculous fertility that children like poets can celebrate. The ten-year-old daughter of a Mississippi tenant farmer put what I am trying to say into words a few weeks before her family was to leave for Chicago: "Everyone says you should leave here, but I don't want to. I know all the people around, and I know all the roads and the fields, and I told my daddy that when we get up there we won't know anyone and it'll be strange as can be up there, and we shouldn't go. But he said we have to, and that's that, and for me to stop bothering him and upsetting myself. But I think he'll change his mind when we leave, and we're far away, and then it'll be too late, that's what I think."

She does indeed know "the roads and the fields." She knows the best spot to be cool and the best spot to see the sunrise and the best spot to see the sunset and the best spot to hide and watch rabbits or skunks and the best spot to hide and listen to them talking, the bossman and the foreman and the assistant foreman — as they are walking along and laughing and kicking stones or smoking or chewing on a piece of grass and saying something like, "The nigger's doing fine, ain't he." She knows where to find water and where to find a soft bed of pine needles and where to find pieces of old, abandoned machinery which are the best playthings she and her brothers have. She knows how "the irrigation" works and how the pesticides work and why the soil needs fertilizer. Put differently, she is informed about things agricultural, and she is protective about the land, her land psychologically if the bossman's legally. Again the contrast has to be made with migrant children, who never really get to know a particular piece of property, but instead experience fields as places that offer a few days of work, but then must be left, and quickly, too.

If migrant children and sharecropper children are alike in being poor and scorned and thoroughly ignored by the rest of us, childhood is different among, on the one hand, a white boy like Tim or the little black girl just quoted, and on the other hand, those migrant children described in the previous chapter. Sharecropper children experience extreme hardships, but they are surrounded by things that give them a tangible refuge, however unpleasant and even stomach-turning some of those cabins can be. In Holmes County, Mississippi, a mother said what I am trying to say: "The kids know everything that goes on you know. Anytime I want to hear about something, I ask them. They sneak around and listen to people, and they're always poking around outside. They'll come in and tell me that the first leaf has turned, and we'll be having cooler weather. They'll come in and tell me that they've seen a little flower sticking its head up from the ground. They'll come in and tell me that the water is beginning to run low or that way over on the other side of the place the crops need more weeding than we thought, or that we forgot to spray a corner of the land, and all like that. You can walk around here and you'll see their marks on the trees and the rocks and you'll see all the huts they've put up and torn down and the other things they've made with the branches and the grass and — well, they've walked over every inch of the farm, yes sir, and probably a million times, I'll bet. If I had to know where the best worms are, I'd go ask them, just like their daddy does. They'll tell you where the best fishing is, and the bossman, you know he takes along one of my kids every time he goes fishing. My boy says the bossman will say it right to him: 'You little nigras, you sure know your fish.' And he'll give them a quarter, if there's a good catch they get. If the fish aren't so good, he'll turn them over to my boy, and then we eat them up for supper, and they always taste good to us, I'll say that.

"If you drove in your car for miles around, my children could show you every bird's nest there is here, and where they're all living, the animals. They keep their eyes on the crops, too. The foreman will always ask them how is everything doing, just like he'll ask me or my husband, and I do believe the children know better than we do. That's why they hate to go over to that school. They'll be sitting there all day, and the teacher will be pushing things on them, the letters and the numbers and like that, and she'll call them the same things the white people do, just as bad, and they'll come home and say they *are* dumb — for going over there and listening to her. They'll tell me they'd rather go out and listen to the animals make noise and help their daddy, if they can, and keep themselves busy and not bother me, than go off there to school and be told all the time that the colored people are no good, and they'll always be like that, because we're working on the land and we're so poor and we don't know how to be clean with ourselves and behave the way we should. Sure enough, it's not a life I'd like for my children, the kind I've had; but if we could make half a living — which we can't, and that's the trouble — then I wouldn't be so sad about anything, and I'd never leave here. You know why? My kids wouldn't let me. Even now they don't want to go — except around mealtime, when I don't give them all they want, because I haven't got it to give, and then they'll change their minds and start telling me we should leave here and go someplace else, where we won't always be afraid there won't be another thing to eat, and come the next time we're supposed to eat, and come the next time after that — until we're so weak we'll never be able to leave here, and that would be the end of us, I guess."

It haunts them, the questions that pose the great alternative. Shall we stay or shall we leave? Shall we keep on fighting a terribly grim and losing battle, in the hope that at least the few years we live on this planet will be spent on familiar and friendly ground, however cold and unfriendly and worse the people are who own that ground, and all the other ground nearby and far away? Shall we, rather, gird ourselves and go — leave as others have left, fearfully, and with all sorts of hopes and expectations? The land restricts and denies. The land awaits and offers up things. The land is someone else's to profit by, but ours to use. The land makes others rich and does little to keep us from extreme and unrelenting hardship. The land is everything we know. The land is, in a way, the source of all our misery. We will miss the land, miss it more than we can ever know — except that even here we *do* know how much our lives are tied to the rhythm of planting and growing and harvesting. We will leave and indeed forget the constant fear, the insults, the hopelessness; we will forget and start again up North, even as our ancestors did centuries ago, when, carried here in chains, they learned how to master the land and make it produce and produce — until white men became rich and proud and cultured and in the end died fighting to keep their land and keep us, their property.

So it goes, I believe, in thousands of minds as men and women mull things over and try to decide whether to continue being sharecroppers and tenant farmers and field hands or whether to make what so often is a fearful and sad as well as a necessary and hopeful break with the past. Sometimes the decision hinges on the children, on how strongly attached they feel to what they already know, on how sick and hungry and tired they are — and in need of help they will never get "nearabouts," as those rural counties are sometimes described. In any event, however the early lives of sharecropper and migrant children differ, one from the other, by the time the children described here and the children described in the previous chapter become eleven or twelve a common fate awaits them, a fate that distinctly overshadows all the differences I have just taken such pains to describe. I am talking about the swift decline of childhood, the abrupt beginning of a working and loving life — all in a matter of months. Then come the responsibilities that go with hard toil and the presence of a woman to feed or a man to cook for and soon, very soon, the arrival of children. At twelve or thirteen, the light and tender moments begin to wane, the world begins to shrink and toughen. Then the wisdom and humor get curbed. Then a kind of battle is joined, and under such circumstances a lot has to be forgotten or taken for granted, rather than enjoyed: the pathways that lead nowhere and everywhere, the rocks hidden all over, the large holes in the ground that indicate rabbits are living nearby, the buttons on the scarecrow, all four of them loose and ready to fall at the slightest provocation, the soil with black ants and toads and caterpillars, and the soil with abundant worms swimming in it, the cool, dry, shaded, restful soil under a pine tree. "You live fast," I often heard from young migrant couples, young migrant parents. Suddenly they were no longer children and all too much the burdened, troubled grown-ups their parents had always been. One can hear the same surprised, puzzled, disappointed remarks from young tenant farmers: "I don't know; it seems yesterday I was just helping out, and now it's all on me, life. My daddy said it was just in time because he fell down and he can't move his left side much, and he came over, the bossman, and said I could take over, if I was planning to stay here, and even if my daddy hadn't gone and fallen sick, I was working along with him, he noticed, and now that I had my woman and all, he thought he might give me a little to do, on top of what Daddy does — some more land to work — and besides that, I can help with driving the truck, if I can learn to tame it. And I can work over in his place where they sort the vegetables and pack them. They pay good there, but it's only a few weeks from the year.

"There was a time I thought I'd never stay here when I got big and could leave, but I guess I'll stay for a little, and see if I like it, now that I'm grown. In a few years they might take me in the Army, and then I'd be able to look over other places to live. Of course, the bossman can tell the Army not to take you, if he wants, because he needs us. He told me if I wanted to go North, he'd let me, but we're to have a child soon, and I have trouble with my eyes, seeing. The bossman said there'd be doctors working for the Army, and they wouldn't let me in. He said one of these days he was going to take me over to his doctor and have him fix up all my ailments, and especially fix my eyes. I said thank you; and I'm still waiting on him, and he's never yet repeated himself or took me over there. But I'll be fine, I hope."

One can only hope, as he does. One can only hope that he will be fine, and his family will be fine and other such families will be fine. One can only hope that his nation keeps on being "fine" — the envy of the world, the pride of the West, the home for hundreds of years, it has turned out, of loyal and resigned young sharecropper men who say that all will go well with them, but know how wicked and cursed the order of things is, know it in ways people like me — however earnest and prolonged our scrutiny — can never really know.

V

HIDDEN CHILDREN

THEY live up alongside the hills, in hollow after hollow. They live in eastern Kentucky and eastern Tennessee and in the western part of North Carolina and the western part of Virginia and in just about the whole state of West Virginia. They live close to the land; they farm it and some of them go down into it to extract its coal. Their ancestors, a century or two ago, fought their way westward from the Atlantic seaboard, came up on the mountains, penetrated the valleys, and moved stubbornly up the creeks for room, for privacy, for a view, for a domain of sorts. They are Appalachian people, mountain people, hill people. They are white yeomen, or miners, or hollow folk, or subsistence farmers. They are part of something called "the rural poor"; they are sometimes called "hillbillies." They are people who live in a "depressed area"; and they have been called part of a "subculture." They have also been called "backward," and more inscrutably, "privatistic."[1] They are known as balladeers and they are thought to have a tradition of music and poems and stories that is "pure" — right from old England and old Scotland and early if not old America.

As for the minds of those mountaineers, the rest of us outside their region are not supposed to have any way of really getting around certain traits that (so it is claimed) make the inhabitants of the hollows hard to reach psychologically, even as their territory and their cabins can be virtually unapproachable. Up in the hollows, the story goes, one finds sullen, fearful, withdrawn men and women who distrust outsiders, shun much of the twentieth century, cling to old and anomalous customs, take to liquor rather freely, and in general show themselves to be survivors of a rural, pioneer America for the most part long since gone. Up in the hollows, one is also told, the worst poverty in the nation exists, with hundreds of thousands of people condemned to a life of idleness, meager employment, long, snowbound winters and summers that can be of limited help to a man who has only an acre or two for planting on the side of a steep, rocky hill. Finally, up in the hollows history's cruel lessons are supposed to be unmistakably apparent: an ignored and exploited people have become a tired people, a worn-out people, a frivolous or unresponsive people, the best of whom, the ones with any life at all in them, continue to leave, thereby making an already dismal situation an almost impossible one.

No one, least of all the people in or near the hollows themselves, would want to deny all of that. Appalachia is indeed cut off in some respects from the rest of us; and the region's people are indeed quiet and reserved and often enough full of misgivings about "city people" and "outsiders," and the declarations of concern and the offers of help that have lately come from "them," whom one mountaineer I have known since 1964 goes on to describe as follows: "They're full of sugar when they come, and they say they want to do something for you; but I can't stand the sight of them, not one of them, because they're two-faced and wanting to treat you like you are dumb, a fool, and someone that needs to be told everything he should do and can't figure anything out for himself."

Yet, that same man, who lives way up one of those hollows (in Swain County, North Carolina) has other things to say about visitors and tourists, and by implication, other things to say about himself and his own kind of people: "A lot of cars come riding through here, you know. Everyone wants to look at the hills, and the bigger the waterfall you have to show, the better. They'll stop their driving and ask you directions to things, if you're down there on the main road, and I always try to help. You see, we're not against those people. It's beautiful here, right beautiful. You couldn't make it better if you could sit down and try to start all over and do anything you want. If they come here from clear across the country and tell you how they love what they've seen and they want to see more, I'm ready to help them, and I always act as polite as I can, and so do they, for the most part. The ones I don't like one bit are different. They don't want to look and enjoy your land, like you do yourself; no sir, they want to come and sit down and tell you how sorry you are, real sorry, and if something isn't done soon, you're going to 'die out,' that's what one of them said. I wasn't there, but I heard he came from Asheville, or from some big city, maybe not in North Carolina; and he was supposed to get us meeting together, and if we did there'd be some money in it for us, and he kept saying we're in bad shape, they tell me he did, and worst of all are the kids, he said, and didn't we know that.

"I didn't hear him or his exact words, of course, but it's not the first time it's happened like that, because a year ago I heard someone talk the very same. He came to the church and we all listened. He said we should have a program here, and the kids should go to it before they start school. He said the government would pay for it, from Washington. He said they'd be teaching the kids a lot, and checking up on their health, and it would be the best thing in the world. Well, I didn't see anything wrong with the idea. It seemed like a good idea to me. But I didn't like the way he kept repeating how bad off our kids are, and how they need one thing and another thing. Finally I was about ready to tell him to go home, mister, and leave us alone, because our kids are way better than you'll ever know, and we don't need you and your kind around here with nothing good to say, and all the bad names we're getting called. I didn't say a word, though. No, I sat through to the end, and I went home. I was too shy to talk at the meeting, and so were a lot of the others. Our minister was there, and he kept on telling us to give the man a break, because he'd come to help us. Now, I'm the first to admit we could stand some help around here, but I'm not going to have someone just coming around here and looking down on us, that's all, just plain looking down on us — and our kids, that's the worst of it, when they look down on your own kids.

"My kids, they're good; each of them is. They're good kids, and they don't make for trouble, and you couldn't ask for them any better. If he had asked me, the man out of the East, Washington or someplace, I would have told him that, too. We all would have. But he didn't want to ask us anything. All he wanted was to tell us he had this idea and this money, and we should go ahead and get our little kids together and they would go to the church during the summer and get their first learning, and they would be needing it, because they're bad off, that's what he must have said a hundred times, how bad off our kids are, and how the President of the United States wants for them to get their teeth fixed and to see a doctor and to learn as much as they can. You know what my wife whispered to me? She said, he doesn't know what our kids have learned, and still he's telling us they haven't learned a thing and they won't. And who does he think he is anyway? I told her it's best to sit him out and we could laugh out loud later when we left the church."

Later, when they left the church, they went home to their children, who were rather curious about the reason their parents had seen fit to go out to a meeting after supper in the middle of the week. There are five of those children and they range from four months to nine years. All the children were born in Swain County, North Carolina, as were their parents and grandparents and great-grandparents going back a century and more. Nor does Mrs. Allen want her children to be born anyplace else, or for that matter, under any other circumstances: "This is good country, as anybody will likely admit once he's seen it, and there's no reason to leave that I can see. You ask about the children I've borne; well, they're all good children, I believe they are. I've lost two, one from pneumonia we thought, and one had trouble from the moment he was alive. He was the only child that ever saw a doctor. We brought him down to Bryson City and there was a doctor there, waiting to see him. The Reverend Mason had called over, and he went with us.

"The doctor looked over the child real good, and I kept on fearing the news was going to be bad, the longer he looked and the more tests he did. Then he said he'd need extra tests, even beyond what he did, and we would have to come back. Of course I told him we'd try, but it's real hard on us to get a ride, and there's the other children I have, and my mother's gone, so they have to be left with one another the whole day, and there's a baby that needs me for feeding. The doctor said he could understand, but he needed those tests, and he was going to have to call some other doctor way over in Asheville or someplace and ask him some things. Mr. Mason said he'd drive us again, and we'd better do what the doctor said. Mr. Mason asked the doctor if there was much hope, even if we did everything and kept on coming back, so long as we had to, and the doctor shook his head, but he didn't say anything, one way or the other. But then my husband, Mr. Allen, he decided we'd better ask right there and then what was happening, and he did. He told the doctor that we're not much used to going to see doctors, and we'd like to know where we stand — it's just as plain and simple as that. The doctor asked if he could talk to Mr. Mason alone, and we said yes, that would be fine by us, but please couldn't they decide between themselves and then come and tell us something before we go back. And they did. They didn't talk too long before they came out, and said they would be honest with us, like we wanted, and the problem was with little Edward's muscles, and they weren't good from the start, and chances are they'd never be much good, and if we come back for the tests we might find out the exact disease, but he was pretty sure, even right then the doctor was, that Edward had a lot of bad trouble, and there wasn't much that could be done for him, and we might as well know it, that he'd not live to be grown up, and maybe not more than a year was the best we could hope for.

"I was real upset, but I was relieved to be told; I was thankful as can be for that. I guess Jim and I just nodded our heads and since we didn't say a word, and it was getting along, the time, the doctor came over and he asked if we had any questions to ask of him. I looked at Jim and he looked at me, and we didn't think of anything, and then Mr. Mason said it was all right, because if we did think of something later, we could always tell him and he could tell the doctor. The doctor said yes, and he said we were good people, and he liked us for being quiet and he wished he could do more. Jim said thank you, and we were glad he tried to help, and to be truthful we knew that there was something real bad wrong, and to us, if there isn't anything we can do, then chances are there isn't anything that anyone can do, even including a doctor, if he didn't mind us saying so. Mr. Mason said he wasn't sure we were in the right, and I said we could be wrong, and maybe they could have saved little Anne from her fever that burned her up — it was the pneumonia, we were sure. The doctor said there wasn't much use going back to what was over and done with, and I agreed. When we left, Mr. Mason said we could take the child back to the doctor anytime and he would drive us, and the doctor told the reverend he wouldn't charge us, not a penny. But Edward died a few weeks later. He couldn't breathe very good, like the doctor explained to us, because of his muscles, and the strain got to be more than he could take, so he stopped breathing, the little fellow did, right there in my arms. He could have lived longer, they said, if we'd have let them take him and put him in a hospital, you know, and they have motors and machines, to work on you. But I don't believe the Lord meant for Edward to go like that, in a hospital. I don't."

Her words read sadder than they sounded. She is tall, thin, but a forceful and composed woman, not given to self-pity. She has delicate bones, narrow wrists, thin ankles, decidedly pale blue eyes, and a bit surprisingly, a very strong, almost aquiline nose.[2] She was thirty and, I thought, both young and old. Her brown hair was heavily streaked with gray, and her skin was more wrinkled than is the case with many women who are forty or even fifty, let alone thirty. Most noticeable were her teeth; the ones left were in extremely bad repair, and many had long since fallen out — something that she is quite willing to talk about, once her guest has lost *his* embarrassment and asked her a question, like whether she had ever seen a dentist about her teeth. No, she had never done anything like that. What could a dentist do, but take out one's teeth; and eventually they fall out if they are really no good. Well, of course, there *are* things a dentist can do — and she quickly says she knows there must be, though she still isn't quite sure what they are, "those things." For a second her tact dominates the room, which is one of two the cabin possesses. Then she demonstrates her sense of humor, her openness, her surprising and almost awesome mixture of modesty and pride: "If you want to keep your teeth, you shouldn't have children. I know that from my life. I started losing my teeth when I started bringing children into the world. They take your strength, your babies do, while you're carrying them, and that's as it should be, except if I had more strength left for myself after the baby comes, I might be more patient with them. If you're tired you get sharp all the time with your children.

"The worst tooth to lose is your first one, after that you get used to having them go, one by one. We don't have a mirror here, except a very small one and it's cracked. My mother gave it to me. When I pick it up to catch a look at myself I always fix it so that I don't see my teeth. I have them in front of the crack instead of the glass. I'd like to have the teeth back, because I know I'd look better, but you can't keep yourself looking good after you start a family, not if you've got to be on the move from the first second you get up until right before you go to sleep. When I lie down on the bed, it's to fall asleep. I never remember thinking about anything. I'm too tired. So is Jim; he's always out there working on something; and so are the kids, they're real full of spirits. No wonder I lost so many teeth. When you have kids that are as rowdy and noisy as mine, they must need everything a mother's got even before they're born. Of course, even now Jim and I will sacrifice on their account, though they'll never know it.

"I always serve myself last, you know. I serve Jim first, and he's entitled to take everything we have, if he wants to, because he's the father, and it's his work that has brought us what we have, all of it. But Jim will stop himself, and say he's not so hungry, and nod toward the kids, and that means to give them the seconds before him. We don't always have seconds, of course, but we do the best we can. I make corn bread every day, and that's filling. There's nothing I hate more than a child crying at you and crying at you for food, and you standing there and knowing you can't give them much of anything, for all their tears. It's unnatural.

That's what I say; it's just unnatural for a mother to be standing in her own house, and her children near her, and they're hungry and there isn't the food to feed them. It's just not right. It happens, though — and I'll tell you, now that you asked, my girl Sara, she's a few times told me that if we all somehow could eat more, then she wouldn't be having trouble like me with her teeth, later on. That's what the teacher told them, over there in the school.

"Well, I told Sara the only thing I could tell her. I told her that we do the best we can, and that's all anyone put here on this earth can ever do. I told her that her father has worked his entire life, since he was a boy, and so have I, and we're hoping for our kids that they may have it a lot better than us. But this isn't the place to be, not in Swain County here, up in this hollow, if you want to sit back and say I'd like this and I'd like that, and you'd better have this and something else, because the teacher says you should. I told Sara there's that one teacher, and maybe a couple more, and they get their salaries every week, and do you know who the teacher's uncle is — he's the sheriff over there in Needmore. Now, if Sara's daddy made half that teacher's salary in cash every week, he'd be a rich man, and I'd be able to do plenty about more food. But Sara's daddy doesn't get a salary from no one, no one, you hear! That's what I said to her, word for word it was. And she sat up and took notice of me, I'll tell you. I made sure she did. I looked her right in the eyes, and I never stopped looking until I was through with what I had to say. Then she said, 'Yes, ma'am,' and I said that I didn't want any grudges between us, and let's go right back to being friends, like before, but I wanted her to know what the truth was, to the best of my knowledge, and nothing more. She said she knew, and that was all that was said between us."

In point of fact Mrs. Allen is usually rather silent with her children. She almost uncannily signals them with a look on her face, a motion of her hand, a gesture or turn of her body. She doesn't seem to have to talk, the way so many mothers elsewhere do, particularly in our suburbs. It is not that she is grim or glum or morose or withdrawn or stern or ungiving or austere; it is that she doesn't need words to give and acknowledge the receipt of messages. The messages are constantly being sent, but the children, rather like their mother, do things in a restrained, hushed manner — with smiles or frowns, or if necessary, laughs and groans doing the service of words. Yet, there are times when that cabin on the side of a mountain will become a place where songs are sung and eloquent words are spoken.[3] Once, after a series of winter storms had worn them all down, Mr. Allen spoke to his wife and children, at first tentatively and apologetically and then firmly: "It's been a tough winter, this one, but they all are until they're over, and then you kind of miss them. You don't get a thing free in this world, that's what was handed down to me by my father. He said if I knew that, I knew all I'd ever have to know. I heard some of you kids the other day wondering if we couldn't go and live someplace else, where maybe there wouldn't be so much snow and ice, and us shivering even under every blanket your mother made and her mother and my mother, and that's a lot of blankets we're lucky to have. I'm sure there's better land than this, better counties to live in. You could probably find a house way off far from here, where they never get any snow, not once in the winter, and where there's more money around for everyone. Don't ask me where, or how you'll get there. I don't know.

"I was out of here, this county, only once, and it was the longest three years of my life. They took me over to Asheville, and then to Atlanta, Georgia, and then to Fort Benning, and then to Korea. Now, that was the worst time I ever had, and when I came back, I'll tell you what I did. I swore on my Bible to my mother and my father, in front of both of them, that never again would I leave this county, and maybe not even this hollow. My daddy said I shouldn't be so positive, because you never can tell what might happen — like another war — and I said they'd have to come up here and drag me off, and I'd have my gun out, and I couldn't truthfully say right now if I'd use it on them or not, but I believe the word would get down to them that they'd better think it over very carefully, if they decide to come another time and take me and others who've given them three years already. Why

do they always want us to go and fight those wars? It wasn't only
the fighting, though. It was leaving here; and once you're over
there, you never see this hollow for months and months and then
you sure do know what you're missing. Oh, do you!

"When you ask me to say it, what we have here that you can't
find anyplace else, I can't find the words. When I'd be in Georgia
and over in Korea my buddies would always be asking me why I
was more homesick than everyone in the whole Army put together. I couldn't really answer them, but I tried. I told them we
have the best people in the world here, and they'd claim everyone says that about his hometown folks. Then I'd tell them we
take care of each other, and we've been here from as far back
almost as the country, and we know every inch of the hollow, and
it's the greatest place in the world, with the hills and the streams
and the fish you can get. And anyone who cared to come and
visit us would see what I mean, because we'd be friendly and
they'd eat until they're full, even if we had to go hungry, and
they'd never stop looking around, and especially up to the hills
over there, and soon they'd take to wishing they could have been
borned here, too."

Mr. Allen never stops saying such things. That is, every week
or so, sometimes every day or so, he rises to the occasion — when
his visitor is still recognized as just that, a visitor. A year or more
later Mr. Allen still will talk affectionately of the hollow he loves,
the county he loves, the region whose hills must be, so he once
told me, "the most beautiful things God ever made"; still, he has
his rough times, and if he bears them most of the time in silence
and even pretended joy, he can slip and come out with urgent
and plaintive exclamations, once he knows a visitor reasonably
well: "Why can't we have a little more money come into these
hills? I don't mean a lot of tourists coming around and prying,
like you hear some people say we need. I mean some work we
could get, to tide us over the winter. That's the worst time. You
start running out of the food you've stored, and there's nothing
you can do but hope you make it until the warm weather. We all
help each other out, of course; but there'll come times when we
none of us has much of anything left, and then it's up to the

church, and the next hollow. Once they had to fly in food, it was so bad, because of the snow and the floods we had. I can't find the littlest bit of work, and it makes you wonder sometimes. They move factories into every other part of the country, but not here. I guess it's hard, because of the hills: We'd be good workers, though. I was taught to work from sunrise to sunset by my folks. You might think this little farm we've got is all that we need, but it isn't. We'd have nothing to eat without the land we plant, but it's money we lack, that's for sure, and you can't grow that. You can pick up a little money here and there — for instance they'll come and recruit you to do work for the county on the roads or cleaning things up. But it's not very much money you ever make, and if we didn't really love it here, we might have left a long time ago. I've been all set to — but then I can't do it. When my kids will ask me if I ever thought of leaving, I'll say no, and why should they ask, I say to them. I guess they know I don't want much to talk about some things, so they never push me too much. I wouldn't let them. They'll find out soon enough — about the misery in this world. The way I see it, life's never easy, and you just have to choose whether you'll stay here and live where it's best to live — or go someplace else, where you're feeling sad and homesick all the time, but they've got a lot of jobs, and you can make good money. I hope my kids think it over real hard before they decide — when they get older."

His children love the hollow, and maybe they too will never really be able to leave. They are unmistakably poor children, and they need all sorts of things, from medical and dental care to better and more food; but they love the land near their cabin, and they know that land almost inch by inch.[4] Indeed, from the first days of life many of the Appalachian children I have observed are almost symbolically or ritualistically given over to the land. One morning I watched Mrs. Allen come out from the cabin in order, presumably, to enjoy the sun and the warm, clear air of a May day. Her boy had just been breast-fed and was in her arms. Suddenly the mother put the child down on the ground, and gently fondled him and moved him a bit with her feet, which are not usually covered with shoes or socks. The child did not cry. The mother seemed to have almost exquisite control over her toes. It all seemed very nice, but I had no idea what Mrs. Allen really had in mind until she leaned over and spoke very gravely to her child: "This is your land, and it's about time you started getting to know it."

What am I to make of that? Not too much, I hope. I was, though, seeing how a particular mother played with her child, how from the very start she began to make the outside world part of her little boy's experience. What she did and said one time she has done and said again and again in that way and in other ways. All of her children, as one might expect, come to regard the land near their cabin as something theirs, something also kind and generous and important. In my conversations with Mrs. Allen I gradually realized just how important the land was to her and her children. I could argue that the land around the cabin helped her mind achieve a certain order or pattern to what I suppose could be called motherhood. From the first months of her child's life right on through the years, she as a mother never lets it be forgotten what makes for survival, what has to be respected and cared for and worked over if life is to continue. And so more than once she fondles her little boy on the hill's earth and tells him how familiar he should get to feel about the little farm, and on other occasions, how fine it is to be where they are and have what they have.

Are such gestures or words nonsense, in view of the hard life the Allens live? Is a mother like her whistling in the dark, and trying to teach her children to do the same? "The first thing I can remember in my whole life was my mother telling me I should be proud of myself. I recollect her telling me we had all the land, clear up to a line that she kept on pointing out. I mean, I don't know what she said to me, not the words, but I can see her pointing up the hill and down toward the road, and there was once when she stepped hard on the earth, near the corn they were growing, I think it was, and told me and my sister that we didn't have everything we might want and we might need, but what we did have, it was nothing to look down on; no, it was the best place in the whole world to be born — and there wasn't anyplace prettier and nicer anywhere.

"To me, your children have to respect you, and look up to you. My daddy never let me talk back and get fresh. My mother was easier with us, but you could go so far and not a step further. She would tell us that we come from Scotland, way back, and we should be proud that our name was McIntosh, and she was one of the McIntoshs too, and we might be having poor times, but we were a large family, and we had neighbors and uncles and aunts and cousins, and we'd stand up for each other. Most of all she'd tell us about the hollow, and who came there first, and who lives in this house and the next one. That was the first learning I got — how to leave the house and walk down the hollow a bit and come back. We were high up, and a little further along there was no more hollow, just woods and the hills. I guess they go on for miles. Once I must have gone in the wrong direction, because I was going higher up and suddenly I could see more than I ever saw before in my life. Now I know what I'd done. I'd gone clear to the top of that hill, and there I was, in that little bit of meadowland there, looking over toward the other hills. The first thing that came to me was that God must be someplace near, and I looked and looked and right then, you know — I'd say I was four — I was sure all I had to do was call on Him, like we're told to do in church, and there He'd be. Instead, a big bird came down, right near me. Oh, it was probably a crow, but to this day I can hear the 'caw-caw-caw,' and he come right at me. He'd probably never seen a child like me wandering up there by herself.

"I guess I thought the bird was preparing the way for God himself, because I got down on my knees and I said, 'Please God, be good to me,' just like I have my kids say now, every evening they do. Well, when nothing happened after a few minutes, I must have figured that something was wrong. I started crying for my mother and my daddy, and when they didn't come I started crying even more. But near the side of the meadow — I'll never forget — I saw a large rock, and I went and sat down beside it, and then I climbed on to it. I must have climbed down and fallen asleep, because the next thing I remembered, my daddy was standing over me, and I was waking up. I thought he was going to be real cross at me, but he wasn't. He said I was a good little girl for not going real wild-like and wandering all over and getting so far away they never could have found me. He carried me home on his shoulders, and I can see me now, riding high on him — he was about six foot four, I think. And I can see my mother coming out to ask me if I was fine or if I was hurting anyplace. After I told her I didn't hurt in a single place, and I just wanted to have a Coke, because I was thirsty, she said I'd been real good and learned my lessons. 'Trust the woods and the paths there. If you ever get lost again, sit someplace, just like you did, in an open spot, and we'll get to you.' She must have said something like that, because that's what I seem to hear her telling me even now.

"I think I try to go along with my folks, the way they used to look at things when we were kids. My daddy, he's seventy and as strong as can be, even if he gets his dizzy spells. My mother died a long time ago, giving birth to my youngest brother — yes, right here in this very room it was. She started bleeding real bad, and it just never stopped. My folks taught us all to be respectful to them and to anyone else we met who was grown up, and I hope my kids will always be like that. I never try to fool myself or the kids, though. I tell them there's a lot of bad people in the world, some of them right here in this county. I don't believe anyone living up this hollow is bad, no sir; but I know for sure some of the people we see in church, they're crooked as the day is long — and that's what my father would say, and he'd point them out to us. I tell the kids they've got to know that the world's not so good, and there's a lot of trouble going on, and you can't be sure of someone until you know him pretty good. But you *can* be polite, and you should be, that's how I feel. You ought to behave yourself with someone, even if you don't much like him. The other thing is, never forget who's your kin, and who you always can trust. When one of my kids starts getting all teary, and there's something bothering him, you know — then is the time for me to help as best I can; and there's nothing that'll work better than getting a child to see if the chickens have laid any new eggs, or to count how many tomatoes there are hanging on the plants, ready for us to pick. I'll take the child up the path and we'll pick a few berries, or do something; it don't make a difference what, so long as I can say how lucky we are to be here, with the land we have. And God forbid a son of mine will be taken overseas to fight like my husband was. But he saw the world, all over he did; and he couldn't get back here too soon, that's for sure."

She loves her children and she loves her property. When she holds an infant in her arms she often will sing. She sings songs about hunting and fighting and struggling, songs that almost invariably express the proud, defiant spirit of people who may lack many things, but know very clearly what they *don't* lack: "I tell the kids there's more to life than having a lot of money and a big brick house, like some of them have down towards town. Here we've got our chickens and we've got good land; oh, it's not the best there ever was, and we could use twice its size, but we get all you can from it, the vegetables, and with the preserves I put up, I make sure we have something right through most of the year. The other day I was trying to get my oldest boy to help me, and he was getting more stubborn by the minute. I wanted him to clean up some of the mess the chickens make, and all he could tell me was that they'll make the same mess again. I told him to stop making up excuses and help me right this minute, and he did. While we were working, I told him that the only thing we had was the house and the land, and if we didn't learn to take care of what we have, we'd soon have nothing, and how would he like that. He went along with me, of course. But you have to keep after the child, until he knows what's important for him to do."

Mrs. Allen's attitude toward the land is by no means rare among the families I have worked with in the Appalachian Mountains. In fact, an observer can make some generalizations about how children are brought up in, say, western North Carolina or eastern Kentucky and West Virginia if he looks at the land as a sort of unifying theme. From the first months of childhood to later years, the land and the woods and the hills figure prominently in the lives of mountain children, not to mention their parents. As a result, the tasks and struggles that confront all children take on a particular and characteristic quality among Appalachian children, a quality that has to do with learning about one's roots, one's place, one's territory, as a central fact, perhaps *the* central fact of existence.[5]

In Wolfe County, Kentucky, I became rather friendly with a whole hollow of Workmans and Taylors, all related to one another. There were one or two other families, whose names sounded different; yet, I came to find out that the wife, in each case, was also a Workman or a Taylor. The Workmans had followed a stream up a hill well over a century ago and are still there, in cabins all along Deep Hollow, so named because it is one of the steepest hollows around. They were the family I lived with the longest there and observed more intensely and casually — in a mixture I can't quantify — than any other. All the time I was there Mr. and Mrs. Kenneth Workman wanted me to be doing something, to be a worker — true to their name — as are all Workmans in that hollow. They asked *me* how things were going, how I felt about the mountains, and how my spirits were now that I was so high up and so near to God. They wanted to know whether one day I might move nearby and give my wife and children "a taste of good living." Yet, I had come to Deep Hollow warned about suspicious, withdrawn people who wanted no part of strangers.

Kenneth Workman is forty as I write this. He is now a small farmer. He used to dig for coal in the mines down in Harlan County, Kentucky, but he was lucky enough to lose his job in 1954. Many of the older men he worked with also lost their jobs around that time, when the mines were becoming increasingly automated, but they came back to Wolfe County sick, injured, often near death. Their lungs were eaten up with "black lung," with pneumoconiosis as doctors call it when coal dust gets into the sensitive fragile organ and progressively kills one section after another.[6] The men were sick on other counts too: their backs had been injured in mine accidents, or their necks, or the muscles and bones of their legs and arms. Some of them had not only "black lung" but tuberculosis too; and years of fear and anxiety while working underground had taken a heavy toll on their minds. Kenneth Workman talks with little prodding about the mines and his fellow miners and Harlan County and Wolfe County — and also about his children, especially if he has a shot or two of the moonshine that he and his brothers and uncles and cousins make out of the corn they all grow: "I never made so much money in my life and I never will again, I'm sure of that. I'd stay there all week in Harlan County, and then I'd drive home to be with Laura and the babies. I was twenty when I got the job; it was in 1950 I believe. They suddenly needed all the men they could get, because the government was building up the Army again, to go fight in Korea, and there was a big demand on the coal mines. The draft people called me, and they said I'd be doing Wolfe County and the United States a bigger favor if I stayed a miner and not go into the Army, and I said that was all right by me — yes sir, it was. My daddy said he was real sorry to see me go down into the mines, but up this hollow we don't see much money. We keep going, and we're not going to be pushed out of here by anyone; but when you get a chance to bring in some money, a lot of it, and regular, each week, you don't mind leaving — and I came back every Friday night. I got a car and paid for it, and I got us things, like the radio and the furniture and the television and the refrigerator. If it hadn't been for those four years, we'd be living a lot poorer, Laura and me and the children.

"I went down the mines for them, for the children, I think I could say that. We had two when I went, and five when I came home. Then came the trouble Laura had, the bleeding, and we lost a baby and then we lost another one and more bleeding and I thought we'd never have a child again. But a few years ago something must have happened inside her, you never know what, and here we are with babies again, and it's like having two families, the older family first, and then we had a little rest, and now the younger one. Maybe if I'd kept on working in the mines, I could have taken Laura to a doctor someplace, and he would have figured out what there was wrong and what we should do. Around here there's no doctor, and who can get up the money they ask, even if we could find one. I saw the first doctor of my life down there in Harlan County. The coal companies have them around, and the union has some of its own, you know. They gave me a going-over before I started working, and they said I needed a dentist, and I had some trouble with my bones here and there, I guess; but I was all right for work, they said.

"As I see it, if I'd stayed in the mines we could have gotten Laura to a doctor, maybe in Harlan County. But I might have had to go to one first. The men I worked with, a lot of them had been down those mines longer than me, and it was a terrible sight to see them — working so hard, and they knew — oh did they! — that they were getting killed by the work they were doing, but they had to do it, because there wasn't any other choice. I'd come back and tell my daddy about what the mines do to you, and he'd say I should stop it and stay here in Deep Hollow. He'd say you can't win everything, that's the most important thing to know, and never forget. If I was to stay a miner, he'd tell me, we'd all be living better, and Laura might see a doctor; but I'd be dead just like those miners are dying. If I was to stop and come back, then we'd be in a lot worse shape about owning what we want to own; but I'd be around to enjoy what we do have.

"Now you ask me what we have. I'd answer you this way: the nicest land in the world, and the nicest people in the world to live on it. That's a lot to have, I tell my kids, when they start crying and bellyaching about something, and they'll ask me why it is the people on the television programs live so rich, and we're not living very good up here — well, it's then I'll tell them they're not seeing the half of it. They're not seeing all the bad things about those cities, and all the meanness you'll find out there. Some of the older miners, they'd been in the war against the Germans and the Japs, and they can tell you and so can my daddy and my older brothers. They've been to those cities. I'll tell my kids that if they don't believe me or anyone in Deep Hollow, then by God I'll take that car sitting out there and somehow I'll make

it work again, and we'll get ourselves over to Harlan County.
There still are some miners there, and I'll let my kids talk with
them and let my kids see how they live, the people who do make
a lot of money! Sure, they have nicer houses than we do, but the
coughing they do, and the spitting up of the black stuff — knowing every second that the coal dust is in you, eating up your
lungs — it's all enough to make you want to turn right around
and come back here, yes sir; and stay here until your last breath
and be glad to be buried right over there."

He would point dramatically when he said something like that,
point with his arm not his finger, with his whole body in fact; he
would even get up and start walking toward the area where
generations of Workmans have been buried by their kin, in
simple caskets made out of wood from Deep Hollow. He never
would go more than a couple of steps, however. In a few seconds
he would be right back in his chair, talking with me and having
himself "one or two more" and insisting that his guest do the
same: "I guess you'd like to know if we raise up our kids some way
that's different from the way other people do. Isn't that it? If you
ask me, I'd say that Laura is real good to the kids and I try to be,
too. We want them to remember their first years later on as a real
good time — when they had a lot of fun, and when they learned
all about the hollow and how to take care of themselves and go
and do things out there up the hill and in the woods and down
by the stream. We want them to be able to say when they're
grown up that they're proud they were born to us, and they're
proud they're living right here in Deep Hollow, Kentucky, yes sir.
And if we're going to be good parents, we've got to teach our
kids a lot about Deep Hollow, so they can find their way around
and know everything they've got to know. It's their home, the
hollow is. People who come here from outside are not likely to
figure out that we've got a lot of teaching to do for our kids
outside of school, and it's not the kind they'll get in books. My
boy Danny has got to *master the hollow;* that's what my dad
used to say to me, all the time he would tell me and tell me and
then I'd be in good shape for the rest of my life."

How does Danny get to master the hollow? For one thing, he

was born there, and his very survival argues well for his future mastery.[7] Laura received no medical care while she carried Danny; the boy was delivered by his two aunts, who also live in Deep Hollow. Danny's first encounter with the Appalachian land took place minutes after he was taken, breathing and screaming, from his mother. Laura describes what happened, and in time goes on to talk about a number of related matters: "Well, as I can recall, my sister Dorothy came over and showed him to me, and then he was making so much noise we knew he was all right. His birthday is July tenth, you see, and it was a real nice day. I'll never forget, because that morning, while I was in pain and hoping the sooner the better, my sister said there wasn't a cloud in the sky, and that meant everything would be fine, and besides she saw two foxes and they were playing nice, and she must have been walking quiet because they didn't pay her any attention, and she said it was good luck when you can just come upon them and they don't get away so fast. She brought me a pail of blackberries that she'd picked and she said they were for later. When Danny was born Dorothy took him over and showed him the blackberries and said it won't be long before he'll be eating them, but first he'll have to learn to pick them, and that will be real soon. Then he was still crying, and she asked me if I didn't think he ought to go outside and see his daddy's corn growing up there, good and tall, and the chickens we have and Spot and Tan, because they're going to be his dogs, just like everyone else's. I said to go ahead, and my sister Anne held me up a little. She lifted up my head so I could see, and the next thing I knew the baby was out there near Ken's corn, crying as loud as he could, bless him, in Dorothy's arms.

"Of course everyone came around to see the child. Dorothy told them all to go back down to her house, but even while I was being delivered they must have been out in the woods, waiting to see what would happen. When she came out with Danny, all my children showed up, and my husband and Dorothy's husband and her children and Anne's husband and her children. They stood around and they said Danny was a red-haired one, like me, and wasn't it good how loud he was with his crying. Ken held him high over his head and pointed him around like he was one of the guns being aimed. I heard him telling the baby that here was the corn, there was the beets, and there was cucumbers, and here was the lettuce, and there was the best laying chicken we've got. Next thing he told the baby to stop the crying and he did, he just did. Ken has a way with kids, even as soon as they're born. He told him to shush up, and he did, and then he just took him and put him down over there, near the corn, and the other kids and my sisters all stood and looked. Dorothy was going to pick him up and bring him back to me, but Ken said he was fast asleep and quiet, and let him just lie there and we should all go and leave things be for a while. So they did; and Ken came in and told me I'd done real well, and he was glad to have a red-haired son, at last, what with two girls that have red hair but all the boys with brown hair. He said did I mind the little fellow lying out there near his daddy's farm, getting to know Deep Hollow, and I said no, why should I, and he's better off there than in here with me, what with being tired and the blood we have to clear away and it was too early for him to touch me, because you know they don't eat too good at first, and only after a week or so do you feel like they're really drawing on you and getting something for themselves, like they should.

"I don't like to feed my baby inside, if the weather holds good on the outside. I'll just go over there under that hickory and sit and rest and the baby will sit and rest and there's a good wind that cools us off. Of course in the winter that's different. In the winter if you go more than a few steps away from our stove, you're likely to get a bad case of the shivers. I sleep near the stove, the baby right beside me. I have him all wrapped up in his daddy's shirt. Yes, I'll put paper around his bottom, to keep the shirts as clean as can be. I have the rope to the paper good and tight, and it's all right on the child, not too tight. It's better in the warm weather. You can just let the child be; you can let him lie in the sun, or so he won't get burned up, you can put him under that hickory — the largest one right over there. A little of the sun dries him out, and the shade of the tree soothes him."

She was talking about Danny, but she was also talking more

generally; for instance, she can remember similar events in the early life of "little Dorothy," who is a year and a half younger than Danny. I have watched her with both Danny and "little Dorothy" or Dottie, named for the aunt who has delivered all Mr. and Mrs. Kenneth Workman's children. I have watched her sun the little boy and soothe him, sun Dottie and soothe her. I have sat nearby as she breast-fed her child quietly, calmly, neither proudly and ostentatiously nor with any shame or worry. Shortly after each child of hers is born, the boy or girl is set down on the land, and within a few months he is peering out at that land, moving on it, turning over on it, clutching at wild mountain flowers or a slingshot, a present from an older brother, or a spoon, a present from an older sister. Next comes crawling; and mountain children do indeed crawl. They are encouraged to crawl. They take to crawling and turning over and rolling down the grass and weeds. They take to pushing their heads against bushes and picking up stones and rocks. They take to following sounds, moving toward a bird's call or a frog's. I have rarely seen mothers like Laura Workman lift up babies like Danny or Dottie and try to make them walk by holding them and pulling them along. No books are read to determine which week or which month should find the baby doing this or that. Life in Deep Hollow and in other such hollows is not lived by the clock or the calendar, by comparisons, by competition, by repeated resort to "authorities" who have something to say about everything. Danny crawled until he stopped crawling and that was that. I happened to watch him stop crawling, start standing himself up in order to walk, and I am sure that I was more moved by these events than his parents — which is emphatically not to say that they had become bored or indifferent. As for Dottie, I saw her begin to crawl, and that evidence of progress *did* get a reaction from her mother: "It's good, because now she'll get to know her daddy's land — where he does his growing and where he keeps his baskets and his tools, and the bushes over there, they'll stop her from getting into anything too steep."

When Danny one day stood up and looked around and plopped himself right down again, his mother said nothing, and when I brought the matter up again, by remarking to Danny's father later that day how sturdy his boy appeared on his two feet, there was only a smile in reply. On other occasions Mrs. Workman did talk about such matters, about the way her children learn to move about: "I guess maybe when they start walking I know they're more on their own. I always hope that by then they've found out all they want to know by peeking into all the places — you know, when they crawl all over and try to see where everything leads to. Yes, if I had to choose a time I like best for them, it might be when they're crawling. That's a good time. I like them up and walking too; but they don't get as much fun out of it themselves, I don't think, as they do when they use their arms and legs like that and just drag themselves here and yonder all day long. When they're starting to walk, they seem to have lost all they've learned while crawling, if you ask me. They'll be walking, and they'll forget about the big rock and fall, and they'll forget the land is on a slope, and they'll forget about the ditches we have near the crops. My husband won't be too patient, either. He'll wish they were either back crawling or up to running all over, that's what you'll hear him say. He doesn't like hearing them cry when they keep on falling, and he thinks they're ·happiest either crawling or when they're older and free to be on their own. When they're starting to walk they get more scared than any other time, and they'll be slower to move. But I never hurry a child. The Lord made them the way He did, and when they're going to do something they're going to, and that's what you have to know."

Certainly she does know that; and she also knows that the chances are her children will leave her very early to wander far over the hills — and in so doing stay close to what she considers "home." When her children grow up, however, she expects they will have little interest in going any farther away than they have already been — even as many other American children, kept relatively close to their parents' small front yard or backyard during early childhood, begin to leave home almost with a vengeance when older. At three Danny had been all over his father's land, and up and down the hollow. He would roam about with his older brother or sister, tagging after them, trying to join in with their work or play. He had learned how to hold onto things and ascend an incline. He had learned how to pick crops and throw a line into a stream and catch a fish. He knew his way down the creek and up the hill that leads to the meadow. He knew about spiders and butterflies and nuts and minnows and all sorts of bugs and beetles and lizards and worms and moles and mice — and those crickets making their noise. He went after caterpillars. He collected rocks of all sizes and shapes; they were in fact his toys. He knew which branches of which trees were hard or soft, unbending or wonderfully pliable. He knew how to cool himself off and wash himself off and fill himself up — all with the water of a high stream. At three he had been learning all that for about a year. He didn't stop crawling and start walking "for serious" until he was two. Once he started walking he was brought to the Workman's outhouse and told what it is for. He was told to use the woods if he had to, but if he could, to wait for the outhouse. Actually, I was present while both Danny and Dottie were being toilet-trained, as we put it, and what they really had to learn quite thoroughly was the importance of *not* "going" in the cabin.

The Workmans, needless to say, have no medical education; they are not aware of the neurophysiological or psychological facts that pediatricians rely upon when they tell mothers how to start "training" their children. Of course in recent decades pediatricians and child psychiatrists have not always been consistent and sensible; they have at one time advocated training children at a year or a year and six months, and more recently relaxed by suggesting parents might wait a year or more longer. Through it all, the shifting currents of "enlightened" middle-class opinion,[8] the Workmans held fast to their old family traditions, the myths and superstitions of their kinfolk. They emerge as rather interesting indeed. Mrs. Workman does not talk easily or at length about such matters, but eventually her remarks tell exactly what she has in mind: "I do with them what my mother told me, and I guess she did like her mother told her. That's what she said to me when she helped me with Alan, our first. She said I should just not fret over him. There's no point doing much until he's old enough to walk and keep walking, that was her advice. The reason is if they can't walk, they can't really take care of themselves that way. She said it was natural for a child who's lying around and crawling around to be messing around, too. Just cover them with paper, or keep them outside where you don't care. That's all. Now, when they start standing up and carrying themselves here and there on their legs, then they're moving on their own, you see, and you can just take them by the hand — their hands at last are free! — and say look child, here's where you do it and there and there and there, but *not here* — you hear? — *not here!*"

She had raised her voice, and she was certainly emphatic as she spoke those last words, so they deserve that exclamation mark. Yet, I also sensed a tone that was remarkably even or flat, remarkably without the veiled anxiety and even hysteria one senses in most mothers elsewhere, particularly, I suppose, those who come to see a child psychiatrist for advice. Moreover, children like Danny and little Dorothy seem to pick up the meaning of that tone rather well, because I watched both of them listen and hear and finally, heed what they were told; and at no time did they or their mother get into states of high tension or alarm. For one thing, as mentioned, the children were old enough to understand what their mother wanted; and beyond that, their mother's requests were rather modest. While they were learning to accede to those requests by day they were given the protection of an old piece of cloth on their bed: "I've used that cloth with all of them. I've washed it and washed it, and still it's good to use. With the small babies, when they're crawling around the house I've tried covering them with paper, so I don't have to keep putting clothes on them, and then they dirty them, and I have to wash them, and then the clothes wear out — and we don't have the money to buy a lot of new clothes, and especially all those clothes they have for babies, and like that. My mother would tell me that when kids are real young it's hard to dress them and maybe it's wise never to dress them at all, except to keep them warm in winter. Even then you're running a risk, you are, with whatever you use, be it a blanket to wrap them, or anything else. I guess I just try to do the best I can, and sometimes I'll do what my mother said, and sometimes what my sister Dorothy says, and sometimes I just go and act on my own hunch — and let me tell you, the children get on all right, and they grow, you know, and before long it's all something that happened back in the past, because they're walking and they're on their own a lot, and they can take care of themselves, yes they can, and there's no trouble with messing or like that. The woods up there is our biggest help, much more than the outhouse, and that's as it should be."

The woods, its earth and its bushes and its grassland were meant to grow things and receive things, she believes, and there is no reason to become worried and self-conscious and fussy. Yet, I do not mean to imply that a mother like Laura Workman doesn't have some very definite and explicit ideas about cleanliness and order and personal neatness, about the way a day should go and the way a child should look and arrange his things and the way, for that matter, a whole hollow should appear: "I try to teach my children to be good to each other and to anyone they meet. They shouldn't be fresh; and they shouldn't speak unless spoken to, not when there are grown-ups around. By themselves, that's different. The important thing for a child to know is that he's reflecting on his mother and his daddy and himself, too; I mean, if he's a mean one, and he doesn't act to help the next person, then it's all of us — the Workman family and the Taylor family, I guess — who's going to pay for it. The minister says the Lord sort of keeps his accounts on how we're behaving, yes; and if we think we can slip by His big net, then we're kidding ourselves real, real bad. I told Danny the other day that there's no reason for him to spill his food on his shirt, and he shrugged back at me. Then I told him it was going to mean that the shirt would look bad on him, and soon I'd be washing it again, and each time, you know, the poor shirt gets fainter and fainter, and pretty soon you won't be seeing the colors, and it'll be thinner, and the holes will come.

"Now Danny's daddy is no millionaire, and he's got to know he can't be causing us to go down to that store and be buying extra shirts, more than is necessary, and trading off the jars of food I've put up. In February we'll miss that food bad, real bad, and they'll be eating it, Mrs. Campbell and her brood at the store, and Danny will be hungry. I'm not going to let all that happen, because if the child learns to mind you, then he'll be doing right, and none of us will be suffering. Every day I have to tell the children that if they don't act more careful about something — there's always temptation around here, like in the Bible — then they're going to pay for it later on, because you just can't help suffering if you go and make mistakes.

"There's a God in Heaven, and He gave us this hollow, and it's the nicest place in His Kingdom, it must be. I want the children to remember that in addition to us owning this, it's God's, so they must not misbehave. Their daddy makes them help with the weeding and we make sure they carry all they pick over to the pile over there. A lot of the trash we'll bury or burn right up and there's no problem. I'll admit the creek down below looks awful bad. The kids will throw things in, and they expect the water to carry everything away. I tell them no until I've about lost my voice, but it's hard; they see the mess all over, and they see the other kids adding to it, and I'll be honest with you, their own kin, right down that hollow, they do the same. Mr. Workman went and spoke to his brother, and they agreed, but his wife, my sister-in-law, she's — well, she's no good at keeping her kids in line, she just can't do it. She'll raise her voice on them, and they'll turn and laugh. Their daddy, that's a different story. One look from him and anyone, no matter the age, would go along and do what he wants. The trouble there is he drinks up too much of his corn liquor, Ken's brother does, instead of selling it, like he ought to do. If we didn't sell what we make, there'd be all that less money and it would be harder than it already is.

"If I was to compare my kids against others in the hollow, like you say, then I'd have to call mine more of their own mind than a lot of the others. Maybe it's because we're just about the last one up here, before the hill reaches the top, so we do things more by ourselves than some below, lower down there in the hollow. Maybe it's me. I think most of the kids in the hollow are God-fearing boys and girls, and if there's differences, they don't amount to much, because we're more alike on most things, I'd say. You go and ask any mother in this hollow, or any of the others in Wolfe County, how their kids are turning out, and they'll say, 'Pretty good.' That's what I'd say about mine. I like for them to obey, and when they're called to do something, to snap right to it, and go ahead. A lot of the time I'm too busy, or I'm not feeling good, and they go ahead and slip up, and they make their mistakes, I know; but I guess we all do. I try to teach Danny to wash his face when he goes swimming in the creek. He'll forget, though. It's only natural. I try to tell little Dorothy that she should act like a lady, and not be always fighting, but I did the same when I was her age — I can even remember doing like her, fighting and raising Hell all day long, to be honest about it. I'd never admit that to her! Most of all I want for my children to be good, and work hard, and like I said before, they should be God-fearing.

"I've sent a lot of children down to our school, and they may not always have the best clothes on, and they may behave real foolish-like some of the time, but I think the teacher would tell you that every one of them is proud of his mother and his father, and proud to be born here in Deep Hollow, and proud of what they've tried to do, small though they are, to be of help to us all — even if they've each given us trouble, as a child always will. Don't you believe they all do, when they're growing up? A child who doesn't give you trouble, there's really something wrong with that child. I think, to be real open now with you, I really think I could have been stricter sometimes with them. I'll talk as strict as I can, but I'm not doing like I preach, and our minister says that's the worst a person can do. Their father, he's as bad. He'll go and tell them to do things for him, then he'll forget, and sometimes he'll ask them why they're doing a chore, when it was *he* that told them to go do it. Another thing: he's been too quick to give the boys that whiskey they make. Our son Alan and his wife — she comes from right near the store, a mile or so, and there's a little money in her family — they both are too independent and full of themselves, and it's telling on their babies, if you ask me. She keeps a poor house, she does. She's spoiled; and he makes it worse with the liquor he takes, and he feeds it to her.

"There will be a time I take some liquor, to ease the pains I get. I get them all over — my chest and my shoulder and my knees and my fingers. I'm getting old, it must be that. But I've got my children to raise up, the last of them, and I don't want them to turn out bad. I'd like them to be sober and know how to take their liquor, so they don't go falling all over and forget the things they're supposed to do. I'd like them to learn the most they can in school, even if there's not much point in spending too much time there, you know, because if you keep your eyes open and your ears, too — well, then, you'll learn most of what you have to know right here, doing the work that you should. My son Tim — you've only met him a couple of times — is probably the best of the children; I mean he turned out best. He has a good job working in a garage over in Campton. It's hard not having him here with us, but he has a car, and it's a good one, and he drives over with his family a few times a week. They have a good place to live, right outside of Campton. He learned how to work on those cars from when he was a boy; I never could figure out how he learned it all so fast. No, he never went beyond the school there near the hollow, but the teacher had him fix her car, and she recommended him to the garage in Campton, and I let him go. He said they'd give him a place to stay a few days of the week, and he could come over and work for them. Then he met a girl over there and the next thing we know that was our second son married, and now we've got grandchildren and they're nice to have, just like your own are.

"Tim disappointed a lot of his kin here in the Hollow. They kept on asking him why did he want to leave us, and aren't we good enough for him. I told them to stop, but I'll admit it, I miss him, too. We can't drive over there to Campton, but he's here in half an hour — maybe less, I think. He's a loyal son, don't get me wrong, but he always was the one who wanted things his way, and not ours, and I had a real fight with him more than one time, oh did I! I told him to stop being so all-certain of himself and listen to me and his daddy. He said I was always telling them, the children, to be sure of themselves, and don't let a soul turn your mind around from what you've made it up to be — so that's what he was trying to do; but you can carry a thing too far, that's what. But he's all right, and we're proud of him. He'll often bring us some money we sorely need, too; and we sure have to be grateful for that. We don't get all that much money, and when your son comes over and gives you five dollars and says there it is, all for you, and not to pay any back — that's a day to go and celebrate, you bet.

"I think we find our times to celebrate anyways, yes. You can't just sit and stare and worry, even if you know you have plenty of reasons to. I'll wake up some of the time, and I'll be scratching myself, asking myself what am I going to give those children when they come and expect a good breakfast, and we don't have the eggs, because there's a limit to what even good chickens can lay, and we're down to the last of the bread and I just don't have one single penny in my house, not one, and I need the biscuits for later, because there's two more meals coming up that day, not to mention the next one. I can't go and catch a little liquor, like Ken does. I have to do the best I can. Most of the time I'll persuade everyone to have some coffee we have and wait until the sun is in the middle of the sky and they're all *really* hungry. You see what I'm doing, don't you? I'm fooling them and I'm coaxing them to be nice and help me and not ask for breakfast; and they know it, but they'll never say they do. The only one that did — I guess it's true — was Tim; he would get himself worked up and tell his father we ought to go and see the county people and demand our rights. Well, *what* rights, their father would say.

"Then they'd start their fighting — Tim would be ten or more, I guess. Tim would tell his father we could do something, and his father would tell Tim to stop looking for trouble, and besides we have the best place in the world up here in Deep Hollow. Ken sometimes would say to Tim that he has a real bad disposition, and he always looks at the black side of the world, like the minister will describe, and that's bad, because you lose your faith that way — in God — and you get sour with people, and Tim could be that a lot, sour. I was fearful for his wife, how she would find him, but she says he's always in real good spirits, and maybe it's because he's got that job he likes so much, over there in Campton. He told his brother Alan to come on over and maybe he could learn to do the work, too; but Alan said no sir, you can have your job, because who wants to go and live in Campton, even if it is in Wolfe County, like you say. So, they never agree with each other. I guess everyone has his different moods, and people see things different, real different, and that's always the case, I believe that — though I think all of us here in this family, and the others in the hollow see eye to eye on most things, if you get right down to it. I'll bet there's not one person here who wouldn't walk up the hill there and look as far as he could and come back and say we're the luckiest people that ever was, to be here; and yes, I'm including Tim, him too."

Everyone in the Workman family, including Tim, does indeed love Deep Hollow; but they all have their doubts and misgivings about the hollow, too — and they naturally would, because they have a tough life, a fact they both recognize and strongly deny. I am not writing about the Workmans in order to show how hurt and impoverished they are, nor to prove them the strongest, proudest, most self-reliant and self-possessed of people. The truth of their lives, as the flow of Mrs. Workman's remarks suggested, can only be found in a mixture. Families like the Workmans are proud, yet feel weak and vulnerable. Such families can be faultlessly neat, yet succumb to disorder and even chaos as they try hard to deal with very concrete and painful circumstances, like hunger that goes unappeased by food, and freezing temperatures that enter and take over a house with only one fireplace and no heating system.

People like Kenneth and Laura Workman struggle with other contradictions, too. They struggle to affirm themselves and not fall victim to despair. Put a little differently, they feel at times energetically ambitious and anxious to accomplish this or that; at other times they feel defeated, so that there seems no point to much of anything. Within the same day, even the same hour, I have heard one or another member of the Workman family insist upon the urgent need to do something, and do it right away; but then declare in a tired voice that whatever is done really means

very little, not only in the long but even the short run of things.
Then, there is always the hollow, and the dozens and dozens of
kin who live in it. One moment I will hear a mother like Mrs.
Workman compare what she thinks and does with what others
think and do, those relatives (primarily) and neighbors who may
live even miles away, yet breathe heavily on each other and make
for a collective social conformity, easily noticed by an outsider
and stoutly defended by mountaineers themselves. At other
times, she and other Appalachian mothers and fathers sound very
much like political anarchists or rebels of a more individualistic
or idiosyncratic kind.[9]

Even more striking with these individuals is the fluctuation in
mood or outlook between seriousness and cheerfulness. I refer not
to something called "manic-depressive" swings, nor indeed to anything psychopathological. Nor do I simply mean that the Workmans and others in places like Deep Hollow, Wolfe County,
Kentucky have their ups and downs; of course they all do, and of
course we all do. I want to point out that in Appalachia a certain
kind of living generates a particular kind of grim but also light-
hearted frame of mind that comes to expression again and again
in the speech and habits of the people.[10] By the same token,
Appalachian mothers demonstrate, as a result of a certain sensibility one meets in those hollows, an equally ironic and at times
unnerving mixture of firmness, even sternness with children,
which is tempered with a generosity that borders, occasionally
more than borders, on indulgence — all logically incompatible,
all of it seemingly inconsistent, but all of it still there, to be
figured out, I suppose, by those whose fate it is to do so.

Again, I have not set up six polarities, six sets of opposing traits
to deny each mountaineer his or her particular fate, which is to
reconcile the conflicts in his or her life — and do so in his own
way, in her own way. These contradictions or ambiguities are
concretely and specifically rooted in Appalachian life and in the
traditions that mountain people call their own. They assert themselves consistently, persistently and confusingly — to a visitor,
and maybe even to people like the Workmans themselves. Per-

haps the word is themes, ones tied to a special history, a very definite kind of experience within and outside of the family. I believe Mrs. Workman's remarks reveal those themes; and I believe those themes go to distinguish the Workmans and other mountaineers described in this book, from the sharecropper families and migrant farm families that also live close to the land, yet under rather different circumstances.

In the case of the Workmans, none of all this was ever explicitly stated or discussed by them, and when I spent time with them I was in fact not myself of a mind to analyze what they said, to break it down into ideas voiced or assumptions held or whatever. I do believe, however, that I can now listen on my tapes to Kenneth Workman or Laura Workman, or I can read the notes and questions to myself written down years ago and see the point of having those themes around in my mind: they help make a little sense of matters that do indeed seem puzzling. Thus, when Mrs. Workman at the end of the long passage above talks about her son Tim's psychological characteristics she is talking about more than one apparently different or unusual child, who has left Deep Hollow, but also comes back. Tim, as presented by her, is only a slightly exaggerated version of everyone else in Deep Hollow. His preferences are theirs; his values theirs; his purposes or goals certainly very much theirs. Often it takes a generalization or a slight overstatement to make the ordinary or the usual a little clearer. Freud knew that patients mirror the rest of us, a bit sharply and even bizarrely, but still recognizably. What they visibly suffer with and from, the rest of us (to varying degrees and in varying ways) manage to hide from others and of course ourselves, too; all of which is necessary — and hardly surprising. An analysis of Tim's struggle to be loyal to his family, yet to remain his own man, should be offered as an effort to understand Tim and others like him as somewhat different from other Americans of their age, but also somewhat the same. No doubt as the "variables" or polarities or ambiguities pile up, we begin to recognize a distinct kind of person, a member of one or another "culture" or "subculture." But there is a danger that we may become so intoxicated with our theoretical exuberance that we allow our formulations to become islands, upon which we settle and isolate a given "group" of people.

At the edge of Logan County, West Virginia, I stayed with and worked with a family whose head, Paul Evans, was by no means "sick" in any psychiatric sense.[11] He did have a noticeably vulnerable quality to him, though; and he had, in his own words, "more of a restless nature than anyone else around." Like Mr. Workman, he had worked in the mines for a while, then left because he was short of breath, coughing, plagued with chest pains, and afraid he might die were he to continue digging coal. He returned to the little town where he and his family have lived for many generations, and for a while he found odd jobs to keep him busy and provide his wife and two sons and three daughters with money. He worked in a gas station. He worked on the roads, digging and helping pave or even rake leaves. He drove a truck. He swept floors, in the grocery store and in several of the churches near the town. Finally he went back home — that is, back up Rocky Creek, so called, I suppose, because there is one patch of fairly large rocks there, some of them half submerged in the shallow water, along with a substantial amount of garbage that also sinks a little and floats a little. Once Paul Evans and I talked about the garbage, and perhaps that point in our conversation is a good one to begin with: "It's no good, all the paper and cans in the creek. A man came from Holden and told us we should clean up every time, and if we did and came together and made ourselves into some kind of organization, or something, then we could get a little money out of those county people over there in Logan. Have you ever been there, in the town, and talked with them? They'll say that we're lazy, that's why there's no work for us — because we don't go and find jobs. Well, I'd like them to come here and find a job. They could look for a million years, and none would come up. If you're going to find a job, you have to know where they're hiring people, and there's no businesses and factories here, no sir — just us and a lot like us up the hollows and the creeks. They'll go on to tell you how dirty you are, and why don't you go and clean up after yourself. The answer is I've been burying our leftovers all my life. My place is covered with garbage that I've put into the land. We have these homes here, there must be ten, I'd say, and we're all burying our garbage and trying to be as clean as we can, and we'll come to church and nobody can say we're not as spotless as can be. My wife is always telling the kids they should look as good and bright as a brand-new penny some of the time, even if they mess around a lot — and messing around is all right too, you know.

"There'll be times, I admit it, when we all lose our patience here in Rocky Creek, and then we'll just go heave something down that stream. It's natural a person will have his temper and then he'll decide there's no use trying to keep the creek in good shape, because there's hardly a dollar that comes in here to any of us, from week to week. We don't *think* like that, though — no, we don't; it just happens, if you ask me. We'll be sitting here on the porch and there's some stuff the wife has for you to go and bury; and you're in a sour mood; and you say to yourself, what the hell difference does it make. Now, that's wrong, I know it. I don't need a minister to tell me that Eternal Damnation business. I was told a long time ago by my daddy to obey the law, and do what's right, even if it's not written up into the law. But Daddy would admit to us that a lot of things just don't make much sense. You want to work all you can, but there's not the work for you to do, except keeping up the place. I take care of my land like it was a baby of mine. I plant the good part and grow enough to keep us out of the cemetery down there in Holden. I have a couple of pigs and the chickens and I make sure they don't go wandering all over. But sometimes I get tired and I'll sit here and rock myself and take a little of those good spirits we make, and before long I'm either all fixed up to go and shoot someone real big and important that's sitting on top of people like us, or I'm ready to go and sleep right through until the next week or the next year or sometime like that. It's then that I'll be seen throwing our stuff into the creek; and of course the kids will take after me and throw their Coke bottles down there, and it all adds up, I guess. If you ask me, one of those county people should go and do something worthwhile; they all get paid more money than you can imagine, and they're supposed to be working for all the people in Logan County. But they're really out for themselves, and if you cross them, you're in real trouble. The bus will stop coming to pick up your kids, and they'll start breathing down your back about the school lunches your kids get, and it becomes so bad, like I say, you want to go and kill them over in the courthouse.

"Most of the time I'm all right; I mean I figure we're better off here than in some big city, where you never lay your eyes on a piece of land, and you're lucky if you see a bird flying. I tell my kids that this is a good place to be born, and not to worry because somehow they'll make it through, like I did. But there will be a minute now and then that I don't believe myself, listening to myself talk, I just don't believe my own words. It's then that I figure it's real bad here, and the only way we can change anything is to go and take away the mines from the owners, and the courthouse from all those people that are running it. Then my wife will tell me to cool off, and she'll say there's no use sounding like some crank who's going to try to take over the government, and like that. She's a hard-praying woman, you know, and she'll start reading the Bible to me, and she'll get my brothers to come on over and tell me to get to my senses. Well, I've half talked them into admitting I'm right in what I say, but I usually agree with them, in that sometimes you may have the right idea, but you can't just go and do what you say you should do, if all that'll happen is you'll go to jail for the rest of your life, and you know that in advance. So, we'll go up the hill there, my three brothers and me, and we'll start shooting, and the one who hits the targets we choose the most, he's the one to pull out some beer for the rest.

"I worry about my kids, I'll be honest and tell you. I'd like for them to have a better life than I ever had, but I don't believe they ever will, and it's too bad. That's why I tell my wife that we can't be too good to them; even when we do have something they want, we've got to let them know that here in West Virginia, in this county, it's not like they see on that television set. Back a while I was making money, you know, in the mines, and I figured we could have all the gadgets we want, and keep on replacing them with new ones, too, like those store people tell you that you should. Then the money stopped, you bet it did. They admitted I should be getting some compensation, because my lungs were starting to go bad, but I wasn't eligible, because neither the company nor the state allows you any money for that. They just tell you it's too bad what you got in your lungs, but don't come to the state of West Virginia; and the companies, well you know them — if they had their way the whole state of West Virginia would be turned into a big strip mine, so they could take out every piece of coal in these hills and make their money. Then, they'd leave and say, so long buddies, nice knowing you, but we've got to go to the next state, and squeeze it dry like we did yours. That's why I tell my kids that they can't have it easy in this world, no matter how nice those hills look, and even though we do have the woods they play in and a lot of other things around here we all would die for, if they tried to come and take them away. A little ways up in that hollow where they did try and take away some people's land the strip mine people started dumping their dirt, and there was a landslide onto a couple of houses, and they were lucky no one was killed. That's where I'd draw the line. That's where I'd take out my gun and use it. I don't care what they'd charge me with later.

"Sometimes when we're arguing I tell my brothers that they're wrong to keep on bragging how lucky a man is to pick his guitar and be living here, where we have some land to our name and crops that we can grow to feed us. That's good, but it's hard to tell your boy, when he asks you why we don't live better — it's hard to tell him that we're living better than anyone in the United States of America, when we damn well aren't. That's what my brothers will tell their kids — that they should be smiling more and not talking about going over to Cleveland or someplace for jobs when they get bigger. Let me tell you, I don't want my kids going over to Cleveland if they could help it, but if they're smart enough to *talk* about going there, then that teacher must be teaching them something smart over there in school. They'll leave for school in the morning and we haven't had enough to give them for breakfast, and thank God they have the hot lunches for them — we had to fight for that, fight and fight — and for supper we're lucky to have good food. When they leave to wait for the bus they'll be nodding to me and their mother, and my little girl — she's in the first grade — she'll be smiling and all. When I feel real down and low, I'll ask my wife why our child smiles like that, the way things are, and she'll say that a mother wants her children to smile, even if there isn't so much to smile about, so the child obliges. I guess that's the correct thing for the child to do, but you're pretty lucky, if you ask me, if your kids believe you, what you say about staying here and being happy in Rocky Creek. We're all happy in Rocky Creek and we love Rocky Creek more than anything. But we're always worrying about the troubles we have, and there'll be a lot of days that I never feel my face smile, not once. That's the truth, yes it is."

The truth Paul Evans tries to spell out for a visiting observer is indeed contradictory, and he has to make sure I realize that. He himself for a long time has struggled with all those contradictions, and expects to continue the struggle until he dies: "I can see myself there on my deathbed: in one breath I'll be telling my family that we've got the best world there can ever be right here in Rocky Creek, and in the next breath I'll be asking each of my kids to promise me that they get out of here, even though it's only for a few years, to make the money they'll need if they're going to come back — and have enough for their kids to eat. I guess what I say with my *last* breath will decide what I believe; but you have to believe what you know is right, and if there's a lot of argument between you and yourself, then that's the way it goes. I once talked to our minister and told him I only half believed what he said, and he smiled and said he was doing pretty good, for me to be going that far along with him. Ever since then I've really liked the way he speaks. I believe that he is as humble as he keeps telling us to be — as if we're not anyway. Once even my older brother lost his patience with a sermon — and of all of us, he's the one who has most of it, patience. After church he went over and told the minister to stop telling us all the time how the poor are going to inherit the world. *Which* world, he asked the minister, and how humble did he want *us* to be — *us*, of all the people on God's earth! The minister didn't know what to say. Then my brother really spoiled it; he said he was sorry, and he didn't mean to go and get him upset after his sermon — and of course the minister said thank you, and he was sure my brother meant no harm.

"Now what do you think of that for getting scared at the last second? Of course, it's not the minister's fault; he's only doing what he's supposed to do. Still, he ought to use his common sense. Once he came to visit us, and he asked me what I thought he should be talking more about on Sunday, and I said about the troubles a lot of us are having in Rocky Creek and other places, just making everything hold together from today until tomorrow. Well, you know he got nervous, I could see, and he said he had to go on to the next house. The poor guy, he's no better off than the rest of us, I guess. And I'll say this to you, he's a fine man, he really is. I'll bet he's better than a lot of ministers. He puts his heart into the job, and he loves us, and we love him. He comes from Logan County, only the city of Logan it is. He's had offers to go to other places, but he wants to stay here in the county, and I don't blame him. I wouldn't go out of this county for a big pile of money; not if they came and put it right before me on this table. I believe that if I left, I'd soon be sick and die. How could I sleep, away from that hill over there? And what would there be to do that would be half the fun of hunting in these woods?"

Like all of us, Paul Evans switches back and forth with respect to a number of "attitudes" he has or "issues" he thinks about. He doesn't give names to his ideas, to his moments of anger or deep and proud enjoyment; he doesn't call what goes through his mind or impels him to speak out (and sometimes, scream out) a "thought" or a "position" or an "opinion." He does, though, recognize some of his own inconsistencies, and he talks about them. Again and again those inconsistencies have to do with Rocky Creek and the Appalachian kind of life — its hardships and its real virtues. Again and again the importance of order and cleanliness is emphasized and the presence of disorder and confusion acknowledged — and stream garbage is perhaps a concrete form of disarray that reflects a much larger uproar and agitation, a social and political rough-and-tumble which a plundered region has to live with, now that so much of its wealth has gone elsewhere. Again and again the questions are raised: should we stay or leave? Should we try to shelter our children as best we can, or speak to them about the especially hard fate that awaits them? Should we teach them the pride we feel in this creek, this county, this state, these familiar, peaceful, lovely hills, or should we come right out with it and admit how fragile is our hold on these hills, in fact on life itself? Finally, ought we tell them how sad and grim all these alternatives are, as they bear down on us, or ought we smile and insist that others before us have survived, so we will, too? Those are the questions and perhaps they are really one question. As Paul Evans sees it — perhaps more clearly than some mountaineers — all those dilemmas lead to this: will life in the Appalachian Mountains ever change so that the thousands and thousands of people who love those mountains, who were born to be part of them, can at last find it possible to keep the homes they love and stay on the land they never, never want to stop loving?

What Paul Evans feels, what Kenneth and Laura Workman feel, their children also feel; more than that, like children anywhere, they face the added struggle that goes with assuming for themselves their parents' struggles. In the case of Appalachian children, the particular tensions and ambiguities that go with a frequently hard but also satisfying mountain life come across repeatedly in the words those children speak and (with unusual, even dramatic clarity) in the drawings and paintings they choose to do. For instance, in Rocky Creek, but a half mile or so away from Paul Evans's house live some of his kin. Paul Evans's mother was a Potter, and her brother is John Potter, a man very much like his nephew, though less fiery and given to speeches. He sulks and broods and then suddenly stops all that and goes hunting and feels better and plays his guitar and feels even better and gets country music blasting loud over the radio and then will even talk about how he feels: "A good hour of music from that little radio and I'm feeling as good as those birds over there, soaring over us and saying to us: catch us if you can, but you won't." John Potter manages as best he can, manages without doctors and psychiatrists and pills of one kind or another; and manages despite a case of "black lung" that makes him suffer much more than Paul Evans does. John suffers silently for the most part. When he is low in spirits he sits and cuts wood and listens to his "hillbilly music" — which at such times doesn't seem to help him feel any better — and stares out at the hills; or he goes to his crops and looks at them and decides what they need and asks his son Billy, aged eight, to "come on over here and lend me a hand."

Billy does just that, and expertly. Billy is tall for his age, with blue eyes and black hair. He has a strong face. His forehead is broad, his nose substantial and sharp, his chin long. Billy is large-boned and already broad-shouldered. He is thin, much thinner than he was meant to be. His teeth are in fearful condition, but his cheeks are red and he looks to be the very picture of good health. His mother knows what ails him though, and she worries: "Billy is a sturdy lad a lot of the time, but he'll fall sick and it's hard to know what's ailing him. He gets pains in his mouth, from the teeth I guess, and his stomach hurts. He has his share of sores, but they don't trouble him any more than they do the rest of us. I worry because he'll be so good and helpful, and you know, I think he's the smartest of my children, I believe he is, and the teacher goes along with me on that; but suddenly he says he's dizzy and he's afraid he's going to pass out, and a couple of times he has. I was afraid he might be having a fit or something like that, you know, but it doesn't last too long — and no, he's never shook, that I could see, or bitten his tongue, no sir. The teacher says he could go on and be good in the regional high school they've built, and even beyond that, but where's the money I asked her, and she shook her head and said yes, she knew. She said it's terrible the way West Virginia's best sons aren't getting all they should be. Billy will be all right, though, even if he doesn't go on in school. He has a good head on his shoulders, and he's nice with the other kids, and he gives his father a big lift, I'll tell you that. His father will take to feeling sorry for himself and for me and for just about everyone in Rocky Creek, and then Billy will come over and practically order his daddy around: tell him to come on outside and help with the corn and the peas, or see if there should be more sawing of the wood, or go see the new litter of dogs we have — it's those things that help snap his dad into a better turn of mind."

Billy is exactly what his mother describes him to be, inventive, imaginative, intelligent, industrious. Perhaps most wonderful of all, he is a truly generous boy. He is generous to his father when he clearly isn't feeling too good about the world, and he is generous to his brothers and sisters and cousins and friends — not *too* generous, not fearfully obliging or nervously amiable, not ingratiating, just directly, openly, unselfconsciously kind, or perhaps thoughtful in the several senses of the word, because he does indeed do a lot of thinking in and around the house as well as at school. Billy has some of his ancestors' fondness for talking, for telling stories — or singing those stories, reciting them in the form of long, drawn-out ballads. Billy can also be stubbornly silent. "It all depends," says his mother, "if he has something that's on his mind, or if he doesn't." Once when Billy and I were talking about his daily life, about what he had to do around "the place," and what he did at school, he suddenly stopped himself in the middle of a sentence and asked me if I knew any doctors nearby. No, I didn't, not near Rocky Creek. How does one become a doctor, was his next question, and is there a medical school near Logan County? I told him I had visited the state's medical school in Morgantown, which is clear across the state from Rocky Creek, in Monongalia County. Is that north or south or east or west from where we were? It is north and east, I said. Pennsylvania is nearby, I added. He'd never been to Pennsylvania, he told me, nor to any other state. He'd never been out of Logan County, for that matter; and he wasn't sure he ever would want to go out — except that he had heard a lot of people talk about leaving, and he knew some that have left, though they try to come back as often as they can, he noticed. As for him, he didn't know. Maybe he would someday like to try another county, or even go over to Pennsylvania and see what it is like. His cousin Stephen Potter has tried Ohio, and doesn't like it one bit there, but he sends home those dollars and they certainly are good to receive.

Billy's father has been out of Logan County, has even lived in Beckley, West Virginia, which the teacher has told Billy is in Raleigh County. His mother, like him, has never left Logan County; and she can remember each time in her life she's left the creek and gone more than the few miles it takes to go to church or shop. Billy knows how far his ancestors traveled to get to Logan County — and not because his teacher emphasized subjects like history. The ballads and songs he has heard since he was a baby remind every listener how hard it once was to penetrate those mountains, survive those winters, stick fast and work upon those small plots of land. If Billy went to Ohio like his cousin Steve, or to Pennsylvania, he might forget those songs, and that would be a shame, or as he put it, "no good." On the other hand, he does want to look at the outside world. Right now Rocky Creek is the whole world for him, but he knows there are other worlds. His teacher keeps talking about those worlds and sometimes his father does, too. Billy once asked his teacher where *she* had been, and she listed the cities for the class: Charleston and Morgantown and Pittsburgh and Beckley and over to Washington, D.C. Billy remembers those, and remembers that there were others, though he forgets the names. Billy also remembers what the teacher said after she enumerated the cities. She told the class it wouldn't be a bad idea if they as a class went over to a city like Washington, D.C., and looked around and saw buildings and monuments and statues and all sorts of things like that. Billy feels she was pushing Washington, D.C., too hard on him and his class. West Virginia is a better place than Washington, D.C., he is sure of that.

For the very reason that Presidents have lived and continue to live in Washington, Billy would be less rather than more impressed with the city, if he ever got there and had a chance to look around. Why? Well, because Presidents must be like those people he hears the men of the creek talking about, the county officials and people like that; they're all quite rich and they're all quite crooked. There are a few good people over there in Logan, the capital of Logan County, Billy knows that, and in fact there have been a few good Presidents, "especially John Kennedy." Yet, on the whole it is the same old story: the rich take away from the poor; the mine owners plunder the land and cheat the people; the sheriffs and people like that push around ordinary people and take their orders from a few, a very few, who really run things. Billy has heard all that many times but he wanted me to know that he wasn't simply mouthing things because he had heard them declared by others. How did Billy let me know that he also had been thinking about some of those things? He did so delicately and discreetly and a little indirectly but also by shifting — rather as many of us do in such moments — to a "larger" or more "general" kind of discussion or analysis: "Ben and I — he's my best friend — decided that one day when we're big we'll go to every city our fathers or our mothers or anyone we know have been to; and then we can see what they're like, and if they're better or worse than what you hear people say. We decided we'd include all the states Mrs. Scott says she's traveled through, and especially Washington, D.C., which she keeps on telling us about in school. I'd like to go in the Army when I get big, and maybe that would be the time. Ben says he'd like to join the Navy, because we've neither of us seen the ocean, except on television, and in the pictures of Mrs. Scott's books. If we became sailors on a ship, we'd go all around the world and then when we got back here to Rocky Creek we'd be able to tell everyone what we saw and if they'd ask us whether there's any better part of the world, we'd say no, nowhere.

"If we joined the Army or the Navy we'd see a lot of people, and they'd be different from us, I know that. Mrs. Scott says we came here first, the people in West Virginia, the people in the mountains here, and then came people from the other countries — from France and like that, or Italy, she said. We don't see them here, but they're in Washington, D.C. I guess, and a lot of the colored people, you'll find them there, Mrs. Scott says. I've never seen people like that in my life, but if I did, I wouldn't act surprised. I'd just try to say hello and ask them what they wanted. Sometimes people pass through here, and they come to the beginning of the creek, just off the road there, and they'll want to sell you something, or they'll be checking up on you for the county, to see if you're hiding something they want, that's what my father will say is the reason they come. Last year the sheriff came and he said we were hiding corn liquor, that's what he kept saying, and everyone laughed and told him to go and search the place up and down and every way he wanted and see if he could find it. He didn't find a thing, because it was buried yonder near that tree, and how could he find it, even if he took himself a whole year to go and try.

"I like to see people that I've never seen before. They're people who are not like us; and you can tell they don't live near here, because they'll have on suits and hats, and they'll talk different; yes, even if they come from over in Logan they talk different. The best thing to do is keep quiet and ask them what their business is here and why do they want to come up the creek. If they're looking for trouble they'll soon find out they're wasting their time, but you should be polite and ask them their intention, and it's only if they don't give you a straight answer that you should go and get the gun and let them see they'd better be careful. I told Ben I wouldn't mind working for the county, Logan County, just for a year or two; then I could get those boots that the sheriff has, and his hat and badge and the pistols — he must have three or four — and the belt and bullets. He's got a car with a red light on it that goes around and around, and he can make more noise with that car than you can imagine. He's on the side of the strip miners. My daddy says so; and all you have to do is listen to him and you can tell. Mrs. Scott had him come in one time and tell us we should mind the law and not get fresh, because it doesn't pay, except if you want to end up in his jail over there in Logan. She asked if any of us had questions to ask him, and one of the bigger kids, Larry, raised his hand and asked if he was working for everyone in the county, equal, or if he got his salary from the people who had all the money. Then Mrs. Scott told Larry to stop with that talk, and he was just like his father, and he was always spouting off, Larry's father.

"The sheriff laughed and said he didn't mind answering; and he was working for everyone in Logan County, that's how he saw it, and the best people in the county, he believes, are the people who run the school, because you need the schools if you're going to learn what you should, and if there's grown people ready to spend their lives making sure Logan County has the right kind of schools and teachers, then they're the best people in the world. He was getting red, his face was, the more he talked, and I could see he maybe wasn't sure of what he said — whether he believed it himself, I mean. You can tell when someone is having trouble persuading you and persuading himself, and maybe that's why he's talking in the first place, to make sure he believes what he says. My daddy says it's not so hard to spot bad people, if you remember to keep your eyes open and your ears. I told Ben I didn't think the sheriff was bad, no; he just does what he's told.

"Afterwards, when he left, Mrs. Scott got real mad at Larry — and she said that people blame the wrong men, the sheriff and the school people, when they're only doing the best they know how, and the trouble lies elsewhere, that's what she kept repeating to us. Then I raised my hand and asked her where that was, 'elsewhere.' She got red like the sheriff, and said we're not in school to go blaming everyone on the whole earth, and that was up to God, and we'd better make sure we study our lessons, so there'd be no one blaming *us*. I had on my tongue to ask her if maybe it was Washington, D.C., where all the trouble came from and the crooks and thieves, but she was looking real wild at us, and more me than Ben or the others, and I thought I'd better not say anything for the rest of the day, and I didn't. Afterwards, Larry came up to me and he said I should be promoted ahead of him in the school for saying what I did; and he laughed and said I should even be ahead of that — I should be the teacher, and teach *her,* Mrs. Scott. Larry said the crooks and thieves came from Logan and from Charleston, where the capital of West Virginia is, and out beyond, too — like in Washington, D.C.

When I came home and told what happened while we were eating supper, my mother and father laughed themselves so much they said I ruined their supper, but they told me it was worth it.

"I'd like to go see for myself when I get bigger, like I said; I mean, I could go and see what people are like in the cities, over there in Logan. I could get a car, if I went into the Army or the Navy and saved up my money like Steve did. I could drive through, and like Mrs. Scott says, you learn that way, just like from reading the books she has for us. If I could choose, like you say, I think I'd do the traveling and then I'd come back here, and I'd try to work in a store, maybe; that way I'd get some more money, and you see a lot of people in the store, and there's food they have, and they'll give you a good meal, I hear say, if you work for them real faithful, like they need you to do. Then after I'd saved a lot, I'd come back here; yes, I sure would, and by then I'd never want to leave the creek again, and neither would Ben or anyone, once they've gone out and looked around. Steve says you have to look around to know what you've got that's so good, and it's right before your eyes. My daddy says that's only half true; he says we've got a lot good here, but there's a lot we don't have, and it damn well should be that we have some money around here for the men who hurt themselves in the mines. That's what he always says if you tell him there's no place better than Rocky Creek."

Billy's Rocky Creek is a scene he can draw and draw and sometimes paint, too — though he is not usually one for paints because they are messy and he also finds the brush hard to control. Not one picture he did of the creek shows a person in it — and in all he did twelve of them with me. He loves to draw trees on the hills or snow up on the hills, or maybe a cabin or two near some hills, or the sky toward which those hills' point. He loves to draw water: the rugged, almost impenetrable land making way for water; or water spilling over the land; or water just sitting there in the form of a lake. In Figure 14 he told me he was going to do the best job possible, "so that Rocky Creek will be there for you, wherever you go, and you can just look at my picture and see it." In Figure 15 he sketched a ravine near the creek and the water that pours out of it — water that often enough has him virtually mesmerized. Billy told me one afternoon that he remembered being very little and asking his dad where that water comes from and how it managed, even over thousands of years, to cut out the ravine — a fact the father had told the son several times, only to be met with a mixture of surprise and disbelief and awe that every parent knows under such circumstances. Apparently, once the question was too much for Mr. Potter, because he told his son God had done it, made the gorge, made the ravine, put the water there, and given it the force it has; whereupon Billy reminded him what he had said, that thousands of years had been required for the slow, erosive process to take place; whereupon the son recalls the father saying, "God sometimes takes it slow in what He does."

The day Billy drew the ravine I asked him, as I have on other occasions, whether he would want to put himself or his father or indeed anyone — say, his dog Speedy — near that ravine, as onlookers perhaps. No he didn't. He just didn't like to draw people or animals he told me, as he had before. He likes to draw the creek and he likes to draw other places he has seen, a nearby hollow, or again, that ravine, or the highest hill he's ever climbed. He likes to draw the moon "almost leaning on a far-off hill." He has seen the moon "leaning" like that from his position on top of a tree halfway up a hill, and it is a scene he likes to see in his mind and reproduce. He wouldn't mind trying to do so with paints, he told me — and in fact a day came when he did (Figure 16).

A little too eager at times, a little unrelaxed when I'm with a child like Billy in a setting like Rocky Creek, I finally did get a picture of the Potter family, or at least some of them, standing near their cabin (Figure 17). I had asked Billy one time too many whether he wouldn't want to show me what his house looks like (as if I didn't know!) or sketch out himself or some of his kin. He had tired of me and my requests — but also tired of saying no. Not that he was seriously annoyed with me; I hadn't been all that forceful or insistent about the matter. I believe now

I had simply been unknowing. I hadn't been able to realize what really mattered to Billy, what experiences and images meant everything to him and were used by him to express himself, if not draw himself. When I worked with middle-class suburban children, they always wanted to draw pictures of themselves or their friends or their parents or their teachers. And often I had tried to get them off that track, tried without success to get them to draw a scene of some kind, a building perhaps, or a yard or street they knew. In contrast, Billy never seemed to forget that he was a small part of a much larger scene. At all times he wanted to take on that scene, do justice to it, and like a Chinese or a Japanese painter, smile benevolently and philosophically at man's relative insignificance in the face of the natural world — hence the way he did choose, finally, to portray his house and kin.

Nor ought an observer conclude that the boy was hiding from himself or fleeing into the woods or up a hill. He was not dodging the issue of his future — by telling me, for example, he couldn't draw a picture of himself grown up. Many children I have worked with elsewhere, well-to-do or poor, respond at once tentatively but with surprising eagerness to the opportunity that a drawing about their future gives them. They can be this or that, live here or there, realize one or another dream or fantasy. But Billy knows exactly where he is and where he will most likely be (if *he* has anything to say about it) and he also knows why his future seems so assured, so concretely before him, so definite. He knows that Potters have been in the creek for generations — and that it was no small job in the first place to get there, to dig in and last and last and last over the decades, which have now become centuries. He knows that ravines take an immeasurable, and incomprehensible length of time to come about, and he sees himself and his family and his kin and his friends as also part of something well nigh everlasting, something that continues, goes on, stays, is *there,* however hard and difficult and miserably unfair "life" can get to be.

Am I perhaps speaking wrongly for the boy? I do not think so. Here is what he said to me about Rocky Creek on the last day of a long stay I'd had with him and his family: "When you come back we'll be here, and you'll know the creek, so I won't have to take you around and show you all over, like before. It'll be the same, because it's only the seasons that change the creek. If you come in the spring or the summer, you'll find it's just like it was this spring, or like it is now, in the summer. If I had to choose a time of the year I like best, then I'd choose the winter. It's hard in the winter, and you're cold and you shiver, even near the fire; but the creek looks the best, and we all have the most laughing and fun then. My daddy says he's in a better mood in winter than any other time, because there's no place to go, and we just get buried in Rocky Creek, and we have the big sled we built and we go hunting, and it's a real job you have fooling those animals and catching them, what with the snow and a lot of them hiding and some of them only out for a short time. A lot of time there's no school, because you can't get in here and you can't get out. We play checkers and cards and we take turns picking the guitar and we have the radio with all the music we want, except if there's a bad storm out there. Daddy teaches us how to cut wood and make more things than you can believe. Each winter he has a new plan on what I'm to make out of wood with my knife. He says he's my teacher when there's no school. But it's a little strange about Daddy, our mother says: he begins to feel bad when the sun melts the snow and it's easier on us to leave the creek. He'll go to church and he'll say he's glad the weather is warming up, and we can leave the creek, but then he'll come home from church or the store over there, where we get the provisions, and he'll get real sad and down, and say he wishes we were back in January, and the whole state of West Virginia was covered with snow, and most of all our creek.

"For me, this is the best place to be in the whole world. I've not been to other places, I know; but if you have the best place right around you, before your eyes, you don't have to go looking. Mrs. Scott says they come from all over the country to look at the mountains we have, and Daddy says he wouldn't let one of them, with the cameras and all, into the creek, because they just want to stare and stare, and they don't know what to look for. He says they'll look at a hill, and they won't even stop to think what's on it — the different trees and the animals and birds. The first thing he taught us was what to call the different trees and bushes and vines. He takes us walking and he'll see more than anyone else. He knows where the animals live and where they're going and why they want to go over here and there. He's taking my brother Donald around now and asking him questions; not like Mrs. Scott does. Then he comes home and tells us that Donald is learning — or else he's not learning all he should. If I left here and went to live in a city, I'd be losing everything — that's what I hear said by my father and my uncle and cousins. We've been here so long, it's as long ago as when the country was started. My people came here and they followed the creek up to here and they named it Rocky Creek; they were the ones, that's right. In the Bible we have written down the names of our kin that came before us and when they were born and when they died, and my name is there and I'm not going to leave here, because there'd be no mention of me when I get married and no mention of my children, if I left the creek. The minister says that all over the country people are moving and moving, and they don't know what to call their home, because they'll no sooner get to a place when they'll be planning to leave because of some reason. But us — well, here we are and here we'll be. And that's the big difference, the minister said; and he's right, he sure is.

"I hope when I'm as big as my daddy I'll know the creek like he does. I hope I'll know his shortcuts and I'll be able to use the rifle as good. He's the best in the creek with his rifle, everyone says so. Mrs. Scott asked me a while back what I was going to do with myself later on, because I was doing good on her tests, and I told her I was going to be as good at hunting and fishing as my daddy, and she said what else was I going to do, and I didn't know what to answer, but I said that was enough right there, it sure was. She said she agreed, but she said maybe I could go on with my schooling and all like that, and I said that sounded good, only if I was going to live in Rocky Creek there wasn't much point to doing so, and it's hard, you know, because we don't have the money for the clothes you need and the books. They'll charge for books and for other things, that's what you hear. Mrs. Scott told me to go home and talk to my parents, and she's told me that a few times, to ask my parents, just outright ask them if I can't stay in school all the way through.

"I went and asked them; I asked if I could go to the high school. And then my daddy answered that about once a month Mrs. Scott gets it into her head to send me to a high school or someplace like that and once a month we've got to let her know that there's more to learn right here in Rocky Creek than any other place in the world including a city up North or even a high school down here. All we need is a little work to do, outside the creek, that's what Daddy says, and we'd be all right for as long as we live, and there'd be the Potter family in Rocky Creek until God decides He's going to call the whole human race up to His throne and judge every last man that ever lived — and then maybe He'll tell us we did good to stay in the creek and believe in Him and do all we could to live good lives here."

On the map Martin County in Kentucky looks a short distance from Logan County, West Virginia, but ordinary maps tell little about high, near impassable hills and mountains and valleys that run north to south rather than east to west — and therefore form a barrier to someone moving across rather than up and down the Appalachians. Marie Lewis is a seven-year-old girl who lives in Martin County, not too far from Inez, the county seat. Marie's father is a good deal better off than Billy's. Mr. Lewis has a full-time job as a bus driver and school custodian. He works for Martin County's school board, and considers himself extremely fortunate to do so. Jobs are short in the county, and a steady job makes one secure beyond the comprehension of outsiders. George Lewis's salary by national standards is low, very low; in 1969 it placed him among the nation's poor, among those who make less than three thousand dollars a year. Yet, as he himself put it: "When others see no money at all, and you get your check every week, you're doing pretty good."

Mr. Lewis worked briefly in a mine but his leg was badly injured, and though he recovered fully in body, his mind never would permit him a return underground: "I could have gone back. They said they'd take me. They said they felt bad about men who get hurt, and if they could find a place for me they would. But I figured I was meant to die that time, and I still can't understand why I didn't. The roof started falling and my two friends were dead inside a couple of seconds. Suddenly my leg was gone. I thought that it was cut off. I was on the ground and I can remember thinking to myself that *I* must be dead, too; just like Davie and Ed, I must be dead. I think I was waiting for God — I mean it — to show up and tell me what the next step was. Then I must have passed out, because the next thing I can recall is Marie, my wife Marie, standing there and a doctor. They said I'd been out for a long time, and my head must have been hit, and the blood I lost must have caused it, too. But Marie said I was going to live, not to worry, and I didn't. Then, like I said, they came to me and told me they'd be taking me back to work, and I could go easy at first and then be right back to my old self, working like before. I said yes, and I sure was grateful to them.

"Then we went back on a weekend visit to my dad's place, here in Martin County, and I'd be waking up every night, hollering and shouting and shaking and coughing and everything (worse than in the day, the cough would be) and no one knew what to do, least of all me. My dad said it had all gone to my head, and so did Mr. McNeil, the minister. I wanted to go back to the mines, because if I didn't we'd starve to death, and there wasn't any choice but that. My father has his place, yes, and they grow what they can. But there are five of us brothers, and we can't all stay there. There were nine to start. We had one sister and she died of pneumonia when she was four. My brother James was killed in the Korean War. My brother Peter and my brother Ronald, they died like our sister; they took ill and all of a sudden they were gone. No sir, there's no doctor we could get them to. We didn't have the money and we didn't have a car, and we were up the hollow, and if you're up the hollow and it's in the winter — well, sir, you're just *up* there, and that's that, it sure is! Even in summer, there's not too many cars, even now, that can get up. I'm about the richest man in my whole family, you know — except for my brother Albert, who's in Cleveland. He's really rich. He makes six thousand dollars a year, or more, but he's wishing to come home someday, and he will. But that's the trouble here; if you want yourself a doctor you're in trouble. Of course, most of the time we get on all right without them, those doctors and lawyers and all the others you'll find in a place like Inez or wherever there's a city.

"When I said I wasn't going back to the mines, when I decided that — after the weekend visit home — my sleep came back to me, sound as can be. Then we didn't know what to do, and if it hadn't been for the help I got from my brother Albert in Cleveland, and my mother's preserves, I admit we might have all disappeared from the face of the earth. But then came a miracle. My wife's kin, they're pretty big, some of them. I mean, one of her cousins has an office over in Inez, and he sells insurance and he owns a lot of land, and he's in a big way with the county people, that run everything here. Marie went over and talked with him and he said he'd come over and talk with me and see what he could do. One day he did; he drove up to see us — we were with my folks — and he asked me if I'd do a good day's work and if I'd mind my business and be loyal to the county, and not cause any trouble to anyone, the county officials and all the others. I said all I wanted to do was work, and if I could work, I'd never stop being loyal to those who give me the work. So, I got the work. I drive the kids to school. I get up at five o'clock and soon I'm on the way. I don't even need the alarm we have. Then when I've driven and driven and I've got them there to the schools — there's two of them, and they're one-room schools, yes both — I go and help out, to make sure everything is right and clean and there's coal and wood for the stoves; and if there's help the teacher needs, the chores to do, then I'm there. Then I have to take the children home again."

Does he worry about the politics of the county, the uses to which certain elected and appointed officials put the school budget? He knows what the question implies, but he is extremely reluctant to discuss such issues: "It's all none of my business. You'll find dishonesty anywhere, I guess. Here you'll find less crookedness, because there's not enough money to make a man lie or cheat. There's no doubt that the school money is the biggest sum of money that's spent in the whole county, and the people who spend it naturally are going to favor the people they know to do the work on repairing the buildings and everything else. Someone has to do the work, though, and I don't see anything wrong in having a friend or your kin do it, so long as they *do* do it. Maybe the school officials and the others *are* too big over there in the county; maybe they do run everything. But if it wasn't them, it'd be some other gang, and what's the difference. They're all the same. They're politicians. My wife Marie says her cousin is the best of them, but she doesn't know what he really does. She doesn't know how he'll stop me from picking up a kid, if his daddy speaks up on something, or talks back to the county people, or if he starts complaining too much about any old thing, even if it's his right to. But the less you know, the better. That's how I look at things. Maybe if we had big factories here, like they do in other parts of the country, the county officials wouldn't be a 'law unto themselves,' that's what I heard one of the teachers say, but she knew she could trust me, and she'll pretend to be as loyal to those county people as I am; we both have to be. So, there's nothing much we can say, no sir. If anyone comes up to me and wants me to start opposing them, the county people in Inez, like you hear it's being done in other counties, then I'll ask them what job they intend for me to have, after I'm fired from this one, and how they expect my kids — little Marie over there, and her brothers — to eat and have a roof of their own over their heads."

Little Marie, as her father calls her, is almost a picture-book child. She has blond, curly hair, blue eyes, a round face with pink cheeks, and a sturdy body, though even at seven she carries herself like a lady — perhaps like the gentle, sensitive school-teacher she wants to be. She has such a teacher in school, and she idolizes her. And if little Marie someday does become a teacher she will substantially consolidate her father's rise in position or class or whatever. Her parents realize this. They see few if any jobs available for their sons, but Marie might indeed be able to become a teacher, unless she marries young, has children and forgets the whole idea. When George Lewis talks about the prospects for his various children, one hears a lot of economics and sociology packed into a few blunt, emotional but well thought-out and considered statements: "My little girl will tell me she wants to be like her teacher, know as much as she does, and give lessons, and have a car of her own. I say that of course, you can, Marie — if you want to, of course. Her mother will tell her the very same thing when she asks. To both of us, it's a relief — a great relief it is! — to be able to listen to your child dreaming of something and talking of being somebody. And it's a relief that we can have the confidence to say yes, that's right, and yes, you go right ahead and keep your sights up like that, and please God you'll go and get what you're dreaming of, someday you will.

"Around here it's the hardest thing for a man to get a job, unless he's got some land or he's lucky like I am. The sons in most families are leaving all the time, even if they hate to, and even if they try to come back later. The daughters have it a little better; they'll get married, of course, or if they don't — even if they do! — they can more likely find a job, if they have the education. A man here can go as far as college and beyond, and then he'll still be looking for work a lot of the time, and finding none. I tell Marie that if she can get to be a teacher it'll be a wonderful thing for her; but it'll help all the rest of us out, too. Yes, she'd be getting a steady wage, and she could help her brothers if they lacked money. I guess one or two of them will have to go to Ohio or someplace and that way they could help the rest of us here; I mean, they could buy a piece of land nearby, even if they lived in Ohio, and later they could build a house on it, and meanwhile some of us would be right where we are, for them to come home and visit. Marie could help them out in other ways too. A job like mine might come up, and she'd be a teacher and working for the county, and she'd know the people over there in Inez, and she could help her brothers by saying a good word for them and they might get jobs, one by one they might. Then they could come home from Ohio and we'd all be sitting pretty, and we'd be a rare family, I'll say that."

While dreams and conjectures are stored up by the Lewis family, little Marie grows and talks and wonders and comes up with one idea, then another. There is, however, a certain consistent mixture of determination and ambition that runs through the conversation one has with her over the months: "I'd like to be a teacher, and my favorite subject to teach would be history, because through that subject you learn more about your ancestors — who came here to settle in Martin County, Kentucky. Then, when a hand is raised you can be ready to answer, like our teacher does. She knows everything there is to know about Kentucky, and the Presidents we've had and the wars we've fought and how they settled the West. They first came here, the pioneers, then some went on to Kansas, I'm sure, and other states, I forget them. She gave us a list, and it's in school; I left it there. The next subject I'd like to teach would be reading and writing, because you can't do anything if you're not fast with reading and if you can't write whatever you want. If something comes to your mind, you should be able to put it down on paper, like Mrs. Wright says. I'm not too good with arithmetic. It's a hard subject. I'm learning all I should be, but I don't look forward to Mrs. Wright telling us to look at the board and start reciting the numbers. We're learning to total them up after her — she'll give you two numbers and then you figure the answer for her. I'll be eight next month, and she says by then I'll be much better at doing numbers.

"Mrs. Wright lost her husband in the war, I think it was Korea. She has a boy, I know that, and he's in another school. He lives with Mrs. Wright's mother, that's what. She has a good drive coming over here to school, Daddy says, but she likes it near us, because her husband's kin, they live a couple of miles away. My mother thinks she doesn't want to teach in the same school her son is going to, and that's another reason for her driving over to us. We can see her passing by in the morning, and I then know it's time for me to get ready. She gets there early, and I guess she waits for us and prepares her lessons, just like we do, my mother says. We're near the road and one of the last stops for the bus, and I'm glad I can sometimes see her in the car, before I even get to school. I really hope I can be a teacher like her when I'm big. My grandma asked what I would do if I couldn't be a teacher, and I said a nurse; but I'd much rather be a teacher, and I've never seen a nurse, except on television and in the books we have in school.

"I'd like to have a family — a girl and a boy; but not a lot of children, like they do up the hollow. We live right at the foot of the hollow, and we see them all going by, and there are too many of them. My daddy says one thing they could do, since they don't have the money, is stop having all those children, one after another. Susan — she sits beside me in school — must have ten brothers and sisters, I think. She says we live in a real fancy house, and how come my daddy gets to make all the money, and I told her he works hard and he's up before all of them in that hollow. Susan says she doesn't want to be *anything*. She just hopes she can marry Jimmie, who lives near her; and she plays with him up the hollow. My mother says they're probably cousins or something. My mother says we should be getting away from our own kin and looking for other people when we decide to get married. She says we have a nice road that you can see from the house, and we should use it and visit Inez and visit other places and not keep asking to go up the hollow, because the further up you go, it gets worse and worse there, and it's very hard on them, Mother says, and they are their own worst enemies, my father says, because they dump their garbage all over and they spend their time making liquor and drinking it and they'll sit around and not take care of their property.

"One man got wild drunk and came down the hollow a while ago, and he had his gun, and he stood in front of our house and said he was going to kill my father, my daddy, if he didn't stop saying bad things about them up there. My mother went out and talked with him — my father was working — and he was real nice and polite to her, as soon as she came out, that's what

Mother told us later. She said she walked up to him and asked him if she could do anything for him and he said, 'No ma'am,' and he just wanted to tell my father a thing or two — tell him right to his face; but he didn't mean to be disrespectful, he said. My mother told him she'd tell my father, and then he went down the road, the highway, to Inez. He said maybe he'd find work there if he kept walking and looking; but he turned around after a while and went home. I told my father that if the man had learned more in school, he wouldn't act like that, but my father said he wasn't so sure, because up the hollow people can't find much work to do, and if you're idle, you're going to get into trouble. A lot of people do."

Marie lives in a modest bungalow, but as she has said, the house is luxurious compared to some of the cabins up the hollow, which rises and rises behind the Lewis's house. Still, the Lewis family is poor. They are not townspeople, but by their own description they are "people just lucky enough to get out of the hollow." They are *at* but not *in* the hollow. They enjoy electricity and a furnace and running water. They have a television set and a radio and a refrigerator and an electric stove. They don't have much money for furniture, nor do they drive a car. They will be paying off the house they have built for years and years and years, and it is all the property they have and hope to have. Kin are nearby, some even up the very hollow that overlooks their home. Indeed, their kin helped them build the house — helped them, but also were paid for work done. Mr. Lewis took a loan and hired his kin, and did a lot of work himself, and emerged as a virtual nobleman of sorts to some of the hollow people, who both admire the house and wish it were theirs, who applaud one man's rise — in this case, it takes the form of a descent — but also wonder whether "lightning will strike twice," as a cousin of George Lewis "up there" in a cabin high along the hollow's path put it.

Little Marie knows all about such social and economic issues — knows them, and as her words show, can in her own way talk about them. She also can put her ideas into drawings and paintings. But for all her precocious verbal ability when compared not only with other Appalachian children, but also with many boys and girls from regions with more "advanced" school systems, Marie doesn't easily put into words things that her pictures repeatedly show. Only after those pictures were completed could I hear her talk about the statements she made with crayons and paints. For instance, in Figure 18 she has drawn a school building and in Figure 19 she has drawn a road, abutted by green hills, two lakes (which seem to be placed right in its way) and an automobile which seems to be at the end of a journey, in view of the arrow's direction. All this does not seem very surprising or unusual, in view of her life and of what we know she has said many times — to me and to others. Yet, the school she drew is not a very imposing one; indeed, the building is a small almost nondescript place utterly surrounded by — one could almost say overwhelmed by — the hills and trees that also appear. Unlike Billy, Marie will gladly draw a building, will draw a few people near it, will draw a teacher — who incidentally looks very much like her pupils, and differs from them only because she is a fraction of an inch taller and wears a hat on her head. Still, not here or any other place does Marie draw a reasonably big school, nor does she supply the school with its (actually quite real and large and pleasant) backyard or front yard or its ornamental garden or bushes. Other children, in other situations, might draw the school differently, but they do not live just outside a hollow in Martin County, Kentucky. Nor do they possess Marie's sense of the pressure and power of those Appalachian hills.

Marie no doubt draws those hills so large and brooding partly because they in fact surround her school and border upon the road she knows so well. But do Marie's pictures have more than a purely descriptive intent? Is she saying something about the relationship between those desires and ambitions she shares with many girls all over America and her particular desires as an Appalachian girl? I find it hard to answer that second question. Perhaps it is phrased much too categorically. As with so many things, the answer is *both* — which is to say that Marie is different because she lives in Appalachia but she also resembles millions of bright, farsighted and somewhat breathless girls (and boys) who want more than they as children happen to have, and who have a good chance of getting what they want — so that *their* children will consequently have different wants and needs and dreams. In any event, Marie's own words have a definite emphasis that has to be respected. In time she does talk about her drawings, and in so doing about herself and her life and her childhood and her hopes and her worries; and I suppose she talks about how it feels to be part "in" and part "out" of a region's "culture" or "subculture" or "social system." I leave the arguments over which is the proper word or words to others.[12] I believe Marie herself knows what part of her life is tied to the hollow and its kind of life and what in her life is more or less shared by millions of Americans, some of whom (be it emphasized) live in the cities of Kentucky or West Virginia as well as New York, Illinois or California.

After Marie drew the picture of the school she spoke to me about her future, as she had on other occasions and would again on still others. That drawing, however, did have a very special meaning for her; it seemed as if she now at last could *see* as well as listen and hear others talk; see as we all see in our dreams, only in this instance not lose such a vision to the morning, but retain the drawing as a lasting bit of evidence that the mind can make its various fictions and fantasies into visible facts: "After I drew the school, I was glad, because it's like I was nearer to being a teacher. I put the other school I drew a few months ago in my room — my mother glued it to the wall — and now I can see it and tell everyone that there's the place I'll be teaching in someday. It's not exactly like the school I'll be teaching in, I know; but there's a resemblance, I'll bet. My mother said if I left and went to a city, I'd be in a different kind of school — the building and everything; but I'd rather live here. My daddy said if you're from somewhere, and you live there, and you get to be a teacher or a nurse or a doctor, then you should stay with your people and try to help them, and not be moving away.

"They say by the time I'm a teacher there won't be too many real small schools left — with one room or two rooms or like that.

The teacher says we'll have big buildings, and they'll be made of brick and have a lot of rooms and we'll be coming from all over, way far off, to the school, just like they do for high school. She said she wasn't sure *all* schools like ours would disappear, though. She said a lot of us really like them and are used to them, and it's hard to move too far because of the mountains, and my daddy has trouble even now picking up everyone that's going to school and getting them there in time, and if he had to drive the bus even further away, he wouldn't get there nearly in time, he says.

"I'd miss the older children, I would, if we only studied with each other. I mean, in the new schools if you are seven, then there only are girls and boys of seven in the room with you. Here the older girls teach me, and the older boys teach the younger boys, and you can learn that way in school, just like outside school. When I become a teacher I'll try to have all the girls and boys feel like they are helping me, and then they won't be surly like the teacher says we get. She says, 'Don't be surly,' and she says if we would 'cooperate' inside school like we do outside, then we'd learn a lot faster, and it would be more fun, school would. She's right, too, because outside school you'll go and help your friend and when you're doing that you're teaching your friend; but in school you sometimes don't pay attention to anyone but the teacher. We've got to act in class like she is invisible and we remember what she's said and taught us, and it's up to us to go and do it together, and we should act as though she was outside the building and up the hill, waiting to hear we'd all done the best job we could. Sometimes she leaves the room — the school, yes — and takes a walk, I guess. She walks fast, up the creek there. She doesn't use her car. Then we all work hard to finish the lessons, and the big kids will help us, and we'll watch them, and it's good when we're there all by ourselves. And when she comes back she's pleased. My daddy said we should go up the creek with her, and she could teach us while we're right near the trees and the flowers and the animals, and then we'd see for real what's in the books and pictures she has; but the teacher says that even if we do know a lot that's in some books, we have to study books that show big cities and foreign countries, where they live different from us. I know the capitals of a lot of the countries and I can point them out on the map we've got.

"When I'm a teacher I'll try to be a good one. I'll try to help out all the kids, especially the real poor ones, the real bad poor ones from way up the hollows. I'd like my school to be near where the children live, so they wouldn't have to ride too long on the bus, and it would be easier for the bus driver. I'd like to have all the food they'd need, those poor kids, and the clothes they'd need, too. Then they wouldn't be ashamed and they wouldn't be so shy, like they are, and so fearful like they are. Daddy says they're 'real bad fearful,' and he's right. They'll come one day and then stay away two or three, that's what the teacher says. You can't keep attendance on them like with other kids. You have to be patient with them, or else they'll run off — go back up the hollow and never come down again. I'd like to have a big television set in school, because some of the kids don't see it much, because the cabins don't have the electricity, that's why; and you need it for television. If they could come to school and see some of the programs, they'd like school better and they'd come more often — they'd just make it their business to. I hear the school people over in Inez are going to get us a big television, but not a colored one, my daddy says.

"I've seen pictures of other schools, yes; and on television sometimes they'll show you them — the classrooms inside, not only the outside of the school. I don't think I would want to teach there, in them. I'd feel strange. I asked my mother, and she said you get used to everything; but if you like it fine where you are, then you should stay there. I'd like us here in Martin County to have more money, like Daddy says, and then more of the kids would come to school more of the time, and they'd stay there longer. The boys wouldn't be laughing and saying you're wasting your time by listening to the teacher and all her talk — that's what they say, she's 'all talk.' She's smart with them, though. She comes up to them with a picture and says, 'I'll bet you don't know what *that* animal is,' and they get real red, because they think they know every animal that ever was, but she's got books about Africa and places like that, and there's animals there you'll never see up a hollow. That gets them going, and they'll study hard to learn what she's showed them, and learn other things. I think the boys like history and geography, and the girls like to help the teacher and do arithmetic and learn how to write good. My mother says I'll have to learn my numbers real good, because most of the time it's the woman who's left to count the change and pay the bills, and the man is only too happy if he has the money, if he makes it. Around here a lot of the men don't make anything, not any money during the whole week."

Marie talks about such somber matters with the seriousness that is appropriate; they are matters, of course, more familiar and less momentous to her than to an outsider, so she can also be a little casual and even humorous as she talks. She can insist upon the things *done* up in the hollow, for all the sadness and misery to be found there. She can point out to her worried and pitying listener that schoolmates of hers, from homes as poor as any in America, nevertheless smile and laugh and jostle one another and get fresh and nasty and tease one another and have fights, "good fights" she calls them, sometimes serious and fierce ones, then make up and become helpful and kind and thoughtful — to everyone, which certainly includes her: "I'd like to marry someone from this county. We have the best people in the world here. The boys can do anything. They can climb every hill in West Virginia, I know they can. They can hunt and fish better than people who live in other places, I know from what my father says. If you go to the cities in Ohio and states like that, you don't know what the people are like. They talk different and they think different. A lot of them don't go to church, and they're mean to you, unless you're in their family; and they don't help you out the way we do here to everyone who comes by, so long as he means well."

An important point. Families like hers, let alone like Billy's, are often called suspicious and distant and aloof and guarded and cut off from the rest of us, and one might presume children like Marie and Billy would begin to learn such attitudes as soon as they are old enough to recognize strangers. Yet, Marie and Billy can be quite friendly to strangers, quite open with them, quite interested in them — as can their parents. Perhaps Marie should speak for herself, this time in connection with her drawing of the road: "I'd like for us to have a wider road, and it could go from Martin County to Frankfort, that's the state capital of Kentucky, and to Charleston, that's the state capital of West Virginia, and to Columbus, that's the state capital of Ohio, and to Washington, D.C., that's the capital of the United States of America. Then if we wanted to go and see the capitals and other cities, we could; and if people wanted to come here they could, and we would do our best to show them around. But if I went someplace, I'd like to get back pretty fast, and I wouldn't want to stay anyplace far away too long. I saw a book with a picture of a highway and there was nothing on either side but some dirt. I saw on television roads with tall buildings near them and factories and other big places. I wouldn't want to live there, where you wouldn't be able to stop and rest and climb up to get some good water if you'd be thirsty — the cool water that runs down real fast, that's the best kind to drink, yes it is. If I had a car and was old enough to drive it, I'd take it on the big highways, but I'd be happiest when I was driving here, and I could stop by the road and look out over the mountains. There's a million views you haven't seen yet of these mountains, our teacher says, and she knows because she's really been all over, up and down our mountains here in Kentucky and West Virginia."

Marie loves to talk about her future, the days ahead of her, the roads she will travel, the places she will see. Always, though, she wants to come back — and not only out of the natural desire any child of seven or eight will have to be close to his or her parents. Actually, Marie does get nervous after she talks an hour or so about distant places; she senses that if the whole world is to be seen and heard and tasted, the home will have to be left, and left for a long, long time. Some homes, of course, prompt the children in them to dream all day long of escapes and rescues, of deliverance and liberation. Marie's home offers no such incentives; her parents love one another and love her, and Marie does not want to get away from them, or at least doesn't want to do so in an overworked, defiant and vindictive way. Like her parents, she wants to stay where she is; yet like her parents, she isn't narrow or confined or parochial or "regional" enough to deny herself an interest in the larger world. Moreover, she knows, however young she is, that her interests and curiosities and appetites are not shared by dozens of children who live near her and sit beside her or in front of her or in back of her in that one-room schoolhouse in Martin County, Kentucky. Like a good social scientist (not to mention a person with common sense), Marie talks about the social distinctions she observes, from the grossly apparent ones to others that are decidedly subtle: "The history book the teacher reads to us says our country is made up of different kinds of people, and they come from all over the world, but then in a book about Kentucky she read to us, it said we're mostly the same here in the mountains. I don't agree we're all the same here, and neither does my daddy, because if you look around in school and in church and if you go with my daddy on the bus when he picks everyone up in the morning, you'll see we're not the same.

"There's a girl Sally who doesn't want to be a teacher or a nurse or anything. She says she doesn't want to come to school, but her mother tells her she should go just long enough to read and write a little, but not too much. There's a girl Betty who is sick, real bad sick she is, and she should go to a doctor in Inez, and Daddy says she belongs in Lexington, where they have a big hospital, but she's never seen a doctor, and the teacher tried twice to have the nurse come over, but each time Betty didn't come to school that day, and the nurse said she couldn't go up the hollow and she didn't know which house it was that Betty lived in, and the teacher didn't know, either. Betty told me one day that the doctors get you sicker, and her daddy has her eating herbs and things, and she'd been prayed over a lot, and she'll be getting better soon, she believes. My mother said it's a shame, and besides Betty being sick there's her whole family: they're all sick with one trouble or another, and they don't have money, and Daddy says they're in the worst shape it's possible to be, and the father is always drinking-mad and fighting-mad, my daddy says. Jamie is her kin, I believe, Betty's kin; and he's maybe nine or ten. He's real good with guns. He can shoot sharper than anyone else, everyone says. Jamie says he's got to know how to shoot, and they're always shooting up there, and not only at animals. They're feuding, feuding real bad all the time, and with liquor it gets worse. They go running up the road and they'll take a shot or two at the first house they come to. They don't dare come down to us and do that, because they know the sheriff would come and have them in jail so fast they wouldn't know what happened to them. Daddy says they fight and drink up the liquor they make because they have to fill up the day, and anyone would surely be unhappy if he didn't have his work and there was no money and all the sickness they have up in the hollow. They're always tossing their mess into the creek — a lot of glass and paper and everything. The dogs go swimming, and they'll get scraps of food if there are any, but food is scarce up there, so they don't throw it away.

"Once the teacher called me over, and she said I was being real nice because I shared my cookies with the kids, and my mother packed me extra ones, because I told her I felt bad eating, when others have nothing to eat. I told her they're hungry from up there, and they need better clothes than they have. I give them the cookies, but they're not going to be saying thank you all the time, and I'm glad they don't! You have to keep your chin up, and not bow and scrape, and people don't like to be asking for favors all the time. Sally said her mother told her not to take anything for free and not to go asking favors of people, and she should have her pride. Sally said her mother told her: 'To hell with people feeling sorry for us, because if they try, they'll get shot real fast around here.' Sally takes my cookies though. We'll eat my cookies and she'll tell me she's glad we live where we do, because our house is a good beginning for the hollow, and we're lucky Daddy has the job he's got. I know that's right, because if I was Sally, I wouldn't be thinking of going on to the high school, either. Sally laughs if I tell her about that. Once she was home with me and she told my mother she wanted to stay with us, and she didn't want to go home. But my mother said she should go home, and finally she did. My daddy was afraid what would happen if she went and told her mother what she told my

mother — that she wanted to stay with us — but my mother said
she wouldn't, and I guess she didn't, because we never heard any
more of it. When they took in their corn, Sally came down with
some, because they grow it and we don't. She said she wanted to
thank us for the cookies at school, and the corn was just picked
and ripe as can be and real sweet, and her mother said they
knew we were good to Sally and they wanted to be good to us.
Later, when she had left, my daddy said I should never forget
that people in Martin County are the best people in the world,
and even if they've got almost nothing except what they grow,
they don't go begging and stealing and they don't do much borrowing either. They'll take something and let a favor be done,
then they'll keep it in their mind, and when the moment is a good
one, then they'll go and pay the favor back. He's told me that a
few times, Daddy has — not to forget Sally bringing up the corn.
I don't. I won't."

What of the Sallys who by the thousands live up those hollows
and creeks, the poorest of the poor, those whose minds and
hearts and souls have significantly given way, having suffered
beyond any reasonable limit, even where people know how to
take hardship in their stride? They are the families and the
children whose extreme condition — of life and limb and spirit —
has been described by Appalachian people themselves, specifically, the people of the hollows and creeks of Kentucky or West
Virginia or western North Carolina. For all their misery they see
quite clearly what is happening to them and others like them.
Sally herself, for example, can spell out unselfconsciously and
even casually some of the distinguishing characteristics that set
her apart, say, from Herbie, a boy of eight who lives not far away
in the same hollow. "Herbie is nice," she has told me many, many
times, and she means it in every sense of the word. That is, she
likes Herbie for his goodness, his largeness and generosity of
character, as it were, his kindness, his pleasing and agreeable
nature, his modest and well-mannered way of getting along with
people: "He's honest; he never will cheat in school or when we
play. They're kin of ours, Herbie's family, but not too close from

what I hear. Herbie's daddy had a job in the mines, but then he got fired because they were closing down the mines, some of them, and laying off people on account of the machines. They had some money during the time he was working, and my daddy says once you've had money you never can forget it. Herbie says his daddy can't recall the last time he saw a paycheck, but you can see his folks went and got things with the money — the television and the stove and the refrigerator. In our place there's no electricity, none — so we couldn't have television or a refrigerator, even if we had the money to buy them. We don't need electricity. We have the stove. All we need is wood for it, and my daddy goes and finds coal up the hollow and digs out the pieces. The trouble is a lot of the time he's under, real bad under, and then we have to do his chores, and my mother will be crying and then we all start and it's then I wish I was staying down the hollow a bit, maybe with Herbie and his folks — they're the best people you could ever meet."

When her father goes "real bad under" he has been drinking too much. Her mother tries hard to stop "the old man's habit," as she refers to him and his drinking. After a while, though, she also starts drinking, first slowly but then with a certain desperate acceleration that strikes terror into the minds of her seven children, who run for cover — to the woods and to kinfolk down the hollow. Sally's parents live as far up the hollow as one can go. From their cabin one can see a truly splendid view of the Appalachians: the hills close by and far; the low-hanging white clouds and the higher gray clouds; the mist or the drizzle or the fog; and, near at hand, everywhere the green of the trees. The cabin is black, tar-paper black, and stands on four cement blocks. The cabin lacks curtains but does indeed possess that old stove, the place where life-giving food is prepared and life-preserving heat is given off. Near the stove there are three beds with mattresses but nothing else. Ten human beings use the mattresses: Sally's grandmother, her parents, and the seven children in the family. The cabin possesses a table but only one chair to go with it, and two other old "sitting chairs," both of which are battered and tattered, with springs in each quite visible.

The children sit and eat outside under the trees, or inside on the floor, or near the house on the ground; or else they walk out in front of the house, in which case they often remain standing and hunch over their food. The children commonly use their hands to eat, or share a limited number of forks (four), spoons (five), and knives (seven) with their parents and grandmother. The children also share clothes: two pairs of shoes, both in serious need of repair, two ragged winter jackets, and three very old pairs of winter gloves. The children, let it be said, also share something else — the hollow: its hills and land, its vast, imposing view, its bushes and shrubs and plants and animals and water and silence and noise, its seclusion and isolation, and also its people, a few families, a few dozen people, but for Sally a whole crowded, complicated sustaining world. Sally at eight talks of that world even as she draws that hollow (Figure 20). She lets me know that she wishes her father didn't lose control and drink so much and take to shooting wildly at animals that no one but he can see. She lets me know that she wishes her mother didn't then begin to weaken and eventually also fall apart. She lets me know that she can imagine a better state of affairs, can for a second or two here and there wish and dream for that, but mostly, for most seconds of most days, she makes do with things as they are. She lets me know that her mother and father, her brothers and sisters, her grandmother, who is weak and pain-ridden and at fifty-two a very, very old woman, all wonder whether the strain and turmoil, the cumulatively devastating episodes of meanness and terror and sorrow and disorder will ever stop and leave a time of peace and plenty.

Sally's eyes and ears notice a good deal more than her school performance would indicate, and her observations about her family and their troubles show once again a mixture of intelligence and hurt that are really inseparable — except in the minds of those who want for their own reasons to dwell exclusively on one thing or another; that is, see in Sally only the grace which goes with suffering that somehow becomes transcended, or see in Sally only evidence of a ravaged and "depressed" and "disadvantaged" and "border-line" mind. I feel that Sally's drawing shows her trying to look beyond, trying to hold on with all her energy to a view, a viewpoint, a perspective. There is nothing sly or quaint or clever about her effort — or about her — and she makes it clear she is not ashamed to be quite firmly, unashamedly concrete: "I like to go up to the field there, on top of the hill, and look over. You can see far, far away. You're closer to the sun. You're near the sky. Once when I was real little my grandma took me up there. My daddy had gone real bad, and he was shooting. My mother was crying so hard I thought she'd turn into water and there'd be nothing left of her. My grandma took me on her shoulder and ran. My brother wouldn't go with her. He said if he was going to be hit, it might as well be a bullet. I don't know what happened to the others. They might have gone by themselves, my older sister and my other brother. Up there we stood, in the field. My grandma put me down and told me what to do — stand there and don't move. She kept telling me things: that there was this mountain and that one, and she'd been told who lived near each one, and if the mountain had a name, what it was. She was listening while she was talking, I guess, because after a while she said we could go back, because it sounded quiet again back there — and we did. I can see her leaning toward me and picking me up. She said she liked carrying me on her back. She told me never to forget that we had this field to go to, and you're able to see as far as anyone on God's earth can, and if you lose your spirits and feel real down, then go up there and talk to God and He'll hear you from that field, if He's ever going to, because you're so near to Him and there's no one else to be bothering Him and asking something of Him at the same time as you are. And I do, I talk with Him. I do."

She does. She goes up there and finds a certain rest, a sense of nearness to Someone or Something that is said to help, that can be called upon and begged and urged to help, that is "up there, where Heaven is," that is waiting and may well take notice. "He'll hear, I know He will," Sally once insisted. Perhaps I did wonder whether she wasn't just a little worried He might *not* hear; but I also have to remind myself that Sally does believe — predominantly and consistently and to her great relief and joy — that He *is* there, and He *will* help, and in *His* way. Why, I came to ask myself when I was with her, do people like me make so very much of the "primitive" and superstitious and "neurotic" quality in the faith of a child like Sally? Why did I look with such suspicion for so long at her flight upward, her flight to the field on top of the hill, her flight to God, her flight, really, for a vision of the widest possible world available? Once when she and I and her little sister and a cousin of hers stood on the top of that hill, for an hour or so the children told me about the mountain "over yonder," and pointed out to me several likely (and utterly lovely) spots God's Spirit might single out for a visit. I shared my doubts and misgivings and suspicions. I asked the children if they thought God's Spirit "really" came to those places they had shown me. Sally in particular smiled and said she didn't know how to answer me. But in fact she did. She quietly and gracefully remarked that "God comes for those who wait for Him," and then she changed the subject.

What have I learned from Sally's life (and her words and her drawings)? The question just asked can be answered quite well by Sally herself. She does not need me to say that a good deal of her life is unsatisfying — to her, never mind me. She does not need me to express her central longing that her family find a more coherent and valuable kind of existence. Sally and children like her made it very clear to me that on the one hand they very much like certain things about mountain living, and on the other hand they are troubled and confused and even badly hurt (yes, they *know* they are hurt) by the hunger pangs they experience, the sickness that goes untreated, and perhaps worst of all, the sight of what their suffering does to their parents. Those Appalachian parents certainly do take notice of their children's suffering — for one reason because they *are* parents, and for another because they are traditionally proud and defiant people. Children notice their parents noticing, and Sally herself can talk about that kind of watching and counter-watching as it goes on among bruised and offended people, unwilling to let go of their sense of dignity and self-respect, and unwilling also to let go of their love for their ancestors, for their homes, their land, their conventions:

"There's nothing that gets my daddy going worse than liquor. Once he told my mother he was going to start drinking because he was upset as bad as he could be, because he'd been down the hollow and over to the welfare people and it was the first time he'd gone and it was going to be the last, even if he starved to death. I guess they didn't give him anything. They said they were sorry. They said there's no money for most people, and that's all they can do in the office there.

"Daddy was more upset that he'd gone over to them than that they had refused him; I know that, because he said so all morning. I've never seen him so fighting mad, and he said he was, and we all got more and more scared. My mother told us we'd better go out to the woods and play, and she would take care of everything. Then before we left he looked at me and my sister and he raised up his hand, and I got scared he might come over and take it out on us — but no, he didn't do anything. He told me I was good and he was glad I was good, and he said the day would come when he'd be able to bring home clothes for us and I'd look pretty. He said I already do, but if you have a dress, it helps. Then he said I could go outside and my mother said to go, and I went. The next thing I knew he was drinking and he started screaming real bad after a while. I believe a lot of the time he gets himself upset on account of us, and then he'll go and take to the liquor he makes.

"I wouldn't want to live any other place. What do you do if there's no hill you're on — if it's flat like they show you in the books in school? If I could change anything I wanted, I'd tear down that place Daddy and his friends use to make the liquor. I'd just have the hill here, where we live, and the other ones, to go and look at. I'd have us living in a different house, maybe like Marie's. Then we'd all be happier, I know that. Then I think my daddy might stop his drinking and never start again, like he'll promise us each time that he's going to do."

Promises, promises — the stuff of hope; though Sally knows enough not to be without skepticism. Nor does Sally's father need anyone to point out his inconsistencies, his mixed feelings: his wish to be sober, to work, to improve his condition and his

family's, to give Sally her clothes and maybe a few good, nutri-
tious meals, and later on, a chance at more schooling and some
good work; and at the same time, his wish to forget it all, the
frustration and futility that cling to his life. Sally's father knows
about those "polarities" I mentioned earlier. Unlike many sharecropper fathers or migrant fathers he owns his land, can feel that
where he is and what he has around him is his and no one else's;
and as a result he has no desire or even willingness to move
anyplace else. Indeed, come what may, he will stay up that
hollow, stay there because his ancestors *chose* to live in that
hollow, and have from generation to generation felt fiercely
possessive of those hills. He would shoot anyone who might dare
suggest that he become a migrant and try to farm for others in
one state after another. Sharecroppers and migrant farmers feel
on their backs the breath of others, men who are powerful and
often enough mean, whereas it can be said that mountaineers
like Sally's father feel their own "hot and bothered" breath. That
is how Sally's mother describes her husband when he takes to
drink: "He gets all excited over nothing that's new, so far as I can
see. He gets worse and worse, and the next thing I know he's
taking one shot of that stuff with his glass, and then another, and
soon you can smell it over to the next hill, and his breath is so hot
and bothered that I wonder how it is the corn we grow right out
there can do that to someone."

Migrants grow up into an increasingly chaotic life — they see
chaos unfolding before their eyes. Sharecroppers grow up into an
increasingly sad life — they see gloom all about them and speak
out (in the blues, for instance) the heaviness of their hearts. But
mountaineers look upon life as a sort of stalemate, in which there
is plenty of good as well as plenty of bad, plenty to hold onto as
well as plenty to wish for, and as a result "an awful lot of plenty"
to be high-strung about, unsettled about, feel torn about. Faced
with such thoroughly mixed feelings mountaineers stand fast and
try to persist. In the words of Marie's father, they "stick it out,
last it out." Stick out and last out *what*, one wonders? Does he
mean the obvious lack of material things and opportunities that

Sally's father knows about but in his way defies? That, yes; but more is at stake than some of us on the outside realize: "As I see it, up there in the hollow it's real bad — yes, with Sally and her people. But there's plenty they just don't want to lose, an awful lot of plenty, I'll tell you. People come in here and they don't know that. I heard on the TV a man saying we're supposed to be suspicious up in the mountains, and we don't trust no one, except ourselves. What a lot of hooey he had in his mouth, saying that. Sure we're not going to like someone if he comes in here and tells us we're a bunch of damn fools, and we should do this and that and everything they want us, and then we'll be all right.

"Hell, this is our country. We made it. We came here and we stayed because we loved it, and no one's going to get us out — except, I guess, if we're going to starve right to death, and then we'll be gone anyway. But I think we're friendlier here than in those cities you see all the time on the TV, where they pay no mind to anyone but themselves. I'm no expert on anything, except driving a bus and making sure those schools stay warm in the winter and as clean as they can, what with all the kids messing things up every day; but you can walk up any hollow or creek in Kentucky and West Virginia and you'll hear the people picking on the guitar and listening to the radio and they'll stop and talk with you, and if you want to stay for supper, that's fine. Now, if you do, they're not going to go and spit on themselves and hold out their hand and say, 'Look here mister, give us a few pennies out of your big fat wallet.' No sir, they're going to put out their best for you, and they're going to show you they've got a lot to put out, that's right. They've got their place, and they've got the food they can grow and all like that.

"Sure, we need more, a hell of a lot more, and you must have figured that out by now. But no one's going to get us feeling kindly by coming on the first thing with a lot of that lousy pity stuff you hear on the TV — about the poor people of Appalachia! Hell on that! Hell on it! They start with that and the next thing I know I'm ready to tell them to take themselves and their charity and go try it on someone else, because that's not what a decent, God-fearing man wants, no it's not. You can bet we get suspicious, like they say we are. The coal people come in here, and they're tearing up everything they can get their hands on, and maybe they'll give you the money, the wages, but sure as hell they get more out of it than all of us ever will, and then the next thing you know they've gone, and all we have for it is that they've torn up a whole mountain and what's left of the mountain is falling down on us in a landslide, and we're supposed to get out, fast. If you don't get suspicious over that, then you're not right in your head, and I say so even if I'm no expert on the mind. Then you know they've been taking our timber away, by the hillfull, since way back, and right in front of our eyes that's what's been happening since I guess Abraham Lincoln or some-one was President. So, why shouldn't we go and tell our children to watch out when some big-smiling city slicker comes here with about a dozen lawyers standing guard over him and they go and hold hands with the county people and fill up their pockets with bribes, and then march on over here, to a place like this, and tell the people they'd better go along and do what's 'legal' or they'll end up in jail.

"It hurts for me to talk like that — I mean, to say what I've just said, because I'm in debt to the county people in my own county, and I guess if you're going to make a halfway decent living in these mountains today, things being as they are, you better *had* be friends of the sheriff and the county people, every one of them. Like they said one time on the TV, and I agree: we need to change the whole thing around, so that there's work here for the people, and they bring home a good wage. And when that happens, if that day ever comes, then I'll tell you no one's going to find us being 'suspicious' like they said, and hard to talk with, and all that. A hunter, he develops a good nose, just like the dogs have. If a man has a good nose he can smell trouble a long way off, but he can smell something good, too. It's as simple as that, if you ask me. Sure we're afraid of them all coming here; we can smell the trouble before it gets to the first hill in Kentucky — or over in West Virginia. But if they came to us and wanted to bring in some work here, and it didn't mean tearing up the whole county, and it didn't mean eating up our lungs, then we'd be just like any American — glad to have a job, you bet your life. We'd want to sit here and be ourselves, of course. We wouldn't want to act like some of the people you see on television. We wouldn't want to dress as they do, and talk as they do, no matter how much money we made. We'd want to live as we do. But we'd be working, and that would sure be a welcome change hereabouts.

"Let me tell you, if you saw some real, reliable, steady money coming in here, then you'd see things change, I know you would. I acted different before I had a good job. You get a job and you want to go and buy things and it makes you feel better all the way around. You still like where you are, but you're more independent, you know. I mean, you can buy your food, so you don't have to grow it — and there's no time for that when you're working every weekday and into the weekends. If you do have some spare moments you like to sit on your porch and walk up through the woods, and you'll hunt and fish as before, but it's not as though you've got to measure everything you do against the weather outside — and your knowledge that if you don't grow food, your children will starve. I guess I could say it this way: you're more independent, like I said, so you're more independent of the land. The hollow, it's still your home, but it's not meaning the difference between life and death to you — the land isn't. And the biggest relief, if you ask me, is your kids; they can like it here up the hollow, but they're not tied to it so much. If you're more relaxed about money coming in, you don't have to worry, and you go and enjoy yourself. Some of the people up there, you'll ask them if everything is going fine, and they say yes, but you know it isn't. All you have to do is look at their kids and you know the truth. Even so, they'll always say, 'It's fine up in the hollow,' and 'It's fine up the creek.' Why shouldn't they? I would. I did. I believe it's fine up in the hollow for Marie, just like for the other kids. The truth is, I think it's Marie who likes the hollow and creeks around here, better than some of the other kids she goes to school with — because all she gets out of them is the good memories, when we're doing something we like. Too many of our children around here, I'll admit it, have a lot of bad memories way up there in the hills and that spoils them on the hollows, even if they're not going to say so and admit it to you, nor themselves either, *nor themselves!*"

At that point the listener had better remind himself that no one alive ever really admits everything to himself. Illusions don't have to be attacked or defended; they exist. Said Sigmund Freud, "I know how difficult it is to avoid illusions; perhaps even the hopes I have confessed to are of an illusory nature."[13] If a man who writes *The Future of an Illusion* can give himself and his readers an inch or two so far as illusions go, Marie's father can be forgiven if he joins their company. Actually, on other occasions Marie's father has shown he will express some of the bitterness and indignation implied in that second, terrible "nor themselves" just quoted: "That may be one of the troubles. They're too good at fooling themselves up there. They're too honest. They're too obliging. They're not suspicious; instead they're trusting, too much so if you ask me. They're *believers.* They believe in God, and they believe in these hills, and they believe in their fellowman. It's a shame, I think — if you stop and consider where it's got them all these years."

Marie's father, for all his relative security so far as life in Martin County goes, cannot himself escape the tensions and contrasts and ironies that surround but do not engulf him. Often in exasperation he despairs. Often in hope he comes forth with a series of specific judgments or recommendations. I can second his estimation of what is wrong in Martin County, and many other counties I know in Appalachia. I can second his plea for the right kind of "intervention" and "assistance" and "change." But I also hope I don't lose in my mind the sight of those mountain children Marie's father so often chooses to mention. They have their "needs" all right, but one need they do not have is an analysis which omits the central, overriding "fact" that the girl Sally, for all the difficulties she has experienced and will experience, nevertheless managed to demonstrate in the picture I have labeled Figure 20. What I call "Figure 20" is nothing less than a clear and forceful demonstration of a mind's ability to perform, to search

FIGURE 14

FIGURE 15

FIGURE 16

FIGURE 17

FIGURE 18

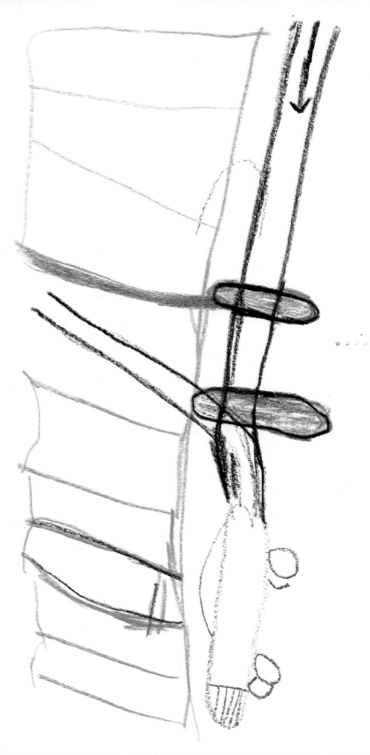

FIGURE 19

FIGURE 20

FIGURE 21

and grope, to gain coherence, to collect itself and master something in the face of innumerable provocations and appalling impediments.

Like the mountaineers, both the children and their parents, I write down my impressions of those hollows with a mixed mind; and perhaps what that tells is somewhat illuminating. Migrants and sharecroppers have comparatively less to offer their children than mountaineers do. They have less of a history, less of what is implied by the word "destiny," less to own and occupy and defend, defend *especially* when there seems to be nothing else left. In other words, it is better to be hidden — from one's enemies as well as from one's friends! — than uprooted or stranded. If no one needs a social scientist to prove so obvious a proposition, I can only say that many of us on the "outside" have yet to convince a man like Marie's father that we really understand what we claim is obvious to us; for he thinks we would only pity him and his kin, even as we pity the children of sharecroppers and of migrant farmers. Our pity, anyway, will give very little to anyone, including sharecroppers and migrants — who need more than pity; and our pity enrages the mountaineers — who know very well what kind of justice they require, and what justice we in America have so far done and not done.

PART THREE

THE WORLD

VI

THE WORLD
OF THE HOLLOWS

T HE children whose early lives I have tried to set forth in
this book belong to particular families and locations. What
makes these children and their parents uprooted, stranded or
hidden has to do with circumstances outside the home, though of
course just about everything in the whole wide world eventually
works its way into the home — everything that takes place in the
political arena, in the marketplace, or even *has* taken place and is
therefore called part of the past, part of history. Migrant children
are uprooted, sharecropper children are stranded, and mountain
children are hidden from the rest of us because a particular kind
of social and economic system permits, even encourages migrant
farmers to wander the land, permits sharecroppers and tenant
farmers to work land that belongs to others for practically nothing in return, and permits mountain families in Appalachia to
live (no matter how they try otherwise) essentially jobless and
literally penniless lives. If all of that is obvious and a matter
of the purest common sense, it is a common sense that has to be
constantly stated and insisted upon by psychiatric workers like
me, because too often we look at minds and even "cultures" or
"social systems" and forget to ask ourselves the plain facts about
who is running whom, who owns what, who hires which people
for what purpose, who prevents what families from living here,
settling down there, working at this kind of job, or indeed working at all.

So, a book by a child psychiatrist about the growth and development of migrant children, sharecropper children, and Appalachian children necessarily must do more than make parenthetical mention of social "factors" or economic "influences." I believe those factors and influences have an observable, palpable existence so far as the children described here are concerned. These children know particular human beings — know those who operate mines or run plantations or transport and put people to work, only to send them off a few weeks later to another county, another state. Who those "bossmen" are — those mine operators and plantation owners and their underlings and crew leaders — and how they all think and feel becomes very much a force in determining who a migrant is, or how a sharecropper child grows up, or what a mountain child comes to think about himself and the larger world, which really is an inseparable part of anyone's particular world, however insistently it is proclaimed to be private or special or different. So far as the children in the foregoing chapters are concerned, the people are very familiar — very much a part of the world uprooted, stranded and hidden boys and girls grow up to find theirs.

1.   *The Miners Need Their Bosses*

Many of the families I have visited in Appalachian hollows are headed by men who once worked in the mines and now don't, or still do but are ailing and expect to stop soon. The children often ask their fathers what coal-mining is or was like, and just as often get sullen, angry rebuffs. It is hard enough to do the work, or to live with the memory of what it was like to do the work; the idea of talking about the experience with wide-eyed, openly admiring children is just too much. Actually, if only they knew how to go about doing so, such children could hear a lot about their fathers and the mines.

In eastern Kentucky, in Perry County or Harlan County or Letcher County, a curious child from up one of the hollows, bent on finding things out, might go and talk to a man who runs a strip mine; the child might, for instance, go and talk to Edward

McCleary, who is a friendly, talkative man, a man quite willing to go on and on about coal mines and the kind of man they require if they are to be made productive. He himself was once a miner. He was born in Perry County, not too far from Hazard, a much written about town which (with nearby Harlan) somehow has come to symbolize the hard and bloody war that had to be waged all over the Appalachian mountains before the United Mine Workers could even begin to bargain effectively with the coal operators. Edward McCleary remembers hearing of the struggle in Hazard and Harlan, remembers the power of the mine owners — remembers them as self-satisfied, ungenerous, and in the clutch even vicious men. He will not defend those men or their cause. He is quite willing to talk about his own origins, his poverty-stricken childhood, his father's struggle to rise up and become better off, a little more secure. At the same time, Edward McCleary believes that those days are gone forever. He will take a visitor proudly through his mines, one classical underground mine and several other so-called "strip mines," which means large stretches of hilly land being worked over, dug into, eviscerated by incredibly powerful and merciless machines that claw and carve and scrape and scoop and gouge — until coal is reached, until the land is made to yield that coal, yield it in abundance. And when the coal is gone, the opened, wounded, bleeding land is abandoned. The wounds are simply left to weaken the rest of the region's body: acid trickles out of enormous craters; landslides come roaring down after rain upon farms and homes and trees and streams and roads, dumping rocks and boulders and thick, unfertile mud upon everything and anyone. Innocent people living up a hollow all of a sudden become refugees, forced to leave or be killed, forced to leave because their land is literally overwhelmed.

To Edward McCleary life is like that: progress entails sacrifices; progress costs money, hurts people, can be painful; but the needs of a whole country go before those of a relative handful — who are, anyway, unspeakably poor (he readily admits) and therefore (he sharply asserts) ought to be elsewhere, in some other section of the nation where, as he puts it, "they won't be sitting and moaning about the twentieth century and living in the nineteenth."

They are his people, he reminds his listener. He is no outsider, no exploiter "from out of Pittsburgh and New York" come to extract then depart, remove coal from the rich land and then go back home. There have been plenty of those, he declares, "plenty of big eastern banks and big eastern companies that have moved in here." He is in fact "tied in" with them, but he is a man of eastern Kentucky, a man who knows what it's like up the hollows, who knows his own people, who suffers with them and for them, even as he feels he knows what they need if somehow things are to get better: "I remember when I was a boy — it was in the twenties after the First World War — my dad used to say Kentucky was a doomed place, this part of the state. My mother would ask him why, and he'd say that the only thing we have here is coal, and when that's gone we'll all starve to death or get out. In a way he's been proven right. We don't need the men we used to need for the mines, and so they've all gone back to the hollows, where a lot of them nearly *are* starving to death. The smart ones have left and gone to Ohio or Michigan to get work for themselves. Sure they come back on weekends, but you notice they leave on Sunday to be back at work up there on Monday morning. I wish I could employ more here, I'd be only too happy to do it. Some of the people up there in the hollows of Perry County think I'm their enemy, but if they got rid of me and everyone who works for me, they'd be no better off. All we'd have here is a few more poor people. That's all."

His father, once a miner, became a foreman; by Edward McCleary's admission the "old man" was tough, extremely tough, but if his son is to be believed, miners need tough men to lead them, miners need bosses, the old-fashioned, strict, no-nonsense kind. Here is why that is so: "Miners need a certain type of foreman, a guy who will tell them what to do and no fooling around — a real boss, you could say. The miner seems independent and he appears as though he's not afraid of anyone, but he's got a hell of a dangerous job, going down there into the mines, and it's like with a good soldier, he needs the good officer to tell him where to go and when and all that. My father was like the best marine officer you'll ever find; he was a real leader, and the company people saw that he was. I guess maybe they figured they'd rather have him on *their* side — otherwise he might become a leader of the workers, and work for the union. And they fought the unions hard, the big coal companies did. After a while Dad was more than a foreman; they had him in charge of a couple of mines, and he was the one who went and talked with the miners and kept them working around the clock and made sure the company had no labor trouble. He was real valuable to them, and they knew it up in Pittsburgh. They told him he was the best man they had, and the reason was he knew how to keep the men working real fast and steady, but he could be friendly with them, too; they'd be angry at 'eastern banks' and not Dad, I guess that was it. But one day one of those eastern bankers, that's what he was, came by and talked with Dad — I think he was on an inspection trip or something — and they became friendly and he was the one who started Dad going with our first mine. I was old enough then to start out with Dad. We only had a part interest, but for all practical purposes it was ours, because we ran it and hired and fired and decided everything. The banker never regretted going in partners with Dad. All the banker had to do was sit and watch his money come in, and send down those lawyers when we needed land to strip-mine, and engineers to help work the machinery and help figure where to dig and what the angle of entry is and all that.

"Dad wanted me to go to engineering school and become a mining engineer, but I followed him. I like running the company; it's a small one compared to the big ones, the giants, but we do right well. You could even say we're rich compared to most people around here — and we didn't start with a lot of money. One thing we've always done is try to be fair with the workers and the people we buy the land from. They'll tell you different, I know. To listen to them, we're the worst people that ever lived. One group came in here to see me about six months ago and they told me I was plundering all of eastern Kentucky and tearing up everything I could get my hands on, and I was as much a mur-

derer as anyone who ever lived. I don't scare easy, though. I
know them, and I know what it would be like here if no coal
company ever came near the whole state of Kentucky to strip-
mine or dig a regular mine. They'd be as sorry a group of people
as they are now; they'd be as bad off, and they know it. At least
the mines give some men work. The mines always have done that
for our men, employ them; and the wages are good. Who wants
to spend his life looking at a hill? They tell me I'm destroying the
scenery, but I wonder who looks at the scenery; that's for tourists
to do, and there's plenty of scenery left for them, and there
always will be. Yes, we've had a few landslides, and I'm just as
upset about that as anyone is. No one's been hurt, though — and
they know in advance, usually, if they're in danger. A lot of the
complaints about strip-mining are bellyaching — by people who
haven't got much of a life, and they see us move up a hill and
they wish they could be working and doing something, like we
are. That's how I see it."

How does he not only see "it" but *them*, those people? In fact,
he has many things to say about life up the hollows: "We've had
people from up the creeks and hollows come down and work for
us all along, and we know their problems. Some of the people up
there are not like my father was. They wouldn't leave home to
work in a mine, even though they're almost starving to death.
Most of them will come, though, if you have the work for them.
We're proud, all of us here are. My dad was probably the
luckiest man who ever lived, and I know it. I'm not going to say
everything we do is perfect, especially the strip-mining. We *do*
tear up the land. You can't help it. How else are you going to get
that coal out? But no one gets his lungs sick that way, and it's a
lot of coal the country gets, and we need that coal. What's the
answer? I don't know. I bleed for my people, sometimes. I'll see
them, and they look sick, you can tell, but they hold on to their
pride. They're not beggars. If I was in Washington and running
the country, and not just a few mines here, I'd take some of that
money we send all over the world and put it right in here, so that
these people could live better. It's a shame. They're not lazy, as
you know. They'll work and work for you. I think more and more

they have started griping and complaining about anything and
everything; but that's because they know how bad their situation
is. Before, we had hundreds of thousands working down in the
mines, and that kept a lot of money pouring into those hollows — money sent there by miners living in the camps. Now we
have fewer and fewer men each year in the mines, because
machines are doing more and more.

"It's very hard to see how they survive up there in the hills, but
they do. They farm a little. They'll have a chicken or two, a pig or
two. They live from day to day, and they're not used to all the
luxuries you and I might consider 'normal.' If you're not used to
something, you don't miss it — and that can even go for electricity and plumbing and heating and everything else you'll find
in a good, modern home. It's not like you see on television —
with the colored people in those big cities; we don't have big
welfare programs here, because we don't have the money they've
got over in the East, and besides, we don't believe in charity
here. A man wants to work here, and if he can't find a job, then
he'll manage to get by somehow. We take care of one another. I
give ten percent of my income to the church, sometimes more,
and you know that goes to feeding people and getting clothes for
them. If it weren't for the church, for the things they distribute to
the poor, we'd have much more trouble on our hands.

"I'm getting old, and I've lived all my life here, and I don't
have the answers. My kids are in college, and they're worried
about us here in Kentucky; they want to know how we can
change things here, and I tell them I'd also like to know. Their
granddad, he wasn't some rich guy that came here and bought
up land dirt cheap from poor unsuspecting farmers and turned
right around and tore up the place for coal. He was a hard
worker, and he moved on up, and he had some lucky breaks, and
he made money, and that goes for me — with me it's just that my
dad was who he was. If he'd been different, I'd be up some creek
now, worrying whether a good supper is coming and probably
drinking that moonshine, because there'd be nothing else for me
to do. Or maybe I'd be dead. Who knows? They live a bad life
up the hollows, a lot of them — hard and mean it is for them. But

they're ready to smile real fast, and even the ones that come in here to this office and start calling me a no-account plunderer — and worse names than that — they do so in a respectful way. We don't have those sit-ins and all that kind of thing down here. Oh, we've had terrible fights in the past, when the unions were getting organized, and lately a few of the radical types — egged on by outsiders, I know it for a fact — have been trying to get the people all stirred up, and they hope they can scare us; but you take the average men here in Perry County or any other part of Kentucky or West Virginia, he doesn't want to do that, parade and demonstrate and like that. He'd rather stay where he is, in his home, and take his chances on getting by, even if he barely makes it. I know it for a fact. Isn't it obvious? Anyone who doubts what I say hasn't been up there to talk with the people, up the hollows and the creeks."

Not for a long time has he been "up there"; for that matter he never really has been "up there," except to supervise what amounts to, really, the destruction of a particular hollow by his machines. As a child he lived the comfortable life of a well-paid executive's son. True, his father was not what we would consider a conventional executive, or perhaps better, his father was indeed a conventional executive — of the old-fashioned kind. His father, in fact, stopped being a miner before his son was born — so that he could direct and watch over miners for a big mining company. And by the time the son was grown up the father had a company of his own for the son to join. Nevertheless, the region's traditions persist over the generations, or so Edward McCleary fervently believes. There is something special about "his" people, and he says they are his not because he lives near them or employs some of them, but out of respect if not admiration: "I can't say I admire the people — if a man is down and out, and living in the worst possible situation, you don't admire him. If he suffers like a gentleman — then at least you can respect him. The people who came to live here never had any idea they'd be the happiest ones in the world; they came here from the East, most of them as poor as could be. They're still poor, and I'm sorry about that. I'd like everyone in the state of Kentucky to live a good, solid life, with enough money so that he could eat well, and have a good roof over his head. But how are we going to get the money, that's what I don't know."

On another occasion he indicates his belief that even if the money *were* available there would be problems: "The poor here in this state who live up the hollows won't take handouts. I mean, they will, of course, because they're desperate; but they don't like the idea, and they wouldn't feel they were getting a square deal if the only thing they could look forward to is one welfare scheme after another. What we need here is factories, lots of them, to give jobs to our people. But the factories don't come here, and with mining no longer a matter of only men, but machines, there's nothing left for people but scratching what they can from the land — or turning to the county welfare system, which is full of all kinds of rotten, dishonest politics. Welfare is a business here, not the right of a citizen who needs help and is entitled to it. No wonder a lot of our people have contempt for welfare, even if they'll accept the money. They know that the county officials use welfare to stay in power, to buy votes and to punish enemies.

"I've thought a lot about all of this, and I've argued with my kids and their friends, back and forth, and I believe there's only one alternative: either the federal government brings in the factories, or a lot of people will just have to go. And they *are* going, of course. More will need to leave, though. We can't have children born up in those shacks, and living the way they do — starving to death, slowly starving. No wonder so many of them die young. The trouble with our people is that they're *willing* to suffer; some of them don't know anything else. All their lives they've been in bad shape, barely getting by from one meal to the next, one day to the next. They think there's no other way, and they're proud they have those cabins in the hills and all the rest. I guess as long as they can shoot some animals and catch some fish and grow some vegetables they'll survive — and they don't need much money. But if more than survival is what you're talking about, then they're in a lot of trouble. The tourists come here in the warm weather, and if they even get near the hollows (which most of them don't) they'll say, 'Isn't that nice, the way they live up there, with a grand view of all the hills.' Of course, they never stop and think what it's like in those cabins in the middle of the winter. A lot of the cabins have no heat or electricity or plumbing. You can't hunt and fish and grow things in winter, like you can in the summer, and there's a limit to what you can both eat and store away during the summer. I guess you know all that. I guess everyone does, if they'd only stop and think.

"To be honest, I don't like to stop and think too much myself. Most of the time I just go along and do my work and try to be as hardheaded as I can. I don't want anything for nothing. I don't want to cause any harm. I try to help out, help other people, when I can. I've enough money so that I could move out of here myself. I could go and live in Lexington, or even up to Cincinnati, and I could have a manager over here, running everything for me. But I love my work, and I love it here, right in Perry County. So does my wife. She's from this county, and she doesn't want to leave. Her kin are nearby. I wouldn't want to tell you how much money we give to our kinfolk, hers and mine. No sir, I wouldn't. Once I mentioned to a cousin of mine — it was at a church fair — that I was thinking of leaving, going over to Lexington, or maybe down to Knoxville for a while and getting a long taste of the city. Well, they got a regular delegation together of our kin and came over to see us, and my wife and I, we felt terrible, real terrible. I told them to stop worrying, and I made sure they could believe me. I took an oath right in front of them. I shouldn't have, but I did. I guess they feared that if I went away, I'd soon stop with the money. But I couldn't do that. A man has to live with himself, you know. A man has to have a good conscience, you know. Sometimes those protesters who shout against strip-mining, they try and get to you. They try and make you nervous. They try and upset you, and give you the idea that you're some kind of devil, and you're not a Christian, and you're breaking God's law, or something like that. I'd never do anything bad, against His law; and like I said, a good lot of the money I make goes out to my kin and to the church, and to helping the colleges my kids go to.

"Maybe I could give more. Maybe it's wrong to send even one man down there underground, or work over the land for coal. I've thought about all that. Like I say, I don't *like* to; I *have* to. You know what I've decided? If I didn't do it, if it wasn't me, why as sure as I'm sitting here talking, there'd be someone else doing exactly what I'm doing, and maybe even worse, maybe cheating on the people by getting their land for nothing, practically, and not paying them a decent price. Maybe someone else wouldn't give a cent to any kin in Perry County, just take it all and spend it in Ohio or Pennsylvania or up there in New York. Now, I'll tell you, that's the *real* shame, that so much of the coal we have here goes to make other people rich, not us. When people come and start criticizing me, I tell them that at least I'm from this part of the country. That doesn't stop them forever, but I notice they slow down on the bad things they say. One of the students that's trying to organize the people up in the hollows, you know what he said to me a few weeks ago? He said this: 'Mr. McCleary, you're a symptom, not a cause. We don't blame you. You're just a pawn in something much bigger. You're caught in this, like the poor people up the hills there.' Well, I asked him what I was a symptom of, and he said 'the system,' and I said I'd rather be my kind of symptom than be a symptom like the poor folks up in the hollow are. And you know what? He said he agreed."

2. *No One Should Be Bossed Around*

Call him an organizer or a member of VISTA or an Appalachian Volunteer or a young activist or an agitator or a troublemaker or an impractical idealist or a wonderful, wonderful, helpful young man; he has been called all that and more, this twenty-three-year-old young man whose first name, like Mr. McCleary's, is Edward, but who has always been called Ned. His last name is Williams, and he was born in Cinderella, West Virginia — which is part of

Mingo County. Ned likes to talk about the various towns in and near Mingo County, towns with names like Bias and Justice and Pie. The county has had a certain notoriety as the locus of long-standing family feuds and thoroughly ingrained political corruption — with dead voters, stuffed ballot boxes, and the outcome of elections a sure thing. Ned describes it all with a mixture of disgust and amusement and half-concealed pride: "You have to hand it to them; they know how to stay in power. It's like with Daley in Chicago or any other boss; it's like the Republican machine they had in Philadelphia for so long. The people who are in power stay in anywhere — until they lose their guts and become too lazy to be efficiently dishonest, or until they get mean enough, flagrantly mean enough, to arouse almost everyone; namely, people from the outside, the state legislators and the federal people, who then come in and supervise things and try to get an honest election held, which in Mingo would strike everyone as a contradiction in terms, I'll tell you.

"It used to be I'd get all worked up about those politicians in Mingo, the courthouse gang and the rest who hang on their tails. Now I think they're just a bunch of small-time crooks, a little more colorful than most, and not half as bad as the *real* crooks in Appalachia. A lot of them don't live here, and never have. They come from the Golden Triangle in Pittsburgh and from Wall Street. A few years ago I would have thought talk like that was crazy; I knew the devils, because I'd grown up in Mingo and seen them with my own eyes. But I didn't know them, not the real ones, the ones with big money and tremendous power — the ones Dad has worked for all his life."

Ned's father is a lawyer, a solid, stable, intelligent lawyer, who for years has represented coal and timber interests. There were the ordinary civil and criminal complaints, too; but Mr. Williams became prosperous because he was a local lawyer who at the same time had national clients. Ned used to rail against his father and the work his father does, but now when he talks about the man (he is near sixty) it is with compassion and charity: "I can't make my father into the monster I used to. He's more a pawn in this whole system than he'll ever know. The truth is that with a couple of bourbons in him he *does* know. Once, about three or four years ago, I came home from college. I was full of bad words about everything in the state of West Virginia, including the university. I wanted to leave Morgantown and go East or West, anyplace but around here. I told my dad this was a wasteland, conquered and plundered by the coal companies and now almost in ruins. He said I was full of a lot of theory, and he was right. He said I was turning my back on the best people in the world, and he was right. He said I wasn't looking at things as carefully as I thought. I recall asking him whether *he* did that — looked at what his job was, and what it meant to the poor people of the state. He fired back his answer: sure, he worked for big, rich companies, most of them out of state. They owned the mines, took the coal out, made the money, and kept it for themselves — in Pennsylvania and New York and New England, where their offices are. The truth is, he told me, there should have been a tax, a deliverance tax, on all coal mined, so that the people who extract coal and transport it out of the state and make huge profits on what they sell pay the state of West Virginia — the *people* of West Virginia — for the removal of their natural resources. First it was timber and now coal.

"I couldn't believe what I was hearing. He saw me looking at the bottle of bourbon and he anticipated me. He knew I thought he was drunk, so he said that you have to separate a man's beliefs from his work. Then he came up with what I now know is the old standby — though at the time I was stunned, absolutely stunned to hear my father talk that way. He just put it on the line: he had to make a living, and that was that. He went on, of course. He reminded me that he came from poor people. His father was a schoolteacher. They sweated a lot to get him through the university and the law school. They wanted him to be more secure than they had been. Most of all, they wanted him to be free of the miserable, rotten, corrupt politics that determines just about everything that goes on in the West Virginia schools. For years my grandfather had to go along with the local political machine, or else he'd have been fired on the spot. He wanted my father to be free of that — and he became free; except that he, too, has had people watching over him and telling him what to do and making him feel compromised. It's tragic, but it's the way the world is. My grandfather had the corrupt county people to face, and my father has had to deal with big banks and big oil companies; he's had to do their bidding, and to be real honest, he's had to be the local front man for those eastern law firms, which send dozens of lawyers here to figure out how to get land and more land from poor, innocent people, who don't have a dime to buy food let alone money for lawyers and are cheated out of everything, their land and their rights of protest, so that strip miners can come in and make millions of dollars — and it all goes out of West Virginia and Kentucky, except for what my father gets and a few others like him.

"My father knows that, but I guess I didn't really think he allowed himself to think about such things, not until we had the talk. Even now I wonder what he actually lets into his mind. He probably can't let himself be too honest; it must be painful. That time, when he was drinking bourbon and I was drinking beer, he let his guard down, but most of the time he won't. Even then he went only so far. He said he had to make a living, then he went off into talk about my grandfather and *his* troubles. How much can a man bear to see? How squarely can a man acknowledge the real purpose of his work? Take me; I've had a good life, and the reason I've had a good life is that my father makes a good living, and the reason for *that* is — well, it goes on and on. I've tried to talk with him about the oil companies and how they now run the coal companies and about strip-mining, and about the black lung that coal miners have been getting all these years — with no compensation once they've become incapacitated. I've tried to talk with him about mine safety and the hazards to the miners, and the accidents, and the hundreds of miners who die every year, while others die more slowly, because the coal-dust level is too high in the mines and gets into their lungs and kills them. He doesn't want to hear about all that. My mother took me aside the last time and she said I should stop and never again go into all that. I'll never forget her words, either; they were like his that time way back: 'Your father knows what you're talking about.

He's been a lawyer all these years, and everything you mention is a legal matter; so he knows.' She knows, and I know too, what went *un*said — that he has been fighting poor, half-dead miners who sue the companies for compensation; and that he has been fighting the people up in the hollows who are trying to get the owners of strip mines to stop causing landslides and stop buying up the options they have on all our land, at prices so low you want to sit and cry, knowing the money those owners make on mining the land, and what they'll do to the whole countryside for miles and miles around.

"I have friends who tell me that the reason I do what I do is because I'm 'guilty.' They say I work up the hollows and try to help communities organize because I know I've profited from the sweat and blood of the poor people in the state. It's true; but I think that's a lousy way to look at a person, and I don't feel so guilty that I let people get away with saying that. I've been to those meetings, where they get you all talking, and before you know it no one has an honest bone in his body, and we're all no good, and we all are corrupt, one way or the other — except the poor man up there in the cabin, way far into the hollow. And naturally if you're really honest and listen to that poor guy, half starving to death, you'll hear that he wishes he and his family could live like yours does, and he wouldn't mind being a lawyer and working for one of the companies. True, some people up the hollows are angry enough to curse the companies every other minute; but a while later, we'll be having a drink, and they'll tell you they wish they had a good job with a coal company — in an office and not down underground. It's easy to concentrate on one thing they say, and forget the other. I guess we're most of us as hung-up in our own ways as my father is."

Over and over again others like Ned try to come to terms with themselves, with our society, with the people whose cause they struggle to uphold — even as they insist it is not up to them, young activists who are outsiders, to uphold anyone's cause, but rather simply help certain people to uphold their own cause. For Ned Williams no amount of time is too much to spend on the question of his motives and the motives or purposes of the mountaineers up in those creeks and hollows. He does get rankled and even outraged by the way some "groups" he has attended make for self-consciousness, make everyone present feel blameworthy, flawed, exploitative and God knows what else — psychologically or politically or both together. Yet, he wants to scrutinize both himself and Mingo County and the state of West Virginia and the Appalachian region and the United States of America just as closely as he possibly can. He wants to be open and candid. Most of all, though, he wants to act — rather than only analyze things and attach explicitly or deviously pejorative labels to this or that person or deed. Still, he is at a loss to know what a person like him from a well-to-do family ought to do; and he is also observant enough to know that those he wants to "help" (he would insist upon the ironic or perhaps sarcastic use of quotation marks) are not quite all that he once thought they are, or even wishes today they might be — even as he would hasten to add that he himself is neither doing what he once hoped to do nor is quite the person he wants to be or thought he might be when he started "organizing."

That word "organizing" is itself a puzzle; it can mean so much and so little, can be argued about intensely, can refer to what seems to be the most casual of occupations. Ned would never try to define the nature of organizing, and when he declares himself to be, calls himself an organizer, he smiles gently and laughs quite uproariously: "It's crazy, a huge joke, real wild, telling people you're an organizer, when your work is to make things different, change things — and so *disorganize* the status quo. When I try to tell people what I do, they say it sounds as confusing as can be; and I myself wonder each day exactly what I've done to earn even one meal. I go up the creek and start sitting — and sitting and sitting and sitting. You know that people around here don't want to talk much — unless of course they *do* want to talk, and then they really can get going. Yesterday I sat with Mr. Butler and Mrs. Butler and their kids for about two hours. I had coffee, and their son Fred picked the guitar and we didn't say much of anything. At the very end, as I was about ready to go,

Mrs. Butler told me word had come from Charleston that her husband's compensation claim was denied. I asked her whether I could see the letter and take it to a young lawyer I know who works for an antipoverty group. She said yes, and gave me the letter.

"Someone who didn't know what 'organizing' is — at least up here in the mountains — might have thought I was wasting my time. The fact is people around here doubt very much that *anything* will really help them, any effort by any person. That's why they don't just go and spill all their worries to strangers, even ones like me who come from the same county or the same state. They're not only proud and suspicious, like all those government manuals for VISTA volunteers say; it's something else — maybe *plenty smart,* that's what they are. My father used those words about a year ago, when I practically recited from memory a description of the 'Appalachian subculture' I'd read in an anthropology and sociology course. The old man took a big puff on his pipe and said it all sounded very nice and important, but if I'd only stop and look at the facts of life around here and give the people credit for doing the same thing, then I'd be able to condense everything the professors say about the people up the hollows into the words *plenty smart.* Then Dad fired one question after another at me, like he was in court. What good would it do them if they *did* hurry, and talk a lot, and go demanding this and that? Do you have any idea what kind of tricky, two-faced people have gone up those hills, trying to sell people sugar pills, fake elixirs, and a share in the state capitol building in Charleston? And what has happened to the men who have left the hills and tried to get a fair deal for themselves in the outside world?

"It was Dad's best moment since the time he drank bourbon with me and talked about himself a little. He wouldn't go any further. He wouldn't answer his own questions. Who needs to answer them? Everyone should know the answers. But he made me realize that you can't understand what goes on up the hollows by reading books and going to those endless discussions with other VISTA people or the community action workers. We all sit around and say: look, they're like this and they're like that, and they've got this hang-up about strangers, and they're a whole 'subculture' and they have five 'traits,' and be sure and know all five if your superior asks you. Even my best friend would think I'm an idiot if I said the people up there in Winding Creek are plenty smart, but if I talked about the 'subculture' and the 'traits,' then I'd be real savvy. It's really discouraging to hear even older men from this county referring to 'traits' and 'subcultures'; I'm talking about intelligent men, but not college graduates, who have thrown their lot in with us, and become organizers, just like I am. There are at least a dozen of them I know in West Virginia and there are more in Kentucky; they are former miners or people from up a creek who are fed up with things and want to see changes take place. You get talking with them, and they tell you they'll help, and they do. But after a while they find it hard to get other people to go along, because people around here are plain scared; they're afraid they'll be cut from welfare, or their kids won't be picked up by the bus, or won't get their free lunch, or a hundred other things will happen that the courthouse crowd can do to you.

"Eventually those men get tired and discouraged, like all organizers do, and soon they start the analyzing routine, just like us students do. You hear Joe King, he's forty-seven and lived here in Mingo County all his life and knows everything there is to know, and he'll suddenly be saying that people are *suspicious* up there in the creek, and it's their *style*, he said last week, and all that kind of talk. But I know why he's begun to talk like that, use those words. He's beaten; the whole rotten system is too much for him — for anyone. When you realize you're up against a stone wall, the way things are now, the only thing you *can* do is adjust yourself to that fact. Since you don't want to get completely demoralized, you start looking for words and ideas that will make it a little easier for you. You shift the burden from the society as a whole and from you as an activist over to the people you're concerned with. Then things become a little easier to live with. Then you can say it's not the social and economic system in America or in Appalachia and it's not me and my moods. No, instead the blame is put on the people up in the hollows; it's their backwardness and suspiciousness and parochialism and resistance to change and rigid adherence to an outmoded kinship structure, and it's their isolation and their refusal to accommodate themselves to a technological society, and it's their fundamentalist religious beliefs and their here-and-now orientation. The words and formulas and theories are a dime a dozen!

"The truth is that the people in this region have tried *everything*. They fought their way out here and adjusted themselves to that. When businessmen came in here and tried to develop the region, use its timber and coal, they adjusted to that. In fact, they adjusted to the most advanced kind of technology — the mines with all their machinery, a lot of it now automated. The people up the hollows even adjusted to the 'war on poverty.' When we told them the war on poverty was geared to 'community participation' and all that, the people got together and did what they thought they should; they met and talked and agreed to meet some more and talk some more, and they decided what they wanted and what they needed, and they voted on every decision and they helped us fill out a million forms and put in a million applications — and of course, the whole thing turned out to be one more bitter disappointment. The other day, up in Turner's Hollow, I heard a mother put it as good as anyone has. She said: 'Ned, they've been tricking you, just like they've been tricking us.' I didn't know what she meant; or maybe I *did* and hoped I wasn't going to hear her say it. Anyway, I asked her what she was trying to say, and she wasn't long in coming up with her answer: 'They told you over in Washington that you should just go and tell those people to organize themselves and decide they're a community, and then they can take advantage of this program and the next one that the government has for communities. So you came and told us, and so did others; and then we did what Washington told us to do. We got a few dollars together, to plan for things, and we met and talked and applied for grants and programs and aid, any aid we could get. But suddenly the war on poverty was over. They told you there wasn't any money, no more of it for us. I hate to say it, but like my husband said, we knew all along that was going to be the way it would come out.' She kept going, and everything she said I'd already thought: that it's cruel to go and tease people, promise them things and when the chips are down have nothing to back up the promises."

He can go on and on, even as the mother in Turner's Hollow can. I have heard both of them do so, and it is hard to forget their indignation. Together they have learned something, the young man and the middle-aged lady, the college graduate and the dropout from a one-room schoolhouse, the son of a solid West Virginia lawyer and the wife of a jobless man who lives "up there" in Turner's Hollow and tries to grow enough on a few acres to keep a family of seven "this side of going without any food at all and dying, that's right, dying." If a mother in West Virginia has to speak that way about her family, a West Virginian youth like Ned has to speak this way about his country and his work: "The country can do anything it wants. The country can take billions and plan with them and spend them so it lands on the moon and dominates the oceans and has the strongest military power the world has ever seen; the country can spend billions under the Marshall Plan to rebuild the whole war-torn economy of Europe. But so far it hasn't done anything halfway significant for the people here, and the people are right, there's no reason to think that anything will be done.

"I was at a meeting last week, and we all got to talking, and they had some 'observers' there. That's what they called them, an expert on 'community action' one of them was, and an expert on 'group process' the other one was. We were all saying the same thing, what a rotten shame it is, the way things have gone in the sixties — the hopes raised and the disappointment. 'You all seem discouraged, depressed' the 'group process' guy said. I didn't say anything. No one did. Then he asked us if we wanted to *talk* about that, our discouragement. I couldn't take it any longer. I said no, I didn't; but I'd like for him to go over to Washington,

D.C., and get the President and some congressmen and ask them if *they* wanted to talk about anything."

When one like me gets to know a young man like Ned or his friends up there in Turner's Hollow, Mingo County, the issue of time becomes all important: what do I consider urgent and what does Ned consider inevitable? Why do my ambitions become translated into achievements, while in Turner's Hollow particular ambitions become gradually abandoned and ambition in general becomes frowned upon and mocked? I have talked with enough children in places like Turner's Hollow to know that, at the age of five or six, mountain children still have their dreams of glory and conquest, of advancement and accomplishment. Soon, though, they "learn," and in this case they learn something "life" teaches rather than schools; that is to say, they learn the futility of learning, the absurdity of ambition. They also learn about the hypocrisy of others and about their own desperate weakness — a vulnerability that will stay with them until they die, no matter what words and slogans and promises are directed their way. Who, then, is to say that such people are "suspicious" or "doubtful" or "egocentric" or "depressed" or "now-oriented," and all the other things they are called? Why don't we simply summarize the problem and call them "realistic," which means smart about the world, plain and simple smart about *their* world? Ned asks himself and others such questions, and in a flash can supply a brief, sharp, bitter reply: "No one wants to see a lot of what goes on in this country. So, if you can call the next guy 'under the weather,' or something that implies he's next to hopeless and always will be, it helps you yourself feel a little better. *He's* backward and discouraged — so that means *you* can go on enjoying your comfortable life and not look the whole, mean, unfair political and economic setup right in the eye. I guess if a lot more of us were discouraged, and as angry as we should be, then there'd be a little chance of changing things; and if things were changed, we'd be surprised at how different these people would act. But that's not the way it's going to be."

Like his friends up in Turner's Hollow, Ned is thoroughly disheartened, is at a genuine loss to know what to do and needs "help," though I do not believe it is clinical help he wants or needs, nor the sort of help that offers social and psychological theories to explain and even justify the existence of problems which in essence have to do with money and power, with the absence of jobs and the presence of joblessness, with the way natural resources are plucked from one region for the almost exclusive profit of a handful who live in another region. People like me are destined (it may be a measure of the futility of *our* lives) to study what happens to the minds and souls of those caught up in such harsh economic and political circumstances, but certainly Ned is right. Our study must constantly specify who is responding to what, lest our readers believe that "traits" or "attitudes" or even things like "subcultures" or "social systems" are givens, with an ongoing life of their own, and not the significant result of a particular kind of history, a particular set of laws, a particular distribution of rights and obligations, and again, in the blunt, earthy way that youths like Ned Williams put it, a particular alignment of both money and power. To Ned, many of the difficult and special attitudes to be found in Turner's Hollow have their origins in the "bossing" that goes on. Ned feels "no one should be bossed around," but Ned knows that hundreds of hollows are full of thousands of people who are bossed around all the time in ways both clear-cut and devious. And that knowledge of his does indeed make for despair — an old-fashioned, nonclinical, nonpsychiatric word which conveys the mixed sadness and bitterness Ned shares with so many mountaineers.

In any event, Ned once proposed a way of resolving some of these philosophical and intellectual and theoretical issues: "This is supposed to be a country where people love to try new things; and social scientists are always looking for new 'experiments' to do. Why doesn't someone bring in *real* opportunities to these people: good jobs and good sanitation and good housing and doctors — in short, tangible evidence of a decent way of life? Then all of you could study the people here, see how 'resistant' they are, and how long it takes them to shake off their backwardness and fatalism and lose their suspiciousness and jump into it — a halfway decent kind of life."

3. *Owning Them*

Again and again in the section devoted to Appalachian children, the officials of county courthouses are roundly denounced — by people who feel aggrieved in general, and in particular feel at the mercy of officials an outsider would simply look upon as men and women elected or appointed to do some of the public's business. For a time I wondered whether those officials weren't mere scapegoats, upon whom the legitimate and accumulated wrath of a confused, hurt and frustrated people could be spent. Maybe in some instances that is precisely what has happened; certainly hungry, jobless people need scapegoats — and in a rural setting those scapegoats may not be so readily available. On the other hand, some county officials have said things to me — not to mention what they have *done* to the people they supposedly represent and work for — that make the resentment and even outrage that they inspire seem rather plausible, to put it mildly.

In a region that lacks a well-developed and strongly diversified economy, a school system can become a major source of money and work and favors, and a sheriff and his men can be a law unto themselves, with few of the checks and balances, sources of protest and pressure and appeal, open to urban residents of, say, Massachusetts or Illinois or California. In some counties of Kentucky and West Virginia one or two families run everything; they control the judge's office and the sheriff's office and they have their man as the superintendent of schools. It is impossible for those who live scattered up the hollows and creeks to defy such "authorities" without paying one or several harsh penalties. As some of our witnesses have already pointed out, the school bus can be diverted, the school lunches stopped, and the sheriff can appear with all sorts of potential complaints on his mind. Still, just as the mountaineers keep on charging various county officials with prejudice and bias, with feathering nests and diverting money from rightful causes to their own causes, certain of those county officials speak openly and directly about the mountaineers. I was inclined to think that the opposite would hold, that sheriffs and school superintendents, who can be incredibly sullen and guarded when even a friendly outsider appears for a more or less conventional visit, would most assuredly have second and third and tenth thoughts about talking at all (let alone at some length) with a doctor from the East who lugs around a tape recorder and (such is the way news travels in Appalachia) has been reported as spending X amount of time with Y people — most of them up in the hollows and creeks. Perhaps it was curiosity, perhaps a desire to set the record straight, perhaps a determination to have one's say, or perhaps it was all of that and a gesture of genuine interest and goodwill; whatever the reasons or explanations, I was given a good deal of time by various county officials, and I heard in substantial detail their views, their likes and dislikes, their worries and fears — yes, fears, hard though it may be for the region's hundreds of thousands of poor people to believe about people so commonly and openly considered the oppressor.

In a county of eastern Kentucky, one like Wolfe County or Breathitt County, I heard this from an important school official: "I know we're not the most popular people, especially with those VISTAS and the others you've been talking with. A delegation of them came over to see me a few months ago and they ended up shouting at me. I hadn't said much of anything to them. They had their list of grievances, and I listened to them. Then I asked them where the *people* were — my people, the people of this county. They jumped on me. What right did I have to talk about 'my people'? Who did I think I was? Where did I get the idea that I owned people, like possessions? They went on and on. I waited and waited, and I was ready to tell them politely that I didn't mean what I said the way they took it, but I was just trying to distinguish between *them* and *us* — and 'us' means me and everyone else who comes from around here and will be around here long after they've gone somewhere else with their 'social uplift' or whatever they want to call it.

"I've never seen the likes of some of these VISTA types and all the other types Washington, D.C., has been paying to come here and go up our hollows and get the people all upset and bothered and scared. They're masters of the big lie. There's no other way to say it. Take that delegation I just mentioned. They said they were in my office because I was punishing people who are working with VISTA, putting the VISTA volunteers up in their homes to live. They said I was rerouting buses and cheating the children on their lunches. That's the biggest lie I've ever heard. Why didn't some of the mothers themselves come over here to my office? My family has been here as long as anyone's. I was elected to serve the people of this county, and that's what I'm doing. They want me to bring Communist literature into the schools. They want us to teach revolution. They want to vote me out and vote in some guy who can barely read and write, on the grounds that he's from the 'people.' They say all we do is bribe people and control them — that's what they've got on their brain, the idea of 'control'; because we pay people salaries for the work they do we're supposed to 'control' them. What do they want me to do, *not* pay salaries? If we pay our teachers and they work all over the county, we're called the 'biggest industry in the county,' and we're supposed to be 'holding on to our power' just because we have jobs and are trying to run a school system for children who need it real, real bad, I'll tell you that.

"I don't know what those 'organizers' are really after. They go around digging into records and asking questions of everybody who will talk to them (and thank God most people won't) and then they write up those things and use their mimeograph machine — which they've got installed in an office the federal government pays for, the government I pay my taxes to — to reproduce all the distortions and made-up stories and rumors and gossip and wild allegations and spiteful accusations they've collected. The worst thing they can say about me, in their estimation, is that me and my family get good salaries, and we're in good jobs, and we live like comfortable people do, and we keep on getting reelected. Now I ask you, what are they really trying to say? What are they trying to get the poor people of this county to believe? I'll tell you. They're trying to destroy this county, and in the long run, they're after the state of Kentucky and all the other states, the whole country. Listen, I'm no right-wing fanatic.

I'm a Democrat. I'm a liberal. I was for Roosevelt; I voted for him the first time I voted — and for Truman and Adlai Stevenson and John Kennedy and Lyndon Johnson. I blame some of this trouble on John Kennedy, though. He trusted a lot of these kids too much. He gave them the idea they could go all over the place and upset whatever they wanted to, and if anyone complains and tries to give them advice, then he's called those names they have; they call me a reactionary, and an exploiter, and they say I'm a feudal baron, and I'm guilty of nepotism. To listen to them I'm the biggest monster the mountains have ever had around.

"I come to work at nine and I'm here until six, and sometimes later. All day I try to make sure this county has a good school system. I try to hire good teachers and fire bad ones. I try to get money from the state government and the federal government — for our teachers, so that we can buy the best equipment and build the schools we need. I try to make sure our buses are as safe as can be, and the drivers are the best qualified we have. I go over the bus routes so we keep the driving time down to a minimum. I go to all the professional meetings I can, and I go visit educators here in Kentucky, in Lexington and Louisville, and also in Ohio. I go to Cincinnati a lot. I try to do reading, all I can; and I encourage my staff to keep up with the latest developments, because we want our little children to get the finest education they possibly can, and we want them equipped to live in the modern world, not only the hollows of this county. I visit our schools all the time, and I keep on telling the teachers and the children that they've got to remember one thing: we're part of something larger; we're living in a big country, and we've got to know all about that country and keep up with what's going on out there.

"When these radical-type men and women come here they tell me I don't know anything about education, and I'm just a politician. Most of them are fresh out of college or still in college, and the ones who are older try to look as if they're college students, the hippie type, who look like the hobos used to look like. These so-called volunteers and 'service corps' types try to pretend they're poor, and they'll tell you they're the ones who represent the poor and speak for them, and should be in charge of what we do for them up in the hollow. I've listened to them. I'm a lot more polite than they are. I've asked them to come and talk with me, and I've sat through their accusations and tried to explain my-self — explain what my responsibilities are. We've met several times, and each time it comes down to this: they say I'm 'run-ning' the county, and my family is, and I'm punishing my political enemies and rewarding my friends with jobs in the schools. I've asked them for the proof. They mention a couple of stories they've heard up a creek or two, and when I try to explain what happened and why, they tell me I'm trying to hide the truth behind 'bureaucratic language.' What can you do with people like that? They've decided that they're the judge and the jury; and when they come here to talk with me, they're not interested in one word I have to say; all they want is to call me names and tell me how bad my family is, and the judge's family — how bad all of us are who work here in the courthouse and the school department offices.

"You know, I agree with them, more than they'd ever believe. I agree with them that the poor we have here are bad off, and we don't have the money to give them. I agree we need help from outside. And I'm opposed to the strip-mining that goes on. I'm in favor of progress — more and better education and medical clinics for those who can't afford to see a doctor. It's on *philos-ophy* that we disagree. They want to turn the whole society upside down. And some of them are the rudest people I've ever met in my entire life. If the people up the hollows heard some of the language I've heard from these so-called leaders, they'd be shocked. We're brought up to be polite, God-fearing people, and self-respecting, too. We don't go around insulting each other and using blasphemous language and flaunting ourselves in public. A lot of these young men and women come from New York and California, and you can see it on them, how *happy* they are — because they've found some poor people up here in the moun-tains and now they can try to boss them around and tell them what they need and what they should say and do. When I finally got them to bring their 'community people' in — that's all they keep on talking about, 'community this' and 'community that' — I noticed the people didn't say hardly one word, not one. They sat there and nodded and said 'yes sir' to everything that bunch of loudmouthed college kids mentioned. Afterwards I went up to them, as they were leaving, and I told them I know them and their kin, and we had a good talk, and one of them looked real sheepish and he apologized to me. He said, 'I'm sorry if you feel bad over all this. We didn't mean to cause trouble.' Then, do you know what the organizers told *him?* They told him, 'If you're going to get any changes around here, you've got to cause trouble, and the more you cause the better.' That's what they said. That's their philosophy — just keep on stepping on people's toes and insulting them and causing trouble on the streets, with the picket signs and demonstrating and all the rest. Well, the country is fed up with them, and so are we, here in this county. The people of Kentucky are conservative people; they like to be kind to each other, even if they come from different backgrounds. We're not going to put up with these types; anyway, after a while it'll turn out they're all leaders and no followers. Up there in the hollows you have a decent kind of person who isn't going to go shouting at others and demanding everything in the whole wide world and *right now* — as if they are kings and queens. No sir, around here each of us knows his place."

He certainly knows his place. He can quite willingly talk about the leadership he must provide, and the "passivity" of most people in the county. When he is not angry and put on the defensive by all those "agitators," he allows himself to be quite open and direct and candid about the "differences" between people, which he firmly believes are there, are inherited, are part of God's way of distinguishing between His millions and millions of children. He states categorically his conclusions, his ideas about the world; and in a way they are very similar to the ones held by those hardy if impoverished mountaineers he seems both to admire and feel just a bit ashamed of. Life is hard; the Lord's ways are inscrutable; a man's fate is largely determined by his family's circumstances; and a man's proper destiny is the fulfillment of that fate in the quietest, most obliging manner possible.

Of course, changes must come, must even be demanded — and not only by those who manifestly need them, but by those few who spend their lives "providing leadership," to use one of his favorite expressions. At heart he seems truly convinced that he does just what such an expression literally means; which is to say he, the leader, looks out in advance and decides what is to be done.

Perhaps all of that smacks of *noblesse oblige,* of paternalism (to use the term so commonly applied to his philosophy by those youths he so dreads) and also of real arrogance and condescension as well as a kind of guileful innocence or naïveté. Perhaps, alternatively, everything he says is meant to deceive a listener like me, or at the very least draw a curtain over and conceal the concrete economic and political issues which those noisy, insistent, indelicate, and utterly determined activists keep harping on. And, far worse, he transforms those activists into "agitators" when they bring up all the unnerving, grisly, embarrassing details that more polished, courteous, and refined people have learned to ignore, indeed actively shun. The youths a superintendent calls with complete disdain "activists" have their counterparts among well-bred people who, as the superintendent would be the first to assert, have an activism of their own: there are some things one simply doesn't think about, nor even mention. If it takes work, painstaking and exhausting psychological *activity,* to make sure the mind does its required job of ignoring such matters, then all to the good, because there is nothing quite as rewarding as an achievement that has cost something. So, an intelligent and industrious school official, a self-declared leader of his people, an important official of a terribly poor and hard-pressed county of a state that is not among the richest in America can earnestly and almost plaintively propose this kind of "solution" to me: "The Bible says we'll always have our poor, and maybe that's true; but I do believe here in the United States we can do a lot for our people, I mean the ones that can't find work. The solution is more education. Don't you think so? If we had these people up in the hollows really educated, then the whole poverty problem would be solved. A man with a good education, he won't sit back and do nothing but grow a few vegetables and make his moonshine and go hunting. He'll want to have a job, a trade, a profession. He'll want to live better. He'll want to be a part of the rest of the world, and not be by himself up there in the hills.

"I hate to admit it, but some of the things said about our 'hillbillies' are true. They *do* behave like little children at times, and often they really discourage their sons and daughters from learning, so our teachers have a very hard time teaching. I once told a group of those VISTA people all that, and they got excited and said I was being 'proprietary' and I was underestimating them — my own schoolchildren, children I've known for over three decades! I answered them right back. I said: a lot of you talk as if *you* have the right to be proprietary to the poor we have here in the county. If I sound proprietary I sound just the way I *want* to sound, because they *are* my children, my schoolchildren. It's my job to make sure they have good schools, and I'm glad I'm proprietary about them. I own them, just like you say, from the first thing in the morning until they go home in the afternoon.

"I figured that was the only way — just answer them right back. Of course, the VISTAS started telling people that I was a slave owner, that I even looked upon myself as one because I talked about 'owning them,' the children. Well, of course I 'own' the children. I'm the head of the whole county school system. My brother is the judge in this county. Between us we've got to feel responsible for these people; a lot of them don't feel responsible for themselves. They don't eat the right food. They waste their money on silly things, trinkets and those guitars they're always playing. They're not economical — and if anybody needs to be economical, it's them. Some of our people have relatives up in Ohio and Illinois, and they get money from them — and it's tragic, I'd say that, *tragic* how they spend the money: on silly, useless gadgets and toys and things like that, a dress or a suit that's too fancy for around here, instead of something they can really use. That's why they need to be educated, you see. When I told what I just said to those college kids — that's what they all are, even if they're thirty and thirty-five and drawing a salary from the federal government — do you know they said I was crazy, out of my head. They said I could educate everyone in the county until they all had their college diplomas, and then there still wouldn't be jobs for them. I replied that they were trying to put the cart before the horse. First we have to educate our people; they're nearly illiterate, the parents of many of our schoolchildren. When everyone in this county is well educated, then they'll go and get jobs; they'll make jobs. They'll attract industry in here. I don't know how; that's not my responsibility. My cousin is on the county's planning commission, and he says you can't beat education. The more educated people are, the better jobs they get. You ask any teacher here, she'll tell you the same thing: our kids need to stay in school longer and not drop out and not be listening to a lot of troublemakers who come in here and promise them quick ways to get rich, when it's the long road of learning that will solve our problem here, and in every other county of eastern Kentucky."

4. Like My Teacher

I did what the county superintendent said I should do; I went to see some teachers, and I asked them questions, asked them about how things go, and what is right and what is wrong — with the schools, with the children, with the county, with "life in general." I had been talking with teachers anyway, but the super-intendent had a very good idea, I came to realize while I was once in his office. His teachers should be given a chance to hear some of his ideas, and perhaps corroborate what he has to say, or differ with him, or in any case let me know what they see and think about the county's social and political setup, and what they think about the way mountain children grow up. (A question about a county's social and political setup at some point always becomes a question about the lives of children, something not all of us observers of children manage to keep in mind.)

The particular teacher I am now writing about, like many who teach mountain children, has for herself alone what some of us might call "eight grades." She doesn't worry about grades or grading, however. She doesn't even want to test her children, "just teach them all I can." Some might consider her school "inadequate"; the building is old, and there are no teaching machines or pieces of "audio-visual" equipment. The books are weathered, their pages well thumbed and often enough torn. The maps aren't up to date, but then which ones are? I guess I would have to say the maps are less up to date than those I've seen in other schools elsewhere. Yet, the children love to look at the maps, probably because their teacher loves maps and always has: "To me a map is the most exciting thing to have on the wall. I can walk over to it and look at it and get talking about a country or a city or a continent or an ocean, and the next thing I know the children are all gathered around me and we're having a wonderful time. They want to know if it's like Breathitt County or Wolfe County, Kentucky, in Bolivia or Egypt. They want to know about mountains especially. Maybe they get to competing in their minds. One child will tell me that there may be bigger mountains in Asia or Switzerland — the children always ask me if I've been to a place when we talk about it — but it's better to live here. I have such fun looking at those places on the map and reading about them with the children in our geography books and the *National Geographic*s we get here, that I frankly think I'd be disappointed if I ever did get to see the places themselves. It's like anything else; you can do a lot better in your imagination than anything real can ever be."

She loves to teach; she loves the children she teaches. She has two children of her own and she taught them too — right in that school of hers. (Two girls, they both are preparing themselves for careers in teaching.) She has seen other schools, has heard how "primitive" and "out of date" and "antiquated" the one-room schoolhouse is. She tires of going to meetings in Frankfort or Lexington or Louisville and hearing those words, and even worse, hearing her fellow teachers apologize for those one-room schoolhouses — "in this day and age," as someone always adds, she says. She has some thoughts about "this day and age." She also has some thoughts about that one-room schoolhouse of hers — that large, large room with the old-fashioned desks, each of them fixed firmly on the floor and all of them lined up in straight rows: "I love this room, this school. So do the children. I don't see why we should apologize for what we have. Before I came here I taught in a 'regular' school, just after I got my degree. My husband was killed in the war, World War Two, and I thought at the time, after the war, that with my mother and my two little girls, the last thing I'd want to do was live out here, where my granddad had his farm. We all wanted to live in the city, and we did, until Granddaddy died, and we thought it was best to come back and stay with my brother and help him out. He was fighting to keep the place, and as a teacher I could help him out, because a steady wage can go a long way here.

"It was strange coming back here at first, and I immediately asked when they were going to put an end to this one-room school and 'regionalize' — that's all you hear at the state teachers' meetings, regionalize, regionalize. Thank God, we've been left alone. The families up the hollow nearby trust me and the school, and the children want very much to come here. They wouldn't send their children far away, they just wouldn't. And no one would ever dare go up those hollows to tell their parents off; no sir they wouldn't dare. Around here parents don't go worshiping at the feet of teachers, or anyone else; but neither do parents go pushing teachers around, and demanding Heaven itself from a poor, struggling teacher. If you're good with the children, the word travels and the children show up regularly, even in the middle of our worst winter storms, which as you know are very, very bad."

She is quite genuinely modest; when I commented on the fact that the children to my eye showed up every single day, she blushed. She had in fact been describing her own ability to reach out and become someone very important to children, but she was embarrassed, and she felt obligated to describe her work as a teacher rather than analyze her own particular qualities. Of course, what makes her the good teacher she is has to do with precisely those personal qualities she possesses in such abundance: enthusiasm, flexibility, warmth, and a kindness that is sure enough of itself to take expression as firmness, even sternness. She is not very interested in political matters, and in fact shuns controversy. She does not even think of her children as "poor" or "disadvantaged" or "deprived." In fact, she gets very proper and formal and a bit officious as she starts talking about some of the same young people her ultimate superior, the county's superintendent of schools, goes on about so critically and at such length. I have to admit that for a long time I was hard put to accept the remarks that follow as coming from the same woman I watched teach so admiringly: "I've met some of the 'volunteer teachers,' I guess that's what they are. They're from VISTA and from various colleges, some of the colleges quite far away. I welcome all the help that I can possibly get. I don't mean to sound ungrateful or petty, and I want you to know that I may be terribly wrong about what I'm going to say. I'm not even sure I should say it; but I will, I think because I *have* to. My mind has been worrying over some of these problems so hard these past few months that I believe it will actually help me to speak out loud what I've kept to myself.

"To be absolutely aboveboard with you, I have found some of these young people, especially the ones from out of state, from the East or the far West, more than a little troubling. They come and say they want to do anything, anything at all to help. They offer themselves to you so fully and generously that I feel like a traitor saying one single disapproving word about them. But I must, because for their own sake they must understand how some of us feel. I'm not worried now about how *I* feel, but how the people near here do, the very people these students and young teachers and lawyers and — community-action experts, is it? — claim they want to help. I spoke to my minister about my reactions to some of them, and I told him that maybe I was just being jealous, the way my girls are of each other and my brother and I still can be. I mean here I am, trying to be a first-grade teacher and a second-grade teacher and on up to the eighth grade, though most of the children around here don't stay in school that long. Then these young people come and say this is wrong and that is wrong, and they're full of ideas and energy, and they have promises about what will happen if the people go and organize and get help from Washington — and perhaps I just resent their knowledge and sophistication. They seem to be so *aware;* they can quote laws to you, and they can tell you what's happening all over the world and make it out to be as though everything happening everywhere is part of what is going on right here, up these couple of hollows that send children to our little school. Let me be clear: I don't disagree with what they say; I just find them — well, it's hard to put into words. I think the word that comes into my mind most often is 'bold,' in the sense, I'm afraid, of being 'fresh' and a trifle full of themselves. My aunt used to tell me when I was young and would tell her she was nice, but she just didn't know all that *I* was learning and knew — she'd tell me to stop being so 'bold' and mind my manners. She meant that before I get too sold on myself, I'd better actually go and find out a little more carefully exactly what she *did* know, and why she acted the way she did and what she believed and wanted out of life. 'We're not as far apart as you think,' she'd also tell me. I think of her sometimes when I talk with these young 'activists,' I guess they like to be known as.

"Let me give you an example. One day two of them came to see me. They'd been living up the creek and were doing a wonderful job helping out the families there. They had helped the children read better, and with their own hands built a fine bridge over the creek. They were tutoring the children and playing games with them all the time and going on hikes with them and really being wonderful to them — and for them. They came to see me to offer their help to me, and I was delighted when they did finally come. I took an immediate liking to them; I'm being honest on that. They seemed bright and sincere and full of more energy than I'd ever before seen in two people. One was a teacher, about twenty-five I'd say; the other was just out of college and told me she wasn't sure what she wanted to do, but she was here because she liked the mountains and the people here, and that was enough for her, and it sounded just right to me. We talked for about an hour, and I was so enthusiastic about them that I was ready to have them join me in teaching, and if they couldn't get any money from the school board I was ready to help them out of my own pocket, if they needed anything extra. They were getting their room and board with the families, and the families were being reimbursed by the program they were part of — so they told me no, not to worry about them.

"We actually sat down to plan our activities — and that was when the trouble began. I had some old *National Geographics* around, as I always do, and one of the two, the older one, the teacher, picked up a copy, and it had something about one of the Latin American countries, I forget which — Brazil or Colombia or Paraguay. She asked me whether the children looked at the magazines much, and I said, 'Oh yes, and so do I.' Then she started in. She began by questioning me. Did I know who 'ran' the magazine and what their political 'orientation' is? Do I think their 'perspective' is the one the children should have? I didn't really have time to answer the questions; they were asked more as a statement, as rhetorical questions I suppose it could be said. I finally did get my few words in. I said I have always loved to get my hands on copies of the *National Geographic*. I said I love the pictures; I love the words, the stories; I love the subject matter. I said I hadn't really thought about the political position of the magazine. To me the magazine brought the whole, wide world right to my small world, here in this county. I said the children waited for copies of that magazine more than anything else and fought with one another over who can have it and for how long. Oh, I said a lot; and it was only in the middle of my speech that I realized I *was* giving a speech, and that I was quite upset and angrier than I recall being in many, many years. When I first started teaching, some of our county school officials, including the superintendent you have met and they so dislike, tried to tell me what I should have in my classroom in the way of pictures and magazines. They visited the school, and believe it or not, *they* were upset over the *National Geographic*, too — and over *Life*. In both magazines there were pictures of natives, scantily dressed, and that bothered the superintendent. He was afraid our children would tell their parents, and trouble would follow. I wondered at the time why they were suddenly so concerned about what the parents might say or do; usually the parents are ignored when decisions are made. If the county officials don't like a certain man, or even a whole hollow full of people, they'll do things like reroute the school bus to get even and keep them in line, the poor people. But suddenly they were worried about the sensitivity of our families!

"Anyway, to get back to the poor old *National Geographic Magazine*, and those 'organizers.' You know that's what they told me they really are, and they're good at that, organizing everyone else. I'm not sure they're as organized themselves, though. I know I'm sounding petty and sarcastic, but I didn't even know what they meant about a magazine being 'reactionary,' a magazine like the *National Geographic*. If they were as good at 'organizing' people as they want to be, they would go slower and not only with me. They've pushed things with some people up the hollow, too — so that they now have their strong supporters and their bitter enemies, and all in only a few months. One of them said it was 'polarization,' and it was to the good and had to happen, but I really wonder. To what effect, for what purpose, does it *have* to happen — polarization? In a place like this, even if everyone were totally behind them there wouldn't be much we could do but march on the county seat. What would happen then? Our county is poor. Our county government only has a limited amount of money. We need industry from the outside — but these people look down on industry as being 'exploitative.' They're not only against the coal companies — so am I, for what they've done to our people and for their callousness, their awful, awful greed — but they're against all companies, all industry. They say so. They want jobs for the people here, but they don't like corporations, wherever they are! They don't even like the *National Geographic Magazine!*

"I had better finish with that subject! I told them I wasn't going to have them talking so critically about me or the children or anything we read. I told them they could hold any political viewpoint they wanted, but to pick up a magazine and start looking at it like they did and making the remarks they did — I just wouldn't sit back and let that kind of behavior go unnoticed. I said more, but I've forgotten exactly what. From that day on we've never been too friendly. I know what they think, because one of them, the younger one, is very open and frank with me. She told me once that she didn't have anything *personal* against me; it's just that I'm part of a rotten, corrupt, exploitative system, and I've had my mind affected by that system, just like everyone else. Perhaps she is right. How can I possibly know? I have no background in politics or economics or whatever they claim to know so much about. But I am a human being, as they are, and I have the right to judge the manners, the attitude, the behavior of other human beings, including these two women I've welcomed here and had teaching beside me these past few months, and including their friends, who come up here from all over Kentucky and West Virginia. And I've gone to some of their meetings, too. I've listened to about fifty of them argue with one another and lead discussions for people like me. What I'm trying to say is this: I find a lot of these young 'organizers' intelligent and idealistic and almost unbelievably self-sacrificing. They want to help people, and no one who has worked with them can honestly doubt that. I have no use at all for what you hear in the county courthouse or from the coal operators, or I regret to say, from some of our newspaper reporters and editors. Thank God for the *Louisville Courier-Journal*. I get it by mail, and it's a fine, fine paper, and an antidote to some other papers in Kentucky! On the other hand, I have to say that I find some of these same young people arrogant, *very* arrogant at times.

"I realize you've heard what I say elsewhere, but I can only tell you how I truly feel. Maybe it's because some of them are young. Actually, I've met a lot of young people in my life, though never, never such a brash, assertive, aggressive and — I'll say it — overbearing type. If they don't agree with what you read or what you say, they'll not hesitate for a minute to tell you that you're part of some terrible 'system,' or you're being used for some God-awful 'reactionary' purpose. The kinder ones, the more likable ones, at least have a sense of humor and really, in my opinion, are more interested in helping people than broadcasting all those political ideas they feel they have to tell you about. But there are some who are as brittle and humorless as anyone I've ever met in my

entire life. They call some of our ministers names, but they themselves remind me of the most unattractive ministers I've met: the
ones full of talk about Hell and Damnation, but without an
ounce of charity and forgiveness and plain, ordinary friendliness
and — well, I don't know what word to use, how to describe
what I'm trying to say, but perhaps *graciousness* is the word.

"I just wish people so determined to help other people would
show a little respect for those people, would see that those people
aren't *only* poor and exploited, and ignorant and manipulated.
I'm tired of hearing about that, about how 'manipulated' we all
are, and how 'clever' and 'calculating' everyone from the editors
of the *National Geographic* to our local officials are. I don't believe people are as mischievous and designing and crafty as these
young organizers say they are. There is a lot wrong with our
country; but there's a lot right with it, too. I've said that out loud
to some of the young activists — we can kid one another a *little*
bit now! — and they always come right back at me. They tell me
I'm well to do; not rich, they'll admit, but on a 'good salary.' I
wish I was making a lot more than eighty dollars a week, after all
these years, but they are right: compared to what so very many
people in this county have, or I should say, *don't* have, I *am* rich.
But does that mean I think like an exploiter and act like one?
Does that mean my every opinion is suspect? Does that mean I
would think differently if I were getting zero dollars a week?
They should actually know better, because there are men and
women up those hollows who would make me sound like a
Communist if they started talking about politics. They are as
poor as anyone can be, but they won't take a cent of welfare, and
they're as proud and independent as can be. They hate the
county officials, but they would also hate people coming up from
Washington and telling them what to do. They talk like Henry
Ford used to talk — yes, I have my children read a book that
portrays him and Thomas Edison and Harvey Firestone as good
and valuable people. My young organizer friends were horrified!

"I guess I'm not making sense. It's hard. I feel close to the
ideals some of these new people advocate — and they *are* new,
new to this region. But they have to convince others than me, and

they have to figure out how to change the whole county, the whole state. I don't think they've succeeded. Maybe our people just won't realize what their own best interests are. Maybe outsiders have trouble knowing us, while there aren't enough 'insiders' ready to go far out on a limb, ready ourselves to be 'organizers' and 'activists,' like my two young lady friends keep on telling me they are, and I am not. I am, as they say, a teacher, and I am like any teacher, like any teacher you'll be talking with here in the mountains. I want my children to get a glimmer of a world I'm afraid they'll never get to know very well. I mean the world of words and drawings, of foreign countries and music. Maybe I *should* start right in with the first graders: tell them how they're going to be used and abused by those 'powerful interests,' tell them how the rich get richer and we stay poor, most of us within sight or sound of this school and all the other schools in the county. But you know, I think my children already are aware of a lot of that. And I'm not saying that because I want to excuse myself. I'm ready to plead guilty to all their charges. Once, at a meeting they had — about twenty of them attended — they called us teachers 'brainwashers' and 'agents of the system,' and at the end of the meeting, the conference, I said it can be reassuring to know how bad you are. That's right! We all feel guilty about things, and we all wonder how bad we are; but after that weekend I *knew* how bad I am, and that's reassuring!

"If some of our idealistic young community organizers would only work as hard listening to children as they say they are working (and I believe they are) to rescue those children from the evils of our society, then it might not be so important to worry about me and my *National Geographic* magazines. I remember the time a second-grade child, a girl of seven she was, pointed out to me a picture in that awful, reactionary magazine. It was, as the two young ladies would say, a rather sentimental picture of very poor people in India and Pakistan. But for all the Kodachrome and the emphasis on Indian clothes and textiles and majestic buildings (temples and a university, I believe) there were still the faces of the Indian people; and a little girl from up our creek — not a very bright girl from not the most alert and intelligent of our families — that little girl saw those faces and sensed something in them that was familiar to her, that was in her also: maybe hunger, maybe a kind of desperation that none of us who are reasonably comfortable will ever really know about, however sympathetic we try to be. Anyway, the girl turned to me and said she thought some of the people there in the pictures were like her daddy. I couldn't for the life of me figure out what she had in her mind, what she was saying; and I was almost afraid to ask. How could some people in New Delhi, or wherever, remind this little girl of her daddy? Well, she told me. She said they 'looked worried,' even if it *was* 'pretty in the picture.' Like any teacher, I tried to point out the difference between our state of Kentucky and the subcontinent of India, and the similarities as well. But you don't forget a moment like that because, like any teacher, you've learned something from one of your children.

"Children teach us all the time. I hope they'll teach some of their new friends, the young people here to help change our society; because like any teacher, any *good* teacher I guess I should say, or any teacher *trying* to be good — it's so hard! — an organizer or an activist ought to learn something every once in a while, and not go from day to day with the idea that he or she is the source of all wisdom, the one who is put here to lift up others, educate them, make them better. I believe I am being the best kind of teacher on a day when a child makes me stop and think and realize how seriously I have overestimated my own importance. I'm afraid those days aren't as numerous as they should be. Like any teacher, or most of us human beings, I'm more often a failure than not. I suppose it's misery that's liking company now, but I do believe what holds for me and other teachers, holds just as much for these fine young people, who want to give so much to our poor people and understand them — but who fail to take enough opportunities to *accept* from these people and *learn* from them and see what they *have* as well as what they don't have, and lack, and need and should get from the society.

"I truly believe what I just said; I think it's what I believe more than anything else. The organizers always talk about the 'ideology' we're all supposed to have, whether we know it or not. Well, what I just said, that's my ideology. I don't care what *they* say my ideology is; to me, that's it. The reason is that I know in my heart how much I've come to learn from these children. Why, they've helped me grow up and be as wise and observant and — yes, grown up — as they are! That's what they can do for you. When I'm not angry at some political outburst from our 'volunteers,' I pray that our children will help them as much as they've helped me. At least these activists are here, living with and working with those children — which is a lot more than I can say for our county officials, who run and just about own our schools and never spend as much as a minute in a classroom, or God forbid, up a hollow. You see, every time I get angry at our radicals, I switch over a few seconds later, when I remember that they are complaining about things I long ago gave up complaining about. What do they call it, the generation gap? We'll always have one, a gap between parents and children; but these young people here, trying to shake us all up, won't let us forget our failures, and if I get angry with them, I want to make it clear I'm more for them than against them. I wish their ideals would come true, and for all their faults, I'd rather have *them* running our school system than our present officials, who may have short, nicely combed hair, and neckties and proper manners — but oh do they rob and cheat our children of what they need and deserve. You question God Himself when you get to know how a few families own everything here — the mines, the stores, the schools, the courts, the police."

5. *God Cannot Be Questioned*

If a schoolteacher can have her moments of religious doubt and skepticism, a minister who lives nearby has no such inclination, or so he emphatically maintains. The teacher and the minister know one another, though she attends a quiet Methodist church in a town, whereas he is an outspokenly evangelical minister whose church is far out of town and draws upon the

people who live up the hollows and creeks. No so-called generation gap separates him from those young activists who have
appeared in the county in recent years; unlike the teacher, he is in
his early thirties and looks to be around twenty-five. He is a tall,
thin man with wavy blond hair and penetrating eyes. (If all fiery
fundamentalist ministers are said to have those penetrating eyes,
only some of them actually do. This young minister, in my opinion, has a thyroid condition.) But there is something more than
what doctors would call an "exophthalmic problem secondary to
goiter" at work in him. He is a fiercely devoted man of God; and
he has energy, enormous amounts of drive and force and will. He
is restless, too; he loves to move from one church to the other on
"temporary stints," even though he does have that one church in
that one county of eastern Kentucky as a main responsibility. He
will dash off here or there in midweek to spread the Word, hold a
revival, feel the "wondrous joy" of souls coming forth and pro-
claiming themselves saved, saved at last — and time is so
precious, he says, because there is so little of it given us: we are
put here for a brief period of testing, and soon, all too soon, we
are called back — by a God who is watching our every move and
mood, our every wink and blink.

The minister's people — and he unashamedly calls them that,
"my people," in a possessive as well as affiliative way — do indeed feel watched by him as well as Him: "I make no effort to
deceive my people into feeling that I'm with them for a couple of
hours on Sunday, and that is that. No, I'm with them all the time,
or at least most of the time. I hope I'm with them when I'm
away, too. I hope they hear my words and heed them. I know
one thing: they say I'm the 'visitingest minister that ever was,'
and I'd like to believe that's true. I try to go up and down the
hollows and creeks; that's where the Lord is, you know. Where
men suffer, God is there. I believe that. He gave Himself over to
the poor, to the suffering. He asked all of us who preach His
Words to live a simple life, and not be like those Pharisees. That's
why I'm not interested in politics and all those social issues you
hear people talking about these days. Jesus Christ knew that
when ministers get involved in politics, when they become men

of money and power, they are Pharisees, corrupt and full of empty, hollow rules. Jesus offers us Life not Death — Eternal Life. If my people spend all their time worrying about this law or that program, they will lose sight of something much more important, Eternity Itself. That's why I make sure I go from home to home during the week; I sit and talk and take out my Bible, and I read a passage or two and when I leave I can see in the eyes of the people a new glow, a happiness. They thank me for coming, but it's not me, it's the Lord Who has come to be with all of us — the people in the family and me and anyone else that's around and comes to be with us. A few weeks ago a woman told me she was at peace, finally, because after we had our visit God appeared to her and told her she was going to be saved, there was no doubt about it. I told her that was wonderful news, and we could all rejoice for her — but there was still no reason for her or the rest of us to sit back and feel the fight is over. We win God every day, and we can lose Him just as fast; it only takes one slip, and you're down again."

So, he is always on guard, lest people fall, lest he himself fall. He is careful about his clothes, careful about his schedule, careful about driving; and he eats only what is good and truly necessary and sleeps only to be refreshed rather than made satisfied and contented. His wife is very much like him in habits and talk, though she has a saving plumpness to her, a softness of the flesh that is a relief to a stranger, and that suggests a spirit of things less righteous and driven than the one her husband's lean frame and bulging eyes manage to inspire. They have twin boys, Peter and Paul, and a psychiatrist can begin to have fantasies when he hears that news — given everything else in the life of the minister. But psychiatrists should keep their fantasies to themselves, and above all distinguish between their fantasies (or their theoretical formulations, the two not being always inseparable) and what can actually be proven. In this case my wildest daydreams were quite forthrightly confirmed, by a man who had no interest in beating around the bush or pretending or deceiving anyone, least of all himself: "To follow God you must try to be like Him. That's not blasphemous, even if it may sound so. I named the boys Peter and Paul because the names are good ones, and they go together; and also, I am reminded of Christ by those names, and we need to be reminded of what He faced when He was among us, and what was left to His disciples, His followers, the Peters and Pauls of this world. We all are potential followers of Christ, you know; but the temptations are great, the worldly temptations of the Antichrist.

"I try to tell the people that the Devil is real, and always ready. I tell them about the Antichrist because they must realize that sins are not committed in a vacuum; when we sin we are fighting against Someone, fighting against the Lord Himself. Many people see the light after a long struggle, and then they remind me of something; they tell me that they have a lot to struggle about here in this county, and when at last they feel they're winning in the biggest struggle of them all, against the Devil himself, then it makes the other struggles a little easier to bear, because hard as it is to get enough food every day and keep warm in winter and get the money to buy the children clothes, all of that is as nothing when there is a good chance a person will be burning forever, burning in the kind of fires no one can imagine, really.

"When I'm asked about God's punishment I try to be true to the Bible, and as honest as I can possibly be. A man might come up to me and tell me he feels he's suffering plenty right here and now, and what could be worse, just what? I don't try to scare him — no, never. A minister who does that is an evil man. I know some do. I've seen them do it; I've heard them do it. I'm no psychologist, but I can see what happens. The people around here are so used to a life of suffering that even if they complain about it, they can't believe there is any other kind of life possible. And as a result, a man who tells them they've got even more pain and sorrow ahead, he'll be believed. Don't you think people become addicted to troubles if they have a lot of them all the time?"

I told him yes, suffering can become a habit. We talked a good deal about that, about suffering, about why it takes place and what it might possibly mean. I held the view that suffering doesn't "mean" much; it just is here, all around us, the result of harsh, unfair social and economic conditions which bring out the worst in people, and consolidate in political forms the meanness and brutishness that, admittedly, seem openly or covertly very much part of every man's psychological makeup. I also held the view that the explicit suffering he and I presumably had in mind, the wretched cabins and faulty diets, the joblessness and want and destitution, the awful presence and even prevalence of utterly avoidable diseases, all of that was needless, shameful, senseless, a comment on man's irresponsible, greedy, mindless ability to ignore and exploit his fellowman. Most of all, I held the view that everything we both knew about and deplored was thoroughly unnecessary, thoroughly remediable. I said that I doubted we would achieve some psychological or spiritual utopia up those hollows or any other place through a mixture of political reform, economic progress, social uplift, and a touch of psychological insight; but liberal ideology aside, I argued the conventional line that held joy and happiness and contentment to be quite possibly elusive or rare, but hunger and idleness and dozens of illnesses to be quite definitely a matter of choice, at least in the United States in the second half of the twentieth century.

While none of that is very original, the minister's response cannot be considered a familiar one to the young activists at work in Appalachia or to most middle-class, "moderate" people in the nation as a whole. I believe that the teacher whose spirit and feelings I have just tried to convey, and the school official and the mine owner, would know better than the VISTA worker (to compare the individuals so far discussed in this section) how the minister replied. His response was a passionate one. Up those hollows and creeks his response would no doubt be taken as God's undeniable, saving message — one which thousands and thousands of people have no trouble comprehending and even enjoying. Indeed, for all that minister's gloomy forebodings, there is a hopeful, flushed, roaring, triumphant quality to his message: "We are here for a second, to quiver with fear, to shake in fear, to know the fear of God. We are here to make a decision, that's what. Nothing could be more simple and more important than that, the decision we have to make after we're born and before we die. A lot of people with a lot of education — the college graduates you know — are always going from one philosophy to another. They say life means one thing, or it means another thing. Today a lot of them say life is without any meaning at all. Then the same kind of people come here and try to tell our people in Kentucky and West Virginia that there *is* a meaning to life, a purpose, and it's to go and get more money from the county and the federal government.

"Don't you think someone who lives up a hollow is smart enough to ask himself a question like this: if these people who come here have had plenty of money and a lot of education and opportunity, and still they are so upset about life and feel so bad about everything, about America and what's going on in the world; and if they're so restless and dissatisfied and unhappy and disgruntled that they leave their homes and their families and their neighborhoods and go wandering all over — there's the Peace Corps and VISTA and a thousand community projects and programs — then what's the point of our fighting and fighting and fighting, just so we can become like them and be as miserable in our minds as they are and be so discouraged and talk with such long faces and with tears practically pouring out of our eyes? I don't believe a lot of people from New England or out there in Los Angeles and San Francisco give our people here credit for being able to stop and think about such things.

"When I preach I'm always carrying on a conversation with the men and women listening; and I'm carrying on another one with myself. I'll be asking myself what have the people before me had to face during the week, and what will they face as soon as they leave and go home. I'll be asking myself how I can console them, give them the consolation our Savior wanted each and every human soul to have, here as well as later, when the chains of the body are finally broken. I'm told by a lot of atheists that people hereabouts are being duped and exploited by capitalists. Everyone is duped and exploited until he becomes part of a larger kingdom that all the money in the world can never build. One man who said he was working to bring these people 'bread and freedom' told me I was a 'drug' to the people. I was in North Carolina, and I'd finished a long sermon, one of the longest I have ever spoken. He came up and said he was a lawyer, a 'poverty lawyer,' something like that. He said that as long as I got people to believe that it pays to suffer and got them all excited over the next world, they'd be easy bait for the crooked politicians and industrialists — the textile people — in this world. That's what he finally said. He started out asking me if we could talk, and before long that's what I was hearing.

"Let me tell you, I turned around and replied to him. I told him I hear people crying and shouting; and I hear how worried they are and frightened, very frightened. I told him I don't mind consoling people, and I told him that because I console them doesn't mean I want them to live as badly off as they do, nor do I want them to *rejoice* in poverty. I want them not to be *destroyed* by it, nor to be overwhelmed and made ashamed by it. A lot of our reformers want to change the world, but they never want to bother with the *people* in the world and with man's *purpose* in the world. They love mankind, but do they care much about these families over here in North Carolina and those over there in West Virginia? You know what I think? They don't even stop and consider individual men, women and children — who have a soul, a God-given soul to save, and not all that much time to save it! No sir, the reformers like to juggle numbers around and come up with a law and a new 'approach.' I'm so tired of hearing about all those 'approaches' of theirs, and the new ideas and the new philosophies. The history of the world is the long, long story of man's vanity, his sinful arrogance. The reformers call me a narcotic and a reactionary, but do they look at how sinful they are, sinful before God? The worst sin is to try to be God, to play with people as if they were subjects to be experimented with. If I become arrogant, I hope the Lord makes me suffer and never stop suffering. I'm sure some of our reformers would laugh at me for saying that; they look up at no one, and they look down upon more people than they realize. That's my observation — and I've preached to the poor for years, so I've met a lot of others who preach to the poor, even if they don't look upon themselves as preachers. Beware of your preacher who thinks he's something else, that's what I have to say, and that's what I told that poverty lawyer in North Carolina."

I can easily reject much of what he says, but there are moments when he comes across exactly right, when he hits home, as it were, when he says in a few direct, forceful sentences what a person like me might not even know about himself, or dare say about others. For all his dogmatism and half-educated theological pretentiousness, he knows how to reach and enliven sad and troubled people; and additionally, he knows that some of his critics also can be pretentious and dogmatic, and are often more ignorant than they can ever acknowledge. He is tough, observant, alternately sympathetic and coldly calculating, ambitious, a fighter for what he believes in, idealistic as can be but also thoroughly practical. How can I possibly distinguish him — having just described him — from many of his mortal enemies, the secular or agnostic "reformers" he keeps on bringing up? They worry him, those enemies of his; they nettle him and threaten him — and he feels it, feels himself being criticized, perhaps scorned is the word. And he is no fool. Because he believes in God and the Devil, in Heaven and Hell, in Christ and the Antichrist, he is aware, if nothing else, of the opposition that anyone (including God Himself) must always face.

Unlike some of his colleagues, he is quite prepared to find opposition in other men, in living form rather than lurking under bushes or in shadows or sprouting from some swamp: "There are superstitious ministers, just like you'll find superstitious doctors and lawyers and teachers. Some ministers tell their people that the Devil is a snake, or he's hiding deep in the earth and comes out at night. I try to tell people that we're all part of the Devil. He has his grip on us, just like he was fighting to make Jesus give up and feel despair. If we would only read the Bible we would know that Christ is no stranger to us; He was poor, and He suffered, and He even doubted, at the end He did. Up here, in the hollows of the Appalachian Mountains, people are near God; they'll tell you how they feel Him — in the woods and up in the sky. I don't discourage them from that, but I try my best to read the Bible to them and let them know that God was a Living God, and He came to us as a Living Man, and He said things, so many things, that we have got to hear and remember. God cannot be questioned; He wasn't a lawyer or a reformer or one of your professors, you know. God wasn't like the people in Frankfort or Charleston or Washington, D.C., though I do believe a lot of them, the lawmakers we have, rather fancy He was exactly like them. Like them, imagine that! He lived a short life, Jesus, and when He died all the important people, the lawmakers of the day, were glad He was gone; they made *sure* He was gone. But He came back, and He came back not to be questioned, not to be told that the world is full of injustice and inequality, but to bring the news, the Good News, that there is something beyond all that injustice and inequality, the same injustice He experienced, the same inequality He saw during His life.

"Up in the hollows people live like He did — in a way they really do. They're born on little farms, almost like in Bethlehem. They live short lives, a lot of them. They're poor. They're despised by their enemies, and sometimes by their friends, too — and you can despise people by the way you go about befriending them, even if you say you're only doing it 'for their own best interests.' I've heard that expression a million times, I'd estimate. Christ must be smiling upon us here, because so many of us have been chosen to live His kind of life, and like I say, die a lot like He did, ignored and looked down upon.

"As a minister I believe in speaking the truth. I pray to my people that they will find the truth and believe it; and that they will feel close to God and feel that His suffering will redeem their suffering. I guess that's the most important thing: life *has* meaning, and so does suffering — through Christ. When a man like that poverty lawyer tells me I'm foolish for glorifying suffering and telling people it's what Christ went through and it'll bring redemption, then I only have this to say: we all suffer, and the poverty lawyers themselves seek out the suffering people — God bless them! We all should want to find the meaning of suffering, whether we're rich or poor. Doesn't a poor man have the right to find some meaning in life, even as a rich man does, or a big thinker does?

"Maybe we're all wrong. Maybe we're all being deceived. I don't know for sure if we are or are not; but I don't *believe* we are, because to me Christ's message makes more sense than anyone else's, and that would include a lot of big-name people that say it's bad for a poor man to pray and have his faith, but it's OK for another man in a college or a mansion to believe in Science and Machines, because they're going to save us, and they should be believed and sold to people as the answers, the solutions to life. To me the solution to the problems of life are to be found *in* life, in The Life, in the Life of our Lord; and His Life is eternal. I believe people here in the mountains, living like they do, so close to the bone, so close to death, so close to the sky, know about that Life. They feel It, somehow; I believe they do. That's how they get their strength. Their strength is phenomenal, we all agree. Their strength is the strength a man gets by worshiping no man, but God, only Him. That's wisdom, and wisdom turns into strength. If you don't fool yourself, and trust only Him, you're not going to become gullible and everybody's fool. These people up here may be weak, weak in a lot of ways, but they're strong folk, too — God-loving, God-fearing, God-abiding folk. God bless them. And I believe He does; I believe He especially blesses them."

6. *The People Are Weak, Weak and Run-Down*

The mountaineers are indeed weak "in a lot of ways," as the minister said: weak politically, weak in something called "purchasing power," weak because the right kind of food and any kind of medical care are not to be had. A grocer, a storekeeper, may not appear to be the likeliest informant for one trying to understand how life goes among people who are up the hills, away from markets, and without cash. Yet the markets do manage to draw the people down from the hollows, and ways are arranged for purchases to be made and eventually paid for. What is more, I have found that storekeepers in Appalachia have shrewd clini-

cal eyes as well as business eyes; in fact some of those storekeepers are an uncanny mixture of the sharp, intelligent observer
and the utterly unscrupulous entrepreneur, who will sell anything
at any price, so long as a huge profit results — and then go on to
denounce the buyer as a fool for making his purchase.

In Appalachia a store is not necessarily part of or very near a
particular community; it all depends on the man who owns the
store, and the location of the store. Some stores have traditionally
been, and still are, gathering places where people enjoy meeting
one another, where they stand or sit and talk, where they pick
guitars and sing songs and listen to country music on the radio,
where they complain about things or rejoice in some good
news, where they leave messages and receive notices and find
out about what happened and might happen. To many mountaineers a trip "down" to the store, like a journey into the county
seat or like the weekly visit to church, means seeing a whole new
world: "I get my children together and I tell them we're going
to the store. Then they get all excited and start jumping and shouting and wondering what they'll see and who they'll see. They
know enough not to ask me what I'll buy for them, because there's
no money for buying things; but we manage, yes sir, we do. The
storekeeper, he slips them something, however little it be, and I
get the money to him eventually, or I bring him the eggs or
vegetables, or best of all he likes my preserves."

So one mother puts it, and if anything she understates the
excitement in the house. Often when I watched that excitement I
wondered what all the observers, including me, who have
written about such families can possibly have meant by words
like "isolated," "withdrawn," "suspicious," or "parochial." These
parents and children alike are looking forward to company, to a
change of scene, to hearing all sorts of stories and joining neighbors near and not so near. If people are truly "withdrawn" and
"isolated" they don't anticipate such experiences, in fact they
shun them rather than perk up at their prospect. Often at the
store (when it is a bit distant) new people are met, in contrast to
what happens at a church located at the foot of a hollow. Here is
the mother again, as she readies her children for the ride, which

an uncle will supply, an uncle just back from Chicago, where he made enough money to buy the car: "I get annoyed with the children because they're hard to keep still on a morning like this. They're talking about the store, the store, and all they'll be seeing there, and the candy they'll get, and most of all they like to see boys and girls they've never seen before — who come in from the town, you know. I don't deny I feel like they do. You wonder about other people, sometimes, and if they're having the same troubles you do, and what's happening over in the town.

"I'm happy where I am, but my brother tells me someday I should go to Chicago, just so I can see for myself the big city. When we go to the store we're mixing with strangers, and you get their ideas on what's happening. The store may not be like Chicago, but it's a change for us, and we enjoy it. The storekeeper lets us stay as long as we care to, and he's nice. He wants his money, or he'll trade with me: a mop for preserves, a toy for some good eggs, a piece of clothing for the vegetables; that's one way he does his business. He gets his food brought in, the boxes and cans, but he also does trading off with us. He's got a sharp eye, and he's in it for the money, but like my husband says, he likes to have us come, and he's a friendly sort, and most of us, we're friendly, too."

I have no doubt she and her husband (and the storekeeper as well) can be unfriendly, can take quick offense to outsiders, and for that matter also get enraged at a few "insiders." (Long before social scientists recorded the "hostility" felt by Appalachian mountaineers to strangers, the region's internecine feuds were legendary.) Perhaps the same mother should be called upon once more: "Sometimes we'll be at the store, and I turn real shy. I can't talk. There'll be some fast-speaking person there, and I get scared. It'll be someone who is too fresh and wise for me; she'll be asking me what I buy, and when I use this or that, and she'll be smart, the real smart type, and dressed up like they do in the city. She'll say she was 'just driving by.' Well, isn't that nice! I'd like to tell her I've been waiting for a month for my brother to come home, so we could take the ride to get to the store; but I'd rather turn away and try to get speaking with another woman.

The good times are when you'll come across a person like yourself, and you may never see her again, but you get to talking, and
she has a real fine recipe, and she'll give you a hint about one
thing or another, and I know when I get home I'll be glad for the
day at the store. I said to my brother the other day that God
wouldn't have made so many people if He didn't believe a lot of
them would turn out good; and even if I don't get to Chicago,
I'm glad I get to leave our hollow some of the time, and I'm glad
to have the store there. There are the goods he has to sell, and we
all feel like we've gone and had a good long trip for ourselves,
and we're ready to come back to the hollow and talk about who
we saw and what we heard. It takes my children a week or so,
you know, to settle down and stop mentioning that this happened and the other thing happened and all that."

Their host, that mother's and her children's, is of course the
storekeeper. He is very, very tall, maybe six feet five. He is very,
very thin — though he is always eating; in between meals he eats
candy and downs pop and chews tobacco and takes a sandwich
and sometimes asks his wife for a "little soup," which turns out
to be the entire contents of a can and an equal portion of water.
He stays thin, though, and in doing so maddens his wife, who
quite reasonably can't understand why she becomes fat so easily,
given the slightest length of an indulgence, while at the same
time, in her words, "he just eats along, hour after hour, and
nothing happens." They run the store together, and have been
doing so for a quarter of a century. They have introduced the
"new lines," the frozen foods and prepared foods, even though
they know full well that many of their most devoted customers
have no refrigerators, let alone freezers. But in fact a variety of
people come into that store: townspeople whose homes are
nearer the store than the center of town, with its several stores;
passersby, some of them tourists, some men on their way north to,
say, Cincinnati, or on their way home from Cincinnati for a
weekend; people from creeks and hollows; and finally, puzzling,
hard-to-describe people — salesmen and organizers and 'government people' and a lawyer or two, a doctor maybe, all of them on
the go, but in need of a place to stop in order to get gas, to get a

little food, to ask something, find out how long the trip will take
or what the road ahead is like.

The storekeeper himself has never left the county in which he
was born — a county way east in Kentucky, a county that abuts
Virginia's long, thin, pointed, western border and also touches
Tennessee's northern territory. His store is a place others seek out
for the sake of company as well as provisions, but the storekeeper sees no reason to go anyplace to meet anyone. In fact, he
grows restless on Sundays; for then the store is closed, and his
wife takes him off to church, where she prays and he sits and gets
drowsy and feels fidgety and wishes it were Monday and smiles
so that he won't offend people, but to himself no doubt thinks
what he is quite willing to say aloud in his own home, which is
upstairs from the store: "I don't get much out of church. I'm a
believer, but it's between me and God. Why do we need to spend
a whole day Sunday, asking all those favors of Him? Why can't
we just pray at home, every day, and maybe He'd like that
better, anyway? If you ask me, the people come to church for the
same reason they come here to my store; they need to have their
meetings. At least when they come here they get something done
in addition. Over in church they put their money into the minister's hat and that's fine for him, but it means less for them, and
they're people who can't afford to give a penny away, if you ask
me, not when they're so short on things."

If anyone knows how short mountaineers are on various things,
the storekeeper is the man. He sells to them, takes their money,
lends them money and, as indicated, does a healthy amount of
trading or bartering with them. He also is watchful, and always
has been. His father had the store before him and trained him,
told him how to keep an eye on other customers while dealing
directly with one particular customer, and told him to stare long
and hard at people and come to some conclusion about them.
Why does he have to do that, judge people, worry about what
they are like? The answer is that a lot of his customers ask for
loans, for credit, for the right to defer payment; and others want
to make promises, which in turn require his trust — promises of
eggs later, venison meat later, a welfare or compensation check

later, a portion of the harvest later. He claims that he is "only a storekeeper," but he also claims he is a "mind reader" and more than that, more grandly and generally, a "judge of human nature." For my part, there have been times when I have found him all he says he is, and certainly better at comprehending human psychology than others who make more elaborate claims in that direction.

For instance, I once asked him to tell me about his customers. He demurred for a moment. They are all different, and which ones did I have in mind? Well, anyone *he* had in mind. Oh, he knew the ones I was "after." He knew what I wanted to know. I tried being evasive; I asked him what he thought I did want to know. Very simple; I wanted to know (he was sure) how poor mountain people get by, considering how hard life is for them; and also I was trying to understand in what ways those people are like him, a reasonably prosperous storekeeper. That was about it, I said. But he had another thought. Maybe I thought they were so special and so different and so "peculiar" that neither he nor I could possibly make sense of it all, of them and how they compared to him or me or anyone else. Now, that idea has been tossed around in considerably more exalted circles and never really settled, as perhaps it cannot be; I mean the idea of the observer and the observed and their different worlds, and the idea of "participant observation" as a very limited way of doing research — because always there is, in example, the mountaineer's "otherness" in contrast to my own "self." Although the grocer left school in the seventh grade to help his father full-time, he also thinks about such anthropological and psychological and existential matters: "I'm me, and they're them, and it's different, being a storekeeper and not being up there in the hills, where it's hard to be much of *anything*, you know. I wouldn't say that to their faces; they're very proud. They hurt, though. If you really know them, you know how they hurt. I get to hurting sometimes when I see them, trying so hard to go along from day to day and from trip to trip down here to the store. I'll ask them how they are, and they tell me they're 'fine.'

"A lot of people in this world feel sorry for themselves; rich people or poor people, they feel sorry for themselves. Half of what I see on television, more than half, it's people feeling sorry for themselves and people asking for things, always asking. The people I know, my customers here, they don't think like that. They don't pity themselves. Or maybe they do. I don't know. One man can never really know what another man thinks. I believe that. But if you stand here all day trying to get for people what they want, so that they can eat and live the best they can, then you get a sense of them, I believe you do.

"The way I see it, a man will come down here from the hollow, and his wife and his children will come, and they will consider themselves the equal of any man alive and second best to no one, and that includes me, even if I'm the one pushing those keys to the cash register and emptying it every night. I've never had a robbery here, never. Doesn't that tell you something? I watch my TV. I know what's happening all over — the stealing and looting. Here, I've never so much as suspected a person of being crooked, not the people I know, poor as they are. Sure some well-dressed fellow in a big car will drive up, and I wonder who *he* is, and what he's doing around here, and what's on his mind. But a man will come down from a creek and I can look at him and see how hard it is for him just to eat, and I'll want to give him the store, every piece of food in it. But will I worry that he's going to try something, go sour on his obligations? No. Never. He'll bring me something — the herbs he'll pick, that I can sell, or meat from what he's gone and shot, or some real good fish. All winter he can't fish or shoot so much, and he can't grow a thing, and they may run out on their preserves. All winter I give them whatever they need. Come spring and summer we get even a little, though it's a big problem for me, because they all at the same time want to give me what they can grow or shoot, in exchange for what they can wear, or for other food, cereal and like that. They have no money. Isn't that something, *no money?*

"But they don't go saying things like that to themselves, how they lack for work and money and how sorry they are for themselves and how they can't get a doctor, no matter how bad off their little boy or girl is. No, they get that ride here — maybe from a brother who is home from Chicago and has a car — and they're full of smiles and talk and they're curious about everything and if they're hungry, it's for what the news is that they'll hear after sitting by the stove and picking the guitar, or sitting out on the porch, of course.

"There will be times, I'll have to admit, that I think they're a little wrong in the head. I'll ask my wife how they can stand it, going without so much, eating only what they can hunt down and grow, and staying so close to their fires and near freezing to death — and starving, too — come winter. She says they're used to it, and of course she's right. But you can be used to something and be unhappy, pretty low in your spirits — and not like them, just as nice and polite and happy as can be. It's a little strange, I find myself thinking, that people so bad off can appear so contented with life!

"My daddy used to give me sermons. He used to say I was one of the most important people in all of Bell County, having this store. He used to say I should remember that no one over there in Pineville, in the courthouse or any other place, means as much to the people near here as we do; we stand for the whole world, so far as they are concerned, up there in the hills, so we've got to be good and gentle with them, and thoughtful, just like they are, and if we treat them the right way, they'll treat us the same way back. That was my father's philosophy. But the fact is, as I've seen it, my daddy was worried about nothing. It's never entered a man's mind hereabouts to treat me, or anyone else, in a bad way. It's true some of them will go and drink too much, and they have their fights, but none of that trouble ever comes into this store, and like I said, it's strange how they keep their head up so high and keep right on going, from visit to visit. Year after year they go along with smiles on their faces, all over their faces; and not just put-on smiles, dishonest ones, but real smiles.

"Now when people are weak, weak and run-down, like they are all over these mountains, and they're still smiling, then I say that you've got a problem on your hands, figuring that out. I'll look at them coming, and whisper to my wife how weak they look, and sick, run-down with an illness. Then they'll be inside here, right by me, right in front of my eyes, and they're as good and friendly as they can be, and they're not asking one thing of you, not a single thing, that they're not going to try and pay for, however they can. You may wonder what it'll be they'll bring, and whether they'll last long enough to bring it, but you say to yourself that these men are great men, and these women are wonderful women, when they can be that weak and run-down and still want to make the promises and then go and keep them. That's something. That's what I can't figure out, their *wanting* to live like they do. They don't stop and think about how bad it is for them — not for long, anyway. No, they don't think like that. They live. Like my wife says, they live and they have a spirit to them. So maybe God *is* watching over them, though it's not every day that I can believe that, I'll have to admit. And maybe I don't know what they *do* think, when I'm not around. And maybe God isn't looking after them, either!"

He is not the first and hopefully he will not be the last man to throw up his hands in perplexity after a hard and prolonged effort to understand such stubborn, defiant, completely challenging people. Like many an "expert" who starts out looking for "answers" and finally realizes there are none, and indeed like some of the very people he describes with such conviction, detail (and ultimately) puzzlement, he always retains the hope that another observer will somehow break through and come up with something: a statement or two, a few conclusions — *anything*, really, that sounds assured, convincing, conclusive definite, clear-cut. So the storekeeper finally acknowledges his exasperation and his sense of mystery and wonder, his admiration tinctured through and through with pity, and tells me: "Go talk with a foreman who works in the mines, who has known them down there, when they worked there; maybe he can tell you what they're *really* like. When a man works in a mine, and he knows he could die any second, the truth of how he feels must come out; then it must, if it ever will."

Yes, I say; yes, I promise, I will. I am trying to reassure him, tell him I value his advice and tell him also that I know, I know how hard it is for any of us to know, *really* to know. I am also admitting to him that, very much like him, I have mixed feelings. Neither of us would want to sit back in comfort and applaud the hard and often desperate life mountain people know; but both of us realize, as we talk and speculate and describe incidents and try to account for things — oh, I guess we realize how very much our mountaineer friends bear and suffer and put up with, but also how long they have lasted, and lasted with their heads up high, most of the time. Mountaineers have abided; and we are at a loss to know what to say, how to speak, in the face of that achievement. We also know how bitter and utterly enraged those same people can feel. Their heads are up, their fists are clenched, their eyes are fixed, their brows are wrinkled, their feet are ready to take up and head for some other place — not too far away, though, if it can be helped; because always, and however awful things are, there is love, love for those hills.

7. *They Near Die Down There, but They Try to Live*

If the hills are loved, they are also hated. They contain coal, and they don't give up their insides without a fight, all too often a mortal fight. Many of the people who come to the storekeeper's place and enjoy themselves there are former miners, men now short of breath and hurting in their backs or their shoulders or their arms and legs. Some who come to buy things still work in the mines; on Saturday they appear, happy at last after a week of pain and fear, happy at last to be in a store with money in their pockets, lots of money and an urge to spend it and enjoy what is bought — for, as they will freely say and literally mean, "life is short, and you never know what tomorrow will bring." Some few who come by are foremen, supervisors, men once miners and now in charge of miners. They happen to live outside the city, near the mines, in sturdy, comfortable ranch houses often right along a main road, but in any case as far removed from hollows and creeks as anyone in Appalachia can ever get, which means always near in miles and sometimes in spirit.

Ben Frazier, for example, is glad now to be living away from a hollow; but he also likes to visit some kin "up there" in what he calls "my hollow." Sometimes when he comes home after such a visit he feels quite unhappy. He has seen misery, and the sight of it troubles him. He is at a loss. Should he blame his own people for "their ways"? (He can say those two words with obvious contempt.) Should he turn on *his* bosses, who have made *him* a boss, and admit that they have in the past squeezed the life blood out of countless men, from all over Appalachia, only to ignore them totally now that there is no need for their labor? Should he call himself a traitor, a man who has gone over to the traditional enemies in order to save his own skin? He is, of course, not beyond any of those responses. He sometimes feels guilty. He sometimes lashes out at the men whose work he supervises. He often has unfriendly, ill-tempered words for his kin, several of whom were badly injured in mine accidents, two of whom died in one of those accidents.

Most of all, though, Ben Frazier is a decent, hardworking man who wants to blame no one, simply survive himself. At fifty he is glad to be alive, and he is fully aware of how lucky he has been. He has been rescued from mines when others have been killed. He has been spared roof falls and explosions when others have suffered serious injuries. He has kept his job when others were discharged, summarily and with virtually nothing in compensation. He has been promoted while others were kept frozen in a large company's hierarchy. As he thinks about all of that, about his personal history and the history of his family and friends and the history of the county in which Fraziers, kin of his, have lived for many generations, he becomes alternately philosophical, troubled, irritated, embarrassed, and perhaps most of all, worried. Where will it all end? Again and again he asks that question, and he has in mind, I am quite sure, nothing less than the whole of Western, industrial civilization — because the storekeeper was right when he said that a man like Ben Frazier sees a lot and has a lot of specific and concrete reasons to mull over what he actually sees.

In a tradition certainly as old as John L. Lewis and his Shakespearean rhetoric, at once a mixture of particular complaints and philosophical pronouncements, Ben Frazier talks and talks and at times comes surprisingly close to tears. He wonders out loud and recalls the past and dreams about a future he knows he will never see, a future he believes his son Ben junior will never see, a future he doubts anyone will ever see: "I wish we could have a really decent and good world, where no one was standing over the next guy, ready to hit him with a pay deduction or get him fired. I wish my son could find the kind of work he wants near the place he wants to live. But we'll never have a world like that. I'm not very religious. I don't believe in all that 'Hell and Damnation' talk, but I'm afraid there's *some* truth to it. We've got to adjust ourselves to the fact that people take advantage of each other, and if they have the power, they use it on the guy who's weak and poor. That's the way it is, and you'll find the same situation in every country in the world, I believe that. Every country has a government, and you can be sure the people in the government live better than the miners or the people who work all day growing food.

"I do think we're moving along, though — to a better kind of world. All I have to do is think back, remember what it was like for me when I started in the mines. I was fourteen years old, and no one asked any questions about my age or my health or anything. I just went and signed up, and they put me to work. They assigned me to a man, and in a few days I was cutting and cutting, all day long. I'd go down first thing in the morning, when it would be dark, and down in the mine it would be dark all day, and I'd come up in the late afternoon, and it would be dark: dark, dark, dark, from late fall to spring. I'd never stand up much, either. All day I'd be on my hands and knees. When I came up I'd try to walk easy and quick, but I couldn't. I felt like a monkey, trying to walk on two legs, trying to be like a man. By the time I'd get home I'd be straightened out, but my mother could tell. She'd pretend; she'd pretend a lot. She'd look at me and try to make me believe that I was her boy, Ben, grown up now and making some money, and so everything was just fine. But I'd catch her looking at me; she'd see the way I walked, and the coal dust working into my skin, finding every line and crease it could, so that I'd look like the rest of them, black as can be, no matter how much soap I used — and of course we didn't have hot water to run from a faucet, or cold water either, unless you went and fetched it. I'm in my early fifties, so you figure out how long ago that was — not very far back, no sir! "You hear people say we should all be grateful for the progress we've made — *some* of us have made. My mother and father never expected anything especially good to happen. They were born up a creek, and they died up there. They never went to a doctor, and they never went over to Pineville to ask for welfare or help of any kind. They never had food stamps, and no one gave us lunches paid for by the government. The teacher would bring us a box of crackers, and we'd bring a little something, or if there was nothing, we'd just not go to school at all. In the winter it's the worst time — the weather, and the food starts running out — so we'd stay away from school then. Come to think of it, we'd hibernate, just like the animals do. We'd go into the cabin and stay there. My daddy would have the wood stored up, and we'd use it, log after log. I recall once there was a warm spell, near Christmastime, and my brother and me, we went out and walked down the creek, and all we could see was a cabin and the smoke coming out, rising up to the trees and the sky, and then another cabin, and the same smoke — but not a person was there, no one in sight. We came back and told our mother that, and she said something I've never forgotten, nor will I. She said, 'Yes, it's wintertime, and everyone in the creek is hiding, and it took you kids to stop and figure out that the weather is warm and good for going outside.'

"Then I asked her why we were all hiding, and that's what she said that sticks in my mind: 'Son, we're hiding because if we don't we'll die. We'll freeze to death, or we'll starve to death, because we only have enough food to fuel a quiet body, and no more, and maybe not even that much.' She wasn't being too sad, and she wasn't feeling sorry for herself; she never cried, and that's what you should know about people around here — no matter how bad off they are, they don't start feeling sorry for themselves. That goes for the miners, and it goes for people up the creeks or the hollows. I don't mean we don't have our faults

here; we do. Instead of weeping over life, we go and drink, a lot
of us do, and we take to fighting and feuding. Sometimes a man
will get real silent, and he won't have anything to say for so long
that it worries you, or he'll start talking strange, about how his
legs won't work, or his arms, and there's something crawling up
his spine. But it's hard to figure out what's wrong with people
here; there's no doctor for most of them, and they don't get the
right food, and where they live, it's either too cold or else it gets
too hot and the flies and mosquitoes practically feed off your
skin. So, it's natural that you'd find people getting themselves
upset and not feeling right some of the time. But even so, we
don't like to cry over ourselves, not around here, and we don't
like to go begging — that's the worst thing in the world to do,
worse than anything.

"I get a little full in the eyes, if I think about it too much —
how a lot of the people live in this county, and others nearby, in
Tennessee and in Virginia and in West Virginia and in North
Carolina. Those are the states, besides this one, Kentucky. I feel
myself starting to melt a little, is the way I'd put it. I can't talk
too good. I'm on the verge of sadness. Usually I can shout; I've
got to, because I have to keep my men in line, keep them getting
at that coal. If I'd be feeling sorry for them all the time, I
couldn't work. There aren't too many jobs a man can find around
here, and I've never been without a job, so I'm probably the
luckiest man you'll meet in the county. I count my blessings, not
every day, but many times, you can be sure. It's hard to talk
about your own work, but I think I've been a credit to the company. They promoted me to a foreman, to supervise the production of coal, because they figured I got along with the men. But I
have to be over them, the way you have to be if you're running a
company for profit. I don't like bossing people, but like I've said,
there will always be the bosses and the people they boss. At least
my men know I'm fair, and I never lose my temper, never. I just
let them know they've got to go along with company policy, as
it's been ratified by the union. The union isn't what it used to be,
but that's a long story. The union is run by bosses, too. And isn't
that the way it goes in this world? Some of the people in the

union, they make more money and they live higher than many company bosses. These poor men here, they work hard and get that coal for us, and then the profits go to the crooked union; it's not only industry that squeezes on the workingman. If you ask me, there's no answer to all of these problems.

"My children have all left here, left the county — and I'm as happy as can be about that, too. My son Ben, he's up in Dayton, learning to be an engineer. I have a boy who's a teacher over near Asheville. I have a girl married to a teacher over in Knoxville. She learned to be a teacher, too. I told my sons never even to think about going down to those mines. I told them if they once even came near the entrance, I'd be standing there, and they should expect me. They'd have to fight me and knock me out, kill me I said, before they could get in. I guess they heard me! If I was to tell you the truth, it would be that I would have been killed at the sight of them going down, even if they never put a hand on me. It's Hell being a miner, that's what. People will never know, because they never see. And us, the ones who *do* know, we won't admit the truth, except to each other, and even then we usually don't. What's the point? The more you talk, the worse you feel, and the harder it is to keep going, day after day. They near die down there, our men, but they try to live; and that's all they want out of life, actually: a chance to stay alive and have a little money in their pockets. If you ask me, a lot of the way miners act can be explained when you stop and think that they are people who are walking on thin ice every second, and they could drown. When you're almost drowning, you don't have time to feel sorry for yourself and you don't talk too much and you go about your business. And if you *like* it here, besides — not in the mine, but in the county, where you've grown up — then you feel even more that it's best to keep your mouth shut and keep from drowning, and then you won't have to go and leave here, because *that's* like drowning, too. You see?"

He was asking me a question, but the look on his face indicated that he was also asking himself the same question. He had struggled with a metaphor to explain what he still felt to be somewhat inexplicable. What puzzled him ought perhaps to continue to puzzle us: how do the mountaineers endure? Observers from near and far are awed that mountaineers appear as thoroughly dignified as they in actual fact *struggle constantly to be*. Perhaps those last italicized words give a hint of how we can look at what happens. Perhaps very hurt people still can work at being something, still can amount to a great deal — in this case, measure up to what they have faced if not surmounted, lived with if not overcome. No one in his right senses wants to let the matter stand there. God knows, those mountaineers want and need a better world, even if they no longer dare or care to say so — especially to those who already have one. Yet, maybe God knows something else, too: what has been the reward as well as the cost of survival; what fierce self-respect can emerge from that continuing struggle for a breath of life, a piece of land, a view of those hills, and perhaps a view beyond.

8. *Hugh McCaslin*

And finally, Hugh McCaslin, who is unforgettable. He has red hair and, at forty-three, freckles. He stands six feet four. As he talked to me about his work in the coal mines, I kept wondering what he did with his height down inside the earth.

Once he must have been an unusually powerful man; even today his arms and legs are solid muscle. The fat he has added in recent years has collected in only one place, his waist, both front and back: "I need some padding around my back; it's hurt, and I don't think it'll ever get back right. I broke it bad working, and they told me at first they'd have it fixed in no time flat, but they were wrong. I don't know if they were fooling themselves, or out to fool me in the bargain. It's hard to know *what's* going on around here — that's what I've discovered these last few years.

"I'll tell you, a man like me, he has a lot of time to think. He'll sit around here, day upon day, and what else does he have to keep his mind on but his thoughts? I can't work, and even if I could, there's no work to do, not around here, no sir. They told me I'm 'totally incapacitated,' that's the words they used. They said my spine was hurt and the nerves, and I can't walk and move about the way I should. As if I needed them to tell me!

"Then they gave me exercises and all, and told me I was lucky, because even though I wasn't in shape to go in the mines, I could do anything else, anything that's not too heavy. Sometimes I wonder what goes on in the heads of those doctors. They look you right in the eye, and they're wearing a straight face on, and they tell you you're sick, you've been hurt digging out coal, and you'll never be the same, but you're really not so bad off, because your back isn't so bad you can't be a judge, or a professor, or the president of the coal company or something like that, you know."

Once Hugh McCaslin asked me to look at an X ray taken of his back and his shoulders — his vertebral column. He persuaded the company doctor to give him the X ray, or so he said. (His wife told me that he had, in fact, persuaded the doctor's secretary to hand it over and tell her boss — if he ever asked — that somehow the patient's "file" had been lost.) He was convinced that the doctor was a "company doctor" — which he assuredly was — and a "rotten, dishonest one." Anyway, what did *I* see in that X ray? I told him that I saw very little. I am no radiologist, and whatever it was that ailed him could not be dramatically pointed out on an X ray, or if it could I was not the man to do it. Well, yes he did know that, as a matter of fact: "I got my nerves smashed down there in an accident. I don't know about the bones. I think there was a lot of pressure, huge pressure on the nerves, and it affected the way I walk. The doctor said it wasn't a fracture on a big bone, just one near the spine. He said it wasn't 'too serious,' that I'd be OK, just not able to go back to work, at least down there.

"Then, you see, they closed down the mine itself. That shows you I wasn't very lucky. My friends kept telling me I was lucky to be alive and lucky to be through with it, being a miner. You know, we don't scare very easy. Together, we never would talk about getting hurt. I suppose it was somewhere in us, the worry; but the first time I heard my friends say anything like that was to me, not to themselves. They'd come by here when I was sick, and they'd tell me I sure was a fortunate guy, and God was smiling that day, and now He'd be smiling forever on me, because I was spared a *real* disaster, and it was bound to come, one day or another. It kind of got me feeling funny, hearing them talk like that *around my bed,* and then seeing them walk off real fast, with nothing to make *them* watch their step and take a pain pill every few hours.

"But after a while I thought maybe they did have something; and if I could just recover me a good pension from the company and get my medical expenses all covered — well, then, I'd get better, as much as possible, and go fetch me a real honest-to-goodness job, where I could see the sun all day and the sky outside and breathe our air here, as much of it as I pleased, without a worry in the world.

"But that wasn't to be. I was dumb, real dumb, and hopeful. I saw them treating me in the hospital, and when they told me to go home I thought I was better, or soon would be. Instead, I had to get all kinds of treatments, and they said I'd have to pay for them, out of my savings or somewhere. And the pension I thought I was supposed to get, that was all in my mind, they said. They said the coal industry was going through a lot of changes, and you couldn't expect them to keep people going indefinitely, even if they weren't in the best of shape, even if it did happen down in the mines.

"Well, that's it, to make it short. I can't do hard work, and I have a lot of pain, every day of my life. I might be able to do light work, desk work, but hell, I'm not fit for anything like that; and even if I could, where's the work to be found? Around here? Never in a million years. We're doomed here, to sitting and growing the food we can and sharing our misery with one another.

"My brother, he helps; and my four sisters, they help; and my daddy, he's still alive and he can't help except to sympathize and tell me it's a good thing I didn't get killed in that landslide and can see my boys grow up. He'll come over here and we start drinking. You bet, he's near eighty, and we start drinking and remembering. My daddy will ask me if I can recollect the time I said I'd save a thousand dollars for myself by getting a job in the mines and I say I sure can, and can he recollect the time he said

I'd better not get too greedy, because there's bad that comes with good in this world, and especially way down there inside the earth."

He will take a beer or two and then get increasingly angry. His hair seems to look wilder, perhaps because he puts his hands through it as he talks. His wife becomes nervous and tries to give him some bread or crackers, and he becomes sullen or embarrassingly direct with her. She is trying to "soak up" his beer. She won't even let it hit his stomach and stay there a while. She wants it back. He tells her, "Why don't you *keep* your beer, if you won't let it do a thing for me?"

They have five sons, all born within nine years. The oldest is in high school and dreams of the day he will join the Army. He says he will be "taken" in, say, Charleston or Beckley — in his mind, any "big city" will do. He will be sent off to California or Florida or "maybe New York" for basic training; eventually he will "land himself an assignment — anywhere that's good, and it'll be far away from here, I do believe that." Hugh McCaslin, with a few beers in him, becomes enraged when he hears his son talk like that: "That's the way it is around here. That's what's happened to us. That's what they did to us. They made us lose any honor we had. They turned us idle. They turned us into a lot of grazing sheep, lucky to find a bit of pasture here and there. We don't *do* anything here anymore; and so my boys, they'll all want to leave, and they will. But they'll want to come back, too — because this land, it's in their bones going way back, and you don't shake off your ancestors that easy, no sir.

"My daddy, he was born right up the road in this here hollow, and his daddy, and back to a long time ago. There isn't anyone around here we're not kin to somehow, near or far. My daddy was the one supposed to leave for the mines. He figured he could make more money than he could dream about, and it wasn't too far to go. He went for a while, but some years later he quit. He couldn't take it. I grew up in a camp near the mine, and I'd still be there if it wasn't that I got hurt and moved back here to the hollow. Even while we were at the camp we used to come back here on Sundays, I remember, just like now they come here on weekends from Cincinnati and Dayton and those places, and even from way off in Chicago. I can recall the car we got; everybody talked about it, and when we'd drive as near here as we could — well, the people would come, my grandparents and all my uncles and aunts and cousins, and they'd look and look at that Ford, before they'd see if it was *us* and say hello to us. I can recollect in my mind being shamed and wanting to disappear in one of those pockets, where my daddy would keep his pipes. My mother would say it wasn't they didn't want to see us, but the Ford, it was real special to them, and could you blame them for not looking at us?

"That was when things were really good. Except that even then I don't think we were all that contented. My mother always worried. Every day, come three or so in the afternoon, I could tell she was starting to worry. Will anything happen? Will he get hurt? Will they be coming over soon, to give me some bad news? No, we had no telephone, and neither did the neighbors. It got so we'd come home from school around two or so, and just sit there with her, pretending — pretending to do things, and say things. And then he'd come in, every time. We could hear his voice coming, or his steps, or the door, and we'd all loosen up — and pretend again, that there was nothing we'd worry about, because there wasn't nothing *to* worry about.

"One day — I think I was seven or eight, because I was in school, I know that — we had a bad scare. Someone came to the school and told the teacher something, whispered it in her ear. She turned into a sheet, and she looked as though she'd start crying. The older kids knew what had happened, just from her looks. Yes, it was a one-room schoolhouse, just like the one we have here, only a little bigger. They ran out, and she almost took off after them, except for the fact that she remembered us. So she turned around and told us there that something bad had happened down in the mines, an explosion, and we should go home and wait there, and if our mothers weren't there — well, wait until they got home.

"But we wanted to go with her. Looking back at it, I think she worried us. So she decided to take us, the little ones. And I'll tell you, I can remember that walk with her like it was just today. I can see it, and I can tell you what she said, and what we did, and all. We walked and walked, and then we came through the woods and there they were, all of a sudden before our eyes. The people there, just standing around and almost nothing being said between them. It was so silent I thought they'd all turn around and see us making noise. But, you see, we must have stopped talking too, because for a while they didn't even give us a look over their shoulders. Then we came closer, and I could hear there was noise after all: the women were crying, and there'd be a cough or something from some of the miners.

"That's what sticks with you, the miners wondering if their buddies were dead or alive down there. Suddenly I saw my father, and my mother. They were with their arms about one another — real unusual — and they were waiting, like the rest.

"Oh, we got home that night, yes, and my daddy said they were gone — they were dead and we were going away. And we did. The next week we drove here in our Ford, and I can hear my daddy saying it wasn't worth it, money, and a car, if you die young, or you live but your lungs get poisoned, and all that, and you never see the sun except on Sundays.

"But what choice did he have? And what choice did I have? I thought I might want to do some farming, like my grandfather, but there's no need for me, and my grandfather couldn't really keep more than himself going, I mean with some food and all. Then I thought it'd be nice to finish school and maybe get a job someplace near, in a town not a big city. But everything was collapsing all over the country then, and you'd be crazy to think you were going to get anything by leaving here and going out there, with the lines standing for soup — oh yes, we heard on the radio what it was like all over.

"It could be worse, you say to yourself, and you resolve to follow your daddy and be a miner. That's what I did. He said we had a lousy day's work, but we got good pay, and we could buy things. My daddy had been the richest man in his family for a while, In fact, he was the only man in his family who had any money at all. After the family looked over our Ford, they'd give

THE WORLD

us that real tired and sorry look, as though they needed some help
real bad, and that's when my daddy would hand out the dollar
bills, one after the other. I can picture it right now. You feel rich,
and you feel real kind."

Hugh McCaslin's life wouldn't be that much better even if he
had not been seriously hurt in a mine accident. The miners who
were his closest friends are now unemployed, almost every one of
them. They do not feel cheated out of a disability pension, but for
all practical purposes he and they are equally idle, equally bitter,
equally sad. With no prompting from my psychiatric mind he
once put it this way: "They talk about depressions in this country. I used to hear my daddy talk about them all the time,
depressions. It wasn't so bad for my daddy and me in the thirties,
when the Big One, the Big Depression, was knocking everyone
down, left and right. He had a job, and I knew I was going to
have one as soon as I was ready, and I did. Then when the war
came, they even kept me home. They said we were keeping
everything going over here in West Virginia. You can't run factories without coal. I felt I wouldn't mind going and getting a
look at things out there, but I was just as glad to stay here, I
guess. I was married, and we were starting with the kids, so it
would have been hard. My young brother, he went. He wasn't
yet a miner, and they just took him when he was eighteen, I
think. He came back here and decided to stay out of the mines,
but it didn't make much difference in the end, anyway. We're all
out of the mines now around here.

"So, you see it's *now* that *we're* in a depression. They say things
are pretty good in most parts of the country, from what you see
on TV, but not so here. We're in the biggest depression ever
here: we have no money, and no welfare payments, and we're
expected to scrape by like dogs. It gets to your mind after a
while. You feel as low as can be, and nervous about everything.
That's what a depression does, makes you dead broke, with a lot
of bills and the lowest spirits you can ever picture a man having.
Sometimes I get up and I'm ready to go over to an undertaker
and tell him to do something with me real fast."

I have spent days and nights with the McCaslin family, and

Hugh McCaslin doesn't always feel that "low," that depressed, that finished with life. I suppose it can be said that he has "adapted" to the hard, miserable life he faces. At times he shouts and screams about "things," and perhaps in that way keeps himself explicitly angry rather than sullen and brooding. His friends call him a "firebrand," and blame his temper on his red hair. In fact, he says what they are thinking and need to hear said by someone. They come to see him, and in Mrs. McCaslin's words, "get him going." They bring him homemade liquor to help matters along.

The McCaslins are early risers, but no one gets up earlier than the father. He suffers pain at night; his back and his legs hurt. He has been told that a new hard mattress would help, and hot baths and aspirin. He spends a good part of the night awake — "thinking and dozing off and then coming to, real sudden-like, with a pain here or there." For a while he thought of sleeping on the floor or trying to get another bed, but he could not bear the prospect of being alone: "My wife Margaret has kept me alive. She has some of God's patience in her, that's the only way I figure she's been able to last it. She smiles when things are so dark you'd think the end has come. She soothes me, and tells me it'll get better, and even though I know it won't I believe her for a few minutes, and that helps."

So he tosses and turns in their bed, and his wife has learned to sleep soundly but to wake up promptly when her husband is in real pain. They have aspirin and treat it as something special — and expensive. I think Hugh McCaslin realizes that he suffers from many different kinds of pain; perhaps if he had more money he might have been addicted to all sorts of pain-killers long ago. Certainly when I worked in a hospital I saw patients like him — hurt and in pain, but not "sick" enough to require hospitalization, and in fact "chronically semi-invalids." On the other hand, such patients had tried and failed at any number of jobs. We will never know how Hugh McCaslin might have felt today if he had found suitable work after his accident, or had received further medical care. Work is something a patient needs as he starts getting better, as anyone who works in a "rehabilitation unit" of a hospital well knows. Hugh McCaslin lacked medical care when he needed it, lacks it today, and in his own words needs a "time-killer" as much as a pain-killer. His friends despair, drink, "loaf about," pick up a thing here and there to do, and "waste time real efficiently." So does he — among other things, by dwelling on his injured body.

He dwells on his children, too. He wants all five of them to leave West Virginia. Sometimes in the early morning, before his wife is up, he leaves bed to look at them sleeping: "I need some hope, and they have it, in their young age and the future they have, if they only get the Hell out of here before it's too late. Oh, I like it here, too. It's pretty, and all that. It's peaceful. I'm proud of us people. We've been here a long time, and we needed real guts to stay and last. Who wants to live in a big city? I've been in some of our cities, here in West Virginia, and they're no big value, from what I can see, not so far as bringing up a family. You have no land, no privacy, a lot of noise, and all that. But if it's between living and dying, I'll take living; and right here, right now, I think we're dying — dying away slow but sure, every year more and more so."

He worries about his children in front of them. When they get up they see him sitting and drinking coffee in the kitchen. He is wide awake and hungrier for company than he knows. He wants to learn what they'll be doing that day. He wants to talk about things, about the day's events, and inevitably, a longer span of time, the future: "Take each day like your life hangs on it. That's being young, when you can do that, when you're not trapped and have some choice on things." The children are drowsy, but respectful. They go about dressing and taking coffee and doughnuts with him. They are as solicitous as he is. Can they make more coffee? They ask if they can bring him anything — even though they know full well his answer: "No, just yourselves."

Mrs. McCaslin may run the house, but she makes a point of checking every decision with her husband. He "passes on" even small matters — something connected with one of the children's schoolwork, or a neighbor's coming visit, or a project for the church. She is not sly and devious; not clever at appearing weak but "manipulating" all the while. She genuinely defers to her husband and his weakness, his illness, his inability to find work — and none of those new medical, social, or psychological "developments" have made her see fit to change her ways. Nor is he inclined to sit back and let the world take *everything* out of his hands. As a matter of fact, it is interesting to see how assertive a man and a father he still is, no matter how awful his fate continues to be. He is *there,* and always there — in spirit as well as in body. I have to compare him not only with certain black fathers I know, who hide from welfare workers and flee their wives and children in fear and shame and anger, but also with a wide range of white middle-class fathers who maintain a round-the-clock absence from home (for "business" reasons, for "social" reasons), or else demonstrate a much-advertised "passivity" while there. Hugh McCaslin, as poor as one can be in America, not at all well educated, jobless, an invalid, and a worried, troubled man, nevertheless exerts a strong and continuing influence upon everyone in his family. He is, again, *there* — not just at home, but very much involved in almost everything his wife and children do. He talks a lot. He has strong ideas, and he has a temper. He takes an interest in all sorts of problems — not only in those that plague Road's Bend Hollow: "My daddy is a great talker. He isn't taken in by the big people who run this country. He's never read much, even when he was young, but he has his beliefs. He says we don't give everyone a break here, and that's against the whole purpose of the country, when it was first settled. You know, there are plenty of people like him. They know how hard it is for a workingman to get his share — to get *anything.* Let me tell you, if we had a chance, men like me, we'd vote for a different way of doing things. It just isn't right to use people like they're so much dirt, hire them and fire them and give them no respect and no real security. A few make fortunes, and the rest of us, we're lucky to have our meals from day to day. That's not right; it just isn't.

"I tell my boys not to be fooled. It's tough out there in the

world, and it's tough here, too. We've got little here except ourselves. They came in here, the big companies, and bled us dry.
They took everything, our coal, our land, our trees, our health.
We died like we were in a war, fighting for those companies —
and we were lucky to get enough money to bury our kin. They
tell me sometimes I'm bitter, my brothers do, but they're just as
bitter as I am — they don't talk as much, that's the only difference. Of course it got better here with unions and with some
protection the workers got through the government. But you
can't protect a man when the company decides to pull out; when
it says it's got all it can get, so good-bye folks, and take care of
yourselves, because we're moving on to some other place, and we
just can't do much more than tell you it was great while it lasted,
and you helped us out a lot, yes sir, you did."

He does not always talk like that. He can be quiet for long
stretches of time, obviously and moodily quiet. His wife finds his
silences hard to bear. She doesn't know what they will "lead to."
Every day she asks her husband whether there is anything
"special" he wants to eat, even though they both know there
isn't much they can afford but the daily mainstays — bread,
coffee, doughnuts, crackers, some thin stew, potatoes, homemade
jam, biscuits. Mrs. McCaslin defers to her husband, though; one
way is to pay him the courtesy of asking him what he wants. I
have often heard them go back and forth about food, and as if
for all the world they were far better off, with more choices
before them:

"Anything special you want for supper?"
"No. Anything suits me fine. I'm not too hungry."
"Well, if that's it then I'd better make you hungry with some-
thing special."
"What can do that?"
"I thought I'd fry up the potatoes real good tonight and cut in
some onions. It's better than boiling, and I've got some good pork
to throw in. You wait and see."
"I will. It sounds good."

He hurts and she aches for him. His back has its "bad spells," and she claims her own back can "feel the pain that goes through his." They don't touch each other very much in a stranger's presence, or even, I gather, before their children, but they give each other long looks of recognition, sympathy, affection, and sometimes anger or worse. They understand each other in that silent, lasting way that defies the gross labels that I and my kind call upon. It is hard to convey in words — theirs or mine — the subtle, delicate, largely unspoken, and continual *sense of each other* (that is the best that I can do) that they have. In a gesture, a glance, a frown, a smile they talk and agree and disagree: "I can tell what the day will be like for Hugh when he first gets up. It's all in how he gets out of bed, slow or with a jump to it. You might say we all have our good days and bad ones, but Hugh has a lot of time to give over to his moods, and around here I guess we're emotional, you might say."

I told her that I thought an outsider like me might not see it that way. She wanted to know what I meant, and I told her: "They call people up in the hollow 'quiet,' and they say they don't show their feelings too much, to each other, let alone in front of someone like me."

"Well, I don't know about that," she answered quickly, a bit piqued. "I don't know what reason they have for that. Maybe they don't have good ears. We don't talk *loud* around here, but we say what's on our mind, straightaway, I believe. I never was one for mincing on words, and I'll tell anyone what's on my mind, be he from around here or way over on the other side of the world. I do believe we're cautious here, and we give a man every break we can, because you don't have it easy around here, no matter who you are; so maybe that's why they think we're not given to getting excited and such. But we do."

I went back to Hugh. Did she think he was more "emotional" than others living nearby? "Well, I'd say it's hard to say. He has a temper, but I think that goes for all his friends. I think he's about ordinary, only because of his sickness he's likely to feel bad more than some, and it comes out in his moods. You know, when we were married he was the most cheerful man I'd ever met. I mean he smiled all the time, not just because someone said something funny. His daddy told me I was getting the happiest of his kids, and I told him I believed he was right, because I'd already seen it for myself. Today he's his old self sometimes, and I almost don't want to see it, because it makes me think back and remember the good times we had.

"Oh, we have good times now, too; don't mistake me. They just come rare, compared to when times were good. And always it's his pain that hangs over us; we never know when he'll be feeling right, from day to day.

"But when he's got his strength and there's nothing ailing him, he's all set to work, and it gets bad trying to figure what he might do. We talk of moving, but we ask ourselves where we'd go to. We don't want to travel a thousand miles only to be lost in some big city and not have even what we've got. Here there's a neighbor, and our kin, always. We have the house, and we manage to scrape things together, and no one of my kids has ever starved to death. They don't get the food they should, sometimes, but they eat, and they like what I do with food. In fact they complain at church. They say others don't brown the potatoes enough, or the biscuits. And they like a good chocolate cake, and I have that as often as I can.

"When Hugh is low-down he doesn't want to get out of bed, but I make him. He'll sit around and not do much. Every few minutes he'll call my name, but then he won't really have much to say. I have those aspirin, but you can't really afford to use them all the time.

"When he feels good, though, he'll go do chores. He'll make sure we have plenty of water, and he'll cut away some wood and lay it up nearby. He'll walk up the road and see people. He has friends, you know, who aren't sick like him, but it doesn't do them much good around here to be healthy. They can't work any more than Hugh can. It's bad, all the time bad.

"We find our own work, though, and we get paid in the satisfaction you get. We try to keep the house in good shape, and we keep the road clear all year round. That can be a job come winter.

"A lot of the time Hugh says he wished he could read better. He'll get an old magazine — the *Reader's Digest*, or the paper from Charleston — and he'll stay with it for hours. I can see he's having a tough time, but it keeps him busy. He tells the kids to remember his mistakes and not to make them all over again. Then they want to know why he made them. And we're off again. He talks about the coal companies and how they bribed us out of our 'souls,' and how he was a fool, and how it's different now. When they ask what they'll be doing with their reading and writing, it's hard to give them an answer without telling them to move. You don't want to do that, but maybe you do, too. I don't know.

"Hugh fought the television. He said it was no good, and we surely didn't have the money to get one. You can get them real cheap, though, secondhand, and there's a chance to learn how to fix it yourself, because some of the men who come back from the Army, they've learned how and they'll teach you and do it for you if you ask them. We had to get one, finally. The kids, they said everyone else didn't have the money, any more than we did, but somehow they got the sets, so why couldn't we? That started something, all right. Hugh wanted to know if they thought we could manufacture money. So they wanted to know how the others got their sets. And Hugh said he didn't know, but if they would go find out and come tell him, why then he'd show them that each family is different, and you can't compare people like that. Well, then they mentioned it to their uncle — he works down there in the school, keeping it in order, and he's on a regular salary, you know, and lives as good as anyone around here, all things told, I'd say. So he came and told us he'd do it, get a set for us, because the kids really need one. They feel left out without TV.

"That got Hugh going real bad. He didn't see why the radio wasn't enough, and he wasn't going to take and take and take. He wanted help, but not for a TV set. And then he'd get going on the coal companies, and how we got that radio for cash, and it was brand-new and expensive, but he was making plenty of money then. And he didn't want to go begging, even from kin. And we could just do without, so long as we eat and have a place to sleep and no one's at our door trying to drive us away or take us to jail.

"Finally I had to say something. I had to. It was one of the hardest things I've ever had to do. He was getting worse and worse, and the kids, they began to think he was wrong in the head over a thing like TV, and they didn't know why; they couldn't figure it out. He said they wouldn't see anything but a lot of trash, and why should we let it all come in here like that? And he said they'd lose interest in school and become hypnotized or something, and he'd read someplace it happens. And he said gadgets and machines, they came cheap, but you end up losing a lot more than you get, and that was what's happening in America today.

"Now, the kids could listen for so long, and they're respectful to him, to both of us, I think you'll agree. They'd try to answer him real quiet, and say it wasn't so important, TV wasn't, it was just there to look at, and we would all do it and have a good time. And everyone was having it, but that didn't mean that the world was changing, or that you'd lose anything just because you looked at a picture every once in a while.

"And finally, as I say, I joined in. I had to — and I sided with them. I said they weren't going to spend their lives looking at TV, no sir, but it would be OK with me if we had it in the house, that I could live with it, and I think we could all live with it. And Hugh, he just looked at me and didn't say another word, not that day or any other afterwards until much later on, when we had the set already, and he would look at the news and listen real careful to what they tell you might be happening. He told me one day it was a foolish fight we all had, and television wasn't any better or worse than a lot of other things. But he wished the country would make more than cheap TVs. 'We could all live without TV if we had something more to look forward to,' he said. I couldn't say anything back. He just wasn't feeling good that day, and to tell the truth TV is good for him when he's like that, regardless of what he says. He watches it like he used to listen to his radio, and he likes it better than he'd ever admit to himself, I'm sure."

On Sundays they go to church. Hugh says he doesn't much believe in "anything," but he goes; he stays home only when he doesn't feel good, not out of any objection to prayer. They all have their Sunday clothes, and they all enjoy getting into them. They become new and different people. They walk together down the hollow and along the road that takes them to a Baptist church. They worship vigorously and sincerely, and with a mixture of awe, bravado, passion, and restraint that leaves an outside observer feeling skeptical, envious and vaguely nostalgic. I think they emerge much stronger and more united for the experience, and with as much "perspective" as others get from different forms of contemplation, submission, and joint participation. Hugh can be as stoical as anyone else, and in church his stoicism can simply pour out.

After church there is "socializing," and its importance need not be stressed in our self-conscious age of "groups" that solve "problems" or merely facilitate "interaction." When I have asked myself what "goes on" in those "coffee periods," I remind myself that I heard a lot of people laughing, exchanging news, offering greetings, expressing wishes, fears, congratulations and condolences. I think there is a particular warmth and intensity to some of the meetings because, after all, people do not see much of one another during the week. Yet how many residents of our cities or our suburbs see one another as regularly as these "isolated" people do? Hugh McCaslin put it quite forcefully: "We may not see much of anyone for a few days, but Sunday will come and we see everyone we want to see, and by the time we go home we know everything there is to know." As some of us say, they "communicate effectively."

There is, I have to emphasize, a certain hunger for companionship that builds up among people who do not feel as "solitary" as some of their observers have considered them. Particularly at night one feels the woods and the hills close in on "the world."

The McCaslins live high up in a hollow, but they don't have a "view." Trees tower over their cabin, and the smoke rising from their chimney has no space at all to dominate. When dusk comes there are no lights to be seen, only their lights to turn on. In winter they eat at about five and they are in bed about seven-thirty or eight. The last hour before bed is an almost formal time. Every evening Mr. McCaslin smokes his pipe and either reads or carves wood. Mrs. McCaslin has finished putting things away after supper and sits sewing — "mending things and fixing things; there isn't a day goes by that something doesn't tear." The children watch television. They have done what homework they have (or are willing to do) before supper. I have never heard them reprimanded for failing to study. Their parents tell them to go to school, to stay in school, to do well in school — but they aren't exactly sure it makes much difference. They ask the young to study, but I believe it is against their "beliefs" to say one thing and mean another, to children or anyone else.

In a sense, then, they are blunt and truthful with each other. They say what they think, but worry about how to say what they think so that the listener remains a friend or — rather often — a friendly relative. Before going to bed they say good-night, and one can almost feel the reassurance that goes with the greeting. It is very silent "out there" or "outside."

"Yes, I think we have good manners," Hugh McCaslin once told me. "It's a tradition, I guess, and goes back to Scotland, or so my daddy told me. I tell the kids that they'll know a lot more than I do when they grow up, or I hope they will; but I don't believe they'll have more consideration for people — no sir. We teach them to say hello in the morning, to say good morning, like you said. I know it may not be necessary, but it's good for people living real close to be respectful of one another. And the same goes for the evening.

"Now, there'll be fights. You've seen us take after one another. That's OK. But we settle things on the same day, and we try not to carry grudges. How can you carry a grudge when you're just this one family here, and miles away from the next one? Oh, I know it's natural to be spiteful and carry a grudge. But you can only carry it so far, that's what I say. Carry it until the sun goes down, then wipe the slate clean and get ready for another day. I say that a lot to the kids."

Once I went with the McCaslins to a funeral. A great-uncle of Mrs. McCaslin's had died at seventy-two. He happened to be a favorite of hers and of her mother. They lived much nearer to a town than the McCaslins do, and were rather well-to-do. He had worked for the county government all his life — in the Appalachian region, no small position. The body lay at rest in a small church, with hand-picked flowers in bunches around it. A real clan had gathered from all over, as well as friends. Of course it was a sad occasion, despite the man's advanced age; yet even so I was struck by the restraint of the people, their politeness to one another, no matter how close or "near kin" they were. For a moment I watched them move about and tried to block off their subdued talk from my brain. It occurred to me that, were they dressed differently and in a large manor home, they might very much resemble English gentry at a reception. They were courtly people; they looked it and acted it. Many were tall, thin, and close-mouthed. A few were potbellied, as indeed befits a good lusty duke or duchess. They could smile and even break out into a laugh, but it was always noticeable when it happened. In general they were not exactly demonstrative or talkative, yet they were clearly interested in one another and had very definite and strong sentiments, feelings, emotions, whatever. In other words, as befits the gentry, they had feelings but had them under "appropriate" control. They also seemed suitably resigned or philosophical — as the circumstances warranted. What crying there was had already been done. There were no outbursts of any kind, and no joviality either. It was not a wake.

A few days later Hugh McCaslin of Road's Bend Hollow talked about the funeral and life and death: "He probably went too early, from what I hear. He was in good health, and around here you either die very young — for lack of a doctor — or you really last long. That's the rule, though I admit we have people live to all ages, like anywhere I guess. No, I don't think much of death, even being sick as I am. It happens to you, and you know

it, but that's OK. When I was a boy I recall my people burying
their old people, right near where we lived. We had a little
graveyard, and we used to know all our dead people pretty well.
You know, we'd play near their graves and go ask our mother
or daddy about who this one was and what he did, and like
that. The other way was through the Bible: everything was
written down on pieces of paper inside the family Bible. There'd
be births and marriages and deaths, going way back, I guess as
far back as the beginning of the country. I'm not sure of the exact
time, but a couple of hundred years, easy.

"We don't do that now — it's probably one of the biggest
changes, maybe. I mean apart from television and things like
that. We're still religious, but we don't keep the records, and we
don't bury our dead nearby. It's just not that much of a *home*
here, a place that you have and your kin always had and your
children and theirs will have, until the end of time, when God
calls us all to account. This here place — it's a good house, mind
you — but it's just a place I got. A neighbor of my daddy's had it,
and he left it, and my daddy heard and I came and fixed it
up and we have it for nothing. We worked hard and put a lot into
it, and we treasure it, but it never was a *home,* not the kind I
knew, and my wife did. We came back to the hollow, but it wasn't
like it used to be when we were kids and you felt you were living
in the same place all your ancestors did. We're *part* of this land;
we were here to start and we'll probably see it die, me or my kids
will, the way things are going. There will be no one left here and
the strip miners will kill every good acre we have. I thought of
that at the funeral. I thought maybe it's just as well to die now, if
everything's headed in that direction. I guess that's what happens
at a funeral. You get to thinking."

VII

THE WORLD
OF THE BLACK BELT

1. The Bossman

NO book about sharecroppers and tenant farmers and hired field hands can escape repeated mention of him. He is a legend of sorts. His name comes up in folk music, is mentioned in blues, has become a part of white, liberal and radical middle-class speech. He is the bossman — originally the plantation owner, but now any exploiter of people. I can't help going back in my mind to the bossmen I have come to know in those long, long conversations (so often with bourbon) that Southerners enjoy and encourage. They *are* storytellers, a lot of those bossmen, right out of Faulkner and Eudora Welty. Another Southerner, the Catholic Flannery O'Connor, would no doubt tell us that, finally, a Georgia bossman's soul is not unlike a Northern industrialist's soul, or a New England lawyer's soul, or a midwestern businessman's soul. Miss O'Connor insisted upon the things that make us all so similar: greeds, lust, envies, resentments, and, conversely if not always commonly, the decency, the grace and charity to be found in unexpected places and under surprising sets of circumstances. I am about to present the words of a boss-man who is proud to be, claims to be a bossman and only a bossman; he will let no one try to mistake him for anything else. They are also the words of a man who has a clear view of what he and his world are about. They are the words of a man who doesn't want and would not appreciate any gentle, ironic, or clever effort on my part or somebody else's to "understand" him, or treat him as a tragic figure, or a benighted one, or a "victim" or a "product" of all those larger social forces people like me are wont to summon.

I have already held off too long from this particular bossman, and perhaps his words will make my hesitations and worries seem plausible. I set forth the hesitations first, because without ever saying so directly to me, the bossman was at times responding not only to the insults he felt have been directed at him by others, but to my own "approach" or "attitude," never explicitly stated, but there — so he felt, as we shall soon see. He has read what various observers have said about him and his kind. He has read the magazine articles and books they publish. He is, among other things, a shrewd observer himself, not likely to miss the difficulties of someone else's position, just as he comprehends his own conflicting entanglements. "Tortured" is the word one looks for to summarize him and his people and their predicament; but that is exactly the word he openly loathes. He senses the implied pity and wants no part of it. He would rather be directly hated, or best of all, ignored. He doesn't mind the melodrama of the word "tortured," and in fact he does feel tortured. He even declares he feels so. But *he* wants the right to apply the word; if others use it, they are in large measure displaying their own compassion, and once again, as so often in the past, taking advantage of the Southerner, exploiting him.

So, we come to the matter of exploitation in a region that still possesses thousands and thousands of stranded, impoverished families such as the tenant farmers and sharecroppers I have already described, a region that provides many Northerners a rallying point for uniting in sympathy for people they most likely will never see, a region whose sins can somehow demand so much attention and outrage from Bostonians and New Yorkers and Californians that none of either is left over for people and conditions far nearer at hand. On this point Mr. Wells, Mr. James Clarke Wells (the three names are inseparable), has more than a few words to say: "Bossman, they call me a bossman, and they're right, I *am* the bossman. What else can I possibly be? I was born into a family that has owned this land for over a century. If I was up North or out West we'd call it our 'property' or our 'ranch,' and the people here would be 'working' for me, and I'd be the owner, the lucky owner, the rich guy, I suppose, that everyone envies. But I'm James Clarke Wells, and I live in Mississippi, and that means that a civil rights worker can wait for me, until he can get close, and shout in his self-righteous Yankee voice that I'm the bossman. 'There he goes, Mr. Bossman,' he said. I had to smile. He probably expected me to get angry, but I had to smile. I stopped the car and said, 'You're right son,' and I guess he was so surprised he didn't know what to say, so he turned around and went back to his people, the same ones I call 'my nigras'! Now I have watched him with them, and he is as *bossy* with them as I'd ever be, more so.

"I want to make it clear, though, that I'm not complaining; I'm not attacking the civil rights people either. One more thing I'm not doing: I'm not trying to 'explain' why we have the system we do down here. I'm sick and tired of our Southern writers going up North (or someone like you, returning to the North) and telling them up there how they've got to 'understand' us, and they've got to realize that we didn't create all this, and we're in an awful predicament, and we're 'tortured,' oh as tortured as hell, and we're victims, too, just like the colored man is. I've been reading that ever since I was in college, and I'm tired of it. I don't feel like a victim. I don't feel tortured. I don't see why it should be said that I never 'made' this society. No one who is born *ever* made the world he's born into. If that isn't common sense, I don't know what is. Why should we people ask for mercy — from those lousy hypocrites up there, who are now beginning to show their true feelings? They don't live near the colored people; they don't want to work with them or have their children go to school with them; but they're ready to tell me I'm terrible for having a plantation, and I'm 'paternal' for giving my workers a home and lending them money to use for food. The unions keep out the black man, then they call us Southern people racist. The people in the suburbs up there keep out the black man, then they say we're a strange breed down here, living in that peculiar region, the South.

"I spend more time with colored people — talking with them and listening to them and as a matter of fact taking their advice — than ninety-nine point nine percent of white American citizens. Yes, indeed, that's the truth. Mind you, I'm not telling you this so that you'll say: 'That guy, James Clarke Wells, he's a mighty fine fellow. He really bleeds for his nigras, and he tries to do the best he can for them, even if he's all caught up in that terrible plantation system they have down there.' And I'm not telling you this so you'll feel I'm one of the 'good guys,' and I'm kind and love the colored — while every other plantation owner here in the Delta and across the Mississippi in Louisiana and over there in Alabama is a no-account Klan type, who beats his workers and squeezes all the work he can get out of them and gives them in return as little as he possibly can. To me, it's like this: the colored people have been here for as long as my family has been here, longer. They don't know how to take care of themselves; they've always worked for the white man. Up in the North I hear tell that in those ghettos, when there's no one like me to 'oppress' nigras, they still don't know how to take care of themselves. They don't learn the way others do. They take more drugs. They haven't the business sense. They don't rise on up like the other 'exploited' people did after they came over here and ended up in ghettos up North. I'm saying this: the colored man isn't the white man, be it down here or up there or anywhere. Look what's happening in England now. Look at South Africa. Look at India, where the high-caste people are lighter than the low-caste ones. If you ask me we're dealing with a problem that won't be solved until people think altogether differently than they do now, and that means this problem of race is going to be around for centuries.

"Now, the truth of the matter is that I have a lot less trouble getting along with colored people than most white people. As I said, I'm with them all the time. They set out my clothes in the morning and they cook my food and they drive me around and they tell me how my business is doing. They wait around to let me know about the weather, what they've heard we're due — rain or a dry spell or strong winds. Last summer, late in the season, we had tornadoes near here. My men heard a tornado might be coming; they were taking the crops to the warehouse and one of the men there must have told them. They came back here and made sure I knew. They didn't have to do that. They could have gone and protected their cabins and themselves as best they could. But they were worried about me and about the 'missus.' They said so; they said they wanted to make sure we both knew there might be 'trouble on the way, tornadoes.' Do you think I dissolved in tears when they left? Do you think I said to myself: 'Those darkies, they're the sweetest, kindest people who ever lived, and they love us, just love Mrs. Wells and me?' Hell no; I know why they came here. They came here because we're *together*, all of us here. We live near to one another and we work side by side, and we're always in each other's way, and it's human, plain human, to go and hold out a hand to the next guy when you're in something as close, when you're tied so close, as we are.

"People can't understand all that about us down here — outside people can't. They think of me as holding a whip or something like that, and the tenant farmers we have here as under some spell or kept against their wishes. No one is living on my land who doesn't want to stay here. We've had some leave, mostly for Chicago. I told them to go if they want to go. I can tell when they are ready to go. They start looking down and away from me even more than usual, and I see them collecting themselves, taking things in the house from outside, things they might want to carry with them. One or two have bought newer second-hand cars, and that's a signal, too. Some slip away in the middle of the night and some come and say good-bye. But most have stayed and are working here and living here, and I'll tell you, liking it here. You don't believe that, I know. You say they're afraid and ignorant and unable to move because they can't even afford the cheapest car or the bus fare. You say they're not telling me the truth; they're telling me what I want to hear, and behaving in front of me one way, then behind my back thinking about a way to escape.

"It's strange how outsiders give our colored people credit for all kinds of cleverness, but assume someone like me is a blind fool. It's also strange how little credit we're *both* given, the colored people who work on a place like mine, and me or my two foremen. We've been talking with our tenants all our lives. We've had some frank moments, a lot more of them than Yankee civil rights people would ever realize. Sure a sharecropper is going to be afraid of a plantation owner; but the plantation owner can have his own reasons to be thoughtful and considerate rather than some tyrant. He needs his work done. He has to live with these people. They help him all the time. The stories about us are ridiculous, if you stop and think about them. They're really stories about slavery, and that's been gone for over a century. They are stories that pit a meek and dumb slave against a cruel, mean master. The fact is that I'm no master at all. I'm a landowner, pure and simple. I have this rich earth here that grows cotton and grain and vegetables, and I can put cattle out to graze on it as well. I can cut down some of its trees and sell the timber. I make money that way. I hire out people to help me. If they don't want to help me, they say no. They leave here, this county, and go to Greenwood or Greenville, or up to Memphis; or God save them, they go North, where they find out how mistaken they've been — to believe that in a ghetto of Chicago there could be a better life than down here in the Delta.

"I know my people. I'm not calling them 'my people' because they work for me, work my land. I'm calling them my people because we're all together here, part of a business, you could call it, and part of something else; I guess the books say 'the Southern way of life.' The colored man is as much a part of that way of life as I am. We've lived side by side for generations, so we really know how to do it — and we know each other. I read in some magazine that the colored man knows his white man all right, better than the white man knows himself. If that's true, then I'd like to add this: the white man knows his colored man, a lot better than the colored man knows himself. I don't say *all* white men do, but any white man who stops and looks and thinks a little, he knows what the colored people are like and what they want out of life. I don't doubt the same holds for a few of our smart nigras; I've seen them watching something or smiling at something, and I've thought to myself — this was long before the Yankee magazines suddenly discovered the colored man in America — that a good, clever nigra — and we have them — gets to know a lot about us white people.

"When you ask me what I think about them, I can answer you like this: I see them trying to live, like everyone else, and doing the best they can to get the best out of life, like everyone else. They're people, human beings. They like to eat and sleep and have children and bring them up and see them grow. They're good with children, you know. They're more like children than the rest of us — and I'm not trying to talk like the Klan people do. I just mean that the colored people aren't as serious and worried as a lot of white people are. They're not caught up in trying to make money, so that they can buy new machines, and then need more money to get more machines, and all that."

He would go on quite a bit in that vein, a mixture of social satire, social condescension, earnest analysis, incurable (it would seem) narrowness, and worse, meanness — some of which he would suddenly and surprisingly admit to me by calling it to his own attention: "I've got my own world here. I can't deny it: I'm what you might call 'provincial,' even if I've been North and I've been to Europe. I have my prejudices, too. I like colored people, but I couldn't take them eating at my table and I couldn't take them being at school with my children. I send my children to private schools. I might be called hard on my workers; but I'm fair with them. I don't cheat them. They work the land, and we divide up the profits. I deduct for the houses and the money I advance them. I buy all the equipment, the fertilizer and seed. I bring in the water for the crops. I do the selling, naturally. I know my tenants don't get a whole lot, but I don't make a fortune here, either. I inherited the land and the house. I inherited an income. I had a decision to make a while back. I could get rid of every single nigra on my land, mechanize completely, or even stop growing altogether and raise cattle and grow only trees, not cotton and other crops. Or I could keep buying machinery, but leave some of the growing to them, the nigras. I know how a lot of people up North would think if they heard me say it, but I know they wouldn't be understanding what I'm going to say: I didn't have the heart to throw these sharecroppers, these tenants of ours, off the land. I grew up watching them work and I hope they'll always be here, just as I hope my family will never leave.

"When I was a boy I'd drive along with my daddy in his Model T. I can recall it, black with the thin wheels and the small gauges and the small steering wheel and the wipers hitched from the *outside* onto the front window. Once we had trouble with the car, right in front of one of the cabins, and the nigras came out and they wanted to help — they wanted to help so bad, you could see it on their faces. My daddy said we could walk to the house and get someone to go fix the car, but they pleaded with him to sit there, and they'd go find someone. Then they asked us if they could go and get some lemonade for us — from our house — or did we want to go back there and get it ourselves after someone came and fixed the car. Imagine that! They were ready to get help for us for the car and they also wanted to go to the house, a couple of miles away, on a hot summer's day, get lemonade for us, and bring it back. My daddy said they'd have done it gladly if he'd have let them.

"I remember the whole thing so very clearly, probably because I asked him why he didn't let them go ahead and do it, and he gave me one of the most serious lectures I ever got from him. He told me the nigras would walk down to the Gulf Coast or to the Pacific Ocean in California if we asked them to, but that was no reason to go and ask them to do it. He said I'd have to learn how to behave with them: treat them firmly but kindly. I'd hear that many times from his lips before he died, treat them firmly but kindly. My mother was stronger on the kindness than the firmness, and they'd have disagreements over that — never fights, no, they never fought, never raised their voices at each other, never once in my memory. Mother would give the *tenants* lemonade and cookies when they came to the house on an errand. And it was our *cook* who didn't like that. Would you believe it?

"I recall one time — I must have been eight or nine or ten, I guess. Thelma was the cook, and she made huge chocolate cakes with either vanilla frosting or chocolate, depending on which one I wanted. She'd come and say, 'Master James, which will it be this time?' I'd always know what she meant. Sometimes after I'd answered her, she could tell I was having a change of mind, so she'd look at me real hard, and say, 'Are you sure?' That would be a signal for me to change, and I always did. Then she'd hurry on out of the room, before I could go back on myself again. Anyway, one afternoon it was exceptionally hot, and some of the tenants had come to the house to help Mother move some furniture around and get ready for a reception they were having for my grandmother, on her seventieth birthday, I seem to recall it was. After they'd done the work, my mother told them to wait, and she sent me in to the kitchen to get some of Thelma's cookies and lemonade. I went there and told her what Mother wanted, and I guess I must have told her what I was going to do with the cookies, though I don't remember that part, actually saying anything to her. Maybe I didn't. Maybe she could just tell by the look on my face. I've never thought about that before, but maybe so! Thelma was upset, *that* I can very much remember. It wasn't what she said, but how she looked. She looked away from me, and she looked down at the floor. To this day I can hear the words she spoke: 'How many of them are there?' I didn't know what to say. I hadn't thought to count them. The next thing I knew she was grabbing her cookies, the chocolate-chip ones, and putting them on a *paper* plate — and making more noise than she ever did. It was the first time I ever saw her use a paper plate outside the kitchen. She used to feed the dogs on those plates! She used paper cups, too, for the lemonade. Sometimes my sister would use them for her doll house — that's the only reason we had them!

"My mind is a blank on what happened, nothing probably. I mean, the nigras had their lemonade and cookies and Thelma went back to the kitchen, and my mother thanked them all and she went upstairs. One thing *did* happen, though, later on. Before I went to bed my mother pulled me over to her and said she wanted to ask me a question. Did Thelma say anything to me in the kitchen before she brought out the cookies and lemonade? No, I said, except that she did ask how many people there were to serve. My mother sat quiet and thought for a second; and then I asked her why she was asking me, and she said she was just wondering. Since I was a curious boy — I was called that many times by my parents — I wasn't going to let her go that easily. I must have sensed the nature of the trouble anyway, because I *told* her, rather than asked her. I said — I can hear me talking — that Thelma was upset, and I knew why: 'She didn't like serving nigras.' Then I asked my mother why one nigra didn't want to serve another one. She waited a while, longer than ordinary, and then she said she didn't think that was the case. She said that Thelma was 'temperamental' and had 'spells.' Well, I knew even then what my mother was doing. She had a wonderful way of getting around an issue she didn't want to deal with head-on. She would slip into talk about 'spells' that people have, or she would say she herself was having one, and she would go upstairs to lie down. So, she told me it was about the hour for *me* to go to bed, and there wasn't any point in talking more and more about Thelma. I could see she knew something or was thinking something she didn't want to talk about with me — children can usually sense a situation like that — and I guess I just went to bed, as she suggested. But you see, the mind won't let go of certain things!

"I'm taking a long time, a long way around, to tell you why I won't push any nigra tenant off this here land of mine. I find it hard to put the way I feel into words. It's very easy for *others* to talk about how a man like me feels. It takes a civil rights person about twenty-four hours in the state to know everything about how everyone here feels — and to say it! And there are those up there in New York who have never stepped a foot below the Mason-Dixon line, but *they* know how we all feel down here, too. I read them in the magazines, full of their moral superiority and their outrage at the terrible 'plantation system,' they'll often call it. They'll go on and on about our sharecroppers and our tenants, our tenant farmers, and what we've *done* to them. If I ever tried to sit down and explain what we've done *for* them, I'd be called 'paternalistic,' or something like that. And if I ever tried to say that Thelma hated her own people a lot worse than I ever have, I'd be called crazy.

"There are a lot of Thelmas around, too; and they're not only working for white people. Last year I saw a nigra kick another one and pull out a gun on him. You should have heard what he called him; the words were so awful I wouldn't want to repeat them. But it's not the unusual situation that I want to make anything special out of; it's what goes on every day in my fields, out there. They won't tell you how they fight and insult each other and waste their money on cheap wine. They're smart enough to bury the bottles, but I've seen them do the drinking and do the burying. I grew up here, and I've lived here with them, and when I was a boy they didn't hide things like that from me — only from my parents, I guess, and the foreman of the place. You see, I'd go out and play with their children; and now they're grown up, like me, and living here on my land. Do you think I'm going to go and turn away a man I knew as a boy?

"One of them came by a month ago and he said his sister and her husband were up there in Chicago, and she was ailing and would die soon, the doctors said. So, he wanted to go see her, but he wanted to come back, and he was afraid that if he went, and if I found out (and he knew I would), then I'd think he was gone for good and would soon be sending for his family, and so I'd throw them off my land right away and burn their house down, like some of us landowners are doing around here. Well, I got very angry with him. I said, 'Lenny, how do you dare come over here and *insult* me?' He looked scared and I could see he didn't know what to make of what I was asking him; he didn't get my point. So, I explained myself to him. I told him that he and I have known one another since we were little, since we were little children not old enough to go to school; and I would come around and play with him and his little sister, the one that went up there to Chicago. I told him he was a good farmer, and I'd just dug a well for his family, so they'd have water to drink nearby from a faucet, and not have to walk over to the other side of the plantation. I told him I'd seen him through good times and bad. When we had a bad drought, before I brought in the water, the irrigation, I fed him and his family, and a lot of others, and I never said a word, and if they so much as started to thank me, to mention anything about what I'd done for them, I told them to stop, and not say another word, or I'd get mad.

"I don't want to lose my shirt on this plantation, but to be honest, I don't need to make a huge fortune on it to get by. And my tenants know that. The days when Mississippi makes all its money on cotton alone are gone. That goes for the whole South. The cows, they're what bring in most of the real profit I make. I barely break even on the land my tenants plow; I'm not saying I give them charity. But it's not their labor that enables me to live a good, comfortable life. I didn't go into all of that with Lenny, but I touched on it. I told him I would stick by him and the other tenants so long as they were here and I was here. I told him there was one thing and only one thing that would turn me sour on everything; and that would be if he stopped trusting me, and I no longer felt I could trust him. By that time he knew what I was getting at. He said he was sorry, and he just wanted me to know what he was intending to do. I said that was fine, and I appreciated it, appreciated it very much. Then he looked right at me, instead of at the floor, and thanked me for talking with him. Then he waited for a second and turned around and was almost out of the room when I told him to stop and wait, please. I left the room and came back and gave him a check for the bus trip and the expenses he'd need, eating and whatever, and thanked *him* for coming over, and before he could start thanking *me* again, I told him I was in a hurry to make a phone call, and I'd see him soon, when he got back, and to please give my regards to Ida Mae, his sister up there, and I hope the doctors find they can help her more than it sounds like they thought they could when they first saw her and took her into the hospital. I left the room fast, and I guess he must have left right after me.

"When I was actually in my study, I found myself looking at the phone and wondering why I had ever said I had to make that phone call in the first place, because there was no call I could think up to make. Maybe I didn't want to hear him thank me and thank me and thank me. Maybe I didn't want him to see how affected I was by the fact that he had come to see me and tell me what he was doing and why. I *did* grow up playing with him and his sister, you know; and when you've lived all your life in a plantation like this, you've spent a lot of time with the nigras, even though you've stopped playing with them since you were old enough to go to school. The other thing to remember is that out here it's not a city; we don't see all that many white people. We don't go much to town. My wife gives the maid a list and she goes. We take trips, to Jackson or Memphis; but a few days of each week it's mostly the tenants I see and talk with — and the foremen, of course. And our tenants don't slink around and run away and hide when I drive up. Their kids rush out, and often I'll give them candy, like I would my own. The tenants will come over and tell me how the crops are going; I encourage them to do that. I'll tell them prices are high up in Memphis, and to keep up the good work. They know they won't get rich, but they'll have money around for Christmas, and there's food at the store for them; I vouch for the food and pay, and then I get repaid later from the profit I make on the crops. They can only charge so much, because I can't afford to buy steaks and lamb chops, expensive things. But they don't have to be told. They love bread, a lot of bread, and they're always cooking up potatoes, boiling and frying them, and there's the bacon and fatback and the greens and soups. They boil up good soups.

"They're in good shape, actually. They keep regular hours. They're up early, they work hard all day, and they retire early; we all do around here. You could fly over this whole county at ten or eleven in the evening, and there might not be a single light to see. They're not crowded together in slums, like you see them up in the ghettos in Chicago. They don't get the welfare down here that they do up there, but stop and think for a minute: most of the welfare goes to pay the huge rents they charge up in those ghettos — Ida Mae wrote to Lenny about that as soon as she got up there. She wrote back one of those short letters they write to each other, because they're not very good at writing. She said she was getting more money than she'd ever seen in her life, but she was spending it just as fast, and in the end, she wasn't left with any more than she had down here. That is about the story, now, isn't it?"

At that point he might have been able to believe himself as he spoke those words; certainly he spoke them forcefully and convincingly. A few months later he had to accept the news that his foreman brought him: Lenny's family was gone. Apparently they had waited until dusk, then vanished. When questioned, the other tenants didn't know anything, hadn't known anything was being planned, could offer nothing in explanation. James Clarke Wells took the initiative in telling me what he had learned and had nothing much to add. He wondered whether Lenny hadn't found it impossible to leave his sister, whether her illness wouldn't in fact last a good deal longer and thus in a way, in a tragic way, keep Lenny in Chicago so long that he (and now his family, called up there naturally by a husband and father very much alone and lonely) would "never be able to break out and get back home." In Mr. Wells's words, "that is about the story." Lenny was indeed unwilling to return, an unwillingness it eventually became my job to document and hear about over and over again, day after day. In Volume III of this work, titled *The South Goes North,* those whose fate parallels Lenny's will give us some idea why they left, why they refused to go back; and yes, why James Clarke Wells is not completely a mistaken, deluded fool, either — because homesickness does occur among people who are utterly glad to have left their "homes."

2. *The Foreman*

He starts out defiantly, bitterly, I suppose my automatic inclination was to think *defensively* — and thereby I am revealed as myself "defensive," because to label someone else can be as "defensive" a way of getting on with the world as to attempt a

kind of self-justification. This foreman of a plantation in northern
Louisiana is a big, blustery, talkative man. He is about six feet
two or three, and heavy, far too heavy. But life is short, he feels,
and death long — and his wife's cooking irresistible.

He was brought up in a Baptist family, which means baptized
in deep water and taught to pray long and hard. As a child he was
given a Bible and made to read it and memorize sections of it. As
a child he was taken to revival meetings, and incidentally, to
meetings of the Ku Klux Klan. As a child he was taught that
Huey Long was a great man and a martyr, that white skin has to
do with being chosen by God, that black skin is linked to Hell
and everything Bad, and that apart from their presence in
unblemished white skin, Good and Virtue can be found elsewhere: in the American flag, in the American Legion, in a hard-
fought football game in his hometown, which is near Monroe,
Louisiana, and in a gun, which he was taught to use so far back
in his childhood that he has no specific memory of learning such
things as how to hold a rifle or aim it or shoot it. Now he carries
one around; there might be a rabbit to shoot or there might be
"an uppity nigger," but most of all, in recent years, there might
be "some wise-guy, nigger-loving Yankee, down here to get these
people of ours on the plantation all excited and agitated up." He
would shoot to kill if that were the case, if such a person showed
up. He is in charge of "these tenants," who in fact are sharecroppers in the old-fashioned, literal sense of the word — they
work land and supposedly split the profits half and half — and
since he is in charge he has his responsibilities, which he insists
on calling his "orders." Certainly he does not own the hundreds
and hundreds of acres that he makes sure all those tenants plant
and cultivate and care for and harvest. The actual owner spends
a fair amount of time in his fine home at the edge of the large
property — but goes for a month or two at a time to places like
New Orleans or Mexico or New York City or San Francisco. The
foreman doesn't mind the trips South (to places as far away as
Brazil, where unbeknownst to him rather a lot of "integration" has
taken place) but he does mind those expeditions northward, even
though during the owner's absence he himself becomes for all

practical purposes undisputed lord and master, with several hundred black men, women and children at his mercy. He can issue threats and back them up with force or, alternatively, demonstrate his "niceness," which is what the sharecroppers call his mixture of attentiveness, assertiveness and sometimes open solicitude.

The foreman talks about on the one hand his own "philosophy" and on the other hand "their psychology," that of the "niggers" he feels he knows better than anyone else, including the plantation's owner: "I'm not out of a college like Mr. Douglas and his wife, too. She's French, from New Orleans. They try to make the whole plantation as perfect as they can; he'll tell you that he wants us to grow the best crops and raise the best beef and he's willing to lose money doing it, because he can get it back on his taxes. He has a lot of money, so he's not here to make money, but build up a fine plantation. But we do make money, a lot of it. I'm not saying it's all due to any one person, but I honestly believe I help out, and I believe Mr. Douglas would agree if you asked him. My philosophy is to keep the niggers working, and to help them out so they know what to do. They're good workers, if they're helped along. They're not bad people. There's where I disagree with your Klan-type person. Mr. Douglas called me in a couple of years ago and he told me he didn't want any trouble here; he didn't want agitating and all that from the 'croppers,' and he asked what did I think. I told him they were good people and not a one of them, a single one, would cause us any trouble, if they're left alone and told what to do. I told him I'd see that is the way it is; and the first civil rights person that comes on our land, he'd be dead before he knew what happened to him. I recommended that we put up signs warning people to stay away — or else. Mr. Douglas agreed and said he was going to leave it up to me to see that things are kept quiet around here; but he told me he wanted to let me know that he is against the Klan, too, and he knows they are strong here in the state. I told him he didn't have anything to worry about, no sir, because I'm also against the Klan. Hell, I work with the niggers, I told him, and I know how good they can be.

"I've seen how some white tenant farmers up in Arkansas live, and my daddy was a tenant farmer, so I guess I'm one white man who's made it good for himself. If you ask me, the colored people are *better* than the whites, much better, so far as taking orders and doing what they're told. Mr. Douglas leaves the niggers to me, and we've never had a single bit of trouble here, no sir, not a thing has gone wrong. I once asked Henry Jones, the smartest of our niggers, if he thought we ever *would,* and he said never in a million years, and I believe him; I believe he's right on the time: a million years. The reason is that Henry and his people are happy here, and they like what they're doing. They have this land to live on and work on, and they've been here for as far back as we have, the white people. We brought them here, didn't we? Everyone will say, according to what you read in the papers, that they're all heading North, niggers from every state in the South are. But there's something funny going on, because as many as are going, we still have them all over the place down here, just like always. I've asked some of our own colored people if they've ever thought of going North, and you know, they give you a look as if to say you're losing your mind for asking them something like that. Henry tells me a few go now and then, ones in the town, but we've not had any of our families leave, not since I've been here.

"I know their psychology. A colored man, he needs to be told what he's got to do, and when he should be doing it. They can't plan ahead, but if you make it clear to them what *is* ahead, then they'll be prepared, and they'll go and follow your directions. I tell my own children that the most important thing in the world is to know how to follow directions. My son Roger gets stubborn and won't listen to me. The other day I told him he'd better watch out, or I'll send him over to Henry Jones and he'll have to live with Henry for a while and learn from him and Leona, his wife, how to follow orders. I guess you might say Henry follows my orders, like I follow Mr. Douglas's orders; except that I'm around here all the time to give orders, and Mr. Douglas isn't.

"I try to help the 'croppers we have. I don't *have* to, you know. It's their land to ruin; I mean for at least one summer it's theirs.

We'd throw them out at the end of the season if they didn't do a good job, and they know it. I've taught them how to plant right and weed real careful-like. I've brought the extension man in from the U.S. Agriculture Department and had him show our people how to spread the fertilizer and take care not to put more than you need. Of course we have good rain here, and that makes all growing that much safer. You have to work not to get a fairly good yield here, but we want better than that, and we get it.

"The colored people are good. They don't complain much. They take care of their sick without making a big fuss. They're as respectful to us as they've always been. I watch the television and I can't figure out where those niggers come from that you see in the pictures, shouting like a bunch of hyenas and trying to take over the United States of America, that's what. None of them could have come from here, not a one of them. You can walk into our town, and they'll get out of your way. They don't want to be pushing on the white man. Here on our plantation we treat them fair. If they bring in a good crop, we give them half of the profits. We have to deduct, of course, but that's for their living in our houses and the advances at the store in winter. Mr. Douglas told the people at the store to sell honest to his people, and to try to get them to eat better. Once he saw Henry's boy sucking on candy and he told Henry it was bad for his teeth. Henry said he couldn't do anything about it, because that was what the boy liked all the time. I told Mr. Douglas there was no point trying to educate them on some things, but he sure disagreed with me on that. He said candy is bad for the teeth, and he told them at the store to try and persuade the families not to buy so much candy. Then he forgot about the whole business, and we were glad. Mr. Perry — he runs the store — said they'd all die, all the little nigger kids, if they didn't have their candy. They like chocolate bars more than anything else in the world. You know what old man Perry also said to me, real quiet-like? He asked whether Mr. Douglas would pay for those kids to go to a dentist. 'If he doesn't like what candy does to their teeth, let him go and have their teeth fixed,' that's what he said, word for word. I said I didn't know but I believe Mr. Douglas never went into the problem too deep with himself. Mr. Douglas will see something and get upset, then he'll forget, and it's up to us to do the best we can and cover his trail, that's the way I see it.

"Besides, the plantation owner doesn't go out there with the colored people. They're living on his land, but that's about it, to be honest. The ones he has up there in his house, they're a different kind. They think they're the most important people in Louisiana, second to their boss and maybe the governor of the state. Talking about your uppity nigger! One of them got wise with me last year. She told me to get out of the way once. I was standing in the door of the big house, waiting for Mr. Douglas. She's a pretty one, and she knows it. She's all full of herself. I guess she must have thought I was eyeing her. She came toward me and made like she was trying to get out, to go on the porch. I thought to myself: now what's her hurry, and where's she going, so fast and nervous-like. There's nothing out there anyway for her to do, not for her. So, I didn't move. That was when she said for me to get out of the way. I grabbed her arm and I told her if she ever *told* me anything again, about getting out of her way or anything, *anything*, I'd make sure it was the last thing she ever said, to me or to the rest of the world. I asked her if she understood what I was getting at, and she didn't answer me. I drew right up to her, about a couple of inches away, and I said she'd *better* understand; then I turned around and told her to look at my little truck over there in the driveway, the pickup truck. I said I keep a rifle in it, because I like to go hunting sometimes, early in the morning. And I said she'd better not forget it, that I was one of the best hunters around. I can shoot anything in sight and never once miss. Then I moved out of her way and she went outside. You know what? I looked at her; I followed her; and sure enough, she went near enough to my truck, so she could look in, and she saw what she was looking for, too. The next time I went up to see Mr. Douglas and she was there, she wasn't so uppity-looking with me. She just moved out of my way real fast, and I thought this to myself: it goes to show you that the only way to treat them is show them you're the one who's got the gun.

"Henry, a fellow like Henry knows better. He'd never try to get in my way or cause me any trouble. Every Christmas I give him ten dollars, yes sir. Every Christmas he tells me he doesn't deserve the money, but I make him take it. He works hard and keeps the others working hard. It's in their own interest to work hard of course; but there's always the danger they'll decide we're fooling, and we'll give them all the food they want and we'll let them stay in the houses, and if they don't get the yield we want and we expect, then we'll not mind, and just let them stay and be here forever. Henry lets them know the truth. I tell him the truth and he tells them the truth. Mr. Douglas doesn't talk like I do; like I say, he's not here all the time, and he's not the one who has to make the whole plantation work right. I say what I know he would say, if he had to do the saying! I just tell Henry to see that the boys keep things working along — or else Mr. Douglas will throw them all off the land and turn it all into meadowland for horses. That scares the hell out of them. I let them know through Henry that we'd burn down their cabins, every single one of them, and I tell them they all owe us money, from over the years, and so they'd be sent off to jail. Every year I get the sheriff to drive up here and make sure they see him. He'll come by to pay his respects to Mr. and Mrs. Douglas and he'll stay and they'll give him some coffee, you know. That's when I tell Henry that the sheriff is a mean, mean man, and Mr. Douglas has to plead with him to keep away from the colored people and not pick them up on some excuse or other and lock them up.

"They don't keep track of anything very much, the nigger people don't. They're better off never seeing *any* money; that's what I truly believe. And mostly they don't. They go all year without a salary, because they're going to get paid at the end of the season. We take care of them. They don't really know how to handle money. They spend it like my children would, on what suits their fancy. I don't blame them, though. You might as well buy what gives you pleasure. Why should they try to be careful and save and all that? Where are they going? They're not going anyplace. They're here. They'll stay here. They've been here all their lives, and they're not going to leave. I don't mean to sound

like I'm jealous of them, but sometimes when I'm sitting with my
wife and trying to pay the bills and make sure we've got enough
for a new television or a chair or a lamp the wife likes, I'll think
to myself that old Henry Jones and his boys, they haven't got it
so bad. Mr. Douglas gave them, a few of them, television sets.
They live in good cabins. They're not the kind of homes you and I
would be wanting, but if you put Henry or the others in our kind
of home, he'd feel uncomfortable. He wouldn't know what to do.
He couldn't relax. Henry will come by to see me and he stands
there, outside or just barely inside, and I can tell he's nervous.
Now, he's not nervous on account of *me*. We're always talking
and working together and we're friends, yes we are. They don't
know about us up North, they just don't. They don't know how
friendly we can be here, the black and the white. If you ask me,
Henry is just made nervous by our kitchen and all the gadgets
and — well, the way it looks, you know. It doesn't look like that
in his place."

Henry Jones does indeed live under circumstances that differ
from those familiar to his foreman — or better, the bossman who
is Mr. Douglas's foreman. Henry Jones lives in an old cabin,
which has electricity and television, but no running water and no
heating and no plumbing. There is a stove, and a mile away, a
well which is far too close to the surface of the land and is
definitely contaminated. The foreman knows that; he was told so
by the county's inspector, who came by and made the judgment
on the well and passed it on "for Mr. Douglas's attention." Yet,
why should Mr. Douglas be bothered by such things, so his
faithful employee thinks, and so he said — to Henry Jones, of
all people! For his part, Henry said this, very tersely but directly:
"I agreed when the bossman told me that the well might not be
giving us the best water in the world; but it's good-tasting water,
and it's nearby, and it would be worse to have to walk another
mile or two." I suppose it can be said that Mr. Douglas and his
foreman and Mr. Henry Jones simply don't "communicate" as
openly and honestly as they claim is the case. Each of them has
his secrets from the other, but each of them can be surprisingly
frank; and that is why generalizations about them and their "rela-

tionships" have to be very cautious, or at least suitably qualified. For instance, I found it almost impossible to describe exactly what goes on between Henry Jones and his foreman, because so very *much* happens as they get along with each other, all of which one gets to see the more time one spends with both of them, the more one follows them about and continues following them about until one's presence is at last forgotten a little. For a stretch of time Henry Jones can be compliant, humble, petulantly obliging. Suddenly he can change, though, and point out something to his foreman, disagree with him, make him change his mind. Nor is Henry Jones a sort of black foreman who *alone* can stand up to Mr. Douglas and his white foreman. Both white men can be found listening to many 'croppers, asking them questions, even asking their permission to do this or that.

When I finally came to know that particular plantation's foreman well enough to talk about some of those ironies or ambiguities, he made a bewildering series of observations: "I'm a redneck, they call us. We're not against colored people. We just want to make sure everyone knows that they're them and we're us. You can't blame a man for wanting that. I try to do a good job here, and a good job means keeping everything running and quiet. I'm happiest when I'm fixing our machinery; I learned to do so during the Korean War. I never take a truck or one of Mr. Douglas's cars to a service station. I've taught Henry a lot about cars, and he's taught me a lot about planting. I was first hired to keep the men in line, the 'croppers, and make sure they didn't just sit out there and let the land be wasted. Mr. Douglas didn't want them back there in the cabins, feeding off the plantation and not doing much. He told me he wanted them at work, doing their share, like they used to — when they *had* to. He meant back when they were slaves! They still *have* to, actually, because he could throw them off his land anytime he wants. But once he told me it wouldn't be a plantation if he didn't have the land under production, and if the tenants didn't work like they used to work. He has all these history books about how the place was run a hundred years ago, something like that, and what everything looked like then. There will be times when I figure all of us,

Henry and his people and me and my family, we're all — I guess you could say ornaments that he has around here, so that when he has a big party and people come, they can say he's got the whole plantation looking like it did before the Civil War. But he wants to make money on the land, too; and he does. He gets money from the government in Washington for *not* planting, and Henry and his people, they bring in those crops, let me tell you.

"I like our nigra people. I'll be there with them, figuring out when to start planting, or something like that, and I'll catch myself looking around at their kids; they're real cute, and it's funny, you don't mind the color on the kids — it even makes them look better than your own kids do. A good nigra, he'll teach his kids manners. Their kids don't always come after them with 'gimme, gimme.' I told my son the other day I was tired of his always asking, asking. I want this. I want that. I want anything I think of to want. That's the white man for you. These colored people, they mind you, and they're quiet, and they're respectful. So long as they don't start getting ideas in their heads, I think they're the best people in the world. Henry will tell me where to go fishing and how to figure out if we're going to have a frost. He knows his land, and he knows the water around here, what's in it and how to fool the fish. Henry has a cousin who's one of the smartest, cleverest men I've ever met. He's a hell of a lot smarter than Mr. Douglas, yes he is. But Mr. Douglas has the money, and that's how it goes. Henry's cousin can start talking about the county and the state and the United States, and before you know it you've got a real teacher beside you, giving you a sermon on how our country is owned, and what made us get so rich, compared to the other countries of the world. I told him, Edward, he should have been a college professor, doing work like that, instead of being here with us; but it's hard for them to get an education. It's hard for us, too; but a white man, it's his country. A black man, he's a stranger, is the way I see it, and he has to wait his turn, after the white man, and take care he doesn't get into trouble. I don't believe it's fair, but hell, nothing *is* fair in this world. There's the rich and the poor; there's those that have good health and those that are always getting sick; and one man will live a good, long life, and another will get killed, like my uncle did, and only thirty-six, in a car accident. I remember I was little, and my mother said to me: don't expect God to be kind to everyone because He isn't. She was right, and the colored people could tell you that even better than my mother, I do believe. But they keep on working along, at least they do here, and so I speak real high of them — because I have a high opinion of them."

An hour or two later I could hear his high opinion suddenly topple disastrously, and all the invective in the world would not have been enough to satisfy his need to "let them have it," which is what he could be heard doing. One of those sharecroppers had faltered; he disobeyed an order without slyly getting the foreman to change or rescind the order. Soon the air was thick with condemnation, and the white skin, as only white skin can, revealed how much anger and rage a man in charge, a foreman, will sometimes feel. Then it was a red-neck who was shouting, a man red with fury and outrage and self-righteousness. Then the world seemed almost ready to disappear in a racial holocaust, instigated by someone who an hour later will have calmed down, will be putting his arm on Henry's shoulder or his hand on Henry's arm, and will be asking him if he won't do something, *please*. And as Henry goes to do what he has been politely asked to do, the warm air receives the particular sweetness of a southern "thank you, Henry, *you hear*," and often enough they both go off, both go to do what the one has asked the other to do.

3. The Teacher

Sharecroppers and tenant farmers like Henry Jones (or that very bright cousin of his who prompts surprise and a touch of envy in the foreman) have almost always had a little taste of school — though I have met many, many children in states like Alabama or Mississippi who get no real experience of any kind with teachers and lessons, with reading and writing, with even a fragment of an education. They are children doomed to be not only "stranded" so far as money and power go, but doomed to the particular weakness and dimness of illiteracy. They are children who have never, I say never, set foot in a school. Among all the children I have described in this book, among migrant farmers and mountaineers as well as sharecroppers, one can if determined enough find parents who don't send their children to school at all. Perhaps they are "retarded," the mother and father — for some reason slowed down and disinclined to have any contact at all with the outside world; or perhaps they live far out of the way, even more so than most such people do; or perhaps a mother or father simply feels there is no point to it all, sending off children who lack shoes or halfway "respectable" dresses or pants to a place they will at best intermittently visit, rather than regularly attend.

I am trying to indicate that over the many decades in which public schools have become taken for granted by millions of American children, some American children almost routinely come to think of the schoolhouse as a place only rarely visited. Sometimes when I hear discussions of "ghetto education" or the "cultural disadvantage" that plagues a certain child or group of children, I find myself wishing I could flick on the switch of a tape recorder and let *this* teacher speak about such things, speak at her most outraged, her most cynical and mocking.

She is a teacher who works south of Montgomery, Alabama, and north of Mobile, Alabama, a teacher who happens to be outspoken, who talks and talks until her listener begins to wonder (as a citizen he is ashamed, as an observer he is overwhelmed) whether she might not be "troubled," because there seems a certain "pressure of speech" going on. Yes, we use that expression, we clinicians do; we have in mind someone agitated and anxious and maybe a little confused and fearful and near the edge of his or her senses. This teacher is all that; she talks fast and almost interminably. Like "manic-depressive" patients, who most often demonstrate "pressure of speech," she is full of agitation and anxiety, confusion and fear; and like those patients she is very near the end of a long, long rope, very near that vague and elusive but in a flash quite definite and obvious "edge" one hears referred to all the time in mental hospitals. Unlike many psychiatric patients, however, she looks at the world around her with utter precision, and has no illusions about the present or the future.

She is tall, very tall for a woman, about six feet. She does literally talk down to a lot of people, and so the thing one hears most about her from white townspeople in Monroe County, Alabama, is that she is one more of those "uppity niggers." She has a habit dangerous in cities like Monroeville and Frisco City and Goodway and Uriah and Mt. Pleasant: she looks right into the eyes of county officials and tells them off. She criticizes and complains and writes notes, memoranda, long letters — "long-winded" ones an official will say when he refers to them. Yet she is tolerated, more than tolerated. Her family is prominent, black but prominent. Her father is one of the handful of black land-owners with substantial holdings in all of Alabama. Not that her father raised her to be as she is, so insistently talkative, so sardonic and even abusive about "the great state of Alabama." (She can do rather a remarkable imitation of the man who likes to use that phrase, the state's sometime governor and the nation's presidential candidate, George C. Wallace.) Her father brought her up to be quiet, obliging and above all disinterested in politics. Her father told her that nothing will ever change in Alabama, not for her and her people, and that even in the rest of the country the changes that take place will "look like more than they are." Her father, for all his rather apparent pessimism, is not a man of cynicism and despair. He works hard, drives himself and his farmhands, takes care to save his money, and over a long life has become by his own description a self-educated man. He never went to school, but he learned to read and write and count, and he has used what he learned, and from year to year learned more.

His daughter acknowledges her father as a better teacher than any she encountered in Monroe County, or for that matter in college, too. He wanted her to be a teacher "from way back," though at the same time he warned her again and again that there was only so much that an education can do for black youth in rural Alabama. In many respects he resembles a certain kind of pragmatic, brooding radical who has little hope of ever witnessing the political and economic changes he advocates. Now in his seventies, he goes on developing his own ideas. He reads everything he can get his hands on, and he keeps up his work on the farm. He is one of the few black farmers who gets help from various agencies of the federal government's Agricultural Department, and also one of the few who is called "mister" in the local stores, in the bank and in the post office and even in the gas station, where he knows particularly rabid segregationists work, even though they are very solicitous when he drives in.

His explanation of this sheds a little light on his daughter's thinking: "They're crackers, red-necks; all over Alabama you'll find them in gas stations, making their remarks about colored people because they're not going very far themselves. I've seen them turn a colored man away, though they regret it, you can see by the look on their faces. But money is money, so they *are* a little different with me, not because they like me personally, but because they are not fools. They know I own land, and I get polite attention from the sheriff and the mayor. They know that I have money in the bank, enough to buy five of their stations. One more thing. They know that I read, that I take both *Time* and *Newsweek*. Now that may impress them more than anything else; they may think that if I subscribe to the magazines, I can write to them and have their reporters down here investigating and causing trouble! Anyway, they're not going to *tell* me why they are so respectful to me and give all the other colored people such a bad time. Do you know what my daughter once said to me? She said they're smart in that gas station. They know I'm the one colored man hereabouts who could start his own gas station. Well, there aren't enough cars, not among colored people, for me to do that, but I do agree with my daughter: the white man, even if he's white trash, doesn't lump every single colored man together, not all the time anyway.

"For years I've been telling my children that if we all became millionaires, we wouldn't get rid of prejudice and hate, but it would be a lot easier for us to live with the white man. But the colored people here in Alabama aren't going to become millionaires; I'm afraid the truth is that most of the colored people in this county haven't had their hands on a ten-dollar bill more than ten times, and they can remember every one of those times. Most of our people here are lucky if they make three or four hundred dollars over a *year's* time. They're tenants, a lot of them, and the truth is they grow crops for the white man and live on his land and in his cabins. He gives them food, not very good food, but food — like he does for his horses and cattle and pigs and chickens; and late in the year, at the end of the harvest, the white man will come over and 'settle up' with them, and like I say, if they get a couple of hundred dollars then, they're very lucky, yes they are, very lucky. A lot of them get nothing, a pat on the back maybe, and a *story*, a big story: about how prices for crops are going down, and how they've been awfully expensive to feed and house, all those tenants, and about how patient and kind the white man should be, but he has to have his limits — and so, look boys, you can do it over again, raise the crops next year, and meanwhile you can stay right here in your cabins, and don't worry, no one is going to bother you or try to get you out, no sir. That's the way the bossmen talk, I've heard them, and that's what my people have to hear — and feel *grateful* for hearing, because the alternative for them is no home, no work, no food, and a trip North, where they can feel it, they can feel it right in their bones, they'll only be a little better off, and still have plenty of trouble. One thing I'm very glad about: none of my children went North, even my oldest daughter, and she's the best educated of us."

His oldest daughter has in fact gone North, but never to stay. Up there she will visit a place, attend a school, stay in a friend's apartment (most of her college classmates have left Alabama), but not for long. She always returns. She likes to teach the children of Alabama's sharecroppers and tenant farmers. She likes to teach them in school, and she likes to go up those paths, not highways and roads, but unmarked and pitted and rutted paths, where she knows she will find children whom no school officials know about or care to know about. What does she do when she finds those children? What can she possibly hope to accomplish on those late afternoons, when she already has a long and difficult teaching day behind her? One might even wonder, as she herself will upon occasion, what she hopes to accomplish in school itself, where the sharecropper children come for a day, miss a day, leave to help in the fields, come back occasionally, and all in all convey to her what she knows is the truth of their lives. Many of us forget how boring lessons were, even to us, who knew there was at least in the future some *point* to it all, some reason to acquire an ability to deal with letters and numbers. Many children in our urban ghettos, however suspicious and contemptuous of teachers and schools, also recognize the relationship between the possession of diplomas and the ease with which jobs are acquired. In Monroe County, Alabama, though, few jobs are to be had, certainly not by black youths, certainly not by the children of black sharecroppers, whatever they may have learned in school. Nevertheless, even if their future is bleak, someone has to teach those children, or so this one teacher believes: "I have no illusions, that is the first thing I want to say. More than anything else I want to make it clear: I'm not teaching because I believe a little more education will mean a little more 'progress.' You can't use a word like 'progress' here; and maybe you shouldn't even use a word like 'education.' Even if the schools here were run by black people, which will be happening more and more in some counties of Alabama and Mississippi and Georgia, states like those three, even so we'll have the same problems here. We'll have the whole system. We'll have tenant farming. We'll have poverty that is unbelievable until you've seen it. We'll have people totally removed from everything.

"I don't believe anyone on the 'outside' knows some of our sharecroppers even exist. I can go to one family after another and no one in the cabin has ever been to a doctor, and no one is registered as a citizen or has a legal address or a phone and all that, like the rest of us have. I will never forget what our school superintendent said, and he thought he was delivering a compliment to me: 'We can't go looking for a lot of these children out in the fields and the woods. They're not like your family. They're like animals; they live like animals. We can't have animals in the schools, and it's best to let them hide and be as they are. You'll find some white families like that, too. They're sharecroppers, the last of the white sharecroppers. There used to be more, but now it's mostly nigras.' That's about what he said — and he added the last part because I think he suddenly realized how enraged I was becoming. I myself didn't realize until much later exactly how enraged I was, and how I must have appeared to him, sitting there and not saying a word."

As I mentioned earlier, silence is uncharacteristic of her; but she knows when to resort to it. She can be very talkative about the reasons she has at one point or another in her life kept her peace, said nothing, been "practical," allowed a particular white man or woman to go on and on, to have their outrageous, insulting, inexcusable say. She can remind me of what she knows I know: how completely even the most prosperous of her people must yield to the white world; and she can indicate how silent whites also have to be, poor and not so poor whites, who have little but their skins to possess. In Alabama some white tenant farmers still go without electricity and running water and decent food, she reminds herself and her listener — and those tenant farmers, like black tenant farmers, have no choice but to grovel before the big landowners and the sheriffs and the state police and all the people who run those counties she knows so well in southern Alabama. She often uses the word "state," uses it when she refers to the physical and mental condition of children, or to their characteristics as pupils. Sometimes in an expansive and yet elliptical frame of mind, she describes her own "state" as well as that of the children, and by the time she has finished, so many connections have been made, so many facts and "states" collected together, one can only join in her judgment — which is that "every person in Monroe County is part of one picture," and therefore it is wrong indeed to talk only about sharecropper children there: "You have to talk about everything here, because everything leads to everything else. I can't see how a study can be done of our tenant farmers and their children without studying the people who run the county system here in Alabama, and the plantation owners and their foremen, and how all of them affect our children. You can be sure that no child you talk with is the way she is, or he is, just because of an accident. In this county and all the others, when you look at the state of the child, you're looking at the state of everything here; and you're looking at what people with money have done to people without money.

"I'm used to a lot of these things, but not all *that* used to them; I can still find myself worked up into such a state that I fear I'll be eligible for one of those strokes my daddy has had, and his two brothers. The doctors told me I'm all right; my blood pressure is normal. But do you know what it feels like to have one of our white doctors, from the great state of Alabama, see you after you've been sitting in his 'colored only' waiting room? 'You're doing fine, *girl*,' he'll say. Girl! I want to say, 'Boy, you're doing fine, too — *little boy*, little, insensitive, mean, thoughtless, arrogant, conceited, unprofessional boy!' I have seen that doctor talking with a white man, obviously a poor one, and he won't call him 'boy,' though he can be just as fresh, just as mean and inconsiderate to his white patients. That's what being a doctor does for you! I don't know why I'm so surprised, though. I don't think a day passes that I'm not wondering how our teachers, our *black* teachers, can behave the way they do toward our schoolchildren. Some of our teachers don't even try. All they do is make critical remarks. If you were to sit and hear them in the teachers' room — so long as they didn't know you were there — you'd be shocked. All you'd hear would be how bad the children are, how bad they look — and dress and behave and talk and eat and do things. They're disgracing us, that's what they're supposed to be doing. Poor us! How terrible that someone might connect *us* with *them* — us nice, well-dressed, overstuffed teachers with those little kids who come to school in a daze, wondering if it's true, that they'll get a lunch here. Of course when they do get lunch they don't really care if they're called animals by those teachers; and sometimes they are. A hungry child wants food, food and more food, and if along with the food come little sermons and lectures and mean remarks — then the child can only sit back and smile and appear cooperative.

"Our children are afraid. They fear that they don't have the right clothes. They fear that they don't know how to say the right thing and do the right thing. They're hungry, and they're afraid they'll be caught at *that*, caught at being hungry! It's hard to believe, I know. They don't know that they have any rights as Americans, and the fact is they don't, not around here. They only come to school at all because, as I said, their parents haven't given up altogether, and there's the promise of milk or a lunch, though they don't always get what they thought they would. We charge them for food, and even if it's a quarter it's too much for some; it might as well be ten dollars so far as they're concerned.

"I often go out to homes where there might be five or six children, and they've never gone to school, not one of them. I go there and introduce myself, or usually I'm brought by someone. I try to persuade them to come to school — persuade their parents to send them. In a few cases I try to teach a little in the home, until it all 'takes,' and the child wants to come and learn. Many of the children don't have shoes; they don't have glasses when they need them, or braces for their teeth — and their teeth are in awful shape. They are tired. They look drawn. Sometimes they are full of curiosity and intelligent thoughts and shrewd ideas, but it's all buried under a veneer, you could call it — of confusion and a sense of futility. I am heartbroken by what I see, the good that goes to waste as much as the bad that gets no attention. I try to spend two hours every afternoon after school, going from home to home. I'll drop by and bring some food and a book or two, and show the children pictures. When it comes time to leave I tell them what I'll be doing tomorrow in school and suggest to them and their parents that they come and try us. I've offered to buy clothes for many children, and I've been taken up on the offer very fast.

"I'm no martyr in all this. I enjoy the children. After all, I have none of my own. I love to go into a cabin out there and spot a sensitive child who is about to perish, mentally as well as physically, and then try to throw a lifeline to him or her. The state of health among the children of tenant farmers is so bad. Their attitudes are also poor; they think they'll always live the way they do, the way their parents do. I wonder how a lot of people in this country would feel if they saw how these children live; but more than that, I wonder how they'd feel if they looked into the eyes of these children and heard what they *think*. They don't very often *say* what they think; they aren't talkative children. I believe they *demonstrate* how they think. They'll turn their head away or down. They'll fidget and then stare off into space, as if to say they appreciate your coming and trying to be of help, but really, there's no point to it. That's what an older child, a ten-year-old girl, said to me a month or so ago. I haven't been able to get her out of my mind. She was as smart as could be, if you stopped and thought about what she said; but she was also illiterate and superstitious and very ignorant. I don't like to call a child 'ignorant'; it's what so many of my friends, our teachers here, say about these children and their parents. But it's true; the children haven't learned how to take care of themselves. They cut and bruise themselves and get infected and are dirty all over. They want Kool-Aid and candy, period. They don't know how to clean themselves. How can they, when they've never felt hot water in their lives, and soap costs money their parents don't have?

"One of these days I'd like to go to a teachers' convention and get up and tell them this one fact: about eighty or ninety percent of the children I teach in school — that's not counting the children who don't get to school at all, or hardly at all — grow up in homes where there is *no* money around, none. Week after week these children don't see a single dollar bill. Their fathers exchange the labor it takes to raise cotton and other crops for the right to live in a cabin and buy certain things, like flour and shortening and candy on loan. That's it; that is how they live and that is what Mr. Wallace's 'great state of Alabama' means. True, the parents raise vegetables, sometimes they do, and they keep chickens and they go fishing. But some of our landowners don't let much of that go on. They want those sharecroppers working on cotton, on what can be sold at the market, not eaten by hungry children. In some cases families are forbidden to plant anything at all for themselves. In other cases, the foreman comes around and makes sure they don't work but a half an hour or so on those little vegetable plots. They don't even let them plant too many flowers, and our people love those zinnias and petunias and most of all the sunflowers.

"You know, the love of beauty, the appreciation for beautiful things — I see those qualities in our children, however ugly and poor their lives. I will come to a home and despair of ever reaching out to anyone in it; everyone seems so dazed and tired and listless, terribly listless. Then we'll be talking, and a child will move a little nearer to me, and I can tell she's getting interested, she's responding — and you know, in a few minutes she'll be pointing to a little rusted can she has, and inside it, in the dirty muddy water, will be a flower, maybe two flowers, just standing there, a little bent over. The flower is the child's pride and joy, her way of touching hope, I guess. I once told what I've just told you to a teacher who has the class next to mine at school, and she said I was going overboard on those kids, and they're really the worst around, impossible to teach. 'They don't learn, they don't learn a thing,' that's what she must have reminded me ten times. I told her that *she* doesn't learn, because she won't open her mind to those children. All she wants to do is teach proper little black boys and girls, whose fathers are the undertaker, the insurance man, and the two ministers.

"A little while ago she came back from a conference in Mobile, and she was all full of herself — what she'd learned about our poor, poor, pathetic children, and all their serious problems. She kept on saying how long it will take to 'lift them up' and how you have to be careful, because you don't want to 'overidentify' with them. *Overidentify!* I glared at her and slipped into dialect. I wanted to embarrass the living hell out of her. I said, 'Why honey child, what you talking about, what*ever* are you coming up with for my ear, huh?' She thought I was trying to be 'smart,' that's what she said, but I told her later what I was trying to do. I told her to come off her high horse and stop feeding me that 'overidentify' business. I said it was nice for her to go down to Mobile and stay in a hotel and eat all she wants and sit and listen to people all day in those nice hotel rooms — at the government's expense. Then she comes back and tells me I mustn't get upset

about our schoolchildren or say they're as interesting and challenging as other children, if you only get to know them — because if I do I'm 'overidentifying.' I'm afraid I 'overidentify'
every day, and so does she, and so do the people who run those
meetings and conferences and institutes because we all just love
what *we* are, what *we* came from, and we 'overidentify' with
ourselves and we can't stand it when anyone tries to say: look,
look at our brothers and sisters, look at how they're trying to live,
too, and how smart they can be, even if they can't read and they
can't write and they can't count.

"The funny thing is that those sharecroppers can't stand being
told they should change their ideas any more than my teacher
friends can stand being told the same thing. I got to know one
sharecropper and his family quite well, but I had to stop coming
there to teach his children and give up on getting them to come
on over to school every once in a while; instead I drop by and we
just talk. Do you know what that man said to me once? We were
talking about reading and writing, and about the value of
knowing how to do arithmetic, when suddenly he stopped the
conversation. He said school was a big waste of time. He said
even if he had the money to dress all his children and drive them
in his own car to school, he wouldn't be very much in favor of it.
I waited for his reasons, but he didn't offer any. I couldn't let the
matter drop there, so I asked him why, what his reasons were.
He moved right toward me and he answered me quickly, as
though he'd been waiting for the chance. He said that it doesn't
help a man like him 'on shares' to be able to read the writing on
a contract, or be able to sign his name instead of an X, or be able
to count up how much money the crops went for and how much
he is going to get and what the difference is. Then he finished
with this: 'The bossman, he has that foreman with those guns
and he can call the sheriff, who has his guns, and it's the guns
that settle things here, not reading and writing and arithmetic.' I
didn't say one more word to him. I got up and told the children
I'd come by soon for another visit and I drove home. It took me a
month to get up the courage to return, and I've made sure we
never have that kind of discussion again."

4. The Sheriff

Those guns that the sharecropper mentioned to the teacher have to be given their significance in what some of us call "child development." Sharecropper children in Monroe County, Alabama, must come to terms with their mothers and fathers and the brothers and sisters that psychiatrists call "siblings"; but in Monroe County a growing child must also learn how to live under the threat of the guns a sheriff and his deputies carry around all the time. The sharecropper quoted just above, that hardworking, terrified, proud, obliging, resentful man, is no child psychiatrist, no authority on "child-rearing practices," but he knows a thing or two about which "factors" influence the way his children's "attitudes" develop: "I try to teach my children all they're *supposed* to know; but most of all I try to teach them what they *have* to know, and sometimes there's a difference. The preacher will come and tell me to get my children to church and to school and all of that; but I know my children have to be here and help me out with the picking, and if they don't the sheriff will come by, and he'll have a different message for me, yes he will. He'll want me to stay on the land and pay attention to the bossman and what he's bargained for with me, or to get the hell off, that's how they'll talk to you; and they're always fingering those guns of theirs when they come here to speak to you.

"Don't you think my boys and girls hear, the same as me, and know what they've got to do, the same as me? My son Elston, he asked me if we would ever have guns, so we could answer them right back. I said to him: 'Elston, they are stronger than us, and there are more of them, and they run the world, and if we get guns they'll come at us with tanks and planes, and if we get tanks and planes, they'll kill us all, every one of us. Don't ask me how, but they will!' Elston didn't like hearing that; but he'd better, he'd better. Elston has asked me if he could go to school and get some learning. I said I didn't have anything against learning, but it wouldn't make any difference, all the learning in the world, so long as there will be the sheriff and his guns. Now maybe if we lived up North it might be different, except that my wife was helping out in the bossman's house, and she heard on the television that up North there are black men who have a lot of education, more than any of us get, and still they can't get the jobs, except a few do. And another time she saw a fight up there, a riot, between the police and the colored, and we lost. I told Elston you don't have to know how to count numbers to see that there are more of the white than you and to see that they have more guns than you."

His son Elston, at that time seven years old, knows the sheriff of Monroe County and his deputy sheriffs and the bossman and the five foremen on the plantation, knows them all as well as many other American children know various teachers and neighbors and maybe a doctor or two and a family lawyer or insurance man. His son Elston knows the sheriff perhaps the way middle-class white children brought up in religious homes begin to know God and the Devil. (I mean nothing sacrilegious or blasphemous here.) I say God as well as the Devil because Elston sees the sheriff as a most fearful, arbitrary, inscrutable, cruel man, but also as a man who has his sudden moments of token generosity.

Ordinarily I have tried to confine the drawings of the children I have observed to the sections of this book where their early lives are discussed, but I believe Elston's drawing of one of Monroe County's sheriffs (Figure 21, facing p. 271) should be mentioned here, because Elston's view of the sheriff and the sheriff's view of him are thoroughly complementary, indeed, are a part of the same psychological story — and there is in Elston's drawing a truthfulness that is rivaled only by the sheriff's various remarks. I would ask the reader to look carefully at Elston's drawing; then go on to the sheriff's honest, inward look — put into words after a year of conversations, some of them pleasant enough, some of them guarded and difficult and extremely unpleasant (for both of us). I happened to ask the sheriff what he thought Elston thought of him, and to my considerable surprise, I heard a virtual torrent of comments without having to do much but listen and occasionally indicate that I did most certainly "get" what was being said: "I know these little nigger

kids. Hell, I grew up with them. Some of those tenants you're
going around visiting are my age; I recall them playing in the
woods and near the grocery store. We'd all go to the grocery
store and try to get the people who owned it to give us candy,
and sometimes they would. Elston's daddy once gave me some
worms; I had run out when I was fishing, and I wanted to stay
longer, and he was with me and he gave me the worms without
my asking him a word.

"They're good people, you know; niggers are good people. I'll
drive by the cabin where Elston lives and I'll get on fine, talking
with his daddy; and I'll always be nice to Elston. I've given him
some of my chewing gum. I gave Elston a whole package of gum
once, and his daddy was nearby, and I told his daddy that I just
got a whole lot of it from the store — the same one we both knew
from a long time ago. Well, it registered with him, because right
in front of me, he told Elston that the two of us — his daddy and
me — we'd go and get some gum for ourselves in that store, but
then it was a smaller store, and the people who ran it were nicer
than the people there now.

"Elston is a nice boy. I don't believe he has anything bad to say
about anyone. He most probably is a little scared when he sees
me; that's how kids are when the sheriff comes around. I'm ready
to believe he doesn't like white people. People always talk about
white people not liking the nigger; but niggers don't like white
people. They'll cuss away at us, worse I'll bet than we do at
them. I can see the hate in their eyes. They'll be looking at you
and saying nothing, just going along doing what you tell them,
but you'll catch a look at them, and they'll be staring at you. I've
never seen more staring than from niggers. Those big black eyes
of theirs, they're always looking at you!

"Elston is one of them that stares. He doesn't talk as much as
his sisters; that's how it is with boys anyway, but there's no one
as silent as a nigger boy, I'll tell you. I know. I know them
backwards and forwards. The trouble with the North is, they
don't know how to take care of their colored people, not the way
we do. Keep them respecting you, and there won't be riots. A
nigger will go crazy and steal and even kill if he gets the idea

he'll be able to. When I get out of my car and come near them, I always put my hand on my gun for a few seconds. You've got to do so, otherwise they'll begin to think you're soft on them, and when that happens trouble is right next door.

"Elston wouldn't answer one way or the other if we asked him what he thinks of the police. I don't believe he's ever talked with his daddy about something like that. Niggers don't talk much, even between themselves. They'll nod and mumble. They have their ideas, of course. I'm not denying that. I've heard them say they think this, or something else, about a subject. But usually they hold their tongues, and that goes for the kids as well as their daddys and mothers. With Elston, you have a pretty smart one; he doesn't have that dumb-looking stare to him. He looks, and you ask yourself what's he thinking. With some of them you think to yourself that they're looking because that's all they know how to do — like an owl, you know.

"Elston probably wishes he could be one of the sheriffs, riding around in a good car. I'll bet he'd like a gun and a badge and a uniform. That's what my own son wants. The difference is, I guess, that Elston knows he can't do it, and he probably stops wanting what he can't get; while my boy, he keeps wanting everything — too much at times, I'll admit. To Elston a white man is no friend; I'd be kidding myself to think otherwise. But he knows me, and he knows that his daddy and I knew each other when we were his age; and he's inclined to give me the benefit of the doubt and think of me as more interested in him and his daddy than most white people.

"Hell, I like niggers. Elston can tell you that. He doesn't run away from me when I come by. He stands still and I'll give him a big smile, like I always do, and look him right in the eye and say hello and ask after his daddy and then go on. Once I even shook his hand. I came over and said to him, 'Elston, you shake your sheriff's hand,' and he didn't right away, but then he did; and I told him it won't be long before he'll be as good as his daddy out there in the field, and he said, 'Yes sir,' and I said, 'Yes sir,' right back. The only time I start hating niggers is when they get pushy and uppity and start asking you for what they have no right having. So far we've had no trouble. Our colored folks are real good. You take Elston's daddy; he's not going to cause any trouble. He knows that he's living over there and no one's bothering him and he gets his food and they have the cabin, and if every nigger in America was as well off, then they'd all be lucky. Up North they live in big buildings and they're packed in like sardines in the can. That's what you hear on television and it's true. I asked Elston if he'd be going North one day, and he said, 'No sir,' and he said he liked it fine here, and I said he was a real smart boy, and he said, "Thank you.' I told him he didn't have to thank me, because I was just telling him the truth, and he said his 'yes sir' again.

"You know, I'd be worried if the boy didn't say 'yes sir.' They've got to know who's sheriff around here and who's the principal of the school or mayor or all like that. A boy like Elston, he's got to respect his daddy and he's got to respect the white people just the same. A lot of the little niggers I see around, they'll be OK with their fathers, but they'll be bad and mean with others, I mean other nigger kids and their parents. With me, with the white man, they're different, though. I guess they know who's the boss around here and who isn't. I've never had to remind them of that, never. If they would be the bosses of themselves, let me tell you they'd be lost. They haven't the brains; they haven't the brains to go and do something on their own. They need to be told what to do. Take Elston, he's not like my boy, the one that's his age. Elston just sits and looks and he tries to oblige, mind you, but he doesn't have the curiosity a white boy will have. I'll be talking with white boys of Elston's age, and they'll ask me questions. They'll want to know how you become a sheriff and what's written on my badge, what it says, and how many bullets are there in my gun and they'll want a ride in my car; everything you can think of, they'll want to know. Elston, he doesn't want to know anything. Like I say, he stares at you and tries to get out of your way, but the truth is he's just a nigger kid, and I guess he must know it. If he's any smarter than the rest of them, I guess he's not going to let me know it. He probably is smarter. He seems to be. But you never know with them, even the kids, what's going through their heads. For all I know Elston thinks I'm a great friend of his, even if he is so shy with me. Maybe he thinks the opposite, that I'm going to shoot him or something. We had a nigger go out of his head here a few years ago; he thought the police were going to hunt him down and kill him, so he was hiding out in the woods saying, 'No, no, no'; all night and day that's what he said. Finally we took him in and brought him over to the state hospital. On the way he asked us to bury him near where his mother is buried and his sister, and when I told him we weren't going to bury him at all, he broke out into one of those crazy laughs. It would scare you, if you could hear it."

As for Elston, he needs no "crazy laughs" to scare him. He is already quite scared — so the sheriff has nothing to worry about. Elston finds the sheriff a big, openmouthed (there are two mouths!) toothy, unsmiling, wide-eyed, large-eared monster of a man, always ready to see something or hear something and then say something that he, Elston, or his daddy can in turn only nod at or agree with. Elston does indeed have questions to ask about that sheriff, as have many other children like him. I have heard those questions, and Elston's are quite representative: "How does he get to be sheriff, that's what I'd like to know. I asked my daddy, and he said he didn't know how. He said probably it was a friend he knew or the governor, or maybe he's a cousin to somebody big. He's not the only sheriff we have; I think he has a boss. Daddy says all the sheriffs and deputy sheriffs are voted in by the white people. A lot of colored people say they will go and vote, but come the day, they decide it's not safe to try. The bossman, he said my daddy shouldn't get into something like that. I guess my daddy agrees. He doesn't vote, he told me. I wish someday there'd be a colored man who would have a uniform like that, and a gun. I asked my daddy if he thought there ever would be, and he said maybe, but if I wanted to be a policeman, I'd do better going to some other place in Alabama, or up North. But I'll stay here with him and help him. I just wish my daddy and I didn't have to watch the sheriffs and the foreman poking into our house here. Daddy says he gets real scared, because he says they'll get themselves full of liquor, and then there's no telling what they'll do. But so far they haven't done anything bad, and that's good. And sometimes the sheriff or the foreman will be real nice; they'll give you candy and gum and ask you how you're doing, and I always say I'm doing fine, and they always smile."

5. The Preacher

He comes to many people each week with his message, *the* message, and he knows full well that but for him many of those people would have very little to fall back upon. He is one of several itinerant ministers, traveling preachers, men of God, that Monroe County's farmhands know and look forward eagerly to seeing and hearing. He is a man who holds forth, commands all eyes as he "does the pronouncing." Most of all, he insists on pronouncing judgments: "Judge not, lest ye be judged," he will cry out, after Christ, then go right ahead and judge and judge and judge. He claims that people need to have someone human to mediate with "the divine"; need tangible evidence that "the Word continues to be flesh — yes, right here in Alabama." To him Christ is very real, very near, unique; but Christ needs His disciples today even as He once needed them, and so he as a "preacher of the Word" is just that, "the Word become flesh."

He is constantly on the move and seems to draw strength and energy and vitality from the active life he leads: "It's all in the Book and what's in the Book is what directs me, yes sir, tells me where to go next and what to say." He never is at a loss for energy or direction or words, so "what's in the Book," his biblical inspiration, certainly works. He sees himself as a "vessel of the Lord," and if that seems self-serving and even a little prideful (the sin of sins), he is at least not compliant or submissive. For hundreds of Southern sharecroppers *he* is virtually the Lord, and those who come to see him and hear him and feel his presence are, like vessels, filled up, made to feel in possession of something nourishing and satisfying and reassuring and comforting. Himself like a vessel, he pours out his admonitions and injunctions, his assurances and promises, his stories and parables — and makes them *his* rather than the Bible's because he takes over what he tells. In fact he sees himself as a leader of sorts, a leader of Alabama's sharecroppers and tenant farmers and field hands — in his words, the state's "poor folk."

They are "good folk," he always says of those "poor folk," but on the other hand, like the rest of us, they can and do stumble and fall. What do they fall into? What can possibly tempt them, penniless as they are? The answer the preacher gives has nothing to do with cheap liquor or cigarettes or promiscuity or foul language. In a curious way he worries about his flock as if they were all thinkers, intellectuals, ideologues — or psychiatric patients. For it is minds that he wants to reach, the minds of the farm workers he sees as he travels from place to place in Monroe County and other counties nearby. In order to be intimate with people he shuns "regular churches." In good weather he prefers "the great outdoors," because God can "hear better," can "come closer," when there is no building to stand in His way. When the rains come and the brisk weather, then the cold weather, he holds forth in cabins scattered over the southern part of Alabama. He has a schedule, and his people have a schedule. Well before he comes they prepare for him. They clean. They more than clean; they scour and scour. They present him with a spotless cabin, a cabin that inside looks simple, bare, unadorned, yet strangely ready for something — perhaps because the room is so exceptionally clean, perhaps because the cross and only the cross stands on the table, or perhaps because some twenty chairs have been gathered together and arranged carefully in a circle around the table.

I have watched families arriving at such a cabin, at what for a whole day will be a house of God rather than a church. (No restrained, pinched, one-hour service will suit Elston's parents.) I have watched the families start from home slow and easy, suddenly speed up as they near the place, then just as suddenly taper off again. Sometimes a family will come to a full stop just a few yards outside, and simply stand there. Are they tired? Are they wondering whether there is any point to it all: the time

spent, the energy spent, the conviction sought after, the doubts
put aside — only to crop up again in some unexpected, devilish
moment? Are they readying themselves for the virtual trance they
will (a good number of them) soon be entering? Are they
expressing in a moment's hesitation the hopelessness they will a
few minutes later try desperately to drown in a torrent of
religious fervor? Who can answer those questions? The questions,
anyway, intrude themselves and suggest once again how ambiguous and contradictory "life," "motives," "reasons" can be.

In a chapter at the end of this book I will try to discuss some
of these questions under the crude title of "Rural Religion." But
this Alabama preacher must speak now because he has thoughts
about the people whose lives I am trying to describe in this
section. To be a preacher to such people calls for a willingness to
understand them as well as exhort them, or so this particular
preacher claims, risking thereby the sin of pride: "If I tell you I'm
supposed to know my people, really know them, besides preaching to them, then you might think I'm prideful, and that's bad, it
sure is. But I do believe I try to understand the men and women
I lead in prayer. I'm not a psychologist, or someone like that, but
I have to talk with my people all the time, and over the years I've
come to know them; I believe I have. Being a Baptist, I believe in
the Bible, every word of it, and I believe if my people follow the
Bible they'll be saved, even though I admit it doesn't look too
good for them here on earth, not for a colored man in comparison
to a white one. That's why the Bible means so much: you learn
it's going to be different when you meet God than it is right
now.

"I believe colored people are the most trusting people in all of
God's Kingdom. I know that sounds a little prideful, and also
boastful; but there are times when, to be truthful, I don't know
how we suffer as we do and never raise our voices. Now, you
may say that we have the civil rights movement; but I must tell
you that the white world doesn't know the colored world. Compared to the thousands and thousands of colored people here in
Alabama who have never raised their voices once in protest over
anything, the civil rights people are a very, very small group, a

handful. The whole world knew about Selma. But did people stop and think that Selma was where thousands of *out-of-state* people of both races from all over the country came? Meanwhile, the people back here in a county like this just go on about their way. Practically none of those tenants on all those plantations and big farms have protested anything; and they won't, either. Outsiders have tried to get the tenants going over in Lowndes County, you know. But I ask you to go there and see how many of my people are marching. They march all right, but to church, and not in front of any courthouse, where the sheriff has his office.

"You ask me what should be done, what they should do, my people. I say they must hope and pray that the answer will be forthcoming, and that one day there will be a better world here as well as in Heaven. But I don't have the answer; only God can provide that. I do not believe that the answer is for my people to rush out of their cabins and embrace the first civil rights worker who comes by here. My people know that civil rights workers come and go; they do their 'organizing,' like they call it, then they leave, because they're tired and they're discouraged and they want to go back home — to New York and Philadelphia and all those cities up there. Who is left here? I ask you. I ask them. I have argued with them, and they have called me terrible names, but I still ask: who is left? I am left, and my people, they are left. I repeat: the black civil rights people come and go, and it happens even faster with the white ones. They call me 'Uncle Tom.' They call me a 'tool' of the landowners, an agent of George Wallace. The truth is I was born in Alabama and I'll die here; and so will thousands of colored people who work hard on the land and don't know anything about agitation and civil rights and all that. They don't know if they can vote or not, and a lot of them don't care. I want them to vote; don't get me wrong. But I want for them to live and feel a little safe and, most of all, be joyous, for a few hours feel joyous — at the good news the Bible has for anyone who listens and says yes, dear God, I am ready, I am ready, even if it don't look very good for me, I am ready to go if You want me.

"In Dallas County some of the civil rights people, while they lasted, took a census. They wanted to know how many houses had good water nearby and how many didn't, things like that. Then I heard them talk about how my people are plundered and exploited and frightened to death; that's what they kept on saying, those three things. Maybe they are right; maybe they are. I just want to add something. I want to say that a lot of my people are going to be *saved*, and that is what really counts. I know I haven't the right to say people are saved. God saves. Only God saves. Man wants to be saved, but God saves. God tells you about salvation, though, and if you believe what He's said in the Bible, you're on your way; and someone like me, he can tell, he can see a person believing — having faith and being saved."

He goes on and on. He repeats himself. He attempts to justify himself in the face of actual criticisms he has heard and in the face of imagined ones, too — of the kind he would hear if he spent more time getting to know even the most moderate of those civil rights groups he mentions, or for that matter almost anyone in Alabama's black or white community who finds fault with the persisting conditions the tenant farmers of the state must endure.

"I know my people," he tells me for the one-hundredth time, and I begin to feel a little drowsy and bored, not to mention angry. He repeats his credentials. He lists once again the virtues of his work. He lists the errors and evils of his opponents. I hesitate to stop him, to tell him he has no right to speak for God and equate his enemies with God's. Presumably, my reason for being there is to hear him out, perhaps to push him a little, but only to elicit from him a more candid expression of *his* views, rather than the predictable responses he makes to the accusations he believes to be leveled against him.

So, I try to pay attention, even though my body slumps a little and I must try harder to keep my eyes open, my ears alerted. I start to daydream; my mind leaves him and Monroe County, Alabama, and goes North. After a while I catch myself, realize to myself that in so doing I have proved him right: like countless others, I have come and soon will go in body, even as in the reverie I had just left. And from the distance of Boston I will, of course, have my angry say against that preacher and his ilk, who do so little to change the world and even arrange to live fairly well with things as they are. Suddenly, though, I am no longer annoyed. He starts to move his eyes. He is alert. He is looking at his dark suit coat; he notices some dust on it, also a spot, and he attempts to clean everything with repeated sweeps of his hand. Then he brings up quite spontaneously other spots, ones he knows are on his conscience: "I lose faith myself many times; more times than my people do. I'll go into some of those cabins after a sermon, because the people want me to, because I know I should, and I near die. I ask myself, after all these years, after all those cabins, after all I've said about the poor inheriting the earth — I ask myself why, *why*. I mean, why does God permit all this? I won't ask why God makes these tenants feel so bad, because no matter what some civil rights organizers say, our people don't feel the way outsiders claim they feel. It's the cabins that get me so upset. It's the cabins that make me start asking the Devil's questions. I'll be in a cabin and I'll start hearing a voice in me; the voice whispers that it's terrible the way the families live, and God has got to, He's just *got* to do something. But the families don't talk like that to me or to themselves, either. Once or twice I've lost my head completely and talked like that out loud, in front of them, and they've looked at me, the tenants have, as if I'd turned into somebody else, and they no longer recognized me, and as if I was now a bad person and not welcome.

"I recall one tenant saying he didn't know what business it was of mine to tell God that something has to be done, because when God wants to do something, He will. Now, what should I have said to him? I don't know. I've tried to tell people that they should be proud of themselves, and that we someday should have a better world, right here on this earth — a world where our people feel they're as good as everyone else and not on the bottom, always on the bottom. Do you know what I've been told when I've said that? They don't answer me back with my words, or even with words out of the Bible. No sir, they speak their own words, and it's hard to put them aside once you've heard them.

They say they've been put here, and they're soon going to go, and all they can do is 'build up a respectable record.' You know what they mean? They mean a record for God, but they also mean a record they themselves can respect. It's hard to believe about a lot of our tenants, because they live so poor and they lack education, but they're very devout people, and they treat each other very, very good. We have some bad ones; I don't mean to deny it. But the tenants are good people, most of them, and it's only when they leave the land and go up to Montgomery and Birmingham or down to Mobile that they turn to sin. I think when they go North they turn to sin also, but I've never been up there, thank God. The white man here in Monroe County leaves the colored man alone, so long as we obey the law. I'm for change, like I say, but as bad as it is for us here, the children are brought up to respect their mothers and fathers and pray to the Lord and be quiet and good.

"In the cities they become lost, our people, lost like the tribes of Israel. I've been in all of Alabama's cities and I've seen for myself: my people look tired and confused; they want to know why they ever left the farms, bad as the cabins are. They don't like the streets and the buildings — where they're pushed together, one on top of the other, with no room for anything. They can't find work, and they miss carrying the water and fishing in the stream and working on the flower garden and the crops they raise. In the cities the police are worse to the colored than any sheriff here will ever be. Here we each of us know the other. I know the sheriff and the deputy sheriffs. I know the judge and the county people, the officials we have. When I drive down to Mobile I feel as if I've gone to a different country. I've gone down there to visit relatives of my people, to report on something that has happened here and to bring back news from there. Let me tell you, they can have the electricity and the city water they get. They can even have the new roads and the new schools. My people say there's no going back once they've moved, but I believe they'd rather be here in Monroe County than in some city. I more than believe it; I know it, because they tell me that.

"I should tell you, and you should never forget — whenever you do your writing about our children — that the colored family out here, working on the plantations and the farms, it's a family that can't afford to make mistakes; so the boys and the girls learn to obey the laws and they don't act mean and sassy and fresh and all the rest. Some of those civil rights people will come by and see our children and they say they're dull, that's what I've heard, and they're scared, and they won't talk, and they're afraid of learning and afraid of the white man and afraid of everything, to listen to these organizers. I'll tell you, they're afraid of civil rights people, and they're afraid of trouble brought in by people who say they are friends but soon will be saying, 'Sorry, I've got to go now.' My people don't spend all their time being afraid. They're not like they're described as being by the people who never see them when they're alone and by themselves and just going along — going from today until tomorrow, you know.

"Children here in this county and the others nearby laugh a lot, even if their daddys are tenants or sharecroppers. Children here have their fun. Children here know where to play and how to help their daddys, or if they're girls help their mothers. Our children are exploited, like they say, but they're brought up to be respectful of their parents. Our children are believers — believers in God and His justice, which will come someday. And our children are brought up to be real close together and to know that all of us here are together, even if we're poor. Now, you go and talk with our children — I do every day — and you'll see them smile and tell jokes on each other, and they can tell you where to go and catch a good fish and where the tallest sunflower in Monroe County is located. They can show you a shortcut to anyplace, and they know how to thin out the crops and weed the fastest way and pick at just the right time. They need more learning, of course they do; but there's a lot they know, and they're not as bad off as people say. A child will bring me rocks he's found, that the Indians used, and he'll be appreciative; he'll comment on the colors and the design. Our children are as good and lively and sweet as any others, and no white man has ever taken that away from them, their disposition. And I'll tell you something else: no white man even knows how our children are getting on. That goes for a lot of rich and fancy colored people in the cities — they don't know, either; and especially I'd like to say that our 'friends,' who are always coming through but never staying for very long, they also don't know."

How long did he want and expect "outsiders" to stay, and anyway, had he actually read what they claimed to know? The answer was that he had no idea how long outsiders ought to stay in a place like Monroe County, nor has he read anything anyone alive has written, because he spends his time reading the Bible and preaching and in between traveling so that he can again preach. Still, he has encountered all those students and organizers and activists, has taken them around the several counties whose roads and people he knows so well, and in so doing heard a lot of opinions expressed, a lot of forecasts made. To him all events are "passing," as are all signs of hope or moments of terror. He is speaking as a minister and theologian when he uses the word "passing," but also as a man who has seen a lot happen and not happen in Alabama, a lot change and a lot stay the same. As a man of God he claims to believe in eternal confrontations rather than temporal ones; and he always stresses the essential timelessness of the rural South: "We've lost some people here, and we've gained some machines, but the families, white and colored both, they're the same as they used to be when I was a child and when my daddy was a child. I mean, we think the same as we did: there's the fields, and there's the crops, and there's the town, where you sell what you've grown and you hope you get a good price; and there's the same God, looking over you. There's plenty of trouble, and there's the good times people have, even if they're poor."

As a citizen, an observer, a man on the moral defensive and on the moral attack, too, he once summarized his outlook this way: "We've had new laws and we've had Dr. King up in Dallas County, in Selma it was, and we've had Governor Wallace, and we've had lawyers come through here from Washington, and about a hundred reporters, and we've had colored agitators and white Northern ones — they're the biggest Mr. Know-it-alls I've ever seen in my life — and if you went and asked a farmer here, a tenant, if it's all made any difference, he would tell you that it's a lot of dust being stirred up, and the dust makes quite a sight for a while, but before long the dust settles down, and here we are, the same old people of Monroe County, the colored tenants and the white farmers, and no one could hardly find a difference between the poor colored and the poor white, and there you have the truth — the truth about Alabama."

6. *The Yeoman Neighbor*

I have indeed heard echoes of that preacher's viewpoint among the tenants he has challenged me repeatedly to seek out and question. Yet, side by side with comments that would sustain his position, one hears remarks, plaintive or belligerent, that utterly contradict it. Things *have* changed, say tenant farmers, who a moment or two later insist that things are just the same. The truth is that both cases can be argued — and have been by the tenants themselves, the sharecroppers who do the same work they always did and get "the same nothing" (as one of them put it to me) they always did, but who also are beginning to vote in a county or two, and win elections and even organize. Occasionally an outsider who is also not an outsider can describe some of those ambiguities very well. The preacher just quoted claims to be one such person; he is black and a native of Alabama, but he is also a traveler, a man with a profession (and a sizable income) rather than a field hand. Another observer I thought it necessary to hear out is, like the preacher, part of Monroe County's rural, tenant-farmer world, but also someone quite apart: he owns the land he works, is white, and is decidedly literate if not, in his words, "too well educated."

He is a yeoman, a strong, hefty, enormously industrious yeoman, who is a neighbor to "all of them, the sharecroppers and the tenants, and the day laborers and part-time field hands." He means by "them" mostly colored farm workers, though he knows what many in his own state let alone elsewhere don't know — that there still are white tenants, white men and women and children who do "a hell of a lot of work in the fields and don't get much out of it for themselves, because someone else owns the land, or loans them money and takes it back when they sell the crops." He himself was once such a person, a white tenant farmer. During the depression he lost his small farm; the bank "came and took it away." He moved into a small town and he "tried to stay alive." (When he uses an expression like that he is being very literal.) He got an odd job or two, but no more than that, and for a time he thought of leaving for Birmingham. He had heard of the factories there and thought he might get a job, any kind of job. He had also heard that the factories were not hiring people, that they were even laying people off. So, he stayed. He and his kinfolk — cousins, aunts and uncles — obtained clothes and food from their church. They moved in with one another, gathered themselves together. They returned to the land that the bank owned but no one used, and they grew vegetables on it. They became tenants. They tried to get by and they did. They lasted. Eventually they were able to purchase the land they cultivated. They had dreamed of a return to farming and now they were back once again on the land, working it over, using it, depending on it, gaining from it, giving themselves over to it, and always, having it upon their minds.

How can one like me, exploring the minds of such people, ever do justice to what the land means to that yeoman and the others mentioned here — the mere handful of people who can be described in one book? This white yeoman once spoke of "the way it gets into your blood, the land." The blood feeds the mind, as D. H. Lawrence knew; and the blood that yeoman speaks of can also echo a "level" of the unconscious that people with minds like mine simply cannot comprehend. Who, after all, in Boston or New York can find it sensible to think of something like land as the source of an "instinct," almost as powerful a "force" as the need for food and the desire for sexual expression and fulfillment or the urge to make one's mark upon the world, often aggressively and at the expense of others? Yet, in the course of speaking about the land, this white yeoman gives an account of the very people and the very historical and political conditions the black minister who precedes him in this book also attempted to characterize: "If you ask me how I like the work, I couldn't rightly answer you. I don't see my land as making work for me, causing me to work. To me the land I have is always there, waiting for me, and it's part of me, way inside me; it's as much me as my own arms and legs, yes, that's how I'd tell it to you. I recall when I came back here, and the bank said they'd forget the past and all I owed and let me start in again, and later if I made some money, I could pay them — well, I remember when we started all over again, right here, and the first day I couldn't keep my eyes dry, no matter how hard I tried, and all I was doing was wiping my shirt, the one sleeve and then the other, and it wasn't hot enough to pretend it was my sweat, and my wife couldn't pretend either.

"We walked up and down and we remembered everything, and it was amazing to us how we did: there were the pine trees over there, and the roots coming up, and the rocks on the other side of the field, and the paths we'd made, and the high land and the low land and the drainage we'd made for the crops; there was everything, and at last we were back here, back with everything that meant something to us — back to ourselves! The first morning I was at work I put my hands into the earth and I picked it right up and I stood there, and then I brought it back to my wife and I said, 'Helen, here it is,' and she said, 'Yes.' There wasn't anything more for either of us to say, and then we got over our being all full of tears and excited, you know, and we just fell into doing like we always did, and ever since then God has been good to us, life has been good to us, and we've had no reason to complain.

"I'm up with the sun and I'm ready to fall asleep when the sun leaves us. I'm always thinking about my crops; I'll be getting ready to take on the weeds, or spray against the worms, or bring in the water or drain it off. The land, it's a friend and an enemy; it's both. The land, it runs my time and my moods; if the crops go well, I feel fine and if there's trouble with growing, there's trouble with me. On Sundays I'm still hoping everything is fine out in the field. We'll go to church and we'll all pray to God, that He look over our soil and keep it strong and good, like it is now.

The land, you need the right amount of sun for it and water for it, and you have to put in good seeds and treat things just the correct way, weeding and putting down fertilizer and killing off the bugs you don't want and keeping those you do. Then you have to cover your soil and give it a rest and nudge it sometimes with the chemicals they have now and tell it to go on and be generous and give you a couple of good crops that year. I'm not a big farmer, just a small one, but I try to keep up with things and talk to the agricultural experts, the agents from Montgomery and the federal government people. They're the only federal people worth a damn. The ones that come here trying to mix the races and all that, I'd shoot them if they ever tried to step a foot on my land. I would. And I'm not exaggerating, mister!

"The niggers around here, they are good people, if they're left alone. They don't own the land, but they know the land, the same as I do. Nigger or white, we're all trying to do the best we can with the land; we all pray for sun and rain and a good, good growing season, that's what we pray for. I had cousins that were on shares, just like some of the niggers still are. One got killed by an auto, and one died in the war over in France, fighting against Hitler. We beat him, but if Mr. Wallace is right, the Russians and the Communist types here at home are still around to bother us. I guess I'm for Wallace. He has the correct view on things. Sometimes I don't like the way he talks; he talks too much and he's too up and down, 'bouncy and little,' my wife says to describe him. I was for Jim Folsom. He was our kind of person; he knew the farmer, and he spoke straight to you. He was easygoing about himself — that's what Wallace isn't. But the other side is that Wallace is fighting to keep Alabama like it always has been, and that's important. I talk with our niggers all the time, and they want what I do. They want good yields on the acre. They want the largest crops that's possible. They want to live good, and they want to *work*. The nigger up North, he doesn't want to work any more. You know why? It would happen with me too: you're good at planting and tending and harvesting, and then you go into a city and you sit and you've got nothing to do, or else you go into a factory and you hate the work. You forget about the sun coming up and going down. You forget about how to use your arms and legs, how to walk up and down and *raise* things, food to eat and cotton that'll lead to clothes. It's no good, taking welfare money or living in a big city where you're no one, just part of everyone.

"I know what I'm talking about. I once visited Birmingham; I went to see a neighbor of ours who'd gone there in 1937. I was thinking of moving there myself; but I'll tell you, I never went. I'm glad now, and so are my sons. They're glad to be here, and soon it'll be theirs, the very same land they've worked on, alongside their father. I hire niggers to help me and help my sons with the harvesting, at that time of the year. They are good workers; I never have had a complaint about them. They are hardworking, and they don't get wise and try asking for every little extra, just to prove they're like the civil rights people, who are causing all the noise and pushing at us for as many favors as they can scare us into giving.

"I can tell you a thing or two you won't hear on that television. I can tell you that I've grown up beside our nigger people, and what they know is what I know: we're all people trying to make Monroe County's land grow; and the more it can grow, the better it is for everyone, and whether you're colored or white doesn't make the slightest bit of difference. I was taught how to use a hoe by a nigger. I've taught niggers how to hoe. I was taught how to space my planting by niggers. I've taught them the same thing. Sure, I'm better off than most of them near here, but I'm a hell of a lot poorer than the white people you see on that television, dressed as they are and acting the way they do on those programs. They're all rich people, the ones you see on television — rich city people. It makes you wonder about America, your own country, where you and your family have been since way back. It makes you wonder, seeing those people on those programs. They look bad, real bad, to us. I'd rather have a hundred niggers around me than some of those white folks you see on television — with the way they look and dress and talk.

They're the worst people ever, the Communist whites that appear on your TV set, and it's *them* that's giving these crazy ideas to the niggers.

"They're quiet people, and real gullible, your nigger is. That's their weak spot. The professors up there in the North, and the bohemian types — whatever they're called now, we used to hear them called bohemians — and the radicals, the Communists — Wallace is right when he says all of them whisper things into a few niggers' ears, and they run wild, trying to do like they're told. It's not our niggers who do that, though. Here in this county all of them are my neighbors, and I know them like they were my own brothers and sisters; and I'll tell you, I'm not ashamed to say it like I just did. They've helped me, and I've helped them. They've never come and demanded anything from me and I've never tried to cheat on them, take anything away from them that was theirs. They don't have much, I know it. But I don't either, don't you see? I only have my land, and the nigger, all he has is our land — the land we have here in this county, and the land that's in the other counties of Alabama."

It took us two years of meetings even to begin talking about that land, which is the single most important thing in his life as a yeoman farmer and yet the one subject he shunned for a long time. What is there to say (he would ask me) about farming and about the "Black Belt"? Some issues are very simple, he would insist; in fact some things can't be talked about because, again, there really isn't much to say. Yet finally he could talk of the land, not in ecstatic or mystical ways, not in ways that seemed sentimental or poetic or even warm and enthusiastic. As I have read his words later on, the real psychological power of the attachment that he feels to the land does come across, but I suppose like all important things in the lives of people, what really matters can at times reveal itself quietly, gently, gradually, almost deviously. I believe that a white yeoman of Alabama and a black sharecropper of Alabama possess quite similar feelings toward that earth, that land they share in common; but I also know I cannot "prove" what I am saying here and in other sections of this book — only offer the words of people and the drawings of children as random testimony. As I indicated at the outset of this book, a yeoman like the one who has spoken the words immediately preceding mine is no "type," no representative of this and that "position" or "view." I can only say, however, that in my experience he is not extraordinary or unusual, either. I can only say that I have talked with others like him, heard those others speak as he has and demonstrate a comparable range of feeling or sensibility. Yet having said that, declared him to be convincing and talkative, even gregarious, I have to go on to say that he is a lonely man and cannot talk about many things. He often changes his mind, and for hours at a time he can be silent, suspicious, aloof. How can this man's loneliness, his crankiness and moodiness, enhance his credibility as a witness? I cannot answer that question, but I feel it necessary to ask the question before going on, because he acknowledges his loneliness and his moods almost in the same breath that he tells of his work on the land. The two "subjects" (the man's inclination to cut himself off and brood, and his love of the land he tames but also stands in awe of and worries about) seem to go together.

"I don't see much of people and don't care to," he will say, then stop cold. We go on and on, and a month later he repeats the terse remark that conveys the obvious, that lets it be known (as if anyone could doubt it!) how much he works by himself on that property of his, that farmland full of cotton, soybeans, and an assortment of vegetables. But despite his apparent sulkiness he can talk and talk, and by doing so virtually refute the substance of his own (self-descriptive) comments: "Like I told you, I don't see too many people; hardly any, if you were to stop and count them — except at church, I guess. I don't do a lot of talking, either. I don't get much out of saying this and saying that. If you want to be near people and talk a lot, you can't work your own farm. That's one thing you have to decide for yourself. There are times I wish I had more money, and I could keep a lot of niggers around me, like they have on the plantations. They can be a lot of help to you, a good nigger — big and strong and half smart — and we have them all over for the asking, you know. Oh, there are the real dumb ones, but strange as it may seem, I don't think they're the ones who are left here. I think a lot of the dumbest left first to go up North. How else can you explain it? A man has to be dumb to leave here and end up in one of those cities you see on the television."

We discuss such matters, politely but with obvious disagreement. My questions become somewhat contentious and his replies are not as impassive as they sometimes can be. Yes, he says, maybe a smart man takes stock and gets out fast, while a slower person waits and waits and hopes in vain. "But," he says, then stops short in his tracks. He has nothing more right at that moment than "but." A little later, though, he lets me know the train of his thought, his objections to my speculations. His argument resembles in several respects, though unintentionally, the position of many contemporary radicals, not to mention old-fashioned southern agrarians: "A man can stay here because he *knows* it's better here, even if he doesn't like it here. I think some of the nigger's friends that come out and say they're for him all the way don't give him half the credit he should get. I keep on telling you I know niggers, have known them all my life. I *talk* with them; I don't talk *to* them, I talk *with* them. I don't try and lead them and get them registered to vote and get them to demonstrate and all those things; but I was born here, like them, and we grew up here, and we're neighbors, and a neighbor is a neighbor, no matter if you're colored or white. I hire niggers every year to come and help me for a while, with the harvest, and they're men I've known all my life. There's one of them, Billy, that's the smartest one of his people you'll ever meet. He'll tell you how he went to Birmingham and came back. He'll tell you how his brother is up in Cleveland, Ohio, and hates it there, real bad. He'll tell you how he's not going to leave here ever, unless he has to. He'll tell you that a man has to be dumb to leave here and go to a northern city and live like a rat in a crowded cage up there.

'Sure, Billy is poor. We all are here, or most of us are. I'm not rich. We have a banker or two, and the few who own big plantations, but that's a small number of people. Most of us work. We don't live fancy. We don't need all the money they use in other places. We grow some food for ourselves, and we help each other out. I have a friend who is in the Klan, the Ku Klux Klan. I've never joined. I've never joined anything except the Army and the church. A lot of people would say he's prejudiced about the colored, but I know better. He gives them food in the winter and clothes from his family. They work for him — he has a farm like I do — and they all get on just fine. He took one of his old niggers down to Mobile, drove him there, to go see a doctor in a hospital there. If you heard him you'd agree with me — that he's *for* the colored man, but he's against forcing us to act in a way that's completely foreign to us. You can't make different people into the same kind of people, that's how we think. Can anyone show us we're wrong? I doubt it. I don't believe so. You ask Billy, and he'll tell you that colored is colored and white is white. Once you accept that, then you can work with each other; and that's what we do. I have known as many of the colored as anyone, and we've kept some of the best colored right down here. And you know what? The smart colored are for the governor, too; they're for Wallace. Yes sir, they are. Now the Yankees don't know that, do they?"

I told him yes, the Yankees don't. I asked him why black people go along with the very person, the very leaders, the very system that keeps them under, keeps them in such bad shape, such outright pain and misery. He had told me that *he* sometimes is in "pain and misery" and he had admitted that his "niggers" also suffer a good deal. I was now giving him back his words, hoping that he would accept them as such and not get too outraged at me. He didn't, not that time. Over the months he had become obviously and explicitly annoyed by my apparent and continuing inability to see what he now would once again patiently explain — this time without shortness of temper or visible bitterness: "Sure they do, niggers have aches and pain and misery like I do. Niggers like Wallace because he speaks right to you, and no phony talk. Niggers don't have to tell me what they think. I never ask them. I never expect them to come running to me with their ideas on politics. But I know that Wallace talks to the ordinary man, whether he'll be colored or white. There are rich niggers, you know, and there are the ones that want to vote, and all of that. They're the ones who go pushing on us, and opening up their homes to those Northern white folks who come here and then go, like the seasons do.

"He came through here, Governor Wallace did, and he came up the road and he joined right in with us. He talked with the colored and the white; we were all here together, working. He talked our talk. He knows what we do. He knows how we live and how we think. A lot of the politicians, they're lawyer types, and you can see by how they dress and talk and act in front of you and on the television that they want to get away fast — with your votes, of course — and join their friends in the country clubs down there in Mobile or up in Birmingham. Some of them talk like they're professors out of the University of Alabama. But Wallace is not one for showing off. Jim Folsom wasn't a high-and-mighty type either. I liked both of them. The colored do, too; *our* colored, around here. I can't say about the ones in the cities. They get all changed around once they get to those cities; and maybe your white people do, the same way.

"Here we like to be alone — and you can't be alone in a city. Here we work by ourselves, or with some help; but it's each man by himself out there, doing the best he can with the crops, planting them and tending to them and taking them in at the end of the season. I'll be out there, and I'll be working hard and praying to God for just a little more rain, or some sun that we need real bad-like. I'll be there, and a nigger will meet me at the end of the row, and he'll tell me he was just praying, too — for the same things. There's only one God, you see; and out there on our land, we're the same, the very same — trying to do a good job and keep the plants growing right and pick them right. And I can't say any more, except what I've said already.

"I get to feeling lonely every once in a while. It's hardest in the spring, when I can't afford any help, and even if I could it's mostly up to me to go and do the best job I can, softening up the land and breaking it up and preparing it, you know, for planting. I'll be honest with you. I miss having the niggers around. They're good to have with you. They're good company — Billy and Jeff and Woody and old Clem, who says he can recall my daddy boasting that I'd be the best man in the county at growing things. He says he and my daddy used to sit and sip a little bourbon and figure out if we'd ever survive what Wall Street was doing to Alabama, to our people down here; and all over it was bad. Well, we did survive; Clem did and I did. My daddy died, and he told me at the end he had a bad life, a lot of it, because of Wall Street and the Republican party we had up there in Washington after the war, the first one with the Germans. I was in the second war. I never have given as much attention to politics as my daddy did. Clem says it's because times are better.

"To be truthful, I don't see much future for the small farmer like me. The plantation boys, the big boys, the ones that own the plantations, they'll be all right. They've got money, all of it they need. Some of them have bought up old plantations like toys, and play with them. The rich get hundreds of colored people to wait on them and pick the crops on the plantations; and the rich look for a man like me to boss the niggers out in the field, to be their foreman. I don't want to be in charge of anyone. I am doing the best I can. I never want to stand over a nigger and tell him to *git*. I hate the rich types as much as the civil rights people.

"If I was in charge of the whole country, like you say, I'd try to be fair. I'd try to help those who work and need a little extra help, a little extra money. I wish I could pay more to the colored. I'd pay them as much as I could afford. I guess I wish there were more of us poor farm people so that the country would be on our side, the side of the man who's growing his crops and minding his own business and trying to do the best he can. I do a lot of thinking while I'll be walking out to my crops or walking over to my house at the end of the day, and there's always just me, you know, and up there is the sky, and God looking down, I guess; and over yonder is my land that I've had all these years, and some pines beyond that, to keep the soil tight and mark off my land from the next fellow's land. I'll be walking and I'll say to myself that I'd a hell of a lot rather be here, even if I just break even and make the little profit I do, than be in a factory down near the Gulf Coast or up there in a steel mill in Birmingham.

You get more money in the factories, but you're no longer yourself any more; you're one of the workers who is hired and fired and told to do this and the next and told off if he doesn't obey. There's no one shouting at me. I wish I had someone I could take a little bourbon with sometime, but I can go and find someone if I want, and it's my time and my day and my week and my life and no one else's. That's what I'd like for you to know, more than anything I could tell you as answers to your questions. I'd like for you to go and tell them, the Yankees and anyone you meet, that this is one man, yes sir, one man who's proud of what he's doing and proud to be where he is. I love my place here, and I'm all for the state of Alabama, over against any other. I can't call in anyone else around here to say he thinks the exact same things I do, but mostly they all do, I just know it, be they white people or the colored. I admit, I'm by myself a lot, but I know how others think; you'll have to take my word for it. What worries me is that I don't believe, I just don't believe that there are many Americans in other parts of the country who want to know what we think, us people here in Monroe County, Alabama. It's not fair that no one listens to us. Can you say it's fair?"

I answered no. I asked him again whether he thought the "colored people" he often mentions would go along with his ideas, and he again answered yes. Are they also lonely, are they also a little cut off from others, as he is? Why, yes, they are. It is how life goes, he reminded me: "Living is working your land — mostly by yourself." I said earlier that this yeoman's loneliness, his sense of the land and its importance to him, his feelings about "the colored" all somehow go together, all somehow strike me as — what word to dare use? Perhaps the word is *revealing*, perhaps *illuminating*. I like somehow a combination of those descriptions, and maybe *revelatory* does it. For it *can* be revelatory, standing out there in the fields of Monroe County, Alabama, and hearing him — an American and a Southerner, a dignified, hurt, sturdy, rather diffident man, a rather gallant if occasionally restless, fidgety, and fearful man. His words reveal how people who are solitary and often desolate nevertheless do come together. His words reveal how men live as workers on the land, as tillers and plowers and harvesters, as yeomen and sharecroppers, as field hands and day laborers. One learns how men challenge the farm's land and how their lives are thereby shaped and affirmed as well as badly warped and wounded. If what I have just said has been worth the learning, I have learned it rather against my will, the product perhaps of too many years spent mastering "disciplines," "methods," "techniques" and over-arching theories — the features, I fear, of my own terrain, my kind of land. What I had to struggle for when I talked with the people whose words I have set down in this section can be called a little awkwardly "the capacity for bewilderment." Bewilder-ment enables its own kind of clarity. Bewilderment tones down the clever man's pride and self-assurance, prompts him to stop asking all those familiar questions, stop cramming whatever is seen and heard into already overstuffed theoretical cupboards which were built far from the site and meant only to accom-modate a particular variety of provisions. Bewilderment is what William Faulkner and James Agee instinctively knew enough to feel in the presence of black tenant farmers or white yeomen; and bewilderment is what a "culturally disadvantaged" observer like me had to be painfully taught, year after year, in those cabins that still stand guard over the rural South's responsive and generous soil.

VIII

THE WORLD
OF THE WANDERERS

THE larger world that migrant farm children come to know
has few people in it; unlike an Appalachian child or a black
child who grows up on a plantation or a white child who grows
up on a yeoman's "piece of land," a migrant child has no community of his own, and often for weeks will see (besides his
parents and the parents of other migrant children) only one
person — the crew leader — for any length of time. Migrants see
people driving along the same roads they use in their trek north
or south and, like tenant farmers and mountaineers, migrants
most certainly have their share of dealings with policemen (in
the North) and sheriffs (in the South) and most definitely with
ministers, as we shall also presently see. Yet, for many migrants,
the Word has become flesh in the person of "the crew man,"
which I say not to be smart and sacrilegious but because over
and over again I hear those crew leaders described as virtual
gods — by people afraid that without crew leaders, without their
guidance and constant help and almost infinite direction, all
would be lost and, no doubt about it, "the earth we work on
would turn on us and would take us back," which is how one
migrant mother dramatically stated the matter.

1. Their Mother, Their Father, Their Everything

The migrant mother quoted above looks upon a crew leader
with almost religious devotion. She sees the earth she helps

cultivate as something fickle, avaricious and consuming, almost as a person in collusion with the powerful crew leader. The migrant mother in question has no time to appreciate such psychological and quasi-theological issues. Her words are as good a way as any to give concrete evidence of what a crew leader "means" to his people: "Without him there would be nothing for us to do." She starts out with that foreboding, nihilistic observation and then gets even more ominous: "I truly believe we'd get stuck someplace and never get away, and we'd have nothing, no food or place to stay. Maybe the earth we work on would turn on us and would take us back, just like you hear the minister says might happen one of these days to the whole world, and everyone in it. The crew leader, he's the one who knows how all the people go about their business, and he talks with the growers, and he'll go and see them, you know, before we ever get to their farm. He's the one who recruited us way back. We tried a couple of times to leave him, but it was bad; we tried to get year-round work and we couldn't and it was either sign up with another crew man or go back to our own. We do know him, we said, and he could be worse — although he could be better, I'll say that. He's all we have, though; and there's something I know — and I tell my children all the time: you can't have any choice about a lot of things if you're down and out and your stomach is beating on you to please, please go and get food, any kind of food, just so it'll stop hurting and you don't fall on your face and soon be dead. Now, the crew leader, he *has* to feed you. He has to make sure you get some food. He needs us alive 'on the season,' not dead. He needs us alive to pick, not dead. You see how it is?"

I am not sure I can ever "see how it is." I believe I was able to appreciate her desperate situation, her awful worries, her restlessness, her dread of no less than imminent and utter extinction. I was not able, however, to dismiss what I suppose can be called my middle-class rationality. Why doesn't she free herself of that crew leader, strike out on her own, as some migrants have? Why doesn't she go back home, return to Mississippi, or veer off into one of those cities she comes so near to — New York or Philadelphia, say, or Rochester? I know those alternatives are not without their drawbacks; but she here implied what at other times she has stated outright, and what I have even heard confirmed by crew leaders themselves: migrants are again and again used and abused by their crew leaders, who often are plunderers the equal of any America has managed to produce and tolerate. Why then, I have felt like asking her, or even shouting at her, does she submit to the crew leader, even welcome his presence as next in importance to salvation itself?

In contrast with me and my stifled questions, the crew leader whose spell dominates her and regulates almost her every move has a very clear idea of what such a woman means, what she is thinking about when she asks me whether I "see how it is." I have used one of his remarks as the title of this section, and perhaps he can help us "see how it is" for migrants as well as himself: "I'm different from the migrant, I know it. I move all over, like them, but they're the sheep and I'm their leader. That's the truth. I try to be good to them. I try to help them out. But I have to shout at them. I have to punish them. They're like children. They're like sheep. It's too bad, how they are. I could have been the same way. The only difference was that one of the growers saw me picking beans, it was about fifteen years ago. I was shouting at my friend, because he was in my way, and I wanted to fill as many bags as I could. The grower called me over and said he liked that, my 'attitude,' he said. He asked me about myself, where I came from and all that kind of thing. So, I told him. It was a story, and I told him all I could remember.

"I told him I was born in Georgia, and my daddy worked on shares, and the bossman one day told us all to get off the land, and fast, because he was turning to cattle, and so we left, as fast as we knew we had to leave. My daddy heard we could get work in Florida, because there are big farms there, so we went there instead of heading for Atlanta, or up to Washington, where his sister and her husband are. My daddy became sick. It broke him, you know, trying to follow the crops. The first year he almost died, and the second year he did die. He loved the work, picking. He never could have lasted a day in a city, sitting there like they do and getting welfare. But he got confused, moving from place to place, and I think he got poisoned by the food in one of the camps, and there was no doctor to come see us. So, I had to take his place, and there was my mother and my two brothers and my two sisters, and we stayed with the crewman that we met when we first came to Florida, and he gave us twenty-five dollars because my daddy died, and he paid to get him buried — it was someplace in Virginia, I think. My mother said she didn't ever want to see the place he's buried, because his soul is gone from the earth, and at least one of us is free of the earth. That was the way she looked at it, you know. She died the next year. I was eighteen then, when we lost her, around that age I think, and I had my younger brothers and sisters with me, and we tried to stay together. Our mother had been sick for a long time before she died, but we never knew from what. No, she never saw a doctor. There was no doctor for us to see in Georgia and once we got on the road the crew leader told us a lot of people have what she had, trouble breathing and the pains in the chest and the stomach.

"The day that grower picked me out to talk to, my mother had been dead a couple of months, I believe. I told him what I've just told you, and he seemed real sorry for me. He asked where my brothers and sisters were. I told him my sister was sick, bad sick, so she was in the camp lying down and the other sister was near her side, trying to give her the help she needed. My two brothers were on the other side of the field, like me, picking beans. He told me I had 'promise.' He told me I was a smart colored man, he could tell. He told me I could be a 'leader,' and I was like him because his mother and daddy died when he was a young man, and they had just come over here from Italy. He said I should stop what I was doing and come and work in the packinghouse. That way I could get a salary, guaranteed every week. Then I could know more about the business; and when it was time to go North, later on, I could take some of the people with me and learn to be a leader. He said he would make sure I went with the best crew leader he knew, better than the one I was working for. He said I could learn from him by helping him. 'You become a

leader by learning how, like everything else.' That's what he said.
I thought I was imagining things, for a while I did. But he went
over and talked to my crew leader and in a second the crew
leader was saying, 'Sure, sure,' and I was riding over in the
grower's truck to the packinghouse.

"That was the start of it. That was the way I began being a
crew man, a crew leader. The grower said you learn to be a
leader, but let me tell you, you have to be lucky to be able to
learn. If God smiles on you, then you get the chance I did. If He
doesn't, you can be the smartest person in the whole world and it
won't make any difference at all. I didn't always pick beans that
fast, the way I did that day when the grower saw me. My sister
Mary was sick that day, like I said, and I wanted to make the
most money I could, so we could get her some milk and extra-
good food. Then he came along, that big guy, and he was
friendly, and he said that he could understand me and he wanted
to help — and he did. That summer when we went up through
Georgia — we came into Echols County and then over to Valdosta right near where we used to live — my brothers and sisters
said it was Momma and Daddy looking down on us that made
me a helper to the crew man and on my way to being one. I said
it was because of the Italian man, the grower; but Mary said no,
it was God's work. Then I told her that if she wanted to think
that way, she could, but not me.

"I'm not very much of a believer. I'll admit to that. I don't
mind those ministers coming around; they quiet my people
down. But can anyone really believe what they say? My sister
Mary, she's dead. My other sister, I keep her home in Florida,
and she's sick. She has tuberculosis. If I didn't have money, if I
was a poor bean picker like my people are, my sister would be
dead — and my brother too. He also has tuberculosis, just like
her! Don't feel sorry for them! They all get one thing or another,
pickers do, the migrant people do. They die because their heads
drown in cheap wine. They die from a venereal disease. They die
because they're drunk, and they fall into a canal or get run over.
They die from the other diseases that migrant people get. Everyone gets a disease and dies, but migrant people, they get diseases

twenty-five years before other people do. I'm glad I make some money, and I know where to go get a doctor and I can pay him, pay him cash. Doctors are like growers; they pay attention to money. If you have money, they'll take care of you. If you don't, they'll tell you to get the hell out of their office. My sister says the doctors are like the ministers, 'God's people,' she calls them. I get a laugh out of that. I say to her, 'God's people,' yes, they're 'God's people' if you have 'God's dollar bill' for them; and if you don't, then they're the Devil — worse than the Devil, because at least the Devil doesn't pretend to be something other than what he is.

"I try to be as good as the ministers say I should, and I try to help people out, like I'd do if I was a doctor. In a way I *am* a minister and a doctor; I'm the only one my people can turn to if they need advice and help. I'm their mother, their father, their everything. And they're my children, my workers, *my* everything! I have two children, but I never let them or my wife come North with me. It would be terrible for them moving from place to place. It's bad for a family, for children especially. We have a nice house in Belle Glade, Florida and, come May or June, I leave and don't come back until September or October. My wife has all she needs: a refrigerator, a freezer and a big car that's air-conditioned. Our house is air-conditioned. You need air conditioning in the summer. When we start on the road I lead, and if there's one of my workers who isn't feeling too good, I have him drive with me in my car, because it's air-conditioned. They all keep in line behind my Oldsmobile; we have four big trucks, and the people can sleep in them or beside the road, whichever they want, and depending on the weather, naturally. A few families — four of them — drive their own cars; and I myself can't figure why those people don't go on their own. If I was them, walking in their shoes, I'd go and get my own deal. They know enough by now where they could go, to what farms, and the money they would make would be all theirs. But they're scared, very scared to be alone. One of them told me last year that every time he thought of leaving us, he got dizzy and things would spin around in his head; so he decided to stay with me.

"Well, I'm glad to be taking care of my people. I do anything you can imagine for them. I wake them up in the morning, or else a lot of them would sleep on and on. I tell them what the weather is going to be like. I take them to the field and get them started. Before that I make sure they've had some breakfast in them. I bring them food to prepare. I tell them where to sleep, and I make sure they don't go and fight with each other. That's the worst problem I have; they fight and fight, all the time they do. When they're not drinking they're cutting up real bad, or they're kicking in a door or breaking something. They are little children — that's what I think; they've just never grown up, the way other people do.

"I agree that if they'd be doing different work and not having to move all over, then they'd be different, they'd act different. But there's no other work for them, and they know that. You go and talk with them; they'll all tell you that they're used to going on the road, and they're satisfied. Maybe they're not satisfied, I'll admit that; but they don't know how to leave, and it doesn't enter their mind to leave, no sir, not even as a thought. I believe that. Once a man told me it was like being hooked, you know. He said he was twice hooked; he was hooked on his needle and hooked on picking beans and tomatoes.

"During the day I have to watch them real close. I take them to the field and leave them off. I always tell them I'll *see them in a few minutes*. With my voice I say it so that they know what I mean: I'm going to get some coffee and then, by God, when I return I want to find them *on their knees,* moving along and picking and piling up those baskets and those bags, as many as they can. Later I'll bring along their food to them, of course. I have a man that works for me; he's very good — he can drive the canteen and cook the food and serve it to them. My people are not good at counting and keeping track of things, and I don't want to give them more trouble than they already have. I've learned to be good with arithmetic. I never had much schooling, no more than my people, but if you have to learn, then you do. You don't need any schooling to know how to keep track of your dollars; no, you just find out how by yourself and consider

yourself lucky for having the chance. Like I said, I make it easy
for my people. I don't give them cards to hand in and have
punched each time they eat. They lose the cards, and since they
pay for them, it means they've lost money. They have to eat, even
if they can't afford to buy the food. Either they eat or they can't
work — and that's no good. So, I tell them they're going to get
three meals every day while we're on the road. I tell them that I
don't care what other crew leaders do; there will be no meal
tickets, no punching of cards before they eat, no paying for
meals. I tell them they're here with me to work, and that means
they've got to eat and sleep, and I'm not going to bother their
minds and mine taking money from them for a place to sleep and
food to eat. That way they can relax and know they'll be OK as
long as we're moving along. That way it's simple and easy for all
of us. I pay all the bills — for gas to move us, and the food and
everything. I get the money from the growers, and I pay all my
bills and expenses, and then I take out my own money, and then
I give the families something, so they won't be going all the way
from Florida up to New York and back without having some cash
left for themselves.

"I'll say this to you, if you want to hear it: I hate to give them
money, any at all, *any*. You know why? They throw it away.
That's what they do. It's the worst thing in the world to see. I'll
hand out the wages to them, and I'll tell them to be careful and
save something. I'll tell them to think about how they're going to
feel, come a few days, when they can't put their hands on a
single cent. They'll one by one say yes sir, yes sir, and there will
be so many yeses you'd think the world was changing. I don't
think they are lying when they say yes; no, I don't. They mean
what they say when they say it, and then they change their minds
later on. Actually, they don't change their minds. They have the
money and they feel thirsty and they're tired, and they think to
themselves that a bottle of wine would be good, so they go and
get the wine and they drink it. Soon their money is gone, and if I
get mad and tell them they're fools, they say yes sir, like always,
and I do believe they mean it, they feel sorry for doing the wrong
thing.

"Our people, the migrants, they're not like others. They have to be *told* what to do. If I didn't act strong with them and keep them moving along and let them know what comes next and what they have to do now, then I'd have them all lying around staring up at the sky, drunk as can be; or if they couldn't get their hands on a bottle, then they'd be sitting around and doing nothing and hoping they'd get their next meal somehow. I don't mean to be so down on them. I like them; they're my people. But you see they've all left their homes, and they don't have anyplace to be but with me; and so it's hard on them, and on me, too. They'll bring me all their troubles, you know. If they're fighting or worried over something or they get fits of crying, crying all the time, then I have to fix them up. Don't ask me how I do it. I don't know. I talk with them. I listen to them until my ears are tired and when I can't hear them any longer, because my head is all filled up, I tell them to get back to the truck and sleep, and the next day when we stop someplace, I'll listen some more. They're very up and down, my people are. One minute they're whistling and singing and they'll do dances, even on the trucks while we're moving up North. The next minute they'll be sitting by themselves, staring off into nowhere. You can't get their attention, it seems, no matter what you do. There are times when I expect them never to say another word to me or anyone else; I expect them to kill themselves, they seem so low. I can't predict how they'll be from one day to the other and even one minute to the other; but I've learned my own kind of psychology, I guess you could call it. I saw on television once a man who said every one of us, no matter who he is and no matter if he has gone to school or not, can learn how to read people and figure out what is on their mind, like a psychologist does. I tell a man that I know there's something bothering him, but there'll be a lot *more* bothering him if he doesn't get his work done. I talk like this to my people: 'You've got your pain now, and I appreciate it; but brothers and sisters, you'll be dead and six feet under if you don't go out there and do your picking. So go and work, and you won't have time for all your pain, and then later we'll solve what's ailing you. We will.'

"They always work. They know I'm telling them what's true. They know that if you stop working — that goes for all of us, right? — you die. I'd die if I didn't keep working. I go nuts sitting at home in Florida. I'm supposed to be resting all the time, because the doctor says my blood pressure is high, way up there on his machine. He told my wife I should stop, and stay home and get rest. I told her that we'd soon be without food, and *then* what would the doctor say. I'm like my people; I've got to keep moving with them. What goes for them goes for me. There's no other way for them to live, nor for me, either. We're all lucky we're even alive. A lot of kids I grew up with there near Valdosta, Georgia, they died before they became men or women, before they knew what life is all about, I'll tell you. Maybe they were lucky. I get to wondering myself, like my people do. They'll come and ask me if there's any reason I can tell them why they should stay alive. I tell them I'd rather be alive than dead, and that's all the 'reason' anyone should need. They start telling me we're all dead, the way we keep going — with no rest, and the work and more work and not much money. Of course they stare into me, right into me, as though I'm getting money even if they're not, as though to say that. I tell them sure, I'm getting more, but a lot of difference it really makes. It means my wife lives better, and I have my big car; but that's all. I'm *with* them, and I'm trying *for* them, to do the best that can be done, so that they can work and eat and not starve to death and not be beggars.

"I'd like to say something about my people. They're like me. They don't want to beg. I never could beg. When I was a kid I asked my daddy once why I couldn't just go over to the bossman who owned the land we lived on and ask him for some money. That bossman always patted me on the head and smiled at me when he came to see us working in the fields, and I guess I thought that if he was nice to me there he'd be nice to me with his money when I asked him for some of it. The only money he ever gave us was a couple of hundred dollars every year just before Christmas. That was for our working on his land and raising cotton for him, enough to make him plenty of money, I know that now. Well, I told my daddy everything I was thinking, and he grabbed me and held on to me and told me I must never think like that again, for the rest of my life. He said to beg is to die. He said begging would kill me like nothing else could. He said he'd sooner kill me than let me beg. I was scared. I was so scared I couldn't answer him back. He shook me, and he asked me if I understood. I nodded that I did. And I did; let me tell you I did. I'm sitting here now, and a lot of years have gone by since then, and I could just as well be back there, looking at him in the face, my daddy, with his eyes looking right into my eyes. I started crying as I left his side, and he came after me. He told me he didn't mean to frighten me. He told me he wanted me to learn it real, real good — learn that people could call us all they wanted, and snicker at us, and treat us like we're mules and like skunks and like the earth of the state of Georgia, but they couldn't turn us into beggars. He said it was one thing if *they* treat *you* bad; it's another when *you* start proving them right.

"I think it was about a year later that he died, my daddy. He was out working with us; we were picking the cotton and he was carrying the sacks, all full, to a cart nearby. All of a sudden he took to shaking and he fell down. The next thing we knew they said he was gone, he was dead. I asked my mother what it was, and she didn't know. She told us afterwards that she was expecting it, though. She said that he had bad pains in his head, and there was something wrong, he knew it, though he didn't know how bad it was. His sister gave him some herbs, and my mother went to see the preacher, and he came over and he told my daddy to pray extra-special hard, and Daddy said he would try and he did, I know he did. My daddy believed in God. He prayed and prayed, every morning and every night; and on Sundays it was all day that he prayed. Even when I was little I used to think he wasn't getting much help back from God, for all the time he was putting into praying to Him, but I'd never have dared talk like that. I remember just once in my whole life when my mother lost her faith. I asked her how old daddy was when he died — it was a week or two, I guess, afterwards — and she said she couldn't be sure; she didn't keep after those years very carefully, but she knew, she'd been told by Daddy, that he was born in 1900, around then, because that's when everything changed, from eighteen to nineteen. I'd gone to school two or three years, and I knew how to figure it, so I said he was about thirty-five — right? — when he died, and she said 'about, maybe.' I recall those two words from her. Then her eyes began to close, and I thought she was going to sleep, but all of a sudden she leaped up from the chair and she said he'd been killed, Daddy had been killed!

"I thought she had lost her mind. I myself saw him take a fit, and no one was near him to hurt him. She explained herself, though. She said all his life Daddy had worked and worked, and if he wasn't owned, like his grandfather, a slave was the only thing he wasn't that his grandfather was, because he *was* a slave, except they don't use the word anymore. She told me I was going to be a slave, too. She screamed a lot; she screamed that every colored man is a slave, and every colored woman. She said there were the red-necks down the road, and they are slaves, too. Her sister was there and told her to stop it, and she did; but before she did she made us promise never to forget that our Daddy could have lived, if he'd only been sent into Valdosta to see some doctor. I guess he went and saw the plantation owner — he was the man I said used to smile at me and pat my head — and he must have done that to my daddy, pat his head. My mother told me that the bossman told Daddy he was all right, and he was doing just fine, and he sent him back to us. That was a month or two before my daddy died. When they buried him there was no one in sight but our own people, our family and people from nearby. But afterwards we were sent ten dollars by the bossman and he came over a day or two later and told us we could stay and my mother could work, and my brothers and me could — but only for a while, because he was getting set to stop growing for a while and try animals, cattle and maybe chickens.

"I'm quick to see if one of my people is sick. I try to quiet them down if they're excited and talking about being afraid. I'm the only one they can call upon, like I said, and I'm there, I'm always there to be of help. There's a limit to what I can do, of course. It's expensive to call a doctor. A lot of the places where we are, there's no doctor for miles and miles around. Even when there is one, they want you to bring the person over, and they can keep you and the sick one waiting all day. I've got the growers pushing on me all the time. In this business, it's rush, rush, everything rush. They want me here and then the next place; they want everything harvested, everything that's been planted, in five days or six or seven — or they'll be ruined, ruined for life, to hear them talk. If I start driving my people to doctors all the time, it won't be long before I'm seeing one myself. I already am. He's the one who told me my daddy died of high blood pressure. He's the one who told me I've got the same thing. Maybe every single migrant has it, for all I know. Sometimes we'll be out there in the field. The grower will be on my back, telling me the tomatoes have to be in by the end of the week or he's through, completely destroyed. I'll be pushing on my people to pull those tomatoes in. The sun will be beating down on us. And I'll be looking at my people and thinking to myself that half of them are in real bad trouble, the men and the women and the children. Maybe *all* of them are in trouble, and I should be taking all of them that day to the doctor. But if we don't get the tomatoes in pretty soon, none of us will be eating three meals a day and then we'll *really* need to see a doctor — and he'll tell us to go and eat! And how, I ask you, how will we go and do that, except by getting those tomatoes in, right on time?

"You see, we're all in trouble, that's the truth. Some of those ministers come over and tell me I'm bad because I steal from my workers. They're from some 'migrant ministry,' some organization like that. They're not like the preachers who want to talk about God with my people; instead, 'migrant ministry' people want to test the water we drink in the fields, and they give me long sermons on how bad it is, what they call 'the migrant life.' I asked one minister a little while ago what other kind of life he thought my people could live. Let those ministers go and get jobs for all my men and see how good the jobs will be. They have a look on them, those ministers, as if they've never had to worry about a meal in their life. They speak good; they talk a good line. They look at you as if you're a crook and you belong in jail. They look at you as if they're the angels and you're the biggest sinner in the whole world. I asked them — they don't scare me — what their fathers did to make a living. They didn't answer me, so I knew I had them. I told them to get out and stop bothering me and my people, or I'd take care of them. I said if they can't even answer an honest question I ask, and instead they keep on asking me things, then they can leave and never come back, *never.* They told me, then they did. One had a father who was a teacher, and the other, his father was a lawyer. Now that's wonderful. I told them, 'That's wonderful.' I wasn't being wise. I mean I was; but hell, I wish my daddy could have been a teacher or a lawyer or something like that instead of a slave — that's what he really was, on a plantation in south Georgia.

"I've argued with those ministers plenty, and with others like them. They're all over the country! I've told them that when they can figure out a way to keep me and my men at work all year around in one place, I'll be the first to sign up, and I'll do anything they want me to do. They say I should be 'nicer' to my men. I'm everything to my men. Like I keep on saying, I have to lead them around and tell them when to do every single thing they do. Like I said I'm their mother, their father, their everything. I'd like to give them, each one, a million dollars and a big home and all the wine they want and people to wait on them. I'd like to. I told the ministers that there are plenty of rich churches, and why don't they go to them and get some money and stop preaching at me because of how bad I treat my people, and instead give them a lot of money, a good fat bundle of cash. One of the ministers told me I was 'evading.' He said I was trying to get out of something, and I should be doing more for my people. Should I? Maybe I should. Where would I get the money, though? I'm not a grower. I'm not a rich man. I make some money, and I do it by working all the time and living here one day and up the road the next day. I leave my family and don't see them for half the year, almost. I have a good car, correct. I have air conditioning in it, correct. I have a good home in Florida, correct. My wife has some nice dresses, correct. I buy my children good clothes, correct. Does that make me into a millionaire? Does that make me a grower, a man who has a hundred jobs to offer?

"What the ministers say is right: we don't live good, we live bad. Why don't they go and talk with the growers, though? Why don't they go and weep on *their* shoulders? You know why? It's because the growers will throw them out without hearing a word from them. It's only suckers like me who listen and listen — until I feel so lousy I'm ready to let those ministers take over. I wish they would. I wish they would come and live with these people here, and not just come around once in a while, checking up on the water and the food and the 'sanitation.' I'm sick and tired of that word they use, 'sanitation.' When they're not complaining on that score, they're telling me I should make my men not drink water from the tap, or I should pay them more. There's always a complaint they have to register. I told them never to come bothering me again; just last week I did. I picked up my gun and told them to leave and not come back. They said I was using my gun on the men; that I was treating them like slaves. What do they know about being a slave? After they left I asked my men if they followed those ministers, if they believed what they said. Not one of my people agreed with them. They all said they never hear them for very long, because they talk too much, and they're trying to stir up trouble. That's what they *are* trying to do, make everyone feel bad and turn us each one against the other. Then the growers would have it even better than they do now. Then they'd have us all on our knees, begging. It's bad enough we're on our knees all day long, picking. I am on my knees, too. I'm on my knees telling my men to work faster, and then I have to stoop over and feel the beans and decide if they are too wet to pick or the time is too soon, all that.

"I beg for my people. I don't only beg for myself but for them. I ask the growers to fix up good cabins and pay the best wages they can. My daddy said never to beg, so I don't, not the begging he spoke of. But I beg. I beg for money, so that the work we do isn't for nothing. I sweat for my people; and they *are* my people. The ministers tell me I have no right to call them that, to call them 'my people.' Whose people are they? You have to belong to someone in this world. I'm *their* crew man, *their* crew leader. They wouldn't leave me for anything, and I wouldn't leave them. I have some money saved up, and I could easily leave. My wife tells me I should. But I won't. Never; I'll never leave my people, and they know it's true, what I'm saying.

"One of my men died a couple of months ago, and I told the others we'd miss him, but we'd keep going; and his brother and his wife, they both came to me and said they wanted to stay with me, and so long as I would keep them, they would stay with me. Then I decided to ask them something. I asked them what they would do if I said no, if I said I was through, and they could go and do what they want and so would I. They didn't answer me. They didn't say a word to me. That's how worried they got. I tried to get them to talk, but they didn't. I asked them if their tongues were all tied down, and they didn't answer me then, either. I asked them if they were ever going to talk again in their whole lives, and they didn't answer me. Then I told them not to worry, and I was only fooling, and there wasn't a chance in the world that I'd give up on them. Right away they started smiling and laughing, and all of a sudden they could talk. They told me I was a great guy, but not to speak like I did, because it made them get scared, and they didn't know what would happen to them if I retired, except that they'd probably end up by the side of the road, dead. Yes sir, that's what they told me; they told me they'd die if I gave up on them. I guess when I do die, they will die. But we all die sooner or later. And in this work, when you go on the road to do harvesting, the chances are it'll be sooner and not later that you die. Even for me, the crew man, that's what the chances are."

I believe I have spent more time talking with him than any other particular person I have met and interviewed in the course of my work with migrant farmers. He is a bundle, a tangle of contradictions. I add tangle to bundle because over time I finally did realize how caught up he is by those contradictions — which can be said to make up his very life. He means just about everything to "his" people, and their extravagant praise of him

more than matches any of his own more grandiose self-evalua-
tions. Yet those same people also doubt him, suspect him, hate
him — all of which in his own indirect way he can acknowledge.
He takes care of dozens of human beings, makes certain that they
eat and work, provides shelter for them, listens to their complaints and worries, offers them advice, interprets things to them,
reminds them of obligations and responsibilities — he keeps in
mind countless birthdays and wedding days and memorial days
— and in general mediates between impoverished, uneducated
(and it can be said), abandoned or wayward people on the one
hand, and the tough, demanding world of agricultural commerce
on the other. Yet he also takes *from* the people he takes care of,
and for all his explanations, whose length and intensity are
remarkable, there is no way he can get around the truth: he rakes
in considerable cash, keeps most of it, gives precious little to the
migrants who work so hard, sends home thousands and thousands of dollars, while at the same time the families whose toil
has produced such an income for him are lucky if they see even
one thousand of those dollars in an entire year. The words can be
summoned forth and pinned upon him, one after the other: he is
protective, shrewd, exploitative, kind-hearted, concerned, evasive, cruel, quite definitely authoritative, even (for these sad and
lost souls) charismatic; he is a confidence man, a manipulator, a
thief, a monster even; he is a middleman in the worst sense of the
word, a living reminder of how awful a society can let things get,
hence force people to become.

What am I to say? I happen to believe he is more tormented
and anguished, more rocked by the awfulness of his life as well
as the fate of his people than he can ever possibly realize.
Somehow, somewhere in himself, he knows how monstrous it is
for everyone — that people should live as migrants do in a
country such as this. He says that, many times he does; he almost
accuses himself, and he of course turns on the migrants, then
rushes to defend them. And I myself rush at this moment to say
something: I am not writing about this tragedy in order to turn
this man into a hero *or* into a sort of terrible gangster. I suppose
if I had to settle on a "position" for myself it would be one that

echoes this man's own plaintive (yes, self-pitying) description of his dilemma: he is bound, confined, and controlled by an evil he turns to profit, but at a price, a price his own conscience cannot quite overlook, a price the United States of America continues to find not unbearable. Perhaps the last word on him and his kind — some of whom are worse, some of whom are better, some of whom are crueler, some more compassionate — ought to be left to the grower we are about to meet, a man who has known and fought with and relied upon this particular crew leader for many years: "Hell, it's a hard, hard world we live in. None of us really are secure, certainly not him. He's trying to keep alive and he knows he has to use his fists to do it, the way things are. But I'll tell you one thing about him: he's the kind of guy who turns around every once in a while to see how the next person is doing and to worry about him, all the guys he's pushing and fighting with. He uses people; but they get to him and they bother him. They do. He'll be talking about them and I can see it in his face, in his look: he worries over them. I can't, I admit it. I don't know the migrants. I just know *him*. I hire him, and he brings them to work here on my land. A man like me can't get to worrying, not over the migrants. I have a million other worries to juggle; and if I don't solve them each year, the migrants would even be worse off than they now are — and so would the crew leaders, and me and my brothers, the growers."

2. *The Growers*

The grower just quoted and his brother are business partners. They own land, thousands of acres of land in central Florida, and they almost fight one another proving which one can extract the most from that land. Neither of them makes an effort to sound anything but determined, tough-minded, and up against difficult odds; though of the two, Philip, the older brother, manages to sound more desperate than his brother Hugh, who is three years younger and some five years further along in education, something neither of the two men ever forgets to mention for one reason or another. They are native Floridians, which in the southern part of the state is no common thing. They were born poor, "dirt poor," but unquestionably the dirt they use to describe their family's earlier social and economic condition eventually made them quite well to do. Others would call them rich, but they do not take to such descriptions. They prefer to think of themselves as hard pressed, in constant danger; their own images have to do with walking on various tightropes or being trapped between several alternatives, each of which inevitably promises at least a few unfavorable repercussions. They also prefer work to play; they let wives and children and cousins enjoy their money, rather like the crew leader just described. It is very hard for an outsider like me to decide whether their almost puritan manner, their self-sacrificing, hard-driving way of working, their constant sense of financial jeopardy are in even remote fact justified "objectively," or rather reflect something people like me call a "psychological problem" — an "insecurity" of some kind.

I have at times found myself the hopeless outsider when confronted with Philip and Hugh Bates; more so, it has seemed, than when I have tried to work my way into that "subculture" in which migrants or sharecroppers are so commonly represented as living. Perhaps I am one of those "academics," impossibly dumb about the business world. All too many people like me make a deliberate and showy habit of ignoring or insulting people like the Bates brothers; for them we have no understanding, no compassion, only scorn and snobbish disregard, or at best a kind of persistent and eagerly acknowledged indifference. Whatever the reason behind my sense that I have not always been able to separate fact from fantasy in the world of Philip and Hugh Bates, and whatever my prejudices, obvious or hidden, I have tried to hear the two men talk, and have on occasion heard from them a kind of eloquence and poignancy that I have to admit, did at first surprise me. Actually, the brothers themselves were surprised, for they weren't in the habit of talking about their work and most especially about the plight of those who work for them. They had to notice that our meetings, at first agreed to casually and with a certain unanxious kind of curiosity, eventually became troubling if not distinctly bothersome — even as they did for me, because after a while I began to realize that my blind spots were as serious as I believed theirs to be, and my rhetoric could be as smug as theirs. I am "against" them and "for" the migrants — and oh, how easy it is to get away with that division of sentiment, that split of advocacy and opposition. I am also convinced that those two brothers, and others like them I have talked with, have a lot to teach an observer, and most assuredly have a right to be heard — and not only out of a convenient and even sly regard for their "helpfulness," which means for what they can tell a particular social scientist.

I know I am getting a little tense about all this, maybe too much so. I know I am struggling with issues that can have no clear-cut resolution, which have been faced and faced again, discussed and discussed again over the ages by those who have been torn between the effort to know particular individuals and judge (as, God knows, it must be done) that larger world called a society. But since Philip Bates, the more talkative of the two Bates brothers, has doubts, misgivings and qualifications as numerous and worrisome as mine (and which certainly gave rise to some of mine), I had best let him talk — "Mr. Bates," as the crew leader invariably calls him, or "Mr. Philip," as his brother Hugh sometimes does: "It's not hard to figure out what psychiatrists are looking for. They want to know about your childhood and how you used to live. I saw on television a movie, and all they kept on saying was that if you had trouble when you were a kid, you're going to keep having trouble; it's as if your head has been branded or something. I've got plenty of reason to be in trouble, if that's how life goes. When we were little boys, Hugh and I, we'd go to bed hungry, yes, we sure would. It's the first thing I can remember about my life. I recall my mother leaning over, and she was trying to quiet me down and tell me to go to sleep. I wouldn't pay any regard to her. I said I wanted something to eat. I guess she had enough of me after a while, because she shouted at me to stop asking her for what she didn't have and go to sleep. I did; I mean I turned over on my other side and waited until sleep came — and I was hungry every second I did the waiting.

"I have another memory in this head of mine. I remember Hugh and me, we were in a grocery store. My mother sent us to get some bread and some coffee. Hugh saw some candy and he put it in his pocket. I did the same. Then I figured I'd try to take something for my mother and my dad, so I put some cheese in my pocket, too. I knew they liked to eat cheese, along with bread. I was even eyeing some bacon. The storekeeper must have been watching us all the time, because he just came over and told Hugh and me to stop it, and go and empty our pockets and pay for the bread and coffee and go home.

"I agree with you, little kids are sometimes likely to steal a little, even if they're from rich homes. My own kids went through a time when they'd be taking things from my bureau and my desk, money and my cuff links and all they could get their hands on, it seemed. But it's not the same. We weren't fooling around, Hugh and me, like our children do. We were dead serious. Do you know what? When we got home we told our mother and father. And you know what they told us back? Our mother told us we shouldn't do things like that, though she knew we meant to do a good deed, and she could see how we'd be tempted, being in that store with all the groceries there. Our dad said he was sorry to hear we almost got caught. Then our mother reminded him that we *did* get caught. The end of it was that they fought over it, and they decided we'd done all right. Our mother and father sat us both down and told us all about Florida and the whole country. They said if you take things and get away with it, you're called good names. If you work yourself to death and don't take but what others will give you, then no one calls you anything. If you get caught taking things, then they'll call you bad. Right this minute I can hear my daddy shouting. He said a lot of rich people, they started out by cheating and double-crossing people and grabbing something from someone and pulling a trick. Then they become rich, and no one dares call them a bad name, and if you call the police against people with money it'll do no good, because the police pick on poor kids, like Hugh and me were. The next day I told my friend Jimmie Wilson what my dad said, and he told his father, and his father said my dad was right. Do you know who Jimmie's father was? He was a policeman."

By now Philip Bates's manner of speaking is perhaps apparent; it is thought provoking, dramatic, ironic — at least to a listener if not a reader. He is six feet four with a full head of brown hair graying at the temples, a strong jaw and nose, blue eyes, ruddy complexion, which he attributes to his constant work outside in sunny Florida, and most noticeable of all, large-boned hands that move and move as he speaks. One more thing: he often gets up to pace about, particularly when he is struggling with a thought, trying to make a point, concerned that his words get understood. At times he would almost seem to carry the words to me, as he started a sentence while sitting, accelerated his speech while getting up, and completed the statement standing — and I mean standing next to me, almost over me, his big ruddy and freckled hands pulling on his shirt-sleeves or rubbing his neck, which is more deeply wrinkled than his arms, hands or face.

The man looks strong. He talks almost coercively, rather than persuasively. He has challenged nature's elements, the market-place, and dozens of competitors, all with a determination that somehow seems very much tied up with his physical brawn, which is definitely shared by his tall, massively built, if quieter and more composed brother. Hugh actually tells things better, less convincingly but more sensibly and without the intimidation his brother can demonstrate himself willing to use. Hugh can also go back to his earlier life and his brother's with a little less rancor. He is bitter, even scarred; but he has mellowed, doesn't have to pace about, needn't use his body so much to declare a last-ditch capacity for brute force, should the need arise in some moment that will most likely never happen but still must be vaguely kept in mind.

"I was born in Marion County, near a little town called Eureka," Hugh says in a matter-of-fact way. His brother was also born there, and it is "up in north Florida," which means the part of the state that is the "real South," and is relatively poor when compared to places like Miami and Palm Beach and Naples.

Hugh and Philip are rather well to do compared to some kin of theirs still up there in Marion County, and after Hugh makes such a comparison he begins to explain the success he and his brother have achieved with pride but without boastfulness. Nor does he utilize Philip's running barrage of denials, apologies and defensive attacks on all sorts of people, places and institutions. If, as his parents once said, and as his crew leader can also say, the migrants are doomed anyway, then those who profit from their labor are part of some larger evil, and are not to be condemned personally.

"In Eureka," Hugh continues, "we were poor, like Philip told you. But even when we were little kids we wanted to get out of there and go and make some money. Our cousins — we had I'd say a dozen of them — thought we were a little off in our heads. Money, money, they'd say we had money on the brain. So did everyone there; they all had it on the brain, but not in their hands. We were so poor my father had to go on relief, and he hated it. He hated the niggers, too. I don't think they could even get on relief. Even some white folks couldn't. Dad knew the mayor and the sheriff.

"Phil and I never went as far as high school. We had to go get jobs. There were no jobs, people said so, but we found jobs anyway. That was the first time we realized how some people sit back and feel bad about what's going on and feel sorry for themselves, and other people say they don't give a damn, they're going to do what they're going to do, even if everyone says it's impossible. I'm not telling you this to brag. I'm not trying to say: look at Phil and me, look at what we did. I'll admit, though, we were proud that we got jobs; and you can't blame a man that's proud of himself for bragging a little, especially when he's a young kid.

"That's what we were, young kids. We got jobs helping a farmer in Marion County. We went and asked him if he had work, and he said no. We told him he must have work; it's money that he lacked to pay people to do the work. He was surprised at the way we talked — it was Phil who did the talking. We said we'd work for him if he gave us some food and a place to sleep.

He said that was fine. We helped him with his planting and weeding. We helped him do the harvesting. We helped clean up his packing place; it was a real small one, and in bad shape. We told him one of us should watch his other help and make sure they did what they were told and kept busy. He had us both do that. He fed us three meals, and all we wanted. He gave us bunks in the shed. After two weeks he came over to us and gave each of us an envelope; it was a Saturday, and we knew we were getting money, but he didn't say it was money, and we just thanked him. The rest of the season he paid us a real good wage. Every Saturday he brought the envelope to us, and we just said thank you. The others were always squabbling with him about how much they'd worked, the exact number of hours, and how much he should be paying out to them. They began to think we were kin to the owner, just because we tried to help him out and didn't fight with him over money. Once a couple of fellows came up to me and asked me how much was I getting paid to spy on them. I thought they'd been drinking. A lot of them did who worked there on the farm. When they pushed me up against a tree and started jabbing at me, I realized they didn't have an ounce of liquor in them. They were sober and they were mean. They said Phil and I were a lot worse than the bosses, the owner and his son. They said we were cousins and agents sent to look around and report back to the bossmen. They told me that Phil and I should leave, and fast, or we'd be sorry.

"We did leave at the end of the season. They didn't make us, but I guess what they said to me started the ball rolling. Sometimes Phil and I wonder if our lives would be the same today if those two men hadn't come up to me and scared me. They scared me a lot more than I ever admitted, but I think the owner of the farm could see the fear in me. We went to see him, not to tell on the guys, but to say we were leaving. We never told him who they were, the two. I wouldn't even tell Phil for a while. It was half that I felt ashamed I didn't fight them back and beat them up, and half that I knew Phil had a temper and I was afraid it would be first him taking after them, and then a whole gang of them jumping on us, and maybe killing us.

"When the owner asked who it was I said I couldn't remember. He knew why I said what I did. When he asked us what we wanted to do, we said leave. He asked why. We said we weren't scared, no sir; but we'd like to go do like he was doing, get some land and grow on it, work on it and take care of it and make it produce for us. Yes, I said that, like I just did to you. He had taught us a lot, just by letting us do chores and errands and putting us to work alongside his men. At that time they were white, you know. It was the thirties, and they were white men, yes sir, tenants from Georgia and Alabama and over in Mississippi and up into Arkansas or Oklahoma who'd had to leave the land. A lot of them went to California; most of them did. But we got some over here in Florida. We also had our own white people here, who'd been doing a little farming; they'd gone broke, and some of them took to picking crops for the bigger farmers. This man we were working for had managed to keep his shirt after the crash, and he was buying up land all during the thirties in south Florida as well as the northern part of the state. He's a million-aire many times now, or rather his son is; he died a few years ago.

"I guess the man liked my brother and me. I guess he saw that we were on his side. When we told him we wanted to leave and do our own farming, but not until his season was over, he came up with an idea, and it was from his idea that everything started for us — really began for us. He said he was a farmer, and he always wanted to be one. He told us he thought the more farmers the better — the more men that owned land in Florida and grew vegetables and fruit. He was buying up land, but there was a limit to how much one man could use, even with farmhands and a few foremen to watch over them. He said he was going to offer us 'real' jobs; we could be foremen, because he was going to open up a whole new tract of land for citrus and tomatoes and beans and even flowers — he was just starting to grow flowers, because there was a big market for them up North. At the time he feared he'd go broke and have nothing for all his dreams and work, but the hope was maybe it would go the other way. He said we'd come to see him when he most needed us, because he could really use us as foremen. But he told us he could see that we were the restless types, and he wasn't going to stop us and interfere with *our* dreams. He was sorry the men had threatened me, but he was also glad, because now I would know that it's *us* against *them*, that's how he saw it — and any grower will tell you that's the truth of things, if you'll only listen and believe us. Today everybody feels bad for the ignorant migrants and believes what the people say who speak for them, like those VISTA kids with their idea that a man should be ashamed because he's working hard and wants everyone else to do the same. And anyway, why don't people listen to us? We have a side to tell and it's an honest side.

"He was right, that old grower was right; he was right about how hard it is to be a grower, and how we have to fight for our rights. Phil and I have come to know that. Back in the thirties when we were talking with him and listening to his offer for us, we weren't so sure. We didn't believe him; I know we didn't. We thought he was too suspicious. We wanted to work the land because we decided we liked doing it and because that way we could make a living. Like I said, I think I'd have gone and shot myself before I started taking charity. My father was never the same after he got those welfare checks; even when he got a job again he wasn't the same. Anyway, as we talked with the grower we were almost ready to say yes to him and join him and work as foremen and stay foremen the rest of our lives. But we didn't say a word, and he went on to tell us that we were 'better than foremen' — those were his words and I remember him saying them and I remember thinking he was going to offer us something that was important. And he did, too. He said we could be tenants like a lot of our ancestors had all been, tenants of his; but this time we could end up owning the land and maybe have some money to spare. He was going to give us some land to use, and help us get started. Later on we could buy the land from him, if we earned enough.

"That was the beginning, in 1937. From then to now it's been more work than anybody will ever know, except Phil and me. We've almost gone into bankruptcy about a dozen times, I'd say.

We started with nothing, and we started back in the thirties, when even we wondered every once in a while how we ever expected to stay out of debt and make a good living by farming. We risked all we had: our time and energy, our whole lives, you could say, our families and our lives. I'm not exaggerating. When the war came in 1941, it got a little easier for us, because the economy picked up and people had more money and wanted more of the food we grew — citrus fruit and vegetables — and the Army did, too; we had an easier life, but it was still rough: we were deep in debt and the weather can destroy you with a bad freeze and the big chain stores push at you to sell for less and less — while they make good profits, of course. Both my wife and Phil's wife said we should do something else after the war, because we started to have a recession then, you'll remember, and we could have gone and got some other job. Industry was coming into the state, and actually we were both offered good jobs by one of the chain stores: to buy produce for them. We'd have really been on Security Street then. We'd have had a solid yearly income and none of our worries: fighting with all the middlemen for a fair price for what we grow; and bargaining with the crew leader, so that labor doesn't get too expensive, which means we're being squeezed out from that direction; and always there's the machinery to buy, the processing plant to keep going, the danger of hurricanes and cold weather and too much rain or not enough rain. People don't know all that. They'll see some documentary on television about a migrant farmer and all of his troubles, but they'll never see us sweating and worrying and gambling — that's it, gambling everything we've worked all our lives to build up, gambling that the weather will come out good, and the market will hold up, gambling that the economy will treat us fine, and that the bankers will give us the money we need for maintenance and replacing machinery, gambling and gambling and gambling.

"We're growers. We're not social workers. We're not doctors. We're not working for the Red Cross or the United Nations or some charity group. My brother and I have some money now. After twenty years of risking all we've got, we have a little to risk — besides our health and the shirts on our back and every ounce of energy we can spend. Now these do-gooders come around and they say we've become rich because we've been 'exploiting' people, taking advantage of the migrant worker. That's what they keep on saying in the newspapers and on the television programs. We've had them come around here, government lawyers and reporters and the investigators that are always trying to expose something. They want to look at where our pickers work and where they live. They want to know how much we pay them and how many cups do we have near the water faucet and do we wash them and what kind of sanitary facilities do we have. They come on your land without asking you for permission, and if you tell them to get the hell off your land, they say you're keeping slaves, you're threatening and scaring your workers, you're treating them like animals — I get sick talking about all the names Phil and I have been called.

"The people who claim they're fair and honest and out to protect the migrants don't really want to speak with me. I've asked them to come and visit my office and hear how we operate; but no, all they want is to go around on their inspection tours and see our packing plant and processing plant and our fields where the workers are and the cabins we have for them. They call themselves 'impartial' or 'investigators,' but they have already made up their minds on what they think. I've let them come here. I've let them see all they want. I've stood by and heard them talking with our workers. The workers don't say much of anything. They're scared — but not scared of me, the way the reporters think, or those OEO people. A migrant farmhand, he's not going to talk with men who drive up here in fancy rented cars, wearing suits, representing the government in Washington, or some Quakers up North, or the minister types that come down here looking for a cause they can find to grab hold of and use to make themselves seem so almighty clean and pure and good. Even when I'm not there, the migrants clam up on them, on all outsiders; but the next thing you hear is that we've been threatening our workers, and they're afraid to talk.

"I think the time has come for us growers to speak up. The

time has come for a lot of people besides us to speak up — the small businessman all over the country who's being attacked from all directions. If you're lazy and on welfare, or if you belong to a street gang in a city, or if you're a draft dodger or a revolutionary who wants to overthrow the government, or if you use drugs, or want people to riot and break into stores and steal — *then* the news media will come to you and talk with you, and they'll put you on television so that you can tell the whole country what you believe and what you want to do. Every night I watch those news programs and I read the papers and the magazines, too. They'll have those radicals, one right after the other, shouting out that this is wrong, and the next thing, and they haven't got one good word for this country and for the guy who's working all day and half the night trying to make his business run and make a decent week's pay out of it.

"Is there something wrong with working like that? That's what I'd like to know. Is there something wrong with a couple of guys like me and Phil, brothers, going out and learning how to farm, and working day and night all year long, with not even a Sunday off, so that we could plant and grow and harvest a crop? Is there something wrong with us because we borrowed money, practically borrowed on our *lives*, to get machinery and the best in fertilizer and bring in irrigation? Sure, we own the land; ten years after we started we got to own it — by paying off our first employer. Sure, we have to watch the wages we pay. What do you want? Do you want us to give the land to the migrants and pay them five dollars an hour — and teach them how to be like us, how to work hard and save money and invest it, rather than work a few hours, spend the money on wine, and then move on and work a few hours more?

"What I'm arguing is that we have our side of the picture. There's always two sides to something, and I don't believe we're getting our side told to people, not one little bit of our side. There will be days when I wonder why we keep going. If people think you're being mean and doing wrong, it's not even worth it; that's how I'll think. But a little while later Phil and I will talk it all over, and we'll decide that we're going to stay right here and do what we've been doing all these years, and the reason is that we're growers, and we love being growers, and we're not going to feel bad because some government official or a holier-than-thou minister comes around and sees only what he wants to and then blames us for a lot of things that have nothing to do with us. The same holds for the reporters and the television people; they can go right on with their stories on the 'poor farm worker.' We've got our problems, the 'poor grower' does, and by God, we're going to stand our ground and live with our problems and complain to no one."

Those two brothers could easily sell their land and make enough money to retire comfortably for life. They could sell to other individuals like themselves, or they could most profitably sell to corporations, agribusinesses as they are more and more called, which are owned by investors from all over and run by managers (and below them, foremen). They could even sell their land to large chain stores, which have also of late taken to growing the food they sell. But the two brothers, like many others, refuse the blandishments of bankers and retailers and conglomerates of one sort or another, even as they refuse the appeals of those who would organize migrant workers or who speak out for higher wages and better working conditions. I do not mean to turn such men into heroes, into brave and courageous men who against great odds are holding on to a certain kind of last frontier — though such a description is not completely inappropriate. Certainly the brothers themselves feel they are last-ditch defenders of a dying order. I have frankly told the brothers how I look at things, what I have seen. I have seen how very well the two Bates families now live, and I have seen how grimly their farmhands live. I have seen how hard those farmhands work, and I have spent afternoons in the offices of Philip and Hugh Bates: air-conditioned, filled with comfortable chairs, covered with good rugs, equipped with electric typewriters and adding machines and an intercom and all the rest that goes to make up a sound, modern, efficiently organized place of business. Mr. Hugh Bates, whose remarks at times seem rather plaintive, goes to a very fine restaurant for his lunch or has very good food brought

in for himself and his visitors while, nearby, dozens and dozens
of migrant farmers do the work of harvesting crops and for lunch
get soda pop and a jelly sandwich, and for water use one cup
that hangs on a single faucet and for a bathroom use some low
pine trees and a muddy tract of land around them.

Mr. Hugh Bates, who cannot understand why so many people
lately have been complaining over so many wrongs in our society,
often speaks of his confusion and annoyance in his home — a
large and modern one, air-conditioned and full of every comfort
and convenience that can be purchased. All the while, not so
many miles away, his migrant field hands live in cabins that lack
running water and effective screens and toilets and sinks and
stoves and refrigerators. Mr. Bates does not want to talk about
such matters, though. He wants to talk about his own struggles.
He wants me to know that he has fought his way "up," has
speculated, tried his luck, taken many chances, labored long
hours, given completely of his mind and body, his time and
energy and concern to a business that only slowly and precariously and somewhat surprisingly became a success — but an in-
secure success, as he frequently and I believe honestly emphasizes, and then goes on to document: "We're a success now, but
we could be wiped out in a year or two by the weather, let alone
market conditions. Five years ago we lost all our savings, and
both of us brothers had to mortgage our homes and borrow real
heavily from the bank. You know why? There was one freeze
after another."

If the listener appears incredulous or unconvinced or even
persuaded but unsympathetic, he will be shown the books and
records and correspondence, cabinets full of them; and he will be
expected to "understand," for the Bates brothers and other
growers want understanding as much as the power and money
they will on one occasion admit to having, or another time deny
having in very significant amounts, or the third time assert is
theirs for sure, but comes by virtue of hard work justly rewarded.
As for those migrant workers, they also work hard. According to
Hugh Bates, they have earned their reward. They make money.
They don't lack a roof over their heads. They eat every day, and

they seem to like what they eat. Above all, they conceivably could (if only they would) go forth and do what Hugh Bates and his brother did, do what others before them have done, do the difficult, do the near impossible, do what requires sacrifice and fearlessness and boldness and intelligence and good, analytic judgment and, very importantly, a considerable measure of good luck, which is mentioned at the end as an aftermath of sorts, a final necessity, as it were. Of course the plain fact is that the migrants are not like the Bates brothers, lack their ambition and stubborn willfulness, or so one of the brothers claims.

Isn't all of that obvious? Can't one observe that, even hear it said by the migrants themselves? Why don't a lot of sympathizers and activists and agitators and bleeding hearts and outsiders who come and go, who excite people and abandon them, lead them on and mislead them, why don't they all truly get to know those migrants, spend years and years with them and thereby appreciate them for what *they* are, which also means what they are *not?* In brief, migrants are not us, not like the two brothers who employ them, and not like other growers, and not like doctors and lawyers, and not like "your factory workers." Migrants go along and have their good times, their bad times, their especially enjoyable times and their tedious times. They are human, but not human in the way a grower is human. God smiles on them, but He wouldn't want to turn them into something they are *not.* (That wouldn't be His way of doing things.) I am, of course, trying to paraphrase, collect together fragments of thoughts and ideas expressed over many months of conversation. I am also trying to cut down into a few sentences long, strongly worded, sometimes bombastic, strident, enormously angry statements directed, I had to feel, at the speaker's conscience as well as at the listener's ears, and at a crowd of like-minded growers or perhaps voters, as much as at an individual sitting there in an office or a living room. Here, for instance, is how Hugh Bates once chose to look at migrant children and their parents: "Migrant people are born different from you and me. I know that. I've spent practically all my grown life with them. Their babies don't move around like our babies do. They just lie there, and their mothers, they don't teach them much of anything, so far as I can see. I want to make it clear: when I call them lazy, I'm not talking against them. I like our farm workers. I find almost all of them the most obliging people you'll want to meet. I have work that I've got to do, and they come here and by God, they do it. I pay them. They're grateful for their wages. They go and spend their money. Then they come back here and are ready to work again. Who could ask for more from a worker?

"They don't want all the advantages others work for. Sometimes I envy them. They want to be left alone. Even the labor organizers that come through here will tell you that. I read in the paper what one of them said just a few weeks ago. He said migrant farm workers are suspicious of labor officials and don't want to join unions. They have to be persuaded, he said, and it's hard to do, he admitted. If I say our workers don't have any interest in labor unions, people will say I'm prejudiced, but there was a labor union man himself saying it. I'll tell you what they do want: they want to work at harvesting crops, because that's all they know; and they want to have someone else taking care of them, that's the most important thing to them. You can see them out in the fields; they ask the crew leader everything, where to go and what to do and what time it is and when they should eat. They are like little children, and their children, in comparison to ours, are sort of grown up. It's strange, isn't it. I mean, the migrants need to be helped out like a baby, and the migrant child, he's quiet and serious a lot of the time, like an old man, and he doesn't take to athletics and games like our children.

"I've seen those children working in the fields beside their parents and I've wondered why. It's not because they need the money. I've asked the parents, and they'll say no, it's not because of money; it's because the children want to, they want to go out there with their mothers and fathers and pick beans, and they even race with them to see who can do the most work. I've told my own children sometimes that they should go and see how hardworking other kids are; but, I'll tell you, it's not long before those same kids are behaving just like their parents. I mean, they take their money and they squander it. They buy one chocolate bar after another and all those Cokes. They learn gambling, at ten years old they do. They don't care about school. My wife has gone and tried to tutor them. Yes, she's gone and worked in a day-care center for the younger ones, and she's tried to teach the older ones. We'd like to do what we can for them, especially the children. But it's hopeless. We've come to see that. We realize now that people are different, and you can't go and impose your ideas and your values on others.

"I've had complaints about how we treat our workers, about the housing and the wages and all that. So, I've gone and asked them — yes, the migrant people themselves; I've gone right out in the fields and asked them, not the crew leader but the workers. You know what they say? They don't say anything at first. They scratch their heads and try and figure out what's the matter with *me*, spending my valuable time out there asking them those questions. Then they tell me that so far as they can see, all is fine. I'll ask them right to their faces if they're satisfied. Are you satisfied with your houses, that's what I'll say. Are you happy working here, and do you get enough money after you've put in your day; I'll say that, too. They don't say yes because they're scared of me. I know a scared man when I see one. I know a man who's trying to give me the answers I want. The workers on my land don't even know me, not the way the crew leader does. They know I'm a businessman — I guess they do — but I don't believe they know who owns all that land. Even their crew leader isn't sure if my brother and I own it, or just manage it for a lot of stock-holders.

"Someone ought to come and ask *me* if I'm happy with the migrants and what they do with my property. I'd answer no, I'm not. They break up the houses. They push in the screens. They tear up everything, their own possessions and things that don't belong to them. They're careless and they don't clean up after themselves. They don't seem to need their things kept in place, like we do. They scatter everything they own all over the map, that's what I've observed. I'll hear them say to each other that they left something up North, or over in the next county, where they were before here. The worst thing I have to deal with is the way they mark up the walls of the cabins, ruin the doors and the windows, spill their garbage and filth all over, ignore the barrels we provide, don't use the privies, but instead the bushes. It's terrible, isn't it? I've tried lecturing them, and my wife has tried teaching their kids. It's no use, though. They'll listen to you real quiet-like, and they seem to be hearing every word you're saying, paying real good attention to you, and not a fresh word comes in return. You leave, and you feel that at long last you've solved the problem; they'll be good from now on, like you've told them, for their own sakes. But a few days later you see them doing the same old thing. It takes a day, maybe two, for them to ruin new screens. It takes a day or even less for them to pull a door off its hinges.

"I don't say all of them are equally bad, but enough of them, enough to make the camps I have for them a sorry mess. I try to clean up after them. When they leave, I hire people to repair the damage they do; but it galls you, year after year, having to put up with that. I once asked some of them if they'd take better care of the cabins if I paid them to do so, and they said they'd try. Do you know what Phil and I did? We gave them an extra allowance, ten dollars a month. It was an experiment. We figured we'd rather give the money to them than to the repair crew we hire. Of course, it was a failure. They took the money and were as messy as ever. The crew leader told us we were wasting our money, and we might be causing trouble for him and everybody, because they'd lose respect for us when they find us giving them money for nothing. They didn't lose any respect; they just kept on with their old habits.

"I'll admit there are bad growers, like in any group of people. We know farms where the migrant worker is cheated out of everything. He works all the time, and he's told that his room and board barely covers the work he does. If he tries to leave, there are guards, and they threaten him — and remember, these are very ignorant people we're talking about. I'm against all of that. I'm for paying them the best wage we can afford to people, in return for an honest day's work. I try to keep their quarters halfway presentable. I can't give them palaces; like I say, they'd

be lost in a home like mine. I can't pay them like they were
princes or experts. I'll grant that we need them, and they *are*
experts of a kind. But we could be rid of most of them right now
if we really had to; there are machines that will do almost anything a man does on a farm. They're expensive, the machines,
and with some crops they prevent you from having a second
growing in the same season. But if worst came to worst, we could
completely switch over, and then we'd no longer have a problem
with the migrant workers. Actually, I'd hate to see them go, in a
way I would. You get attached to them, after all these years you
do. As I said, they're like children; and you get attached to
them."

3.   Guarding the Animals and Children

It is not possible to dispute that grower's acknowledgment;
thousands of migrant farm workers do indeed live under awful,
shameful conditions — in effect, a continuing form of peonage.
The facts are as the grower knows them and describes them:
men, women and children are recruited in, say, rural Alabama or
Louisiana or Texas, or brought over the border from Mexico, and
then carried in buses and trucks or cars to southern Florida.
The men who find such people and promise them high money,
easy work, comfortable rooms and first-rate food are, needless to
say, the crew leaders — and from the moment of recruitment
until most probably the migrant's dying moment the crew leaders
are always there, promising and promising, pledging and cajoling
and, if need be, threatening, coming down hard with curses and
warnings of the ugliest sort. Behind those crew leaders, the obviously vicious ones and also the kind ones, stands a virtual army
of assorted private guards, "hired men," supervisors, foremen,
"patrol men," who in turn can usually depend upon sheriffs and
their deputies — and in addition the informally and quickly
deputized "auxiliary" police who in many rural counties rally to a
threat from "outside." The names that growers give to the men
who protect and defend their property are not very important;
however diverse those names the work itself is constant and uni-

form — the work of watching, the work of driving along in trucks that have racks inside filled with rifles, and the work of standing still, standing under a shady tree, say, and looking at migrants, making sure they keep to their job of picking, keep to their cabins, and in general stay where they are supposed to be, keep at what they are supposed to be doing, and most of all, "keep the attitude they should have." The men who guard some of those farms ("look over" them is perhaps the most common way of putting it) will gladly talk about their work — if, that is, a particular grower, who is their boss, tells them to go ahead and do so. I say "tells" them rather than "lets" them because such men both respond to authority and convey it; indeed, for some of them there seems to be nothing else that matters very much.

I have noticed that those guards whose minds have a clear-cut, unambiguous, and relatively uncomplicated notion of what is to be done talk about migrants as if they were animals; whereas the guards who are struggling with mixed feelings, who worry about the people they guard and feel sorry for them and even at times get sick (nausea and headaches are often mentioned) at the sights to be seen, those are the guards who usually don't talk about their charges as animals — but as children. The guards who sound the worst, who use the cruelest, most appalling imagery are found in a way more acceptable by migrants than the others, who can be fitful, unreliable, and confusing. It would be easy to describe this latter group of somewhat troubled and even tormented men from a migrant's point of view; but I have found that a good number of guards themselves are comparatively aware of the various pulls and tugs on them. Indeed, it is all too tempting for me to spend hours trying to comprehend the shades of sentiment or awareness in a particular farm worker — and then brush off a guard as an impossibly sullen, mean and disagreeable man, maybe an *animal* of sorts. To do that is to bring name-calling around at least one full circle. The fact is that certain men I had called "animals" in my mind (for thinking of migrants as animals) eventually directed strong and pointed English at me, and thereby showed how at least in that respect I misjudged them.

I misjudged, for instance, the man whose words I am about to present. The several inconsistencies that come up in his remarks ought to remind one just how difficult it is to make a sweeping, unqualified description of anybody, anywhere. In one afternoon's talk he surprised me by asking me if I had ever had to protect somebody. He wasn't being nasty or cynical or argumentative. He wanted to know the answer to a question that clearly meant a good deal to him. I told him I believed I had protected certain people and still do feel protective toward those people. He went on to say that he also has protected people, and still does. He does so not as a private person, but as a worker — which he insisted is what distinguishes him from me. Then he explained himself: "I know what people say. They had an article in the newspaper about a year ago, and it talked about 'camp guards' beating up the workers here on the farms. The district attorney looked into it, and he said there wasn't any evidence of that, and he couldn't understand why someone is always coming around here ready to insult us and write the worst things about us. All I do is make sure that people hired to work *work* and don't go around destroying property. Is there anything wrong in that? The trouble here is that you've got a type of people, the migrant people, who aren't like other people. They are more like animals. I don't mean them harm when I call them animals. I believe you've got to say the truth. If people would come here and see what I see, they'd know what I am talking about. They'd understand why Mr. Warren has to hire me and a lot of other guards. If he didn't he'd have his whole operation, everything, destroyed in no time flat. In the cabins they live like pigs. They throw things all over. When they're not being pigs they're being wild like a wild animal is — tearing up whatever we've built for them. In the fields they turn lazy on you. They want to sit and talk, and you have to keep watch over them. In the packing plant they'll get sloppy and stop sorting right. Then they'll go and drink at night and if you don't keep them here on the property, they'll get lost and never show up again. A lot of them get killed. They fight when they drink; they pull razors and knives on each other or they stumble into the path of a car on the road. Some of them drown; they'll be walking along and end up in the canals we have here all over the county.

"That's why I look on my job like this: you've got a lot of people who can't do anything without being told. Mostly they'll act like animals unless they're made to shape up and do what they should. My job is to be sure that they obey — and they *do* obey. If they don't, they've got my gun in their ribs so fast they can't figure how it could have happened. I'm just around, pushing them along with the gun. I never hide the gun and then surprise them with it. They see it all the time, so they know what a pistol looks like. When they start getting too noisy and they're not following orders, I'm right there; it's the *sight* of the gun that works. Like I say: with animals, you have to train them. You can't talk with them and explain yourself. The same way with these people. If you ask me — I'm no expert, but I've been working here for ten years — there's so much difference between the way a picker behaves and other people that you can't just say we're all the same before God. There must have been some reason God had when he made people like these; they may look like us, but they're a different type. If I ever sank that low, I'd hope someone *did* shoot me. There are times when I figure death would be the best thing for them, because it would take them out of their misery. They don't live a very good life. They move all over, and you feel sorry for them, if you let yourself. But I don't agree with some of my buddies; I don't agree it's all this 'poverty' business that's at fault.

"I have a friend Paul; he does the same work I do, but he and I are always arguing. Paul says the migrants are like children and I say they are much more like animals. It's not a joking matter, either, because he tries to be nice to them, then after a while he can't take it any more, the way they behave in spite of all he does for them, so he explodes at them and he really starts kicking them around and punching on them, and I've heard him tell them he'll kill them. Boy, do they obey him then! But a while later, after he's cooled off, he'll feel sorry for what he's said, and he'll come and tell me we should quit, and try guarding money in a bank. I tell him he's crazy, that's his problem. He's crazy to go soft on them in the first place — be so worried over them. That's letting them get under your skin. He says yes, but I guess he can't help himself. When I say you've got to adjust your mind, so you remember you've got a couple hundred animals here on this farm, and they're depending on you to keep them straight and make sure they eat and know the right place to sleep and how to work — when I say that to Paul, he gets so excited and tells me I've got no heart inside my chest. The fact is I'm easier with my children than he is. I go out and hunt and fish with them; my boys and I, we're real good friends. With Paul it's different. He says he doesn't want his boys handling guns and shooting and anything like that. He wants his boys to get all the education that's possible and be teachers, I guess, or lawyers — something big. It's not the money, though. With him it's because he says we don't do good work, and he wants his boys to go and help people out, you know. I think he's crazy, like I said.

"I'm the biggest help in the world to these people. There isn't a day that goes by when I'm not thanked and thanked and thanked by them. They'll thank me for telling them to speed up on the picking — of course it's only after they collect their money that I'll hear the thanks. They'll thank me for keeping them out of the lousy bars in town, where you lose your shirt paying big prices for the cheapest wine that was ever made. They'll thank me for breaking up their fights. If I didn't separate them with my gun, they'd disappear from killing each other off. They run to me when there's trouble, you see. They run and say Mr. John this is wrong, and Mr. John can we go and do this, and Mr. John what time is it, and when do we start and when do we stop — everything! Paul says it proves they're children, but for me it proves they're talking animals. Hell, a kid *grows*, a kid *learns*. A kid becomes a *man*, a *woman*. These migrant people, they never change. With them, it's the law of the jungle, like you read in the books. If the crew leader and me, if we didn't have our pistols and the rifles around — which they can see, just like we can — then it would be worse than over in the Everglades, where all kinds of animals live off one another. The migrants would be running around wild and turning on each other and killing each other off."

The one guard is quite correct about the other guard, so the other guard willingly admits. It is a matter of outlook, of philosophy, and no amount of discussion has budged either of the men — though to look at them from hour to hour they seem very much alike in the way they go about their daily tasks. "It's only on little things that we differ," Paul says, an observation which probably does explain their similar outward appearance, the slightly rigid posture they both demonstrate, the mixture of boredom and impassivity that both of their faces exhibit — that is, when the two men are not thoroughly alert and angry. Paul is rather introspective, and even introspective about the causes of his tendency to look inward. Paul and the other guards are in different "spots," of course, as they do their work. Often Paul dozes or eats some food he has brought along or shouts at some harvesters across the field. He believes that his job encourages him to think over things: he is alone so much, the hours go slowly, and his job's grimness apparently gives him cause to wonder, to pause and ask himself why — why are human beings treated like animals. "They are treated like animals," I hear him say. His friend declares migrants to be animals. I mark his friend in my mind as brutish, if not actually animal. Now Paul calls the *treatment* a group of people receives animallike. It is time, I sense, to bring the subject up again and give voice to what I have been thinking. Paul himself invites that, invites whatever openness one can manage. He himself can be a polite, respectful man, given to a kind of self-examination that theologians and philosophers and psychologists all consider either necessary or virtuous or both. He welcomes a chance to say what is on his mind: "John and I don't agree on what is right and wrong. He says I'm soft; and I say he's too hard. Actually, we're both the same most of the time. We have work to do, moving the pickers along and keeping them where they're supposed to be, and we just go ahead and do it. But there will be plenty of times when each of us works differently. I'll ask. He'll shout. I'll remind them. He'll order them around. He'll practically order *me* around. He'll say I'm dumb, treating them as if they're as smart as us. I'll come right back and let him know how I feel: to me these are just the poorest of the poor, and if I'd been born into what their life is like, I'd be acting just like them; I'd be one of them. That's the real argument. John says no. He says I couldn't be one of them, whether I wanted or not. When I tell him that *he* could be, that's too much for him to hear. He gets red and starts telling me I need a rest, because I'm letting the people here get to my head.

"I'll admit, they *do* get to my head. I think about them. The way they live, it *makes* you think. I couldn't tell John I spend some of my time thinking like that, because he'd probably say I was losing my mind. But, you know, I think even he will stop and wonder about all this, though he wouldn't admit it in a million years. Most of the day we're just standing here; and the poor people, they are beaten down and they have learned to give us no trouble. John has his transistor radio, and I have one; but you have to put them off after a while or you get dizzy from listening to them. A lot of the migrants really like their little radios. I encourage them to save and go buy one. They work better to music. They work hard. If it helps them to listen to people playing and singing those songs, I'm all for it, even if I can't take to the same music they like. I like regular songs — popular music, you might say.

"There are times, naturally, when I have to get tough. I can lose my temper. I have a real mean temper. I explode. I can't even recall what I say later on. I know that when my temper is going I'll agree with John; and I'll tell *them* that, too. I've called them 'animals' right to their face, many times in the past few years. I'll say this about John; he'll never do that, never call them anything like that. He'll treat them like that — he says we have to — but he won't call them to their faces what he says they are behind their backs. I try to be easier on them, but when I've gone and lost patience with them I'm full of cusses, and they must think I'm the worst guard we have here. Later on I feel bad, and I'll come home and tell my wife that we should get out of here, leave Florida and look for a different kind of work, the kind where you don't see such miserable people all day long. My boys ask me why. They want to know why they're miserable, so many migrants, and why we can't do anything about it. *We,* why can't *we* do something about it, they want to know! I don't know where to begin — with a question like that you could start with Adam and Eve and go all the way down through the whole history of the world, because that's the way it is: there's always the guy who has the gun and the guy who's looking down the barrel, the guy who owns the land, and the one who works for him, the men who have money, and those who don't. I don't guess that will change and, to be honest, I have to admit I'd rather be a guard here than be picking those beans the way they do. It's a hell of a lot better here under the shade than under the sun. And I'm sitting and they're all bent over. And I have my own water cup, and look at them, lining up there to use that dirty old cup we have here for them."

As he says, "that's the way it is": like him, many of us who are more "fortunate" often alternate in this life between general outrage at the way things are around us and the specific contentment our particular lives happen to offer; or perhaps, again like him, we move from a specific outrage we feel about one or several matters to a more general sense of contentment with the "progress" we choose to see and emphasize in our minds. And finally, like him, we move from an understanding of large-scale historical trends to an unnoticing, even blind immersion in those trends — an immersion which amounts to the everyday continuity of our lives.

4. Selling Gas to the Children

One has to be careful to emphasize that not all of us go through the motions I have just mentioned. If Ed Bryan, the owner of a gas station in Florida, had his way, no such ponderous, mealy-mouthed backing and filling would ever be said to characterize *him.* A lot of talk and analysis are good for nothing, Ed Bryan feels. The business of reflecting and speculating inevitably leads to preachy self-righteousness: "Hell, you can use a lot of words to talk about these people, but why bother, I say. It's all a lot of fancy lies, what you hear from nigger lovers and the college people. They don't know these people, but they'll bend your ear for a week talking about them and half the time you can't even understand what they're saying. They're full of themselves. They think they know everything. I saw one of those agitators, beard and all, on the television a few months ago, saying we don't treat our poor people right. Well, why in hell don't our poor people go and treat themselves right? Why don't they work, like I do?

"Yes, sure the migrants work. They should. They have it pretty good. I've been putting gas into their cars for years, so I should know. There are some stations that won't let them even go near them. If they so much as drive an inch on their cement, the owners will shoot to kill. They don't want the fancy tourist trade from up North being put off by any animals; that's what they are. To me a dollar is a dollar, even from animals. To me there's no difference between Yankees coming down here for the winter, and these migrants going North for the summer. If they come into my station and ask for gas and have the money to pay for it, I'll sell it to them. The only thing I ask — I see to it! — is that they stay out of my rest rooms and stay in their cars and get the hell out of here as fast as I've filled up their tanks and gotten my money.

"I haven't a lot of degrees. I never finished high school. One thing I know, though, is how to judge a person. When you wait on them all day, the poor ones and the rich ones, niggers and white people, your own folks from Georgia and the goddam Yankees with their Buicks and the plates from New York and Pennsylvania, on their way to Miami Beach — is this the right way, they're always asking — then it's not so hard to figure out what's on the mind of people. I can figure them all out. I can tell who's going to ask for a dollar's worth, and who wants the tank filled up, and I can tell the strangers from our own people without even looking at the license plates or hearing them speak. It's in their faces, what they are. You know what these migrant-work people are? They're the dumbest people you'll ever meet. I don't have it against them, like with the welfare-type niggers — who are a bunch of lazy troublemakers. At least the migrants try to work. Of course, a lot of them are niggers and some are the Mexican types. I've even seen some white people come through, vegetable pickers. But they're all the same, no matter what their race. Like I say, the niggers who are migrants aren't really niggers. They're more migrant-work people than niggers. You see? Well, if you don't I don't know how I can make you see. The only way I know of putting it is that they're like the circus people we used to see come through here. No more, though; they've stopped coming. I mean, the migrants don't live like we do, in a home. They seem to enjoy themselves, moving up North and coming back. I'll get them going both ways, on their way up and on the return. Like it is with your birds and animals, they make their home all over, and they don't stay in any one place more than a week or two.

"You can feel sorry for them; my wife will. Sometimes you look in the car or truck and see the children they have, and you start asking yourself why in hell it is that people decide to live like that. I guess the reason is simple: they just do, because that's how they're made. They're made the way they are just like we're made the way we are. When you see a bird flying, you don't ask why she doesn't sit right where she was, on that tree yonder. When you see those little squirrels and chipmunks running all over the place, coming together and then scattering, you don't ask why they're behaving so strange. It's in their blood — in their blood to behave like they do. That's how it is with the migrant-work people, too. They're like the circus people, born to be itchy and move. They leave a mess after them. They would mess up my station if I let them. But I don't. I sell them gas and then they leave. They can tell by the way I treat them that they'd better go, *fast*. I admit, it's a good thing they're around. They pull in the crops each year. That's about all they're good for, and if we didn't have them doing the work I think we'd have a lot of trouble from them. They'd have nothing to do to keep them busy. They'd probably join the civil rights people, and we'd have to mobilize the National Guard to keep the peace. I don't believe you can teach migrant people. You can only make sure they mind you. Yes, like I said, I sell them gas. Why not? The green stuff is the green stuff. I need every dollar I can get my hands on. If an alligator came up from the Okeefenokee Swamp and offered me a dollar for some gas, I'd sell it to him. I'd just make sure he didn't hurt me. I make sure the migrant people don't ruin my station. I hear tell they carry diseases with them, dirt and plenty of diseases. You have to be careful in this world, that you don't catch other people's diseases."

5. *Teaching the Wanderers*

A sensitive teacher who works with migrant children said to me almost word for word what I have just quoted from that owner of a gas station — who is proud to call himself a "redneck," proud to be an inhabitant of what is called Maddox Country, proud to call "them" by their God-given name, niggers. (So I was once told, amid the foulest of language — that "niggers" is the way God Himself would refer to "the colored.") The teacher has a master's degree in education, comes from New Jersey, has devoted fifteen hard, frustrating, lonely years to migrant children in Florida, where they spend most of the year. She has even followed them North, and in doing so come within a few miles of the town in which her parents used to live — it is in southern New Jersey, near Delaware and near Pennsylvania. In other words, she has taught migrants in the winter as part of her regular job in Palm Beach County, then taught them as a volunteer in the summer. She loves migrant children, and she certainly knows them; but she has her grave doubts about them, and out of context one can quote her in such a way that she sounds like a complete supporter of the gas station owner. She has several times said what he once said: "I don't believe you can teach them."

To be sure she *does* believe most of the time that those children can be taught; she has taught them a lot, and she knows it. Because she knows what the future holds for migrant children, she concludes that all they learn they also unlearn — or, put differently, that her teaching cannot "take" because it is undone by one set of circumstances after another. She can put her doubts into a series of those unanswerable educational and philosophical questions that in her case are not rhetorical: "What is the point of teaching at all, if the teacher knows the children she has in her classroom haven't any chance at all of moving into a society where education means anything? Can it be said I've *taught* children when they soon learn to forget what they learn? I wonder whether I should be a teacher at all, a teacher of migrant children. Perhaps I should be ringing doorbells in Washington, D.C., though I doubt many people there would answer. I've written my share of urgent letters to congressmen and federal officials. It doesn't take long for them to reply — with form letters or those stupid, composed ones that say nothing in polite and hypocritical terms. I'd like to bring some of Florida's congressional delegation to the migrant camps near here and see what the reaction of those high-minded men is. Oh, they'd have their pious phrases! I will say this to you and anyone else: I prefer the worst rabble-rousing mob to the hypocrisy some of our elected officials display and to the hypocrisy I've encountered in those government bureaus up there in Washington."

She has gone there, gone to Washington; she has also gone to Tallahassee. She would not want to be known as an "activist," though. She belongs to no political organization, and she is not even very well-read on current events. She prefers novels. She likes to read Edith Wharton and John Galsworthy and Willa Cather and Elizabeth Bowen. She majored in English, once thought she might want to teach English in a college or university. But by accident (or was it design, she will wonder aloud?) she "came upon the migrants." How did that happen — and what made her stay with them so long, in view of her despair, so often avowed — her conviction that her efforts do not accomplish very much at all? She is far from a talkative person, which is no great disadvantage to a teacher who works with migrant children. It is hard for such children to comprehend those who (out of whatever helpful motives) come across as wordy, as loud and strong and confident. Migrants have learned to fear and respect authority and to expect very little from people like teachers. A sincere, idealistic, rather voluble teacher (like some VISTA workers or other volunteers) can be confusing, puzzling, even threatening — or so a number of veteran teachers claim. Many migrant children are reluctant to say anything out loud in school, perhaps because they see so many schools or indeed so very few. Here is how this teacher talks for a moment or two about those children: "Many of the children I teach will be with me a month or two, then leave. They will go on to another school, or they won't. Some have never been in school consistently for any continuous period. I've become close to some crew leaders, so they bring the children to *me*, not to the school here. I am lucky to have a principal who is flexible and lets me make these private arrangements. After school I go out to the camps and have another class there, and the children really mob me then. But even there, in the middle of the camp, I find the children very quiet and reserved. I am a stranger, and they know it — a nonmigrant, a part of another world. Perhaps if I worked in the camps all the time the children would feel different.

"I've thought of doing just that, but I can't. I get too upset by the conditions I see there. I worry for the children, feel awful for them. I try not to show my feelings to the children, because I know it doesn't help them to have me virtually in tears. But it's hard, that hour in the camp, and I guess I need the protection of the school building. I come into the building and I feel safe; when the children come into the building they feel as if they are in real danger, and many children never even go near a school building, not once in their lives. I wonder how people would feel all over America if they knew how these children live, and if they knew that hundreds and hundreds of them, I know from my own observations, *never* go to school. They aren't registered anyplace, and they just grow up illiterate. They start working in the fields with their parents when other children start kindergarten and the first grade. And no one cares; the growers don't, nor do a lot of the crew leaders. The city and county officials here in Florida don't see their job as one of going way out up the dusty roads to find migrant children, and they would really have to *look* to find those children, because they are out of the way, way out of the way.

"I didn't come here to work with migrant children. I came here because my father was ill and had to leave New Jersey and go South. We didn't have much money, so we stayed clear of places like Miami and Palm Beach. Even if I had a million dollars I'm not sure I'd like to live in those places. They're full of glitter and polish and cheap extravagance; and I become enraged now when I go near them and my mind thinks of our migrant families — so nearby, only forty or fifty miles away from each of those cities. We originally stopped in a motel near Belle Glade, and it seemed like a nice city. Little did I realize how my life would be changed. I had planned to leave my parents and return to New Jersey, where I was teaching the second grade in a pleasant suburban town. But my father became even sicker, and I decided to stay with them, all that winter. I also decided to get a temporary teaching job, if at all possible, and that was the beginning — and I have to be honest and say it, there are times when I think it was also the end. I've loved teaching migrant children, but I've become so discouraged I hardly know what to do. There are times when I want to go up to Washington and New York and tell everyone important there that it's criminal beyond any words I can use, *criminal* how we let children live this way, in a country like this. I turn on the television and hear that we're doing all these things on every continent for the sake of 'freedom,' and I begin to wonder whether they actually realize what these young children have to face in their lives, even before they get to school.

"As for the schools, there's very little we can do when a child is moving around so much. I keep teaching them because I have a certain faith. I believe that maybe two or three children each school year hear something I've said and won't forget it. Maybe, just maybe, a chain of circumstances will be set in motion — and those children will escape from the migrant stream. I know I may be foolish to hope for that, but I do. I tell each class several times a day that, bad as things are, an effort can lead to change. I sound like a minister, I know; but the children listen, and maybe a few will remember. Some *are* reached, I know that, because they come up afterwards — it breaks my heart — and ask me how, *how* can they and their families ever get to settle down and live in the same place, so that — bless them! — they can stay here, stay in my class. I try to reassure them. Things will improve, I tell them. They know better, though. I feel like a liar who for her own sake has to keep on going through the motions — of lying. I suppose *I* feel better for being able to offer the children encouragement. It is awful. I find it hard to talk about.

"In my class I'm not one for much talking. I try to get the children to *do* things. Migrant children, a lot of them, are very good with their hands. I suppose I should say that they have good 'motor skills and coordination.' I like to emphasize what they can do, rather than cram a few facts into their heads. The beautiful moments are when I can get a quiet, frightened migrant child teaching himself, or teaching one of our regular children from a very comfortable home. You see, migrant children learn to pick beans and tomatoes, which means they learn to control the movements of their hands so as to exert just the right force on the vine. They can also be very imaginative children; they love to use scissors and cut out things and paint, and they love to use a hammer and nails. They make wooden cars and trucks. They draw trucks. They cut trucks out of cardboard or drawing paper. Oh, some of them will do nothing, absolutely nothing. I'm afraid they are gone, gone for good. But enough of them are still alert and responsive, and it's harder, in a way, when they are. There are days when I firmly believe that it would be better for them all, those thousands of boys and girls, if they were dull and dazed beyond all pain, beyond all recognition of the world they live in. It's not right to talk that way, I know. I should have a 'positive attitude.' That's what I hear from the young college students who come around here and want so desperately to help out. I love them. I'm all on their side. There are few of them, few compared to the need, and the few we have give of themselves totally, completely. But I fear they are as naïve as I once was.

"Oh, I hate to talk like I've just been talking. I know I sound like an old, tired, fussy, cranky teacher, who has given up a long time ago. But I believe we will never be able to do much educationally for these children until they stop traveling and learn what roots are, what it's like to stay in one place and grow there. The government has been spending more and more money these past few years to provide us with all the best teaching equipment and materials for migrant children, and they are trying to offer migrants some medical services, too. I'm for that. Who wouldn't be? Plenty of people, actually, or we would have had that kind of assistance a long time ago. But even with the improvements I know that many migrant children don't *ever* go to school and *never* get near a health clinic, whether it's mobile or in a permanent building. They just don't. They live out there up those unpaved roads, away from everyone, and they are slaves, that's what I am going to call them — their fathers and mothers are worked like slaves, and they don't dare raise their voices. If they did, if they got 'uppity', they would be thrown in jail for 'owing money' to the crew leader or the grower. The children start working as soon as they can stand and walk and have the necessary use of their hands. If the children fall sick, they either live or they die; no doctor comes to help, one way or the other. As for schools, what possible use are *they?* That is the question so many migrant parents ask themselves. I ask you, is it an unreasonable one?

"I met an official from the government, from the Office of Education I think it was, and he was full of wonderful ideas. He wanted us to have machines and newsletters and new curricula and everything, and he said he could help us pay for it. I asked him why the government didn't stop these children from moving up and down the Atlantic coast and working ten and twelve hours a day. He said that wasn't his business. He said that wasn't an 'educational matter.' Well, I don't mean to be fresh, but it *is* an educational matter. Of course, I don't blame *him* or our college students or anyone, no *one* person. I do blame my country, though. I can't believe that the United States has to allow such things. Until the migrant people are able to organize and bargain with the growers, until they have a place to live in and an income through the year, then they'll keep on wandering, and their children will be hurt, hurt so very much, hurt I believe beyond repair. They tell me how they 'live all over,' the children do. And the truth is they are wanderers, sad and aching little wanderers. I tell myself not to get all worked up over them; it'll do no one any good, and certainly not me. But as I have said to you several times, I want to scream sometimes. Most of the time I guess I do just the opposite. I keep my mouth firmly shut and try the best I can to be a good teacher. Sometimes, though, I'm ready to start a revolution in this country. I am a law-abiding person, but I see injustice all around me, and the people who represent me in Washington work for the rich, not the poor. What is one to do?"

6. Saving Their Souls, Their Damned Souls

Two kinds of ministers look after the spiritual needs of migrant farm workers: one kind only prays for their souls, the other kind also works passionately to educate the public and change the laws. The migrants themselves know the difference between the two kinds of ministers and don't really as a rule prefer one sort to the other. Social activists are of course quick to pour scorn on evangelical, fundamentalist ministers. Conservatives have a similar contempt for liberal ministers who supposedly care not at all about God, only about the minimum wage law or the Office of Economic Opportunity. Migrants have needs, more unfulfilled needs perhaps than any other American citizens, and so they are glad to have a man of God arguing their cause with the growers. They are also glad to hear the Lord God besought on their behalf with ringing, evocative phrases. I have already mentioned that the next and last section of this book contains a discussion of "rural religion"; here I simply want to say a few things about those ministers, whether liberal or thoroughly fundamentalist, because they are frequently so important a part of the migrant farmer's world; I also want to set down the way some of them think and feel about their harassed and afflicted parishioners, who come and go, attend a service, then are soon hundreds of miles away and at another service.

Whatever the theological viewpoint of the minister, each one will go on at great length about the miserable living conditions migrants must accept. After that central fact is acknowledged, however, a distinct difference of opinion begins to emerge — when one asks the question "What is to be done?" From an intense, fast-thinking, warm, compassionate, impressively self-sacrificing and generous minister — out of an Ivy League school and Union Theological Seminary — comes one answer: "What is to be done? I'll tell you what is to be done. Only when the migrants are organized will anything be done. I look upon myself as an organizer, a man of God, yes, that too, but an organizer most of the time. I would like to help migrant workers get more power; it's as simple and direct as that. I'd like them to have the political clout that businessmen have and other workers. I want them to have more money, more economic power. I want their entire manner of living changed. They have to become part of us, not a totally removed and exploited subculture. I conduct services, religious services, but I also hand out leaflets and go from camp to camp, trying to encourage leadership and the organization of the workers. And when I'm not here, working with migrants, I'm in New York and Washington, trying to squeeze out money from people who don't know anything about these conditions, or trying to buttonhole congressmen, so that maybe one of these days we'll get migrants covered by the laws Roosevelt got passed to protect other workers.

"As for the migrants themselves, I think they could do a lot for themselves — if they once would start pulling together. They cling to the crew leader because he's their lifeline, at least they *think* he is. They are uneducated and mostly from an isolated, farm-type background. Their fathers were sharecroppers or tenant farmers, or they were themselves, and failed at it. I've spent hours trying to teach them — teach them, for instance, how dishonest crew leaders are, and how exploited the farm worker is. I know I come on like a typical middle-class intellectual on all this, but what am I supposed to do, sit back and 'appreciate' all the fears and hang-ups of these people, their 'social problems' and 'cultural attitudes' — and never try to get some *change* going? I believe in a social gospel, and if ever there was a group that needed a social gospel, it's the migrants. Yet, they are the hardest people in the world to reach. They want me to pray for them. When I tell them they ought to be getting a quarter more an hour (a dollar more would be better!) they shrug their shoulders. Sometimes they look at me as if I'm a little disturbed up in my brain. Sometimes I think I *am*, too; because it's discouraging, and we don't see much progress from month to month, even year to year. In school, at Union, I'd read about Damnation; now I know what it means to be cursed and exiled — to be damned. They are damned, migrants are, and as Christ points out all through His parables, so are we, the rest of us, because we allow such things to exist; we are indifferent; we couldn't care less."

In decided contrast to such despair is the philosophy of another minister who also spends his working life with migrants. He is hardworking, and like his colleague, intelligent and high-minded and kind. He is more outgoing and talks more rapidly, but he is not a shallow man — though his ideas would probably command little attention at, say, Harvard or Yale or Princeton *or* Union Theological Seminary. Still, as he himself points out, people up in those schools aren't exactly worried about the fate of migrants, spiritual or otherwise, even if a few from those "fancy Northern schools" do "come through." They don't stay long, he insists, and in many cases he is right. His recital of the reasons those ministers (or others from such universities) don't stay long tells a lot about his own way of thinking, and of course, gives us yet another view of migrant farm workers: "I don't have to say very much about my liberal church brethren from up North. They are fine men, and I wish them well. I wish them every success in what they are trying to do. I don't happen to agree with them, that's all. They want more money for the migrants. So do I. They want more education and health services — the whole liberal package, is what I call it. But what has all that education and medical care brought the rest of us who are not migrants? I ask you that. I ask you. Talk with them, talk with *them* — not the migrants, but our liberal crusading ministers, who want to change the world. They want to make migrants part of their world, but in the next breath they condemn their world, call it every name in the book — and I agree with them. I wish they'd think out their position. To me it's rather simple: God put us here, and He'll take us away, and we'll suffer, every one of us, each in his own way. I don't *want* the migrant to suffer — what nonsense! — but I don't believe an increase in the minimum wage, even a big increase, will make the migrant worker the full, happy man those colleagues of mine keep on talking about. If they want to argue, as *citizens,* for a change in the laws, that's fine. What bothers me is when they mix up their religion with their social conscience. They are two separate things.

"I'm here to try to do the Lord's bidding, in the best way I know how. I'm here to try to save souls for Him. We are either with Him or against Him, you know. We will either be saved or lost — lost forever. The rich don't get saved because they've got money, and the poor don't get saved because they haven't a cent to their name; I believe that. God will save a banker and a poor migrant farmer — if they both have faith in Him, and not in presidents and kings, in Mammon or machines. There are times, I admit it, there are times when I want to stop preaching and get some good food and clothes for some of these migrants, especially their children. I've done that, actually — though I don't advertise it, like others do, and I don't get prideful over it, like they do. But you have to be strong. You can't be sidetracked from the Lord's work. These children here need food and clothes, I agree; but of what use will all that be if they're abandoned to the Devil and left for an eternity in Hell? We can all be saved or we can all be lost. Maybe migrants are nearer damnation than most people. Their souls are in danger of being lost, and when a soul is lost, that's the biggest tragedy possible. No laws and giveaway programs can reverse that! But I agree, I do, that our growers are in danger, too. They need to pray for forgiveness, just like the migrants do. God wants us all to be saved, if we would only hear Him and join Him. If not, we'll burn a long time — and Damnation will be a lot worse than picking beans up and down the coast."

One wonders, one really wonders, without any blasphemous or sacrilegious intent, whether in fact *anything* real or imaginary could be much worse than the lives some American migrant children continue to live. Are they already irreversibly damned, the souls of those children? Perhaps so; perhaps they are cursed and condemned in ways hurt and hungry children know, but do not talk about. And so in a curious way the contempt a guard or gas station owner or crew leader may express for those children (They are no damned good! They are damned fools! Damn them!) somehow expresses the gospel truth, terrible and apocalyptic in its finality. Since most of us manage not to know a single thing about the children whose souls that fundamentalist minister spends all his time trying, apparently against insurmountable odds, to save, we are hardly in a position to dismiss him and his ideas. Again and again I have heard him express (yes, and demonstrate) the care he feels toward those migrant children. Meanwhile, millions who would laugh derisively at his religious beliefs are nowhere to be seen and heard by a man who feels lonely and isolated and hopelessly frustrated in the face of the problems of his people. Sometimes I have heard him even turn to blasphemy, use the verb damn, the adjective damned, but not in connection with migrant children.

PART FOUR

THE RURAL LIFE

IX

THE RURAL MIND

THE thing I least want to do in the concluding section of this book is to announce a lot of "traits" or "attitudes" or "variables" which could be grouped under a convenient and catchy rubric like the title of this chapter. In the course of writing up this work I believe I have learned more about my own mind than anyone else's — learned how narrowly I viewed people, how set I was in *my* psychology or personality, or in my professional ways. I was at times ready to do things like compare migrants with sharecroppers, and sharecroppers with mountaineers, and mountaineers with the middle class I guess most of us belong to (though, God knows, there are plenty of "subgroups" in *that* category) and set forth with long lists of similarities and differences.

In this section I mean to summarize what I *at last* found out. After a decade of work I began to see two aspects of the "rural mind" — its unyielding, hesitant side, and its generous, affectionate side. And if those adjectives seem contradictory, it is because I have at last given up trying to fit stubbornly various and particular lives into the authoritarian needs of one or another theory. Perhaps all that a book like this can do is to require the writer, and reader, to look inward as well as feel more informed about all of "that," all of "them" living out "there" — way out there in the United States of America.

1.   Whose Strengths, Whose Weaknesses

They would be sitting or standing there in front of the cabin, or peering at me from the inside, and I would start slowing myself down. I always needed the extra seconds that a few more steps provide. I would hold my head bowed or pretend to notice something up there in the sky or over toward the plantation proper. That way their eyes and mine didn't connect, and I didn't have to smile and start saying hello before they could really hear me. That way I could get my mind set for the purpose of my visit, the discovery of certain things, the unearthing of information I thought I ought to possess.

In the beginning ritual masked fear on both sides. I noticed how quiet they all were. My car's noise was a signal to them. They usually heard the car before they saw it because of a sudden turn in the road that made us visible to one another only at the very end of a mile-long unpaved, dusty road. By the time I was in sight they had taken up their positions. They seemed rooted. They never looked at me. Or rather, they looked at me when I would not notice. At times I thought them wooden, impassive — and, of course, frightened. When the day came that *I* was not so frightened, their eyes caught mine. I remember being close to grateful that I had someone else's nervousness to observe. Fear has power; power seeks to affirm itself by exertion. And so the edgy, responsive dark irises and white eyeballs belied the calm, the silence. I looked on feet crossed, making still circles out of many legs, and knees crossed, enabling worn, mud-caked shoes to point, but not move an inch. Hungry for the truth about "the sharecropper's mind," I found my answers in movement. The eyes did, after all, move and the eyes, my mother told me, were the "windows of the soul." What is more, I thought (or had to think) I saw dilated pupils, which every doctor knows to be a telltale sign that all is not well inside, below, underneath, wherever. (And haven't we learned in this century that any truth that is worthwhile has to be buried, concealed, and apparent *only* to the well-trained, in contrast to the well-educated or the desperately or naturally sensitive?)

I now realize that my movements and postures underwent the same careful scrutiny that theirs did. Five years later we could reminisce: "I don't believe we knew what you were after. I thought maybe you was here to spy on us, or to sell something.

But my sister, she said there was nothing around here to spy that they didn't already know, the bossman and all. And we don't have the money to buy nothing, so no one could be wasting his time every week for that, to sell. Well, we thought there was no harm just waiting to see. Before long you find out everything you ask about — that's what my daddy used to tell me, and he's right.

"Now, with you we figured you was too slow to be with the sheriff, and not sure of yourself, not enough. And my little boy, James it was, he said, 'Mama, the man doesn't always know what to say.' I think maybe that was the first time any of us, we'd seen a man in a suit be shy — I mean be shy himself and be shy with words, too. Then, when you switched to regular clothes, the summer pants and no more of the tie and like that, well then we decided you might be from up there in Washington, and the government. You know, they're trying to be for us, on our side. I tried to tell people you are a doctor with a college, but they said doctors don't go around the country sitting and talking here and there.

"No, I can't say I ever have been to a doctor's office. They ask you to pay first, and we can't, not first or later. So, it's just as well. They'd give us medicine, if they agreed to see us, and then the next thing you knew there'd be the sheriff here, and we'd be hauled off to jail for not paying the doctor's bill."

But before we came to that kind of mutual confession — in which I replied in kind, my thoughts about their thoughts, and finally, my thoughts pure and simple — there had to be one long stretch of coming and going, of sly and bewildered talk, of muscles relaxed a bit, quickly tightened up, then once again allowed to slacken, each time for a little longer. They began to realize that I was in fact an oddball — who belonged to no recognizable part of their world. And after much too long a period of time I began to realize — an important first step — that they were not the helpless, pitiable objects of study I have to admit I predominantly felt them to be. Oh, it was never necessary to be that blunt. Instead of calling them the wretched of the southern earth, I could lash out at the South itself: the region's blacks are terribly poor people; they are mercilessly exploited by the individual bossmen, often "managers" or "foremen" who do the rough and tough work, the squeezing dry of lazy bodies, the extraction of ergs from machines that are running at a caloric loss. (But aren't millions of people in other countries and continents even worse off?) And finally, they are badly educated people, barely literate or for all practical purposes illiterate.

All that is true, I thought to myself in the beginning, but someone has to be hardheaded enough to document what oppression does to its victims, how degraded they actually become. Cannot relentless psychological scrutiny turn into the sharpest kind of social criticism? Romantics may speak of a "culture" that peasants have, or include them in some "agrarian tradition"; but I came to them armed with both Marx and Freud and so, in a way, any desire to cover up their "condition" and my account of it with soft, understated, merely allusive or (worst of all) ambiguous language was doubly suspect. I knew enough to ask myself whether I was beholden to the "power structure" — perhaps one I simply don't care to recognize myself, let alone acknowledge to others. I knew enough to ask myself whether sharecroppers, simple sharecroppers, vulnerable sharecroppers, made me feel scared and to blame for something. And of course I knew that we are all afraid; we all feel at fault; everyone has "work" to do, fears and guilts to understand and "resolve."

So, it is better to be blunt, I decided as I started visiting them. They are "deprived" and "disadvantaged" and all the rest. They need "higher horizons." They should go North. They need "enrichment programs." They are eligible for every "title" in every federal law; and they need more laws with more "titles." Headstart is only a beginning. Leap is a drop in the bucket. Upward Bound is not "relevant," not to people so badly off, so out of things, so firmly, almost intractably part of — what is it called? — the *lumpenproletariat*. The only things that will help them, change them, make them part of America, are "massive programs," a "frontal assault" on their poverty, a "basic restructuring" of our society, a "planned attack" on — well, everything "socioeconomic" and "psychosocial" and "sociocultural" that amounts to their very bad lot.

And here are some of the things I found — in one family from the Mississippi Delta — that go to make up that bad lot. The cabin has no heat, no running water, although three miles away there is a faucet and "all the water you can tote." (Not every family in that "area" is that lucky.) None of the seven children was born in hospitals; none was delivered by doctors; none has ever seen physicians; none has taken vitamin "supplements" as infants or vitamin pills as children; none is without evidence of illness; and none has any clothes that can be called his, his alone.

"The children, they're the most trouble when they're by theirselves. Most of the time they're together, though. And then I know it's okay." They are indeed together. They sleep together: four in one bed, three in another, all in one room. The other room belongs to their parents and also serves as the kitchen — and living room and dining room. They share not only space and time but clothes and plates and forks. There are three pairs of shoes to go around, so only certain children can fight their way into them, or fight to fill them up — and then go to church or, yes, to school. (And, naturally, it is the absence from school that bothers us secular, twentieth-century Americans, for whom education is sacred, a way to virtually everything, at least on this earth.) As for the children in that cabin, church wins over school hands down. They fight to go with their parents on Sunday, "to walk with them" as one boy put it, and to sit there and see and hear "everyone get to talking and have a real good time." Those who stay at home are sad, but they turn happy on Monday if spared school because they still don't have those shoes, or because they feel tired and sick, or because they have to mind the younger ones and help around the house — which means in the fields or around "the place." (It is no mansion. It has no columns, not even a magnolia tree. It is a substantial house, nondescript in style, painted white with green shutters and a green door.)

I don't know what the United States Census Bureau did with

the information they obtained from the parents of those seven children. Are they classified sharecroppers or tenant farmers or field hands or employees or retainers or servants or just plain slaves? Are they listed as educated up to this grade or that one? Are they called citizens of this country, or aliens? Or were they overlooked and not counted at all? The census questions that you and I answer every decade can be very embarrassing, although not to "us."

"No sir, I can't say I've ever voted," said the father one day when I got around to that issue. "Yes sir, I think I know what you mean. [He knew damn well what I meant.] They have the law now, that says we can go vote. Some are trying it, and some aren't. I'm afraid I haven't got around to it, yet. But I hope to, before I die I hope to. Right now I guess I've got some other things to do."

Well, what other things? (Those are the good moments, when the observer is practically invited to ask something.) "I don't know — things like where to live, you know. We're thinking of going North. My sister is up there, in Chicago, and she keeps telling us to leave. But we're afraid to. They don't need a lot of us here, but I hear they don't need us there, either. We don't know what to do. We work on the crops part of the time, but the machines do more and more. There's some cotton they can't get, and there's the cattle and a few vegetables we have. I've got the chores to do. And my wife helps out in The House."

His father "worked on shares." Put differently, his father produced cotton and gave it over to the present bossman's father, and in return they continued to live side by side, the share-cropper and the bossman — on the bossman's land. He gave the sharecropper a few hundred dollars to spend during the course of the year, and The House sent over some food and some outgrown and secondhand clothes. The man I know grew up and became a field hand. There was no point getting credit for seed and tools and living quarters and food, and then working the land and receiving a share of the crop's value, minus charges for all the credit advances, including the money required for drainage, for irrigation, for fencing: "The bossman, he came and told me that with my daddy it was one thing, but times are changing, and a lot of the sharecroppers, they're not needed, and he was switching. I could work for him and in return I could live in the house and he would make sure that I never starve to death. And even with the machines coming, we could stay, because my wife is such a good help and especially her cooking."

His wife's cooking: until then I thought I knew everything about her cooking. In the morning she makes breakfast. She fries up some grits and they are washed down with either a Coke or some coffee. There is no such thing as lunch. The children have another Coke, and some very cheap candy like licorice or sugar-coated gum, which they chew and chew and chew dry and take out of their mouths and stretch and tear into fragments and laugh over and play with and stick upon one another. The parents also have another Coke and some candy, which they eat with greater reserve. Supper is the main meal. It is served early, about half-past four or five, and includes without exception fried potatoes and more grits and greens, and bread with peanut butter sometimes, and fatback sometimes. Every once in a while a stew appears, made of potatoes and gravy and pork. Even more unusual is a soup, the product of boiled bones and potatoes and greens. For dessert there is another Coke, and maybe more candy.

I asked about cooking and I heard this: "We have practically no money, so it's hard to get by. We grow a little, but we haven't much land to do it on, and the bossman wouldn't want us spending too much time on that. My kids grow some flowers, the zinnias. You can't eat zinnias, I know it, but you can like them — just like you can rest beside a sunflower. We get our greens from the yard, and some tomatoes, though they don't last long. We don't have the money to buy the food stamps. We get the commodities, and that's how we live. We'd be dead right now without the lard and flour they give, the government. Yes sir, everyone of us would be dead. I try to fill my kids' stomachs up as best I can. I figure if they doesn't hurt them too much, their stomachs, well then, that's good. They gets their energy from the candy and the Coke. They take a drink and bite on the licorice, and I know they've got their sugar in them and can keep going."

But her husband was talking about the cooking she did for the bossman. I asked her about that and she told me: "Oh, yes. I've been helping her out for years. I go up there and do what she tells me. I don't plan anything. She always says to me: 'Ruth, I've planned today's menus out.' Then she lists what I've got to do and I go ahead and get to work there."

She gets to work in a spacious, well-equipped kitchen. The sink is stainless steel. The stove is an electric range. The refrigerator is huge, and next to it stands a freezer, and next to *it* stands a washing machine and then a dishwasher. ("I do the dishes and some laundry, too.") Obviously, she has a few minutes to relax, because there is a small television set on one counter — and also a waffle iron, and a toaster, and a mixer for "working up" cakes, and an electric knife sharpener, which also takes care of pencils. I never would have seen all those electrically run gadgets had I not decided to compare her place of work with her place of residence. I knew her bossman well, and, in fact, once heard him say this about Ruth: "She's a fine woman, and so is her husband a fine man. They do an honest day's work, and we'll never let them go without a roof over their heads. I'm going to build them a new place, as a matter of fact. We're letting a lot go, though a lot of them don't want to. I tell them they may as well go North. We can't use them here. One by one they slip away; but you know, we have quite a few still here, right on our land. Eventually I suppose we'll only have maybe five families left here. Imagine that! It's hard for me to believe, after all these years with about a hundred or more. But I sure hope Ruth never leaves. I told my wife I think we'd near starve to death. She's the best cook in this county, easily."

I discovered what he meant. I had lunch with him and his wife. I had a big lunch, that started with a glass of tomato juice and a neatly cut piece of lemon. Then Ruth served us hot diced chicken and rice with raisins mixed in and peas and chutney on the side. And finally we had deep-dish apple pie and ice cream and coffee. It was all tasty, all neatly and attractively presented. The rice was fluffy and warm and covered with butter and seasoned just right. The chicken was cut perfectly, not too small and not too large. The peas were not overcooked; they were fresh, not frozen or canned, and like the rice, delicately salted. The pie had a light crust, and inside were warm tart apples, neither too syrupy nor dry. I was afraid I was going to be told that the ice cream was homemade, but no, it was store-bought: "It used to be we'd make our ice cream here, when I was a child. But you know it's too easy to buy it, and I think Ruth has enough to do as it is." I had commented on how good the ice cream was, and on how good the ice cream was at a nearby (and larger) plantation, where it was a bit ostentatiously, if generously, handed over with the hostess's advice from across the table that "Mary-Jean makes it, fresh every day." Ruth's mistress had been there many times — and clearly regretted the unfavorable comparison that I suppose I had unwittingly made.

When I left the house my stomach was filled with Ruth's food, and my mind was finally brought up short, the way it should have been months before. I kept on thinking of Ruth and that kitchen and of all the Ruths in America, but guilt masks many things, one of which is pride. My guilt so far had been the kind I easily notice in both myself and in patients: we have so much; others have so little. The guilt I began to feel for the first time after that lunch was something else, though; it had to do with the recognition of a willful kind of ignorance and blindness — mine. For a long time I had known that Ruth worked for the bossman's wife — cooked and cleaned and dusted for her, looked after her clothes and her dishes and her bedroom and bathroom. I knew all that, but I never really allowed my imagination to go any further; in fact, to bridge the two worlds that Ruth bridged every day. It was all right, of course, for *me* to bridge those two worlds; but Ruth in my mind had to be a sharecropper's wife, pure and simple. (And don't thousands of them work in those big houses in one capacity or another?)

The search for order and clarity can often help a case of the nerves, can help a person come to terms with his worries and fears as well as his "methodology." Somehow a confusing, am-

biguous, irony-filled world becomes a little more manageable
when this man is distinguished from that one; and if they both
can be placed on a graph or two and made part of a few
percentages and made to possess a few "attitudes" and "beliefs"
and "habits" and "problems" — well then, all the better. Ruth
and her mistress live worlds apart on that plantation. I was busy
finding out precisely how far apart. Every liberal bone in my
body, I assure you, was full of the proper mixture of outrage and
pity and sadness. In my cool, farsighted, evenhanded moments I
felt sorry not only for Ruth but for her mistress, a kind, soft-
spoken woman who speaks ill of no one and at moments can
challenge my stereotypes as significantly as Ruth eventually did:
"I have a lot of respect for Ruth, and you know we have many
like her in Mississippi. She is a good person, and we have never
had cause to complain about her. I never made this world, but
I'll admit there are times when I say to myself that there but for
the grace of God go I. What I mean is that I do believe Ruth has
the same intelligence we do, and if things were different — well,
I think she could be, well, I think she could be just like me, more
or less. She could run the house, I'm sure, and plan things and
make sure everything goes according to schedule."

When I heard that, I was in danger of being a very smug
listener. I felt like getting up and screaming at the polite and
honorably frank speaker. I felt like telling her that Ruth already
was running her house, that without Ruth the house would be
messy and disorganized, and its occupants would find mealtimes
a lot less pleasant. But I was agitated, really, because I was
hearing from someone else a very familiar kind of condescension,
one that I fear is all too much the property of people like me.
Neither she nor I — although I have to say, she a little better
than I — seemed able to talk about the extent of Ruth's social
and cultural achievement. Yes, we know that she is a good cook;
and her mistress *senses* (and perhaps does not dare let her mind
become more explicit) that without such "nigra help" life would
be far different. All along I had known, prided myself on
knowing, that Ruth is a fine, hardworking, reliable person who is
exploited and appreciated only in ways that don't cost a cent. But

in the last unsparing analysis I had to conclude that Ruth lacked dignity, even as her mistress knows that Ruth is only potentially capable of being dignified. And, needless to say, I had set out to study the consequences of the indignity America has visited upon people like Ruth: what happens to a woman who is stripped of her legal rights, her rights as a citizen, and kept socially apart as well as miserably poor.

I think it was the array of electric appliances in the kitchen that first made me stop and think and realize how much had been escaping my notice. Ruth was the master of all those machines. She was a gracious hostess, who served fine meals. She knew better than I where on the table a lot of those extra forks or spoons go. She knew her spices. She knew how to take care of the finest, most expensive clothes. She knew which plants needed a lot of water, which very little. She knew how to arrange flowers. I remember my mind latching on to that last fact. I remember deciding to ask Ruth about those flowers: "Well, she likes her flowers. She grows a lot of them, and there will be times when she has to send for them, from the store, you know. I fix them up. I know which vases to use for which flowers, and how she likes them. She used to say 'good'; but now she just expects it, I guess — that I'll do right. You see what I mean?"

Of course I hadn't been seeing; that is the point. I had been figuring out how Ruth lives and how her mind deals with "reality" and what psychological "defenses" she used. I had been developing a very clear idea of the hardships she faces every day, and even the stubborn persistence she possesses. I had declared her in my mind a desperate but inventive woman who somehow, beyond all explanation, endured. I was not so sure that she would, as Faulkner predicted, prevail; but I was prepared to say it was possible. I had at least shaken off the simpleminded view that the poor and even persecuted people are *only* hurt, sad, beaten down in spirit, deracinated, and branded with the unforgettable "mark of oppression." I was not going to become a "romantic" about Ruth and her family, but I would no longer be a slobbering, so-called reformer who needs the people whose cause he espouses to be as down and out, wretched and shattered as possible. Life is hard and even brutal for Ruth, and to survive has cost her a lot. But she is shrewd and ingenious, I had gradually persuaded myself; in the words of contemporary psychoanalysis, her mind has learned to be "adaptive" — and so has her overworked, tired body.

For all that, I had failed miserably to realize that Ruth is a *cultured lady,* a woman who knows her cuisine and her horticulture. Her manners are impeccable, her sense of timing in polite company faultless. She knows what people want and need and deserve and she gives it all to them. She is intuitive and sensitive. Her sensibilities are refined; and she even is at ease with our reigning technology. Her hands deal with the racks of the dishwasher, the shelves of the freezer, the clocks and pointers of the stove — and the pencil sharpener. ("The mister, he taught me how, and now missus gives me the pencils every once in a while, from all over the house. She says the noise of the machine gets to her; it makes her nervous. So she has to leave the room before I start.")

I am not saying that suddenly my mind came to its senses and fought its way to a more accurate and honorable picture of Ruth and her family. But over time, starting with that lunch, I did come to comprehend more and more of Ruth's life. The more I saw the more difficult it was to fit her into the convenient categories I had brought with me when I first met her. She is still poor. She is still disenfranchised. She continues to speak ungrammatical English, and so I have to edit her remarks. To this day she needs a doctor, a lawyer, a teacher — as do her children and her husband. She has no more money now than she ever did. And *she* would like a different life — so who am I to wax ecstatic over the countryside of the lovely Delta, the trees and flowers near her cabin, the rich, productive land, the mighty and almost mythic river that she can see by taking a good long walk for herself. Yet, on the other hand, who am I to deny her life its achievements, its ironies, its ambiguities, to refuse to credit her mind with the sense of style and the subtlety it surely demonstrates all the time?

At times I am pleased with my own ability to leave Cambridge, Massachusetts, and somehow come to a reasonably strong and valuable "relationship" with a family like Ruth's. I am not so pleased, however, when I remind myself how long it took me as an anthropologist or psychiatrist or whatever, to recognize *Ruth's* experience and competence. She, too, goes back and forth between two worlds; and she does so every day. She, too, watches others and tries to help them out. She, too, takes away burdens from people and makes them feel less harried, less at the mercy of this and that. Like a "trained mental health professional," she adjusts herself to the problems and the needs of others. She doesn't get "overinvolved." When she and they part company, she knows how to go back to her own life and live it. If she has any "fantasies" about life over there in The House, she controls them, buries them or, more likely, lets them quietly come and quickly go. ("Oh, every once in a while I ask myself why God did things the way he did and made me me and her her; but pretty soon there's the next thing I have to tend to.") Ignorant and barely literate, she is sophisticated and worldly; and as the bossmen in my profession say about precious few of us, she has "very good ego defenses." She has taught me a lot I rather expected to find out; but most of all she has taught me about the weaknesses in my way of thinking that prevented her various strengths from being immediately and properly obvious to me. The arrogant man wants to make his world the whole world. He pushes himself ahead of anyone in sight and blinds himself to all sorts of things that he might see in others. When he is safely up front he may mellow, and here or there grant a few favors; but without prodding, I fear, only a few.

2. A Proud and Fierce Spirit

Starting in the seventeenth century and continuing especially in the eighteenth, men from the Atlantic seaboard, sometimes alone, sometimes with their families, forced their way inland toward the Appalachian Mountains until, finally, an almost impassable stretch of woods, hills, and treacherous mountains yielded to their passage. The explorers found their way into the valleys, places of quiet and almost awesome beauty, and settled there. Some of them fought their way up the hills, and on their sides built cabins here and there, so that each home commanded a view of the vast countryside. While many of these pioneers continued west, into the flat, rich lands of Missouri and the central Plains states, others stayed on; and they gradually became sealed off in the very territory they had opened up and conquered. As we have seen, in the nineteenth century the land became valuable: its trees for the lumber they provided, its lower depths for the coal they held. Towns gradually developed, as well as mining and lumbering camps. In point of fact four different kinds of communities developed in the region. First there are the hollows, with scattered pockets of people up in the hills — people usually related to one another, and people with little to do but farm and hunt. Serving a number of these hollows is usually a larger community, far less remote geographically, able to offer the surrounding area a crossroad store, a post office, a school, and perhaps some police protection. Then there are the towns — mill towns. Here lumber and coal are gathered and loaded on their way out of the region. The town is likely to be a county center, with a courthouse whose offices are occupied by men of real political and economic power in the region, unlike one in a Northern city or suburban town, where there are many and competing sources of power. The mill towns have a number of stores and are actually regional centers. Some of them remind the visitor of New England towns: grimy, busy in a casual way, filled with an odd mixture of stores, railroad tracks, and churches. Finally, there are the real urban centers. They are usually prosperous, and again, able to draw upon the wealth of the region's forests and mines, only in some cases not merely as stopping places on a journey elsewhere but as centers whose factories will process or use what has been cut or dug many miles away.

Indeed, the contrast between these large towns — they are proper cities — and the small communities makes plain the fact that even within the Appalachian region there is a struggle, a clash of values and modes of living. In the urban centers the frontier man encounters the city man, the rural man encounters the factory worker or middle-class business and professional man. If the people of the hollows are isolated and tied to their families and their neighborhoods, the people in, say, Beckley, West Virginia, are very much like the people of other American cities — dependent on "the economy" rather than their own land, relatively free of cousins and next-door neighbors. This is not to say that bonds of kin are easily broken by those mountain families who move to cities, within or without the region. Often those who move out of the region, to Cincinnati and Dayton, to Chicago and Cleveland, to Detroit, have first moved to a city in Kentucky or West Virginia but found lacking there the jobs they wanted and needed.

Today Appalachia is not a stable, rural region, but a region of mixed city and farm people, with a good deal of movement — out for jobs, back in for visiting, or return from an outside found unbearable. In some areas the people live very much like those in other American cities, but in many other areas they live under circumstances that are all their own — and with values similarly a product of a special kind of existence. It is safe to say that the region as a whole has had to face a harsh fate: difficult terrain that has not made the entry of private capital easy, progressive deforestation, land erosion, periods of affluence when "coal was king," followed by increasing automation of the mine industry (and a decreasing national demand for coal), pollution that has ruined some of its finest streams so that strip-mining can go full speed ahead. In a curious way the people of a region called "backward" face the particularly cruel burdens of an advanced, technological society.

No psychiatrist studying the people who live in the region can overlook what such a state of affairs can mean to the human mind. Fiercely individual men have had to confront over the generations an increasingly conspicuous poverty in territory they love. A tradition of independence and strict personal honor has to contend with a harsh and mean struggle for arable land, food, and whatever cash can be gained from jobs that are scarce. Men have to accept welfare, from Washington or from local sources. The most stubbornly aloof and out-of-the-way region in the country eventually becomes represented (unfairly so in many respects) as the nation's most dependent and needy area. Those who have to fight harder, on their own, for a survival that is at least of their own doing, become ironic fatalists, resigned to what will come because year after year there is little else to do. Such ironies are not unlike those which must have constantly challenged W. J. Cash as he struggled to complete *The Mind of the South,* an extraordinary study of Southern customs and attitudes that showed how rewarding it can be to draw from many fields of inquiry in looking at human behavior. He tried to show that a region, like a person, can have a character all its own, shaped by historical events, by facts of money and power, by facts of geography.

In my work in the South and in Appalachia I have come to hesitate a long time before making any psychological generalizations — because, frankly, I have made too many mistakes when I have tried to do so. Negro children in Louisiana faced terrible mobs and danger, only to survive handily — and without the psychiatric symptoms I expected them to develop. Whites whom I interviewed repeatedly over several years broke with a wide variety of conventions which they had once proclaimed to be simply impossible to abandon, regardless of what new laws were written and enforced. The most hateful and angry people I have ever seen would appear in one city, yet be nowhere evident in another — not because they were unavailable, but because they were not allowed to assemble to heckle and assault children.

In some instances what I as a child psychiatrist interpreted as a stress, the children in fact experienced as an opportunity. "We have trouble all the time," one Negro boy from Asheville, North Carolina, told me when I asked how he felt being alone in a white school. But he continued: "At least now the trouble is good, because it'll accomplish something, and I'll get someplace, and so will my friends if they come next year." One has to give people — most of them — credit for a rather considerable emotional leeway. Fantasies or dreams cannot fully explain what goes on in the street or the marketplace. We know more about what people *think* than why they *act* as they do.

If the southern white is indiscriminately called racist, the southern Negro frightened and unimaginative, the migrant farmer shiftless and indigent, then the Appalachian mountaineer is likely to be quickly labeled sullen, suspicious, backward and apathetic. Often enough the breezy visitor's conclusions are made somehow worthier or more valid by resorting to the language of the social sciences. Appalachia is a "subculture." The people are inordinately "passive-aggressive," prone to fits of alcohol and violence that alternate with longer episodes of inertia, resignation, and depression. The social structure of the region is rural, rigid, closed, excessively traditional.

I have no intention of adding yet another conceptual generalization to those already made about Appalachian people. An observer has a responsibility to categorize when it is necessary to do so, but he also has a responsibility to fit in the special, the different, the particular with the everyday and even the universal. The Appalachian Mountains may be high, but they are not high enough to have cut off those who live near them from their very humanity.

A baby born to a woman who lives in the Appalachian region is less likely to get constant medical scrutiny, with vitamins, fluorides, inoculations, and immediate tests or treatment for metabolic or congenital diseases. He is more than likely a child whose growth and development is not followed closely before birth by an obstetrician, nor after birth by a pediatrician. He may well be delivered at home, and in some cases that holds even in the towns. In my first extended exposure to an Appalachian family (in North Carolina) I was struck by the unharried, informal, and relatively casual attitude of the pregnant mother. In labor she was noticeably stoic, much less prone to cry and complain than either the middle-class white women or the rural Negro women I have known in the South. As I watched her later with her growing infant girl I again had to compare her kind of mothering not only with that of middle-class, suburban mothers, but with what I saw happening between mothers and children in southern rural homes, both Negro and white.

From the very start this mother seemed to me at once close to the child and yet detached from it; close, because she held it with obvious warmth and delight, and breast-fed it with pleasure whenever it cried for milk; detached, because the baby's presence, its notions and noises, did not command from its mother a continuing attention or at least an obvious concern. In sum, the mother seemed less anxious to make her new child (it was her third) the temporary center of her life than many others I have seen. If she was not always attentive, she was consistently unworried and placid in the good sense of the word — unalarmed by screams and calm at the sight of rashes or insect bites. In this respect I would contrast her to the well-to-do suburban mother for whom child-rearing is a *very* serious (and sometimes anxious) business; also, I would contrast her to the Negro mothers I know, who immediately upon the child's birth establish an almost devotional closeness to him; and finally, I would contrast her to the rural white mothers of the South, who I think are less intimate with their children than their Negro counterparts, and far more casual toward them (if that is the word, and I am not sure it is) than the Appalachian mothers I have observed.

A colicky infant, for example, recently fed but still crying loud and strong will be held and held by his Negro mother; he will be held, then put down by his southern white mother, who nevertheless will be made fretful and irritable; he will be alternately held and put down by his middle-class suburban mother, while, you can be sure, a doctor will be called, a book read, or perhaps some medicine or pacifier given. In the case of the Appalachian mother, the child's cry will be heard but somehow accepted as (so I've heard several women say) "the way it goes for a while." Of course I do not mean to be rigid about these distinctions. They merely represent certain general trends, the product, no doubt, of complicated historical, social, cultural, and psychological influences which in given locations among certain people sort themselves out into particular patterns. Just as it is not at all irrelevant to remember that Negro mothers once (not so long ago) had to surrender their children to the demands of slave markets — and thus have good historic reason to keep close to their children now — so it may well be that a mother herself born and reared in a region whose fate seems unshakable will find the vicissitudes of the growing baby to be yet another reflection of just that fate. (I again warn that these are at best suggestions, or possible and only partial explanations for some mothers.)

What can be said about the way Appalachian children are characteristically trained and taught at home — about the way they learn their rights and wrongs, learn to see the world about them and get along with their parents, their brothers and sisters, their neighbors and relatives? In the outlying valleys and hollows, where plumbing may be virtually nonexistent, one can see an almost uncanny mixture of the tidy, the orderly, the neat and the messy, the littered and the unkempt. Among migrants and sharecroppers I have come to expect a pervasive lack of interest in the house, its appointments and appearance. "We leave them, one after the other," a migrant farm worker once told me when I asked whether he ever tried to give his home the same scrubbing he was then giving his car. (We knew one another well, and I think he knew by my manner that I was curious, not critical or especially worried.) Likewise among tenant farmers in the rural South I have seen a similar indifference, with shrugged shoulders, or even less than that, the response to a child's unruly assault upon what meager, already damaged furniture there is.

I need not describe the prevalent American middle-class regard for antisepsis, luster, newness, and property that is "kept-up." I judge Appalachian mountain parents somewhere between their rural neighbors to the South and their urban neighbors both inside and outside the region. Children are trained to use the woods or an outhouse at a time many city doctors would today call rather early — before the third year begins — and they are trained to do so by mothers who appear anxious and determined enough to have reminded me more of my hometown, Boston, than of migrant labor camps or Mississippi Delta towns. Migrant farm mothers quickly and decisively manage to teach their children to use as a toilet whatever field is nearby. Mountain women stay put on their land and therefore want an outhouse used, not the territory nearby. They thus spend more time getting the child to comply with their wishes; they start earlier than do other rural women; and they themselves become angrier and more upset while doing the job. Yet, in contrast to many comfortably urban housewives, mountain women are permissive in one respect: their children are often allowed to be quite thoughtless and even destructive within the home, crashing about and creating disorder not in a "playroom" but anywhere they please.

The mountain child is allowed a good deal of freedom with his body, his legs and arms, as he learns to explore, climb, run, and strike out. Brothers and sisters are likely to be much closer to one another; indeed, they live and play together without evidence of the charged, defiant "individuality" one finds so often in middle-class city homes. I am not saying that there is no "sibling rivalry," no tension and envy between the children of the hollows, but I am asserting a greater sense of family, of shared allegiance to parents and grandparents, that somehow makes for relatively more cooperative activity, frolic (and eventually), work than one sees among many other American children.

Appalachian boys and girls are not given individual rooms, but sleep together, often as if a community themselves, bed beside bed, not always with one occupant to each mattress. Families tend to be large, and there is just so much time a mother can have for any one child. Beyond that, however, is the more positive value of kith and kin, of doing things together — particularly since there are only a limited number of people around at all. Outside a town north of Knoxville I heard the following from a father, in reply to a comment I made about how well his four sons and two daughters managed with one another: "I tell them they've each got to be the best friend to the other, because they'll grow up and they'll learn you can walk a long way hereabouts and find no one." I asked his wife how she felt, because the littlest ones, I told her, seemed already quite a bit friendlier than many children of their age are apt to be. "Well, they're together always, and I have them feed one another, and they're in bed side by side, so I guess they know they're all mine, and I like them as a family better than one by one, you might say."

Toys, reading matter, or coloring sets are of course far less in evidence than the child's very real and very actual engagement with indoor and outdoor tasks. While migrant children of five or six are often taken to work and left beside the fields to play, and while sharecropper children may be left at home with a grandparent, mountain children are set to work, doing errands, helping about the home or the land, learning what often is far more important to them than school — how to use one's hands in farming, in caring for animals, or in fetching water or preparing food. The knife is mastered by boys, and perhaps a guitar. Dogs are companions, and help in hunting. Girls also learn to work the land and look after animals. The mountain child does not spend much time with books, or listening to stories, or hearing fantasies of one kind or another, so familiar an experience to some American children. There is adventure enough, there are good times enough, but these usually occur in the midst of doing things, going somewhere, or trying to start or finish something: "The kids relax together after they've done their chores, and I tell them they have to, because there are more to come." Those words from a mother in Tennessee reminded me that play can only be an interlude, never a goal in itself.

For children of the hollows school is also an interlude. The relationship of the rural schools of the region to its family life is no easily discussed matter. Particularly the one-room schoolhouse, but also the larger schools, are frequently the only buildings whose activities and functions unite in a personal way people spread over considerable distances. For millions of American children elsewhere the first day of school marks a decisive break with the past, and a nervous entrance into an important unknown. There are tears, from both parents and the young, and enough anxiety in some of them to forebode a variety of future difficulties. Indeed, while there are not more than a few hundred child psychiatrists in this nation, I daresay all of them find that the so-called "learning problems" or "school phobias" make up a very large part of their practice. In contrast, I have seen few of these neurotic problems in mountain schools. The teachers report retarded children, or what they call "slow children," but they do not describe (and I have not seen it in my classroom or home observations) that particular mixture of ability and nonperformance, of anxious effort and surprising collapse, of earnest desire and almost retaliatory reluctance that characterizes the child with a "learning block." Appalachian children often play near their schools and may go to visit them with their brothers or sisters before they ever enroll themselves. The teacher is, of course, a neighbor. The school emphasizes what the home teaches the mountain child: the definition of the community. If there are any American children who understand the meaning of territoriality, as it has been recently described by ecologists, they are to be found in the hills of Appalachia. What city folk call a "neighborhood school" is, in comparison to the one-room schoolhouse — and even the regional schools — a no-man's-land crowded with strangers. In a sense, the mountain school emphasizes the relative isolation of the child by bringing together those whose fate is similar.

It is during the first years, anyway, that the child begins to learn almost hungrily about the larger world that exists outside his home and backyard. For the majority of American children of five to ten, both people and machines appear as constant sources of confusion, fascination, instruction, and possible danger. The body's natural urge to move and exercise its growing bones and muscles comes into conflict with the limitations of an exceedingly complicated human and technological world. The child learns about streets and traffic, property limits and restrictions, the laws of entry and exit in buildings. If he is a black child there is a whole additional world of special rules and fears to master and have at one's command — yes, fears, because without fear a black child in the South may eventually lose his life: "We have to teach our children to be afraid, or they'll get themselves beaten up so bad, expecting the white man's justice and his rights instead of ours."

What one finds in mountain children, in contrast, is their developing intimacy with the soil and land surface and its variations — its changing height, its bodies of water, its ability to nurture food or supply ore. Mountain children live closely together, but have wide distances to travel or use for play —

always defined, it must be added, by the hills or mountains that for them are genuinely impassable. If cars come, they do so as an event, and animals are as familiar as the automobile engine. What animals teach children, and how children use animals is itself a subject for an essay — though since psychiatrists seem to live in cities, I doubt that it will be written. Sex may be a mystery to large numbers of middle-class children whose parents are "inhibited," whose lives are sheltered and heavily weighted toward "privacy"; but not so for boys and girls who live intimately with horses and dogs, chickens and pigs. Children learn to care for animals, to feed them and clean up after them, to help them in sickness and profit from the various rewards they offer, to have them as company, a kind of uncomplicated nonhuman company — perhaps more easily loved or abused than humans.

Young Appalachian children's drawings show how very different their world is from the one I have seen painted or sketched by middle-class children from either the city or the suburbs. Land, trees, flowers, animals, the sky and the sun appear regularly, and not as some decorative afterthought. Indeed, it is buildings and machines, roads, traffic, and sometimes even people that I find lacking in the pictures of mountain children.

Next, what of the adolescent in western North Carolina or eastern Kentucky? At that time, when youth looks both backward and forward with a special intensity (and vulnerability), the young man or woman learns what the society (as well as his or her body and daydreams and nightmares) has to say. In times of crisis — and adolescence is likely to be such a time — what might otherwise go unnoticed becomes rather apparent. Coming of age in the mountain families I have studied is, literally, growing up in a family — not leaving it conclusively, rebelling from it dramatically, scorning it eagerly, or doing anything possible to make its life hard and troubled.

Even before adolescence, mountain children learn that a family is no laughing matter — no temporary arrangement, characterized by divorce, constant movement, and a strictly limited membership, lucky to include anyone outside a set of parents and, most likely, a matching set of children. Kin — relatives of one sort or another — have a real and well-known meaning in the region, but I am not sure the psychiatric implications of that meaning have been thought through. American child psychiatrists tend to treat children whose loves and hates are narrowly confined to a mother and a father and perhaps one or two brothers or sisters. When I left such work I gave up a position in a children's hospital in Boston to work in the South with white and black children going through the social crisis of school desegregation. I had to accommodate myself to children who grew up in homes where fathers were often absent, and more children were present. In particular, grandmothers were extremely important figures, even among white families in the rural South. Yet, nowhere down there did I meet up with a real *sense* of family, only a change in the nature of the family. It was in western North Carolina that I began to see what a difference aunts and uncles and cousins can make to a growing child — I mean such relatives when they are felt to be a real part of the family, not vaguely connected to it.

The intensity between parents and children can be attenuated when there are many children and many "parents" — grandparents, great-aunts and great-uncles, aunts and uncles, or older cousins who in fact are parents themselves. Children in the hollows are very conscious of who they are, of what their name means, of who is kin to them, of what blood means. "Who am I?" one hears from our middle-class college youth so often. In fact, Erik H. Erikson's work on identity has achieved prominence in this country for a very good reason: immigrant groups have come here and spread over the land, all too commonly surrendering themselves and their children to the dispersal that our expansive technological society seems to press on its members. If there are advantages — money, comfort, success, the new roots of California or the eastern suburbs — there is also a price to pay in feelings of rootlessness and an almost desperate need for attachment to a plot of land, to the house on the land, to those few who live in the house. The rivalries and fears, the "blocks" and terrors in mountain children are of a different order than those I once treated in Boston; and certainly the intense private relationship between the growing child and his parents is far less prevalent than is the case in Boston, or perhaps any region of the country outside Appalachia.

For the adolescent, home always becomes a touchy subject, but again I must emphasize the difference between a youth who may have "little" (in the economic sense) ahead of him, but who can be sure of exactly who he is, where he comes from, and even what he would like to have (if it were possible to have it), and a youth who has "a lot," though he is uneasy about how he will keep it, and about where he will have to go next or what it is he will have to do. It is absurd to turn the harsh destiny that many Appalachian youths constantly must face into a story of serenity and joy, but it also gets us nowhere to see only the weakness, the gloom and frustration because of the scarcity of jobs throughout a region that is abandoned only reluctantly, and always with the hope of returning.

We must ask how mountain youths handle the tensions that go with little or no work and with a family life that is cherished but nevertheless deprives its young members of considerable freedom and independence. There is an ironic mixture of isolation and intimacy in these lonely hill people — and among the youths in particular one can see how the dangers of individual loneliness or anxiety are countered by the formation of cliques, perhaps ever so small and innocuous in comparison to those seen in the city, but nonetheless vital and helpful to the young men involved.

Young women, of course, tend to stay nearer home, and help in the daily chores of rural living. The division of labor between men and women can be dramatically sharp, but also blurred, particularly where farming is done. Certainly a number of young women find their way into teaching or nursing, and often emerge the mainstay of their future family, psychologically as well as economically. Yet, the kind of matriarchy that observers describe among lower-class Negroes is not the rule in Appalachia. I once asked a woman, a schoolteacher, about the problem — as it happens, she is about the strongest mother and wife I have met in the region: "Well, our men have a terrible time getting a job, lots of them do, and so it's hard for them to be happy with themselves. At least that's the way I figure it. That's why we have to be understanding, and the woman is lucky if she can step in and do something to make it easier.

"It's hard, though, when you do. I was brought up to be soft-spoken, and my mother told us girls — there were four of us, and five boys — to mind our tongues. We each of us girls expected to get married and have a lot of children, as has always been the case. But I was good in school, and I went to high school because there wasn't anything else to do. My daddy needed the boys, and the ones he didn't he told them to go get work in the mines, the way you used to be able to do. So, they never got to go to school, and I did. That's the way it happened, and that's how I came to get a college degree.

"So, when I married, my husband was just like my brothers. He couldn't find any work, not on the land and not underneath it, either. I had to keep working if I could, and we had to have my sisters help out with the kids. I think that's why I don't have more than three of them. We've learned to think a lot before letting me miss any time from work."

I wanted to know, later, how she thought her husband managed under such circumstances: "He doesn't like the way it is, but neither do I, or anyone. He's here, and he takes care of the kids and does work around the house. I think not having a job causes him a lot of pain, but it's silent pain, because he never talks much about his feelings. He'll drink, though, and more than he should, I know that. I try to say something every once in a while, but I know how he feels, and there isn't much else for him to do but drink and talk with his friends, and go visit his family, and my family." (The two families are distantly related.)

That teacher's husband is by no means down and out. He is at least *present*, around his home with his wife and children; and he is loyal to them, regardless of how "useless" he feels. I asked him one day whether he ever had the urge to leave, to pick up his roots and go — either with or without his family. He was surprised at the question, on both counts: "I like it here, and I know I'll never like it better any other place. I want my children to grow up here, and not in some big city, even if I could get a job there and sweat it out all day for a few dollars. Mind you, I'd like to have a job, but not enough to ruin everyone's life, not only mine. And I'd sure never go anyplace without my family. To tell you the truth, I wouldn't even want to try moving to another county, even to a valley nearby. It's different, and you get tired and mixed up, trying to figure everything new out again, all over."

In fact, for all the isolation one sees in those mountains, homes separated from homes by miles of woods, hollows virtually oblivious to the outside world, mountains sealing off whole towns from all but the most determined technological attack, the youth of Appalachia impress me as far less distrustful of one another than those I have seen in other rural communities, whether white or Negro. The elderly are usually spared that final sense of abandonment and uselessness so commonly the fate of the middle-class suburban aged. Life goes on within the family for young adults and older ones: work or idleness, hunting and fishing, church, sitting, meeting up with neighbors, an unhurried life, both formal and informal in its emotional tone.

I have emphasized the relatively quiet, unassuming quality of the Appalachian people, their reserved, almost shy demeanor often masking a wry acceptance of hardship rather than a devotion to it as a virtue in itself — though I have admittedly met some Calvinistic mountaineers. With regard to sex, the subject is not often mentioned, but clearly the practice continues! Families are large and, from what I have seen, within the family sex is simply performed, not constantly hinted at and turned to increasingly bizarre humor. In that sense I judge America's upper-middle-class sexual morality far more Victorian (in an inverted fashion) than Appalachia's willingness to ignore the subject and take the action as it comes.

Freud talked of sex and aggression as two important forces working on the mind's life. It is perhaps easier to deal with the sexual life of Appalachian people than with either their reputed or their real violence (the two being not necessarily the same). If the youth of the region learn about sex naturally but unostentatiously, they also grow up familiar with guns and knives, and in some counties, are heirs to longstanding feuds. While the violence in the region probably will never even approach what one sees in our cities, including the affluent small towns that surround them, a certain violence does exist, and its nature and causes are not, in my opinion, tidily explainable.

There is, of course, a tradition that encourages the use of both guns and liquor. There is, in addition, a tradition of self-sufficiency, with individuals and communities alike taking up arms against any "threat" — and an offer of aid, particularly if it is presented as "charity," can offend a people's sense of self-sufficiency as much as an explicit attack or direct demand upon them. There is also a conflict within the traditions of the region: one must not get too far ahead, surpass others, become the different brother, sister or cousin who leaves behind (to some the word is "betrays") the common, shared experience of the ridge, the valley or the hollow. Yet, one has (or aims to have) property and possessions, and if they can be increased and transmitted over the generations, then one is all the more successful, at least by general American standards. It is hard to reconcile an ethic of sharing with one of acquisition, and the tension in doing so may well spill over into deeds of spite and revenge.

Anyway, in an area where there isn't much at all to go around, where land and money are precious, even as families are large, where work is by no means to be taken for granted, what there is either must be regulated, apportioned and transmitted by firm habit or law, or a struggle may likely arise. One does not have to spend too much time in a hollow to see and hear the people struggling with one another in those half-concealed ways they do everywhere, but especially so when the stakes are virtually for survival. Jokes and contests, drinking bouts, or dances and socials all provide avenues of "release," especially so in a tightly knit, circumscribed community. As one man in a hollow told me recently: "It's a good thing we have drinking to do sometimes, because we tell one another off, and we're all equal again, until things build up the next time." I thus feel that the so-called "factionalism" one finds in some counties of the region stems from a combination of causes, and certainly is not the result of a "personality type" to be found in the region.

Nor do I think the apparent "apathy" or "gloom" one sees is a deep-rooted product of early childhood influences. I know how many people in the region (in towns as well as villages or sparsely settled valleys) dislike "change," fear "outsiders," resent "assistance," and even refuse to avail themselves of hospitals or schools when they are available. I know that the hills contain for the most part Anglo-Saxon families, deeply attached to the old ways. I know they go to churches that stress the sin and evil of this world, its hopelessness except for what the next world can promise, and they cling to values that preclude the bouncy, "adaptive" and hungry search for more and better things, wherever they are and at whatever price. Yet, there is also among these people a respect for work and a loyalty to routine, to daily effort: "We raise our children up to behave themselves and keep themselves as busy as they can be," a mother in Tennessee told me several years ago, when I first started getting to know families like hers. "They *need* to stay busy," she added, and then she told me why: "Without anything to do, they just linger about, and there's no telling what they'll do, usually nothing that's good for them or anyone."

I believe the ordinary men and women who live in the remote areas of this range of mountains that has figured so prominently in our nation's history are quite like that mother psychologically — that is, able to respond to any reasonable and consistent opportunity that comes their way. That would hold for the region's city people, too, and its people who live in camps, once mining camps, now often enough camps of the jobless. Too often observers who are social scientists force upon the observed all the negative and derogatory labels they themselves have learned to shun — all done under the guise of pity or "understanding." There is ample spirit in Appalachia's people; indeed their style of life and their values have conserved a good deal of the spirit that once prompted men of courage and daring to leave the Atlantic seaboard and fight their way into the region against almost incredible odds. Psychologically, the people of this region are fighting a last-ditch battle for survival. They do not need welfare to confirm their defeat. They need the resources that capital investment (public *and* private) provides. Their minds are quite able to handle those resources.

3. *The Mind of Christ in Their Heads*

Lorrie is an eight-year-old girl who has traveled widely and knows quite a bit about life and what sustains it. She was born in the hill country of Arkansas and lived there a solid two years. However, since then she has never lived anywhere more than six months, and at times she will spend more days of a month moving about with her family than settling into some kind of home life.

Lorrie looks at first glance to be a pretty, blond girl with light blue eyes and a fetching smile that would seem to caution any social reformer against too grim a view of her life. True enough, she commonly takes her meals by hand rather than with fork or spoon, and on the floor (or whatever nearby field is her temporary backyard) rather than on a table, but she eats lustily and with no evidence of dismay at her family's living conditions. I am sure many middle-class children could envy her the sticky mess she can regularly make of a meal, pushing her fingers at will through pork fat, potatoes, gravy, and wet, spongy bread, staining her faded denim dress with them all. That dress was made for an older girl: it reaches down to her shins and looks as if it had fallen upon her, hanging out of balance, her left shoulder bare, her right one covered halfway up the neck.

When I first saw Lorrie's smile I noticed her poor teeth. When she walked I noticed the toughened but still bruised and infected soles of her feet. Her unkempt hair was dry and stringy; she had sores on her body; her eyes hurt in the sunlight; her skin was coarse, some of it blistered, some of it decisively marked with lines of dirt or old scars. My sons might wish that they, like Lorrie, never would see a dentist or a doctor, though I doubt they would want to pay the price she has.

Lorrie's school habits are another source of possible envy to children like mine: she goes to school only occasionally, sometimes missing classes altogether for several weeks, at other times going to them days and even weeks in a row. When she *wants* to go to school, and when there is a school available, she will go. But when she feels vaguely hesitant about leaving home or is interested in staying home with her brothers and sisters to work in the fields with their mother at gathering a particularly lush harvest, there is no question about her sovereign right to make her own choice.

Migrant farmers, like sharecroppers, are essentially the rural poor who have shunned becoming the urban unemployed. They are people who know a great deal about how to survive on little money — one has to keep on emphasizing that many of them see less than a thousand dollars a year. They know how to buy stale bread at low cost, or soda pop instead of milk for their children. They know that candy takes you a long way on its calories and that, for a pittance, fat, which subdues hunger, can be obtained. They know enough not to worry about changing clothes or looking at them too fondly; pants or dresses are simply to cover you when you leave home to work or travel or walk the road to a store. They know enough to sleep together when it is cold or outside when it is warm. Finally, they know that children are born and children die, even as they themselves are lucky to have lived to the working age of ten or twelve, the marrying age of fourteen or fifteen. Owning little else, they cherish their infants and want more of them, in the fearful expectation that not all those conceived, born, or even reared through infancy will live long enough to start their own families. And again, they belong to no particular, geographically fixed community.

Not only our political life is grounded on the laws of the local community. Our educational system consists of thousands of separate systems, and what coordination they have is supplied (and limited) by the individual states. Lorrie's family travels from state to state, and Lorrie as a child comes under the jurisdiction of many schools.

How might we come to find and educate children like Lorrie?

In order to be of help to people who often are not actively seeking it (and are suspicious when help comes), those in a position to be of service must try hard to learn the assumptions which they as middle-class citizens do and do not share with the poor and the needy. The experience of many ministers, doctors, social workers, and nurses indicates that it is not always easy to obtain the gratitude and cooperation of such people, even when cooperation would seem to be to their evident advantage. Well-intentioned efforts to treat sick people, or change their diet for the better, have been seen by migrants as senseless intrusions at best; often they are feared and rejected outright as harmful. To a migrant, for example, the presence of a doctor may imply the increased likelihood of death. Similarly, the desirability of sending children to school is by no means apparent. And as we have seen, migrant children do not escape the doubts, fears, and suspicions held so fixedly by their parents.

Lorrie's sister is not illiterate. At ten she can print her name and she knows about half the letters of the alphabet. A word or two come readily to her as she tries to read, but reading is generally tough going. Like her parents, who also had a sporadic kind of education, geared to accomplishing a signature and a rather limited recognition of words, she now knows more than she will know in the future; older migrants soon slip back when it comes to reading and writing. In the words of Lorrie's mother: "I learned the writing and reading in school, but I left off when I was old enough to work steady and not be bothering my folks. Now, to tell the truth, I've forgotten all I learned. We don't have no use for writing and reading."

Lorrie's drawings, or those of her sisters and brothers, show quite clearly what she expects of life. I repeatedly asked her to draw a school. She responded with silence and a few aimless gestures of the crayon in her hand. She could draw woods and fields, birds and a nearby lake, but not a school building. Nor could she easily draw her home; she told me directly that there were many homes, and asked me casually which one I had in mind. Eventually she was able to draw one, a composite of many nondescript cabins she knew. Nearby, indeed touching the home, was a car. She clearly intended to let me know that the car, too, was her home. I was struck at how naturally she could draw the terrain on which the house stood; the house itself was sketched quickly and very poorly, then ignored — as if she had obliged me at the price of her own annoyance. "I'd rather sleep outside than in the car," she told me as she pushed the drawing in my direction. I was being pointedly told that the family car really meant more to her than the succession of temporary shacks I might call her various "homes"; and, in any case, she was more tied to the outside world than *any* quarters.

The school building Lorrie finally managed to draw was distinctly small, dwarfed by a giant pine tree and off to one side of the paper. Lorrie drew it hastily, as she had the house. She used a black crayon and supplied no windows or doors. In fact it was an isolated box, essentially irrelevant to the carefully drawn landscape.

Lorrie's view of both home and school is, as I have indicated, shared by the other migrant children I have come to know. Moreover, the drawings of these young boys and girls contrast markedly with those I have accumulated over the years from children from middle-class suburbs, or black and white children attending newly desegregated schools in the South. Comparing the sheaves of drawings collected from migrant farm children with hundreds of others reveals how specifically children learn to define the makeup of their world. Those from comfortable, suburban neighborhoods lavish attention on the homes they draw, fill their pictures of schools with windows and doors, plants and flags, people and books; for that matter, they sometimes sketch pictures within pictures, so that the corridors of the buildings will faithfully resemble those real ones they daily walk. Even the very poor black and white children in cities like New Orleans and Atlanta see their homes and schools as central to their lives, worthy of concern and care in representation.

Migrant farm children, in contrast, see schools as ultimately irrelevant to their future. As we have seen, so do many of the earnest, hardworking teachers who watch them come and go. Those windowless, doorless schools in Lorrie's pictures tell the observer that for such a child there is little connection between anything that happens in school and the events of the world.

People who spend their lives growing and harvesting food see little use for education. The world for them is one of sunrise and sunset, seeds becoming plants, plants producing vegetables or cotton, to be picked by their hands. Children for them come into the world as it is and are expected to live or die in that same world. "Low is de way to de upper bright world," I've heard sharecroppers say, but they do not have themselves or their children in mind.

Many of these rural children are sick in body, uneducated in mind, yet quite strong and effective psychologically, so long as their strength and capacity to manage their lives are judged by the standards — the obligations and challenges — of their own world. One migrant put the issue quite directly to me: "I don't care about books for my kids. If it would be different, they could need them, but not now." A black man, he had fled the South to find his social and political freedom in Chicago. Eventually, faced with the alternatives of the ghetto and the relief rolls, he decided that seasonal farm work, mostly in the South, offered a better life: "It's hard, I know; but we can do as we know how to, and I believe it's better on you than being in the city, sitting yourself on the stairs all day."

Such people are stubborn, as human beings often are when confronted with the grim alternatives of life and death, endurance or surrender. They may even be suspicious, defiant, and almost mischievously aloof in the face of our occasional generosity — those sudden, good-spirited moments when we send parcels, medicines, books, and our own high intentions.

I think hundreds of thousands of rural parents and children want a better life, *as they know life*. They want steady work at higher wages, a chance to live in homes that are theirs, on land they know, near towns and people they know. Many of them picture their children going to school someday, learning those numbers and letters which — they vaguely know it — lead to an improved kind of existence. However, they picture that day in the *future*, and they have learned to be circumspect — even harshly doubtful — when that future approaches the present. Too many valuable announcements have already come their way, only to no effect: roads bringing the traffic of people and progress, electricity lighting up the countryside, or Social Security deductions promising a retirement with at least some income — which few migrants live long enough to collect. It would be a further irony if more schools were built in rural areas, yet migrants and sharecroppers found their hand-to-mouth existence untouched.

Over and over one asks what is to be done. Our cities need no more refugees, candidates for the wasted, heavy hours of the slums. Our farms will need less and less labor as machines gradually replace hands in harvesting. Still, for some years to come, sharecroppers and migrant families will continue to live on farms. It is their children who are going to require the kind of education that will enable them to achieve a different, kinder world, but their parents never really dare imagine such a world near at hand. I once heard a migrant mother tell her child, "Someday the sun will shine on us all day; but that's off from now. I want my boy to go plumb through school, but if he does, *then* what will he do?" That is the problem facing us: only when that mother and her child find a sensible connection between what happens in school and in their lives will they be interested in classrooms.

Until now only a few impressive and lonely ministers, teachers, or public health workers (doctors, nurses, social workers, dieticians) have cared much for the welfare of these people and earned their respect. There is no reason why more of us cannot join their company. Mobile teaching units — I once worked on a mobile medical unit — can go to people quite afraid to ask for help, quite unaware that such help might be forthcoming. Schools can be established on the basis of the needs and lives of these people, rather than the habits and interests of the rest of us. It scarcely makes sense, for example, to expect people chronically on the move to respect the primacy of the town school. On the contrary, regional networks of schools are badly needed, many of them mobile, all staffed by teachers specifically concerned with the customs and beliefs of the rural poor, white and black.

Of course, more generally we need something good schools alone cannot provide; we need a nation that in dozens of ways gives the mother just quoted answers to that question: *"then what will he do?"* We need an end to the politics of indifference, greed — and yes, fitful pity. In this chapter I am trying to point out how responsive even our most hurt and burdened people might be — given a society *responsive to them.* True, among the rural poor one sees backs broken, spirits destroyed, minds numbed. But one also sees tenacious and willful people, as I hope by now I have made clear.

"We have the mind of Jesus Christ in our heads," a migrant farm worker told me; the year was 1963, I was beginning to know him, and I wondered whether he was drunk or crazy or delirious or slow of thought — all the things a doctor has to let run through *his* mind. Several years later I could write notes to myself about the man's searching, compelling eloquence. Many who have gone through these pages this far and may be more than ready for some handy summary of "the rural mind" might indeed think of how Christ wandered, knew pain, received scorn, experienced isolation, suffered loneliness, and at the end, doubted himself and almost everyone or everything, including God's purposes and intentions. Even so we believe He rose and lives on, and even so that migrant's "mind" will persist and make do — and might achieve its own kind of ascendance, were we to believe in, which means act on behalf of, the people we now cast aside.

X

RURAL YOUTH

O NE would scarcely believe it — to hear some self-consciously young Americans dwell on *their* generation — but "age" has its limits as a "common denominator," an explanation of things. It may be that generational tensions and outright warfare are not so explicit, so prevalent, so talked about, so fussed over and even deliberately cultivated everywhere in the United States, let alone abroad. It does seem fair to ask *which* American youths think of themselves as "young"; which ones don't trust people over thirty, and conversely, which ones even take any notice at all of that age; which young men and which middle-aged men stand or don't stand glaring at one another across "the generational gap."

1. Winston

Winston, for example, is twenty years old. He was born near Itta Bena, Mississippi, and he will die there. He is already a sharecropper, and so without any worry about his future "career." Yes, he knows about his age; in fact he keeps track of time rather more closely than many of his "peers" elsewhere.

"I was born on Thanksgiving Day — yes sir, in Leflore County, that's right — but that day changes, so it's not like having Christmas to celebrate your birthday then. The war was over, and my daddy came home, and I was the first one after the war, my momma used to tell me. She used to say the war meant a lot, because people around here, it was the first time they got outside of the state of Mississippi, and so it was bound to change one

517

day, because of that. And when the Korean War came, she said the same thing to my uncle when he went — but he never came back, and he was buried there, they told us.

"Well, I can't say I've had it too bad, though I wish my momma was right and the wars did make a difference here in Leflore County. I was lucky, I'll have to admit. My daddy kept sending me to school. He took me there when I was little and said he wanted me to go get my education, and it didn't make any difference if I couldn't work in the field with him, because if I could just do my reading and my writing, then I could go up to Memphis, maybe, and get a good job. They say there's factories coming in there all the time.

"So I kept in school until — I think — it was about seven or eight years ago or maybe nine, that I just left. It was one thing to go to the school nearby and you could help out with the planting or the rest early in the morning and later in the day; but then they said those of us who wanted more schooling would have to go to high school, and that was way into Itta Bena, and they didn't close it down for harvesting, and besides, you have to be a rich colored man, that's what my daddy said, to go right through and try to finish everything and get the degree from them.

"Well, I did a lot of learning, and I can sign my name and I know my numbers good. Yes, and I could read if it came to it, but I can't say we do much of that here, I'll have to admit. It's mostly taking care of the bossman's land, and I help him out in the house, too. His wife has to have the errands done, and there's lifting sometimes, and I help with getting the supplies. Mostly these days they're trying to cut down on us, and they say the cropper's day has gone in Leflore, and even the whole state of Mississippi; but we are lucky, and our man, he's always been good to us. I hear some of the white folks, they call him a 'nigger-lover,' and he's 'soft' on us, they say. But you can't tell if what you hear is true, you know — because black people, they do a lot of talking about the white man, and what they say to each other, and probably it's some exaggeration.

"I used to look at the map. I remember that map in school. We used to get things pointed out. The teacher would put the stick on here in Leflore and then she'd move it up through Clarks-dale — I have some uncles and aunts up there, and I was carried there once when I was real small, so I don't remember. Then she'd move on up to Memphis and tell us that we was out of Mississippi, and you could vote and things like that. But it was still the South, so she'd push on up to Chicago, and that was where the North was. You know, next thing she'd ask us if we wanted to go there, and we all said no, because she told us we shouldn't, because it was cold, cold up there, and you weren't any better off, for all your moving and moving. 'It's even worse, it's even worse,' she said, and I hear tell she's right, if you look at it one way. Of course I wouldn't mind having a vote in things and not having that sheriff to face every time you cross a white man wrong, even if it's only his word, and it's not true. But I can't truly say I want to leave here, so long as we can keep going and we have food to eat and a roof over us, and for the most part — you know — they leave us alone. That's my opinion.

"Yes sir, I got married a while back; I don't think I can tell you for sure the day, but it was nineteen hundred and sixty-four, and a week or two beyond Easter, on a Sunday. We are believers, especially my wife, she is, and we told the minister we wanted a long time there in church, because it'd be plenty long outside afterwards, and if we got tempted to make a mistake here and there, it's best to clear the air beforehand and do a lot of praying. You see what I mean? We go every Sunday, and my son and my daughter, they've been baptized all right. I sure do hope they'll do even better than us; and what with the changes as they keep coming, even in my lifetime, I think they will.

"During the day? During the day I work; yes sir, all day long. It starts with the sun on one side, and by the time the sun's ready to take a rest, well, so am I. A couple of my older brothers left us, and they're in Detroit; and they came back twice and said you work eight hours there, if you work. I figure that's about half the length of my time each day. But I'm happy to keep going. The bossman is OK with me and Leona — she's my wife — she thinks it's better all the time. You can go get the food, the commodities, if the worst come to the worst, and most of the time we just get up and go right along the day, and come nighttime, well, to tell the truth we're glad to be here and so tired we just goes off, until the next light comes up, and it's time to start again.

"The thing I'd like most would be some animals, chickens maybe, to help out with the food, and maybe to give me a little independence, yes, that. We could have the eggs and keep the chickens going, and we'd be better off. But I have all I can do taking care of the crops and catching up after the machines and doing what they should do in the odd places they can't reach, and I help around the place, in their home, as I said. So that's what's 'most on my mind,' like you said I should tell."

2. Myrna

Myrna is eighteen. She spends her winters in Florida, her summers in Long Island and New England. She even travels in between: there are the Carolinas in May, at their loveliest, and often she stops in Virginia during October on her way South.

"Yes, eighteen is right. That's my age, and I can prove it, because I was registered, and my sister Laura keeps the important papers with her. She lives in Macon, Georgia — you know where that is? — and she's always trying to get me and Lonnie to settle in with her and stay around. Once we tried it, and it was bad, I'll tell you. There wasn't a job around — nothing. They live near the edge of the city, but they can't do anything with the land, because it's not theirs to touch. They have to sit around and get a little something to do now and then, but mostly they just 'gets by,' that's what my sister calls it. Only I know what she does, and she can't fool me. She says she'd rather give herself over a few times a week to a man and have a *home* than be like me, and I tell her she can have her Macon and her lousy, rotten life — that it is, I'll say. She's just three years older, twenty-one.

"We were close together, I mean we were *real* sisters. I have five other sisters, but that's different. There's the blood we have together, but I didn't know them real well when we were kids, and now three of them have took to Cleveland, Ohio, and they're near to one another, we hear. My sister Laura, she's my only real

family that I know and where I can go, even if it's been a year
since I've seen her. No, there's no parents left for us. My mother
died giving birth to our last sister — she's Shirley, and she's in
Cleveland, living with my sister Annette. My grandmother, she's
our mother, and she's in Cleveland, too. And my daddy, he got
killed a couple of years ago. They say he was fishing, or trying to,
and he fell in and drowned. I don't know. He did a lot of
drinking.

"That's what worries me and Lonnie about Laura. She always
has a bottle around, and the men bring her one if she doesn't.
One day she'll have only bottles and no money, and that will
drive her to the street, and then she'll be like Daddy, wandering
around always. She says she has to do it, to get her some money,
but I'd rather walk a thousand miles than that.

"Me? How did I 'go on the land'? Well, we had an uncle —
Daddy's brother — and he was down in Florida, working the
crops there, and one day he showed up. We were living in Valdosta, Georgia, as I recall, and that's only a few miles from
Florida. He said he was on his way North, but only for the
summer, to get some money, and he'd soon be back in Florida.
We were hurting bad, then. We had moved into Valdosta from
near Thomasville. My granddaddy, he was a tenant — not on
shares, no. He paid his rent every year, and he as much as owned
the land after that, because it was his to do what he could with
and get out of it all there was to get. That's what he did; and he
learned how from *his* daddy. So, you see, we've been in Georgia
a long time, and been tenants on the land for as far back as
anyone can remember, except when we were slaves, I guess, and
then no one wants to remember *that*.

"But it all fell to pieces in my daddy's time, when he was
young and growing up. You couldn't break even to save your
soul, and you kept going and piling up the debts and hoping that
maybe the owners and the store people were in the same boat
with you, so they'd have more patience and more patience and
more. And then, they just had to tell us to go. They took the land
and started planting trees on it, or something, and they said a big
company would use it, and maybe for cattle, too — and that's

how we came to Thomasville, and later my daddy moved us over to Valdosta, which is where I was growing up.

"Now, when my uncle came by I was fourteen, I think. I wasn't in school no more, just hanging around and helping out and taking care of the baby and another one next door. I'd make some money for my time with that child. It was getting bad, then, real bad. Daddy was no good. He grew up expecting to work on the land, and we didn't have any no more. His daddy died of a broken heart, and my daddy caught it from him, and my grandma — she's my mother's mother — she didn't have much patience with either of them. She'd been in the city, in Valdosta, since a child, and that's why we came up there in the first place. My mother met my father when she took a trip over to Thomasville to see her cousins and other family. My grandma couldn't understand all that 'crying about the land' — is what she used to say.

"Well, you see, it's a long story. But when my uncle came, I was going with Lonnie and we were set to do *something*. We just had to, we figured. Lonnie is my age, a year older in fact. He couldn't see anything ahead of him, nothing, and he was thinking of trying Atlanta, or maybe New York, as long as it would be a big city. But he was scared, too. You hear tell that you go up there, and it's all real swell at first, but in a while it gets worse and worse, and soon you're dead up there, like you never can be down here. No one knows you, and you're dead. Even right next door, people, they'll cut you down and look right through you — colored I mean, not white.

"And that's why it sounded good about Florida and working there on the land. Lonnie said he itched to use his hands, and I said let's go, because there's no future here, and I'd rather go farther South than North.

"So, one day we told everyone we're getting married and expecting, and we're going to Florida. My uncle had left us with the name of a man down there in Bean City who does the hiring, and he said, 'You just go there and look him up, and you'll be picking beans and cutting celery before you know it, and the work comes in day upon day.' So, we had the paper with the name, and we had the car that was supposed to be junk, and Lonnie had fixed it up to go. And we left one day.

"The families like the idea? Yes and no. I don't think they wanted to see us go, but they figured we were heading for *work*, and not just taking off into nowhere, so that was good. And Lonnie and I, we showed them by our faces that we were happy.

"My girl was born in Florida, and my boy up North in New Jersey. We've been harvesting three years now, I think. I lose track of time. I don't like the moving up and down, but we stay in Florida a full half of the year, and we can keep a good car going. We hope to find a job someday that will keep us in one place all the time, but until then, it's better this way than staying in Valdosta, or like my sister is in Macon, and I think even it's better than my family in Cleveland, where they don't work much, I hear. The nurse from the Public Health, she told me that the migrant people someday would stop moving because of the machines, and I agree with her, but I hope we can find something to do then, and I'd rather it be near the land. And I hope my kids can know a place to call their own, but it'll be near the land, too. And since I didn't go to school hardly at all, I hope they can have that, too."

3. Ronald

Ronald is named after his father, and his father will tell a visitor that there has been a Ronald in the family for many generations. ("Perhaps we're Norwegian, underneath our Scotch blood.") All those Ronalds have lived in eastern Kentucky for a couple of hundred years — "easily," says young Ronald, rounding off the estimate. Additional evidence for a Nordic strain in the Anglo-Saxon lineage can be found in young Ronald's hair; it is orange-yellow in winter and in the summer it borders on a very light, almost white blond.

"Hereabouts you don't plan too far ahead. I'm twenty-two, and I hope to get married one day, but I don't know who she'll be, yet. There are a couple of girls I know, and sometimes I see myself married to them; but you never can really decide a thing like that until you're ready, and I'm not ready now. My father was thirty-four when he got married, and he likes to tell me that he was reluctant, even then, though my mother says he went about the country having a first-class time for himself, and then got tired — 'more tired than he knew,' is how she puts it — so they got married and he settled down.

"Of course, one problem they had was where to live. They couldn't really stay with their folks. My grandparents are still going pretty strong; they're seventy-eight and eighty. They still work. My grandpa takes care of his land, and my grandma cooks and cleans up like she used to. The boys have left except for my Uncle Jim and his family. They help. My father was supposed to stay, but I guess he really was a wanderer, like he says, and he wanted to do things on his own. When he came back from the war everyone thought he'd never stay here in Wolfe County, Kentucky; but he did, somehow. He said he was glad when I was born, a boy he could give his name to; and he wasn't going to take us up to Dayton or Detroit or Chicago for any amount of money.

"That's the reason I've never been outside. It takes a war, I guess. We have one now, but I'm not eligible. I had a rheumatic heart and there's still a murmur, the doctors say, so I can't go. I'm sorry, I'll admit. I don't think I'd want to go over to Vietnam, to Asia. I'd rather see Europe or out West. But if they sent me, that'd be OK. It's only a year, and from what I hear, time goes a lot faster in the service than around here. And you have a lot to talk about when you get back.

"They do a lot of farming over there, from what I see on TV, except for Saigon. That looks like New York or someplace, I imagine. I'm going to come over to Lexington someday; we know people near there. I've just never had occasion to try it, the city.

"It's OK here. I like it. Oh, I wonder about other places. Isn't that natural? But I think we're pretty well off here — I mean it could be worse. Sometimes it's bad, I'll have to admit; but what can you do? My father was lucky; he got a job in the garage. He learned a lot about cars in France in the war; they were always getting stuck there. The weather is worse than here. Now I've been helping him out, though they don't need me full time. If I were going off on my own, I'd have to have something to do, or else I'd have to have decided it didn't make any difference, and I could stay here and get what relief you can, and an odd job here and there, probably.

"Now I help my dad, and I help my grandpa, too. I have my own time, too. I have a car, and I work on it. I keep it in top shape — I'll bet I could sell it for a lot in the city. They don't know how to care for cars there, I'll bet. I've got two or three real good friends and a lot of guys I hang around with. Some have gone into the service, but a lot have deferments. They got sick or something back-away. We were always coming down with something wrong in school, I remember; so I guess it affects you later, so far as the Army people go. But I feel in real good health, and I'll bet I could be the equal of anyone, if they once let me into the uniform.

"I like to watch TV. We get good programs here, especially the Westerns, and you get a real good look at other people. My mother says she don't know how she ever grew up without it. You can look on over the hills and see outside, but you can stay here, too — and not get in all the trouble and confusion out there. It's good here, I think.

"Yes, I go hunting a lot, and fishing. That's right, and I read some *Popular Mechanics;* I have a subscription to that. There's a lot there to keep your mind real busy. I went through the school here, and then I went to the consolidated school some, but it wasn't really doing much for me, and I figured the extra year or two in school wouldn't make that much difference, not around here. If you're planning to go on, or move, that's different. But you have to have money or you have to be real clever, and I never was, where schoolwork was concerned. The teacher said she couldn't in all fairness encourage every one of us, and no one of my real best friends finished school. My brother Richard says he aims to, and we'll see, I tell him. I'd be glad if he did.

"Me and my folks get along real fine. My mother is a real friendly sort; no one could deny that. She could almost be your friend, even if you're a man. She would humor us, instead of getting mad at us, and I think we all have good dispositions on account of her. Sometimes, I think I can talk to her better than my father; but he's OK, more of a quiet person, and he works hard all day and is tired when he comes home. He used to eat supper with us and then fall right off to sleep, but now he takes it a little easier, and he doesn't seem to need the sleep he used to. He and I, we do a lot of hunting, and my two uncles come along. We have kin all around, and they're liable to join — it depends on the time. We go see the families, my mother's and my father's; they're up the road a bit, and it's a good change for us. And like I said, me and my friends will go to the store and stand around. They've got a good machine there, and we lose our money to it, but it's worth it — the music is good, and you relax some.

"No, we don't try to keep to ourselves, by age — as you say. There'll be some of us who are my age, and there'll likely be older and younger. I don't know everyone's exact age, but I can say that they're not little kids in the store, unless they come with their parents, and they're not real old, except if they come to buy something, mostly. Those of us who sit and do the listening and fool around, we're twenty or thirty, more or less, I'd say.

"If I could, I'd like to go visit Chicago — we have kin there. But they always come home and say if it wasn't for the money, they'd be back here for good — and someday they *will*. I'd go there and look around, and maybe stay a while, and then come back here. There's nothing wrong with it here, except that work is hard to find, and I think if you'd go asking all the people how they liked it, they'd say, 'Fine,' even the sorriest ones up the hollow would — even if they scarcely have anything. They make you feel real bad when you see them coming down for water. I wish we could do something for them, but it's hard to know what."

Winston and Myrna do not think of themselves as "young"; they are long past being children and all too taken up with making things just barely work from day to day. Indeed, Winston has summarized his particular youthful preoccupations in one terse sentence: "Every morning I start trying to make sure we'll be around to see another morning." Ronald is a little less desperate — and Myrna maybe more desperate, but what has to be emphasized is the speed with which these still young but in ways quite old men and women have come to be workers, people who have assumed responsibilities of a kind that are utterly crucial: if they are met, certain lives will persist, however tentatively; if not, those lives will flicker out.

"Flicker out" is an expression I heard Ronald once use. We were talking about the evenings; Ronald wanted to tell me how much he likes the quiet that comes with sunsets, the hush over the land, and then suddenly he had to say more: "At the end of the day the shadows really come over the valley. When I was a little boy my daddy used to come and tell me not to worry, because there'd be light in a few hours. I guess I was scared. Now, I like the quiet and the dark; it's restful. The day flickers out; you can see it happening. It's time to ask yourself if you did all you should have, if you did the work that needed to be done so you'll get your money and be able to eat good and have some to spend on yourself and give some to your folks, of course. That's what people do around here, they take to resting their tired bones, come the end of a day. Once in a while, because of all you see on the TV, I guess, I'll try to figure out what I'd be doing if I was living in some other country, or maybe up in one of our cities, in our own country. I can't come up with much, though. It would be different, a lot different, I can guess that. I wonder if a fellow my age, one like me, over in another state than this one — I wonder if he would like to watch the sun go down, just lose its strength, minute by minute and flicker out, like a candle that's lost all its wax and is going away, is disappearing."

He wonders whether others of his age feel themselves so much a part of nature — its days and nights, its light and shadows, its water or heat or coldness, its various rhythms. He also wonders what tomorrow will bring, and he means tomorrow literally, tomorrow concretely. He can talk about long-range plans, about marriage and the dread possibility that he or his friends may have to move up to Chicago or some such place, but most of all there is the here and now, the work to do, the family to be with, the guitar to pick, the errand to do, the "special girl" to see. The children I have described in the first section of this book have always been right there, near their parents working, near their kin talking, near other children — who also travel North to help parents harvest crops, or who also live on the plantation, or who also, like Ronald, live near or up a hollow. If Winston's parents stay where they are, and can possibly stay alive, Winston will stay with them. If Winston's parents stay, but stay on the condition they sit in a cabin (owned by their bossman) and virtually starve to death, or barely stay alive — by growing a few vegetables and getting "packages" from "the lady" and maybe a few, very few dollars of relief from the county — then Winston might well leave, head for a city, and feel as sad as he is hopeful.

I hope to convey, in Volume III of *Children of Crisis*, what actually happens to the Winstons of this world when they go North. Yet, even when the subject of "rural youth" is being discussed, the reveries and daydreams of a youth like Winston ought to be summoned. Since Winston in fact was one of the first children I met in the course of this work, I have some of those reveries in several different forms — not only as remembered and expressed by someone twenty years old, but as spoken by a boy of twelve, or a youth of twelve, or a young man of twelve, or a hardworking field hand of twelve, who at that age had already begun to sleep with a girl he had known since "before either of us can remember," and whose life has not changed much from what he described to me a week after his twelfth birthday: "There's work the bossman wants of me, for me to do, apart from my daddy and his chores, so I doubt I'll be going back to school. The bossman says I've got a good back and strong arms and my hands are big. He really looks you over. He said I could always get a job being a mover, picking up furniture he means, if I went up to Chicago. He says he wants me to stay right where I am and be of help to him. He says if a lot of the niggers go and move North, it'll be better for the rest of us who stay here. Yes sir, I guess he means the colored man. It's always good for the white man, I believe it is, whether the colored move out or not.

"I help with the land, fixing it up so we'll be ready for the planting, so we'll have a good, clean field. I help in his storage place, yes sir, the warehouse. He's always finding a job for me to do, he and his foreman both. I heard him say once that Mississippi still needs niggers real bad, but not as many as before. He was talking to the sheriff, and the sheriff said yes. I asked my daddy last year, I think it was, if I could become a sheriff if I stayed in school and got the degree that they give at the end. He said I should stop trying to be smart, and then I knew I shouldn't ask him any more of those questions. My mother says there are some questions you don't ask, and they're the ones she calls 'those questions,' that's right.

"I'd like to be a sheriff, because they have a car with that light, and there's the uniform they get with the job. I'd like to be an airplane pilot; they fly over here and spray our fields. I'd like to run the train that comes through, that would be a good job. But seeing how I'm me, I'll just work here, like my daddy, and it's just as well. Daddy says we eat, so far we still do; and some people don't know if they'll have anything to eat from meal to meal. My mother asked him how he got that idea in his head, since he's never been anyplace but right here. He said he heard the bossman say it was like that, and he said there's no reason for the white man to be feeling bad because we're eating, the colored people are — the ones he has on his place I guess he was meaning. I'd sure hate to work all the long day, like I do now, and then be staring at an empty table, with nothing on it to eat, and a lot of hungry eyes and a lot of hungry hands. My mother says I should be glad for what we have; that's what she says when I want something extra to eat. I'll tell her that my belly isn't full, and it's wanting more, and she says it'll just have to be like it is, no matter what I ask for.

"I know a lot of girls. They all tell me they'd like to be with me, and they'd like to be out of their mother's way and cooking for themselves and their man. But you know, they'll soon miss their mothers, I know that. It's not natural to leave your mother and not miss her. I've never been a day away from my mother, nor my daddy. My grandmother, she's always been around, too. She

gets sick now, but we take her up the road a little, past the gas
station and then some, too. There's a healer, there. She gets you
feeling better real fast. I was told I couldn't go see her until I was
older; I was told so when I was a real little boy. Now I'm bigger,
getting bigger almost right in front of my own eyes, my grandmother said; now I can go there. I've been there twice, and not
once did I get scared. It used to be they thought the healer
would make me cry. Last year my daddy said if I was old
enough to do real good work helping him, and old enough to go
with the girls, then I could take my grandmother and hold her
hand and keep her company, walking to the healer. She showed
me how to get there, and now I know.

"It's very quick with the healer; she tells you that if you're
going to be healed, you're going to be healed because you really
want to be healed, and no fooling, not any fooling. Then she goes
and heals you. She mixes up something she has, leaves and
powder and all, and tells you to take it and not say a word, not
make a sound. If you do, you'll be sent home and you'll be in real
trouble, my grandmother says. Then she has you close your eyes,
and she walks around and around, and you're there, sitting there,
and she's saying things. I couldn't tell you exactly what she says,
no sir, I couldn't. The first time I went I asked my grandmother
what it was that the healer said, and my grandmother said no
one knows, except the healer does. I heard her say 'devil,' and I
heard her say 'curse,' and I heard her say 'get better,' but it was
the in-between that you can't make any sense out of. After she's
circled the room a few times and done her talking, she stops right
in back of you and touches your head and tells you to open your
eyes, but still not to say a word. She didn't touch my head, but
she said I should open my eyes, because she didn't tell me to
close them anyway, but I did. Then we shouldn't turn our heads,
she said, not the slightest little bit, she said. So, we didn't. We
looked at her pictures, one of the Lord Jesus Christ and one of
her teacher. My mother says that God was a healer, Jesus Christ
was, and He came down here to talk to people and try to make
them better — but He sure didn't convince everyone, and in a
while they crucified Him, the bossmen did. My mother doesn't

know who the healer's teacher was, but from her picture she looks like a smart woman: her eyes are big, and she wears something wrapped over her head, so you can only see her face and none of her hair.

"It must be a little while only, but it seems to me you're there all day before she tells you, all of a sudden, that you've been healed, and you'll find out pretty soon. Then you pay her and leave. Walking back, both times, my grandmother said she didn't feel any different than she did before; but then all of a sudden she did. She stopped and grabbed me and told me it's getting better, what's been bothering her, and she started singing her song, to thank the healer and thank Jesus Christ and thank the healer's teacher, who's in the picture. Then she told me I'm all grown up now, because I'm talking deeper, because my voice is growing up, and I'm near as big as I'll ever be. Yes, I say yes to all she says. You can't disagree with her. You don't want to. She gets real upset. She'll shout you down. She'll pick up a stick and come after you. On the way home from the healer's she's good, though. She takes me around and wants to hold on to me after she's finished her singing. She says I should stay in good health and not be sick, but if I do get sick, go to the healer. She says I should go visit her all by myself, and when I meet a girl I'm going to stay with, and there'll be children, then I'd better go and see the healer and get on her good side, because she can put a curse on you, and that's real bad. She can say that she's putting her hand on you, and you're in trouble, bad trouble. She told my grandmother that someone must have gone and put the hand on her, someone bad, and she was taking it off, the healer was, and she'd try and make sure it stays off. My mother doesn't have the pains, as much of them, as my grandmother, but she does have the miseries, and they say you just have to live with them. I'm always having my teeth hurt, and my belly, and my arm was hurt bad, but you can't expect to be in Heaven when you're down here being tested, like the minister says we are.

"I asked my daddy if the healer is better than the doctor that comes to see the bossman. I helped the doctor with his car, when it broke down; I helped to move it and change the tire. The doctor said I was a smart little colored boy, and I should stay in school. I told him I was leaving, and he said that was fine, and I should go and get work as fast as I can. He was changing his mind on me, but I didn't say anything to him. He said if I got sick to come and see him, and I said yes sir, I would. Daddy says that we can't go to see him, because he's for the white people, and if a colored man goes to see him, he's got to have more money than we ever see, one big pile of it. But I can't see how anybody can cure you better than the healer. She comes from near here, though she's been up to Memphis and done a lot of studying up there. If you're on her good side, she'll leave her place and come with the midwife and she'll be there to see there's no hand put on the woman, when she's pushing out the baby. I saw her for the first time then, near my mother. I wasn't supposed to be watching, because I was a little one then, but I did, and when my daddy saw me, he said he'd tell no one, meaning my grandmother. I have two girls I like to be with, and they'll each say to you they wouldn't know what to do if the healing lady turned against them, and they're right. She's no one to be an enemy of yours, and the best one to have for a friend.

"The older people do a lot of singing. I'm no good at singing — not like them. They'll go out and pick the crops, even my grandmother does, and they'll have their songs and they go from one song to the other. I'm learning some now, because I'm old enough to leave school and be all grown up. The healer said I looked to be turning into a man, and my grandmother said yes, she was right. I've seen the healer a few times in the gas station, buying her groceries. I'll never be able to call upon God the way my daddy's uncle does, and my mother and my daddy, they can sing, too, but they say voices aren't what they used to be, and today you're glad to have the work, and you don't do your singing and talking to God except in church and not out there working the bossman's land. But I've been listening, and my daddy's uncle told me I was big now, big enough to come and learn from him how to play the banjo. He said he'd teach me how to sing, and then I'd know the songs. I'm afraid I'll forget the words, but he says no, I'm big enough, I'm grown enough. I guess I am."

At twelve he was indeed "grown enough"; he was even then a full-fledged and full-time handyman — and field worker and errand boy, which is exactly what he'll be called at sixty, if the bossman has anything to say about it, and if there are no more changes in Itta Bena, Mississippi, during the next half century than there have been over the last half century. Winston didn't find such a state of affairs ironic or sad or outrageous — that, for instance, he should come of age, and that others should acknowledge it by calling him an "errand boy" rather than a "nigger child." Winston at twelve had an almost detached manner about him, and not one simply put on for my benefit. Within only a decade he had found out all he needed to know about the facts of life; for him those facts are not the mystery of sex, but of a whole society and its various customs — all backed up, in the clutch, by plenty of policemen or sheriffs. Sex for Winston had long been no strange or "forgotten" or discreetly overlooked matter; years before he could do anything about sex, at least anything that would lead to children, Winston saw his parents sleeping together, moving and thrashing about with each other, doing what Winston knew led to his brothers and sisters. No one had to sit down and "explain" all of that to him. No one had to teach him things in school about "the biology of reproduction." He knew at twelve what he had seen happening all his life, and also seen happening between animals.

Nor did his parents decide he either should or should not go out on "dates" or take this or that girl here or there. He and his girls, the girls he used to tell me he "goes with" or "is with," would walk and make love and go back to their homes; they went to no restaurant or club, nor did they seek out movie houses or share hobbies. They did enjoy listening to the radio, and they talked a lot about relatives and friends — and about the various white people they know. Leona, eventually Winston's wife, was always a "big talker" and also had a fine, fetching voice, as Winston can reminisce years later, when he is twenty: "Leona was my favorite, even when I had several girls I was weighing, deciding which would be the best, which I could last with. Leona made it easy for me: I'd sit out there near the big pine tree, and she'd talk herself half asleep, filling up my ears with everything she'd heard since the last time we'd been together. Then she'd sing the songs she'd learned, from the radio and from church and from her daddy, and I'd say to myself, 'Leona, she's the one'; and you know, even back then, I think if anyone would have said to me, 'Winston, are you going to marry Leona?' I would have said yes."

He is vague on exactly when he did get married, or why. Leona wanted a marriage. He felt that it was time to go see the bossman and ask for a cabin; and there are always cabins around — vacant, waiting, reminders of how many more share-cropper families once lived in the Delta. He remembers deciding Leona was "the one," a decision made when he was about fifteen. Eventually Leona persuaded him that they had to go to church and in his words "spend a half a day praying over ourselves." So, they did. As I quoted him saying earlier in this chapter, the day was in the spring of 1964, and he can talk about that spring, that year, as though it were a quarter of a century ago or more. When he says that he has been married "quite a while," he doesn't think of the time as a few short years ago, but as a long stretch of sea-sons that lead back into his youth, I suppose, his short-lived youth, a time when decisions were made even as they are by middle-class youths, but made in Winston's case rather concretely and quietly and without much self-consciousness, without a million discus-sions and announcements, without preparations and more prepa-rations. Winston, that is, graduated from nowhere; moreover, he and Leona did not decide they would go to church, would get married, until after they were in fact living together in a cabin — he working, she with a child — and they decided to do that "a week or two" beyond Easter, "when Leona really had a mind to, and I said yes to her, I would."

To be sure, Winston's life and Leona's both differ from Myrna's and Ronald's. Migrant children live more chaotically, more hurriedly, and become youths (and old) without those trips to a healer, and often enough without resort to a marriage ceremony. I have in the first part of this book suggested how early most migrant children start working, and also how early young mountain children start helping their parents cultivate the land or go find herbs to sell. (Until only a few decades ago, mountain children worked in the mines, too — as Lewis Hine has unforgettably documented with his camera.) I think I am trying to say that there comes a time, a point, a certain moment, when a sharecropper, a migrant worker, or a mountaineer begins to think of his child as no longer that, as grown. The child's body has become a man's or a woman's body. The child may have been working for some time, as a harvester or an "errand boy," but now he is a man working, she is a woman working, and he or she is accepted as such, treated as such. So, Winston goes to the healer with his grandmother, begins learning to sing work songs and the blues, begins playing a banjo, has his girl friends to visit, becomes a father and gets a cabin of his own, and gets to be considered a full-time, regular worker by the bossman, who stops calling him a "nigger child" and starts calling him an "errand boy," which, to that bossman, Winston will be at the age of ninety.

As for migrants, the child turns into a grown-up when he or she becomes visibly a man or a woman. Then young migrants stop giving their earnings to their parents. Then they are no longer called "little" but "big." Then the records blare, and the radios; then the young people dance and kiss and go off together and have their beer and make love. Then their parents, their weary, exhausted parents, go to sleep and wonder how it can be that someone can work all day under the hot sun, picking and picking those beans or cukes or tomatoes, and still have the energy for "carrying on," an expression which by no means has to imply disapproval. Here is what "carrying on" means to a migrant mother — who without pedantry articulates a valid psychological and anthropological description of "adolescence," of growing up in a particular social and cultural setting: "Lilly became a woman a few months ago, and now she's carrying on. I tell her I know it's natural, and she should, but to get the sleep she needs, because she's got to be out in those fields come morning, like her boyfriend and me and everyone else. It's all right by me for her and her man to go off. It's what happens to you, inside you. She's no longer little. She's big. I saw it happening. She was getting taller and taller, and you know, her hair was starting to grow on her, and like that. Then she started with the bleeding, and I was glad. She'll pick a man and stay with him, and I only hope they have an easier life than I've had up to now.

"When she started looking big and becoming a woman, she started acting like one, that's how I'd say it. She wanted to go on her own to church sometimes, and I let her keep what she made at work, so she could get a nice dress that fitted her good. You need a new dress or two for the good times when you become a grown woman. We still work together, but she doesn't lean on me as much; and I don't tell her it's time for food or time to get out of the way of the sun. She turns and tells *me* that, and I figure to myself that Lilly's all big now, and thank God she's lived this long, and I hope she finds a man who treats her right. My son, my son Frank, he's big too, and I hope he treats his woman right. He's fifteen, and he works real hard. The crew leader told me that he's got real energy, that son of mine does. I hope he finds his way to leaving this work and staying in some city. But he'd need someone to help him, or else he'd never know what to do in those cities. We pass near them, and one sight of them makes me scared. But I'll bet if my son grew up there, he might still be in school, and he'd be with me and his brothers and his sisters and not by himself. I don't want to keep him tied to me, and I know he's all big, all grown, but I'll look at him sometimes and I'll ask myself where it all went, the time, and he'll still seem a boy of mine, playing here near me, in the field, and helping me with the picking."

Like many mothers she bows to the inevitable, accepts what has to be, and has her moments of recall, of yearning, of sadness and regret. She knows what growing up means: the body is ready, the society is waiting, always waiting for those vegetables and, anyway, there is no real alternative. What one sees in her behavior, hears in her words, is the accommodation a parent makes to a physiological fact, an economic situation, and a set of social circumstances. Her children work as children; youth for them is not taking on a job for the first time. Her children play with one another and sing and have their intimacies, their games that revolve around touching and feeling; youth for them is not suddenly, for the first time, meeting a boy or a girl and becoming close, real close. (Myrna and Winston as children slept side by side with brothers and sisters and knew sex as part of the rhythm of things, as part of their parents' activities, as part of what happens at night between a man and a woman, with children nearby, able to watch and listen — though often enough, over time, not looking much and not hearing much.)

What *is* youth, then, for Myrna and Winston? I suppose it is what they both say it is, and their parents say it is: the continuation of what was and the beginning of something new. Youth for Winston and Myrna can be staying with the parents and working alongside them but going off a few hours, or bringing in a companion or a wife. Youth can be keeping money, the little that is earned, or for the first time getting a dress — not something called clothes, but a dress. Youth can be a migrant learning to drive a car — yes, sometimes being taught to do so by a crew leader in a tender and even fatherly way.

In Appalachia youth can mean a whole range of things started, allowed, encouraged — but again, with considerably less formality and fuss than many young Americans experience at the hands of their parents, their schools, their relatives and neighbors. A boy or girl in Appalachia does, however, grow up somewhat more gradually than is the case in many parts of the "Black Belt" or among migrant families. I did not know Ronald when he was still a child, when he was, like Winston, twelve years old and, at least in body, going through marked, if not dramatic changes; but I did meet Ronald when he was a little over eighteen and his brother David was just fourteen and his sister Clara was in between at sixteen. The three of them at that time were quite grown up and responsible for themselves and for work they had to do every day; but they were still rather like children, like *youths,* as we outside of Appalachia call so many of our freshly grown-up people. In eastern Kentucky, where Ronald lives, one can be that — a youth, a young man, a person neither altogether a child nor altogether an adult, and certainly one can be called the equivalent of a youth: a "young one," a "grown young man," a "grown young lady."

Ronald has all along had his friends, and they have not been much older or much younger than himself. He and David and Clara know they are not like their young brother of seven or their young sister of six; nor did they yet, when they were eighteen and fourteen and sixteen, consider themselves quite through with growing, quite ready to give up some of their childlike ways and take on the manner and bearing of completely grown men or women. At times they did indeed look upon themselves as thoroughly grown, as independent, as proudly themselves. At times, though, they felt anxious about themselves; they wondered where they were going or might have to go — I mean "where" literally, because many thousands of young mountaineers reluctantly leave what they love for northern, industrial centers. What Ronald and his brother and his sister have never relinquished is their attachment to their family, to their homestead, to their whole way of life. Ronald's remarks about his age and his past and his future show particularly well how a regional "culture" or a kind of sensibility manages to influence, indeed give striking shape to, a young man's sense of himself and his purposes. So, if there is no doubt that some of Ronald's life has resembled Winston's and Myrna's — all of them live close to the land, left school at an early age after a somewhat casual record of attendance, live uncertain and relatively impoverished lives, have been working long and hard from their earliest years — there is also no doubt that the Ronald speaking below could not be Winston or a brother of Myrna's: "I'm just eighteen, and it's a good age. Like I say, you're really on top of things. You can walk anyplace and not get tired, and your back doesn't hurt and all that. I hate not having a job I can do all on my own, apart from Dad. He keeps on telling me how lucky we are, that neither of us is down in the mines working; but the pay miners get is real good, even if it is dangerous work. I never want to leave here, but sometimes I think maybe I should; not only so that I could get a job and save money, but so that I could see someplace else, and then be absolutely sure that this is the best county in all of America. I know it is — you see tourists come through here from everywhere to look at our mountains — but sometimes you just plain forget.

"When I think back at being younger, I recall my dreaming that I'd be big and able to shoot, and go shooting by myself and learn to drive a car and all that. That's how I knew I was growing up and becoming a man, yes sir. The first thing was that my dad said if I wanted to leave school, it was all right by him, since I was never a great learner. I liked the teacher, I always did; and when I started growing up, and all like that — well, I took to noticing the teacher even more, and the girls around, too. The girls were getting ready to leave. I recall one *had* to leave. She was about a year or two older than me, maybe about fourteen or fifteen, and she started getting fatter and fatter, and finally we figured out what was going on. A lot of us left around then. She left for her reasons, but we left too, because it wasn't for us to stay and stay in school. There isn't a future in school, not around here. When I was ten, around then, my dad took me out hunting and gave me a gun and said it was mine, and not just one of his that I have to ask for, to borrow. And later, around when I was fifteen or sixteen, he got me into his car and started showing me how to drive it and how the motor works, and he had me come and work beside him. It wasn't long before I could go around any curve we have in the county.

"One day I feel I'm just like I was a long time ago. I'll wake up and I'll be lying there, waiting for my mother to come over and say, 'Ronald, it's time.' She never had to say much to get us going, but she did have to say something. The next day I'm feeling exactly the other way. I wish I'd be in a different home, then — in my own place. The trouble with getting married and setting up your own place around here is that there's not much work around. I guess you know that from your studying us; but it's hard if you know about it because it's you and your whole life ahead of you and your future that's going to be ruined. I knew I was *really* growing up when my dad took me aside one day and told me I should come and work with him, and if I didn't, I'd have nothing for a job. At first I wasn't too happy. You like to do your own work. He had to show me so much, teach me so much, that I thought I was back to the first day of school. I'd get silent on him, and he'd say I should liven up and stop being so quiet. Then one day he told me he knew how I was feeling, but even so if we could just divide up what there was to do, it would be easier for him and better for me, because I'd have some money in my pocket. Ever since I started working, I've had the money, though I don't keep it all that long. I'm paying on my guitar. I've been learning how to play it, not just fool with it. I've been learning the songs. My uncle knows more of them than any other man in the country, he says; his father, my grandfather, used to pick up some money singing ballads at the fair they have for the tourists each summer. I'd hate to do that, go and sing just to make money. I like to sing, though, and I like my guitar; it's one of the best you can buy around here. My dad says I have a gift for the strings. He says when you get big and your hands are as long as they'll get, and as nimble, you either can play or not, and I turned out to have the right kind of ear and fingers and voice; it's those three things that you have to call upon.

"Since I've been working with Dad all the time, since I've been fourteen, I think it was, I've had my money, like I said, and I've tried to give a regular amount to the church, just like Dad does. The first time I got paid for working all week, Dad said that we owe God some; we owe him a regular amount. So I said I'd sure oblige, and I have. My friend John doesn't even want to go to church. He and his girl made a bad mistake; she's got her baby, and her father never wanted John for a son-in-law. Her father said John is no good. John can't find a job. He says he may go to Chicago. He was going to go there when the trouble happened, when he was fifteen I guess, and he was going to take Mary Alice with him. But being under sixteen and all, everyone told him he'd run into trouble up there — they'd both run into trouble — because they'd need to prove they're over sixteen, and they couldn't. Then, when John got to being sixteen he decided to stay here a little longer, and he's still here.

"John helps with moonshine, with making it. His dad has a still. We're not supposed to know, but of course we do. Dad says that sooner or later the federal agents will come by, and then they'll send John to jail, and his father and uncles. John says it's better to eat and maybe go to jail someday than starve to death a free man with no record of trouble before the law. My friends will try hard liquor, but they much rather would have beer, except that the cost of beer mounts up. That was when I knew I was getting real old: I stopped school, started work, shared a beer with my dad, started picking on that guitar all the free time I had, and was soon driving and hunting almost as good as Dad. I knew how to shoot long before then, as far back as I can recall, but when I was learning to drive, Dad said if my mind could concentrate on the road, it could make me hold the gun steady and shoot good, and not go hitting wild. So, you see, one day you're little, the next you're big; but a year or two later after you've grown up, you can find yourself wishing that you were back in school and sitting there, with the teacher trying to be nice to you and at the same time get you to do what she wants. She used to tell us that the day would come when we'd wish we were still in school, and she was right. But mostly I don't think of school; I just go ahead and work. Like my dad says, we're lucky no one is standing over us, ordering us around and telling us what to do and where to go and when we can eat and rest and breathe and everything. A boss is worse than a teacher will ever be, Dad says, and he's got to be right — because our teacher was good; I wouldn't mind taking orders from her. I remember I did cause her trouble, though. She said I was a 'stubborn kid,' that's what she called me. She said I wasn't reared to take orders like I should. I got to obeying her, though, after a while I did. It was just a short time ago we were all there in that school, and it seems at times like so long ago that I can't remember much of what we did."

Ronald knows how lucky he is, as do many Appalachian

youths, even as they all struggle hard to make ends meet. Unlike Winston or Myrna, there is no plantation owner, no grower, no crew leader to take him in hand and make sure he knows how to follow orders without hesitation or qualification. Ronald is much more his own person than Winston or Myrna can hope to be, though his seemingly less compelled and driven life actually is not all that "free" or spontaneous or the result of his tastes and preferences and his alone. Like all of us, Ronald and his family respond to long-standing social customs, which in fact largely determine how young people assume various obligations and become "adults" in their eyes and in the eyes of others. For Winston, being a youth means getting ready fast, very fast indeed, for the demands of that foreman, that bossman. For Winston, being a youth means picking a woman to live with and staying with her and starting to work and settling into life, with all its constant and unremitting demands. For Myrna, being a youth means being a full-fledged picker, being a migrant, and alas, being other grim and sad things, too. For Ronald, being a youth means becoming a mountaineer by stages, which means he has a certain margin that does resemble, in form at least, the margin middle-class youths have. In the long run, of course, because mountain life is not suburban, Ronald will be a man of the hills, the land, the woods, the sparsely settled, often un-settled, countryside; and like Winston and Myrna he will know how to deal with the land, grow crops, fetch water, hunt and fish for survival's sake rather than out of choice or out of pleasure. Still, he will have come to all that, come of age, rather more gradually and less frantically than the children of many share-croppers or migrant farmers.

Certainly Ronald will not ever talk as a cousin of Myrna's does. Albert is Ronald's age, but by his early twenties he looked as if he were nearing forty, maybe forty-five or fifty. At eighteen Albert said this about his life, his childhood and youth and adolescence and years of growing up: "What does it mean, a birthday? I don't have any, I really don't, not one that I know. I've been told I was born in May, but who can bother remembering the days? One day is like another. All days are the same. I have three children and I don't teach them their birthdays. I don't know their birthdays. All I know is that my wife has had a bad, bad time. She has lost two children. She loses half her blood, it must be that much, when she gives birth to a baby. She suffers the worst pain, and her mother can't quiet her down. I'm afraid each time she'll lose her mind and never get it back. The crew leader said the next time he'll personally take over; he'll see to it she gets to have a doctor. But last time he said he'd do that, and he didn't.

"I look at them, when they're born, and I say to them that I'm sorry; it's too bad they can't have a better place to enter the world than out here in the field or the camp. You don't choose your parents, though, and you don't choose if you'll live a long life or a short one. To me, you either have a lucky star looking down on you or you don't. My wife believes the stars tell you everything, if we could only figure out the message they have. There's a woman who does, who knows where the stars are going to take you over the years you have to live. You give her a dollar and she'll read you. She reads my wife and tells her if the crops will be good and we'll make a little money, or if the crops are going to be real poor and we'll have to tighten our belt.

"My wife and I were born almost on the same day, so what the stars say about her, they also say about me — that's what I heard. When we were small we belonged to the same crew leader; he'd take our families up North, and we'd work right along with the big people. I can think back to when I thought of a man like me as a 'big person,' a 'big one,' that's what we'd call them. I first thought of myself as being a 'big one' a long time ago, maybe ten years ago. I was ten, maybe that, or twelve. I started growing hair, you know, and I could do it, I could be a man like the men my mother has, one and then another. There was this girl, she was a twin, and she had a sister who looked exactly the same; anyway, she was the one, the first one I had. She was ten or eleven, and so was I. Then I took up with her sister, her twin: Ruthie and Marie they were called — first it was Ruthie and then Marie I went around with. We'd go to a 'platter party,' you know, in Belle Glade. There would be the records and we'd dance and dance and then go off by ourselves. I knew a good spot. In the morning we both had to be out in the fields. We wouldn't feel much like talking back and forth then. Even on the trucks, when we'd both go out together to a farm to pick beans and like that, we'd not say a word to each other — Marie or Ruth to me and me to them. What is there to say? You're tired at five or six when you get up, and you're tired all day. You just hope the sun will go as fast as it can from one side of the sky to the other. You look up at that sun and you curse it for taking its time. I like the stars, even if they don't do all that my wife and that fortune lady say they do; at least stars come out in the night, and they don't beat on you and squeeze out all your energy and leave you with a dry, dry mouth and dizzy and sick to your stomach, and your head as sore as can be.

"My wife was a friend of the twins. She knew both of them. She might be related to them. They all came from the same place, from Georgia. So do I; that's where my people are from, going back a long time. Don't ask me how we got to this life. I know, but I hate to mention it — because it's no favor the stars did us, if they were the ones that persuaded my daddy and momma to join up with the crew leader and become his property. That's what we are. I'll go and admit it to you, I will. The crew leader wouldn't even be angry if he heard me talking like that — no sir, he wouldn't. He wants us to talk, to say how nice a man he is, and how absolutely, completely, one hundred percent he owns us. He was the one, the crew leader was, who told me I should pick a girl and stay with her and not go from one to the other. I was thirteen or fourteen, I don't know which. Maybe I was fifteen. What difference does it make, how old you call yourself? Here, out in the fields, you do the picking, no matter how old you are. Then you go to sleep, no matter how old you are. When you're on the road, going up North, you're crowded into the crew leader's truck, no matter how old you are. Like I say, what difference does it make if you're sixteen or twenty-six? I don't think I was a kid, a baby, for more than three or four years, maybe five or six. I never count things up like that. All I know is that one day I was working, and if I stopped, if I was ever to stop, I'd have had no place to stay and no money and nothing to eat. *You stop, you die* — that's what we say when we need to remind ourselves about the kind of life we have ahead of us. And if we forget to remind ourselves, the crew leader won't; he won't forget to tell us the score. That's what he'll say, 'You know the score.' He doesn't have to say another word.

"I listened to his advice; I chose my girl, my wife. She is a good woman. She's always been good. She's nice to be with. She loves me. She tries to be a good mother. I love her. I'd die without her. We'll be moving on up to the next farm, and I'll feel sick. I put my head on her shoulder, and I feel better, all of a sudden; it's like there's been a miracle. She says I make her feel good. She says if it wasn't for me and the children, she'd have died a long time ago. To tell you the truth, I don't know how we all have lived so long. I'll be twenty-five soon, I guess — which is a lot of time."

He goes on. He tells how he once tried to break away from the crew leader, how he failed to do so. The sheriff came and arrested him for owing money, for disturbing the peace, for drinking too much, for possible thievery of one or another kind. It was all faked, all trumped up, but the point was made, and he was quickly released — into the hands of his accuser and long-time "friend," the crew leader. He was at the time a young adolescent, as we would put it. He was, that is, "about fourteen."

His wife, who is his age, remembers all of that, among other things: "It seems a long, long time ago — to think back to the time when I first met him. It isn't so long that I can't come up with the answers — the month and the year — but it's hard just keeping up with each day. I try never to look ahead too much, and I don't want to go back much, either. My children ask me questions about what we used to do and where we used to live, a lot of questions. I tell them it's always been the same, as long as I can remember it's always been the same. They stop asking you if you tell them that. If you let them go, let them ask more and more questions, you'll soon get sad; that's the trouble.

"I was never so scared as when they took my husband and put

him in jail. He never did a thing wrong. The crew leader heard we were both planning to leave him and try going to a city and see what we could find there. We figured we'd get married, and we'd stay in one place. I was expecting to have a baby, and I wanted to be in a hospital then, so my baby would be born safe, and me too. My mother died before they could get her to a hospital. My grandmother told us hospitals are no good, and they don't want the migrant people, but I've always thought that my mother would have lived if she'd seen the doctors and not the fortune lady with the spells that she tries to put over you. That lady knows I don't follow her. She says I'm the devil, and she won't come near me. I've taken my kids to the public health place, the truck they have that comes to the field. There they have needles to stop sickness from coming.

"We never got to a city. We never got away from the crew leader. It seems like we were born to be with him and do the work he takes us all over to do. My little girl, the smallest one, says he's our daddy, 'the daddy of us all,' she said. She sure is right. A child can say something like that, even right to the man's face. Soon she'll be helping us out in the field, and she won't dare talk so much then. But at least he pays us. He gives us enough to eat, and he makes sure we live in places where the screens keep out the mosquitoes and no one sleeps on the floor. I heard him having a big fight with one grower. He was saying we're not animals, and the grower said he can't be spending all his money on fixing up the damage we do. Then the crew leader said we are good people, and if he didn't want us to come, then we'd leave and never come back. Then the grower told him to settle down and not get excited — and then they saw me listening! The crew leader told me later that I mustn't be like a child, sneaking up to hear what people are saying. I believe that was a long time ago, when that happened, yes sir. I was carrying Albert junior — and he's seven. I must have been fifteen, maybe less; but not more, I don't think more."

Youth for Albert and his wife was a short-lived time; youth for them was working the way they had done for years as "children," but working now as a man and a woman who were sleeping together and were about to have a child and planning to travel "all over" together — though they thought of themselves as "young," and just "catching on." Now, to what were they just "catching on"? They were catching on, of course, to what they had already seen and come to know, even as later their young daughter and son will begin to see things and know them and comment on them. They were catching on to the life they had lived and were about to see lived by a new generation — which includes in it their children. They were catching on to experiences, to sexual experiences, to the experience of becoming a mother and a father, to the singleness of purpose, really, that will characterize their lives: work, travel, much needed if fitful rest, sex, food, more work, more travel — and the children to be borne and fed and put to bed for some rest and carried "all over," and, soon, set to work. The arrival of children, in a way, marks the end of a migrant youth's youth: "I was having a good time with the girls," Albert once said, "but then I heard she was expecting a baby. I said to myself, you'll be a father soon. Soon I was, and that was the end of fooling around. Now I'm doing just what I used to see my folks do, and I'm no longer a kid, but as big as they were — as big as they were when I was a kid and looked up to them."

By fifteen, all of that had happened to Albert; and by thirteen or fourteen other migrant youths are going through what he described. They are getting ready to surrender a certain exhilaration, a curiosity of mind, a kind of youthful intensity, an inclination to experiment and dream and speak out — and escape. Whatever all of those words and more mean to us, Albert once told me what they mean, or more properly, meant to him: "I was a kid, then I became like I am: I work, and I have my family. Once I tried to break away and take my woman with me, before we had our family. If I'd been able to, I would have started on a new life. I would have been my own man and said only what I believed. But maybe you can't have but one kind of life, at least here on this earth — especially if you're like us migrant people. I guess those few weeks, when we were dating and figuring out our plan to break away — I guess that was when we were young, when we could hope for a good break. You could say that was true; I think you could."

I do not know how to improve upon such a description. The man did indeed make his terse summary, describe that brief spell, that interlude, really, in his life. I can make no generalizations that would tidily lump together Albert's youth and Myrna's and Winston's and Ronald's. I have tried to show the differences that such youths demonstrate: ultimately their differences are closely tied to matters of region and occupation. I have also tried to indicate certain common themes in the lives of such youths: they are poor; they are struggling to survive in rural sections of America; they are relatively without self-consciousness; and they quietly and patiently try to get on with life, with its chores and tasks, its hard work, its severe demands, its limited successes. Perhaps these rural youths, even the more fortunate of them, are not destined for the great and important things many middle-class urban and suburban parents in twentieth-century America want for their children. Perhaps these rural youths just "don't count," because (unlike other youths) they are weak and isolated and unable to call attention to their views and complaints. Nevertheless, to repeat what I mentioned at the beginning of this chapter, it is instructive to see how some literally extraordinary Americans live at fourteen or sixteen or eighteen; among other reasons, it is instructive because many of "our" young people want to help "them" — youths like those whose experiences I perhaps vainly submit to what may well be the futility of words. Ronald once told me how hard it can be to get those words we use to convey what goes on inside us: "I can't say it, how I kept learning all I did after I left school. In school we'd recite and recite, say out loud everything we learned. Out of school I just learned things, and I changed a lot — but I never thought to recite it all to anyone. I was my own teacher, I guess, and maybe I was whispering to myself now and then. But if I was, I never listened much. I just went on doing what I should — working, you know."

He still is working, and he still is learning, and in 1970 I still see him in my mind, at twenty, as a relatively young man; but I do not believe he would want me calling him that, a "youth" or a "young adult" or someone just out of something called "adolescence." He is Ronald and no one else, even if he is in many respects like others in a particular county in Kentucky. "When I was ten or fifteen, and when I'll be forty or seventy," he once insisted, "I'll be *Ronald*, not a ten-year-old one or a fifteen-year-old one, or someone who is forty years old or seventy years old." How certain Ronald was of himself when he gave me that message — certain of something *about* himself, *in* himself, that transcends all "ages," those groupings of years with which some of us constantly concern ourselves. We are not supposed to "romanticize" the Ronalds of this earth. But occasionally, thank God, a person can defy all efforts to analyze him and look at his life critically. Occasionally a person whose life is full of uncertainties and severe stresses nevertheless can prompt in an observer a touch of wonder, if not of envy — and I felt both when I heard those words of Ronald's.

XI

RURAL UPHEAVAL

THE rural South and Appalachia have exerted enormous influence on our nation's recent political climate, an exaggerated influence if only the population of both regions is considered. It was in Little Rock and New Orleans that schoolchildren faced mobs, and through television did so before the eyes of millions of Americans in California, Illinois and New York. It was in Montgomery, Alabama, that Rosa Parks said she would not move to the rear of a bus. And it was in that same city that Martin Luther King — a young Negro Baptist minister "out of Atlanta" — came to her side. It was in Greensboro, North Carolina, that four students staged a sit-in; and if they failed to get any of Woolworth's coffee for their effort, they had the eventual satisfaction of seeing a random act of theirs in 1960 become an example to thousands of other nonviolent demonstrators. Freedom rides, marches, statewide summer projects — the South experienced them all, and so did the rest of the country when newspapers and cameras covered the news that was made.

In 1960 John F. Kennedy went before Appalachia's poor rural Protestant people to ask their help in his quest for the presidency. They said yes to him, those "hillbillies" did, with their long bodies and craggy faces and their Protestant Anglo-Saxon heritage. The young Catholic aspirant, out of Boston and Harvard, drew them down in large numbers from the hollows. Each one of them seemed at first glance shy and sad, perhaps members of Lincoln's family still in mourning. At first glance, they also seemed impossibly unwilling to commit themselves, content merely to stand and watch, listen and on occasion faintly smile. They nevertheless knew a winner, and they knew that they needed him to be *their* winner. John Kennedy worked hard in West Virginia and never quite knew while there to what avail. From what I have heard these recent years from people in the region, he was the prototypal "community organizer" from the "outside." He came in to offer help and, admittedly, to be helped himself. He was "different," a stranger. He didn't talk the right way: in every promise of assistance, a prickly, oversensitive ear could detect an implied criticism. Still, the mountain people were in trouble, and this man from "over there in Massachusetts" offered help. Despite any misgivings the Appalachian people may have had and any mistakes in their dealings with a "special sub-culture" made by John Kennedy and his aides, an alliance was forged. To this day, I find the former President's picture on the walls of cabins that lie in the remotest hollows imaginable.

It is possible, then, for isolated rural people to reach and be reached; it is possible for them to affect significantly, even momentously, the populous cities and to respond more quickly to urban influences than some observers would seem to think. It can be argued that the South's villages and small towns provided the atmosphere of clear-cut contrast, of total black subservience and total white control, that made the civil rights struggle so appealing to the entire nation. (I fear the word "appealing" may be just right in its implication of something that calls for an almost self-serving kind of sympathy rather than active, dedicated, and sacrificial involvement.) Yet, something contagious happened in the South in the early 1960's, something that for a while began — and only began — to make a difference elsewhere, in more ambiguous situations. It is possible to see the War on Poverty as a direct aftermath of conflict in the South and of the "new" interest in Appalachia that developed after 1960 (and perhaps culminated so far as the public is concerned in the famous CBS documentary "Christmas in Appalachia").

Many of our present urban problems are in essence rural ones that have been exported. The sharecroppers and tenant farmers, the migrant farmers and Appalachian people I have studied these past years all have their kin in Chicago, New York or Detroit. Some of them have gone North and stayed, so that I now am studying not their rural lives but their lives in transition, their lives as immigrants — from two very distant regions that both, perhaps, qualify as nations within a nation. We in the cities are beginning to learn about what life *was* like in the Delta or in the mountain hollows of Kentucky and West Virginia. The presence among "us" of thousands of confused and virtually penniless exiles from "the land" makes the problems of, say, McCormick County, South Carolina, the very real problems of New York City. For example, I am appalled at the poor health I find among ghetto children, and I am also puzzled when a Negro mother I know refuses to avail herself of the medical services of a city hospital that was built and is run to provide people like her and her children free medical care. Yet that mother has only recently come to Boston from McCormick County, South Carolina. She is thirty-five and has seven children. Except for the three times she was taken to Augusta, Georgia, to have her baby in a hospital, she has never seen a doctor in her life. (Her other children were born at home.)

Here are the "facts," the raw medical information that might be called the "background" to her current "attitudes" toward doctors and hospitals. (The welfare woman who visited the mother asked me to look into her client's "fears" and "anxieties," so that four boys and three girls would receive the attention and care they needed, the inoculations and vitamin supplements, the corrective surgery and eyeglasses, the dental care.) There are exactly two (white) physicians in McCormick County, South Carolina. When they are called for help, they ask for a fee, and that is known by the mothers and fathers who are farmhands, occasional harvesters, or out of work altogether. In 1961, the infant-mortality rates in McCormick County were as follows: for white children, 208 per 10,000; and for Negro children, 1,073 per 10,000.[1] Those terrible numbers, comparable to what comes forth from government bureaus in New Delhi,[2] have a far wider, greater, and more persistent "meaning" than the most covetous statistician could ever wish or dream. "In McCormick County we learned to do without doctors, because there just wasn't none around," said our welfare worker's troubled Negro mother recently. Then she went on: "Now up here, they tell us they're here, waiting. But I get the shakes every time I think of going near the hospital, and I don't know how to stop them, the shakes. If you're brought up to have them, you can't just stop because you've moved up the road, no matter how far."

Actually, several months later she did go to the Boston City Hospital, and since then she has overcome her childhood inhibitions, perhaps more directly and easily than some of us. I mention her experience not only to make the obvious point that lives in their continuity transcend abstractions like "rural" or "urban," but also in order to introduce her younger brother, whose activities I believe have helped make poor people all over America more bothersome — if that is the word — to the rest of us.

He is twenty-six, Peter, and it is hard to know what to "call" him. There are words, but none of them quite fit. In the early sixties he was "simply" a civil rights worker, a young Negro college student who worked with Dr. Martin Luther King's organization in rural Georgia, not too far from his home county of McCormick, South Carolina. In 1965, he became a "community organizer" for a brief period. The work was in Washington, D.C., where he hoped to gain some "techniques" and "skills" that he could put to use in what he then called "the rural situation." (He had already learned a good deal of jargon when he arrived in Washington.) He lasted three months in the city, then went "home" — his way of describing the return South. And he went South with a vengeance — to the Mississippi Delta, where he became involved in the now rather famous Child Development Group of Mississippi (CDGM). Without enumerating the historical and political details of the group's brief existence,[3] I can say that the "operation" was designed to reach the poorest children of that very poor state and to educate them (through Headstart programs) to learn not only their "letters and numbers" but something about *themselves* — children of the Delta, poor Negro boys and girls who need better food, a doctor, clothes, and perhaps most of all a sense of what a future can be, one that is not an endless repetition of the past. CDGM was started in 1965 and funded by the Office of Economic Opportunity (OEO). Many of its leaders were white "outsiders," though fairly soon Negroes from Mississippi became not only recipients of the "benefits" of Headstart programs but, by design, active in planning the organization's purposes and activities. Peter was one of the early "organizers" who helped shape the philosophy of what might be called, with no exaggeration, the nation's most forceful and unusual preschool "program."

"I think of myself when I'm with these kids," he says repeatedly. He even tells the children about his own life and does so in a direct, open way that commands the extraordinary gift of silent attention from five-year-old boys and girls: "I come from nothing, the way white people would call it, and black men, too, the few of us that have got a lot of money and put on airs like the white man. No one in my family ever went to school except a few weeks here and there, you know, when there was no work to do in the fields or around the house. The white people, they didn't care — they didn't even want us to take school too seriously. And our colored teachers, they wanted us all white and starchy, neat and obedient. They knew they couldn't get what they wanted — us to be little angels for them — so they called us all kinds of names, right to our faces, and pushed us around. We felt lousy before them — afraid and no good, no damn good. I recall when I was about five or six I'd hear from them that niggers were no good, most of them, and they were poor because they didn't know how to take care of themselves. So, I'd go home and tell that to my mother, and she got so nervous she didn't know what to say. Sometimes she would shake her head, but agree. Sometimes she would say it wasn't so, but tell me to mind the teacher and try to follow what she says, so that I wouldn't have to work the white man's land. Most of the time, though, she didn't say a word. Nor did my daddy. They were too tired, and maybe too confused. I don't know the truth, even today.

"Well, actually, I owe a lot to one teacher. She gave me a test when I was in the third grade, or the fourth — it didn't make any difference, it was just a one-room school. She said I was a genius or something from the results and I must have cheated somehow. How's that for building up a guy's confidence about himself! So they sent me over to Columbia, South Carolina, or someplace for another test, and they watched me like hawks and police dogs and everything. And I broke the bank again.

"So, they gave me a special plan, they called it. They asked my parents to keep me in school all the time, no matter what, and they said they'd even send me over to Greenwood, South Carolina, for a special class they had for smart little colored children who knew how to behave and had a lot of brains. They even brought in white teachers every once in a while to give us a special talk. As I recall, we'd spend most of *that* hour or so just looking, not listening. If they had asked me what I learned after a white lady's talk I'd have had to tell them nothing, except what she wore, and how she was made up, and how her hair looked, and the way she talked, and the jewelry she had on, and all that. I'd go home and tell my mother about all that, and she'd tell me that 'white folks sure can look pretty' — meaning *we* can't. I remember learning that over and over again when I was five or six — how pretty white people are and how useless and hopeless it is for us to try to be pretty or good-looking or whatever. It's not the words, it's the feeling, you know. My parents never came out and told us that 'white' meant 'beautiful,' or 'black' meant 'ugly' or 'menial.' They made us *feel* all that — and you never forget it that way.

"That's what CDGM is about. We want to help these kids, the poorest kids in America, feel some self-respect, feel that there's a chance for them, on their own, as black kids from the 'Black Belt,' as farm kids, the sons and daughters of sharecroppers. We want them to feel they can stay here, as well as go North to Chicago — and be *men* and *women,* wherever they go, wherever they live. You talk about poverty; you could give a lot of these people here — maybe a lot of Negroes everywhere — a million dollars and they'd still feel so low and scared before the white man that they'd feel poor, even with color television in every room of a twenty-five-room house.

"We try to show them that we respect them, as children, as

human beings. We aren't forever comparing them to some white face in a white child's book. We show them the strength and value of their *own* words, their own tradition — they are the children of workers who built this whole state with their sweat and tears and shortened lives. We tell the kids that, and they listen."[4]

In 1965 I heard him tell children just that, and they did listen, much more attentively than I might have believed had I not seen them listen to him again and again. He would stand before them and talk, much as he did with me, and then show them pictures of white suburban homes near Jackson, pictures from books used in both the Negro and white schools of Mississippi, pictures of their own homes. He would emphasize the *reality* of their condition, but insist on the possibilities that nevertheless exist: "We have to learn, not because the white man is embarrassed if we can't sign our name to prove we owe him everything. We have to learn *who* we are and *where* we're going and *what* we want." He would say it over and over to the children, that last sentence, and I would later hear them reciting their who's, where's, and what's to one another. They would also carry the message home, to the cabins and huts, up the alleys of the small towns, or alongside the cotton fields.

In one home that I had been visiting for years before CDGM came into existence, I heard this from the mother of one of Peter's students: "That teacher must be sent down here from Someone Big, I'll say. If I didn't think all the disciples of Jesus were white, I'd begin to wonder. He talks like he knows everything and isn't one bit scared. He talks different from those civil rights ones, too. They'll tell you not to be afraid to follow them, their lead. He says go be yourself and don't be afraid of that, being who you are. I tell my boy I don't understand it, to be honest, but it sure sounds different, I'll have to admit. Of course, what should we do next, that's what I'd like to know, and that's what I'd like to ask him, Mr. Peter."

Mr. Peter, like all good modern teachers, wants to bring the home into the school, the school into the home. After he had figured out what he was going to say to his young students, how he was going to hold their interest, he did indeed visit their parents and get them to ask him the questions he knew they had in mind anyway: "I try to tell them that we've got to stick together and *do* something. At first a lot of them would give me that blank stare, or the sly look. Some still do, but a lot of them have changed. Especially they pay attention when I remind them that the only way to change things is *acting* — even when it seems hopeless. I must have told the story of Rosa Parks in Montgomery a million times in the past few months. She reaches them, and the story of the freedom rides. I tell them that everyone said they were wrong, the freedom riders, or they were foolish, or they weren't doing the right thing in the right way at the right time. Even our 'friends,' I tell them, said we should 'take it easy,' and not do too much marching and too much demonstrating and too much protesting. 'You have to pace yourselves,' we'd hear from the conservative Negroes, and 'not so fast you don't bring along the rest of the country' from the liberal whites.

"Then I tell them what *happened* — because we didn't do the 'right' thing, the 'sensible' thing, the 'smart' thing, the 'practical' thing. They *know* what happened, but I remind them, about five times each visit. And before I leave I tell them what *they* can do: support us, CDGM; send their children to a Headstart center that means business; go register to vote; tell the bossman they want more money. I know the last thing isn't likely to happen — they'll be thrown off the land first. But they're going to be thrown off anyway — and even *they* know there's no point going North now. All that's up there is welfare and rats, and what happens in Watts is what they'll be traveling two thousand miles to see. So, we've got to stay here, and organize here, and make it work down here. It's our state, as much as whitey's, and we'd better let him know it, and let the people in Washington know it. They can invest in dams and conservation and foreign countries; let them invest in us, right in this place, and they'll be helping their cities in the bargain, I'll tell you."

They nod, the people he visits, and I've seen some of them give him an unbelieving smile that I suppose someone like me has to call "hostile." They sometimes escort him to the door as if he were a white insurance salesman; it's an ingratiating "yes" and "yes" and "yes" until he has left — when you know that they will laugh scornfully and bitterly. The mother in the family I knew best put it this way: "I don't see what they're talking about. There's nothing, absolutely nothing, we can do, except be as always — and hope somehow it'll change. He can't fool me, that man Peter, he can't even fool himself. I can tell that he doesn't know what to do any more than I do."

Yet, her children were excited by what they learned, and they were getting the best meals they ever had — and all at government expense. What is more, she and other parents were coming together and talking — about their children, yes, but about other matters, too. From visit to visit I could watch a federal anti-poverty program — a unique one in a uniquely difficult situation — take root in the mind of an individual mother. Coming together with others prompted this observation from her: "I've never done that, sat and talked about anything with people. At first you don't know what there is to say, and then you find you've been thinking about this and that and the other thing, and you start in."

She would come home and talk to her husband and to her neighbors about the meetings. She began to tell her older children that there were other ways to learn, other things to learn, than those provided by the state of Mississippi and their county's board of education. She would also become downcast and have no reply to make when her husband pointed out that good ideas were useless in the face of a sheriff's gun. But she would go to the next meeting and bring up *that* subject for discussion: "My husband says for me to think about the sheriff and the policemen and what they'll do when we start getting more and more ideas in our head and then talk out loud about them in front of the courthouse. There won't be one of us left here, he says. We won't have a job among us; we won't have a cent in welfare money; we won't have our homes; we'll have to run for our lives, clear out of the state. And my brother tried that and went up to Cleveland,

Ohio. Now he sits all day in a store to keep from the snow, and he hides from the welfare lady, so that his wife Martha can collect her check. He says it's like a real good job down here, being on welfare is, because they give you enough to pay the rent and eat. But he says there's not a thing for him to do, and he gets tired, and he thinks he's getting sick from sitting around all day. Sometimes he wishes he could just do some chopping and go get the water like in the old days down here — but he'd never want to come back, you can be sure, just to do that. So, if we're going to leave, all of us, then OK. But if we plan to stay we'd best be careful, that's what my husband says. And isn't he right?"

They weren't at all sure her husband was right. One or two mothers nodded their heads, and another one paid her recognition to the length and ardor of the statement she had heard by saying, as if in church, "Yes, you're right." Peter was there as an observer and a teacher. He wanted to know what others thought. For a minute and ten seconds there was silence, and the chairs squeaked with shifting bodies. I used the movement in my watch as an excuse to avoid looking around, and all the while I expected *Peter* to come up with something, to break the impasse and send us along a more hopeful road. Suddenly, one of those enormous women I have sometimes seen at such meetings stood up. I had seen her at several earlier gatherings. She always wore large printed dresses full of flowers and bold colors as if she long ago had decided to enjoy her fat. She regularly sat in the rear, on a long bench, for which she seemed grateful. She had a habit of putting her right hand through her hair as if she were looking for something, then inspecting her palm and fingers when she was through, and finally resting the entire arm on the back of the bench — where no one else sat. The fingers would soon be moving again and one could safely bet everything in the world that the hand would soon be raised again, the fingers soon be weaving and scratching their way on the top of her head.

She had immediately commanded everyone's attention by her move. They heard her get up and move two steps forward. She hesitated. She seemed voiceless. She seemed ready to sit down again. Peter stood up, nervous and ready to have his say. Suddenly the woman spoke: "I have two children here in Headstart. I have older ones, and they're not eligible for anything as I see it. I have three of them younger, and God knows if the government up there in Washington will desert us after a while. But I plan to stay here, and if for no other reason just to hear my boy, he's five, and my girl, she's six, come home and talk to me the way they do. They say I'm a fool and I've been a fool all these years, putting up with things. I ask them what 'things,' and they can't answer except to show me that they can fill in the picture books they're given at school — and the pictures show us with our heads looking up and real proud-like.

"So I think we should stay right here and keep our poverty program going the way it is, and if the state police come and try to break it up and scare us to death, then we might as well fight them over this than anything else. To me it don't matter if we vote or not, because we can't seem to win even if we do vote, from what I hear, like up there in the North. But the children, they're learning how to spell right and speak right and, most of all, learning about themselves and us, the colored people and what we've gone through these past ten thousand years — and every year is a century to you and me — and what we've done for the country — build all that's important, I think, if you would ask me."

She opened her left hand and released, for her own use, a small handkerchief. It was a child's. She didn't wipe her brow, but patted it. She moved back to the bench without turning her back on the others, and then she sat down. The impact of her body on the bench could be heard and so could the sound of the wood accommodating to the new weight. Peter looked around, curious about what would happen next. I thought to myself that the woman had succeeded in triggering off a series of similar exhortations that would come one after another for at least an hour. And to myself I made a reassuring analysis: they were nervous, and they felt stymied; there was just so far they could go, and they knew it; they were becoming "organized," but they were also becoming afraid — and aware of their own weakness; they were now "supporting" one another with brave speeches, but they were also ready to run, and they knew it, and Peter knew it.

In point of fact, it was the state of Mississippi that became afraid; eventually, the federal government began to look very warily at the workings of CDGM, to investigate it from top to bottom. Its "management" was declared poor by Washington; its purposes and goals obviously offended the governor's mansion in Jackson. In 1965, I was asked by officials of OEO to evaluate and help improve the medical program that had to be a significant part of a rural Mississippi Headstart program. My impressions were welcomed and later that year submitted to the Senate as it prepared to finance the War on Poverty for yet another year. In 1966, quite a different set of circumstances prevailed. A beleagured CDGM had to fight what seemed like a hopeless battle; the state of Mississippi was its avowed enemy, and as for the federal agencies — well, I'll let another mother I heard speak out at a meeting make her summary: "The government people up there in Washington, D.C. — they're more afraid than we are. We must have gone through a lot down here when the day comes that the people representing the United States are more scared than we are. It used to be they'd come down here and tell us *we* shouldn't be afraid. 'There's *nothing* to be afraid of,' I heard one of them government lawyers tell the NAACP man. 'This is still America, and if they go too far, we can take them all into *court*.' I was standing there on the street, and they were coming out of the church they burned down that he was referring to, but I came home and said to my mother that it was the biggest joke I'd heard in thirty-seven years of living — as if the white man doesn't own the courts! And my mother is sixty-four, and she said it wasn't so special, that kind of talk. She said they're always doing that, the outsiders: they come here and tell us to stand up and do this and do that, and then they go away. And who's left? Who's here to have 'nothing to be afraid of'? It's us, and we don't own anything, and with nothing yours, there's a lot to be afraid of. That's the way my mother saw it, truly, and she never went to school a day in her life. That's the truth. But she knows about things, everything there is to know, I believe.

"And now it's changing. It must be when I have to go tell my mother that *we're* not scared, but *they* are, in Washington, D.C. I guess they gave up on us a long time ago; so when they gave us the Headstart program they thought it would be a real quiet-like thing. But we have some real good people teaching our children, and they give us food for them, and a woman like me, they've given me a job, not sweeping after Mrs. Charley for five dollars a week and maybe a piece of donut I'd get to share with the dog and the coffee that otherwise would be spilled out, but a *real job* and one that pays me good *to do what's important for me and my family.* I never believed there were jobs like that, where you could get paid a good salary to spend your time helping your own children and your people's children, instead of the white man's kids. I help serve cookies and juice, and I arrange things and clean up after the kids and help them go take a nap and wake up and things like that. They call me an 'aide' and pay me, but I'll tell you I'd do it for nothing, the way I feel.

"It didn't take them long to figure out we was up to no good, no good at all. We was being 'uppity.' And we're scaring the colored as well as the white. 'An uppity nigger will get shot sooner or later, and mostly sooner' — that's what I used to hear my granddaddy say. Well, his daddy was a slave, I think, or the son of one, so you could understand his thinking. But here I am, and born only thirty-seven years ago, and I believed the same thing until last year. Now isn't that something! And if you had known me five years ago — well you couldn't, because I'd have been afraid to look you in the eye, or let you get within a mile of our house, for fear of being shot dead talking to a man from Massachusetts who is white.

"It was the way they went about doing this that got us feeling drawn to it, I'd say. They made us feel it was *ours*, and we were somebody, and not people they'd throw something to, so that they could go home and feel better. And I mean the colored as well as the white. Have you ever seen a rich colored man telling his 'brothers' how bad off they are, and how he's going to give them five dollars, not one but five United States dollars — if they'll be real good and nice?

"They probably saw that they got us going too fast, and that we'd be real, honest-to-goodness practicing citizens of the USA, and they never have allowed that here, and maybe up in Washington they're not ready for it either."

What has surprised not only me, but even a veteran civil rights activist like Peter, comes across in that woman's words, and even more in the insistent, assertive, defiantly wry quality to the delivery of those words. Peter and I both remember the apathy and fear that one met in Delta Negroes, without exception. Whether the "projects" were limited and conservative in aim, or far-reaching and "radical," they invariably came to a gradual halt when ideas planned in New York or Atlanta or even Jackson had to face the "reality" of a sharecropper's life or a tenant farmer's life in Itta Bena, Louise, or Sidon, Mississippi. No matter how clever and persuasive the "fieldworker" was, the "people" shunned him or accepted him with fear and open distrust. Nor in many cases was "time" the answer. In time, the outsider — darkskinned, sincere, earnest, full of ideas and plans — can become familiar and likable. What else can he become, though? Does he bring bread or enough men and guns to change things, really change them? Does he bring work or land that he owns and wants worked? Does he bring anything but trouble? And trouble for what? So that I, James, called a "boy" all my fifty-eight years, can go put my "X" by some politician's name — and of all crazy things, go get some coffee in one of those Holiday Inns in Greenwood or someplace like that? Even if he laughs with me about all those *other* organizer types, what has *he* got to offer, really?

Well, he's got plenty of talk about how bad every white man is, but we've always known that. He's got his idea that we should all be like him and be together, and that would create new power, black power, and change things. But when and how would it change things? And what about the beginning, the dangerous, terrible, awesome first steps when we're so naked and weak, so exposed to those gruff, stocky, beefy, red-faced sheriffs, with the *two* guns they carry around their waists and the cars they drive with the lights whirling about on top of them? What are we supposed to do when the plantation owner or his managers (they do the "dirty work" and they're often the real mean ones) come around and tell us to "get away," to "move on" real fast — if we want to stay alive, that is? And then there would be the storekeeper who'd be after us for all we owe. What do we tell him — that we're together, the poor black people of Mississippi, and let him, or the Mississippi Highway Patrol, try to bother us?

Those are the questions that aren't asked right away. Without words, but in a stare, a long silence, a gesture, they can be conveyed to the visitor. Then, in time, they are put to words — eloquently, vividly, pointedly. By then it is perhaps too hard for the visitor, the organizer, the "worker" to reply at all. Someday, when all the accounts are settled and regions like the South or Appalachia have at last achieved the kind of democracy we assume America is all about, a historian or two will need to know about the despair of "outsiders" like Peter, as it grew out of the apathy felt by the "insiders," the isolated, lonely farmhands who knew too concretely the meaning of abstractions like "power" or "class" or "race."[5]

In 1966, more than a year after CDGM had proved it could work by inspiring the lives of the most "backward" and "remote" farm people, I heard this summing up by Peter: "I never would have believed we could have done it. The whole thing doesn't make sense according to every idea and slogan we believe in these days. Here was a program devised by white liberals from New York and a few civil rights people. We were looking for the *real* poor, and the ones way out in the countryside as well as in the towns. We were running nursery schools, mind you — of all things. I would have laughed at the idea a few years ago.

"But we had money, enough money to give people who need food, need clothes, need all kinds of advice, some real, tangible help. That was one thing that made a difference. The other was our approach. We wanted them to feel it was theirs, their program to do something with and feel proud of. If they owned nothing else, they could own those Headstart centers. They could see that the books were specially designed for them and their kids, that they were the staff, that the 'experts' admitted how much they had to learn and didn't know. We could offer them doctors for their kids and good food. We could bring them together to talk about something *real*. The checks came to the centers, and poor people who never had seen a check in their lives got them — for working as 'aides,' for cooking and cleaning and 'minding' their *own* children, for a change.

"That's what got to them, money and a chance to join in together. But the third thing that glued this operation together, if you ask me, was opposition. We never had it easy, even when the War on Poverty was going strong nationally and they were sending all sorts of visitors down here to see how even Mississippi was in the 'war.' The state caught on to us right away, even if Washington didn't. They knew we were interested in the families of children, not only in five-year-old children, and they knew we considered the words 'health' and 'preschool education' to be much broader than a lot of politicians would like. So a federal agency was giving us money, and we were trying to let people know — as many as we could afford to let know — that they were actually a little free, to come together and speak out and have their children taught what mattered to *them* and what *they* thought important and desirable. Of course we were subversive. How subversive could you get?

"Now no one in power in this state and no one representing this state in Washington can afford to ignore something like that, a program like that; and they didn't. The more they attacked, the stronger we became with the people. It was beautiful: they couldn't really burn down our centers as if they were churches in the old days. We were connected to the federal government, and anyway the state of Mississippi has learned it can't let that kind of thing happen too often any more. They couldn't stop us from functioning either. We had the money, for at least a year we did. Talk about 'education,' it was the greatest education these parents ever had. They saw their own strength, their own power, in daily operation — against the white man's opposition. They never had gone through anything like that before, and I doubt they can ever be the same afterwards.

"You should see the letters they sent up to Washington, and the petitions they wrote, and the statements they issued — to one another. And when we thought that we were through, that we had had it, that we were getting no more money — well, they knew about it, and they stuck together. They were fighting for *theirs*, for a paycheck, against the bosses — like in the old days of the labor-union movement. From isolated, unorganized people — at the mercy of every sheriff, every plantation owner, every redneck in the state — they became tied together as 'members of CDGM,' that's what a lot of them called themselves spontaneously, 'members.'

"You know there were a dozen or more critical moments when the whole thing could have collapsed. From the very beginning Washington and Jackson pushed us here and there. They'd want a compromise on this issue, a little ground given on something else. Sometimes they seemed to want to bribe us to surrender! If we'd only move our headquarters, or fire so-and-so, who is too 'radical,' or too much an 'open civil rights type' — like me! If we'd only stop letting the children and their parents know that just about all other Americans are richer; that is, they have more money and don't want to share it with a few million Negroes. If we'd only use those nice, sweet middle-class 'farm books' and stop telling it like it is, which is called being 'inflammatory.' We say to a woman who practically never sees money at all that she is being exploited by the white plantation owner and the white political system that won't let her vote and won't give her the kind of food and medicine and education her kids need; and for that we're accused of turning a preschool program into a 'political' program. We're called agitators. And when they call us agitators in Jackson — when the governor does and *his* representatives in the Congress do — then believe me the bureaucrats in Washington listen, even in the 'flexible' agencies, the ones full of imagination, like the OEO.

"So we'd go tell the people *that*, as if they didn't know in their own way. During one bad time, when they had inspectors all over the place and they were telling us in Washington we'd have to 'slow down,' clean house, and — really — stop being so successful at organizing poor people, I heard a woman get up at a meeting of Headstart parents and say: 'If we do like they want us to, we'll turn into nothing. If we make a fight of it, we'll win even if they cut off the money, because for the first time we'll stick together and stand up to them. And maybe when they see we're doing that, it'll be them who'll back down. They won't know what to do with us behaving that way.'

"She was right. Even *we* were surprised, the so-called 'leaders.' Those people were determined to have their kind of Headstart program, and if we wavered because we knew 'the facts,' they kept on telling us that they knew everything *had* to turn out right, even when the checks stopped coming, and we reminded them about the threats coming down upon us.

"Yes, I suppose they were 'naïve.' But they also were 'involved,' really so. And their attitude gave us strength even when we didn't admit it. You can persuade yourself to be 'realistic' — in fact, to sell out a good and decent program when the people in it are only halfhearted members. It's a little harder to do so with a really emotional and enthusiastic group — who talk a lot about the Bible and God and make you feel like a two-bit Judas for entertaining ideas of being 'practical' and 'realistic' and giving in to the politicians."

The encounter between rural "innocence" and American *realpolitik* had been stated rather well. It was an encounter that to some extent took place inside him. Yes, he was for "the people," for CDGM, and against the whole social and political system that keeps those people in their present circumstances; but he was also part of that system, perhaps more than he cared to realize. I was myself awakened, even stunned at some of the introspection and self-scrutiny that emerged in those moments of "struggle" with the state and federal governments. We had the same all-night "soul sessions" I had once heard civil rights workers "conduct"[6] or unwittingly slip into. ("Like, man, we've spent the whole night talking and taking ourselves down until there's nothing left, and no one knows how it all got started.") A young man like Peter — of the people, for the people, with the people — had to face his own "distance" from "them." It wasn't only that he had gone to college, or even that he had worked at "community organization" or in a protest movement. It wasn't only his "savvy," his political shrewdness, his canny understanding of what in the news was "really" significant — his "worldliness," it used to be called by cloistered men and women. What separated him, finally, from the ranks of the "poor" — so he began to believe and say — were the assumptions he took for granted and ordinarily never questioned or indeed thought about. When he was literally penniless these past years, he had not been "poor"; and when he was fighting hardest alongside the tenant farmers or the abandoned mothers and their children, he was not struggling the way they were. Even when he tried to forget everything he knew, everything he had ever learned, he could not achieve their ignorance, their vulnerability, their concrete, earthy vision — both idealistic, shattered, pitiful, foolish, and at times enormously, powerfully convincing.

"You look at me, at my life, someone like you could, and you'd think I could really 'make it' with these people." Then Peter went on: "The truth is that I'm miles from the very people I'm 'from' and now working 'for.' It's not my education, and it certainly isn't my 'background.' It's hard to put into words, but I think something happens to you, no matter how 'radical' you are, when you work to change a political system. Some of the system's values rub off on you — you can't help it — even when you're fighting it. It happens to all of us. In fact, in a way the *more* you fight, the more you become entangled in what you're fighting, and the more it all becomes part of you. I remember when I was in SNCC, I'd go up to Washington — in 1962 or 1963. We'd meet all those government people. I remember the time I went into Bobby Kennedy's office. I thought to myself, here I am, Peter Woods, from McCormick County, South Carolina, a southern nigger from the backcountry if ever there is backcountry, and I'm standing in the office of the attorney general of the United States. Of course I said to myself, 'Watch yourself' or 'Beware,' as my mother used to say it, 'Beware of evil.' Well, you know what the greatest evil is? Every little colored boy in McCormick County knows that the sin of pride is the worst of them all. My mother used to tell me it didn't matter what the white man had, the property and cash and everything; he has pride, too — the sinful kind, and so he'll burn while we stand by and watch. Later on, of course, is when he'll burn, the time will be later on, and it won't be here on this earth. Our bones will be lying around, tired as usual, but at least getting a rest; and the white man's will be lying comfortable in a satin coffin. But up there it will get reversed — because of pride and its temptations.

"Well, you can only be tempted so many times, and even if you resist it every time, you've tasted it and smelled it and felt it and learned about it. We'd leave Washington all heady and walking on air. Each of us knew enough not to show how we felt to the other. We'd try to be real suspicious and angry — and we *were* suspicious and angry. I'm not telling you that we 'sold out' or were 'conned' or 'had,' nothing like that. It's not even that we were so impressed and excited; if that was all, we'd just be ordinary tourists. The point is that we were fighting something, and we left still fighting it, but we also left just a little more a part of what we were against. *We* began to think about this group and that one, and the pressures here and there, and what might happen if we did one thing or another one. *We* began to worry about what one group would do, or another. *We* began to realize how difficult everything was, and complicated and involved and hard to solve. We'd leave Washington telling one another how unmoved we were, how unimpressed we were with all the people there and the offices they had and the flunkies around them — United States power!

"Then we'd get home and the next thing you'd hear, when we were talking about *our* strategies, *our* tactics, we'd begin sounding like *them* when we spoke to one another. I remember a guy saying to me, 'What's got into you?' when I said something to the effect that we had to 'think our options through carefully.' Then the guy said: 'If we had thought like you during the last three years, there wouldn't be any movement to worry about. We wouldn't have had the sit-ins, or the freedom rides, or the projects in Alabama or Mississippi. We'd have had nothing but a lot of talk, a lot of meetings and discussions and plans that are so well thought out that they lead you nowhere — which is exactly where they're supposed to lead you.' I blew up at him and told him it was easy to demonstrate and much harder to figure out what was happening in the country. But as soon as I said that I knew I was a fool, and I apologized to him. The fact was that the more we sat around and worried about a lot of 'effects' and 'potential reactions' or 'responses' to what we did — well, the less we would do.

"What I mean is that we were trying to change things, but in this country it's hard to keep your momentum going. You try to change things, and the first thing you know you're being wined and dined, and the TV people are hanging around you, listening to your every word, and people write newspaper columns about you, and kids come from every campus in America, to 'help' you, and a million journalists and political scientists and sociologists and psychologists — cats like you — try to figure us out and study us and write about us — and make their living off us, make money from what we *do*. Pretty soon *we're* making money, too. There's plenty of it around, and people will give it to you. Then *we* become worried about our 'image,' and *we* become interested in the 'larger picture' — until that's about *all* we're doing: trying to 'mobilize public opinion' by saying things that 'get across' or doing things *because* they'll 'get across,' worrying about our telephone lines, our lines to the 'power structure,' rather than what's going on between us and the people in the Delta.

"So, that's it. You're with the people here, a guy like me, but you're somewhere else, too. That's all right though, so long as you don't forget the difference, and so long as you stay here and do what you can. I believe a lot of my friends have left because they're further removed from life down here than they can allow themselves to admit. So they find excuses, and they leave. I'm not criticizing them. I'm not. They're — a lot of them — city boys, black boys from the ghetto. They want to go back. I may want to leave, too; but for me to go 'back' means McCormick County,

South Carolina. So I'm removed from the scene here because I'm 'wise' to a lot of things, but I'm also close to the scene — out of my life, man. You know?"

In Appalachia I have seen the very same struggle take place among those who "work" there with the poor and among the poor.[7] Peter's struggle comes to my mind often when I hear an Appalachian Volunteer,[8] a middle-class college student, talking about his effort to "reach" the "people" in a particular hollow and "do" something for them — teach their children, take stock of their medical problems, join them in their battle with a county courthouse or a strip-mining company that wants to devour their land.

Yet, the War on Poverty (insofar as it brought on a number of skirmishes in the Appalachian Mountains during the mid-sixties) was remarkably able to "penetrate" all the cultural "resistances" and demonstrate one more time that loyalty to a particular kind of past[9] can live side by side with a willing and even eager acceptance of new opportunities and possibilities. The terribly private, solitary man of the hollows — so out of the world, so out of the way — feels the lure of bread and medicine, work and money. He does more; he abandons in their wake some of the social and psychological characteristics that people like me take pains to observe, analyze, and fit into one or another "frame of reference." He does so almost unnervingly, but only when the "change" makes real sense for him. Here is a man in Wolfe County, Kentucky, speaking: "I don't know about all these college kids coming in here, wanting to do things, all kinds of things — you wonder how they think up so many ideas at the same time. They tell us they want to be here with us and be our friends, and I wonder what about their friends back home where they come from. Do you think they don't have any there? But I don't care. They say they'll go fix our bridge and help us with the road we've been meaning to lay down for — I'd say ten years, I guess. There's enough of them to go do it, too. They'll hurt themselves a little, I think — some of them don't look too strong to me — but they'll do the work, I can tell. And they're good with the kids. The kids like them. My wife says they tickle my son and my daughters, and they're real nice with them.

"They've got some money to bring here, and that's welcome, let me tell you. The kids get a good lunch, and if we put up a volunteer, they pay us out of the government's pocket. The one with us, his name is Richard, and he comes from someplace near New York, I think outside the city there. His mother writes him these letters and tells him to be real careful and not to get sick. You'd think he was someplace over in China. But he's OK. We've never before met anyone from where he comes, or like him, but he's good to have around. I think he's taken to my wife's food pretty good, and he likes the singing we do. He's a little jittery, we notice. He can't sit for too long. He has to be doing something or moving about. I guess that's his way. A while back I never thought we'd see people like him hereabouts — ever. But I've lived to see them. First it was in the Army, where you meet all types, and we got sent over there to England and France. Yes, and it's television, too. I've never seen so much in all my life as TV brings into your home. It's the thing that my kids pay most attention to — more than to me or their mother, even. Nowadays they've seen everything before a father has a chance to talk.

"Of course Richard is in the flesh, not on a program. My daughter Jeanne, she said he's really cute, and she was sure he was like two or three people she'd seen on TV. He talks like them, and he wears the same kind of clothes. I can't figure why he came all the way down here to be with us, even for a summer. And now I hear him talking about staying here for a while and working with us on a couple projects they have in mind, the AV's.

"There's plenty for them to do. They say we can fight the mine strippers. I think they'll find out different, but let them go try. I don't mind someone coming in here so long as he tries to do what needs doing and not what *he* wants. You know some of the people who used to come through, back in my daddy's day and way before, too, they'd be a certain kind of minister or a teacher maybe — for a disguise — and they'd want to change *us*, not the things that these kids do. They'd preach at us; but these kids, they don't say a bad word about us, and it's pretty clear that they're trying to be of some help, and they want to do some building or clearing or whatever there is. Now that's a difference. Of course you don't really give yourself over to them. Why should you? Some are a little too one-sided for me. You know what I mean? They're so all-fired serious, and they want to make over the hollow and the county and the whole state of Kentucky, for all I know. I told one the other night to just relax and not lose so much sleep on things, the 'poverty' as she keeps calling it. Sure it's bad down here, and elsewhere from what you hear, but these mountains have been here for a long time, and so have we, and you can't just dissolve the world's misery in your own time.

"I'm glad they're here, though — on the whole. One or two may be a nuisance to us, but they're workers, and that's what counts. And they have money to bring in here, and that's the scarcest thing around. And they don't hand it out, they ask us for help, for their room and food, and to work with them, so it's not something that's welfare and charity. We have to take *that,* too — but no man like me wants it. If there were jobs around here, I'll tell you, none of us would be sitting around trying to get a handout here and there from anyone he can. Not our people. We want work."

A year later, he and others were more wrought up than I ever thought possible. Those "kids" — some of them were well into their twenties — had done a quiet, respectful, but clear-cut job of bringing together people whom tradition, geography, and a sense of futility had long kept apart. Moreover, the volunteers were increasingly coming from within the region, even from local people who were not students, but unemployed men whose sharp, well-articulated sense of what is "wrong" with the Appalachian region often surprises the well-meaning and arrogant outside observer. While "we" — student activists and people like me who "observe" them — have come to accept the "wisdom" that relatively uneducated poor people have, it still comes as a surprise to hear an unemployed former coal miner, or even a "dirt farmer" from one of the Kentucky hills, give a sharp and comprehensive analysis of the social and economic system in the United States.

As a matter of fact the repeated irony has been inescapable: it is not due to the reluctance of the hidebound, the "hillbillies" of the backwoods, that the War on Poverty in Appalachia turned out to be a limited one; rather, the issue has been resources. How much can come into the region, after all, to a people largely willing to take what they can get, what they need, and be grateful? "Yes, we get annoyed at some of these people who come in here," I heard one man from near Beckley, West Virginia, say to a group of "outsiders," some of whom, I knew, did indeed annoy him. "But if they bring the bacon in with them, well that's what counts."

In Kentucky and West Virginia both I have seen virtual mob scenes unheard of in "mountain history." That is, "community organization" has worked. People have come together because they have been led to believe that it pays to do so, that jobs and various "improvements" will result. Even more interesting and potentially significant, once a number of people have "organized" themselves, they are newly sensitive and newly prepared to act when confronted with an insult, a rebuff, an assault of one kind or another. "The best thing that can happen to bring one of these mountain communities *really* together is a strip miner coming along." The owner of a gas station in a small West Virginia town told me that — as a criticism, actually, of the federal government's community-action program. He went on, though: "People around here are to themselves, mostly; they know their kin, and they don't have much to do with others. Maybe it's that way in the city, too — except you notice it more here. Actually, they're friendly to one another here, but they don't work together. Why should they? In the city, they probably do — one man by the other on the assembly line, I guess. Now all this 'community action' they talk about, I don't think it means much. I guess the people down here will go along, of course. They'll go along with practically *anything* if it means more food and money and a new road put in and some water from the hills brought under control.

But I have noticed that if a stripper comes along now, they'll be in a better position to fight him, the people in the 'action program'; and they do so much talking when they meet that I think they're all primed up and *looking* for trouble, for something to go fight and win, if you ask me. I admit we have plenty of things to fight about down here, but it's not so easy to find who the enemy is. From what I see, if they can't find a mine stripper, they turn on the school people or the mayor or on the federal government, who's paying to 'organize' them in the first place. It all goes round and round from what we can figure out. Now they're talking about marching on the state capital, and Washington, and letting the whole country know about conditions down here. So, you see, they don't just sit together and talk; they look for trouble and go out and make it when they can't find it, and they won't adjust themselves to the real situation around here, but they have to go find someone to have a duel with."

In his "community" he is rather well to do. His gas station is also a grocery store, and he has the local post office in his quarters, too. In other words, he is a shopkeeper, a member of the bourgeoisie if there ever was one. I think he deserves to be credited with a keen eye for the principles of "group psychology," though he denies himself and his listeners any "formulation" of what he sees. He knows that Appalachia, *his* Appalachia by virtue of property as well as birth, is not for long going to "stay put." Ironically, the region is not only "backward" but also plagued with the "posttechnological" unemployment that comes with automated (mining) industry. The new roads will bring in outsiders — and for a gas station owner like him, more money. Television sets have already brought him and his neighbors face to face with the rest of the country. Most unsettling of all, however, are "those VISTA types" and "the people who are always talking about organizing, organizing, organizing." He thinks they are looking for trouble, the organizers, volunteers, and activists of all descriptions. He knows there is trouble to be found. He is afraid they will persist long enough to make more trouble for him and for the order of things he has always taken for granted. He once put the whole issue very clearly: "I believe you have to bend with the wind and give way sometimes. But there's just so much giving you can do and still have something yourself. If they keep on telling us this is wrong, and that, and something else, we'll have to *draw the line,* draw it firm, and say: 'What are you trying to do, change the whole society on us?' "

It would seem that those who give and those who demand, those who accommodate and those who confront, may yet have to find out whether in fact there has to be a line drawn, a decisive struggle waged, or whether in America, somehow, the blurred limits of our enormous, confusingly disparate but nonetheless real "middle class" will be yet again stretched, reluctantly or hospitably. I don't frankly know whether this nation at this particular stage in its history will choose to make the political choices, the social and economic changes, that are needed if a vulnerable and relatively powerless and isolated minority is to be made — in essence — wealthier and stronger. In the thirties, the poor, the downtrodden, were everywhere — visible victims of a "system" that clearly was in trouble. Today, the country as a whole is prospering, as people in the Delta or in Appalachia know better than we may suppose. Yes, some exceptional and highly publicized atrocity — to a civil rights worker, to mountain land by a strip-mining company — can command a certain indignation from the rest of us. Is that kind of response enough, though, to get a national legislature to initiate the kind of planned economic investment that will reach our rural areas and make them reasonably self-sufficient and capable of keeping people who don't *want* to go to urban ghettos but feel they *must* go? Right now we seem committed to a patchwork of doles, commodity food programs that leave children on the brink of serious malnutrition, humiliating "happy pappy" programs that are susceptible to the worst sort of political control and welfare payments that are disgracefully inadequate and given or held back in the most inhumane and arbitrary way.

If I have learned anything from the work I've done with migrant farmers, sharecroppers, tenant farmers, and mountain families, it is that the people "we" consider so distant, removed, backward, illiterate and passive may well be more capable of changing themselves than our nation is of changing itself. Of course, people cower and appear dumb, stony, impassive, inert when they face gun-wielding sheriffs with implied and covert power. Of course, "outsiders" and their "help" are spurned by people who are shrewd enough to appraise that help and see it for what it is — and isn't. Of course, despair and "hostility" appear regularly among people who are hungry or have no significant work. Yet, given a chance, "they" don't have to be that way. Perhaps one of America's achievements is that its rural "proletariat" is not, in psychological and social fact, a *lumpen-proletariat*, a truly and fatally disorganized "mass." The next few years will probably give us the answer: whether or not this country will be persuaded to concern itself seriously with people who are all too conveniently kept out of sight and deprived of just about everything the rest of us enjoy and ask the world to emulate.

XII

RURAL RELIGION

PERHAPS nothing is more difficult for the "outsider" to comprehend than the deep and abiding religious faith that is to be found among black sharecroppers and white tenant farmers, among migrant farmers who, again are white or black (or sometimes Mexican-American) and finally, among the mountain people of Appalachia. A psychiatrist is trained to look for rational and reasonable behavior or irrational and fearful behavior.[1] These days we are likely to talk about the "adaptive" value of religious faith — though we are less willing to talk in a similar vein about the dozens of secular ideologies that command from well-educated and well-to-do people compliance, belief and, not uncommonly, real zealotry. For a long time I found myself — in the midst of a service, say, in a Holiness Church near a mountain hollow — thinking about the "context" of the passionate and fundamentalist faith being shouted and sung and affirmed: simply affirmed in the faces and the eyes of the parishioners, directly affirmed in their voices and words and, if it has to be said, affirmed by and large without anxiety or fear. At first I supplied the "context" for such devotion and faith by dwelling upon the satisfaction and the relief thereby afforded. Then I reminded myself how much desperation had to be somehow dealt with by these far from confident and certainly vulnerable people. Finally I ended up turning on them in those churches: what they said is not what they meant; what they appeared to feel was not what they *really* have going on within themselves.

Now, migrant workers and sharecroppers, and mountaineers

obviously have "problems." So do I, though. Generally I have problems because I am a human being, one who is capable of his own kind of proprietary and uncritical faith, his own reassuring beliefs, his own convictions that have an "adaptive" purpose and no doubt a "context" also. As an observer I have the additional and more specific problem of coming to terms with the faith of "poor, wretched believers," which is the way I once heard a sharecropper woman describe her family — and clearly the third word made the first two insignificant to her, if not to me. The observer's problem is how to come to terms with something called "rural religion" without making caricatures of individuals who have been worked with, without turning them, people with sincere opinions and passionate beliefs, into opiated and deluded victims, or into philosophically duped and neurotically afflicted patients. I will try, though; I will try to hint at — maybe this is the way to put it — the animated spirit of the Spirit, as one like me has happened to see and hear and feel that Spirit become active, become an event. It *is* an event: something happens, something takes place; the worshiper feels taken over, feels no longer a person who only talks about the Spirit, who only uses that word, but rather, one who at last is on the way, at last is set to *do* something, I would even say *go* somewhere. In rural churches one is moved and transported, one is elevated and summoned, one uses the arms and the hands and the legs, one bends and straightens out and twists and turns, and yes, finally yes, gets there, *arrives*. A woman in Mississippi, a mother of a share-cropper's five children, talks about those Sundays, and why she picks herself up to go to church, and where it takes her, the praying and more praying, the kneeling and sitting and standing and leaning and bowing and bending and finally the taking leave, the final bowing, the bowing out, the turning around and the returning from a moment with Him to this cursed earth: "I wait all week for Sunday. That's the day that counts, you know. It's the only day of the week for me, the only one when *we* count, because then God is there, beckoning you, telling you it's all right, just come on over and be with Me, be with Me for a few minutes, yes sir. If you *do*, if you *go* to Him, if you *be* with Him then, like He says, you'll be all right. When you go back home, you'll be good again."

Those verbs — do, go, be — what are we to make of them, virtually marched out in formation one right after the other and stated so easily and unselfconsciously and knowingly (it seems) by that thoroughly uneducated woman — no doubt rash about what she says, no doubt given to thoughtless conjectures stated as uncontrovertible facts, no doubt full of "illusions," dozens of them, having to do with "my being a child of His, just like every-one else"? To her, the idea of a church, a Christian church, means exactly what she says: doing, going and being. Church does *not* mean sitting nearly inert and hearing and watching and maybe singing a hymn or two and maybe reading (or more likely whispering, and even that with embarrassment) a few prayers. Church does not mean following orders, following a routine, doing what the printed program of the day tells one to do. Church does not mean going to a building, staying for an hour or so, and then leaving. Church does not mean attending something, taking part in a *service*. The idea of service, of course, is rather familiar to that woman. She talks in quite another fashion about God's intentions for her and her family: "If you ask me, the Lord must be wanting us to be true to ourselves with Him, and not treat Him like the bossman over there in town, who comes out here and tells us we should do this now and the next thing later and something again in the afternoon. No sir, He wants the truth, like the man says, the minister; and He knows the truth when it's before Him and He knows a lie when it's before him. I'll be saying one thing to the bossman and under my breath another thing to myself, but in church I let myself go and Lord, it all comes out, my faith in Him does, and I don't hold back on it, no sir, because you do that all the time — you have to — and on Sunday comes the time for the truth, and He is there, listening and wanting you to be as honest as you can, because if you'll be that way, He can trust you and you'll go and be saved, yes you will, you'll go and be saved from all the bad things going on in this world."

She says that a time *comes*, a time of truth, a time when one *goes* to be saved, when faith *does* something. Oh, there is an orgiastic quality to her kind of worship, no one these days would care to deny that, least of all her. Others besides twentieth-century doctors and social scientists knew about the passion that faith can not only mask but also *be*. Freud, versed as he was in classical literature and mythology, not to mention Shakespeare's plays, knew that the passions he described had been seen by others, lived by others, were known to others.[2] The history of theology is full of books in which religious passions are un-ashamedly, indeed proudly, connected to man's physical and psychological nature, his lusts and urges and wants and needs.[3] Precisely what else *are* they to be connected to, those religious passions? Of course some of us agnostic ascetics or religious puritans want faith to be "pure"; or we take peculiar pleasure in finding faith "impure," — lusty, driven, sensual, *physical*. For that woman in Mississippi a church is initially a destination, a place over there that requires the physical effort of attendance — which means hundreds and hundreds of steps taken. The passion behind all those steps, the force of mind and heart that makes them possible, becomes obvious perhaps only when an observer witnesses the effort of traveling, down the Appalachian hollows, across the Delta's mud, away from cabins in migrant labor camps to a nearby town or simply to an open field, this time not so that crops will be harvested, but so that legs can be bent, bodies made to kneel, kneel as on weekdays, but now for a different purpose: "I kneel all week long with the beans, but on Sunday I kneel to speak with God, and He makes my knees feel better, much better. I'll be walking over to the field where he comes, the minister, and I'll say to myself, Sally, you're doing better today than yesterday, you're feeling real better, and thank God for that. So I speed up and get myself there right in time for the first prayer. I'm ready to speak then, to speak my heart to my God."

She is possessive, excessively possessive about God, not quite as ready to share him as all other things must be shared: "All week I try to be good and do the picking and take care of the children, you know, and help us all stay in good shape for the next trip coming up. On Sundays I have to go thank Someone, thank Him for giving me the strength. He must want you, He must be thinking of you, not only everyone else, or how could I still be going, going as strong as I am?"

She does keep going, up and down the Atlantic seaboard, all the time harvesting those beans; and on Sundays she is still going, moving herself — as she sometimes puts it, "carrying" herself to a location where an event unfolds, minute by minute, with her and others like her very much *doing* things and *becoming*.

Afterwards, right afterwards, one can hear the sense of achievement, of victory at last grasped — because things that a woman like Sally senses deeply all week become spoken, finally, on Sunday: "I've got to go back, and we'll be out in the fields this afternoon, because we've got to get the crops in by next week or else they'll be gone, yes sir, on their way to being rotted. I've got myself rested and strong now, because God will refresh you if you ask Him, if you only ask Him. I'll be talking with the Lord, and all of a sudden I know He's touched me and given me a little of His strength, so I can go on. That's why I'll say thank you, thank you to Him, for coming to us here and recognizing us, yes sir, recognizing us, just like the others. When you've been recognized, you can feel up in spirits, way up, and you leave and go about your work, fall to doing what you've got to do."

She means, naturally, by "fall to doing" something like "get to doing," though one always wonders what she *does* mean, a woman like her, who does indeed, every day, fall to the ground in order to work, in order to pick at those bean plants. Ask her and she replies; she says she means she'll "soon" be doing something when she "falls to doing" something. But she gets the irony, just like any proud, linguistically sensitive listener does: "I know what you mean. I'm always falling on my knees to go up and down those rows. I have the rubber pad, of course, and it protects you from the mud and the water and it makes it easier on your knees — but there's just *so* easy it can be on your knees, with the kneeling all the time. The only time I feel really rested on my knees is when I'm on them praying. Then they feel real quiet-like and calm and they get stronger, they seem to, while I try hard to pray the best I can."

How is one to make neurophysiological (not to mention psychological) sense out of all that? Does she somehow virtually hypnotize herself? Is she what psychiatrists call a "hysteric," that is, someone who profoundly ignores important facts and feelings, and accordingly seems indifferent or even at peace, when in fact turmoil would be found were one to look "underneath" or wherever it is we keep our emotions? Really, does she not know better, know that whistling in the dark is what she is actually doing? Dozens of times I have asked myself questions like those. I have given up looking for answers. Ought I do a thorough medical examination on her, especially a neurological and psychiatric "evaluation"? Ought I ask her, right to the point, whether she sometimes doesn't have her misgivings, her doubts about God and His churches and in fact those ministers who from time to time take so much money from poor migrant workers? Am I to assume I cannot ask her such a question — because she is almost illiterate and weak and fearful and superstitious and in need of whatever "support" she can find? Am I best advised to take a different line of reasoning, to see the wonder of what occurs when devotion is brought into a building or a place and is given expression, is rewarded by uplift? (And I mean by uplift a lot more than a moment of euphoria or self-satisfaction, more than a "shot in the arm" or a temporary boost of self-confidence.)

"Uplift" is in fact what the woman I have just quoted talks about. She has obtained the word from a minister, who perhaps (to be grim and cynical and appropriately suspicious) teaches his parishioners to use the word as if it were a thing, a piece of property, for them to want and then to get and then gladly, proudly own. What is more she talks about *finding* her "uplift" and *keeping* it, almost like a consumer. She talks about a lot more, though, and she gives one like me, if not answers to what must finally be considered unanswerable questions, at least pause for thought. Here she is — very much dressed up that day and resembling neither a mother nor a wife in appearance or manner — talking before she departs to walk to church, which means two miles under a hot, hot sun: "I know it'll be worth it, because it always is. I get tired, and my feet are aching bad — the shoes, you know — but once I'm there I can forget me and my feet and everything, because there's Someone up there, and He's bigger than all of us, and if you know that, once you do, then you're on your way, and it won't be long before every one of us will be there, meeting Him, and what He decides is what counts and nothing else. I get discouraged a lot by things; there'll be this to bother you, or something else again. You're not put here to have an easy time, I guess. When I'm low, I'll wonder if there's any point — you know, to going on. But that's only temporary. I'll be sitting there and hearing the minister, and we'll be singing, and all of a sudden there's God talking to me; I know He is. It's not that He'll say anything special, no sir. It's just that I can feel the truth; it's there, and it's enough big that I can rely on the message.

"God's message is that we should try to be patient. Maybe He means for us to be patient with Him. I don't mean to be fresh, like it sounds. I mean, He is testing you, and if you don't wait for him to finish, then you're rushing it, trying to be too fast for your own good. It's like out in the field: on a wet morning, you have to let the beans dry before you rush down the rows, trying to pick them. Sure, you'd like to get as much done as you can before the sun is high and right over you and beating down and drawing all your strength right out of your legs and your arms, and just weakening you all over. But you can't forget the moisture on the plants, and so you've got to take your chances and hope that even with the sun you'll get a good day's picking done. Now, with God it's us He's got out here all over the world, and He can't be rushed either, because there's all the other people and not just yourself, and if you come to Him and always say, 'Look at me, look at me, and see what I want from You and see how I believe in You,' well, He's going to turn His back on you, yes He will. He'll tell you, God will, that it's not what He's trying to do, give you a lollipop, like you do with the kids if they mind all you say and don't get into trouble — and they'll be telling you they're good, the kids, so you get them the candy. But to me church isn't where there's candy, no it's not.

"To me, church is where you meet God, where for a little while you find Him and keep Him, where He tells you that it's all right, and it's going to be all right, and no matter what, you'll come out on His side — if you want to and set it on your mind that you will. A lot of times I have to do something, and I'll be tired, real tired, and I'll wonder if there's any use; it's then that I say to myself that I will, I just will — I mean I *will* get to the end of the row, and I *will* get us ready to go on the road again. You see? But you get weak on a lot of days, and your head hurts and your feet, from the top to the bottom. Then you're in trouble, because you start having bad thoughts, one after the other, until you've lost everything, all your belief in God, and you just want to go sit someplace and fill yourself up with all the wine you can find, and steal some if you haven't the money to buy it, and then you're glad when you start going under and you get dizzy and if you go to sleep you hope it lasts and lasts. There have been times, no fooling, when the last thing I could recall was myself saying it would be nice if I slept and slept and *never* woke up. I ask you, can a person justify himself before God, doing that? The minister will tell you no, but I'll let you in on a secret: it's not him, the minister, who does the convincing of me. It's God, and how He does it, I don't know. I mean I won't be so good on some of these Sundays, and I'll go, but I'm not expecting much, and then I all of a sudden get the uplift. It's not like you've made a good wage this week, and you've got yourself the best food there is and eaten all you could possibly put down you. It's not that someone has come along and promised to help you out. I guess if I had to say — it's hard to say these things, you know — then I'd say it's like you're under a cloud, a real bad one, and the sun is gone and it's raining and maybe some thunder and lightning are there — but all quick-like, you see the sky clear up, and not only is there the sun to see, but it's cool too, at the same time, and you've got a nice friendly world around you — over you — protecting you and keeping you warm, but you don't go and get too warm, and the crops, they're growing like mad, and they'll be easy to pick, because they'll get nice and dried out. So, you feel good, and you know you've found a place; you've found your rest. And you look around and you see there's others; they've been saved, too.

"I don't know much about being saved, I mean if you're saved every week, or if God makes up His mind only at the end, when you have to face Him; but there will be a little while on Sundays — not all Sundays, no, but some of them — when I feel real good. The uplift, it's got me hoping. I'll be hoping the week will be better, and I'll not have the pains I get in my stomach; but mostly it'll be I'll have a better spirit about everything. 'All things come to the one who waits,' is what you learn from the Bible, and I'll tell you something, either you know that or you don't, and if you don't, then you're in more trouble than you'll ever know, because you'll go running all over and getting cross at your husband and your children, and worse it is when you get cross at yourself. But if you can just remember to catch yourself and be patient with God, and if you know He's coming upon your life, to look it over and do like that, then you won't be killing yourself with the wine and with shouting at everyone when the least little thing goes wrong. That's how I think."

What do I think about how she thinks? I can take note of, in the first place, her mixed feelings, her faith that turns to despair, her high hopes that become a grim low point, full of what some call nihilism or depression, still others religious doubt. I can take note of her stubborn, quarrelsome spirit, which returns almost weekly to the struggle. I can also mention, even as she did in her own way, the various things that happen to her — I say again, the things that *happen* to her rather than the things that religious faith and attendance at church do *for* her. The point is that she actively takes on something or Something when she goes to church. It seems to me, having been with her on those Sundays, that she is taking on all of her life and all of everyone's life, all of *life itself* perhaps, though believe me I am not one bit sure. I am fairly sure, however, in all my talks with other migrants, and with sharecroppers and mountain people about the religious experience, I am hearing not about isolated episodes or scattered incidents but about events that live on and on and have a continuity. To draw upon an Appalachian father this time: "A real time of it we have, and once it's over, we know we've been through something, yes, indeed we have, and that means we'll be thinking of it, what we've been through, and remembering that we found God and hope never to lose Him." I presume that is what some of us from more "fortunate" backgrounds call an "experience." I presume, also, that some of us sorely miss what that man and others quoted here have and describe, a conviction that we are not alone, that through constant effort and dedication we can find meanings that last longer than a moment or two — meanings that will lead us to bigger meanings, to Meanings, if not to God.[4]

Worship means prayer and supplication, means the acknowledgment of faith, means the protestation and affirmation of beliefs; but a mind that is worshiping is also at work in other ways. There is the coherence sought and found so helpful, and the reassurance that somewhere one is being noticed and somehow does matter, after all. There is also the achievement of a purpose in what may seem a purposeless existence, though obviously one has to distinguish between a philosophical sense of purposeless futility and the purposeless misery and hurt these extremely poor and hungry and worried American citizens confront every day of their lives.

Finally, a man or woman at worship obtains a perspective, a "real sense of things" in the words of a retired miner from eastern Kentucky.[5] Put differently, time and space are both rendered comprehensible: "You go down and sit there in the chair — we sit around in a circle all the time — and he'll be talking, the reverend, and it takes about an hour or more, but every time it happens I say to myself: here you are, Donald Samuel McCallum, and it's today and the year is 1966, or some other year, you know, and I'm here in this little church, listening to him talking, the reverend, and there's my wife, and there's my oldest son, and there's my youngest one, and these are the three boys in between, and now I've got a real sense of things. Most of the week I'm going along and I don't stop and think much at all, but by Sunday at suppertime I know when I'm living and where I'm going, come the next world. Then you get to thinking and counting the years and asking yourself what's ahead and how you'll spend the time and where you'll spend it — and it's for sure that some are leaving here, more and more, it seems. You'll wonder if you should live like you've been living or maybe change something around; and sometimes you end up changing a habit you have."

So, standards come to mind in those churches. Comparisons are made with what was and what might be. Things fall in place. A sense of sequence emerges. The self becomes felt — and I know full well how hard it is to define words like the "self," and how hard put I would be to "prove" exactly when and in what form one "feels" that "self." Yet that miner knows what it is about — suddenly and for a moment to be agitated and excited, to blush and flush or turn pale, to heave and tremble and warm up, and finally, as he says it, "to get thinking about yourself." He cannot, any more than I can, "define" himself, his self, after he has done all that thinking, but he can say a few things which indicate his experiences and questions to be not so unlike those of sophisticated theologians: "I don't ever 'see' God, the way some people say they do. He comes to me, though — I guess His Spirit is what comes. I don't hear His voice, not like others will. I guess I'm not the kind. All I know is that before I go to church I'll be in a bad mood, maybe, or worried about something — the usual things you worry about. Then I'll leave church — not always, but sometimes — and I've changed my outlook. I'm ready to be more patient, like the minister says — but it's not because I'm paying attention to him and listening to him and obeying him. It's because we'll be singing, you know, or praying, and I feel myself changing, yes sir, and I'm more awake, that's the only way I know how to tell you. Then I'll recall other times, when I'd be in trouble here or there, and how we managed to keep on going, and I'll recall my dad, his telling me that God is watching over us, and when He wants us, He'll come and get us, and there's no point trying to figure out the time, because it's not our decision to make, but His. My dad also said the thing you have to remember is that each day might be the last one, and if you can just live like that, as though you knew that, then you'd probably end up all right before Him, God.

"Of course, you never can be perfect; I mean you'll have the best intentions — and when you're in church and you get all taken up with the Spirit, that's the time you have the best intentions, but there will be backsliding, there always will be. I don't think a man is a man if he doesn't some of the time lose his temper and be — well, unfair to those around him. All I know, though, is that sometimes over there in that little church of ours I feel there's forgiveness in this world, and the good Lord, He's near us, and He isn't going to let us get completely taken over by the bad in the world, the bad that's in yourself and the bad that's in others. But like the Bible will tell you, it's a big struggle, and no matter if you're high or low, you're going to be fighting the struggle all your life, and a lot of the time you'll be near to losing, with the devil just about to claim you his property, but then you'll be singing a hymn or like that, and you'll turn around and realize you're in danger and get saved in the nick of time, yes sir, right in the nick."

The devil is there in him, then; and the devil must be exorcised. Temptations are to be expected, and they must be challenged, though not with the idea there is any decisive victory to be had, at least in this life on this earth. Fear and trembling, the very kind Kierkegaard knew, and before him St. Augustine, are also very much a danger and (as this miner more suggests than explicitly declares) are a constant source of temptation. Indeed, among the poor and weak there are plenty of reasonable grounds for fear and for trembling, so the line between justifiable fright and apprehension on the one hand and self-pitying panic on the other becomes necessarily blurred. Moreover, that miner, and others like him, and many sharecroppers I have met and this migrant worker whose words I am about to set down know rather a lot about the so-called "aesthetic aspect" of religious activity,[6] as I rather belatedly began to realize when I heard these remarks: "We're on the move a lot, and I guess even in church we can't sit completely still. When the minister comes to us in the field, I don't want to do much but listen to him, and a lot of the time I don't hear him too good. But in Belle Glade it's different, because there's a good church there. I can come in and sit down, and the seat is good and we all sit down and like it. I can get rest; but it's not that I feel tired and go off to sleep, no sir. I feel comfortable, that's how I feel; and I like to look at the windows they've got, with the pictures of Jesus Christ and His men, who were with Him when they were hunting Him down — and they got Him and killed Him.

"Once my wife said she'd like to stay in the church all the rest of her life and not move from it; but I told her you can't. Church is for Sundays, and that's the way it has to be. I'll be out there picking beans, and I'll be real worn down, and ready to quit. Then I'll think of the church there in Belle Glade, or the others we know when we're out of Florida and up in Virginia or New York, and once I've thought of them, I'll feel better. In my mind there will be the benches and the pictures on the walls and the windows and the altar with the flowers and most of all Him — and you know, you have to remember that the Lord God Himself didn't have a much better life than we do, and maybe worse, much worse.

"The singing is what my kids like, and so do I. With the songs you find yourself getting real close to Him. Sometimes I'll be singing, or the chorus will be, and the organ is going, and I get to feel weak and I'm soon acting like my wife — I mean, I'll get to have some tears, and I can't for the life of me tell you why. I'll say to myself: now why are you crying, and no answer comes to me, so I don't know the reason. When I was a boy my mother would take us to church, and my father would be sleeping — usually because he drank a lot on Saturday nights, and so he couldn't get up. She'd cry, my mother. She'd be singing and my sister would poke me and I'd look up and see her cheeks all wet, and then my sister would start, and I would try real hard not to, but sometimes you can't control yourself. It's a bad time we have, as bad as my father did in his life. I don't drink anything, no wine or beer — nothing that will get me drunk. It's not what the minister says that stops me. To be honest it's that I can see my dad lying there dead-drunk on Sunday morning, and my mother crying later in church. Maybe that's why I still cry; it's a habit you can't shake off.

"I like it best when we all stand up and say what we think, and then the minister and the people next to you, they'll talk and talk and give you the strength to go on. Mr. Thomas is the best of all the ministers. He can shout and he can sing and he can pray and he can speak right to you. He'll leave that altar over there in Belle Glade and come down the aisle and he'll look into you — into your eyes — and stare and stare until you're all shaking and trembling and you're afraid you're going to fall on the floor or go run and hide. He's after the truth, that man is. He wants to find you out and tell God about you and tell you about God. He'll get us singing and get us talking and get us confessing, and pretty soon you won't know if you've been there a day or a week. All you know is that you're paying attention, because it's the most important thing in your life to do so, and it's what counts.

"You have to have Someone who will save you. A man like me works all the time and crosses all over the country trying to get by — he's going to need the Lord. I tell my kids every day that the Lord had troubles, just like ours. I tell my kids every day that they shouldn't forget that in God's eyes we're better people than those growers think, or the sheriff. To hear them, we're no good, not one little bit good; but if you pay attention to what the Bible says, then you *are* good — a lot better, maybe, than all the rich folks. I wouldn't mind having the money, mind you; I certainly wouldn't. But if we're never going to live an easy life, at least we can stop right still, come Sunday, and take ourselves to hear about Him and all they did to Him and how He never did have the big people, the rich people, the important people, out there helping Him, and they killed Him, that's what, and you know the sheriff and the growers would as soon do it to us, the same way, if they didn't need us to pull in all the crops and to separate everything out in the packing plants and all like that.

"If you don't feel you're all alone, you and your people, then you can go on better, and that's why you'll see a lot of us come to the church and pay attention, because in our religion, it's God who is on our side, not on the side of the foreman and the bossman over him and the police who always are patrolling the camp, and they call us every bad name you can think of. My little girl, she went out and held a picture of Jesus Christ up right before their eyes, for them to see. They said she was out of her mind, and they grabbed the picture and told her she'd better watch out, being fresh like that, and 'playing around.' That's what they said: 'playing around with pictures of God' — and where did she get the picture, they wanted to know. My girl was afraid to say anything. She told me later she was all set to tell them — that it was at church where she got the picture, and she wanted them not to forget what the minister said, how God is looking down upon us and He sees everything that happens. I'm glad she didn't, though. I'm glad she didn't start anything with the police — because you know we'd all be in jail, the child and the rest of us. They'll do that; they'll say either you do what they want or everyone goes in the cell until the police decide to let them out. Oh no, no sir, it never gets to any judge. The police do what they want. They are the judges. They'll take you in and let you sit there in a cell, and by that time, after sitting there day and night, you'll say anything to be let out.

"Once the police picked me up and told me I was drinking too much. I hadn't touched anything like beer or wine, but I was talking to the others and saying we should ask for more money, and I had the picture cards they give you at church, of Jesus Christ on one side and on the other the name of the church and a message from the Bible. They came and grabbed the cards and they thought I was handing out 'Communist stuff,' they said. I didn't know what they were talking about and I still don't, except that you can figure it out: the growers don't want us to become part of a union, and the police work for the growers. The foremen call the police, and they come. And when they're poking you with a gun, it helps if you know that Jesus Christ, the Son of God, was also dragged away and put in jail, or someplace like it, and before He could have known what to do, they were calling Him all the bad names, like they do us, and telling Him either he went along and didn't cause them the trouble, or they'd go and sentence Him — and they did, and they didn't give Him any mercy, none at all."

No, they didn't; nor does this worker get much mercy from those who herd him and his family all over the nation, and pay them sums like fifty or sixty cents an hour for stoop labor. Yet he knows the word mercy, knows what it means, has experienced mercy, the kind a tired and hurt person receives when he learns that Almighty God Himself was also tired and hurt and repeatedly betrayed. It was merciful of God to appear among men as a humble man, a lonely man, an exile and a wanderer, abused, insulted, mocked, condemned, and eventually tortured and killed. And when one is living an extremely humble life oneself, when one knows from daily experience how arbitrary and mean high and proper people can be, when one has heard again and again about lynchings or has been pushed and shoved and threatened by the gun-carrying guards of migrant camps — then it does come as rather a surprise, as rather extraordinary, as almost unbelievable, that God actually saw fit to be as merciful as to choose the kind of life He did.

The more one listens to migrant farmers and tenant farmers, to self-described "mountain people" in western North Carolina and to self-described "hill people" in, say, the southern part of West Virginia, the more one understands of what theologians conceptualize as "grace" and "charity" and the "forgiveness of sins" and "the mystery of faith" and "redemption through faith." The people described in this book by and large know the Bible, know some kind of church, know what it means to pray long and hard.[7] They also know in their bones what others talk about and speculate upon; they know and live out "resignation" and "estrangement." They feel a certain soreness of mind and body. They know what it is to feel cursed by the rest of mankind. They know what self-doubt is and abandonment. They sometimes wonder whether they are not now, right now, in Hell. Heaven is to them a constant vision — even as water is to a thirsty man crossing a desert. Here is how the wife of a sharecropper in Alabama[8] makes that last comparison. She reminds me that her life and Christ's are not unlike, which is not a presumptuous or blasphemous thought for her and her minister to have, but rather something for all of us to wonder about and maybe get nervous over, as perhaps Jesus Christ originally intended: "I truly believe if God didn't have a purpose for us suffering here in Alabama, we wouldn't be. That's what I believe. If you don't believe that, then you're denying God, aren't you? You're saying He overlooks some of His children, and He lets some of His children go and be mean, real bad mean to others of His children, which is the way it is now — right? The only way you can make sense of this world is by thinking like the minister does, the reverend, and he's correct, real correct. He says, 'The last are going to be first,' and he says Jesus said that, and He meant it, and that's why He came down here, to prove it to us with His example.

"A lot of the time I'll be thinking that there's no point in going on. Then I'll remind myself that I may feel bad and I may feel sorry for myself, but there's the sky up there and there's the next day coming, and just like there's the next day there's the next life, and that's when the Judgment Day will be, and we won't be so bad off then, like now. I truly believe so. It's not for anyone to speak for God, I know that; but He did His speaking, and you mustn't ever forget what He said. I think we're born to be tested, and we're always being tested around here, that's for sure. In the same way Jesus was being tested all the time. They'd ask Him this and they'd ask Him that, and a lot of people just didn't believe Him, and they didn't like Him and they got Him after a while, they killed Him, and it was terrible.

"I'll wake up sometimes and I'll ask myself whether it's going to be today that something real bad will happen. Some days just go fast and nothing real bad happens, but all of a sudden we'll get a lot of troubles come our way, and it makes you wonder if you can last. It's then that you stop and remind yourself the Lord is up there, and He doesn't miss a single trick. I mean, how could He? No sir, He's not about to let the bossmen get away with things. Someday they'll be up there, all those bossmen, and they'll be standing in line, waiting on God's decision. The bad people we've got here, who own everything and give the poor folk nothing, they'll be sent down to Hell, right direct to the place, and no place to stop on the way, and no escaping — no sir, no escaping what He decides. Of course, I admit that every once in a while I catch myself getting worried. That's when I'll say to myself that maybe *this* is Hell, right where we are, right here.

And it's not a good thought to have. It's a bad one! But sometimes you can't help yourself. Sometimes you get to thinking."

There it is, faith and doubt, utter conviction and skepticism, resigned acceptance of God's will and His mysteries and a gnawing suspicion that maybe justice might *never* be done, here or "up there" or anywhere. Those sentences, those avowals and disclaimers and questions and self-supplied answers demonstrate the loneliness before God and passionate acceptance of Him that have alternated in saints and sinners throughout the centuries. If I were asked to summarize what the churches "do" for those who live up the Appalachian hollows or in the Mississippi Delta or around Florida's Belle Glade and Bean City and Pahokee, I would begin by emphasizing that the churches provide a sanctuary. In Europe some (but by no means all) churches have traditionally provided sanctuary to outcasts, fugitives and vagabonds, wanderers and runaways. Today in America the sanctuary a church might offer is thought about often — by those who in fact might have few conventional religious loyalties. The poor rural people I am writing about find in those churches, mostly small and simple, a real chance for escape, for haven, for respite from a tough daily life. Yet sanctuary is not the only thing found. There is also the joy that comes with listening to music, with praying, with singing, with *saying things* — for when things go unspoken too long moroseness and despair result. A tenant farmer in North Carolina apologetically but earnestly described the way it can get for him: "God forgive me, I sometimes can't say a word and I don't believe in God or anything — only in the mean, mean bossmen; they're always around, and you can depend on them to be watching you."

If the expressiveness of religious services helps foster joyfulness, helps also release bottled-up resentments and fears and qualms, the same quality of those services brings peace and calm as well as excitement or relief. What is more, people constantly hard pressed, unable to do much more than live from minute to minute and day to day, can for a few minutes of at least one day sit down and ponder things and find in life a little structure, a little shape. Also to be found is an answer to isolation, a sense of belonging. Much is made today of the word "community," but in 1962, near Burnsville, North Carolina, I watched a rural mountain community begin to appear and assemble in front of a church and later that day I heard the meaning of the word discussed: "We're a community, and on Sunday you know it most, that's when. You come down from the hills and there she is, our church, that we built with our own hands. We want to see each other, now that the whole week has gone by, and we want to tell the news and have the day of rest and visiting we need — one out of seven! If we didn't go to church, we'd not be neighbors to a lot of people. There are kin I see only on Sundays, only then. It's the one day I can put on that suit of mine, and see my wife real dressed up, and the kids dressed up, too; and we look like we're out of the catalogue that tries to sell you on those clothes. It's the way you *should* look, going to the Lord's house, and being serious about it. I know, like the reverend will say, that you shouldn't let your pride run away with you and look too fancy, when it's the praying that's the important thing; but like he says, there's nothing wrong with looking real good for Jesus Christ, and if you come dirty-looking, why that's disrespectful. So I try to be as clean and fresh as I can on Sunday morning."

Thus does a man describe the genuinely felt communion of a group of parishioners; and as well, the formal and neighborly quality to those Sunday mornings, the *occasions* that they are. He and others all over feel stronger on late Sunday afternoon for what they have gone through on Sunday morning. They also feel more in touch with things, more aware of what is happening about them, and better able to face the next day, the next week. Perhaps most of all, such people feel they have somehow obtained *sanction*. Again and again I have heard from them, all of them mentioned and described in this book and many others, a virtual cry for approval, for authorization of sorts — and here I feel the awkwardness of language: "I come out of there and I'm taller. I'm feeling bigger. I feel God has taken me to Him. He put His hand on my shoulder, and said, 'Brother John Wilson, the reason that I want you praying to me is so you won't be looking at yourself and feeling so low. Brother John, it stands to reason that if I'm going to be looking after you, then you're OK, yes you are, and don't let anyone tell you otherwise.'

"The reverend tells us to listen to God all the time, but you don't need him to tell you, because you know you should. My daddy used to tell me when I was a boy that he didn't want my spirit to go and break, and if I prayed to God, He'd keep me strong, and I'd never lose my spirit, no matter how bad they treat you, and no matter what words they call you, the bad words — and Lord, you sometimes wonder where they get all those swearwords for a colored man, and here I am, working on their land, their own land, and planting for them and harvesting for them. But like Jesus Christ learned when He was here on earth, if you don't have respect for yourself, then no one's going to go and give it to you, and that sure goes for us here. That's why I'll have my time of praying, and I'll feel like it says in the Bible, a new man — because He's nodded at me and given me His blessing and said, 'Brother John, you're an all right man, even if you do slip and stumble every once in a while. So you keep right on going, and I'm right up here, looking down on you, and it'll be OK. Bad as it is, you'll come through, yes sir.' That's what He might be saying to me — to us. I sure hope so, that He's on our side."

Although migrant farmers, sharecroppers and the mountaineers of Appalachia are in many ways quite different and distinct groups of people, they have in common not only their closeness to the land but their closeness to God's Word, to churches and the life that goes on inside a certain kind of church. I am talking about a faith that is fundamentalist, that has no desire to reinterpret Scripture in the light of nineteenth- and twentieth-century scientific discoveries. I am talking about people who hear the Bible and memorize its words much more than they read it. I am talking about people who see no reason to worry and fret because there are inconsistencies and contradictions and ambiguities in that Book — and contrary to what many of us may believe, those contradictions, those "troubles" I once heard them called up in Swain County, North Carolina, do not go unnoticed. The churches I have attended with the people who speak in this book have been Baptist churches, Pentecostal churches, Holiness churches — and often enough they are churches best described in long sentences by the minister himself and the worshipers themselves, rather than by the use of denominational labels.

In my experience there is nothing about the life of rural people that is less understood by their city-bred sympathizers and advocates than the nature of so-called fundamentalist religious faith. The social, economic and political condition, not to mention the medical and psychological problems of, say, sharecroppers, all command wide and sympathetic interest from well-educated people who are truly horrified that America continues to allow some of its people to live in a state of near peonage. Every effort is made by liberals and progressives to comprehend the so-called life-styles of the rural poor, and often enough those efforts are made in a sensitive and fair spirit that shuns condescension and patronizing pity. Nor do we merely try to understand; we proudly consider ourselves supporters, well-wishers, champions of the poor and the miserable, of America's version of Frantz Fanon's "wretched of the earth." The language of tenant farmers, the traveling and living habits of migrants, the music played and sung up in the hollows — all of that we can look upon with discernment and insight and (we hope) not a little compassion and empathy. But our forbearance wears thin at the church door. True, the aesthetic side of religious practice may enlist a spark of recognition and interest and acceptance in us, but to fundamentalist theology we can only say no. As for the social and political "effects" of all that prayer, we are likely to think this way: what hardships they face, in return for a promise that another world will redeem this one's evils! And what energy and imagination and combativeness is week by week drained away, carried off in a noisy, superstitious tide of prayers and hymns, all meant to make people compliant, slightly dazed, and ridiculously hopeful — in the face of the awful circumstances that characterize their "objective condition"!

In reply many poor people working on plantations or on small farms up along the Cumberland Mountains or the Allegheny Mountains might say, "True, true," an expression that is used by just about all the people I have worked with in the rural areas east of the Mississippi. As I indicated earlier, those same people are not quite so oblivious to the intellectual and political critiques some of us would make of "churchgoing among the rural poor." After a few years of visiting some of the people described in the earlier sections of this book I finally was able to summon enough courage to present a few of my own doubts and suspicions — to people whom I had badly underestimated. In Martin County, Kentucky, I heard the reply of "true, true" after I had cautiously joined in when an entire family began to register objections to a minister's line of thought that Sunday. The minister had pointed out how "transient" and "temporary" all our "worldly ills" are, and the father of the house, a onetime coal miner now injured for life and barely able to live off the small farm he has, said at suppertime that "temporary" could be a long, long time, it seems.

I knew the man's laconic, proud, understated ways, and so I was particularly moved to hear him speak — as he sat before a meal of cornbread, pork that was just about all fat, and coffee without milk. I also felt the need to say something myself, so I did. I remarked upon the nice car the reverend drove and observed as quietly as I could that maybe a new car helps one take the long view, helps make life's serious problems seem like nothing, nothing at all. "True, true," he replied, and then hesitated, while I thought he was only agreeing with me: "I'll wonder a lot about God, and if he meant for us to get near Him by going to church and listening to ministers. We get them one after the other as they come through. Then they go on to the next church and the next one — their circuit, you know. I don't have anything against them, though. They're no better or worse than the rest of us. They come here and tell you to take heed of God and the really important things, the salvation of your soul; so if they'll say some silly things in the bargain, then what can you expect but that?

"When we were down in the mines, cutting away there, and with every cut facing a landslide and death so swift you'd not know what hit you — well, it was then that we'd get to talking about God and about going to church and about what it means:

life and living and dying, I guess. A lot of us would laugh at the
talk you hear in church, about salvation coming only to the weak
and the meek and the poor and the humble. We'd say we'd like
to be the owners of those mines and be sitting up in the offices
where the bosses are, and then we'd take our chances with going
to Heaven or Hell. It's not that we were being disrespectful, don't
get me wrong. We hated being down there, more than you ever
can admit to yourself while you're there. We'd hear the same
thing we hear now — in the church that stands there right beside
the mine. The minister would tell us we were so lucky, being
poor, because we'd be going to Heaven, while the rich fellow,
he'd never go any place but Hell. The way I see it, you don't hold
it against the Bible, because it says that. The Bible is trying to tell
you the truth, and the truth is that the mine owners are sinners,
every one of them, for the way they treat us and sit back and let
us get killed in those mines — while they take in the fat profits
and send them up to Pittsburgh and New York and wherever the
money goes, everywhere but here in Kentucky. The Bible says a
man who lets another man die while he goes and lives off the fat
of the land, that's a man who God wouldn't want around Him.
And the Bible is right. But God can't come down here and run
the show; if He could, the world wouldn't be like this. I mean to
say, God may be on our side, but we're going to have to fight for
ourselves; and the reason we pray to Him, that's what I believe,
is to get the strength to fight for ourselves. If you really believe
that God is on your side, then you'll go and fight all the harder
for your rights. At least that's what we used to say down there in
the mines.

"I'll admit there are times I wonder about things. I ask myself
why don't all the ministers go and call on the mine owners and
people like that and tell *them* they're sinners. A lot of good it
does *us* to know that! Maybe some ministers do that, but I've
never heard of it. You can tell that the minister in the church near
our mine is all cozy with the owners. He'll never say anything out
of line. The ones that come through here, the ones that go on the
circuit from one church to the other, some of them are better
than others. But I don't believe we're supposed to believe every-

thing that ministers say. Only the Bible. They'll read the Bible, and sometimes I can go along real good, and sometimes I'm not clear on what it all means. I ask myself questions a lot of Sundays. I'll be there in church, sitting and praying, and I'll get ideas in my mind. I'll say to myself, why *are* we here, and what's it all mean? If God knows in advance how it's all going to turn out, then why does He bother putting us through this?

"I remember once when we were all trapped, twenty-eight of us, and we thought for sure we were gone. We held on to each other and waited down there, and we gave ourselves maybe a minute, maybe ten minutes. During the war, the Second World War, they talked about there being no atheists in the foxholes. I remember that; I'm old enough to remember. Well, we turned pretty fast; I mean we were atheists one second and believers the next. First we wanted to know how God could let something like that happen. Then one guy, my friend Allen McGuire, spoke up — and you know, a year later he got killed, in a second he was killed by a landslide down that same mine. Allen said we should pray to God and stop complaining and calling Him and everyone else names and doubting Him. Another guy, I think it was Bob Smith, said he agreed we should ask why God let these things happen, but he said it wasn't God's business to tell us how we should do things, run the coal mines and like that, and we should look to Him for guidance, but we're the ones that have to figure out how to act. We ended up sitting there, every minute expecting to die, and talking about what a good Christian is, just like the minister talks on Sundays. I'll never forget that time down there. I think it made a better Christian out of me. I know it's not for me but God to decide who's a good Christian, but at least I'm no fool, expecting Him to come and make life easy for us and get even with the coal companies and those politicians. I think a lot of ministers could have learned something if they'd heard Bob Smith talking, yes, they would. That's where I think you can go wrong on Sundays, expecting a few hours of prayer to change the state of Kentucky, or this country here. No sir, that's never going to happen.

"I get real discouraged a lot of the time, I admit. I'll be sitting

around here and wishing I had my health back and wishing I
could find a job and wishing I'd at least have obtained a pension
and some insurance money instead of that thousand dollars they
awarded me, the company did, for being 'temporarily disabled,'
they said. I'm 'temporarily disabled' all right. I can barely plant a
row of corn without having to sit and catch my breath for an
hour. That's why I didn't like the reverend talking about how fast
your life goes compared to eternity. To me, eternity is now. It's a
long, long time from sunrise to sunset when you're having trouble
catching your breath, and you don't have the money to get the
food you need for yourself and your family, and let me tell you,
it's a long time from sunset to sunrise, too. I'll be tossing and
turning there in bed and wondering what will be the end of it:
the trouble I have, and the troubles the kids have — the ailing
they do. I know if I had the money I could get them to a doctor.
Here up in the hollow if we need a car ride, it costs almost as
much as I'll spend on food, unless your kin can help. We don't
have a car, except for my oldest boy, and he's in Ohio — Dayton,
it is. He'll be of help to us after a while. He's just gone there. It's
awful bad, knowing your child is the one who's going to make
the difference, bail you out of a million troubles. Of course, he
shouldn't have to do so. He has his own life.

"In the night I'll think of God, and what He'd like for us to do.
I'll think of what we've heard in church. I'll think of my father.
My father was a real proud man; he hated to leave here and go
work in those mines, but the money was too much to resist. He
left after a while; he said he either would leave or one day he'd
be buried down there. A month after he left, there were forty-
eight killed all of a sudden, including my father's brother, and
they used to work together. My father believed in God. He knew
how to read the Bible; that's all he knew to read or ever did read.
He could recite passages by heart. He'd do that in one breath,
and then he'd tell us that a lot of ministers are holding the hands
of the mine owners and getting paid to do nothing much except
tell us to be quiet and law-abiding. Ministers will tell you that, to
be calm and not go getting violent. My father said that even so
we should go to church, and the church belongs to God, and

He'll have his bad ministers, like there are bad in every type of person. He was betrayed by one of His disciples, way back there, and it still happens.

"The way I see it, on Sunday you get a chance to go together, the whole family, and collect yourself, that's how I'd put it, *collect* yourself — and you're doing it right before God. If the minister says something foolish, which he'll do from time to time, then he's going to have to square himself before God, too — and I'll bet a lot of those reverends, they've got some explaining to do before Him, God. You could say I learned that from my father, and I've never forgotten it, how it's not the minister who is God, but God who is God. And down in that mine, when we thought we'd all be killed pretty soon, I believe that's what we all knew. We all said if we were going to be called by God right there and then — well, that's all right, but we didn't want to hear that because we're poor and the next guy is rich, that's fine and God wants it like that or else He'd come and change things. No minister could tell me that and have me believe him."

He wants and needs an explanation not only for his acknowledged misery but for a million injustices he knows exist all over the world: up and down the mountains and in cities — indeed, wherever there are people. He is not willing to accept what he is told by a particular minister, and he even senses but doesn't talk about some of the tensions and contradictions that preoccupy more theological minds than his. Implicitly, though, he makes his point: there is God and there is the church and there is man. The minister is a mediator between man and God — through an institution, which is the church. As for the Bible, it is God's Word — but heard and written down by men. Does that mean he really dares question God's Word as revealed by the Bible? If so, can he not be considered a free-thinker, a corrupted modern man — like so many of us? He seems not to worry about such things. He reads the Bible, and in so doing becomes stronger, speaks louder, feels more certain about things. Something happens to him that is physical; I have seen it happen as grace is said over a meal the vast majority of American citizens would find hard to eat, let alone say grace over. He would indeed like more food, different kinds of food, especially milk for his children, but he is not about to be pitied, and he would rise in anger at anyone who wanted to lecture him on the sad, sad life he and his kinfolk must live.

Proud, defiant, and independent, he can speak like a prophet, like Isaiah and Jeremiah. He can denounce evil and treacherous people who seem to be everywhere and know in his bones that there is a *point* to denunciation, that Someone is listening, that voices of lamentation and exhortation will be heard by Him, the voice of voices. And such conviction must certainly constitute the very heart of religious faith.

I am reminded of Kierkegaard's formulations (in *Fear and Trembling* and *Repetition*) because like him this mountaineer in essence demands a *particular* relationship with God, one that in the clutch will gladly dispose of all intermediaries, be they ministers, politicians, secular propagandists, wise neighbors and friends — and yes, overbearing would-be advocates and helpers. What is more, signs of resignation appear again and again in his words and sentiments — and I say resignation, not depression or despair. He knows what Kierkegaard knew[9] and spent a short lifetime attempting to describe: the wishes and dreams that men have during their brief time on this earth are not the stuff of faith, but rather are obstacles to faith or distractions from it. Yet, again in company with Kierkegaard, the mountaineer understands that he is human, that he is bound to demand and expect the impossible (from himself, from others and from God) but that ultimately whatever goes on between him and Him, as it were, is mysterious and beyond rational calculation or analysis. "Who can ever think he's got God's design figured out but a fool?" I once heard that mountaineer ask. No doubt the tormented Danish theologian would have smiled, had he been there to listen.

Whether the miner or others like him ever come to the point of Kierkegaard's *teleological suspension of the ethical*, as in Abraham's willingness to sacrifice his son to God, if need be, no man can ever determine. I have often wondered, though, as I talk with miners about to descend into the bowels of the earth, whether in some fashion many of them haven't in their ordinary, everyday lives made some of the "motions of faith" or "movements of the spirit" that Kierkegaard writes about at such length. Life to those miners (and to so many migrants and sharecroppers) is comically and tragically absurd, yet has to be confronted and not only lived but in so far as it is possible, understood. If life is absurd, then faith can easily become one more hopeless effort to make sense of the absurd — which is *not* what that miner wishes to do. The paradox of faith always has to do with transcendence, with the mind's ability to see what prompts it to faith (one need not be a psychiatrist for that kind of self-awareness; indeed, many psychiatrists sorely lack it) and then go on to renounce precisely that kind of faith — because such faith becomes recognized as an expression of man's sinfulness, and so one more reason for him to be forgiven, especially by a Christ Who went through the same sort of experience on the Cross, when for a moment He felt abandoned and forsaken and knew not why, in view of *His* explicitly avowed and undeniable faith.

All of this gets complex and unfathomable, which is just the point, because a simpleminded "give-and-take" religiosity (in contrast to religiousness) is exactly what makes the miner and Kierkegaard both shudder. I am good, so be good to me, dear God — in a sentence like that one can summarize the pharisaical pieties that so many of us manage to embrace at one time or another. If any group of people could perhaps be forgiven such a direction of thought and belief, these people here in this book are the ones. Yet, I see little of that kind of religious bargaining among them, perhaps just because they know the concrete experience of hunger and pain and solitariness and abandonment. These people know "existential despair": the assaults of what seems like the entire universe rain upon them and their children all day and in the many waking moments of the night, when the empty stomach intrudes upon the brain's consciousness and those sores and injuries and illnesses conspire to say no, you cannot possibly escape from the pain and fear and sadness we impose, not even in your sleep or your dreams. It was Kierkegaard who insisted that men caught up in despair, in "fear and trembling," are not bargain-hungry, churchgoing burghers, and maybe for that reason are nearer to God's Spirit.

The wife of one of the tenant farmers I came to know had her shrill and bombastic times with the language of the Christian religion, but as with the miner, I think she was struggling for something, and out of the hard, tangible, dreary particulars of her life she came up with what she called "a religious philosophy." I have to acknowledge the times I concluded she was offering me examples of "peasant wisdom," which means, I now realize, she was closer to Bethlehem and Galilee and Nazareth than I fear people like me will ever get, certainly as long as we look upon people like her with that peculiar kind of pride that variously masks itself as effusive pity or clever abstractness: "Every time I open my eyes in the morning, the first thing and right away, I whisper to God, thank you. My husband has got used to it. There was a time he'd ask me what I'm talking about, but then I told him. Now he'll join me every once in a while, and add his thank you to Him, to God. We're not expecting much, mind you; I know He isn't going to come down here like someone out of Washington, D.C., and start telling the plantation-owner people to stop driving us, and give us some more of the money from what our land makes each year. The people out of Washington talk a lot, but they don't do all that much, from what we can see. I guess they're afraid of our Mr. Wallace. I remember him, you know, when he was a boy. He was always getting into things, and he still is.

"You know, don't you, that God has His own purpose, it's a 'design,' like you hear in church, and it's not for us to figure out. But there's one thing I know after all this living — yes sir, after all this living — and that's how foolish you are if you start the day, or the year even, waiting for the good Lord to come into the state of Alabama and straighten everything out and make us all be good to each other. My mother prayed harder than anyone I ever knew. There was one day when my older brother asked my mother a hard question. He asked my mother why she did the praying, because when she'd get through she would still have to tell us we can't have much for dinner, and things are real, real bad for us. Then my mother turned on Edward, and I thought she was going to hit him hard, real hard, but instead she just pulled him up to her, real close, and said what she had to say. She told Edward and all of us listening that we don't pray to God so He'll change the people of Alabama. She told us that the people of Alabama will meet God, one of these days, the governor and all of them, the sheriffs and the others, and even if we'd like to be around to see what happens, it's God's business what happens and no one else's. He's not up there to settle things between those bossmen and us. He's not there to make white folks and black folks come together.

"Like you hear when the preacher reads to you from the Bible, Jesus Christ had to suffer all the time. The Lord God, did He come rushing over there to where His only Son was and stop them all and tell them to leave Him alone? No sir, He didn't, and I'll tell you why: because we're here on trial, and how we behave is up to us, and if we're rich or poor, it's up to us, the way we treat each other. True, later on, we're going to be judged, yes sir, we are, but that's not going to take place in Alabama. So, if the police and the governor want to come and be mean to us, and if the plantation owner wants to squeeze us and take our money away, as much of it as he thinks he can get, then God Almighty can't do a thing about it, not during our lifetime He can't. It was a long time ago, like the preacher says, that God told us we're all going to be left alone here to be good and be bad, and He's stuck by His decision ever since, I think He has. That's how my mother saw it and that's how I see it.

"My mother taught us to think like that. She taught Edward and me and the rest of us. She never convinced Edward; no sir, he went unpersuaded, I'll tell you — and as soon as he could, he left us. My mother told him he was hunting after something he'd never get, because up North they're no better people than down here, but Edward told her she was as wrong as can be, and now he sends us the money he makes in Detroit, working on those automobiles, and he tells us with his notes that we're crazy to stay here. My husband agrees with my mother, with what she used to say, and so I guess that's why I'm still here. I'd leave if he wanted to. I was closer to my mother than Edward, and even though she's gone now two years I can still hear her voice, saying this and saying that. There'll be a time in church when I get the Spirit in me, and later I don't even recall what happened or what I said, but my husband does, and he claims it's hard to understand some of it, but a lot of it is my mother talking, her and no one else. He says it's not just the words, it's her voice, and he says I keep on saying what she used to say, about Alabama and God and us here on the plantation, and then I'll go on to something else, and then he says I'll lose him and all the others, and the minister says it's the Spirit, the Holy Spirit, taking over and making me talk, you know. I can't tell you any more, because I don't know any more."

I suppose, like her husband, I am left to say what I have observed and heard during the times I have gone with the family to the small church about three miles from their home. On Sundays they go there for the whole day. They start at nine-thirty and stay till about one in the afternoon. They break for food, which they have brought to the church, and at about three there are further prayers spoken, hymns sung, and spirituals cried out — with foot-stomping and arms held up and bodies not infrequently bent forward and then backward. By six or seven they are all home, tired, "cleaned out" in soul and heart, but also "real freshened up" in soul and heart. During that long day what does the tenant farmer's wife do, besides repeat her mother's advice and warnings, given long ago and remembered so vividly? Often I have heard her begin what I suppose can be called "glossalalia" or "speaking in tongues" with the phrase "after all this living." What follows is, of course, largely incomprehensible, if very emotional, eye-catching, exhausting, confusing — and at times alarming, at times utterly compelling. So, I cannot answer the question I just asked. I cannot even put down in rough, unedited form much of what I hear her say when she "goes off," as her husband describes it. But I can observe that there came a point in most of her "episodes," as I guess I came to think of them when my mind at last stopped counting, counting this and analyzing that and waiting, always waiting, attentively waiting — for something intelligible, something that can be explained, fathomed, held on to, turned into "material" for formulations. Often in that church I felt quite alone as well as anxious, and my loneliness and anxiety took such disguised forms as concern for a person's health or worry over the possibility he or she might be having a seizure, a stroke, a mental "break" of some sort — or God knows what. I mean no sarcasm, nor do I intend to indicate my confusion or ignorance, when I resort to the expression "God knows what." Who but He can possibly comprehend what is, anyway, claimed to be just that, His Spirit, the Holy Spirit, coming to its own, dark, cryptic and baffling expression? Still, she cannot, even when "going off" manage to forget "all this living"; and it is exactly that living which provides her with what I can only call the "substance" of her faith. Put differently, the source of her particular prayers, of her worship, of her emotionally religious allegiance is her life itself, her life as a black Alabama tenant farmer's wife.

In a nearby county I have come to know (and go to church with) a white tenant farmer's family, and heard from the wife of that tenant farmer rather similar religious concerns and convictions. White or black, tenant farmers in Alabama or Mississippi or North Carolina are all hard pressed, are all at the constant mercy of uncertain and mostly unsympathetic "forces." All of them are people who live intimately with the land — God's earth, they feel it to be, seized perhaps by greedy owners and manipulators, but ultimately a creation of His. The white woman, in many respects a counterpart to the black woman, says much of what I want to say rather more directly than I seem able to do: "We're God-fearing, yes, we are. I was told I'd better be by my daddy and my mother, and they were right. God isn't going to appear one of these days and save you from all your worries; no, He's not. He's up there, and He's waiting. So long as you're alive and struggling to make ends meet, all you can do is pray and try to get as close as you can to Him, and then struggle along here

with the crops and with the people who own all this land — and
they drive a hard bargain, I'll say that about them, and my
husband has told you so a thousand times, I know.

"Sometimes I lose myself in church, and my husband does the
same way. I don't recall what it is I'm saying, except one thing I
can recall, and it's in my head a lot of the time: I'm standing on
our land, with my feet in it, far enough so you can't see my
ankles even, and my knees are where I'm above the ground. It's
as though I was becoming a carrot or a beet or like that. I'm
trying to speak with God, to say something to Him; I think
mostly, though, it's that I want *Him* to speak to me, to say
something to me. Well, the next thing I know, I'm coming out of
a faint, and I guess the Spirit has taken over me. It's hard to
know why one Sunday it'll happen, and then not for maybe a
couple of weeks. There are some people who go in and out;
they're always seeing something or hearing the voice of God's
Spirit. With me, I'll be sitting and listening or praying, and lo
and behold, I'll be wandering back to our place, in my thoughts,
and there I am, maybe standing near our corn and our tomato
plants, or the hay we have, and the next thing I'm sinking in and
going to sleep, sort of, but it's not anything that would frighten
you, no — not one little bit do I get scared. Of course when I'm
back to my old self I'll ask the kids, sometimes, if they could hear
what I said and if it meant anything to them, and they always
smile and say no, not so far as they can reckon."

Like her children, I have listened hard and come up with
nothing, except that she mingles her babbling, murmuring talk
with spells of mild coherence, with an intelligible phrase here
and an understandable exclamation there, and yes, a plea every
once in a while — that too, and that almost defiantly: "Please,
dear God, please shine upon us. We need your sun, and we need
your rain. We need the sun and the rain for your land. It *is* yours.
It was yours before it was ours, that's for sure. We'll never stop
knowing that, God. The land is yours, and we're here but for a
second on it. Make sure we never forget, we never stop knowing
that."

I have often wondered whether she is *only* addressing God

when she asks Him to make her remember, and make her not forget. In a way, blunted social criticism is what she comes forth with; amid stretches of "glossalalia" she bitterly and imploringly asks all near to know and never stop knowing Who really owns Alabama's land, Who made it and Who one day will descend from Heaven and take possession of the whole world, let alone the rural South. She is heard by no landowners, by no plantation owners, by no stockholders in those enormous "factory farms" that have moved into the South from the West and Midwest. It would be too much to ask that they hear her, and no doubt were she confronted with them there would be her quiet, silent, abiding, completely shy and respectful self — to make them feel as confident and as proprietary as ever. Still, as we have learned in this century, the mind is driven by knowledge it both possesses and fears. Driven minds eventually become vocal, because a human being wants to state things, give them the force of utterance — all of which she tries to do, it seems to me, on those long, long, hot, clammy Sundays, when a voice both soft and drawling yet in a flash high-pitched and sharp and fierce with agitation and earnestness declares Alabama's rich black loam God's, once God's and eternally God's. And alas, it is *we* who stand between now and eternity: that is, she, and the landowners to whom she and her husband are tenants, and those politicians she and others like her talk about, and in fact, the whole struggling, sometimes decent, sometimes indifferent, sometimes harsh and unjust world.

Churchgoing is a very serious matter for all three of the groups I am attempting to describe in this book, but if the three groups are compared, migrants go to church less, miss church more, and produce not more skeptics but more people relatively uninterested in religion. Fundamentalist, Pentecostal religion, like all church life, falls back on the rhythm of the worshiper's life. Many migrant families can't attend the same churches week in and week out: "We have to catch our praying on the go," one migrant farmhand told me, and his wife added a few more observations that have to do with their very special kind of fate, which inevitably makes for a special way of "facing God," as she put it when she started explaining to me, very intensely, how, for all the obstacles of migrancy, her children do indeed have direct meetings with God, almost confrontations with Him, it seems: "I want my children to go and face God. If they're not going to be facing God every week, then how will He ever see them? We're always moving, from one place to the other we move, and if we keep slipping by, and no one sees us except the crew leader, then God could easily miss us, I'm afraid He could. One minister, from the 'ministers for migrants,' I think he said he was, told us not to worry, because God sees *everything*. I hope He does. I believe He does, most of the time I do. Sometimes I'm not too sure, though. I admit it. I told the minister I was glad He was looking out for us, God was, but I wish sometimes He'd go ahead and *do* a little bit for us. But I know it's not going to be like that, because God does things later, after we're gone and died, gone up to Him.

"My husband is not so good about his religion. He'll come with me to church, but he gets real mad a lot of the time. He doesn't like ministers telling us we should be patient — that's the message you'll hear from a lot of them. Of course there are the other kind, and they'll go and fight so you can get better wages. They are our true friends. Last year we went to a little church in New Jersey — we were picking mostly beans and radishes — and I was afraid we'd all be put in jail, the whole family, and it was because of what my husband did. We had all our children there, the baby included. The Reverend Jackson was there, I can't forget his name, and he told us to be quiet, and he told us how glad we should be that we're in this country, because it's Christian, and it's not 'godless.' He kept on talking about the other countries, I forget which, being 'godless.' Then my husband went and lost his temper; something happened to his nerves, I do believe. He got up and started shouting, yes sir. He went up to the Reverend Mr. Jackson and told him to shut up and never speak again — not to us, the migrant people. He told him to go on back to his church, wherever it is, and leave us alone and don't be standing up there looking like he was so nice to be doing us a favor. Then he did the worst thing he could do: he took the baby, Annie, and he held her right before his face, the minister's, and he screamed and shouted and hollered at him, that minister, like I've never before seen anyone do. I don't remember what he said, the exact words, but he told him that here was our little Annie, and she's never been to the doctor, and the child is sick, he knows it and so do I, because she can't hold her food down and she gets shaking fits, and then I'm afraid she's going to die, but thank God she'll pull out of them, and we've got no money, not for Annie or the other ones or ourselves.

"Then he lifted Annie up, so she was higher than the reverend, and he said why doesn't he go and pray for Annie and pray that the growers will be punished for what they're doing to us, all the migrant people. The reverend didn't answer him, I think because he was scared, and then my husband began shouting some more, about God and His neglecting us while He took such good care of the other people all over. Then the reverend did answer — and that was his mistake, yes, it was. He said we should be careful and not start blaming God and criticizing Him and complaining to Him and like that, because God wasn't supposed to be taking care of the way the growers behave and how we live, here on this earth. 'God worries about your *future*'; that's what he said, and I tell you, my husband near exploded. He shouted about ten times to the reverend, 'Future, future, future.' Then he took Annie and near pushed her in the reverend's face and Annie, she started crying, poor child, and he asked the reverend about Annie's 'future' and asked him what he'd do if he had to live like us, and if he had a 'future' like ours. Then he told the reverend he was like all the rest, making money off us, and he held our Annie as high as he could, right near the cross, and told God He'd better stop having the ministers speaking for Him, and He should come and see us for Himself, and not have the 'preachers' — he kept calling them the 'preachers' — speaking for Him.

"I thought he was going to drop Annie, I truly did. I wasn't worried about the reverend; it was Annie I was worried about, and of course my husband. I thought he'd been drinking, that's what I thought, and I couldn't figure out why, because he never does, he never does on Sunday. He takes a few drinks on Saturday night, but he never will before church time on Sunday. But he didn't drink, you know; I found out later he was as sober as he'd ever been in his life. He stopped after he'd finished talking about the 'preachers,' and he came back to us, and there wasn't a sound in the church, no sir, not one could you hear — until a couple of other men said he was right, my husband was, and so did their wives say so, and then I figured maybe he *was* right. I'd been scared, but now I wasn't. My friend Caroline came over and said she wanted to hug my husband, and she said first I should, and I did, and everyone clapped their hands and I felt real funny. I was a little ashamed and worried, on account of the reverend — he just stood there looking out at us, yes — but I was proud of what had been said and spoken by my own husband. Later on I asked him — it was a few days afterwards, I think — if he still believed what he said, and you know he answered yes, he did; he said he believed in God, but he believed God wanted us to stop moving all over and to settle into one place and live there and get some money each week, like the rest of the people do, enough so we can stay alive and not be hungry. That's what he says he believes, and so do I. The reverend, he said he agreed with us, too — and he was sorry we'd misunderstood him, that's what he said happened, and he'd try to make himself clearer, he said. But I don't know if he will or not. If we come back there next summer, I don't know if I'd want to go back to the church. He might even call the police on us, you know; though I don't think so. No, I hope he wouldn't."

Unquestionably, not all migrant workers feel so specially, defiantly religious, and so puzzled and perplexed by the ironies that plague man the believer — man the worshiper of a "just God," as He is described by "preachers" like the one denounced just above. Yet I have found among migrants particularly a rather intense mixture of faith and doubt, of prayerful religious devotion and outright scorn of prayer, of loyalty to the church and deliberate, angry avoidance of ministers. Sharecroppers and mountaineers find in the church a *place* — a place to go and meet neighbors who in fact don't live so near and kin who live a good distance away, especially for people without automobiles. Migrants live abroad the land and have no such sense of place;

indeed, they have an opposite sense, of drifting and wandering, something that has by now no doubt become rather clear to the reader. What has to be stressed here is that the religious beliefs of a particular people respond closely to a whole range of other beliefs, not to mention experiences. The migrant woman whose husband behaved so scandalously believes in God all right, but also believes in the unrelenting depravity of the "world." For her the world is no harmless abstraction, nor is it one of a series of ritually descriptive words, such as "the world, the flesh and the devil." For her and her husband all the terrors of Hell itself are real, living, daily matters — again, matters of the world, this very world. She needs no long poem of Dante's to spell out how diabolical and even grotesque it can *eventually* be for doomed people; she knows *right now* what the word *infernal* means — hellish in the colloquial sense of disgusting and awful and mean and brutish.

Obviously, she and her husband have "mixed feelings" or "ambivalence" toward what they seem to take seriously and embrace wholeheartedly, namely the church, the value of prayer, and above all, the glory of God. Still, it surprised me (and that minister) to know how fully thought-out some of those hesitations and misgivings can be and how forcefully upon occasion they become expressed, perhaps most forcefully when people like me (and the minister, too) are nowhere near. Nor are such doubts and moments of defiance absent among Appalachian families or tenant farmers, for what binds all these people is "angst," as some theologians and existentialist philosophers and psychologists put it — in this case an angst that is not elusive or metaphysical or associated only with unconscious mental conflicts, but a kind that is thoroughly clear-cut and specific and apparent and very much tied to the same "everyday life" Freud had in mind when he gave a title to his great book on psychopathology. The rural people I have worked with, in some fourteen states, simply cannot be overawed by references to the terror ahead after death. For such people the apocalyptic struggle, the ultimate encounter between Good and Bad, between God and the Devil, has an almost prosaic counterpart in the daily struggles they as field hands and farmhands, barely alive and always at the edge of what agricultural economists call "subsistence," constantly wage and often enough lose. (Little Annie died at the age of three; we did get her to a hospital but she was badly malnourished, epileptic, and had a kind of congenital heart defect that ought to have been operated on shortly after she was born.)

In any event, they fight on, the people I have been writing about, and they continue to pray — most often very earnestly indeed. They forthrightly and with not a little desperation ally themselves with Him Who offers them hope, redemption and another, sorely coveted chance. They have by and large little inclination to express open social protest, to denounce aloud those they know exploit and abuse and cheat them — though in prayer and song they again and again speak and sing as allegorically as the rest of us do. To "them," to the people who appear in this book, God's suffering requires no complicated explanation, nor does Christ's pain and humiliation, His harassment and exile, His final disgrace at the hands of His persecutors, all of whom were avowedly high-minded, powerful, practical, and full of pieties. Christ's suffering, God's suffering is Annie's suffering, is her parents' suffering. Meanwhile, small rural churches continue to receive multitudes. The mystery of God and the world persists. Life for these uprooted and stranded and hidden children of His goes on as well as is possible. Muted protests continue to take place in those churches, but minds also become refreshed, relieved, newly at ease in those churches. Not least important, those churches are places where enjoyment is had, even entertainment of the kind that is an expression of seriousness and devotion and loyalty on the part of people not likely to be taken with the idea (if anyone were to put it that way to them, and certainly they themselves never would) that God is dead.

No, God lives for migrants, lives for sharecroppers, lives for mountaineers, difficult though that fact may be for some of their distant friends and allies to accept and believe. Once again we have to take note of the tension between the outside sympathizer (with his kind of faith) and the recipients of that sympathy —

often enough it is a kind of sympathy which stubbornly and even arrogantly dwells upon exteriors, upon the dreadful surfaces of life, the lack of plumbing and electricity and furniture and money. I can only at this point bring up the words of Annie's father — and he certainly is no apologist for murkiness, self-deception or religious opiates: "That minister should go and pray for us. He should ask God to give us what we deserve. He should ask God to make him a better minister, so that he'll be able to talk with us and, you know, be more a part of us — know us and not always be giving us those lessons on what *we* should do and how *we* should live. *He* should do some things, too — so *he* can be better and live better, because it's not just us that have to change our thinking, like he keeps on telling us to do. How does he know what I'm thinking? Has he ever asked me? And has he asked himself — asked himself what *he's* thinking, and if *he* should go and change anything in *his* thinking? He says he wants to help us, but he doesn't really want to see the world as we do. Maybe he should do us a favor and hear us for a change, and then go back to his side of the fence and ask himself if the people over there have anything more important to say."

Then I felt close to that minister — and rightly warned.

REFERENCES

CHAPTER II

1. I ended Volume I of *Chidren of Crisis* with a quotation from James Agee's *Let Us Now Praise Famous Men* (Boston: Houghton Mifflin, 1941). I can only mention that book again — and say that in rural Alabama it is still possible to find some utterly poor white yeomen like those Agee and Walker Evans saw and tried to understand, write about, and (in photographs) present to their readers. Nor is George Orwell's *The Road to Wigan Pier* (New York: Harcourt, Brace and World, 1958) altogether out of date. His descriptions of miners and the mines, of company towns, of men robust and weary, of women devoted and sad, of children lively and canny and fearful, still apply to parts of Appalachia. Before Orwell, we had Emile Zola's *Germinal* (New York: Boni and Liveright, 1924) with its vivid portrayal of miners; and long before Agee, Dostoevski knew how to convey the gentleness and brutishness that exist side by side in "Poor People," published in *The Gambler and Other Stories* (New York: Macmillan, 1923), and *The Insulted and Injured* (New York: Macmillan, 1956). I mention such writers simply to remind all of us that social scientists have a larger historical past to summon than some of them (and the rest of us) may care to remember.

2. Southern writers, as Flannery O'Connor has insisted in *Mystery and Manners, Occasional Prose,* selected and edited by Sally and Robert Fitzgerald (New York: Farrar, Straus & Giroux, 1969) are not simply dealers in the grotesque and bizarre, though ignorant and self-righteous Northerners would have it so. Writers like William Faulkner and Eudora Welty draw upon Mississippi rather as any novelist draws upon what is familiar — in order to illuminate larger, more universal themes. Both Malcolm Cowley in *The Portable Faulkner* (New York: Viking, 1946) and Cleanth Brooks in *William Faulkner: The Yoknapatawpha Country* (New Haven: Yale University Press, 1963) have stressed the "brooding love for the land" that one finds in *Sartoris,* in *Sanctuary,* in *The Hamlet,* in *As I Lay Dying.* Robert Penn Warren agrees, and in his fine essay "William Faulkner" takes particular pains to describe the surroundings Faulkner both knew and constantly evoked: "No land in all fiction lives more vividly in its physical presence than this county of Faulkner's imagination." See *Selected Essays* (New York: Random House, 1958). If Faulkner was among other things a nature poet in the tradition of Wordsworth

(which Cleanth Brooks argues convincingly) he was also another Southerner who knew his kin, his neighbors, his land — and those places and situations and conditions no road, let alone map, ever reveals to an outsider. I believe southern writers persist in capturing our interest and imagination because they really do have stories to tell, adventures to relate, mysteries to unfold which entice us urban people (who read all those books). And the tradition of concrete descriptive writing in the South, tied always to the land, whether in the form of essays or novels, goes way back. Augustus Baldwin Longstreet wrote *Georgia Scenes* in 1835; Alice Walker, a black woman born in Eatonton, Georgia, to sharecropper parents wrote *The Third Life of Grange Copeland* (New York: Harcourt Brace Jovanovich) in 1970.

3. Erik H. Erikson has struggled for many years to cross all sorts of professional boundaries, yet preserve intact his own particular outlook as a psychoanalyst. His *Insight and Responsibility* (New York: W. W. Norton, 1964) is an especially rich resource for those of us who try to remain loyal to our clinical training, yet learn how life goes for men and women and children who are by no stretch of the imagination "patients." In this regard, two of that book's essays, "The Nature of Clinical Evidence" and "Psychological Reality and Historical Actuality," are of landmark importance. I have gone into Erikson's influence on psychoanalytic and psychiatric "field workers" in *Erik H. Erikson: The Growth of His Work* (Boston: Atlantic–Little, Brown, 1970). In a paper I wrote about Anna Freud's work, "The Achievement of Anna Freud," *The Massachusetts Review*, VII (Spring, 1966), I tried to indicate how she, too, has made every effort to observe children outside as well as inside the so-called "clinical situation." Her study, in collaboration with Dorothy Burlingham, of *War and Children* (New York: International Universities Press, 1944) shows what two psychoanalysts could do to make sense of the responses young English children demonstrated during the Second World War — when death fell down from the skies. And her book *Normality and Pathology in Childhood* (New York: International Universities Press, 1965) emphasizes something a clinician become social observer must never stop reminding himself: it is no easy, clear-cut task to distinguish the "normal" from the "abnormal." If that holds in clinics and hospitals and in the doctor's private office, one can only imagine how careful a doctor must be as he works in a particular neighborhood of a southern town or up an Appalachian hollow.

4. In the midst of the work that preceded the writing of this book I found myself struggling with this issue, and wrote about it in "Psychiatrists and the Poor," *The Atlantic Monthly*, CCXIV (July, 1964).

5. I refer the reader to a section on "Method" in Volume I of *Children of Crisis*, subtitled *A Study of Courage and Fear* (Boston: Atlantic–Little, Brown, 1967). In that section I tell how I became involved with the children who initiated school desegregation in the South and with the youths who waged sit-ins and freedom rides and more generally carried on a widespread social and political struggle.

6. The first report of that work was delivered to the American Psychiatric Association at its annual meeting in May of 1965 and published as "The Lives of Migrant Farmers" in *The American Journal of Psychiatry*, CXXII (September, 1965). A somewhat different report was issued by the Southern Regional Council as a monograph titled "The Migrant Worker" in the fall of 1965.

7. I reported upon that work to the American Orthopsychiatric Association in the spring of 1967. The paper was published as "American Youth in a Social Struggle: The Appalachian Volunteers," *American Journal of Orthopsychiatry*, XXXVIII (January, 1968).

8. If muckraking journalism and testimony before Senate committees qualify as an effort "to change things" I can cite "Peonage in Florida," *The New Republic*, July 26, 1969, and a long summer morning that same month before the U.S. Senate Subcommittee on Migratory Labor. (See U.S. Congress, Senate, Subcommittee on Migratory Labor, *Hearings*, "The Migrant Subculture," Washington, D.C., July 28, 1969). I must admit that more emphatic pressure than any people like me are likely to muster may well be the only way those "things" I just mentioned will indeed change.

9. At times I believe the only way to do justice to the black man's language is through his music: his songs, his spirituals, his blues, his "hollering." I find myself fiddling with phrases and sentences and paragraphs — with a whole afternoon of conversation — and I realize that the "translations" I make for a book like this, the grammatical and idiomatic and metaphoric demands I make, may also be considered an insulting straitjacket. And what I come up with may be terribly misleading too, because the spirit and power and force of what I hear, the "soul," just doesn't make it across the barrier of language — hence, both writer and reader still do not understand, still get the wrong "message." In any event, let me recommend LeRoi Jones's *Blues People: Negro Music in White America* (New York: Morrow, 1963) for its analysis of the words and rhythms sharecroppers and tenant farmers have called upon over the centuries; also *American Negro Folklore* by J. Mason Brewer (Chicago: Quadrangle, 1968), and Paul Oliver's first-rate *The Story of the Blues* (Philadelphia: Chilton, 1969). Oliver recommends many records; I want to mention especially "The Sound of the Delta" (Testament Records T–2209), and George Mitchell's two unforgettable volumes, "Delta Blues" (Arhoolie 1041 and 1042). With respect to mountaineers the same problem holds. I strongly urge a look at Wylene P. Dial, "Folk Speech is English, Too," *Mountain Life and Work*, XLVI (February, 1970), and by the same author, "The Dialect of the Appalachian People," a publication of the Appalachian Center of the University of West Virginia.

10. See "Students Who Say No: Blacks, Radicals, Hippies" in Volume VII of *International Psychiatry Clinics*, Dana Farnsworth and Graham Blaine, eds. (Boston: Little, Brown, 1970); also "Serpents and Doves: Non-Violent Youth in the South" in *Youth: Change and Challenge*, Erik H. Erikson, ed. (New York: Basic Books, 1963); and "Social Struggle and Weariness," *Psychiatry*, XXVII (November, 1964).

CHAPTER III

1. There is a medical literature that in a dry and restrained way can be devastating. One can feel the pediatricians and obstetricians and public health doctors struggling to be objective and thorough scientists — but struggling too with the appalling conditions it is their fate to observe, and within the limits of their resources, try to correct. See Earl Siegel, "Migrant Families: Health Problems of Children," *Clinical Pediatrics*, V (October, 1966), and, in addition, G. Delgado, C. L. Brumbeck, M. B. Deavor, "Eating Patterns Among Migrant Families," U.S. Department of Public Health Report 76 (1961); Florida State Board of Health, Bureau of Maternal and Child Health, "Migrant Project 1959" (Jacksonville, Florida, 1959); H. L. Johnston, "Medical Needs and Responsibilities for Children of Migrants," *Medical Responsibilities for the Displaced Child*, Report of the Forty-third Ross Conference on Pediatric Research (1963); A. L. Turri, H. L. Johnston, D. Harting, "Adapting Immunization Programs to Special Groups," U.S. Department of Public Health Report 72 (1957); T. J. Northcutt, R. H. Browning, C. L. Brumbeck, "Agricultural Migration and Maternity Care," *Journal of Health and Human Behavior*, IV (1963); and G. Reich, J. Davis, J. Davies, "Pesticide Poisoning in South Florida," *Archives of Environmental Health*, XVII (November, 1968).

2. In "The Lives of Migrant Farmers," *The American Journal of Psychiatry*, CXXII (September, 1965), I try to discuss some of the puzzling and ironic psychological issues migrant families present to a psychiatric observer. There is every reason to keep in mind that the particular stresses migrant children face are not swift and sudden and unexpected, but emerge for them as part of a life they and their parents live. For comparative purposes the reader may want to look at James Anthony's "Stress in Childhood" in *The Nature of Stress Disorder* (London: Hutchinson Medical Publications, 1959). Also of interest is "The Reaction of Infants to Stress" by M. Leitch and S. Escalona in *The Psychoanalytic Study of the Child*, Volume III/IV (New York: International Universities Press, 1949).

3. In recent years psychoanalytic observers and theorists have grown commendably wary of a strictly psychopathological view of human development. The Ego has been given (by Heinz Hartmann, Anna Freud, and Erik H. Erikson) growing authority and leverage. I am trying to emphasize in this chapter the tension between "integration" and "disintegration" that takes place among children who live in a harsh environment. Bruno Bettelheim's recent observations in Israel, in *The Children of the Dream* (New York: Macmillan, 1969), are not without significance to this study. In the kibbutzim, families are less "nuclear," more "extended" — indeed, more than "extended" in the traditional anthropological sense of the word. Under constant threat (political and environmental) and in the face of fear and privation, children grow up in a certain way — different from ours, stronger and more resilient in some ways, less responsive and less imaginative in other ways.

4. If the United States government has done relatively little to improve the migrant worker's political and economic situation, various federal agencies have done an excellent job of documenting that situation. See, for example, "Economic and Social Characteristics of Hired Farm Workers" (October, 1969) and "Manpower Implications of Fruit and Vegetable Mechanization" (December, 1969) in *Farm Labor Developments*, published by the U.S. Department of Labor. See also the "Yearbook of Agriculture" (especially the 1964 issue, *Farmer's World*) put out by the U.S. Department of Agriculture, which from time to time discusses "labor problems." Best of all are the various reports of the U.S. Senate Subcommittee on Migratory Labor — in particular, "Migrant and Seasonal Farmworker Powerlessness" (July, 1969).

5. Unknown as migrant children are to most school systems (including those which ought to be urgently concerned with such children), there is a small "literature" on the subject. Anthony F. Pinnie has collected articles from many sources in *Educating the Migrant Child* (Philadelphia: Temple, 1969). Two other fine books are Shirley E. Greene, *The Education of Migrant Children* (Washington, D.C.: National Education Association, 1954), and Elizabeth Sutton, *Knowing and Teaching the Migrant Child* (Washington, D.C.: National Educational Association, 1960). I will also mention two of my own articles: "Journey into the Mind of the Lower Depths," *The New Republic*, February 15, 1964, and "What Migrant Children Learn," *Saturday Review*, May 15, 1965.

6. One thinks of Anna Freud's observations of those who survived concentration camps. The price of the willfulness is a sadness so "deep" and pervasive that it informs everything in the person's life — yet may also be less explicit or clear than the "depressions" or "moods" others face. It is as if a person gets *so* devastated he dare not let his guard down at all. See Anna Freud's "An Experiment in Group Upbringing" in *The Psychoanalytic Study of the Child*, Volume II (New York: International Universities Press, 1946). See also Maria Piers's and my account of Miss Freud's work in our book *Wages of Neglect* (Chicago: Quadrangle, 1969).

7. I have to compare these boys and girls with the children I worked with in New Orleans and Atlanta and other southern cities — children who had a purpose, a cause, a sense of destiny, and so could endure mobs and violence as they initiated school desegration in the South at the end of the fifties and during the sixties. See *Children of Crisis: A Study of Courage and Fear* (Boston: Atlantic–Little, Brown, 1967).

8. The reference to Joseph Conrad is for me important. He long ago knew how to observe what meanness and greed can do to people — to those who profit from the exercise of those passions as well as those whose lives become literally sacrificed. (In this regard, "Heart of Darkness" comes immediately to mind.) Conrad also knew how history lives vividly in particular lives; more than that, he described what he saw and felt in unforgettably concrete stories. He was passionately detached but never ethically indifferent, not an easy "position" to keep, but one that enables him to reach and unnerve many otherwise hard-hearted or blind readers.

9. There is a fine tradition of reportage on migrant farm workers — which suggests that they are out of our sights and minds only because we have chosen to ignore what first-rate social observers have insisted upon calling to our attention. In 1939, Carey McWilliams described the migratory labor problem in California in *Factories in the Field* (Boston: Little, Brown); in 1942, he extended his observations to other migrants in *Ill Fares the Land* (Boston: Little, Brown). Then there was Paul S. Taylor's brilliant and moving pamphlet *Adrift on the Land* (New York: Public Affairs Committee, 1940), and his *An American Exodus: A Record of Human Erosion in the Thirties*, which includes his wife Dorothea Lange's photographs (New York: Reynal and Hitchcock, 1939; and New Haven: Yale University Press, 1969). More recently, we have had *The Harvesters* by Louisa R. Shotwell (New York: Doubleday, 1961), *They Harvest Despair* by Dale Wright (Boston: Beacon Press, 1965), and Truman Moore's *The Slaves We Rent* (New York: Random House, 1965). A particularly moving account of the so-called "eastern stream" of migrants has been written by Earl L. Koos, a public health doctor: *They Follow the Sun* (Jacksonville, Florida: Florida State Board of Health, 1957). See also Zora N. Huston's haunting novel *Their Eyes Were Watching God* (Philadelphia: Lippincott, 1937) as well as John Steinbeck's better-known *Grapes of Wrath* (New York: Viking, 1939). A book which describes the physical setting of south-central Florida, where I have done most of my work with migrants, is *Lake Okeechobee* by A. J. and K. A. Hanna (Indianapolis: Bobbs-Merrill, 1948). Another fine monograph by public health doctors is *On the Season* (Jacksonville, Florida: Florida State Board of Health, 1961). The authors are R. H. Browning and T. J. Northcutt, and they are disciples, so to speak, of Earl Koos.

10. In the first volume of *Children of Crisis* I described the differences between the drawings and paintings of middle-class children and those done by some of the poor and black children I have worked with. There are a few good books which show how and what children draw at various ages. *Group Values Through Children's Drawings* by Wayne Dennis (New York: Wiley, 1966) and *Young Children and Their Drawings* by Joseph H. DiLeo (New York: Brunner-Mazel, 1970) are especially good and important. Also, see *Children's Drawings as Measures of Intellectual Maturity* by Dale Harris (New York: Harcourt Brace and World, 1963), and *Psychological Evaluation of Children's Human Figure Drawings* by E. Koppitz (New York: Grune and Stratton, 1968).

11. Here I think of Simone Weil's *The Need for Roots* (Boston: Beacon Press, 1952). Nor do I believe the "association" is farfetched. She saw how desperately the poor struggle to belong, to affirm one another — even as members of the bourgeoisie do. Migrants create what "communities" they can as they wander over our land. Meanwhile, so many of us "dig in," buy homes and acreage, accumulate "property," but trust practically no one — neighbors, business "associates," or even at times relatives. A migrant mother once told me she thought the well-to-do farmer she worked for about a month out of each

year "doesn't trust his own shadow." He too is adrift in America. He too lacks the kind of "roots" Miss Weil had in mind when she wrote in her own terse, compact, suggestive, epigrammatic way about our crying need for a community of trust and shared passion.

CHAPTER IV

1. It is no news that the number of sharecroppers has been steadily declining all during the twentieth century. In 1930, the South possessed some seven hundred and seventy thousand sharecroppers and over seven million tenant farmers. In 1950, the total number of sharecroppers and tenant farmers was down to about a million. In 1960, there were an estimated one hundred and seventy thousand — though the number of hired farm workers was actually rising. In Mississippi, for instance, the number of sharecroppers fell — between 1954 and 1959 — from one hundred thousand to forty-five thousand, but the number of hired farm workers rose by 77 percent, from eighteen thousand to thirty-one thousand. See the report "Sharecroppers in the Sixties" (New York: The National Sharecroppers' Fund, 1961). The families I am writing about in this chapter include sharecroppers, tenant farmers and hired farm workers. Indeed, one learns that *in fact* the distinctions blur: by the time profits and losses are settled it makes little difference to the men and women and children who work the land whether they are "on shares" or "renting" or "working for the bossman." But the historical development of sharecropping (and tenant farming) is quite another matter. Slaves became utterly dependent sharecroppers after the Civil War — whereas tenant farmers were much more independent, though still at the mercy of the uncertainties and disasters which plagued the cotton market. Interested readers can find an excellent historical account of sharecropping and tenancy in the various volumes that make up the "Social Study Series" of the University of North Carolina — written in the twenties and thirties by men such as Rupert Vance and Howard Odum, scholars unafraid to demonstrate in clear, literate prose both compassion and a capacity to tolerate and describe life's complexities without reducing them to the simplifications of ideological rhetoric. See Rupert Vance's *Human Factors in Cotton Culture* (Chapel Hill: University of North Carolina Press, 1929) and *Human Geography of the South* (Chapel Hill: University of North Carolina Press, 1935). Also of interest in that series is *Negro Workaday Songs* by Odum and Guy Johnson (Chapel Hill: University of North Carolina Press, 1926), and *Southern Pioneers in Social Interpretation*, Howard Odum, ed. (Freeport, New York: Books for Libraries Press, 1967). A good historical and economic analysis of the South's agricultural system can be found in Frederick Shannon's *The Farmer's Last Frontier* (New York: Holt, Rinehart and Winston, 1963). Lowry Nelson's *American Farm Life* (Cambridge, Massachusetts: Harvard University Press, 1954) is also of value, as are the more sociological books, *Deep South* (Chicago: University of Chicago Press, 1944), whose authors — Allison Davis, Burleigh Gardner and Marty

Gardner — were a productive "team," and *Blackways of Kent* (Chapel Hill: University of North Carolina Press, 1955) — a fine book indeed.

2. In this regard one keeps coming back to the writers, to novelists and short-story writers and social or literary critics, none of which the South has lacked. Besides Faulkner and Eudora Welty, besides the "fugitives" (Allen Tate, Robert Penn Warren, Donald Davidson), there have been Erskine Caldwell's evocation of rural Georgia, Katherine Anne Porter's portrayal of what can be called southern sensibility, and Carson McCullers's efforts to capture the spiritual loneliness that bears down so heavily on that "beautiful" southern landscape. And then there are essayists like William Alexander Percy, whose *Lanterns on the Levee* (New York: Knopf, 1941) is a moving description of the world a sensitive planter's son both took for granted and questioned closely. Also of value is *South: Modern Southern Literature in its Cultural Setting*, Louis Rubin and Robert Jacobs, eds. (New York: Doubleday, 1961). On the black side, Richard Wright's *Native Son* (New York: Harper, 1940), and Ralph Ellison's *Invisible Man* (New York: Modern Library, 1952) are indispensable. And, again, I mention Alice Walker's *The Third Life of Grange Copeland.* For the people themselves, the "voices" of sharecroppers and tenant farmers and "poor rural folk," one can turn to *These Are Our Lives: As Told by the People and Written by Members of the Federal Writers' Project of the Works Progress Administration in North Carolina, Tennessee and Georgia* (Chapel Hill: University of North Carolina Press, 1939). Also see Josephine Carson, *Silent Voices: The Southern Negro Woman Today* (New York: Delacorte, 1969). James Agee and Walker Evans in *Let Us Now Praise Famous Men*, op. cit., have once and for all set down the white tenant farmer's "inner" and "outer" worlds. As for the black people of the rural South, I know of no one who has captured their spirit better than novelist and playwright Paul Green. See his *Lonesome Roads* (New York: McBride, 1926) and *Wide Fields* (New York: McBride, 1928). And sometimes in a publication like *The American Ecclesiastical Review* one comes across a small gem of an article like "Rural Blacks and the Cooperatives" by Father A. J. McKnight, CLX (March, 1969). All of this is by way of suggesting that what I describe myself as having "noticed," the reader can approach through a whole tradition (powerful and rich and continuing) of stories, novels, essays, plays, and autobiographical statements. I have no doubt that someone like me has his job to do, his particular observations to record — but oh, how often do we psychiatrists and social scientists blindly and smugly forget all we have to fall back upon, all that has been done in the name of the writer's craft rather than "science."

3. And why should such parents have the kind of "conviction" I mention — when in county after county their annual income is well below a thousand dollars a year. In several articles on the rural South of the late sixties, Harry Huge and I tried to blend federal government statistics with our own observations. See "We Need Help: A Message from Mississippi," *The New Republic*, March 8, 1969; "In Jamie Whitten's Backyard," *New South*, XXIV (Spring, 1969); and "Thorns

on the Yellow Rose of Texas," *The New Republic*, April 19, 1969; "Peonage in Florida," *The New Republic*, July 26, 1969; "A Cry from the Delta," in the monthly bulletin of the Southern Regional Council, *The South Today* (July, 1969).

4. The blues range wide; some dwell on women, some on work, some on one or another disaster, some on sheriffs and their gun-happy deputies. They range from "Spoonful" and "Shake It" and "Break It" to "Mississippi Boll Weevil Blues" to "High Sheriff Blues" to "High Water Everywhere," which tells of the disastrous flood of the Mississippi River in 1927.

5. No one has a monopoly on sadness or despair — or "depression," as clinicians are used to putting it. Again and again in clinical conferences or meetings of psychiatric and psychoanalytic societies I have been asked about the "deep depression" which poor rural blacks "must" experience. And no doubt they do — as do so many well-to-do and well-educated white people who live in Boston or New York or San Francisco, and who perhaps have less sturdy and effective means of giving expression to (and thereby loosening the grip of) *their* "blues." See *The Meaning of Despair*, Willard Gaylin, ed. (New York: Science House, 1968). Psychoanalytic theorists have struggled valiantly and intelligently with the mind's continuing capacity for (some would say predilection toward) self-laceration. The poorest of our poor often manage to see a brighter life in store for them in some Heaven, and yet on this earth manage to cry their hearts out, resorting to a complicated musical and literary tradition (work songs, "the hollers," jazz, the blues, spirituals, the signifying and reciting and testifying that take place in churches). That being the case, one has to be careful about saying a particular sharecropper child (let alone all sharecropper or tenant farm children) is "depressed" or headed for "despair," pure and simple.

6. Neither Martin Buber nor Sören Kierkegaard had anything to do with the rural South, but both men know how to get epigrammatically at the center of man's various dilemmas — rather as Eddie "Son" House from Lyon, Mississippi, did when he sang:

> It's a dry ole spell, everywhere I been,
> I believe to my soul this ole world is bound to end.
> Lord, I stood in my backyard, wrung my hands and screamed
> And I couldn't see nothin', couldn't see nothin' green.
> Oh Lord, have mercy if you please
> Let your rain come down and give our po' heart ease.

7. I must refer the reader here to *Still Hungry in America* (New York: New American Library, 1968), which documents observations made in the course of my work with rural children. In this regard, an excellent medical article with a good bibliography is H. P. Chase and H. Martin, "Undernutrition and Child Development," *New England Journal of Medicine*, April 23, 1970. Also of value is *Poverty and Health*, A. Antonovsky and J. K. Zola, eds. (Cambridge, Massachusetts: Harvard University Press, 1969).

8. An interesting book that documents the "world view" of these (rural, black) children is *Sweet Pea* by Jill Krementz (New York: Harcourt, Brace and World, 1969) with a short but precise introduction by Margaret Mead emphasizing both the sad and joyful sides of the black child's words and the accompanying photographs. Needless to say, a generation of psychologists and psychiatrists have tried to describe how children grow up. There is, for the "normal" child, Lois Murphy's fine *The Widening World of Childhood* (New York: Basic Books, 1962), not to mention Erik H. Erikson's *Childhood and Society* (New York: Norton, 1950). For emotionally disturbed children, there is Rudolf Ekstein's *Children of Time and Space, of Action and Impulse* (New York: Appleton-Century-Crofts, 1966). For poor children, a comprehensive book (among others) is *Social Class, Race, and Psychological Development*, M. Deutsch, I. Katz, A. K. Jensen, eds. (New York: Holt, Rinehart and Winston, 1968). Piaget's work is of course indispensable; see, for example, his *The Child's Conception of Time* (New York: Basic Books, 1969). I mention such books because I have tried in Chapters III, IV and V to convey how rural American children, both black and white, get their very special sense of time and space — and indeed, grow into their very own world. And I have tried at certain points to make comparisons between, say, Delta children and migrant children or children from Kentucky's hollows. I have also, from time to time, tried to draw upon my clinical experience with middle-class urban children — hence some of the references in this footnote. I am concerned that the reader not forget what the "children of crisis" share with other children — even as we are aware that a field hand's child growing up in rural Alabama or Mississippi has his or her quite special way of seeing things and comprehending the "environment."

9. The South's rural schools have been in the past neglected by state legislatures and the federal government, but not by certain meticulous scholars. See Horace Mann Bond, *Negro Education in Alabama* (New York: Atheneum, 1969). An old classic, well worth tracking down, is W. E. B. DuBois, *The Negro Common School* (Atlanta: Atlanta University Press, 1901). Also valuable is Charles S. Johnson, *Shadow of the Plantation* (Chicago: University of Chicago Press, 1934).

10. What has the ordinary white man of the South obtained — for all the hate he has been prompted by various people to indulge? Hate has in a way bound the two races together — hate and the guilt of the haters, hate and the resentment and bitterness and fear of the hated. The South's "poor white" haters and black slaves or black field hands have long been analyzed by historians, both traditional and "psychological-minded." And the "literature" is impressive. C. Vann Woodward's *Tom Watson: Agrarian Rebel* (New York: Oxford University Press, 1963) is biography become sweeping social analysis, as is T. Harry Williams's *Huey Long* (New York: Knopf, 1969). Nor can anyone who wants to understand the region our "stranded children" still live in do without Woodward's *Origins of the New South, 1877–1913* (Baton Rouge: Louisiana State University Press, 1951)

or *The Strange Career of Jim Crow* (New York: Oxford University Press, 1957). Another sensitive and indeed brilliant historian is David Potter. His *The South and the Sectional Conflict* (Baton Rouge: Louisiana State University Press, 1968) is an important contribution, as are William R. Taylor's fine book *Cavalier and Yankee* (New York: Braziller, 1961), and social historian David Bertelson's *The Lazy South* (New York: Oxford University Press, 1967). I cannot recommend too strongly Eugene Genovese's *The World the Slaveholders Made* (New York: Pantheon, 1969). In a sense, part of this book tries to show what that "world the slaveholders made" came to — in the form of particular lives now being lived. Another good book is *Scottsboro: A Tragedy of the American South* by Dan Carter (Baton Rouge, Louisiana State University Press, 1969). Though Mr. Carter is concerned with the fate of particular black Alabama men accused of raping white Alabama girls, the fear and hysteria that millions of both races share is powerfully evoked. A little-known book that specifically describes the plight of both black and white sharecroppers is *The Forgotten Farmers: The Story of Sharecroppers in the New Deal* by David Conrad (Urbana: University of Illinois Press, 1965). I need not repeat, in this or any other footnote, the value of *Let Us Now Praise Famous Men* as a study of the South's white yeomen and tenant farmers. John Dollard's *Caste and Class in a Southern Town* (Garden City, New York: Doubleday, 1957) shows what it was like for those "famous men" and what it continues to be like for *Children of Bondage,* whom Dollard and Allison Davis wrote about (New York: Harper and Row, 1964). A recent sequel to *Children of Bondage* is Anne Moody's *Coming of Age in Mississippi* (New York: Dell, 1968). And republished of late is Charles Johnson's classic *Growing Up in the Black Belt: Negro Youth in the Rural South* (New York: Schocken, 1967). One can only wonder how it has been possible for so many extraordinarily eloquent and powerful books, all so carefully written and meticulously documented, to avail so little against what I once heard a white tenant farmer in Alabama call "the powers that be."

CHAPTER V

1. Here is Arnold Toynbee in *A Study of History* (New York: Oxford University Press, 1947): "In fact, the Appalachian 'mountain people' today are no better than barbarians. They have relapsed into illiteracy and witchcraft. They suffer from poverty, squalor and ill-health. They are the American counterparts of the latter-day white barbarians of the Old World — Rifis, Albanians, Kurds, Pathans and Hairy Ainus; but, whereas these latter are belated survivals of an ancient barbarism, the Appalachians present the melancholy spectacle of a people who have acquired civilization and then lost it." At another point Toynbee calls Appalachia's mountaineers "ci-devant heirs of Western civilization who have relapsed into barbarism under the depressing effect of a challenge which has been inordinately severe."

2. She reminded me again and again of Dorothea Lange's photograph

entitled "Woman of the High Plains, Texas Panhandle," taken in 1938. The South's and Appalachia's poor white and black rural people have been captured in a manner beyond the descriptive power of words in *Dorothea Lange,* with an introductory essay by George P. Elliot (Garden City, New York: Doubleday, 1966) and also in *An American Exodus* by Dorothea Lange and Paul S. Taylor, op. cit.

3. The music of the Appalachian region, the stories, the language — in other words, the social and cultural traditions mountaineers claim as theirs and no one else's — have been written about in book after book, article after article, over the decades of American history. In 1913, Horace Kephart published *Our Southern Highlanders* (New York: Outing Publishing Co.). In 1921, John C. Campbell wrote the classic *The Southern Highlander and His Homeland* (New York: Russell Sage Foundation). Now reprinted with a foreword by Rupert Vance (Lexington: University of Kentucky Press, 1969), Campbell's book is an example of what can be done by a clear-headed, literate observer who is not tempted to burden his readers (or those written about) with overworked and murky theories. A particularly helpful book is Robert Munn's *The Southern Appalachians: A Bibliography and Guide to Studies* (Morgantown: West Virginia Library, 1961). Recent and important additions to the literature not listed in Mr. Munn's comprehensive bibliography are Harry Caudill's *Night Comes to the Cumberlands* (Boston: Atlantic–Little, Brown, 1962), and Jack Weller's *Yesterday's People* (Lexington: University of Kentucky Press, 1965). Less known than those two, but really fine books are *Neighbor and Kin: Life in a Tennessee Ridge Community* by Elmora Matthews (Nashville: Vanderbilt University Press, 1965); *Stinking Creek* by John Fetterman (New York: Dutton, 1967); and *Shiloh: A Mountain Community* by John Stephenson (Lexington: University of Kentucky Press, 1968). A most wide-ranging and fairly well-known effort is *The Southern Appalachian Region,* Thomas Ford, ed. (Lexington: University of Kentucky Press, 1962) in which the region is thoroughly surveyed, its economy analyzed, and its social and cultural traditions examined. Nothing since has measured up to this book — and alas, the problems emphasized in its pages remain.

4. There are some fine books about Appalachia's land written with naturalists in mind — or indeed, children — and they can be both informative and thoroughly refreshing. I have in mind Maurice Brooks's *The Appalachians* (Boston: Houghton Mifflin, 1965) and Thomas Connelly's *Discovering the Appalachians* (Harrisburg: Stackpole, 1968). Rebecca Caudill's books for young readers are a joy — and tell a lot about the region's terrain. My three boys have doted on them. Favorites of theirs are *Schoolhouse in the Woods* (New York: Winston, 1949), and *A Pocketful of Cricket* (New York: Holt, Rinehart and Winston, 1964). In addition, Rebecca Caudill has written a fine social document in *My Appalachia: A Reminiscence* (New York: Holt, Rinehart and Winston, 1966).

5. See Elmora Matthews's book *Neighbor and Kin,* op. cit., for its first-rate explanation of the mysteries and complexities of "kith and kin."

Of course, Appalachia is not nearly as homogeneous as some suppose. Many outsiders and even a few who live in Kentucky and West Virginia don't know that immigrants from Ireland and Spain, Italy, Austria, Poland, Greece, Russia and Turkey penetrated West Virginia's coal fields and Kentucky's hollows in the twentieth century — intent on work in the mines. Those people also have had their traditions; and they also develop tight patterns of association. A fascinating book that shows how such "non–Anglo-Saxon" people contributed their fair share to West Virginia's cultural heritage is Ruth Musick's *Green Hills of Magic: West Virginia Folktales from Europe* (Lexington: University of Kentucky Press, 1970). From the other end of history's spectrum, one can read about the first mountaineers and what happened as they settled West Virginia in the eighteenth and nineteenth centuries in *The Allegheny Frontier: West Virginia Beginnings, 1730–1830* by Otis Rice (Lexington: University of Kentucky Press, 1970).

6. Harry Huge and I tried to describe the disease to the general reader in "Black Lung," *The New Republic,* January 25, 1969. The interested reader should consult more technical papers: L. E. Kerr "Coal Workers' Pneumoconiosis," *Industrial Medicine and Surgery,* XXV (April, 1956) and, very important, D. Rasmussen, W. Laquer, and P. Lutterman, "Pulmonary Impairment in Southern West Virginia Coal Miners," *American Review of Respiratory Disease,* 98 (July, 1968).

7. Again, a lot has been written, yet the rural poor in Appalachia, as in other sections of the country, get inadequate (if indeed *any*) medical services. See "Crisis in American Medicine," *The Lancet,* March 16, 1968. See also "Low Income Barriers to Use of Health Services," *New England Journal of Medicine,* March 7, 1968. In *The Southern Appalachian Region,* op. cit., C. Horace Hamilton has written an excellent section on "Health and Health Services." As for Danny's "survival," and for those children who don't survive, I can only recommend Diana Hunt's "Health Services to the Poor: A Survey of the Prevalence and Causes of Infant Mortality in the United States" *Inquiry,* VI (August, 1969). And, alas, she offers at the end of her paper no less than fifty-one medical references, many of them papers and articles whose contents ought thoroughly to shame this rich nation.

8. Anna Freud soberly and most persuasively has shown how psychoanalytic theories have been used in a succession of ways by nervous, eagerly submissive middle-class urban parents — who want, no doubt, *everything* for their children, including that elusive and often banal thing known as "mental health." See *Normality and Pathology in Childhood* (New York: International Universities Press, 1965).

9. There is a lot in Appalachia's history that invites comparison with the kind of rebelliousness and social struggle that E. J. Hobsbawm has described in *Primitive Rebels* (New York: Norton, 1959). The "social bandit" Professor Hobsbawn writes about is no stranger to the hollows of Kentucky or West Virginia — where exploitative industry and county corruption are countered by outbursts of populist anger, often futile, but just as often pointed and violent. Needless to say, the United Mine Workers did not just appear out of the blue; nor were they

granted immediate recognition by "social-minded" or "progressive" coal companies or the steel industry. "Bloody Harlan" stands for one more moment of pain and suffering in American history. By the same token the subsistence farmers of the rural South and the Appalachian high-lands had their own sad, hungry time — and upon occasion have shot it out with sheriffs, or drunk themselves to oblivion, or "picked up" and moved west. All "Okies" did not come from Oklahoma. Los Angeles and its environs contain many families who "hail" from Alabama or Tennessee or (eastern and western) North Carolina. I cannot in a book like this write about the history of farm labor organizing or, for that matter, union organizing among the miners, but there *is* such a history, and I would like to refer the reader to those who have written it — and to those who have done a similar job of documenting the plight of the English farmer and the English worker. British social historians are a magnificent lot, and their books are so suggestive that they deserve constant scrutiny, even if an Appalachian miner or a southern share-cropper has a quite different "past" to fall back upon — or escape, as the case may be. Of great value is *Farm Labor Organizing, 1905–1967: A Brief History* (New York: National Advisory Committee on Farm Labor, 1967). Also of interest is the U.S. Department of Labor, Bureau of Labor Statistics, Bulletin No. 836, "Labor Unionism in American Agri-culture" (Washington, D.C.: Government Printing Office, 1945). Again, I mention Carey McWilliams's *Factories in the Field*. More generally, America's agricultural growth and development is chronicled in *Farmers' Frontier, 1865–1900* by Gilbert File (New York: Holt, Rine-hart and Winston, 1966). For what happened across the Atlantic in Eng-land one can turn to *The Agricultural Revolution, 1750–1880* by J. D. Chambers and G. E. Mingay (London: Batsford, 1966). A fascinating volume is *Captain Swing* by E. Hobsbawm and G. Rude (New York: Pantheon, 1968). The rising discontent of England's rural poor is vividly portrayed — and the individual farmers somehow come wonder-fully to life. On the industrial side, I would recommend E. P. Thomp-son's *The Making of the English Working Class* (New York: Pantheon, 1963). In that book one meets up with this: "If we stop history at a given point, then there are no classes but simply a multitude of individuals with a multitude of experiences. But if we watch these men over an adequate period of social change, we observe patterns in their relationships, their ideas, and their institutions. Class is defined by men as they live their own history, and, in the end, this is its only definition." I suppose it can be said that in the several volumes of *Children of Crisis* I aim to describe some of the "individuals" and "experiences" Professor Thompson mentions — and by following particular families over the years, indicate how difficult it has been for certain Americans to de-velop the kind of class-consciousness he refers to in this quotation.

10. For this way of looking at mountain children I am clearly indebted to Erik H. Erikson — who has never shunned contradictions or tried to wipe them away with unequivocal theoretical formulations. See *Child-hood and Society* (New York: Norton, 1950).

11. There is a "literature" of sorts that deals directly or indirectly with

the psychological troubles of Appalachian people. The best writing on the subject is not by a psychiatrist, and it is concerned with the past, not the present. I have in mind Arthur K. Moore's *The Frontier Mind: A Cultural Analysis of the Kentucky Frontiersman* (Lexington: University of Kentucky Press, 1957). The author teaches English, and has written an unsentimental and at times harsh book about Kentucky's early settlers; but at least he does not gratuitously pin medical and psychiatric labels on his "subjects," and though I do not agree with his somewhat one-sided portrayal of the "frontiersman" (who is still around in parts of Kentucky) I find the severe, unromantic look cast by the author valuable indeed. Less impressive, but to be expected these days, are papers such as Carl Wiesel and Malcolm Arny, "Psychiatric Study of Coal Miners in the Eastern Kentucky Area," *American Journal of Psychiatry*, CVIII (February, 1952); Walter Smitson, "The Group Process in Treating Culturally Deprived Psychotics from Appalachia," *Mental Hygiene* (January, 1967); G. D. Looff and M. Smith, "School Phobia in the Southern Appalachian Region: Crucial Importance of Early Treatment," *Southern Medical Journal*, LXII (March, 1969); and finally, E. Weinstein, R. Eck and O. Lyerly, "Conversion Hysteria in Appalachia," *Psychiatry*, XXXII (August, 1969). One reads about a "miner's syndrome" — the men complain about aches and pains and develop a "passive dependent attitude." One reads that "the first important characteristic of the disadvantaged person in our society is his lack of participation in group activities" or that "there is little or no fighting spirit left" in mountaineers, who are elsewhere called "illiterate, clownish and grim." It is dangerous indeed to write about people whose central preoccuptation is survival itself in a way which relies so persistently on clinical concepts derived from a particular kind of work with particular (middle-class, so-called "neurotic") patients. One can write pages and pages on this matter. I would mention an article I did write: "Psychiatrists and the Poor," op. cit. In *Erik H. Erikson: The Growth of His Work*, op. cit., I go into the "problem" at great length. But to end on a positive note, and thus indicate the valuable work that *can* be done, I will mention Rex A. Lucas, *Men in Crisis: A Study of a Mine Disaster* (New York: Basic Books, 1969). I have written about this fine book in the *American Journal of Psychiatry*, CXXVI (May, 1970). Also of value is U.S. Department of Health, Education, and Welfare, Public Health Service, "Mental Health in Appalachia" (Washington, D.C.: Government Printing Office, 1965).

12. The literature on this subject is enormous. I would mention Oscar Lewis's crucial essay "The Culture of Poverty" in his *Anthropological Essays* (New York: Random House, 1970). The same book contains some short but splendid essays on rural America, including the edge of the South's "cotton country." The more one writes about the "mind" of a particular group of people the more he has to watch his step, as I think I have tried to warn both myself and the reader from time to time. Often I wonder (with regard to Appalachians, for instance) why a particular mother wants fewer children than *her* mother had, or why an older person up one hollow thinks as he does, in contrast, say, to

an older person I might meet up another. And then there are the children and their idiosyncrasies or (seeming) patterns of behavior. Gradually, I have taught myself to look for help from sensitive sociologists or essayists, who don't automatically leap to exclusively psychopathological explanations. For example, Gordon DeJong has written a provocative book called *Appalachian Fertility Decline* (Lexington: University of Kentucky Press, 1968) in which he shows how subtle (as well as large-scale) geographic "moves" within the region can affect a mother's notion of what size her family ought to be. And E. G. Youmans has edited a fine book on *Older Rural Americans* (Lexington: University of Kentucky Press, 1967) in which the actions and thoughts of a wide range of elderly citizens are described in rich detail — and in all the normal variety that psychiatrists ought to know about before they discuss the "abnormal," not to mention (in the case of Appalachians) the "passive dependent" or "apathetic" or "depressed." As for children, I strongly recommend, along with the writings of Erik H. Erikson and Anna Freud, a volume titled *Children Under Stress* by Sula Wolff (London: Allen Lane, The Penguin Press, 1969). The author looks sensitively at all the "normal" psychological stresses and strains of childhood and offers a good number of clinical examples — which deserve careful attention from any child psychiatrist out in the "field."

13. Sigmund Freud, *The Future of an Illusion* (New York: Liveright, 1949).

CHAPTER XI

1. These were the figures given in a report on rural medical problems to OEO by the Tufts University Department of Medicine in 1966.
2. The infant mortality rate in India in 1966 was 831 per 10,000 according to *The United Nations Demographic Yearbook.*
3. Excellent historical accounts of CDGM have been written by Pat Watters, Director of Information of the Southern Regional Council. See "CDGM: Who Really Won," *Dissent* (May-June, 1967) and *New South* (Spring, 1967). Mr. Watters makes quite clear what the political and economic stakes were (and are) in the struggle between an exceptional Headstart program and the "local authorities" in Mississippi.
4. I have tried to write about some of my own experiences as one who had occasion to observe the Child Development Group of Mississippi in the summer of 1965. See "The South, The South" in *Harvard Educational Review*, XL (February, 1970), and a review of Polly Greenberg's *The Devil Has Slippery Shoes* (New York: Macmillan, 1969) in *Social Casework*, LI (July, 1970).
5. In 1964 I tried to describe some of the weariness and despair felt by youths like Peter in "Social Struggle and Weariness," *Psychiatry*, XXVII (November, 1964). See also the discussion of civil rights workers in *Children of Crisis: A Study of Courage and Fear.*
6. See R. Coles and J. Brenner, "American Youth in a Social Struggle: The Mississippi Summer Project," *American Journal of Orthopsychiatry*, XXXV (October, 1966).

7. See R. Coles, "Mountain Thinking," Appalachian Review, I (Summer, 1966).

8. For an extended analysis of the work done by the Appalachian Volunteers see R. Coles and J. Brenner, "American Youth in a Social Struggle (II): The Appalachian Volunteers," American Journal of Orthopsychiatry, XXXVIII (January, 1968).

9. There is an extensive literature on the Appalachain "subculture," much of it discussed and listed in the paper mentioned in the preceding footnote as well as in the notes for Chapter V of this book. See also R. Coles, "Childhood in Appalachia," Appalachian Review, II (Summer, 1967).

CHAPTER XII

1. I fear that on the whole, psychoanalytic psychiatry has had a rather narrow and deterministic view of what "religion" amounts to. Freud (in The Future of an Illusion) saw worship as, at best, essentially a maneuver of the mind — and most likely a neurotic device meant to appease the conscience and, to a degree, deceive one's rational side. And many of his followers simply cared little and knew little about the various "meanings" of religious belief. In contrast, Jung abstained from reducing religious concerns to this or that "conflict"; instead, he saw in man's various faiths evidence of his most civilized and important strivings. See Modern Man in Search of a Soul (New York: Harcourt, Brace, 1934). Erikson's approach to Luther and Gandhi, both of them spiritual leaders, is of course free of psychiatric and psychoanalytic labeling. I have at length discussed his way of responding to Luther's spirit to Gandhi's challenge, in Erik H. Erikson: The Growth of His Work.

2. I suppose it can be said, has been said, that Freud was more deeply influenced by various religious and philosophical traditions than he ever realized (or could bear to realize). A most suggestive book is David Bakan's Sigmund Freud and the Jewish Mystical Tradition (Princeton: Van Nostrand, 1958). Certainly in Freud's New Introductory Lectures on Psychoanalysis (New York: Norton, 1933) a messianic and utopian strain comes across again and again. One has a vision of a psychoanalytic "elite" of sorts, whose members like prophets will "go forth" unto the needy, which in this case means the unanalyzed, who are presumably prone to irrational and "destructive" behavior.

3. In example, see St. Augustine's Confessions, not to mention Pascal's Pensées or Kierkegaard's On Authority and Revelation, and of course Either/Or. More recently, Jacques Maritain (A Preface to Metaphysics [New York: Sheed and Ward, 1948] and Man and the State [Chicago: University of Chicago Press, 1951]) in the Catholic tradition and Reinhold Niebuhr among Protestant theologians have unashamedly broken with the more puritan and punitive elements in the Christian tradition, which can be not only implacably deterministic, but ascetic in the extreme and (of interest here) utterly abstract and apparently unconcerned with the ongoing life of human beings. See especially

Reinhold Niebuhr's *The Nature and Destiny of Man* (New York: Scribner's, 1949); and *Moral Man and Immoral Society* (New York: Scribner's, 1932).

4. There is something special about "rural religion," something in the atmosphere of those churches and the villages they so often dominate, that Georges Bernanos has captured once and for all — and I believe for most countries and continents, even if his "locale" is so thoroughly the French countryside — in *The Diary of a Country Priest* (New York: Image, 1960). Simone Weil, also in France, saw what "peasants" possess in the way of faith (and also need, and lose when they go to the city). The "sanctity" she seems to have struggled for, and almost against her will found, is perhaps very much present in some of the "witnesses" I call upon here. Like Miss Weil, they know *The Need for Roots*, op. cit., and are *Waiting on God* (New York: Putnam's, 1951). In our country three religiously sensitive and spiritually powerful writers with a special concern for the South are: Flannery O'Connor (see especially *A Good Man Is Hard to Find* [New York: Harcourt, Brace and World, 1955] and *The Violent Bear It Away* [New York: Farrar, Straus and Giroux, 1960]); James Agee — in *Let Us Now Praise Famous Men* and *The Morning Watch* (Boston: Houghton Mifflin, 1951); and finally, Cormac McCarthy — in *The Orchard Keeper* (New York: Random House, 1965), and *Outer Dark* (New York: Random House, 1968).

5. An excellent account of contemporary religious developments in Appalachia may be found in Earl Brewer's essay, "Religion and the Churches" in *The Southern Appalacian Region*, op. cit. Also of value is Elizabeth Hooker's *Religion in the Highlands* (New York: Home Missions Council, 1933). Of interest is the minister Jack Weller's book *Yesterday's People* (Lexington: University of Kentucky Press, 1965). At times I feel the religious "spirit" of the people up those hollows defies all words, be they tape-recorded or from a gifted novelist's soul. Perhaps a photographer like Eliot Porter in *Appalachian Wilderness* (New York: Dutton, 1970) or yes, a composer like Igor Stravinsky (in *The Rite of Spring*) manages more successfully to capture the land's power or nature's rhythms — and man's religious response in the face of light, darkness, beauty, mystery.

6. The religious "practices" of migrants have not been extensively documented; however, two books already cited are helpful here: Zora Huston's powerful novel *Their Eyes Were Watching God*, and E. L. Koos's *They Follow the Sun*.

7. It is no secret that the South is still very much loyal to various Protestant sects. Liston Pope's *Millhands and Preachers* (New Haven: Yale University Press, 1942), a study of Gastonia, North Carolina, offers a thorough and tactful look at the ways organized religion fits into the lives of Southerners, many of them not that long "off the farm."

8. To understand the sociological and historical background of religion, as sharecroppers and tenant farmers and field hands have experienced it, one should turn to E. Franklin Frazier's *The Negro Church in America* (New York: Schocken, 1963); see also W. E. B. DuBois, *The Negro*

Church (Atlanta: Atlanta University Press, 1903) and Carter G. Woodson, *The History of the Negro Church* (Washington, D.C.: The Associated Publishers, 1921). For a view of both black and white "rural religion" in the South, I recommend Frank Alexander, "Religion in a Rural Community in the South," *American Sociological Review,* VI (April, 1941). Of interest in this regard is *Small Town in Mass Society, Class Power and Religion in a Rural Community* by A. Vidich and J. Bensman (Princeton: Princeton University Press, 1948). Also of value is Harold Kaufman, *Mississippi Churches, A Half Century of Change* (Hattiesburg: Mississippi State University Press, 1959).

9. In Kierkegaard's last work, *Attack Upon Christendom,* Walter Lowrie, trans. (Princeton: Princeton University Press, 1946) the reader is presented with an uncanny analysis of (and expansion upon) "sayings," popular stories, and what is sometimes referred to as "peasant wisdom." There, and in the earlier *On Authority and Revelation,* Walter Lowrie, trans. (Princeton: Princeton University Press, 1955), the Danish theologian and Christian psychologist shows how much he understands an emotional, struggling, almost rambling "approach" to God — an approach strong on the heart's lyricism, the brain's need to give forth its mad and irreverent and skeptical side as well as its fearful, awestruck but only somewhat silenced side. Again, I believe Kierkegaard might find a "Holiness Church" in Appalachia, or a "One and Only True Church" among migrants, or a Pentecostal Church in Mississippi's Delta congenial, spontaneous, startling, surprising and unnerving — not fossilized like more conventional religious institutions.

INDEX

Accommodation, 129
Activism, political and social: in Appalachia, 285–297, 571–577; school official's reaction to, 300–305; schoolteacher's reaction to, 308–316; minister's reaction to, 316–317; to help the migrant, 468–473, 474–475; southern black, 553–571. *See also* Antipoverty program
Adams County, Mississippi, 14
Adaptation, 53–54, 347; of the sharecropper, 492; and religion, 578
Adolescence, 190–192, 517–549; in Appalachia, 503, 505, 507, 523–526, 537–542; and the sharecropper, 517–520, 528–535; and marriage, 519, 522, 533–535, 545, 546; and the migrant, 520–523, 534–537, 543–548; and migration (leaving home), 524–525, 528–529; brevity of childhood, 526–527, 535, 541, 546–547; desperation, 527; and arrival of children, 547
Agee, James, 25, 26, 421, 619, 626, 636
Aggression, *see* Violence
Agriculture Department, U.S., 376, 385
Alabama, 9, 12–13, 38, 148–150, 156, 159, 186, 362, 414, 419, 570, 593, 606–611; sharecropper education in, 382, 384–385, 387–389, 391; revivalists in, 400–409; and Wallace, 412. *See also* "Black Belt"

Alcohol (wine, whiskey, moonshine), 420; and the migrant, 81, 85–86, 99, 112, 426, 428, 429, 430, 459, 461, 521, 590, 613–614; and the mountaineer, 194, 209, 211, 219, 220–221, 222, 227, 237, 250, 258–259, 261, 262, 265, 266, 281, 338, 497, 506, 508, 541; and the miner, 342, 343, 348; and the sharecropper, 369, 585, 586; and the sheriff, 400
Alexander, Frank, 637
Allegheny Mountains, 6, 598
American Orthopsychiatric Association, 621
American Psychiatric Association, 621
Anthony, James, 622
Antipoverty program, 290–291, 293–294, 551; hostility toward workers of, 300–305; in rural South, 558–560, 561–571; opposition to, 565; federal warnings to slow down in Mississippi, 566–567; distance between workers and the poor, 568–571; in Appalachia, 571–577
Antonovsky, A., 627
Anxiety, 505
Apathy, 111, 563; of older migrant children, 81–83, 85; of the mountaineer, 497, 509
Appalachia, 11, 22, 33–34, 38, 193–271; isolation of, 194; coal miners of, 193, 208–211, 268, 334–358; and federal government, 226, 244, 247–248, 251, 268, 283, 293–295, 298–299, 309; and unemploy-

639